critical theory and

international relations

critical theory and international relations

A READER

EDITED BY Steven C. Roach

Routledge
Taylor & Francis Group
New York   London

Routledge
Taylor & Francis Group
270 Madison Avenue
New York, NY 10016

Routledge
Taylor & Francis Group
2 Park Square
Milton Park, Abingdon
Oxon OX14 4RN

© 2008 by Taylor & Francis Group, LLC
Routledge is an imprint of Taylor & Francis Group, an Informa business

International Standard Book Number-13: 978-0-415-95419-8 (Softcover) 978-0-415-95418-1 (Hardcover)

Library of Congress Cataloging-in-Publication Data

Critical theory and international relations : a reader / edited by Steven C. Roach.
    p. cm.
    ISBN 0-415-95418-5 (hardback : alk. paper) -- ISBN 0-415-95419-3 (pbk. : alk. paper)
    1. International relations. 2. Critical theory. I. Roach, Steven C.

JZ1242.C77 2007
327.101--dc22
                                                              2006009323

Contents

Acknowledgments

This reader grew out of my early ruminations and conversations with several critical theorists in Berkeley, California, during the early 1990s. Such ruminations would continue during my formal training in international studies (Ph.D.), where many proved instrumental in shaping the ideas that would serve as the conceptual foundation of the book, including Micheline Ishay and Jack Donnelly, among others. I benefited a great deal from the suggestions and comments of the reviewer, Bernd Reiter and the former senior editor, Rob Tempio, who helped to further broaden the book's scope. I am also indebted to my wife, Erica, for her invaluable assistance with the editing of the book and in securing the permissions to reprint material.

Accordingly, I would like to express my gratitude to the following publishers for allowing me to reprint the following materials.

Chapter 2 reprinted from *Kant's Political Writings*, edited by Hans Reiss. Copyright © 1991 by Cambridge University Press. Reprinted with permission of Cambridge University Press.

Chapter 3 reprinted from *Kant's Political Writings*, edited by Hans Reiss. Copyright © 1991 by Cambridge University Press. Reprinted with permission of Cambridge University Press.

Chapter 4 reprinted from G.W.F. Hegel, Hegel's *Phenomenology of Spirit*, with permission of Oxford University Press. Copyright © 1977 by Oxford University Press.

Chapter 8 reprinted from Antonio Gramsci, *Prison Notebooks* (New York: International Publishers, 1971), "Hegemony and Problems of Marxism," pp. 257–264, 409–414, with permission from International Publishers. Copyright © 1971 by International Publishers.

Chapter 9 reprinted from Georg Lukács, *History of Class Consciousness*, with permission from Ms. Erzsébet Panuska, c/o MIT Press. Copyright © Erzsébet Panuska.

Chapter 10 reprinted from *Civilization and its Discontents* by Sigmund Freud, translated by James Strachey. Copyright © 1961 by James Strachey, renewed 1989 by Alix Strachey. Used by permission of W.W. Norton & Company, Inc. Sigmund Freud © Copyrights, The Institute of Psychoanalysis and the Hogarth Press for permission to quote from *Civilization and its Discontents* from the *Standard Edition of the Complete Psychological Works of Sigmund Freud* translated and edited by James Strachey. Reprinted by permission of the the Random House Group, Ltd.

Chapter 10 reprinted from *The Birth of Tragedy and the Genealogy of Morals*, by Friedrich Nietzsche, translated by Francis Golffing. Copyright © 1956 by Doubleday, a division of Random House, Inc. Used by permission of Doubleday, a division of Random House, Inc.

Chapter 11 reprinted by permission from the University of California Press, from Max Weber, *Economy and Society*, Vol. 2. Copyright © 1971 by the Regents of the University of California.

Chapter 13 reprinted from Max Horkheimer, *Critical Theory: Selected Essays*, by permission from The Continuum International Publishing Group. Translated by Matthew J. O'Connell; English translation by © Herder and Herder Inc.

Chapter 14 reprinted from Max Horkheimer and Theodor W. Adorno, *Dialectic of Enlightenment*, by permission from The Continuum International Publishing Group. Translated by John Coming; English translation © 1972 by Herder and Herder Inc.

Chapter 15 reprinted from Theodor W. Adorno, *Negative Dialectics*, by permission from The Continuum International Publishing Group. Translated by E.B. Ashton; English translation © 1973 by The Continuum International Publishing Group.

Chapter 16 reprinted from Herbert Marcuse, *One-Dimensional Man*. Copyright © 1964 by Beacon Press. Reprinted with permission of Beacon Press, Boston.

Chapter 17 reprinted from Friedrich Pollock, "State Capitalism and its Possibilities," by permission from The Continuum International Publishing Group. Copyright © 1982 by The Continuum International Publishing Group.

Chapter 18 reprinted from *Soviet Marxism*, by Herbert Marcuse. Copyright © 1979 by Columbia University Press. Reprinted with permission of the publisher.

Chapter 19 reprinted from *The Theory of Communicative Action, Volume 1: Reason and the Rationalization of Society* by Jürgen Habermas. Introduction and English translation Copyright © 1984 by Beacon Press. German Text: Copyright © 1981 by Suhrkamp Verlag, Frankfurt am Main. Reprinted by permission of Beacon Press, Boston.

Chapter 20 reprinted from Jürgen Habermas, *Between Facts and Norms*, translated by William Rehg. Copyright © 1996 by MIT Press.

Chapter 21 reprinted from Axel Honneth, *The Struggle for Recognition: The Moral Grammar of Social Conflicts*, with permission from Polity Press. Copyright © 1995 by Polity Press.

Chapter 22 reprinted from Nancy Fraser, "From Redistribution to Recognition? Dilemmas of Justice in the Post-Socialist Age," with permission of *New Left Review*. Copyright © 1997 *New Left Review*.

Chapter 23 reprinted with permission by *Millennium: Journal of International Studies*, from Mark Hoffman, "Critical Theory and the Inter-Paradigm Debate," Vol. 23, No. 1 (1994): 109–118. Copyright © 1994 by *Millennium: Journal of International Studies*.

Chapter 24 reprinted from Mark Neufeld, *The Restructuring of International Relations Theory*. Copyright © 1997 Cambridge University Press. Reprinted with Permission of Cambridge University Press.

Chapter 25 reprinted with permission by *Millennium: Journal of International Studies*, from Andrew Linklater, "The Question of the Next Stage in International Relations Theory: A Critical Theoretic Point of View," Vol. 21, No. 1 (1992). Copyright © 1994 by *Millennium: Journal of International Studies*.

Chapter 26 reprinted with permission by *Millennium: Journal of International Studies*, from Mervyn Frost, "The Role of Normative Theory in IR," Vol. 23, No. 1 (1994): 109–118. Copyright © 1994 by *Millennium: Journal of International Studies*.

Chapter 27 reprinted with permission by *Millennium: Journal of International Studies*, from Robert Cox, "Social Forces, States and World Order: Beyond International Relations Theory," Vol. 10, No. 2 (1981): 16 pp. Copyright © 1981 by *Millennium: Journal of International Studies*.

Chapter 28 reprinted from Justin Rosenberg, *The Empire of Civil Society*, pp. 129–35, with permission by Verso Press. Copyright © 1990 by Verso Press.

Chapter 29 reprinted from Claire Cutler, "Locating Authority in the Global Political Economy," *International Studies Quarterly*, with permission by Blackwell Publishing. Copyright © 1999 by Blackwell Publishing.

Chapter 30 reprinted with permission by *Millennium: Journal of International Studies*, from Stephen Gill, "Globalisation, Market Civilisation, and Disciplinary Neoliberalism," Vol. 24, No. 2 (1995): 17 pp. Copyright © 1995 by *Millennium: Journal of International Studies*.

Chapter 31 reprinted with permission by *Millennium: Journal of International Studies*, from Christian Heine and Benno Teschke, "Sleeping Beauty and the Dialectical Awakening: On the Potential of Dialectic for International Relations," Vol. 25, No. 2 (1996): 404–423. Copyright © 1996 by *Millennium: Journal of International Studies*.

Chapter 32 reprinted from *Power/Knowledge* by Michel Foucault, edited by Colin Gordon, Copyright © 1972, 1975, 1976, 1977 by Michel Foucault. Preface and Afterword © 1980 by Colin Gordon. Bibliography © 1980 by Colin Gordon. This collection © 1980 by the Harvester Press. Used by permission of Pantheon Books, a division of Random House, Inc.

Chapter 34 reprinted from Jean-Francois Lyotard, *The Postmodern Condition*, translated by Geoff Bennington and Brian Massumi, with permission by Minnesota University Press (1994). English Translation and Foreword copyright © 1984 by the University of Minnesota. Original French-language edition translation copyright © by Les Editions de Minuit.

Chapter 35 reprinted from Richard Ashley and R.B.J Walker, "Reading Dissidence/Writing the Discipline: Crisis and the Question of Sovereignty in International Studies," *International Studies Quarterly*, with permission by Blackwell Publishing. Copyright © 1995 by Blackwell Publishers.

Chapter 36 reprinted from Jens Bartelson, *A Genealogy of Sovereignty*. Copyright © 1995 Cambridge University Press. Reprinted with permission of Cambridge University Press.

Chapter 37 reprinted with permission by *Millennium: Journal of International Studies*, from Christine Sylvester, "Empathetic Cooperation: A Feminist Method for IR," Vol. 23, No. 2 (1994): 321–334. Copyright © 1994 by *Millennium: Journal of International Studies*.

Chapter 38 reprinted with permission by *Millennium: Journal of International Studies*, Richard Devetak, "The Project of Modernity and International Relations Theory," Vol. 24, No. 1 (1995): 27–51. Copyright © 1995 by *Millennium: Journal of International Studies*.

Introduction: From Critical Theory to Critical IR Theory

Dialectic and Kant's Legacy

If critical social theory offers us a logical avenue for understanding social change, then the term "dialectic" can be seen as the vehicle for maneuvering our understanding along this avenue. In modern critical social theory, dialectic serves as a scientific and holistic method of analysis. Its purpose(s) is to investigate the social forces of political order and transformation in terms of the relational oppositions and historical contradictions between the individual and society and to examine the meaning of reason (*Vernunft*) and rationality in the social context of ethical, economic, and political struggles for justice and freedom. The dialectic in this sense is both inspired by and derived from the writings of Kant, Hegel, Marx, and Habermas, among others. And, unlike ancient theory, which explores the dialectic as an "art of defining ideas related to the method of determining the interrelation of ideas in the light of single principle," a modern conception of dialectic emphasizes the historical and social (scientific) dimensions of societal change. Thus, dialectic, as understood here, can be employed in a variety of ways to explain societal transformation(s) in the contemporary world, including the emergence of human rights (gender and indigenous groups), new institutional norms and forms of citizenship (EU), and global ethics.[1] As such, one encounters different modern conceptions of dialectic, ranging from Marx's dialectical materialism ("the progressive unification through the contradiction of opposites") and Habermas's hermeneutical dialectic (intersubjective interaction or communicative action) to Adorno's negative dialectics, which conceives dialectic as an inherently subversive element of reason and rationality.

In recent years, however, a pervasive skepticism has emerged concerning the dialectic and its role in advancing the emancipatory project of modernity (emancipation that is guided by the principles of reason, rationality, justice, and societal and political integration). Such skepticism reflects what Richard Bernstein argues is a tension between the modern and postmodern (*Stimmung*). As Bernstein notes, "[*Stimmung*] is an amorphous, protean, and shifting [force] but which nevertheless exerts a powerful influence on the ways in which we think, act, and experience."[3] In his view, such skepticism explains why postmodernist and modernist thinkers seek to address the political and ethical consequences of their theory. Confronting such consequences, as he insists, is not simply "contingent" or "accidental," but "a dialectical consequence of the questions that they raise themselves."[4] We might therefore see the bond between postmodernists (Baudrillard, Lyotard, Derrida, Foucault, and Delueze) and modernists in terms of the mutual struggle to locate the meaning of freedom and justice at the margins. Having said this, though, it is important to note the critical source of tension between these schools, especially as it concerns the dialectic and social totality. For postmodernists, dialecticians reinforce exclusion and oppression by conceiving social integration and societal relations in holistic terms, that is, as an unfolding social totality. Not only does the dialectic engender an essentializing logic that privileges Western-empowered notions of universality; it also ignores the relativization of truths/values and social fragmentation, or what Jacques Derrida refers to as the "indestructibility of otherness." To affirm this indestructibility is thus, on the one hand, to valorize difference and to resist hegemonic practices.

On the other hand, affirming the relativization of truth fails to provide constructive criteria for promoting social and political integration. While we need to be concerned with the problematics of power and sovereignty, it is equally important that we address the constitutive aspects of knowledge building, consensus formation, and social empowerment. The question that arises, then, is whether the permanent dismissal of the dialectic undermines the principles of solidarity, equality, and tolerance. How, in other words, should we conceive critical social thought as a steering mechanism that is capable of guiding our investigation into and understanding of societal and political change at the domestic and global levels?

The comprehensive approach of this reader addresses these questions by focusing on the changing and evolving features of dialectical thought. Its primary aim is to provide the heuristic tools for charting the evolution of critical theory into the global realm, through the writings of Kant, Hegel, Marx, the Frankfurt School and critical IR theory. In this way, it seeks to bridge an ongoing gap in critical IR studies between the tradition of critical theory and critical IR theory, and to encourage IR scholars, students, and practitioners to see the global realm as a new context for applying and engaging dialectic to understand social change. Given these objectives, it becomes important to inquire into the modern origins of critical social thought.

We can begin our inquiry in this case with Kant's distinction between experience and cognition, or how the understanding does not begin with experience but arises out of it. It is this distinction that reveals the autonomous capacity of reason and rational understanding and that reaffirms the role of dialectical criticism by prioritizing the distinction between the "is" and "ought" in our theory of knowledge. In this way, Kant's philosophy created a new moral foundation for inquiring into the limits of nature (experience) and the transformative possibilities of a moral civil society.[5] A key construct of this new foundation was speculative reason. Kant thought of this dimension of reason as providing a space for directing our thoughts toward the future possibilities of regulating and promoting human conduct. For him, this dimension necessitated an open-ended view of society, whose immanent task was to (re)orient our thoughts, ideas, rational judgments and concepts toward the rule of law. Kant in this sense shows us that dogmatism and orthodoxy are never too far away, and that we need to orient reason toward the universal or ethical ends of moral freedom as a way of transcending the irrationalism of the (political) passions. This moral requirement might well explain Kant's paradoxical intellectual debt to David Hume, the Scottish Enlightenment philosopher (empiricist skeptic) who, as Kant remarked, had "interrupted my dogmatic slumber."[6]

Hume, of course, is not the only philosopher who deserves credit for inspiring Kant's modern formulation of dialectical criticism. Equally essential are the ancient philosophers, in particular, Plato, whose Meno dialogue addresses the dilemma of how we can know something of which we have no knowledge. What this problem (*aporia*) suggests is that in acquiring knowledge of something, we also fail to grasp its essence. Another way of putting this idea is to say that our deeply embedded ethical convictions can and should always take the form of the following permanent questions about our political existence: What is the role of the state? What are my moral duty and responsibility for promoting civil society? Addressing these questions requires us to overcome the presumption that there are permanent answers to life's greatest problems.

Inquiring, then, into the sources of authoritarianism constitutes one of the core tasks of critical theory. Because political leaders can use their power to manipulate the rules of institutions and the system, they can also subjugate the individual to the state. Thus, the reason why speculative reason is so important in this respect is that it stresses the immanent tensions between the state (society) and individual; it treats, in other words, these tensions as existing, albeit changing constructs of our moral understanding. In this way, speculative reason is predicated on the following question: How do reason and dialectical thought enable us to challenge and overcome dogmatism and barbarism?

Hegel's and Marx's answer to this question involved elaborate and systematic attempts to historicize and materialize the dialectic. Hegel, for instance, conceived the dialectic in terms of the historical unfolding of the absolute spirit and knowledge, or the grand reconciliation between freedom and the state (*Aufhebung*); while Marx built upon Hegel's dialectical project by theorizing about the class conflict between the proletariat and bourgeoisie and how this conflict would be resolved through the dissolution of capitalism (private property and the bourgeois state). In this way, Marx, perhaps more than any other social theorist, revealed the practical qualities of dialectical thought. His influence on the Frankfurt School's critical theory would lead some to label the Frankfurt School as a "second stage of Marxism."[8]

A central question for critical IR theorists, then, is how [an extended] critical theory exposes the dogmatism and orthodoxy of militant ideologies. Here, though, we need to be careful about how we approach the word "extension." What exactly are we extending? And how does the extension of dialectical criticism qualify the international principles of justice or global forms of citizenship? To address these questions, we need to examine the core concepts and aims of critical theory.

Why Critical Theory?

The Frankfurt Institute of Social Research (The Frankfurt School) officially coined the term "critical theory" in 1937.[9] Its formulation of critical theory would incorporate a wide range of ideas, including those of Kant, Marx, Hegel, Nietzsche, Freud,

Weber, Lukács and Gramsci. As such, critical theory reflected a synthesis of various traditions of modern theory, including German Idealism, Historical Materialism, Modernism, and Psychoanalysis. Max Horkheimer, one of the founders of the school, saw the mission as one of investigating the relationship between reason and authority.

But attempts to synthesize the traditions failed to produce a cohesive theory. Stephen Bronner, for instance, argues that critical theory, while shedding much needed light on the emancipatory project, remains an amalgamation of competing normative and sociological concerns.[10] The reasons for this lack of cohesion are not clear-cut. But it is possible that the project of the Frankfurt School remained too ambitious; that synthesizing so many differing strands of thought had compromised their focus, and allowed the deep skepticism or pessimism of Freud's and Nietzsche's writings to filter into their views of the Enlightenment's legacy. As we shall see, Horkheimer's and Adorno's critique of instrumental reason—which held that scientific and technical rationality had outstripped the progressive elements of reason—was emblematic of this deep skepticism. For many, however, Habermas's critique of this critique would motivate many to rethink the legacy of the Enlightenment or the project of modernity. His theory of communicative action, for instance, would convince many to reconsider the progressive aspects of the Enlightenment's ideals of reason and rationality.

Nonetheless, the main reason why we study the Frankfurt School, whether it is Habermas's theory of communicative action, Horkheimer's and Adorno's critique of instrumental reason, or Herbert Marcuse's one-dimensional man, is that critical theory offers us a key set of insights into the changing dynamics of dogmatism and authoritarian political structures. From this vantage point, critical theory not only encompasses the objectives of critical thinking (reasoned argumentation and deliberation); it also reflects the process of learning to do theory in the sense of becoming aware of one's changing ties to (identity with) society. Critical theory, therefore, provides us with a holistic deliberation approach to studying state authoritarianism, one which is comprised of the following four central tenets.

First, critical social theory addresses the reflexive dimension of an individual's theory/ideas, or the intrinsic link between one's actions and values and his or her ideological orientation. Here ideology shapes one's underlying preferences, and is the lens through which one understands his or her environment.[7] One's knowledge and the tools he or she uses to acquire specialized knowledge are always being shaped by historical and social circumstances.[11] Theory, in this respect, is both holistic and practical in its undertaking, since it concerns the need to investigate the social genesis of facts and the emerging social and political trends in society. Accordingly, to be self-reflexive is to be conscious of the social origins and conditions shaping the content of these facts. In this way, critical theory opposes positivism, or the employment of deductive, inductive and empiricist methods to objectify social phenomena. For critical theorists, social values inhere in our practical and theoretical understanding; they are, in other words, immanent to our action (praxis) and knowledge of society.

Second, critical social theory focuses on the mutability of political structures. It seeks, in this way, to demonstrate how political power and ideological controls can foster the perception of the permanence of political and economic structures.

Such reified thinking characterizes the Nazis' use of heroic and naturalized symbols of blood and soil to champion the eternal greatness of the German (Nazi) state. Marx, Lukács and the Frankfurt School theorists, for instance, drew on the oppressive practices of capitalism to establish the link between reification and oppression/authoritarianism. By reification we are referring to the false conversion of something into its concrete form, that is, the false identification of the authenticity and social content of this form or product. Thus, for example, Georg Lukács conceives the reification of consciousness in terms of the inert immediacy of social facts (the proletarian victory in the Soviet Union). When we critically assess the falseness of political structures in relation to the changing social circumstances of society, we also seek to expose the dogmatism of these structures. For Horkheimer and the rest of the Frankfurt School theorists, such dogmatism symptomized humankind's desire to dominate nature; it showed, in other words, why some chose to use naturalized and eternal symbols to dominate and oppress other peoples.

Third, critical social theory is an open-ended interdisciplinary approach rooted in both ethical concerns and social and economic relations of production. In Gramsci's writings on the dialectical interaction between civil society and the state, ethics and cultural concerns remain immanent to social progress and equality. Here, cultural concerns refer, in part, to the the role of organic intellectuals in educating the masses. For some critical IR theorists, such a project, when extended to the global level, underscores the immanence of exclusionary and inclusionary modes of citizenship and political participation in the global civil society. This project, in turn, rejects any Archimedean point of reference by which to measure or validate the universal value of rights and goods. As noted above, the normative dimension of critical theory assumes that an individual's ethical responsibilities are always being shaped by changing social circumstances. For this reason, our knowledge is never complete per se, which is to say that we can never have the final say over what does and does not constitute absolute or permanent moral knowledge. We can only assume that the conditions that shape our knowledge claims also [permanently] presuppose the tensions between societal change and our moral convictions. What becomes important, then, is the need for an interdisciplinary and pliable theory to explain this complex theoretical task.

Fourth, critical social theory is an integrative analysis of social reality. It provides "guides to social reality, producing models and cognitive mappings of societies, and the 'big pictures' that enable us to see, for example, how the economy polity, social institutions, discourses, practices, and culture interact to produce a social system."[12] In this case, critical social theory offers a big picture of the changing contours of the international and/or global realm, whose main features include the counter-hegemonic efforts of international social movements, NGOs, new forms of citizenship, and new supranational institutions (EU, ICC, etc.). This is one main reason why, as we shall see, that many critical IR theorists have claimed that critical theory offers a new paradigmatic approach of international relations theory.

In sum, critical social theory remains both relevant and applicable to understanding the complex interaction of identities, practices, and institutions at both the domestic and international levels. As the fourth tenet suggests, the extension of critical theory into IR theory reflects a progressive, albeit problematic theoretical development in IR theory.

The Extension of Critical Theory to Critical IR Theory

THE IR DIMENSION

Turning to international relations theory we encounter three so-called great debates (accompanied by a recently emerging fourth) regarding the scientific and theoretical parameters of the discipline. The first debate between idealism and realism arose out of E.H. Carr's *Twenty Years Crisis, 1919–1939*.[13] This was eventually followed by the second debate between scientific methodology and history (1950s and 1960s), which culminated in Kenneth Waltz's *Theory of International Politics*. By the 1980s, the emergence of an inter-paradigm debate between structuralism, pluralism and realism gave rise to a third debate between positivism and post-positivism. Here we can point to the following two ways in which critical theory initially entered into international relations theory: (1) an internalized approach that works within realism or conventional IR approaches in order to formulate a critical realist theory; and (2) an externalized approach that works within the critical theory tradition to posit a self-standing theoretical approach, equipped with the methodological tools and governing principles to compete with other IR research programs or approaches.[15]

Realism in IR consists of a long tradition of ideas dating back to ancient times. The key concepts of realism include the balance of power, hegemony, and power politics. (see Thucydides, Machiavelli, Hobbes and Hans Morgenthau). In IR theory we distinguish between a political and a structural realism. The former, for instance, focuses on the functional components of the balance of power and the operational and ethical parameters of foreign policy decisions. Meanwhile, structural realism is more rigid and processual in its approach to the international system. It uses scientific variables (distribution of capabilities across states) and establishes continuous patterns in IR to measure the causes and effects of state behavior.[16] Thus, structural realism turns on sharp and often rigid dichotomies between objectivity and subjectivity, ontology and epistemology, and state and nonstate actors. Not only does it reduce the variability of state behavior to the ontological realm of anarchy, but it also ignores the role played by history in explaining the political transformation of the international system.

In his 1981 article on political realism, Richard Ashley attempted to move beyond these rigidities of parsimonious theory, by distinguishing between a practical and a technical realism. Drawing on Habermas's communicative action theory, he argued that structural realism failed to show how the competitive power interests of states were constituted by social interaction or the intersubjectivity of values, norms, and interests. In this sense, Ashley was not simply concerned with developing a critical theory of IR per se, but with restructuring realism in a way that internalized the ethical and political content of the power and competitive interests of states.[17] Yet precisely because Ashley sought to internalize the shared power interests of states, he failed to adequately expose the ideological dimensions of the interstate system. As Mark Hoffman notes, Ashley overlooked the fact that realism "performs an ideological function in legitimising an order in which only certain interests are realised—the technical and practical interests of states and the state system. This leaves it void of emancipatory interests, of the humanist element that is central to critical theory."[18]

Nonetheless, it is important to stress that by working within the realist paradigm, internalized approaches staticize the political and social structures of the international system. As such, they contradict one of the fundamental aims of critical theory: to demonstrate how the ideological elements of political structures subjugate and threaten human reason, freedom, and equality. This is one of the main reasons why critical IR theorists have strongly criticized Alexander Wendt's social theory of international politics; in particular, his "thin constructivism," which retains the state centric assumptions of realism in order to formulate a scientific realism based on three cultures of anarchy: namely, Hobbesian, Lockean, and Kantian.[19] Certainly it could be said that Wendt's theory steers a path between the limits of realism and postmodern relativism, offering what Samuel Barkin aptly describes as "realist constructivism."[20] However, Wendt's theory also allows the scientific variables of realism to limit analysis of the structural influences of NGOs and other nonstate actors.

By contrast, then, an externalized approach seeks to devise an alternative theory to conventional IR approaches. Not only does it critique the limits of conventional approaches, such as realism and neo-institutionalism, it also reflects the antipositivist orientation of critical theory and the attendant possibilities of drawing on the critical theory tradition to restructure the IR discipline. As one of the first critical theorists of the international political economy, Robert Cox distinguished between problem solvers and those who employ the scientific or positivist methods to measure and predict the recurrent effects of state power and interests; and critical theorists, who interpret the social forces of world order in terms of ethics and the mutability of structures (the internationalization of the state).[21] His efforts to develop a critical theory approach to the international political economy would ultimately inspire Andrew Linklater to formulate a critical IR theory, which placed the emancipatory project at the core of international theory.[22] Linklater's principal aim, as we shall see, was to position critical theory in IR by building on Mark Hoffman's earlier claim (1987) that critical theory had emerged (out of the inter-paradigm debate) as a new, albeit undeveloped paradigm of IR theory. Accordingly, by the mid- to late-1980s, the evolution of critical theory into IR theory marked an important feature of the transition from the inter-paradigm debate of IR theory to the third debate.[23]

Facilitating this transition was a series of transformative events including the dissolution of the Soviet Union, the rapid advancements in informational technology (e.g., satellite technology and the Internet), and the effects of these advancements on the erosion of state sovereignty. More than anything, these events helped inspire a renewed and sustained focus on ethics and morality, while also challenging the reductivist and deterministic approaches of structuralism and positivism. As such, they raised several normative and empirical questions regarding the changing global order. Are states really the exclusive or primary actors/agents of the international system? If realism and rationalism have ignored the ethical and moral implications of power (war), how do we explain the state's obligation to resolve inter-communal conflict? Moreover, what is the normative connection between this trend and the emergence of global governance (not world government), in which NGOs, social movements, environmental and peace movements, and private actors have come together to influence decisionmaking at the global level? And how do these nonstate actors influence and explain the emergence of the World Trade Organization (WTO), Kyoto Protocols, and the International Criminal Court (ICC)?

As we shall see, however, critical theory in IR addresses each one of these questions. Here, we should also note the important contribution of international political theory, in particular Charles Beitz's work on international ethics.[24] Beitz, for instance, analyzed many of the key features of international society, including liberal cosmopolitan right, global justice,[25] and global responsibility. Beitz formulated, among other things, a global original position (via John Rawls' *Theory of Justice*[26]) in order to address general problems in normative IR theory (including an equitable global distribution of social goods). In doing so, however, he also exposed the problem of championing the tradition of rationalism, which, as Nicholas Rengger notes, "ultimately 'squeezes out' non-rationalist normative voices that address crucial problems in IR."[27] Whether or not Beitz's analysis squeezes out non-rationalist perspectives, it is important that we realize that the inclusion of more critical perspectives will continue to allow IR theorists to address new problems in global politics, while also exposing the limits of conventional IR theories.

In short, both international political theory and critical IR theory stress the role of history, ethics, and social and political integration. Yet, in doing so, they also draw attention to the important challenge posed by radical IR approaches (e.g., postmodernism, feminism and other critical theory approaches): namely, the need to focus on the dark side of reason, universality, and rationality, or the systemic effects of oppression, patriarchy, marginalization and racism. If critical IR theory is to move beyond this challenge, then it must become a self-reflexive theory that can accommodate the concerns of the postmodernists. This task, however, raises the following question: How should we address this dark side of the Enlightenment's legacy (the promotion of its signature ideals of reason, rationality, freedom, justice, solidarity and equality) within a reflexive, yet pluralistic theoretical framework that does not allow an anything-goes approach (pure relativism)?

Critical IR Theory and The Third and Fourth Debates: Challenges and Prospects

To address this question, let us examine some of the central issues surrounding the "third debate" in IR theory. As noted earlier, the debate pits positivism against postpositivism and seeks to promote a methodological pluralism that "will lead to the reexamination of scientific dissensus and its relationship to scientific progress."[28] As such, it focuses attention on the value of difference and a plurality of voices in the field, and exposes the points of crisis in the discipline by actively interrogating the hegemonic practices in international relations (sovereignty).[29]

Accordingly, by the early to mid-1990s, the third debate encompassed a range of interpretive modes of analyses, including postmodernism, feminism, critical IR theory, constructivism, post-colonialism and Neo-Gramscian approaches to the international political economy. Within this cluster of theories, several competing claims to knowledge emerged, including, among other things, the need for articulating a social dialectic to explain the trajectory of IR,[30] the governing forces and principles of inclusion and exclusion within and outside the discipline,[31] the arbitrary meaning of territorial boundaries or state sovereignty,[32] and the role of gender, individual private actors, NGOs, social, environmental and peace groups in IR.[33] While such approaches focus much-needed attention on many long-neglected and newly emergent social movements, they also reflect a difficult tradeoff between a plurality of competing critical theory approaches and the loss of a set of governing assumptions that can direct and guide the discipline along a coherent path. Perhaps an apt metaphor that captures the complexity of this tradeoff is constellation, which Adorno borrowed from Walter Benjamin to describe the increasing fragmentation of modern society. As he states, societal relations are "juxtaposed rather than an integrated cluster of changing elements that resist reduction to a common denominator, essential core, or generative first principle."[34]

Still, few will argue that an open-ended methodology of some kind is needed, especially given the complexity of global issues and the need to devise imaginative theoretical approaches to reflect upon and resolve these issues. What remains unclear, however, is whether we can develop an empirical and policy-relevant critical IR theory. It is precisely this issue that lies at the core of what some are referring to as a fourth debate. In a recent special issue of the *Review of International Studies*, for instance, several leading critical IR theorists were asked to discuss the implications of Jürgen Habermas's discursive ethics for a "practical"[35] critical theory of international relations. In his article on dialogical politics, for instance, Linklater argued that IR theorists needed to address the problematic limitations to Habermas's proceduralism and to see its procedural limitations as a necessary precondition for further accommodating relativist claims.[36] Others have drawn on Axel Honneth's theory of the struggle for recognition to articulate the empirical prospects of a critical IR theory. For instance, Jürgen Haacke states that Honneth's account of the struggle for recognition "would not appear to exhibit the same tension as is inherent between Habermas's discourse ethics and his analysis of contemporary (international) politics."[37]

In sum, we might point to three important focal points of the fourth debate and beyond. First is the ongoing and unmet need to bring together history with a philosophy of science, or rather, as Fred Halliday insists, of treating the philosophy of social science as heuristic tools for advancing the IR discipline.[38] Here, it is critical that we engage critical IR theory as an emerging whole, that is, to critically analyze the logical and historical implications of the ideas found in the modern or derivative texts of critical IR theory, such as Kant, Hegel, Marx, Weber, Nietzsche, Adorno and Habermas. Second, critical IR theorists will need to develop a practical and policy-relevant critical IR theory rooted in the discursive link between policymaking and the theoretical abstractions of identity and political will formation. And, lastly, critical IR theorists will need to reexamine the diverse dialectical traditions of critical social thought, perhaps with a view to imagining new ways of formulating a reflexive dialectic, including the counterposing of negative dialectics (Adorno) to positive dialectics (Hegel, Marx and Habermas). In this way, it will be important to return to the debate on the dialect initiated by Christian Heine and Benno Teschke in the mid-1990s.[39] The two, as we shall see, posited that dialectic could, if properly understood, offer the methodological steering mechanism for IR theory.

Whether this latter focus will expose the dialectical interaction of critical theory and postmodernism is certainly an intriguing methodological issue. But it is also true that fundamental tensions continue to divide normative and structuralist-oriented critical theorists (international political economy). And while it is possible that these strands of political and economic thought may evolve into a major disjuncture within the sub-field of critical IR theory, as some have pointed out, it is important to realize that this challenge will require a deeper appreciation of the extension of critical theory into the global realm.[40]

Given these tensions, it should be emphasized that while this reader is intended to be comprehensive in scope, it does leave out certain critical perspectives on IR, most notably constructivism and post-colonial approaches. This is not to say that constructivists and post-colonial writers (subaltern) are not critical theorists. Rather, in excluding these perspectives, this reader seeks to focus on a particular historical lineage of critical social thought.

A Historical Approach

In providing a framework for studying the evolution of critical theory into critical IR theory, this reader adopts a historical method (periodization) to understand the philosophical underpinnings and emergence of critical IR theory. The primary aim is to expose the social and political tensions that have helped to extend critical theory into the global sphere (e.g., regional integration and global forms of communication). Three historically based criteria will serve as the basis of investigation. First, what are the main ideas of abstract universalism; and how do these ideas engender a historical materialist interpretation to counter the oppressive forces of industrialization? Second, how do the extreme ideological dimensions of the totalitarian state expose the limits and problems in our understanding of social change? And third, how does technological rationality, or the Frankfurt School's views on the authoritarian state, give way to a revolutionary, hermeneutical interpretation of constitutional law and world society; namely, the liberating and oppressive forces of globalization?

In this way, this reader offers a detailed, historical lineage of critical theory: from German Idealism to the critical theory debates of IR theory. Accordingly, there are four phases of critical theory in which changing social and economic circumstances have helped engender critical and revolutionary insights into the laws and dynamics of society. These include the early/abstract phase, 1800–1865; the historical materialist phase, 1866–1914; the critical synthesis phase, 1915–1965; and the globalization phase, 1966–present.

As such, each of these periods reveal the impact of the changing social conditions on the evolution of critical IR theory: from a purely abstract universalism to a hermeneutical understanding of global society. Together, they allow us to see critical IR theory as constituting an open-ended dialectical project of critical theory, in which the opposing meanings of society and state have given way to a deeper understanding of the oppressive and liberating forces of world society. Such periodization is also intended to facilitate our understanding of the primary tasks of critical IR theory, which, as Richard Devetak points out, "is to reflect on the possibility of extending the rational, just, and democratic organization of politics to the entire species;"[44] and, as Andrew Linklater states, "how critical theory continues to evolve beyond the paradigm of production to a commitment to dialogic communities that are deeply sensitive about all forms inclusion and exclusion—domestic, transnational and international."[42]

Endnotes

1. Raymond Williams, *Keywords* (Oxford: Oxford University Press, 1975), p. 106.
2. Or, as Engels would later state, "the science of general laws of motion, both of the external world and human thought—two sets of laws which are identical in their substance but differ in their expression." Quoted in Ibid.
3. Richard J. Bernstein, *The New Constellation: The Ethical-Political Horizons of Modernity/Postmodernity* (Cambridge, MA: MIT Press, 1993), p. 11.
4. Ibid.
5. Immanuel Kant, *Kant's Political Writings*, edited by Hans Reiss (Cambridge: Cambridge University Press, 1989).
6.. Immanuel Kant, *Prolegomena to any Future Metaphysics,* translated by P.G. Lucas (Manchester: Manchester University Press, 1962), p. 9.
7. See Plato, *Protagoras and Meno* (London: Penguin Classics).
8. See Andrew Arato and Eike Gebhardt (eds.) *The Essential Frankfurt School Reader* (New York: Continuum Press, 1982).
9. The Frankfurt School was established in 1923, and later moved to New York City (Columbia University) in the 1930s to escape Nazi persecution. It would not move back to Germany until the 1950s. For an excellent historical overview of the Frankfurt School's first generation of theorists, see Martin Jay, *The Dialectical Imagination: The History of the Frankfurt School and the Institute of Social Research, 1923–1950* (Berkeley: University of California Press, 1973).
10. See Stephen Eric Bronner, *Of Critical Theory and its Theorists*, 2nd Edition (New York: Routledge, 2002).
11. Thus, as Tim Dant explains, "critical theory does not seek to objectify distance but aims to be adopted as a mode of knowledge and action by all human beings so that their decisions shape their history, rather than their actions following mechanically those of a system." See Tim Dant, *Critical Social Theory* (London: Sage Publications, 2003) p. 136.
12. Steven Best and Douglas Kellner, *Postmodern Theory: Critical Interrogations* (New York: The Guilford Press, 1991), p. 260.
13. E.H. Carr , *The Twenty Years Crises: 1919-1939,* 2nd Edition (London: Macmillan, 1946), p. 236.
14. Kenneth Waltz, *Theory of International Politics* (Palo Alto, CA: Addison-Wesley, 1979).
15. I derive these two ways from Mark Hoffman's distinction between internal and external critical theory approaches to IR. See Mark Hoffman, "Critical Theory and the Inter-Paradigm Debate," *Millennium: Journal of International Studies*, 16(2) (1987), pp. 231–249.

16. For an excellent overview of realism, see Jack Donnelly, *Realism and International Relations* (Cambridge: Cambridge University Press, 2000).

17. Richard K. Ashley, "Political Realism and Human Interests," *International Studies Quarterly*, 25(2) (June 1981): 204–236.

18. Mark Hoffman, "Critical Theory and the Inter-Paradigm Debate," *Millenium* 16(2) (1987): 238.

19. Alexander Wendt, *Social Theory of International Politics* (Cambridge: Cambridge University Press, 1999).

20. Samuel J. Barkin, "Realist Constructivism," *International Studies Review*, 5(3) (2003): 325.

21. Robert Cox, "Social Forces, States, and World Order: Beyond International Relations Theory," *Millenium* 10(2) (1981).

22. Andrew Linklater, "The Question of the Next Stage in International Relations Theory: A Critical Theoretic Point of View," *Millennium: Journal of International Studies*, 21(2) (1992): 77–98.

23. Yosef Lapid, "The Third Debate: On the Prospects of International Relations Theory in a Post-positivist Era," *International Studies Quarterly*, 33(3): 235–254, 1989.

24. See Charles Beitz, *The Political Theory of International Relations* (Princeton: Princeton University Press, 1979).

25. It should be noted that whereas political theory remains rooted in domestic conceptions of justice and freedom, international theory, by contrast, has traditionally oriented itself to principles of power and interests, which provide the means and ends to regulate state conduct.

26. See John Rawls, *Theory of Justice* (Cambridge, MA: Harvard University Press, 1971). For an excellent introduction of the normative approaches to IR theory, see Chris Brown, *International Relations Theory: New Normative Approaches*. Third Edition (New York: Columbia University Press, 2003).

27. Nicholas Rengger, "Political Theory and International Relations: Promised Land or Exit for Eden?," *International Affairs*, 76: 769, 2000.

28. Yosef Lapid, "The Third Debate: On the Prospects of International Relations Theory in a Positivists Era," p. 244.

29. See Steve Smith, Booth Ken, Zalewski, Marysia, eds. *International Theory: Positivism & Beyond*. (Cambridge: Cambridge University Press, 1996).

30. Christian Heine and Benno Teschke, "Sleeping Beauty and the Dialectical Awakening: On the Potential of Dialectic for International Relations," *Millennium: Journal of International Studies*, (1996), 25(2), pp. 399–423.

31. See Andrew Linklater, "The Changing Contours of Critical International Relations Theory," in Richard Wyn Jones (ed.) *Critical Theory and World Politics* (Boulder, CO: Lynn Reinner Publishers); *op. cit. The Transformation of Political Community* (Cambridge: Polity Press, 1998).

32. See, e.g., Richard Ashley, "Living on Border Lines: Man, Post-structuralism, and War," in James Der Derian and Michael J. Shapiro (eds.), *International/Intertextual Relations*. (New York: Lexington, 1989).

33. Sylvester, Christine, "Empathetic Cooperation: A Feminist Method for IR," *Millennium: Journal of International Relations*, 23(2): 324–334, 1994.

34. Quoted in Bernstein, *The New Constellation*. p. 42.

35. Thomas Diez and Jill Steans, "A Useful Dialogue? Habermas and International Relations," *Review of International Studies*, 31 (2005), 127.

36. Andrew Linklater, "Dialogic Politics and the Civilising Process," *Review of International Studies* 31(1) (January 2005): 141–154.

37. Jürgen Haacke, "The Frankfurt School and International Relations: On the Centrality of Recognition," *Review of International Studies* 31(1) (January 2005): 189–194.

38. Fred Halliday, "The Future of International Relations: Fears and Hopes," in Steve Smith, Ken Booth, and Marysia Zalewski (eds.) *International Theory: Positivism & Beyond* (Cambridge: Cambridge University Press, 1996), pp. 318–327.

39. Christian Heine and Benno Teschke, "Sleeping Beauty and Dialectical Awakening: On the Potential of Dialectic for International Relations," *Millennium: Journal of International Studies*, 24(2): 404–423, 1995.

40. Richard Wyn Jones (ed.) *Critical Theory and World Politics* (Boulder, CO: Lynne Rienner Publishers, 2001).

41. Richard Devetak, "The Project of Modernity and International Relations Theory," *Millennium: Journal of International Studies,* 24(1): 48, 1995.

42. Andrew Linklater, "The Changing Contours of Critical International Relations Theory," in Richard Wyn Jones (ed.) *Critical Theory and World Politics* (Boulder, CO: Lynne Reinner Publishers, 2001); p. 25.

Part I

Abstract Universalism and the Critique of Reason

1

The Roots of Critical Theory
German Idealism

Introduction

This first chapter focuses on the foundations of critical theory (1800–1865). For many writers at this time, the events of the French Revolution (1789–1799) served as a reminder of the volatility of human passions, and the consequent failure to preserve the ideals of freedom, justice, equality, reason, rationality and solidarity. Here, I have included Kant's essays on the "Groundwork of the Metaphysics of Morals" (1785), "The Metaphysics of Morals, Theory of Right (1797)" and "Idea for a Universal History with a Cosmopolitan Purpose (1784)," as well as selections from Hegel's *The Phenomenology of Spirit* (1807) and *The Philosophy of Right* (1821).

Kant conceived politics in terms of the tension between human nature and the civil laws of the state (social contract). It was this antagonism that constituted man's *asocial sociability*, and represented, as Kant states, "a great tendency to live as an individual, to isolate himself since he also encounters in himself the unsocial characteristic of wanting to direct everything in accordance with his own ideas." In his essay on "The Metaphysics of Morals," Kant theorized that civil society (*Civilis-Communitas*) reflected the balance of constitutional rules and state coercion, or "the harmonization of public wills." Here he situated the moral autonomy of the individual (the self-legislating individual) within the antinomies of practical (moral) and pure reason (universal), and experience and understanding. In this way, our understanding was not simply conditioned by passions (happiness and sympathy); it operated independently of the passions, that is, through our reasoned capacity to act in accordance with universal maxims or imperatives.

Following Kant, Hegel showed how this tension could be transcended through the absolutization of spirit. Here he conceptualized the dialectic in historical terms: as the unfolding of absolute freedom or the immanent reconciliation between reason and freedom (*Aufhebung*). In *The Phenomenology of Spirit*, Hegel theorized about the self's struggle to become conscious of itself through various stages or historical moments. The most important [stage] involved the struggle between Lordsman and Bondsman, in which the slave's or bondsman's struggle for freedom became a concrete metaphor for realizing the idea of freedom for and in itself. In *The Philosophy of Right*, the historical struggle entailed the movement through and ultimately beyond the civil society institutions of the German state to one in which the German state would serve as the final concrete expression of the idea of freedom. For as Hegel notes, "the state is the actuality of the ethical Idea."

Despite its profound and lasting influence, Hegel's theory of the state failed to take stock of the persistent tensions between changing societal realities and state power. In the end, Hegel's abstract idealism seemed to cast a veil between the social deprivation of the workers and the economic practices of the bourgeoisie, whose exploitative practices contradicted the (bourgeois-controlled) state's role in preserving individual freedom. How these growing social and economic disparities drove the class struggle for freedom was as much a cognitive idea as it was a material one. It would be this material contradiction that would provide the basis of Marx's seminal analysis of historical materialism.

Endnotes

1. Immanuel Kant, "Idea for Universal History with a Cosmopolitan Right", in *Kant's Political Writings*, Hans Reiss (ed.) (Cambridge: Cambridge University Press, 1989), p. 45.
2. Georg Wilhelm Friedrich Hegel, *The Philosophy of Right* (Oxford: Oxford University Press, 1967), p. 155.

Immanuel Kant, Selection from *Groundwork of the Metaphysics of Morals*

[Imperatives in General]

Everything in nature works in accordance with laws. Only a rational being has the power to act *in accordance with his idea* of laws—that is, in accordance with principles—and only so has he a *will*. Since *reason* is required in order to derive actions from laws, the will is nothing but practical reason. If reason infallibly determines the will, then in a being of this kind the actions which are recognized to be objectively necessary are also subjectively necessary—that is to say, the will is then a power to choose *only that* which reason independently of inclination recognizes to be practically necessary, that is, to be good. But if reason solely by itself is not sufficient to determine the will; if the will is exposed also to subjective conditions (certain impulsions) which do not always harmonize with the objective ones; if, in a word, the will is not *in itself* completely in accord with reason (as actually happens in the case of men); then actions which are recognized to be objectively necessary are subjectively contingent, and the determining of such a will in accordance with objective laws is *necessitation*. That is to say, the relation of objective laws to a will not good through and through is conceived as one in which the will of a rational being, although it is determined by principles of reason, does not necessarily follow these principles in virtue of its own nature.

The conception of an objective principle so far as this principle is necessitating for a will is called a command (of reason), and the formula of this command is called an *Imperative*.

All imperatives are expressed by an '*ought*' (*Sollen*). By this they mark the relation of an objective law of reason to a will which is not necessarily determined by this law in virtue of its subjective constitution (the relation of necessitation). They say that something would be good to do or to leave undone; only they say it to a will which does not always do a thing because it has been informed that this is a good thing to do. The practically *good* is that which determines the will by concepts of reason, and therefore not by subjective causes, but objectively—that is, on grounds valid for every rational being as such. It is distinguished from the *pleasant* as that which influences the will, not as a principle of reason valid for every one, but solely through the medium of sensation by purely subjective causes valid only for the senses of this person or that.

A perfectly good will would thus stand quite as much under objective laws (laws of the good), but it could not on this account be conceded as *necessitated* to act in conformity with law, since of itself, in accordance with its subjective constitution, it can be determined only by the concept of the good. Hence for the *divine* will, and in general for a *holy* will, there are no imperatives: '*I ought*' is here out of place, because '*I will*' is already of itself necessarily in harmony with the law. Imperatives are in consequence only formulae for expressing the relation of objective laws of willing to the subjective imperfection of the will of this or that rational being—for example, of the human will.

[Classification of Imperatives]

All *imperatives* command either *hypothetically* or *categorically*. Hypothetical imperatives declare a possible action to be practically necessary as a means to the attainment of something else that one wills (or that one may will). A categorical imperative would be one which represented an action as objectively necessary in itself apart from its relation to a further end.

Every practical law represents a possible action as good and therefore as necessary for a subject whose actions are determined by reason. Hence all imperatives are formulae for determining an action which is necessary in accordance with the principle of a will in some sense good. If the action would be good solely as a means *to something else*, the imperative is *hypothetical*; if the action is represented as good in *itself* and therefore as necessary, in virtue of its principle, for a will which of itself accords with reason, then the imperative is *categorical*.

An imperative therefore tells me which of my possible actions would be good; and it formulates a practical rule for a will that does not perform an action straight away because the action is good—whether because the subject does not always know that it is good or because, even if he did know this, he might still act on maxims contrary to the objective principles of practical reason.

A hypothetical imperative thus says only that an action is good for some purpose or other, either *possible* or *actual*. In the *first* case, it is a *problematic* practical principle; in the second case, an *assertoric* practical principle. A categorical imperative, which declares an action to be objectively necessary in itself without reference to some purpose—that is, even without any further end—ranks as an *apodeictic* practical principle.

Everything that is possible only through the efforts of some rational being can be conceived as a possible purpose of some will; and consequently there are in fact innumerable principles of action so far as action is thought necessary in order to achieve some possible purpose which can be effected by it. All sciences have a practical part consisting of problems which suppose that some end is possible for us and of imperatives which tell us how it is to be attained. Hence the latter can in general be called imperatives of *skill*. Here there is absolutely no question about the rationality or goodness of the end, but only about what must be done to attain it. A prescription required by a doctor in order to cure his man completely and one required by a poisoner in order to make sure of killing him are of equal value so far as each serves to effect its purpose perfectly. Since in early youth we do not know what ends may present themselves to us in the course of life, parents seek above all to make their children learn things *of many kinds*; they provide carefully for *skill* in the use of means to all sorts of *arbitrary* ends, none of which can they be certain that it could not in the future become an actual purpose of their ward, while it is always *possible* that he might adopt it. Their care in this matter is so great that they commonly neglect on this account to form and correct the judgement of their children about the worth of the things which they might possibly adopt as ends.

There is, however, *one* end that can be presupposed as actual in all rational beings (so far as they are dependent beings to whom imperatives apply); and thus there is one purpose which they not only *can* have, but which we can assume with certainty that they all *do* have by a natural necessity—the purpose, namely, of *happiness*. A hypothetical imperative which affirms the practical necessity of an action as a means to the furtherance of happiness is *assertoric*. We may represent it, not simply as necessary to an uncertain, merely possible purpose, but as necessary to a purpose which we can presuppose *a priori* and with certainty to be present in every man because it belongs to his very being. Now skill in the choice of means to one's own greatest well-being can be called *prudence* in the narrowest sense. Thus an imperative concerned with the choice of means to one's own happiness—that is, a precept of prudence—still remains *hypothetical*: an action is commanded, not absolutely, but only as a means to a further purpose.

Finally, there is an imperative which, without being based on, and conditioned by, any further purpose to be attained by a certain line of conduct, enjoins this conduct immediately. This imperative is *categorical*. It is concerned, not with the matter of the action and its presumed results, but with its form and with the principle from which it follows; and what is essentially good in the action consists in the mental disposition, let the consequences be what they may. This imperative may be called the imperative of *morality*.

Willing in accordance with these three kinds of principle is also sharply distinguished by a *dissimilarity* in the necessitation of the will. To make this dissimilarity obvious, we should, I think, name these kinds of principle most appropriately in their order if we said they were either *rules* of skill or *counsels* of prudence or *commands* (*laws*) of morality. For only *law* carries with it the concept of an *unconditioned*, and yet objective and so universally valid, *necessity*; and commands are laws which must be obeyed—that is, must be followed even against inclination. *Counsel* does indeed involve necessity, but necessity valid only under a subjective and contingent condition—namely, if this or that man counts this or that as belonging to his happiness. As against this, a categorical imperative is limited by no condition and can quite precisely be called a command, as being absolutely, although practically, necessary. We could also call imperatives of the first kind *technical* (concerned with art); of the second kind *pragmatic* (concerned with well-being); of the third kind *moral* (concerned with free conduct as such—that is, with morals).

[How are Imperatives Possible?]

The question now arises 'How are all these imperatives possible?' This question does not ask how we can conceive the execution of an action commanded by the imperative, but merely how we can conceive the necessitation of the will expressed by the imperative in setting us a task. How an imperative of skill is possible requires no special discussion. Who wills the end, wills (so far as reason has decisive influence on his actions) also the means which are indispensably necessary and in his power. So far as willing is concerned, this proposition is analytic: for in my willing of an object as an effect, there is already conceived the causality of myself as an acting cause—that is, the use of means; and from the concept of willing an end, the imperative merely extracts the concept of actions necessary to this end. (Synthetic propositions are required in order to determine the means to a proposed end, but these are concerned, not with the reason for performing the act of will, but with the cause which produces the object.) That, in order to divide a line into two equal parts on a sure principle, I must from its ends describe two intersecting arcs—this is admittedly taught by mathematics only in synthetic propositions; but when I know that the aforesaid effect can be produced only by such an action, the proposition 'If I fully will the effect, I also will the action required for it' is analytic; for it is one and the same thing to conceive something as an effect possible in a certain way through me and to conceive myself as acting in the same way with respect to it.

If it were only as easy to find a determinate concept of happiness, the imperatives of prudence would agree entirely with those of skill and would be equally analytic. For here as there it could alike be said 'Who wills the end, wills also (necessarily, if he accords with reason) the sole means which are in his power.' Unfortunately, however, the concept of happiness is so indeterminate a concept that although every man wants to attain happiness, he can never say definitely and in unison with himself what it really is that he wants and wills. The reason for this is that all the elements which belong to the concept of happiness are without exception empirical—that is, they must be borrowed from experience; but that none the less there is required for the Idea of happiness an absolute whole, a maximum of well-being in my present, and in every future, state. Now it is impossible for the most intelligent, and at the same time most powerful, but nevertheless finite, being to form here a determinate concept of what he really wills. Is it riches that he wants? How much anxiety, envy, and pestering might he not bring in this way on his own head! Is it knowledge and insight? This might perhaps merely give him an eye so sharp that it would make evils at present hidden from him and yet unavoidable seem all the more frightful, or would add a load of still further needs to the desires which already give him trouble enough. Is it long life? Who will guarantee that it would not be a long misery? Is it at least health? How often has infirmity of body kept a man from excesses into which perfect health would have let him fall!—and so on. In short, he has no principle by which he is able to decide with complete certainty what will make him truly happy, since for this he would require omniscience. Thus we cannot act on determinate principles in order to be happy, but only on empirical counsels, for example, of diet, frugality, politeness, reserve, and so on—things which experience shows contribute most to well-being on the average. From this it follows that imperatives of prudence, speaking strictly, do not command at all—that is, cannot exhibit actions objectively as practically *necessary*; that they are rather to be taken as recommendations (*consilia*), than as commands (*praecepta*), of reason; that the problem of determining certainly and universally what action will promote the happiness of a rational being is completely insoluble; and consequently that in regard to this, there is no imperative possible which in the strictest sense could command us to do what will make us happy, since happiness is an Ideal, not of reason, but of imagination—an Idea resting merely on empirical grounds, of which it is vain to expect that they should determine an action by which we could attain the totality of a series of consequences which is in fact infinite. Nevertheless, if we assume that the means to happiness could be discovered with certainty, this imperative of prudence would be an analytic practical proposition; for it differs from the imperative of skill only in this—that in the latter the end is merely possible, while in the former the end is given. In spite of this difference, since both command solely the means to something assumed to be willed as an end, the imperative which commands him who wills the end to will the means is in both cases analytic. Thus there is likewise no difficulty in regard to the possibility of an imperative of prudence.

Beyond all doubt, the question 'How is the imperative of *morality* possible?' is the only one in need of a solution; for it is in no way hypothetical, and consequently we cannot base the objective necessity which it affirms on any presupposition, as we can with hypothetical imperatives. Only we must never forget here that it is impossible to settle *by an example*, and so empirically, whether there is any imperative of this kind at all: we must rather suspect that all imperatives which seem to be categorical may none the less be covertly hypothetical. Take, for example, the saying 'Thou shalt make no false promises.' Let us assume that the necessity for this abstention is no mere advice for the avoidance of some further evil—as it might be said 'You ought not to make a lying promise lest, when this comes to light, you destroy your credit.' Let us hold, on the contrary, that an action of this kind must be considered as bad in itself, and that the imperative of prohibition is therefore categorical. Even so, we cannot with any certainty show by an example that the will is determined here solely by the law without any further motive, although it may appear to be so; for it is always possible that fear of disgrace, perhaps also hidden dread of other risks, may unconsciously influence the will. Who can prove by experience that a cause is not present? Experience shows only that it is not perceived. In such a case, however, the so-called moral imperative, which as such appears to be categorical and unconditioned, would in fact be only a pragmatic prescription calling attention to our advantage and merely bidding us take this into account.

We shall thus have to investigate the possibility of a *categorical* imperative entirely *a priori*, since here we do not enjoy the advantage of having its reality given in experience and so of being obliged merely to explain, and not to establish, its possibility. So much, however, can be seen provisionally—that the categorical imperative alone purports to be a practical *law*, while all the rest may be called *principles* of the will but not laws; for an action necessary merely in order to achieve an arbitrary purpose can be considered as in itself contingent, and we can always escape from the precept if we abandon the purpose; whereas an unconditioned command does not leave it open to the will to do the opposite at its discretion and therefore alone carries with it that necessity which we demand from a law.

In the second place, with this categorical imperative or law of morality, the reason for our difficulty (in comprehending its possibility) is a very serious one. We have here a synthetic *a priori* practical proposition; and since in theoretical knowledge there is so much difficulty in comprehending the possibility of propositions of this kind, it may readily be gathered that in practical knowledge the difficulty will be no less.

[The Formula of Universal Law]

In this task we wish first to enquire whether perhaps the mere concept of a categorical imperative may not also provide us with the formula containing the only proposition that can be a categorical imperative; for even when we know the purport of such an absolute command, the question of its possibility will still require a special and troublesome effort, which we postpone to the final chapter.

When I conceive a *hypothetical* imperative in general, I do not know beforehand what it will contain—until its condition is given. But if I conceive a *categorical* imperative, I know at once what it contains. For since besides the law this imperative contains only the necessity that our maxim should conform to this law, while the law, as we have seen, contains no condition to limit it, there remains nothing over to which the maxim has to conform except the universality of a law as such; and it is this conformity alone that the imperative properly asserts to be necessary.

There is therefore only a single categorical imperative and it is this: '*Act only on that maxim through which you can at the same time will that it should become a universal law.*'

Now if all imperatives of duty can be derived from this one imperative as their principle, then even although we leave it unsettled whether what we call duty may not be an empty concept, we shall still be able to show at least what we understand by it and what the concept means.

[The Formula of the Law of Nature]

Since the universality of the law governing the production of effects constitutes what is properly called *nature* in its most general sense (nature as regards its form)—that is, the existence of things so far as determined by universal laws—the universal imperative of duty may also run as follows: '*Act as if the maxim of your action were to become through your will a universal law of nature.*'

[Illustrations]

We will now enumerate a few duties, following their customary division into duties towards self and duties towards others and into perfect and imperfect duties.

1. A man feels sick of life as the result of a series of misfortunes that has mounted to the point of despair, but he is still so far in possession of his reason as to ask himself whether taking his own life may not be contrary to his duty to himself. He now applies the test 'Can the maxim of my action really become a universal law of nature?' His maxim is 'From self-love I make it my principle to shorten my life if its continuance threatens more evil than it promises pleasure.' The only further question to ask is whether this principle of self-love can become a universal law of nature. It is then seen at once that a system of nature by whose law the very same feeling whose function (*Bestimmung*) is to stimulate the furtherance of life should actually destroy

life would contradict itself and consequently could not subsist as a system of nature. Hence this maxim cannot possibly hold as a universal law of nature and is therefore entirely opposed to the supreme principle of all duty.

2. Another finds himself driven to borrowing money because of need. He well knows that he will not be able to pay it back; but he sees too that he will get no loan unless he gives a firm promise to pay it back within a fixed time. He is inclined to make such a promise; but he has still enough conscience to ask 'Is it not unlawful and contrary to duty to get out of difficulties in this way?' Supposing, however, he did resolve to do so, the maxim of his action would run thus: 'Whenever I believe myself short of money, I will borrow money and promise to pay it back, though I know that this will never be done.' Now this principle of self-love or personal advantage is perhaps quite compatible with my own entire future welfare; only there remains the question 'Is it right?' I therefore transform the demand of self-love into a universal law and frame my question thus: 'How would things stand if my maxim became a universal law?' I then see straight away that this maxim can never rank as a universal law of nature and be self-consistent, but must necessarily contradict itself. For the universality of a law that every one believing himself to be in need can make any promise he pleases with the intention not to keep it would make promising, and the very purpose of promising, itself impossible, since no one would believe he was being promised anything, but would laugh at utterances of this kind as empty shams.

3. A third finds in himself a talent whose cultivation would make him a useful man for all sorts of purposes. But he sees himself in comfortable circumstances, and he prefers to give himself up to pleasure rather than to bother about increasing and improving his fortunate natural aptitudes. Yet he asks himself further 'Does my maxim of neglecting my natural gifts, besides agreeing in itself with my tendency to indulgence, agree also with what is called duty?' He then sees that a system of nature could indeed always subsist under such a universal law, although (like the South Sea Islanders) every man should let his talents rust and should be bent on devoting his life solely to idleness, indulgence, procreation, and, in a word, to enjoyment. Only he cannot possibly *will* that this should become a universal law of nature or should be implanted in us as such a law by a natural instinct. For as a rational being he necessarily wills that all his powers should be developed, since they serve him, and are given him, for all sorts of possible ends.

4. Yet a *fourth* is himself flourishing, but he sees others who have to struggle with great hardships (and whom he could easily help); and he thinks 'What does it matter to me? Let everyone be as happy as Heaven wills or as he can make himself; I won't deprive him of anything; I won't even envy him; only I have no wish to contribute anything to his well-being or to his support in distress!' Now admittedly if such an attitude were a universal law of nature, mankind could get on perfectly well—better no doubt than if everybody prates about sympathy and goodwill, and even takes pains, on occasion, to practise them, but on the other hand cheats where he can, traffics in human rights, or violates them in other ways. But although it is possible that a universal law of nature could subsist in harmony with this maxim, yet it is impossible to *will* that such a principle should hold everywhere as a law of nature. For a will which decided in this way would be in conflict with itself, since many a situation might arise in which the man needed love and sympathy from others, and in which, by such a law of nature sprung from his own will, he would rob himself of all hope of the help he wants for himself.

[The Formula of Autonomy]

This principle of humanity, and in general of every rational agent, *as an end in itself* (a principle which is the supreme limiting condition of every man's freedom of action) is not borrowed from experience; firstly, because it is universal, applying as it does to all rational beings as such, and no experience is adequate to determine universality; secondly, because in it humanity is conceived, not as an end of man (subjectively)— that is, as an object which, as a matter of fact, happens to be made an end—but as an objective end—one which, be our ends what they may, must, as a law, constitute the supreme limiting condition of all subjective ends and so must spring from pure reason. That is to say, the ground for every enactment of practical law lies *objectively in the rule* and in the form of universality which (according to our first principle) makes the rule capable of being a law (and indeed a law of nature); *subjectively*, however, it lies in the *end*; but (according to our second principle) the subject of all ends is to be found in every rational being as an end in himself. From this there now follows our third practical principle for the will—as the supreme condition of the will's conformity with universal practical reason—namely, the Idea *of the will of every rational being as a will which makes universal law.*

By this principle all maxims are repudiated which cannot accord with the will's own enactment of universal law. The will is therefore not merely subject to the law, but is so subject that it must be considered as also *making the law* for itself and precisely on this account as first of all subject to the law (of which it can regard itself as the author).

[The Exclusion of Interest]

Imperatives as formulated above—namely, the imperative enjoining conformity of actions to universal law on the analogy of a *natural order* and that enjoining the *universal supremacy* of rational beings in themselves *as ends*—did, by the mere fact that they were represented as categorical, exclude from their sovereign authority every admixture of interest as a motive. They were, however, merely *assumed* to be categorical because we were bound to make this assumption if we wished to explain the concept of duty. That there were practical propositions which commanded categorically could not itself be proved, any more than it can be proved in this chapter generally; but one thing could have been done—namely, to show that in willing for the sake of duty renunciation of all interest, as the specific mark distinguishing a categorical from a hypothetical imperative, was expressed in the very imperative itself by means of some determination inherent in it. This is what is done in the present third formulation of the principle—namely, in the Idea of the will of every rational being as *a will which makes universal law.*

Once we conceive a will of this kind, it becomes clear that while a will *which is subject to law* may be bound to this law by some interest, nevertheless a will which is itself a supreme lawgiver cannot possibly as such depend on any interest; for a will which is dependent in this way would itself require yet a further law in order to restrict the interest of self-love to the condition that this interest should itself be valid as a universal law.

Thus the *principle* that every human will is *a will which by all its maxims enacts universal law*—provided only that it were right in other ways—would be *well suited* to be a categorical imperative in this respect: that precisely because of the Idea of making universal law, it is *based on no interest* and consequently can alone among all possible imperatives be *unconditioned*. Or better still—to convert the proposition—if there is a categorical imperative (that is, a law for the will of every rational being), it can command us only to act always on the maxim of such a will in us as can at the same time look upon itself as making universal law; for only then is the practical principle and the imperative which we obey unconditioned, since it is wholly impossible for it to be based on any interest.

We need not now wonder, when we look back upon all the previous efforts that have been made to discover the principle of morality, why they have one and all been bound to fail. Their authors saw man as tied to laws by his duty, but it never occurred to them that he is subject only to *laws which are made by himself* and yet are *universal*, and that he is bound only to act in conformity with a will which is his own but has as nature's purpose for it the function of making universal law. For when they thought of man merely as subject to a law (whatever it might be), the law had to carry with it some interest in order to attract or compel, because it did not spring as a law from *his own* will: in order to conform with the law, his will had to be necessitated by *something else* to act in a certain way. This absolutely inevitable conclusion meant that all the labour spent in trying to find a supreme principle of duty was lost beyond recall; for what they discovered was never duty, but only the necessity of acting from a certain interest. This interest might be one's own or another's; but on such a view the imperative was bound to be always a conditioned one and could not possibly serve as a moral law. I will therefore call my principle the principle of the *Autonomy* of the will in contrast with all others, which I consequently class under *Heteronomy*.

[The Formula of the Kingdom of Ends]

The concept of every rational being as one who must regard himself as making universal law by, all the maxims of his will, and must seek to judge himself and his actions from this point of view, leads to a closely connected and very fruitful concept—namely, that of *a kingdom of ends*.

I understand by a '*kingdom*' a systematic union of different rational beings under common laws. Now since laws determine ends as regards their universal validity, we shall be able—if we abstract from the personal differences between rational beings, and also from all the content of their private ends—to conceive a whole of all ends in systematic conjunction (a whole both of rational beings as ends in themselves and also of the personal ends which each may set before himself); that is, we shall be able to conceive a kingdom of ends which is possible in accordance with the above principles.

For rational beings all stand under the *law* that each of them should treat himself and all others, *never merely as a means*, but always *at the same time as an end in himself*. But by so doing there arises a systematic union of rational beings under common objective laws—that is, a kingdom. Since these laws are directed precisely to the relation of such beings to one another as ends and means, this kingdom can be called a kingdom of ends (which is admittedly only an Ideal).

A rational being belongs to the kingdom of ends as a *member*, when, although he makes its universal laws, he is also himself subject to these laws. He belongs to it as its *head*, when as the maker of laws, he is himself subject to the will of no other.

A rational being must always regard himself as making laws in a kingdom of ends which is possible through freedom of the will—whether it be as member or as head. The position of the latter he can maintain, not in virtue of the maxim of his will alone, but only if he is a completely independent being, without needs and with an unlimited power adequate to his will.

Thus, morality consists in the relation of all action to the making of laws whereby alone a kingdom of ends is possible. This making of laws must be found in every rational being himself and must be able to spring from his will. The principle of his will is therefore never to perform an action except on a maxim such as can also be a universal law, and consequently such *that the will can regard itself as at the same time making universal law by means of its maxim*. Where maxims arc not already by their very nature in harmony with this objective principle of rational beings as makers of universal law, the necessity of acting on this principle is practical necessitation—that is, *duty*. Duty does not apply to the head in a kingdom of ends, but it does apply to every member and to all members in equal measure.

The practical necessity of acting on this principles—that is, duty—is in no way based on feelings, impulses, and inclinations, but only on the relation of rational beings to one another, a relation in which the will of a rational being must always be regarded as *making universal law*, because otherwise he could not be conceived as *an end in himself*. Reason thus relates every maxim of the will, considered as making universal law, to every other will and also to every action towards oneself: it does so, not because of any further motive or future advantage, but from the Idea of the *dignity* of a rational being who obeys no law other than that which he at the same time enacts himself.

[The Dignity of Virtue]

In the kingdom of ends everything has either a *price* or a *dignity*. If it has a price, something else can be put in its place as an *equivalent*; if it is exalted above all price and so admits of no equivalent, then it has a dignity.

What is relative to universal human inclinations and needs has a *market price*; what, even without presupposing a need, accords with a certain taste—that is, with satisfaction in the mere purposeless play of our mental powers—has a *fancy price* (*Affektionspreis*); but that which constitutes the sole condition under which anything can be an end in itself has not merely a relative value—that is, a price—but has an intrinsic value—that is, *dignity*.

Now morality is the only condition under which a rational being can be an end in himself; for only through this is it possible to be a law-making member in a kingdom of ends. Therefore morality, and humanity so far as it is capable of morality, is the only thing which has dignity. Skill and diligence in work have a market price; wit, lively imagination, and humour have a fancy price; but fidelity to promises and kindness based on principle (not on instinct) have an intrinsic worth. In default of these, nature and art alike contain nothing to put in their place; for their worth consists, not in the effects which result from them, not in the advantage or profit they produce, but in the attitudes of mind—that is, in the maxims of the will—which are ready in this way to manifest themselves in action even if they are not favoured by success. Such actions too need no recommendation from any subjective disposition or taste in order to meet with immediate favour and approval; they need no immediate propensity or feeling for themselves; they exhibit the will which performs them as an object of immediate reverence; nor is anything other than reason required to *impose* them upon the will, not to *coax* them from the will—which last would anyhow be a contradiction in the case of duties. This assessment reveals as dignity the value of such a mental attitude and puts it infinitely above all price, with which it cannot be brought into reckoning or comparison without, as it were, a profanation of its sanctity.

What is it then that entitles a morally good attitude of mind—or virtue—to make claims so high? It is nothing less than the *share* which it affords to a rational being *in the making of universal law*, and which therefore fits him to be a member in a possible kingdom of ends. For this he was already marked out in virtue of his own proper nature as an end in himself and consequently as a maker of laws in the kingdom of ends—as free in respect of all laws of nature, obeying only those laws which he makes himself and in virtue of which his maxims can have their part in the making of universal law (to which he at the same time subjects himself). For nothing can have a value other than that determined for it by the law. But the law-making which determines all value must for this reason have a dignity—that is, an unconditioned and incomparable worth—for the appreciation of which, as necessarily given by a rational being, the word '*reverence*' is the only becoming expression. *Autonomy* is therefore the ground of the dignity of human nature and of every rational nature.

Immanuel Kant, Selection from *The Metaphysics of Morals*

Introduction to the Theory of Right

§A

Definition of the Theory of Right

The sum total of those laws which can be incorporated in external legislation is termed the *theory of right* (*Ius*). If legislation of this kind actually exists, the theory is one of *positive right*. If a person who is conversant with it or has studied it (*Iuriconsultus*) is acquainted with the external laws in their external function, i.e., in their application to instances encountered in experience, he is said to be *experienced in matters of right* (*Iurisperitus*). This body of theory may amount to the same as *jurisprudence* (*Iurisprudentia*), but it will remain only the *science of right* (*Iuriscientia*) unless both its elements are present. The latter designation applies to a *systematic* knowledge of the theory of natural right (*Ius naturae*), although it is the student of natural right who has to supply the immutable principles on which all positive legislation must rest.

§B

What is Right?

The *jurist*, if he does not wish to lapse into tautology or to base his answer on the laws of a particular country at a particular time instead of offering a comprehensive solution, may well be just as perplexed on being asked this as the logician is by the notorious question: 'What is truth?' He will certainly be able to tell us what is legally right (*quid sit iuris*) within a given context, i.e., what the laws say or have said in a particular place and at a particular time: but whether their provisions are also in keeping with right, and whether they constitute a universal criterion by which we may recognise in general what is right and what is unjust (*iustum et iniustum*), are questions whose answers will remain concealed from him unless he abandons such empirical principles for a time and looks for the sources of these judgements in the realm of pure reason. This will enable him to lay the foundations of all possible positive legislations. And while empirical laws may give him valuable guidance, a purely empirical theory of right, like the wooden head in Phaedrus' fable, may have a fine appearance, but will unfortunately contain no brain.

The concept of right, in so far as it is connected with a corresponding obligation (i.e., the moral concept of right), applies within the following conditions. *Firstly*, it applies only to those relationships between one person and another which are both external and practical, that is, in so far as their actions can in fact influence each other either directly or indirectly. But *secondly*, it does not concern the relationship between the will of one person and the *desires* of another (and hence only the latter's needs, as in acts of benevolence or hardheartedness); it concerns only the relationship between the will of the first and the *will* of the second. And *thirdly*, the will's *material* aspect, i.e., the end which each party intends to accomplish by means of the object of his will, is completely irrelevant in this mutual relationship; for example, we need not ask whether someone who buys goods from me for his own commercial use will gain anything in the process. For we are interested only in the *form* of the relationship between the two wills, in so far as they are regarded as *free*, and in whether the action of one of the two parties can be reconciled with the freedom of the other in accordance with a universal law.

Right is therefore the sum total of those conditions within which the will of one person can be reconciled with the will of another in accordance with a universal law of freedom.

§C

The Universal Principle of Right

'Every action which by itself or by its maxim enables the freedom of each individual's will to co-exist with the freedom of everyone else in accordance with a universal law is *right*.'

Thus if my action or my situation in general can co-exist with the freedom of everyone in accordance with a universal law, anyone who hinders me in either does me an injustice; for this hindrance or resistance cannot co-exist with freedom in accordance with universal laws.

It also follows from this that I cannot be required to make this principle of all maxims my own maxim, i.e., *to make it the maxim of my own actions*; for each individual can be free so long as I do not interfere with his freedom by my *external actions*, even although his freedom may be a matter of total indifference to me or although I may wish in my heart to deprive him of it. That I should make it my maxim to *act* in accordance with right is a requirement laid down for me by ethics.

Thus the universal law of right is as follows: let your external actions be such that the free application of your will can co-exist with the freedom of everyone in accordance with a universal law. And although this law imposes an obligation on me, it does not mean that I am in any way expected, far less required, to restrict my freedom *myself* to these conditions purely for the sake of this obligation. On the contrary, reason merely says that individual freedom *is* restricted in this way by virtue of the idea behind it, and that it may also be actively restricted by others; and it states this as a postulate which does not admit of any further proof.

If it is not our intention to teach virtue, but only to state what is *right*, we may not and should not ourselves represent this law of right as a possible motive for actions.

§D

Right Entails the Authority to Use Coercion

Any resistance which counteracts the hindrance of an effect helps to promote this effect and is consonant with it. Now everything that is contrary to right is a hindrance to freedom based on universal laws, while coercion is a hindrance or resistance to freedom. Consequently, if a certain use to which freedom is put is itself a hindrance to freedom in accordance with universal laws (i.e., if it is contrary to right), any coercion which is used against it will be a *hindrance* to a *hindrance of freedom*, and will thus be consonant with freedom in accordance with universal laws—that is, it will be right. It thus follows by the law of contradiction that right entails the authority to apply coercion to anyone who infringes it.

§E

In its 'strict' Sense, Right can also be envisaged as the Possibility of a general and reciprocal Coercion consonant with the Freedom of Everyone in accordance with Universal Laws

This proposition implies that we should not conceive of right as being composed of two elements, namely, the obligation imposed by a law, and the authority which someone who obligates another party through his will possesses to coerce the latter into carrying out the obligation in question. Instead, the concept of right should be seen as consisting immediately of the possibility of universal reciprocal coercion being combined with the freedom of everyone. For just as the only object of right in general is the external aspect of actions, right in its strict sense, i.e., right unmixed with any ethical considerations, requires no determinants of the will apart from purely external ones; for it will then be pure and will not be confounded with any precepts of virtue. Thus only a completely external right can be called right in the *strict* (or narrow) sense. This right is certainly based on each individual's awareness of his obligations within the law; but if it is to remain pure, it may not and cannot appeal to this awareness as a motive which might determine the will to act in accordance with it, and it therefore depends rather on the principle of the possibility of an external coercion which can coexist with the freedom of everyone in accordance with universal laws.

Thus when it is said that a creditor has a right to require the debtor to pay his debt, it does not mean that he can make the latter feel that his reason itself obliges him to act in this way. It means instead that the use of coercion to compel everyone to do this can very well be reconciled with everyone's freedom, hence, also with the debtor's freedom, in accordance with a universal external law: thus right and the authority to apply coercion mean one and the same thing.

The law of reciprocal coercion, which is necessarily consonant with the freedom of everyone within the principle of universal freedom, is in a sense the *construction* of the concept of right: that is, it represents this concept in pure *a priori* intuition by analogy with the possibility of free movement of bodies within the law of the *equality of action and reaction*. Just as the qualities of an object of pure mathematics cannot be directly deduced from the concept but can only be discovered from its construction, it is not so much the *concept* of right but rather a general, reciprocal and uniform coercion, subject to universal laws and harmonising with the concept itself, which makes any representation of the concept possible. But while this concept of dynamics (i.e., that of the equality of action and reaction) is based upon a purely formal concept of pure mathematics (e.g., of geometry), reason has taken care that the understanding is likewise as fully equipped as possible with *a priori* intuitions for the construction of the concept of right.

In geometry, the term 'right' (*rectum*), in the sense of '*straight*,' can be used either as the opposite of '*curved*' or of '*oblique*.' In the first sense, it applies to a line whose *intrinsic nature* is such that there can be only *one* of its kind between two given *points*. But in the second sense, it applies to an *angle* between two intersecting or coincident *lines* whose nature is such that there can be only *one* of its kind (a right angle) between the given lines. The perpendicular line which forms a right angle will not incline more to one side than to the other, and will divide the area on either side of it into two equal parts. By this analogy, the theory of right will also seek an assurance that each individual receives (with mathematical precision) *what is his due*. This cannot be expected of *ethics*, however, for it cannot refuse to allow some room for exceptions (*latitudinem*).

(Editor's Note: Kant then adds some remarks on "equivocal right." He does not mean right in the strict sense, but in the wider sense of the word. Only two aspects of right arise here: equity and the right of necessity. Kant remarks of equity that it concerns only such cases as are outside strict right, i.e., where there is no case in law at all. The right of necessity applies to cases where one acts against someone else (for instance, by taking someone else's life because one's own life is in danger). A man cannot be punished with any greater punishment than the loss of life itself. There can be therefore no law punishing a man who acts out of necessity. Kant explains the division of the theory of right into private and public right. He also distinguishes between innate and acquired rights. In his view, freedom (i.e., independence from the coercive will of another), in so far as it can co-exist with the freedom of everyone else in accordance with a universal law, is the sole original right. It belongs to every man by virtue of his humanity. Equality, honesty, and the right to act towards others in such a way that their rights are not infringed all derive from this right of freedom. Kant also provides a general division of the metaphysics of morals, distinguishing between those duties which are duties of right and those which are duties of virtue. In the first section of *The Metaphysical Elements of Right*, Kant deals with private right which is concerned with property. There are two kinds of property: property which one possesses directly through physical possession and property which one only possesses indirectly. Kant examines the philosophical foundations of the law of property, deducing it from the idea of original communal possession of the soil. He also argues that external possession of things of which we are not in physical possession is possible only because we are noumenal beings, not necessarily bound by the limits of mere empirical (phenomenal) possessions. Kant goes on to argue that external possessions are possible only in a state of civil society, whereas, in a state of nature, such possession can have only a provisional character. Subsequently, Kant deals with the right of acquiring things and with various other rights, such as the rights of persons, marriage, parentage, landlords, contract, money, books, inheritance, etc. His discussion of the theory of private right is followed by a discussion of the theory of public right, which is printed below.)

The Theory of Right, Part II: Public Right
Section I: Political Right

§43

Public right is the sum total of those laws which require to be made universally public in order to produce a state of right. It is therefore a system of laws for a people, i.e., an aggregate of human beings, or for an aggregate of peoples. Since these individuals or peoples must influence one another, they need to live in a state of right under a unifying will: that is, they require a *constitution* in order to enjoy their rights.

A condition in which the individual members of a people are related to each other in this way is said to be a *civil* one (*status civilis*), and when considered as a whole in relation to its own members, it is called *a state* (*civitas*). Since the state takes the form of a union created by the common interest of everyone in living in a state of right, it is called a *commonwealth* (*res publica latius sic dicta*). In relation to other peoples, however, it is simply called a *power* (*potentia*—hence the word 'potentate'); and if it claims to be united by heredity, it may also call itself a *congeneric nation* (*gens*). Within the general concept of public right, we must therefore include not only *political right* but also *international right* (*ius gentium*). And since the earth's surface is not infinite but limited by its own configuration, these two concepts taken together necessarily lead to the idea of an *international political right* (*ius gentium*) or a *cosmopolitan right* (*ius cosmopoliticum*). Consequently, if even only one of these three possible forms of rightful state lacks a principle which limits external freedom by means of laws, the structure of all the rest must inevitably be undermined, and finally collapse.

§44

Experience teaches us the maxim that human beings act in a violent and malevolent manner, and that they tend to fight among themselves until an external coercive legislation supervenes. But it is not experience or any kind of factual knowledge which makes public legal coercion necessary. On the contrary, even if we imagine men to be as benevolent and law-abiding as we please, the *a priori* rational idea of a non-lawful state will still tell us that before a public and legal state is established, individual men, peoples and states can never be secure against acts of violence from one another, since each will have his own right to do *what seems right and good to him*, independently of the opinion of others. Thus the first decision the individual is obliged to make, if he does not wish to renounce all concepts of right, will be to adopt the principle that one must abandon the state of nature in which everyone follows his own desires, and unite with everyone else (with whom he cannot avoid having intercourse) in order to submit to external, public and lawful coercion. He must accordingly enter into a state wherein that which is to be recognised as belonging to each person is allotted to him *by law* and guaranteed to him by an adequate power (which is not his own, but external to him). In other words, he should at all costs enter into a state of civil society.

    The state of nature need not necessarily be a *state of injustice* (*iniustus*) merely because those who live in it treat one another solely in terms of the amount of power they possess. But it is a *state devoid of justice* (*status iustitia vacuus*), for if a *dispute* over rights (*ius controversum*) occurs in it, there is no competent judge to pronounce legally valid decisions. Anyone may thus use force to impel the others to abandon this state for a state of right. For although each individual's *concepts of right* may imply that an external object can be acquired by occupation or by contract, this acquisition is only provisional until it has been sanctioned by a public law, since it is not determined by any public (distributive) form of justice and is not guaranteed by any institution empowered to exercise this right.

    If no-one were willing to recognise any acquisition as rightful, not even provisionally so, before a civil state had been established, the civil state would itself be impossible. For in relation to their form, the laws relating to property contain exactly the same things in a state of nature as they would prescribe in a civil state, in so far as we conceive of this state only in terms of concepts of pure reason. The only difference is that in the second case, the conditions under which the laws are applied (in accordance with distributive justice) are given. Thus if there were not even a *provisional* system of external property in the state of nature, there would not be any rightful duties in it either, so that there could not be any commandment to abandon it.

§45

A state (*civitas*) is a union of an aggregate of men under rightful laws. In so far as these laws are necessary *a priori* and follow automatically from concepts of external right in general (and are not just set up by statute), the form of the state will be that of a state in the absolute sense, i.e., as the idea of what a state ought to be according to pure principles of right. This idea can serve as an internal guide (*norma*) for every actual case where men unite to form a commonwealth.

Every state contains three powers, i.e., the universally united will is made up of three separate persons (*trias politica*). These are the *ruling power* (or sovereignty) in the person of the legislator, the *executive power* in the person of the individual who governs in accordance with the law, and the *judicial power* (which allots to everyone what is his by law) in the person of the judge (*potestas legislatoria, rectoria et iudiciaria*). They can be likened to the three propositions in a practical operation of reason: the major premise, which contains the *law* of the sovereign will, the minor premise, which contains the *command* to act in accordance with the law (i.e., the principle of subsumption under the general will), and the conclusion, which contains the *legal decision* (the sentence) as to the rights and wrongs of each particular case.

§46

The legislative power can belong only to the united will of the people. For since all right is supposed to emanate from this power, the laws it gives must be absolutely *incapable* of doing anyone an injustice. Now if someone makes dispositions for *another* person, it is always possible that he may thereby do him an injustice, although this is never possible in the case of decisions he makes for himself (for *volenti non fit iniuria*). Thus only the unanimous and combined will of everyone whereby each decides the same for all and all decide the same for each—in other words, the general united will of the people—can legislate.

The members of such a society (*societas civilis*) or state who unite for the purpose of legislating are known as *citizens* (*cives*), and the three rightful attributes which are inseparable from the nature of a citizen as such are as follows: firstly, lawful *freedom* to obey no law other than that to which he has given his consent; secondly, civil *equality* in recognising no-one among the people as superior to himself, unless it be someone whom he is just as morally entitled to bind by law as the other is to bind him; and thirdly, the attribute of civil *independence* which allows him to owe his existence and sustenance not to the arbitrary will of anyone else among the people, but purely to his own rights and powers as a member of the commonwealth (so that he may not, as a civil personality, be represented by anyone else in matters of right).

Fitness to vote is the necessary qualification which every citizen must possess. To be fit to vote, a person must have an independent position among the people. He must therefore be not just a part of the commonwealth, but a member of it, i.e., he must by his own free will actively participate in a community of other people. But this latter quality makes it necessary to distinguish between the *active* and the *passive* citizen, although the latter concept seems to contradict the definition of the concept of a citizen altogether. The following examples may serve to overcome this difficulty. Apprentices to merchants or tradesmen, servants who are not employed by the state, minors (*naturaliter vel civiliter*), women in general and all those who are obliged to depend for their living (i.e., for food and protection) on the offices of others (excluding the state)—all of these people have no civil personality, and their existence is, so to speak, purely inherent. The woodcutter whom I employ on my premises; the blacksmith in India who goes from house to house with his hammer, anvil and bellows to do work with iron, as opposed to the European carpenter or smith who can put the products of his work up for public sale; the domestic tutor as opposed to the academic, the tithe-holder as opposed to the farmer; and so on—they are all mere auxiliaries to the commonwealth, for they have to receive orders or protection from other individuals, so that they do not possess civil independence.

This dependence upon the will of others and consequent inequality does not, however, in any way conflict with the freedom and equality of all men as *human beings* who together constitute a people. On the contrary, it is only by accepting these conditions that such a people can become a state and enter into a civil constitution. But all are not equally qualified within this constitution to possess the right to vote, i.e., to be citizens and not just subjects among other subjects. For from the fact that as passive members of the state, they can demand to be treated by all others in accordance with laws of natural freedom and equality, it does not follow that they also have a right to influence or organise the state itself as *active* members, or to co-operate in introducing particular laws. Instead, it only means that the positive laws to which the voters agree, of whatever sort they may be, must not be at variance with the natural laws of freedom and with the corresponding equality of all members of the people whereby they are allowed to work their way up from their passive condition to an active one.

§47

All of the three powers within the state are dignities, and since they necessarily follow from the general idea of a state as elements essential for its establishment (constitution), they are *political dignities*. They involve a relationship between a universal *sovereign* (who, if considered in the light of laws of freedom, can be none other than the united people itself) and the scattered mass of the people as subjects, i.e., a relationship of *commander* (*imperans*) to him who *obeys* (*subditus*). The act by which the people constitutes a state for itself, or more precisely, the mere idea of such an act (which alone enables us to consider it valid in terms of right), is the *original contract*. By this contract, all members of the people (*omnes et singuli*) give up their external freedom in order to receive it back at once as members of a commonwealth, i.e., of the people regarded as a state (*universi*). And we cannot say that men within a state have sacrificed a *part* of their inborn external freedom for a specific purpose; they have in fact completely abandoned their wild and lawless freedom, in order to find again their entire and undiminished freedom in a state of lawful dependence (i.e., in a state of right), for this dependence is created by their own legislative will.

§48

The three powers in the state are related to one another in the following ways. Firstly, as moral persons, they are co-ordinate (*potestates coordinatae*), i.e., each is complementary to the others in forming the complete constitution of the state (*complementum ad sufficientiam*). But secondly, they are also *subordinate* (*subordinatae*) to one another, so that the one cannot usurp any function of the others to which it minis-ters; for each has its own principle, so that although it issues orders in the quality of a distinct person, it does so under the condition of a superior person's will. Thirdly, the combination of both relationships described above assures every subject of his rights.

It can be said of these powers, considered in their appropriate dignity, that the will of the *legislator* (*legislatoris*) in relation to external property cannot be reproached (i.e., it is irreprehensible), that the executive power of the supreme *ruler* (*summi recto-ris*) cannot be opposed (i.e., it is irresistible), and that the verdict of the supreme *judge* (*supremi iudicis*) cannot be altered (i.e., it is without appeal).

§49

The *ruler* of the state (*rex, princeps*) is that moral or physical person who wields the executive power (*potestas executoria*). He is the *agent* of the state who appoints the magistrates, and who prescribes rules for the people so that each may acquire some-thing or retain what is his by law (i.e., by subsuming individual cases under the law). If the ruler is taken to be a moral person, he is called the *directory* or government. His *commands* to the people, the magistrates, and their superiors (ministers) who are responsible for *administering the state* (*gubernatio*), are not laws but ordinances or decrees; for they depend upon decisions in particular cases and are issued subject to revision. A *government* which were also to make *laws* would be called a *despotic* as opposed to a *patriotic* government. This is not to be confused with a *paternal* govern-ment (*regimen paternale*); the latter is the most despotic kind of all, for it treats the citizens like children. A patriotic government (*regimen civitatis et patriae*) means that although the state itself (*civitas*) treats its subjects as if they were members of one family, it also treats them as citizens of the state, i.e., in accordance with laws guar-anteeing their own independence. Thus each is responsible for himself and does not depend upon the absolute will of anyone equal or superior to him.

The sovereign of the people (the legislator) cannot therefore also be the *ruler*, for the ruler is subject to the law, through which he is consequently beholden to *another* party, i.e., the sovereign. The sovereign may divest the ruler of his power, depose him, or reform his administration, but he cannot *punish* him. (And that is the real meaning of the common English saying that the king—i.e., the supreme executive authority—can do no wrong.) For to punish the ruler would in turn be an act of the executive power, which alone possesses the supreme authority to apply *coercion* in accordance with the law, and such a punishment would mean subjecting the execu-tive power itself to coercion, which is self-contradictory.

Finally, neither the sovereign nor the ruler may *pass judgement*; they can only appoint judges as magistrates. The people judge themselves, through those fellow-citizens whom they have nominated as their representatives, by free election, for each particular juridical act. For a legal decision or sentence is a particular act of public justice (*iustitiae distributivae*) by an administrator of the state (a judge or court of law) upon a subject; i.e., one who belongs to the people, and it does not carry the necessary authority to grant or assign to the subject that which is his. Now since each member of the people is purely passive in his relationship to the supreme authority, it would be possible for either the legislative or the executive power to do him an injustice in any decision it might make in a controversial case involving that which belongs to the subject; for it would not be an action of the people themselves in pronouncing a fellow citizen *guilty* or *not guilty*. After the facts of a legal suit have thus been established, the court of law has the judicial authority to put the law into practice and to ensure, by means of the executive authority, that each person receives his due. Thus only the *people*, albeit through the indirect means of the representatives they have themselves appointed (i.e., the jury), can pass judgement upon anyone of their own number. Besides, it would be beneath the dignity of the head of state to act the part of a judge, i.e., to put himself in a position where he could do some injustice, and thus give cause for an appeal to some higher authority (*a rege male formato ad regem melius informandum*).

There are thus three distinct powers (*potestas legislatoria, executoria, iudiciaria*) which give the state (*civitas*) its autonomy, that is, which enable the state to establish and maintain itself in accordance with laws of freedom. The *welfare* of the state consists in the union of these powers (*salus reipublicae suprema lex est*). But this welfare must not be understood as synonymous with the *well-being* and *happiness* of the citizens, for it may well be possible to attain these in a more convenient and desirable way within a state of nature (as Rousseau declares), or even under a despotic regime. On the contrary, the welfare of the state should be seen as that condition in which the constitution most closely approximates to the principles of right; and reason, *by a categorical imperative*, obliges us to strive for its realisation.

Immanuel Kant, "Idea for a Universal History with a Cosmopolitan Purpose"*

Whatever conception of the freedom of the will one may form in terms of metaphysics, the will's manifestations in the world of phenomena, i.e., human actions, are determined in accordance with natural laws, as is every other natural event. History is concerned with giving an account of these phenomena, no matter how deeply concealed their causes may be, and it allows us to hope that, if it examines the free exercise of the human will *on a large scale*, it will be able to discover a regular progression among freely willed actions. In the same way, we may hope that what strikes us in the actions of individuals as confused and fortuitous may be recognised, in the history of the entire species, as a steadily advancing but slow development of man's original capacities. Thus marriages, births, and deaths do not seem to be subject to any rule by which their numbers could be calculated in advance, since the free human will has such a great influence upon them; and yet the annual statistics for them in large countries prove that they are just as subject to constant natural laws as are the changes in the weather, which in themselves are so inconsistent that their individual

---

* A passage printed this year among other brief notices in the twelfth issue of the Gothaische Gelehrte Zeitungen, based, no doubt, on a conversation of mine with a passing scholar, calls for the present elucidation, without which the passage referred to would be unintelligible.

occurrence cannot be determined in advance, but which nevertheless do not fail as a whole to sustain the growth of plants, the flow of rivers, and other natural functions in a uniform and uninterrupted course. Individual men and even entire nations little imagine that, while they are pursuing their own ends, each in his own way and often in opposition to others, they are unwittingly guided in their advance along a course intended by nature. They are unconsciously promoting an end which, even if they knew what it was, would scarcely arouse their interest.

Since men neither pursue their aims purely by instinct, as the animals do, nor act in accordance with any integral, prearranged plan like rational cosmopolitans, it would appear that no law-governed history of mankind is possible (as it would be, for example, with bees or beavers). We can scarcely help feeling a certain distaste on observing their activities as enacted in the great world-drama, for we find that, despite the apparent wisdom of individual actions here and there, everything as a whole is made up of folly and childish vanity, and often of childish malice and destructiveness. The result is that we do not know what sort of opinion we should form of our species, which is so proud of its supposed superiority. The only way out for the philosopher, since he cannot assume that mankind follows any rational *purpose of its own* in its collective actions, is for him to attempt to discover a *purpose in nature* behind this senseless course of human events, and decide whether it is after all possible to formulate in terms of a definite plan of nature a history of creatures who act without a plan of their own.—Let us now see if we can succeed in finding a guiding principle for such a history, and then leave it to nature to produce someone capable of writing it along the lines suggested. Thus nature produced a Kepler who found an unexpected means of reducing the eccentric orbits of the planets to definite laws, and a Newton who explained these laws in terms of a universal natural cause.

First Proposition

All the natural capacities of a creature are destined sooner or later to be developed completely and in conformity with their end. This can be verified in all animals by external and internal or anatomical examination. An organ which is not meant for use or an arrangement which does not fulfil its purpose is a contradiction in the teleological theory of nature. For if we abandon this basic principle, we are faced not with a law-governed nature, but with an aimless, random process, and the dismal reign of chance replaces the guiding principle of reason.

Second Proposition

In man (as the only rational creature on earth), *those natural capacities which are directed towards the use of his reason are such that they could be fully developed only in the species, but not in the individual.* Reason, in a creature, is a faculty which enables that creature to extend far beyond the limits of natural instinct the rules and intentions it follows in using its various powers, and the range of its projects is unbounded. But reason does not itself work instinctively, for it requires trial, practice and instruction to enable it to progress gradually from one stage of insight to the next. Accordingly, every individual man would have to live for a vast length of time if he were to learn how to make complete use of all his natural capacities; or if nature has fixed only a short term for each mans life (as is in fact the case), then it will require a long, perhaps incalculable series of generations, each passing on its enlightenment to the next, before the germs implanted by nature in our species can be developed to that degree which corresponds to natures original intention. And the point of time at which this degree of development is reached must be the goal of man's aspirations (at least as an idea in his mind), or else his natural capacities would necessarily appear by and large to be purposeless and wasted. In the latter case, all practical principles would have to be abandoned, and nature, whose wisdom we must take as axiomatic in judging all other situations, would incur the suspicion of indulging in childish play in the case of man alone.

Third Proposition

Nature has willed that man should produce entirely by his own initiative everything which goes beyond the mechanical ordering of his animal existence, and that he should not partake of any other happiness or perfection than that which he has procured for himself without instinct and by his own reason. For nature does nothing unnecessarily and is not extravagant in the means employed to reach its ends. Nature gave man reason, and freedom of will based upon reason, and this in itself was a clear indication of nature's intention as regards his endowments. For it showed that man was not meant to be guided by instinct or equipped and instructed by innate knowledge; on the contrary, he was meant to produce everything out of himself. Everything had to be entirely of his own making—the discovery of a suitable diet, of clothing, of external security and defence (for which nature gave him neither the bull's horns, the lion's claws, nor the dog's teeth, but only his hands), as well as all the pleasures that can make life agreeable, and even his insight and circumspection and the goodness of his will. Nature seems here to have taken pleasure in exercising the strictest economy and to have measured out the basic animal equipment so sparingly as to be just enough for the most pressing needs of the beginnings of existence. It seems as if nature had intended that man, once he had finally worked his way up from the uttermost barbarism to the highest degree of skill, to inner perfection in his manner of thought and thence (as far as is possible on earth) to happiness, should be able to take for himself the entire credit for doing so and have only himself to thank for it. It seems that nature has worked more with a view to man's rational *self-esteem* than to his mere well-being. For in the actual course of human affairs, a whole host of hardships awaits him. Yet nature does not seem to have been concerned with seeing that man should live agreeably, but with seeing that he should work his way onwards to make himself by his own conduct worthy of life and well-being. What remains disconcerting about all this is firstly, that the earlier generations seem to perform their laborious tasks only for the sake of the later ones, so as to prepare for them a further stage from which they can raise still higher the structure intended by nature; and secondly, that only the later generations will in fact have the good fortune to inhabit the building on which a whole series of their forefathers (admittedly, without any conscious intention) had worked without themselves being able to share in the happiness they were preparing. But no matter how puzzling this may be, it will appear as necessary as it is puzzling if we simply assume that one animal species was intended to have reason, and that, as a class of rational beings who are mortal as individuals but immortal as a species, it was still meant to develop its capacities completely.

Fourth Proposition

The means which nature employs to bring about the development of innate capacities is that of antagonism within society, in so far as this antagonism becomes in the long run the cause of a law-governed social order. By antagonism, I mean in this context the *unsocial sociability* of men, that is, their tendency to come together in society, coupled, however, with a continual resistance which constantly threatens to break this society up. This propensity is obviously rooted in human nature. Man has an inclination to *live in society*, since he feels in this state more like a man, that is, he feels able to develop his natural capacities. But he also has a great tendency to *live as an individual*, to isolate himself, since he also encounters in himself the unsocial characteristic of wanting to direct everything in accordance with his own ideas. He therefore expects resistance all around, just as he knows of himself that he is in turn inclined to offer resistance to others. It is this very resistance which awakens all man's powers and induces him to overcome his tendency to laziness. Through the desire for honour, power or property, it drives him to seek status among his fellows, whom he cannot *bear* yet cannot *bear to leave*. Then the first true steps are taken from barbarism to culture, which in fact consists in the social worthiness of man. All man's talents are now gradually developed, his taste cultivated, and by a continued process of enlightenment, a beginning is made towards establishing a way of thinking which can with time transform the primitive natural capacity for moral discrimination into definite practical principles; and thus a *pathologically* enforced social union is transformed into a *moral* whole. Without these asocial qualities (far from admirable in themselves) which cause the resistance inevitably encountered by each individual as he furthers his self-seeking pretensions, man would live an Arcadian, pastoral existence of perfect concord, self-sufficiency and mutual love. But all human talents would remain hidden forever in a dormant state, and men, as good-natured as the sheep they tended, would scarcely render their existence more valuable than that of their animals. The end for which they were created, their rational nature, would be an unfilled void. Nature should thus be thanked for fostering social incompatibility, enviously competitive vanity, and insatiable desires for possession or even power. Without these desires, all man's excellent natural capacities would never be roused to develop. Man wishes concord, but nature, knowing better what is good for his species, wishes discord. Man wishes to live comfortably and pleasantly, but nature intends that he should abandon idleness and inactive self-sufficiency and plunge instead into labour and hardships, so that he may by his own adroitness find means of liberating himself from them in turn. The natural impulses which make this possible, the sources of the very unsociableness and continual resistance which cause so many evils, at the same time encourage man towards new exertions of his powers and thus towards further development of his natural capacities. They would thus seem to indicate the design of a wise creator—not, as it might seem, the hand of a malicious spirit who had meddled in the creators glorious work or spoiled it out of envy.

Fifth Proposition

The greatest problem for the human species, the solution of which nature compels him to seek, is that of attaining a civil society which can administer justice universally.

The highest purpose of nature—i.e., the development of all natural capacities—can be fulfilled for mankind only in society, and nature intends that man should accomplish this, and indeed all his appointed ends, by his own efforts. This purpose can be fulfilled only in a society which has not only the greatest freedom, and therefore a continual antagonism among its members, but also the most precise specification and preservation of the limits of this freedom in order that it can co-exist with the freedom of others. The highest task which nature has set for mankind must therefore be that of establishing a society in which *freedom under external laws* would be combined to the greatest possible extent with irresistible force, in other words of establishing a perfectly *just civil constitution*. For only through the solution and fulfillment of this task can nature accomplish its other intentions with our species. Man, who is otherwise so enamoured with unrestrained freedom, is forced to enter this state of restriction by sheer necessity. And this is indeed the most stringent of all forms of necessity, for it is imposed by men upon themselves, in that their inclinations make it impossible for them to exist side by side for long in a state of wild freedom. But once enclosed within a precinct like that of civil union, the same inclinations have the most beneficial effect. In the same way, trees in a forest, by seeking to deprive each other of air and sunlight, compel each other to find these by upward growth, so that they grow beautiful and straight—whereas those which put out branches at will, in freedom and in isolation from others, grow stunted, bent and twisted. All the culture and art which adorn mankind and the finest social order man creates are fruits of his unsociability. For it is compelled by its own nature to discipline itself, and thus, by enforced art, to develop completely the germs which nature implanted.

Sixth Proposition

This problem is both the most difficult and the last to be solved by the human race.
The difficulty (which the very idea of this problem clearly presents) is this: if he lives among others of his own species, man *is an animal who needs a master.* For he certainly abuses his freedom in relation to others of his own kind. And even although, as a rational creature, he desires a law to impose limits on the freedom of all, he is still misled by his self-seeking animal inclinations into exempting himself from the law where he can. He thus requires a *master* to break his self-will and force him to obey a universally valid will under which everyone can be free. But where is he to find such a master? Nowhere else but in the human species. But this master will also be an animal who needs a master. Thus while man may try as he will, it is hard to see how he can obtain for public justice a supreme authority which would itself be just, whether

he seeks this authority in a single person or in a group of many persons selected for this purpose. For each one of them will always misuse his freedom if he does not have anyone above him to apply force to him as the laws should require it. Yet the highest authority has to be just *in itself* and yet also a *man*. This is therefore the most difficult of all tasks, and a perfect solution is impossible. Nothing straight can be constructed from such warped wood as that which man is made of. Nature only requires of us that we should approximate to this idea. A further reason why this task must be the last to be accomplished is that man needs for it a correct conception of the nature of a possible constitution, great experience tested in many affairs of the world, and above all else a good will prepared to accept the findings of this experience. But three factors such as these will not easily be found in conjunction, and if they are, it will happen only at a late stage and after many unsuccessful attempts.

Seventh Proposition

The problem of establishing a perfect civil constitution is subordinate to the problem of a law-governed external relationship with other states, and cannot be solved unless the latter is also solved. What is the use of working for a law-governed civil constitution among individual men, i.e., of planning a *commonwealth*? The same unsociability which forced men to do so gives rise in turn to a situation whereby each commonwealth, in its external relations (i.e., as a state in relation to other states), is in a position of unrestricted freedom. Each must accordingly expect from any other precisely the same evils which formerly oppressed individual men and forced them into a law-governed civil state. Nature has thus again employed the unsociableness of men, and even of the large societies and states which human beings construct, as a means of arriving at a condition of calm and security through their inevitable *antagonism*. Wars, tense and unremitting military preparations, and the resultant distress which every state must eventually feel within itself, even in the midst of peace—these are the means by which nature drives nations to make initially imperfect attempts, but finally, after many devastations, upheavals and even complete inner exhaustion of their powers, to take the step which reason could have suggested to them even without so many sad experiences—that of abandoning a lawless state of savagery and entering a federation of peoples in which every state, even the smallest, could expect to derive its security and rights not from its own power or its own legal judgement, but solely from this great federation (*Fœdus Amphictyonum*), from a united power and the law-governed decisions of a united will. However wild and fanciful this idea may appear—and it has been ridiculed as such when put forward by the Abbé St Pierre and Rousseau (perhaps because they thought that its realisation was so imminent)—it is nonetheless the inevitable outcome of the distress in which men involve one another. For this distress must force the states to make exactly the same decision (however difficult it may be for them) as that which man was forced to make, equally unwillingly, in his savage state—the decision to renounce his brutish freedom and seek calm and security within a law-governed constitution. All wars are accordingly so many attempts (not indeed by the intention of men, but by the intention of nature) to bring about new relations between states, and, by the destruction or at least the dismemberment of old entities, to create new ones. But these new bodies, either in themselves or alongside one another, will in turn be unable to survive, and will thus necessarily undergo further revolutions of a similar sort, till finally, partly by an optimal internal arrangement of the civil constitution, and partly by common external agreement and legislation, a state of affairs is created which, like a civil commonwealth, can maintain itself *automatically*.

Whether we should firstly expect that the states, by an Epicurean concourse of efficient causes, should enter by random collisions (like those of small material particles) into all kinds of formations which are again destroyed by new collisions, until they arrive *by chance* at a formation which can survive in its existing form (a lucky accident which is hardly likely ever to occur); or whether we should assume as a second possibility that nature in this case follows a regular course in leading our species gradually upwards from the lower level of animality to the highest level of humanity through forcing man to employ an art which is nonetheless his own, and hence that nature develops man's original capacities by a perfectly regular process within this apparently disorderly arrangement; or whether we should rather accept the third possibility that nothing at all, or at least nothing rational, will anywhere emerge from all these actions and counter-actions among men as a whole, that things will remain as they have always been, and that it would thus be impossible to predict whether the discord which is so natural to our species is not preparing the way for a hell of evils to overtake us, however civilised our condition, in that nature, by barbaric devastation, might perhaps again destroy this civilised state and all the cultural progress hitherto achieved (a fate against which it would be impossible to guard under a rule of blind chance, with which the state of lawless freedom is in fact identical, unless we assume that the latter is secretly guided by the wisdom of nature)—these three possibilities boil down to the question of whether it is rational to assume that the order of nature is *purposive* in its parts but *purposeless* as a whole.

While the purposeless state of savagery did hold up the development of all the natural capacities of human beings, it nonetheless finally forced them, through the evils in which it involved them, to leave this state and enter into a civil constitution in which all their dormant capacities could be developed. The same applies to the barbarous freedom of established states. For while the full development of natural capacities is here likewise held up by the expenditure of each commonwealth's whole resources on armaments against the others, and by the depredations caused by war (but most of all by the necessity of constantly remaining in readiness for war), the resultant evils still have a beneficial effect. For they compel our species to discover a law of equilibrium to regulate the essentially healthy hostility which prevails among the states and is produced by their freedom. Men are compelled to reinforce this law by introducing a system of united power, hence a cosmopolitan system of general political security. This state of affairs is not completely free from *danger*, lest human energies should lapse into inactivity, but it is also not without a principle of *equality* governing the *actions and counter-actions* of these energies, lest they should destroy one another. When it is little beyond the half-way mark in its development, human nature has to endure the hardest of evils under the guise of outward prosperity before this final step (i.e., the union of states) is taken; and Rousseau's preference for the state of savagery does not appear so very mistaken if only we leave out of consideration this last stage which our species still has to surmount. We are *cultivated* to a high degree by art and science. We are *civilised* to the point of excess in all kinds of social courtesies and proprieties. But we are still a long way from the point where we could consider ourselves *morally* mature. For while the idea of morality is indeed present in culture, an application of this idea which only extends to the semblances of morality, as in love of honour and outward propriety, amounts merely to civilisation. But as long as states apply all their resources to their vain and violent schemes of expansion, thus incessantly obstructing the slow and laborious efforts of their citizens to cultivate their minds, and even deprive them of all support in these efforts, no progress in this direction can be expected. For a long internal process of careful work on the part of each commonwealth is necessary for the education of its citizens. But all good enterprises which are not grafted on to a morally good attitude of mind are nothing but illusion and outwardly glittering misery. The human race will no doubt remain in this condition until it has worked itself out of the chaotic state of its political relations in the way I have described.

Eighth Proposition

The history of the human race as a whole can be regarded as the realisation of a hidden plan of nature to bring about an internally—and for this purpose also externally—perfect political constitution as the only possible state within which all natural capacities of mankind can be developed completely. This proposition follows from the previous one. We can see that philosophy too may have its *chiliastic* expectations; but they are of such a kind that their fulfilment can be hastened, if only indirectly, by a knowledge of the idea they are based on, so that they are anything but over-fanciful. The real test is whether experience can discover anything to indicate a purposeful natural process of this kind. In my opinion, it can discover *a little*; for this cycle of events seems to take so long a time to complete, that the small part of it traversed by mankind up till now does not allow us to determine with certainty the shape of the whole cycle, and the relation of its parts to the whole. It is no easier than it is to determine, from all hitherto available astronomical observations, the path which our sun with its whole swarm of satellites is following within the vast system of the fixed stars; although from the general premise that the universe is constituted as a system and from the little which has been learnt by observation, we can conclude with sufficient certainty that a movement of this kind does exist in reality. Nevertheless, human nature is such that it cannot be indifferent even to the most remote epoch which may eventually affect our species, so long as this epoch can be expected with certainty. And in the present case, it is especially hard to be indifferent, for it appears that we might by our own rational projects accelerate the coming of this period which will be so welcome to our descendants. For this reason, even the faintest signs of its approach will be extremely important to us. The mutual relationships between states are already so sophisticated that none of them can neglect its internal culture without losing power and influence in relation to the others. Thus the purpose of nature is at least fairly well safeguarded (if not actually furthered) even by the ambitious schemes of the various states. Furthermore, civil freedom can no longer be so easily infringed without disadvantage to all trades and industries, and especially to commerce, in the event of which the state's power in its external relations will also decline. But this freedom is gradually increasing. If the citizen is deterred from seeking his personal welfare in any way he chooses which is consistent with the freedom of others, the vitality of business in general and hence also the strength of the whole are held in check. For this reason, restrictions placed upon personal activities are increasingly relaxed, and general freedom of religion is granted. And thus, although folly and caprice creep in at times, *enlightenment* gradually arises. It is a great benefit which the human race must reap even from its ruler's self-seeking schemes of expansion, if only they realise what is to their own advantage. But this enlightenment, and with it a certain sympathetic interest which the enlightened man inevitably feels for anything good which he comprehends fully, must gradually spread upwards towards the thrones and even influence their principles of government. But while, for example, the world's present rulers have no money to spare for public educational institutions or indeed for anything which concerns the world's best interests (for everything has already been calculated out in advance for the next war), they will nonetheless find that it is to their own advantage at least not to hinder their citizens' private efforts in this direction, however weak and slow they may be. But eventually, war itself gradually becomes not only a highly artificial undertaking, extremely uncertain in its outcome for both parties, but also a very dubious risk to take, since its aftermath is felt by the state in the shape of a constantly increasing national debt (a modern invention) whose repayment becomes interminable. And in addition, the effects which an upheaval in any state produces upon all the others in our continent, where all are so closely linked by trade, are so perceptible that these other states are forced by their own insecurity to offer themselves as arbiters, albeit without legal authority, so that they indirectly prepare the way for a great political body of the future, without precedent in the past. Although this political body exists for the present only in the roughest of outlines, it nonetheless seems as if a feeling is beginning to stir in all its members, each of which has an interest in maintaining the whole. And this encourages the hope that, after many revolutions, with all their transforming effects, the highest purpose of nature, a universal *cosmopolitan existence*, will at last be realised as the matrix within which all the original capacities of the human race may develop.

Ninth Proposition

A philosophical attempt to work out a universal history of the world in accordance with a plan of nature aimed at a perfect civil union of mankind, must be regarded as possible and even as capable of furthering the purpose of nature itself. It is admittedly a strange and at first sight absurd proposition to write a *history* according to an idea of how world events must develop if they are to conform to certain rational ends; it would seem that only a *novel* could result from such premises. Yet if it may be assumed that nature does not work without a plan and purposeful end, even amidst the arbitrary play of human freedom, this idea might nevertheless prove useful. And although we are too short-sighted to perceive the hidden mechanism of nature's scheme, this idea may yet serve as a guide to us in representing an otherwise planless *aggregate* of human actions as conforming, at least when considered as a whole, to a *system*. For if we start out from *Greek* history as that in which all other earlier or contemporary histories are preserved or at least authenticated, if we next trace the influence of the Greeks upon the shaping and misshaping of the body politic of *Rome*, which engulfed the Greek state, and follow down to our own times the influence of Rome upon the *Barbarians* who in turn destroyed it, and if we finally add the political history of other peoples *episodically*, in so far as knowledge of them has gradually come down to us through these enlightened nations, we shall discover a regular process of improvement in the political constitutions of our continent (which will probably legislate eventually for all other continents). Furthermore, we must always concentrate our attention on civil constitutions, their laws, and the mutual relations among states, and notice how these factors, by virtue of the good they contained, served for a time to elevate and glorify nations (and with them the arts and sciences). Conversely, we should observe how their inherent defects led to their overthrow, but in such a way that a germ of enlightenment always survived, developing further with each revolution, and prepared the way for a subsequent higher level of improvement.

All this, I believe, should give us some guidance in explaining the thoroughly confused interplay of human affairs and in prophesying future political changes. Yet the same use has already been made of human history even when it was regarded as the disjointed product of unregulated freedom. But if we assume a plan of nature, we have grounds for greater hopes. For such a plan opens up the comforting prospect of a future in which we are shown from afar how the human race eventually works its way upward to a situation in which all the germs implanted by nature can be developed fully, and in which man's destiny can be fulfilled here on earth. Such a *justification* of nature—or rather perhaps of *providence*—is no mean motive for adopting a particular point of view in considering the world. For what is the use of lauding and holding up for contemplation the glory and wisdom of creation in the non-rational sphere of nature, if the history of mankind, the very part of this great display of supreme wisdom which contains the purpose of all the rest, is to remain a constant reproach to everything else? Such a spectacle would force us to turn away in revulsion, and, by making us despair of ever finding any completed rational aim behind it, would reduce us to hoping for it only in some other world.

It would be a misinterpretation of my intention to contend that I meant this idea of a universal history, which to some extent follows an *a priori* rule, to supersede the task of history proper, that of *empirical* composition. My idea is only a notion of what a philosophical mind, well acquainted with history, might be able to attempt from a different angle. Besides, the otherwise praiseworthy detail in which each age now composes its history must naturally cause everyone concern as to how our remote descendants will manage to cope with the burden of history which we shall bequeath to them a few centuries from now. No doubt they will value the history of the oldest times, of which the original documents would long since have vanished, only from the point of view of what interests *them*, i.e., the positive and negative achievements of nations and governments in relation to the cosmopolitan goal. We should bear this in mind, and we should likewise observe the ambitions of rulers and their servants, in order to indicate to them the only means by which they can be honourably remembered in the most distant ages. And this may provide us with another *small* motive for attempting a philosophical history of this kind.

Georg Wilhelm Friedrich Hegel, Selection from *The Phenomenology of the Spirit*

Self-Consciousness

Self-consciousness exists in and for itself when, and by the fact that, it so exists for another; that is, it exists only in being acknowledged. The Notion of this its unity in its duplication embraces many and varied meanings. Its moments, then, must on the one hand be held strictly apart, and on the other hand must in this differentiation at the same time also be taken and known as not distinct, or in their opposite significance. The twofold significance of the distinct moments has in the nature of self-consciousness to be infinite, or directly the opposite of the determinateness in which it is posited. The detailed exposition of the Notion of this spiritual unity in its duplication will present us with the process of Recognition.

Self-consciousness is faced by another self-consciousness; it has come *out of itself.* This has a twofold significance: first, it has lost itself, for it finds itself as an *other* being; secondly, in doing so it has superseded the other, for it does not see the other as an essential being, but in the other sees its own self.

It must supersede this otherness of itself. This is the supersession of the first ambiguity, and is therefore itself a second ambiguity. First, it must proceed to supersede the *other* independent being in order thereby to become certain of *itself* as the essential being; secondly, in so doing it proceeds to supersede its *own* self, for this other is itself.

This ambiguous supersession of its ambiguous otherness is equally an ambiguous return *into itself.* For first, through the supersession, it receives back its own self, because, by superseding *its* otherness, it again becomes equal to itself; but secondly, the other self-consciousness equally gives it back again to itself, for it saw itself in the other, but supersedes this being of itself in the other and thus lets the other again go free.

Now, this movement of self-consciousness in relation to another self-consciousness has in this way been represented as the action of one self-consciousness, but this action of the one has itself the double significance of being both its own action and the action of the other as well. For the other is equally independent and self-contained, and there is nothing in it of which it is not itself the origin. The first does not have the object before it merely as it exists primarily for desire, but as something that has an independent existence of its own, which, therefore, it cannot utilize for its own purposes, if that object does not of its own accord do what the first does to it. Thus the movement is simply the double movement of the two self-consciousnesses. Each sees the *other* do the same as it does; each does itself what it demands of the other, and therefore also does what it does only in so far as the other does the same. Action by one side only would be useless because what is to happen can only be brought about by both.

Thus the action has a double significance not only because it is directed against itself as well as against the other, but also because it is indivisibly the action of one as well as of the other.

In this movement we see repeated the process which presented itself as the play of Forces, but repeated now in consciousness. What in that process was *for us* is true here of the extremes themselves. The middle term is self-consciousness which splits into the extremes; and each extreme is this exchanging of its own determinateness and an absolute transition into the opposite. Although, as consciousness, it does indeed come *out of itself*, yet, though out of itself, it is at the same time kept back within itself, is *for itself*, and the self outside it, is for *it*. It is aware that it at once is, and is not, another consciousness, and equally that this other is *for itself* only when it supersedes itself as being for itself, and is for itself only in the being-for-self of the other. Each is for the other the middle term, through which each mediates itself with itself and unites with itself; and each is for itself, and for the other, an immediate being on its own account, which at the same time is such only through this mediation. They *recognize* themselves as *mutually recognizing* one another.

We have now to see how the process of this pure Notion of recognition, of the duplicating of self-consciousness in its oneness, appears to self-consciousness. At first, it will exhibit the side of the inequality of the two, or the splitting-up of the middle term into the extremes which, as extremes, are opposed to one another, one being only *recognized*, the other only *recognizing*.

Self-consciousness is, to begin with, simple being-for-self, self-equal through the exclusion from itself of everything else. For it, its essence and absolute object is 'I'; and in this immediacy, or in this [mere] being, of its being-for-self, it is an *individual*. What is 'other' for it is an unessential, negatively characterized object. But the 'other' is also a self-consciousness; one individual is confronted by another individual. Appearing thus immediately on the scene, they are for one another like ordinary objects, *independent* shapes, individuals submerged in the being [or immediacy] of Life—for the object in its immediacy is here determined as Life. They are, *for each other*, shapes of consciousness which have not yet accomplished the movement of absolute abstraction, of rooting-out all immediate being, and of being merely the purely negative being of self-identical consciousness; in other words, they have not as yet exposed themselves to each other in the form of pure being-for-self, or as self-consciousnesses. Each is indeed certain of its own self, but not of the other, and therefore its own self-certainty still has no truth. For it would have truth only if its own being-for-self had confronted it as an independent object, or, what is the same thing, if the object had presented itself as this pure self-certainty. But according to the Notion of recognition this is possible only when each is for the other what the other is for it, only when each in its own self through its own action, and again through the action of the other, achieves this pure abstraction of being-for-self.

The presentation of itself, however, as the pure abstraction of self-consciousness consists in showing itself as the pure negation of its objective mode, or in showing that it is not attached to any specific *existence*, not to the individuality common to existence as such, that it is not attached to life. This presentation is a twofold action: action on the part of the other, and action on its own part. In so far as it is the action of the *other*, each seeks the death of the other. But in doing so, the second kind of action, action on its own part, is also involved; for the former involves the staking of its own life. Thus the relation of the two self-conscious individuals is such that they prove themselves and each other through a life-and-death struggle. They must engage in this struggle, for they must raise their certainty of being *for themselves* to truth, both in the case of the other and in their own case. And it is only through staking one's life that freedom is won; only thus is it proved that for self-consciousness, its essential being is not [just] being, not the *immediate* form in which it appears, not its submergence in the expanse of life, but rather that there is nothing present in it which could not be regarded as a vanishing moment, that it is only pure *being-for-self*. The individual who has not risked his life may well be recognized as a *person*, but he has not attained to the truth of this recognition as an independent self-consciousness. Similarly, just as each stakes his own life, so each must seek the other's death, for it values the other no more than itself; its essential being is present to it in the form of an 'other', it is outside of itself and must rid itself of its self-externality. The other is an *immediate* consciousness entangled in a variety of relationships, and it must regard its otherness as a pure being-for-self or as an absolute negation.

This trial by death, however, does away with the truth which was supposed to issue from it, and so, too, with the certainty of self generally. For just as life is the *natural* setting of consciousness, independence without absolute negativity, so death is the *natural* negation of consciousness, negation without independence, which thus remains without the required significance of recognition. Death certainly shows that each staked his life and held it of no account, both in himself and in the other; but that is not for those who survived this struggle. They put an end to their consciousness in its alien setting of natural existence, that is to say, they put an end to themselves, and are done away with as *extremes* wanting to be for *themselves*, or to have an existence of their own. But with this there vanishes from their interplay the essential moment of splitting into extremes with opposite characteristics; and the middle term collapses into a lifeless unity which is split into lifeless, merely immediate, unopposed extremes; and the two do not reciprocally give and receive one another back from each other consciously, but leave each other free only indifferently, like things. Their act is an abstract negation, not the negation coming from consciousness, which supersedes in such a way as to preserve and maintain what is superseded, and consequently survives its own supersession.

In this experience, self-consciousness learns that life is as essential to it as pure self-consciousness. In immediate self-consciousness the simple 'I' is absolute mediation, and has as its essential moment lasting independence. The dissolution of that simple unity is the result of the first experience; through this there is posited a pure self-consciousness, and a consciousness which is not purely for itself but for another, i.e., is a merely *immediate* consciousness, or consciousness in the form of *thinghood*. Both moments are essential. Since to begin with they are unequal and opposed, and their reflection into a unity has not yet been achieved, they exist as two opposed shapes of consciousness; one is the independent consciousness whose essential nature is to *be for itself*, the other is the dependent consciousness whose essential nature is simply to live or to be for another. The former is lord, the other is bondsman.

The lord is the consciousness that exists *for itself*, but no longer merely the Notion of such a consciousness. Rather, it is a consciousness existing *for itself* which is mediated with itself through another consciousness, i.e., through a consciousness whose nature it is to be bound up with an existence that is independent, or thinghood in general. The lord puts himself into relation with both of these moments, to a thing as such, the object of desire, and to the consciousness for which thing hood is the essential characteristic. And since he is (a) *qua* the Notion of self-consciousness an immediate relation of *being-for-self* but (b) is now at the same time mediation, or a being-for-self which is for itself only through another, he is related (a) immediately to both, and (b) mediately to each through the other. The lord relates himself mediately to the bondsman through a being [a thing] that is independent, for it is just this which holds the bondsman in bondage; it is his chain from which he could not break free in the struggle, thus proving himself to be dependent, to possess his independence in thinghood. But the lord is the power over this thing, for he proved in the struggle that it is something merely negative; since he is the power over this thing and this again is the power over the other [the bondsman], it follows that he holds the other in subjection. Equally, the lord relates himself mediately to the thing through the bondsman; the bondsman, *qua* self-consciousness in general, also relates himself negatively to the thing, and takes away its independence; but at the same time the thing is independent vis-à-vis the bondsman, whose negating of it, therefore, cannot go the length of being altogether done with it to the point of annihilation; in other words, he only *works* on it. For the lord, on the other hand, the *immediate* relation becomes through this mediation the sheer negation of the thing, or the enjoyment of it. What desire failed to achieve, he succeeds in doing, viz. to have done with the thing altogether, and to achieve satisfaction in the enjoyment of it. Desire failed to do this because of the thing's independence; but the lord, who has interposed the bondsman between it and himself, takes to himself only the dependent aspect of the thing and has the pure enjoyment of it. The aspect of its independence he leaves to the bondsman, who works on it.

In both of these moments the lord achieves his recognition through another consciousness; for in them, that other consciousness is expressly something unessential, both by its working on the thing, and by its dependence on a specific existence. In neither case can it be lord over the being of the thing and achieve absolute negation of it. Here, therefore, is present this moment of recognition, viz. that the other consciousness sets aside its own being-for-self, and in so doing itself does what the first does to it. Similarly, the other moment too is present, that this action of the second is the first's own action; for what the bondsman does is really the action of the lord. The latter's essential nature is to exist only for himself; he is the sheer negative power for whom the thing is nothing. Thus he is the pure, essential action in this relationship, while the action of the bondsman is impure and unessential. But for recognition proper the moment is lacking, that what the lord does to the other he also does to himself, and what the bondsman does to himself he should also do to the other. The outcome is a recognition that is one-sided and unequal.

In this recognition the unessential consciousness is for the lord the object, which constitutes the *truth* of his certainty of himself. But it is clear that this object does not correspond to its Notion, but rather that the object in which the lord has achieved his lordship has in reality turned out to be something quite different from an independent consciousness. What now really confronts him is not an independent consciousness, but a dependent one. He is, therefore, not certain of *being-for-self* as the truth of himself. On the contrary, his truth is in reality the unessential consciousness and its unessential action.

The *truth* of the independent consciousness is accordingly the servile consciousness of the bondsman. This, it is true, appears at first *outside* of itself and not as the truth of self-consciousness. But just as lordship showed that its essential nature is the reverse of what it wants to be, so too servitude in its consummation will really turn into the opposite of what it immediately is; as a consciousness forced back into itself, it will withdraw into itself and be transformed into a truly independent consciousness.

We have seen what servitude is only in relation to lordship. But it is a self-consciousness, and we have now to consider what as such it is in and for itself. To begin with, servitude has the lord for its essential reality; hence the *truth* for it is the independent consciousness that is *for itself*. However, servitude is not yet aware that this truth is implicit in it. But it does in fact contain within itself this truth of pure negativity and being-for-self, for it has experienced this its own essential nature. For this consciousness has been fearful, not of this or that particular thing or just at odd moments, but its whole being has been seized with dread; for it has experienced the fear of death, the absolute Lord. In that experience it has been quite unmanned, has trembled in every fibre of its being, and everything solid and stable has been shaken to its foundations. But this pure universal movement, the absolute melting-away of everything stable, is the simple, essential nature of self-consciousness, absolute negativity, *pure being-for-self* which consequently is *implicit* in this consciousness. This moment of pure being-for-self is also explicit for the bondsman, for in the lord it exists for him as his object. Furthermore, his consciousness is not this dissolution of everything stable merely in principle; in his service he *actually* brings this about. Through his service he rids himself of his attachment to natural existence in every single detail; and gets rid of it by working on it.

However, the feeling of absolute power both in general, and in the particular form of service, is only implicitly this dissolution, and although the fear of the lord is indeed the beginning of wisdom, consciousness is not therein aware that it is a being-for-self. Through work, however, the bondsman becomes conscious of what he truly is. In the moment which corresponds to desire in the lord's consciousness, it did seem that the aspect of unessential relation to the thing fell to the lot of the bondsman, since in that relation the thing retained its independence. Desire has reserved to itself the pure negating of the object and thereby its unalloyed feeling of self. But that is the reason why this satisfaction is itself only a fleeting one, for it lacks the side of objectivity and permanence. Work, on the other hand, is desire held in check, fleetingness staved off; in other words, work forms and shapes the thing. The negative relation to the object becomes its *form* and something *permanent*, because it is precisely for the worker that the object has independence. This *negative* middle term or the formative *activity* is at the same time the individuality or pure being-for-self of consciousness which now, in the work outside of it, acquires an element of permanence. It is in this way, therefore, that consciousness, *qua* worker, comes to see in the independent being [of the object] its *own* independence.

But the formative activity has not only this positive significance that in it the pure being-for-self of the servile consciousness acquires an existence; it also has, in contrast with its first moment, the negative significance of *fear*. For, in fashioning the thing, the bondsman's own negativity, his being-for-self, becomes an object for him only through his setting at nought the existing *shape* confronting him. But this objective *negative* moment is none other than the alien being before which it has trembled. Now, however, he destroys this alien negative moment, posits *himself* as a negative in the permanent order of things, and thereby becomes *for himself*, someone existing on his own account. In the lord, the being-for-self is an 'other' for the bondsman, or is only for him [i.e., is not his own]; in fear, the being-for-self is present in the bondsman himself; in fashioning the thing, he becomes aware that being-for-self belongs to *him*, that he himself exists essentially and actually in his own right. The shape does not become something other than himself through being made external to him; for it is precisely this shape that is his pure being-for-self, which in this externality is seen by him to be the truth. Through this rediscovery of himself by himself, the bondsman realizes that it is precisely in his work wherein he seemed to have only an alienated existence that he acquires a mind of his own. For this reflection, the two moments of fear and service as such, as also that of formative activity, are necessary, both being at the same time in a universal mode. Without the discipline of service and obedience, fear remains at the formal stage, and does not extend to the known real world of existence. Without the formative activity, fear remains inward and mute, and consciousness does not become explicitly *for itself*. If consciousness fashions the thing without that initial absolute fear, it is only an empty self-centred attitude; for its form or negativity is not negativity *per se*, and therefore its formative activity cannot give it a consciousness of itself as essential being. If it has not experienced absolute fear but only some lesser dread, the negative being has remained for it something external, its substance has not been infected by it through and through. Since the entire contents of its natural consciousness have not been jeopardized, determinate being still *in principle* attaches to it; having a 'mind of one's own' is self-will, a freedom which is still enmeshed in servitude. Just as little as the pure form can become essential being for it, just as little is that form, regarded as extended to the particular, a universal formative activity, an absolute Notion; rather it is a skill which is master over some things, but not over the universal power and the whole of objective being.

Reason

In grasping the thought that the *single* individual consciousness is *in itself* Absolute Essence, consciousness has returned into itself. For the Unhappy Consciousnessness the in-itself is the beyond of itself. But its movement has resulted in positing the completely developed single individual, or the single individual that is an *actual* consciousness, as the *negative* of itself, viz. as the *objective* extreme; in other words, it has successfully struggled to divest itself of its being-for-self and has turned it into [mere] being. In this movement it has also become aware of its unity with this universal, a unity which, for us, no longer, falls outside of it since the superseded single individual is the universal, and which, since consciousness maintains itself in this its negativity, is present in consciousness as such as its essence. Its truth is that which appears in the syllogism whose extremes appeared as held absolutely asunder, as the middle term which proclaims to the unchangeable consciousness that the single individual has renounced itself, and, to the individual, that the Unchangeable is for it no longer an extreme, but is reconciled with it. This middle term is the unity directly aware of both and connecting them, and is the consciousness of their unity, which proclaims to consciousness and thereby to itself, the consciousness of the certainty of being all truth.

Now that self-consciousness is Reason, its hitherto negative relation to otherness turns round into a positive relation. Up till now it has been concerned only with its independence and freedom, concerned to save and maintain itself for itself at the expense of the *world*, or of its own actuality, both of which appeared to it as the negative of its essence. But as Reason, assured of itself, it is at peace with them, and can endure them; for it is certain that it is itself reality, or that everything actual is none other than itself; its thinking is itself directly actuality, and thus its relationship to the latter is that of idealism. Apprehending itself in this way, it is as if the world had for it only now come into being; previously it did not understand the world; it desired it and worked on it, withdrew from it into itself and abolished it as an existence on its own account, and its own self *qua* consciousness—both as consciousness of the world as essence and as consciousness of its nothingness. In thus apprehending itself, after losing the grave of its truth, after the abolition of its actuality is itself abolished, and after the singleness of consciousness is for it in itself Absolute Essence, it discovers the world as its new real world, which in its permanence holds an interest for it which previously lay only in its transiency; for the *existence* of the world becomes for self-consciousness its own *truth* and *presence*; it is certain of experiencing only itself therein.

Reason is the certainty of consciousness that it is all reality; thus does idealism express its Notion. Just as consciousness, that comes on the scene as Reason, possesses that certainty *directly* in itself, so too does idealism give direct expression to that certainty: 'I am I', in the sense that the 'I' which is an object for me is the sole object, is all reality and all that is present. Here, the 'I' that is object for me, is not merely an *empty* object in general, as it is for self-consciousness as such, nor is it, as in free self-consciousness, merely an object that withdraws itself from other objects which retain their worth *alongside* it; on the contrary, it is for self-consciousness an object such that any other object whatever is a *non-being*. But self-consciousness is all reality, not merely *for itself* but also *in itself*, only through *becoming* this reality, or rather through *demonstrating* itself to be such. It demonstrates itself to be this *along the path* in which first, in the dialectic movement of 'meaning', perceiving and understanding, otherness as an intrinsic being vanishes. Then, in the movement through the independence of consciousness in lordship and bondage, through the conception of freedom, through the liberation that comes from Scepticism and the struggle for absolute liberation by the consciousness divided against itself, otherness, in so far as it is only *for consciousness*, vanishes for *consciousness itself*. There appeared two aspects, one after the other: one in which the essence or the True had for consciousness the determinateness of *being*, the other in which it had the determinateness of being only *for consciousness*. But the two reduced themselves to a single truth, viz. that what *is*, or the in-itself, only *is* in so far as it is *for* consciousness, and what is *for* consciousness is also *in itself* or has *intrinsic* being. The consciousness which is this truth has this path behind it and has forgotten it, and comes on the scene *immediately* as Reason; in other words, this Reason which comes immediately on the scene appears only as the *certainty* of that truth. Thus it merely *asserts* that it is all reality, but does not itself comprehend this; for it is along that forgotten path that this immediately expressed assertion is comprehended. And equally, anyone who has not trodden this path finds this assertion incomprehensible when he hears it in this pure form—although he does as a matter of fact make the assertion himself in a concrete shape [i.e., the assertion is implicit in his behaviour].

The idealism that does not demonstrate that path but starts off with this assertion is therefore, too, a pure *assertion* which does not comprehend its own self, nor can it make itself comprehensible to others. It proclaims an *immediate certainty* which is confronted by other immediate certainties, which have, however, been lost on that same path. With equal right, therefore, the assertions of these other certainties, too, take their place alongside the assertion of that certainty. Reason appeals to the *self-consciousness* of each and every consciousness: '*I am I*, my object and my essence is *I*'; and no one will deny Reason this truth. But in basing itself on this appeal, Reason sanctions the truth of the other certainty, viz. that there is for me an 'other'; that an other than 'I' is object and essence for me, or, in that I am object and essence to myself, I am only so by drawing back from the 'other' altogether, and taking my place as an actuality *alongside* it. Not until Reason comes on the scene as a *reflection* from this opposite certainty does its affirmation about itself present itself not merely as a certainty and an assertion, but as truth; and not merely alongside other truths but as the sole truth. Its *immediate appearance* on the scene is the abstraction of its *actual presence*, the essence and the *in-itself* of which is the absolute Notion, i.e., *the movement which has brought it into being*. Consciousness will determine its relationship to otherness or its object in various ways, according to the precise stage it has reached in the development of the World-Spirit into self-consciousness. How it *immediately* finds and determines itself and its object at any time, or the way in which it is *for itself*, depends on what it has already *become*, or what it already is *in itself*.

Reason is the certainty of being all *reality*. This *in-itself* or this *reality* is, however, a universal pure and simple, the pure *abstraction* of reality. It is the first *positivity* in which self-consciousness is in its *own self* explicitly *for itself*, and '*I*' is therefore only the *pure essentiality* of the existent, or is the simple *category*. The category, which formerly had the meaning of being the essentiality of the existent—and it was *undetermined* whether of the existent as such, or of the existent contrasted with consciousness—is now the essentiality or simple *unity* of the existent only as a reality that thinks; in other words, the category means this, that self-consciousness and being are the same essence, the same, not through comparison, but in and for themselves. It is only the one-sided, spurious idealism that lets this unity again come on the scene as consciousness, on one side, confronted by an *in-itself*, on the other. But now this category or *simple* unity of self-consciousness and being possesses difference *in itself*; for its essence is just this, to be immediately one and selfsame in *otherness*, or in absolute difference. The difference therefore *is*, but is perfectly transparent, and a difference that is at the same time none. It appears as a *plurality* of categories. Since idealism proclaims the simple unity of self-consciousness to be all reality and *immediately* makes it the essence without having grasped it as the absolutely negative essence—only this has negation, determinateness, or difference within it—this second assertion is even more incomprehensible than the first, viz. that in the category there are *differences* or *species* of categories. The assertion as such, as also the assertion as to any *specific number* of species of categories, is a new assertion which, however, itself implies that we no longer have to accept it as an assertion. For since the difference originates in the pure 'I', in the pure Understanding itself, it is thereby made explicit that the *immediacy*, the making of assertions and [mere] finding of differences, is here given, and we begin to *comprehend*. But to pick up the plurality of categories again in some way or other as a welcome find, taking them, e.g., from the various judgements, and complacently accepting them so, is in fact to be regarded as an outrage on Science. Where else should the Understanding be able to demonstrate a necessity, if it is unable to do so in its own self, which is pure necessity?

Now, because, in this way, the pure essentiality of things, like their difference, belongs to Reason, we can, strictly speaking, no longer talk of *things* at all, i.e., of something which would be for consciousness merely the negative of itself. For to say that the many categories are *species* of the pure category means that this latter is still their *genus* or *essence*, and is not opposed to them. But ambiguity already attaches to them, since in their *plurality* they possess otherness in contrast to the pure category. In fact, they contradict the pure category by such plurality, and the pure unity must supersede them in itself, thereby constituting itself a *negative unity* of the differences. But, as *negative* unity, it excludes from itself both the differences as such, as well as that first *immediate* pure unity as such, and is a *singular individual*; a new category which is consciousness as exclusive, i.e., consciousness for which there is an 'other'. The singular individual is the transition of the category from its Notion to an *external* reality, the pure *schema* which is both consciousness, and, since it is a singular individual and an exclusive unit, the pointing to an 'other'. But this 'other' of the category is merely the other first-mentioned categories, viz. *pure essentiality* and *pure difference*; and in this category, i.e., just in the posited-ness of the 'other', or in this 'other' itself, consciousness is equally itself. Each of these different moments points or refers to another; but at the same time they do not attain to otherness. The pure category points to the *species*, which pass over into the negative category or singular individual; this latter, however, points back to them. It is itself pure consciousness which is aware in each of them of being always this clear unity with itself, but a unity which equally is referred to an 'other', which in being, has vanished, and in vanishing also comes into being again.

Here we see pure consciousness posited in a twofold manner: once as the restless movement to and fro through all its moments, aware in them of an otherness which is superseded in the act of grasping it; and again, rather as the *tranquil unity* certain of its [own] truth. For this unity that movement is the 'other', while for this movement that tranquil unity is the 'other'; and consciousness and object alternate within these reciprocal determinations. Thus on the one hand consciousness finds itself moving about searching here and there, its object being the *pure in-itself* and essence; on the other hand, it knows itself to be the simple category, and the object is the movement of the different moments. Consciousness, however, as essence is this whole process itself, of passing out of itself as simple category into a singular individual, into the object, and of contemplating this process in the object, nullifying the object as distinct [from it], *appropriating* it as its own, and proclaiming itself as this certainty of being all reality, of being both itself and its object.

Its first declaration is only this abstract empty phrase that everything is *its own*. For the certainty of being all reality is at first [only] the pure category. This Reason which first recognizes itself in the object finds expression in the empty idealism which grasps Reason only as it first comes on the scene; and fancies that by pointing out this pure 'mine' of consciousness in all being, and by declaring all things to be sensations or ideas, it has demonstrated this 'mine' of consciousness to be complete reality. It is bound, therefore, to be at the same time absolute empiricism, for in order to give filling to the empty 'mine', i.e., to get hold of *difference* with all its developed formations, its Reason requires an extraneous impulse, in which first is to be found the *multiplicity* of sensations and ideas. This idealism therefore becomes the same kind of self-contradictory ambiguity as Scepticism, except that, while this expresses itself negatively, the former does so positively; but it fails equally with Scepticism to bring together its contradictory thoughts of pure consciousness being all reality, while the extraneous impulse or sensations and ideas are equally reality. Instead of bringing them together, it shifts from one to the other, and is caught up in the spurious, i.e., the sensuous, infinite. Since Reason is all reality in the sense of the abstract 'mine', and the 'other' is for it something indifferent and extraneous, what is here made explicit is that kind of knowing of an 'other' by Reason, which we met with in the form of 'meaning', 'perceiving' and the 'Understanding', which apprehends what is 'meant' and what is 'perceived'. Such a knowing is at the same time pronounced by the very principle of this idealism not to be a true knowing, for only in the unity of apperception lies the truth of knowing. The pure Reason of this idealism, in order to reach this 'other' which is *essential* to it, and thus is the *in-itself*, but which it does not have within it, is therefore thrown back by its own self on to that knowing which is *not* a knowing of what is true; in this way, it condemns itself of its own knowledge and volition to being an untrue kind of knowing, and cannot get away from 'meaning' and 'perceiving', which for it have no truth. It is involved in a direct contradiction; it asserts essence to be a duality of opposed factors, the *unity of apperception* and equally a *Thing*; whether the Thing is called an extraneous impulse, or an empirical or sensuous entity, or the Thing-in-itself, it still remains in principle the same, i.e., extraneous to that unity.

This idealism is involved in this contradiction because it asserts the *abstract Notion* of Reason to be the True; consequently, reality directly comes to be for it a reality that is just as much *not* that of Reason, while Reason is at the same time supposed to be all reality. This Reason remains a restless searching and in its very searching declares that the satisfaction of *finding* is a sheer impossibility. Actual Reason, however, is not so inconsistent as that; on the contrary, being at first only the *certainty* that it is all reality, it is aware in this *Notion* that *qua certainty*, qua 'I', it is not yet in truth reality, and it is impelled to raise its certainty to truth and to give filling to the empty 'mine'.

Georg Wilhelm Friedrich Hegel, Selection from *The Philosophy of Right*

The State

The state is the actuality of the ethical Idea. It is ethical mind *qua* the substantial will manifest and revealed to itself, knowing and thinking itself, accomplishing what it knows and in so far as it knows it. The state exists immediately in custom, mediately in individual self-consciousness, knowledge, and activity, while self-consciousness in virtue of its sentiment towards the stale finds in the state, as its essence and the end and product of its activity, its substantive freedom.

The *Penates* are inward gods, gods of the underworld; the mind of a nation (Athene for instance) is the divine, knowing and willing itself. Family piety is feeling, ethical behaviour directed by feeling; political virtue is the willing of the absolute end in terms of thought.

The state is absolutely rational inasmuch as it is the actuality of the substantial will which it possesses in the particular self-consciousness once that consciousness has been raised to consciousness of its universality. This substantial unity is an absolute unmoved end in itself, in which freedom comes into its supreme right. On the other hand this final end has supreme right against the individual, whose supreme duty is to be a member of the state.

If the state is confused with civil society, and if its specific end is laid down as the security and protection of property and personal freedom, then the interest of the individuals as such becomes the ultimate end of their association, and it follows that membership of the state is something optional. But the state's relation to the individual is quite different from this. Since the state is mind objectified, it is only as one of its members that the individual himself has objectivity, genuine individuality, and an ethical life. Unification pure and simple is the true content and aim of the individual, and the individual's destiny is the living of a universal life. His further particular satisfaction, activity, and mode of conduct have this substantive and universally valid life as their starting point and their result.

Rationality, taken generally and in the abstract, consists in the thorough-going unity of the universal and the single. Rationality, concrete in the state, consists (*a*) so far as its content is concerned, in the unity of objective freedom (i.e., freedom of the universal or substantial will) and subjective freedom (i.e., freedom of everyone in his knowing and in his volition of particular ends); and consequently, (*b*) so far as its form is concerned, in self-determining action on laws and principles which are thoughts and so universal. This Idea is the absolutely eternal and necessary being of mind.

But if we ask what is or has been the historical origin of the state in general, still more if we ask about the origin of any particular state, of its rights and institutions, or again if we inquire whether the state originally arose out of patriarchal conditions or out of fear or trust, or out of Corporations, &c, or finally if we ask in what light the basis of the state's rights has been conceived and consciously established, whether this basis has been supposed to be positive divine right, or contract, custom, &c.—all these questions are no concern of the Idea of the state. We are here dealing exclusively with the philosophic science of the state, and from that point of view all these things are mere appearance and therefore matters for history. So far as the authority of any existing state has anything to do with reasons, these reasons are culled from the forms of the law authoritative within it.

The philosophical treatment of these topics is concerned only with their inward side, with the thought of their concept. The merit of Rousseau's contribution to the search for this concept is that, by adducing the will as the principle of the state, he is adducing a principle which has thought both for its form and its content, a principle indeed which is thinking itself, not a principle, like gregarious instinct, for instance, or divine authority, which has thought as its form only. Unfortunately, however, as Fichte did later, he takes the will only in a determinate form as the individual will, and he regards the universal will not as the absolutely rational element in the will, but only as a 'general' will which proceeds out of this individual will as out of a conscious will. The result is that he reduces the union of individuals in the state to a contract and therefore to something based on their arbitrary wills, their opinion, and their capriciously given express consent; and abstract reasoning proceeds to draw the logical inferences which destroy the absolutely divine principle of the state, together with its majesty and absolute authority. For this reason, when these abstract conclusions came into power, they afforded for the first time in human history the prodigious spectacle of the overthrow of the constitution of a great actual state and its complete reconstruction *ab initio* on the basis of pure thought alone, after the destruction of all existing and given material. The will of its re-founders was to give it what they alleged was a purely rational basis, but it was only abstractions that were being used; the Idea was lacking; and the experiment ended in the maximum of frightfulness and terror.

Confronted with the claims made for the individual will, we must remember the fundamental conception that the objective will is rationality implicit or in conception, whether it be recognized or not by individuals, whether their whims be deliberately for it or not. We must remember that its opposite, i.e., knowing and willing, or subjective freedom (the *only* thing contained in the principle of the individual will) comprises only one moment, and therefore a one-sided moment, of the Idea of the: rational will, i.e., of the will which is rational solely because what it is implicitly, that it also is explicitly.

The opposite to thinking of the state as something to be known and apprehended as explicitly rational is taking external appearances—i.e., contingencies such as distress, need for protection, force, riches, &c.—not as moments in the state's historical development, but as its substance. Here again what constitutes the guiding thread of discovery is the individual in isolation—not, however even so much as the *thought* of this individuality, but instead only empirical individuals, with attention focused on their accidental characteristics, their strength and weakness, riches and poverty, &c. This ingenious idea of ignoring the absolute infinity and rationality in the state and excluding thought from apprehension of its inward nature has assuredly never been put forward in such an unadulterated form as in Herr von Haller's *Restauration der Staatswissenschaft*. I say 'unadulterated', because in all other attempts to grasp the essence of the state, no matter on what one-sided or superficial principles, this very intention of comprehending the state rationally has brought with it thoughts, i.e., universal determinations. Herr von Haller, however, with his eyes open, has not merely renounced the rational material of which the state consists, as well as the form of thought, but he has even gone on with passionate fervour to inveigh against the form and the material so set aside. Part of what Herr von Haller assures us is the 'wide-spread' effect of his principles, this *Restauration* undoubtedly owes to the fact that, in his exposition, he has deliberately dispensed with thought altogether, and has deliberately kept his whole book all of a piece with its lack of thought. For in this way he has eliminated the confusion and disorder which lessen the force of an exposition where the accidental is treated along with hints of the substantial, where the purely empirical and external are mixed with a reminiscence of the universal and rational, and where in the midst of wretched inanities the reader is now and again reminded of the loftier sphere of the infinite. For the same reason again his exposition is consistent. He takes as the essence of the state, not what is substantive but the sphere of accident, and consistency in dealing with a sphere of that kind amounts to the complete inconsistency of utter thoughtlessness which jogs along without looking behind, and is just as much at home now with the exact opposite of what it approved a moment ago.

The Idea of the State

(a) has immediate actuality and is the individual state as a self-dependent organism—the *Constitution or Constitutional Law*;
(b) passes over into the relation of one state to other states—*International Law*;
(c) is the universal Idea as a genus and as an absolute power over individual states—the mind which gives itself its actuality in the process of *World-History*.

Constitutional Law

The state is the actuality of concrete freedom. But concrete freedom consists in this, that personal individuality and its particular interests not only achieve their complete development and gain explicit recognition for their right (as they do in the sphere of the family and civil society) but, for one thing, they also pass over of their own accord into the interest of the universal, and, for another thing, they know and will the universal; they even recognize it as their own substantive mind; they take it as their end and aim and are active in its pursuit. The result is that the universal does not prevail or achieve completion except along with particular interests and through the co-operation of particular knowing and willing; and individuals likewise do not live as private persons for their own ends alone, but in the very act of willing these they will the universal in the light of the universal, and their activity is consciously aimed at none but the universal end. The principle of modern states has prodigious strength and depth because it allows the principle of subjectivity to progress to its culmination in the extreme of self-subsistent personal particularity, and yet at the same time brings it back to the substantive unity and so maintains this unity in the principle of subjectivity itself.

In contrast with the spheres of private rights and private welfare (the family and civil society), the state is from one point of view an external necessity and their higher authority; its nature is such that their laws and interests are subordinate to it and dependent on it. On the other hand, however, it is the end immanent within them, and its strength lies in the unity of its own universal end and aim with the particular interest of individuals, in the fact that individuals have duties to the state in proportion as they have rights against it.

The actual Idea is mind, which, sundering itself into the two ideal spheres of its concept, family and civil society, enters upon its finite phase, but it does so only in order to rise above its ideality and become explicit as infinite actual mind. It is therefore to these ideal spheres that the actual Idea assigns the material of this its finite actuality, viz. human beings as a mass, in such a way that the function assigned to any given individual is visibly mediated by circumstances, his caprice and his personal choice of his station in life.

In these spheres in which its moments, particularity and individuality, have their immediate and reflected reality, mind is present as their objective universality glimmering in them as the power of reason in necessity, i.e., as the institutions considered above.

Mind is the nature of human beings *en masse* and their nature is therefore two-fold: (i) at one extreme, explicit individuality of consciousness and will, and (ii) at the other extreme, universality which knows and wills what is substantive. Hence they attain their right in both these respects only in so far as both their private personality and its substantive basis are actualized. Now in the family and civil society they acquire their right in the first of these respects directly and in the second indirectly, in that (i) they find their substantive self-consciousness in social institutions which are the universal implicit in their particular interests, and (ii) the Corporation supplies them with an occupation and an activity directed on a universal end.

These institutions are the components of the constitution (i.e., of rationality developed and actualized) in the sphere of particularity. They are, therefore, the firm foundation not only of the state but also of the citizen's trust in it and sentiment towards it. They are the pillars of public freedom since in them particular freedom is realized and rational, and therefore there is *implicitly* present even in them the union of freedom and necessity.

But mind is objective and actual to itself not merely as this necessity and as a realm of appearance, but also as the ideality and the heart of this necessity. Only in this way is this substantive universality *aware* of itself as its own object and end, with the result that the necessity appears to itself in the shape of freedom as well.

This necessity in ideality is the inner self-development of the Idea. As the substance of the individual subject, it is his political sentiment [patriotism]; in distinction therefrom, as the substance of the objective world, it is the organism of the state, i.e., it is the strictly political state and its constitution.

The political sentiment, patriotism pure and simple, is assured conviction with truth as its basis—mere subjective assurance is not the outcome of truth but is only opinion—and a volition which has become habitual. In this sense it is simply a product of the institutions subsisting in the state, since rationality is *actually* present in the state, while action in conformity with these institutions gives rationality its practical proof. This sentiment is, in general, trust (which may pass over into a greater or lesser degree of educated insight), or the consciousness that my interest, both substantive and particular, is contained and preserved in another's (i.e., in the state's) interest and end, i.e., in the other's relation to me as an individual. In this way, this very other is immediately not an other in my eyes, and in being conscious of this fact, I am free.

Patriotism is often understood to mean only a readiness for exceptional sacrifices and actions. Essentially, however, it is the sentiment which, in the relationships of our daily life and under ordinary conditions, habitually recognizes that the community is one's substantive groundwork and end. It is out of this consciousness, which during life's daily round stands the test in all circumstances, that there subsequently also arises the readiness for extraordinary exertions. But since men would often rather be magnanimous than law-abiding, they readily persuade themselves that they possess this exceptional patriotism in order to be sparing in the expression of a genuine patriotic sentiment or to excuse their lack of it. If again this genuine patriotism is looked upon as that which may begin of itself and arise from subjective ideas and thoughts, it is being confused with opinion, because so regarded patriotism is deprived of its true ground, objective reality.

The patriotic sentiment acquires its specifically determined content from the various members of the organism of the state. This organism is the development of the Idea to its differences and their objective actuality. Hence these different members are the various powers of the state with their functions and spheres of action, by means of which the universal continually engenders itself, and engenders itself in a necessary way because their specific character is fixed by the nature of the concept. Throughout this process the universal maintains its identity, since it is itself the presupposition of its own production. This organism is the constitution of the state.

(1) The abstract actuality or the substantiality of the state consists in the fact that its end is the universal interest as such and the conservation therein of particular interests since the universal interest is the substance of these. (2) But this substantiality of the state is also its *necessity*, since its substantiality is divided into the distinct spheres of its activity which correspond to the moments of its concept, and these spheres, owing to this substantiality, are thus actually fixed determinate characteristics of the state, i.e., its *powers*. (3) But this very substantiality of the state is mind knowing and willing itself after passing through the forming process of education. The state, therefore, knows what it wills and knows it in its universality, i.e., as something thought. Hence it works and acts by reference to consciously adopted ends, known principles, and laws which are not merely implicit but are actually present to consciousness; and further, it acts with precise knowledge of existing conditions and circumstances, inasmuch as its actions have a bearing on these.

The state is universal in form, a form whose essential principle is thought. This explains why it was in the state that freedom of thought and science had their origin. It was a church, on the other hand, which burnt Giordano Bruno, forced Galileo to recant on his knees his exposition of the Copernican view of the solar system, and so forth. Science too, therefore, has its place on the side of the state since it has one element, its form, in common with the state, and its aim is knowledge, knowledge of objective truth and rationality in terms of thought. Such knowledge may, of course, fall from the heights of science into opinion and deductive argumentation, and, turning its attention to ethical matters and the organization of the state, set itself against their basic principles. And it may perhaps do this while making for this opining—as if it were reason and the right of subjective self-consciousness—the same pretentious claim as the church makes for its own sphere, the claim, namely, to be free from restraint in its opinions and convictions.

This principle of the subjectivity of knowing has been dealt with above. It is here only necessary to add a note on the twofold attitude of the state to this opining. On the one hand, in so far as opining is mere opining, a purely subjective matter, it is without any genuine inherent force or power, plume itself as it may; and from this point of view the state may be as totally indifferent to it as the painter who sticks to the three primary colours on his palette is indifferent to the academic wisdom which tells him there are seven. On the other hand, however, when this opining of bad principles embodies itself in a general organization corrosive of the actual order, the state has to set its face against it and protect objective truth and the principles of ethical life (and it must do the same in face of the formulae of unconditioned subjectivity if these have proposed to take the starting point of science as their basis, and turn state educational institutions against the state by encouraging them to make against it claims as pretentious as those of a church); while, vice versa, in face of a church claiming unrestricted and unconditional authority, the state has in general to make good the formal right of self-consciousness to its own insight, its own conviction, and, in short, its own thought of what is to hold good as objective truth.

Mention may also be made of the 'unity of state and church'—a favourite topic of modern discussion and held up by some as the highest of ideals. While state and church are essentially one in truth of principle and disposition, it is no less essential that, despite this unity, the distinction between their forms of consciousness should be externalized as a distinction between their special modes of existence. This often desired unity of church and state is found under oriental despotisms, but an oriental despotism is not a state, or at any rate not the self-conscious form of state which is alone worthy of mind, the form which is organically developed and where there are rights and a free ethical life. Further, if the state is to come into existence as the self-*knowing* ethical actuality of mind, it is essential that its form should be distinct from that of authority and faith. But this distinction emerges only in so far as the church is subjected to inward divisions. It is only thereafter that the state, in contrast with the particular sects, has attained to universality of thought—its formal principle—and is bringing this universality into existence. (In order to understand this, it is necessary to know not only what universality is in itself, but also what its existence is.) Hence so far from its being or its having been a misfortune for the state that the church is disunited, it is only as a result of that disunion that the state has been able to reach its appointed end as a self-consciously rational and ethical organization. Moreover, this disunion is the best piece of good fortune which could have befallen either the church or thought so far as the freedom and rationality of either is concerned.

The constitution of the state is, in the first place, the organization of the state and the self-related process of its organic life, a process whereby it differentiates its moments within itself and develops them to self-subsistence. Secondly, the state is an individual, unique and exclusive, and therefore related to others. Thus it turns its differentiating activity outward and accordingly establishes within itself the ideality of its subsisting inward differentiations.

1. The Constitution (on its internal side only)

The constitution is rational in so far as the state inwardly differentiates and determines its activity in accordance with the nature of the concept. The result of this is that each of these powers is in itself the totality of the constitution, because each contains the other moments and has them effective in itself, and because the moments, being expressions of the differentiation of the concept, simply abide in their ideality and constitute nothing but a single individual whole.

In our day there has come before the public an endless amount of babble about the constitution, as about reason itself, and the stalest babble of all has been produced in Germany, thanks to those who have persuaded themselves that they have the best, or even the sole, understanding of what a constitution is. Elsewhere, particularly in governments, misunderstanding is supposed to reign. And these gentlemen are convinced that they have an unassailable justification for what they say because they claim that religion and piety are the basis of all this shallow thinking of theirs. It is no wonder that this babble has made reasonable men just as sick of the words 'reason', 'enlightenment', 'right', &c., as of the words 'constitution' and 'freedom', and a man might well be ashamed now to go on discussing the constitution of the state at all! However, we may at least hope that this surfeit will be effective in producing the general conviction that philosophical *knowledge* of such topics cannot arise from argumentation, deduction, calculations of purpose and utility, still less from the heart, love, and inspiration, but only from the concept. We may also hope that those who hold that the divine is inconceivable and the knowledge of truth a wild-goose chase will feel themselves bound to refrain from taking part in the discussion. The products of their hearts and their inspirations are either undigested chatter or mere edification, and whatever the worth of these neither can pretend to notice from philosophy.

Amongst current ideas, mention may be made of the necessity for a division of powers within the state. This point is of the highest importance and, if taken in its true sense, may rightly be regarded as the guarantee of public freedom. It is an idea, however, with which the very people who pretend to talk out of their inspiration and love neither have, nor desire to have, any acquaintance, since it is precisely there that the moment of rational determinacy lies. That is to say, the principle of the division of powers contains the essential moment of difference, of rationality *realized*. But when the abstract Understanding handles it, it reads into it the false doctrine of the absolute self-subsistence of each of the powers against the others, and then one-sidedly interprets their relation to each other as negative, as a mutual restriction. This view implies that the attitude adopted by each power to the others is hostile and apprehensive, as if the others were evils, and that their function is to oppose one another and as a result of this counterpoise to effect an equilibrium on the whole, but never a living unity. It is only the inner self-determination of the concept, not any other consideration, whether of purpose or advantage, that is the absolute source of the division of powers, and in virtue of this alone is the organization of the state something inherently rational and the image of eternal reason.

How the concept and then, more concretely, how the Idea, determine themselves inwardly and so posit their moments—universality, particularity, and individuality—in abstraction from one another, is discoverable from my logic, though not of course from the logic current elsewhere. To take the merely negative as a starting-point and to exalt to the first place the volition of evil and the mistrust of this volition, and then on the basis of this presupposition slyly to construct dikes whose efficiency simply necessitates corresponding dikes over against them, is characteristic in thought of the negative Understanding and in sentiment of the outlook of the rabble.

If the powers (e.g., what are called the 'Executive' and the 'Legislature') become self-subsistent, then as we have recently seen on a grand scale, the destruction of the state is forthwith a *fait accompli*. Alternatively, if the state is maintained in essentials, it is strife which through the subjection by one power of the others, produces unity at least, however defective, and so secures the bare essential, the maintenance of the state.

The state as a political entity is thus cleft into three substantive divisions:

1. the power to determine and establish the universal—the Legislature;
2. the power to subsume single cases and the spheres of particularity under the universal—the Executive;
3. the power of subjectivity, as the will with the power of ultimate decision—the Crown. In the crown, the different powers are bound into an individual unity which is thus at once the apex and basis of the whole, i.e., of constitutional monarchy.

The development of the state to constitutional monarchy is the achievement of the modern world, a world in which the substantial Idea has won the infinite form of subjectivity. The history of this inner deepening of the world mind—or in other words this free maturation in course of which the Idea, realizing rationality in the external, releases its moments (and they are only its moments) from itself as totalities, and just for that reason still retains them in the ideal unity of the concept—the history of this genuine formation of ethical life is the content of the whole course of world-history.

The ancient division of constitutions into monarchy, aristocracy, and democracy, is based upon the notion of substantial, still undivided, unity, a unity which has not yet come to its inner differentiation (to a matured, internal organization) and which therefore has not yet attained depth or concrete rationality. From the standpoint of the ancient world, therefore, this division is the true and correct one, since for a unity of that still substantial type, a unity inwardly too immature to have attained its absolutely complete development, difference is essentially an external difference and appears at first as a difference in the number of those in whom that substantial unity is supposed to be immanent. These forms, which on this principle belong to different wholes, are given in limited monarchy the humbler position of moments in a whole. The monarch is a *single* person; the *few* come on the scene with the executive, and the *many* en masse with the legislative. But, as has been indicated, purely quantitative distinctions like these are only superficial and do not afford the concept of the thing. Equally inadequate is the mass of contemporary talk about the democratic and aristocratic elements in monarchy, because when the elements specified in such talk are found in a monarchy there is no longer anything democratic or aristocratic about them. There are notions of constitutions in which the state is portrayed from top to bottom as an abstraction which is supposed to rule and command, and how many individuals are at the head of such a state, whether one or a few or all, is a question left undecided and regarded as a matter of indifference. [E.g.:] 'All these forms', says Fichte, '…are justified, provided there be an ephorate' (a scheme devised by Fichte to be a counterpoise to the chief power in the state) 'and may…be the means of introducing universal rights into the state and maintaining them there.' A view of this kind—and the device of the ephorate also—is begotten by the superficial conception of the state to which reference has just been made. It is true enough that in quite simple social conditions these differences of constitutional form have little or no meaning. For instance, in the course of his legislation Moses prescribed that, in the event of his people's desiring a king, its institutions should remain unchanged except for the new requirement that the king should not 'multiply horses to himself...nor wives...nor silver and gold'. Besides, in a sense one may of course say that the Idea too is indifferent to these forms (including monarchy, but only when it is restricted in meaning by being defined as an *alternative* on a parity with aristocracy and democracy). But the Idea is indifferent to them, not in Fichte's but in the opposite sense, because every one of them is inadequate to it in its rational development and in none of them, taken singly, could the Idea attain its right and its actuality. Consequently, it is quite idle to inquire which of the three is most to be preferred. Such forms must be discussed historically or not at all.

Still, here again, as in so many other places, we must recognize the depth of Montesquieu's insight in his now famous treatment of the basic principles of these forms of government. To recognize the accuracy of his account, however, we must not misunderstand it. As is well known, he held that 'virtue' was the principle of democracy [and rightly], since it is in fact the case that that type of constitution rests on sentiment, i.e., on the purely substantial form in which the rationality of the absolute will still exists in democracy. But Montesquieu goes on to say that in the seventeenth century England provided 'a fine spectacle of the way in which efforts to found a democracy were rendered ineffective by a lack of virtue in the leaders'. And again he adds 'when virtue vanishes from the republic, ambition enters hearts which are capable of it and greed masters everyone...so that the state becomes everyone's booty and its strength now consists only in the power of a few citizens and the licence of all alike'. These quotations call for the comment that in more mature social conditions and when the powers of particularity have developed and become free, a form of rational law other than the form of sentiment is required, because virtue in the heads of the state is not enough if the state as a whole is to gain the power to resist disruption and to bestow on the powers of particularity, now become mature, both their positive and their negative rights. Similarly, we must remove the misunderstanding of supposing that because the sentiment of virtue is the substantial form of a democratic republic, it is evidently superfluous in monarchy or even absent from it altogether, and, finally, we may not suppose that there is an opposition and an incompatibility between virtue and the legally determinate agency of a state whose organization is fully articulated.

The fact that 'moderation' is cited as the principle of aristocracy implies the beginning at this point of a divorce between public authority and private interest. And yet at the same time these touch each other so directly that this constitution by its very nature stands on the verge of lapsing forthwith into tyranny or anarchy—the harshest of political conditions—and so into self-annihilation. See Roman history, for example.

The fact that Montesquieu discerns 'honour' as the principle of monarchy at once makes it clear that by 'monarchy' he understands, not the patriarchal or any ancient type, nor, on the other hand, the type organized into an objective constitution, but only feudal monarchy, the type in which the relationships recognized in its constitutional law are crystallized into the rights of private property and the privileges of individuals and Corporations. In this type of constitution, political life rests on privileged persons and a great part of what must be done for the maintenance of the state is settled at their pleasure. The result is that their services are the objects not of duty but only of ideas and opinions. Thus it is not duty but only honour which holds the state together.

Another question readily presents itself here: 'Who is to frame the constitution?' This question seems clear, but closer inspection shows at once that it is meaningless, for it presupposes that there is no constitution there, but only an agglomeration of atomic individuals. How an agglomeration of individuals could acquire a constitution, whether automatically or by someone's aid, whether as a present or by force or by thought, it would have to be allowed to settle for itself, since with an agglomeration the concept has nothing to do. But if the question presupposes an already existent constitution, then it is not about framing, but only about altering the constitution, and the very presupposition of a constitution directly implies that its alteration may come about only by constitutional means. In any case, however, it is absolutely essential that the constitution should not be regarded as something made, even though it has come into being in time. It must be treated rather as something simply existent in and by itself, as divine therefore, and constant, and so as exalted above the sphere of things that are made.

Mind is actual only as that which it knows itself to be, and the state, as the mind of a nation, is both the law permeating all relationships within the state and also at the same time the manners and consciousness of its citizens. It follows, therefore, that the constitution of any given nation depends in general on the character and development of its self-consciousness. In its self-consciousness its subjective freedom is rooted and so, therefore, is the actuality of its constitution.

The proposal to give a constitution—even one more or less rational in content—to a nation *a priori* would be a happy thought overlooking precisely that factor in a constitution which makes it more than an *ens rationis*. Hence every nation has the constitution appropriate to it and suitable for it.

Part II

Historical Materialism

2

Internationalism, Hegemony, and Orthodoxy

Introduction

The extension of Hegel's and Kant's moral ideas to social theory represents the second period of the evolution of critical theory, or the phase of historical materialism (1867–1914). As is well known, Marx sought to overcome the unresolved tensions of Hegel's and Kant's abstract idealism by formulating a social theory of class conflict. In his critique of Hegel's absolutization of the spirit (1844 manuscripts), Marx argued that Hegel's idea of the absolute spirit failed to account for the constitutive material elements of property rights and class relations. Against Hegel's abstract and mystical analysis of societal relations, Marx theorized that class struggle was the driving force of history: the product of class antagonisms which had fueled the evolving transformation of societal relations (within the modes of production, from communalism and feudalism to capitalism). For him the task of social theory was to first interpret the oppressive laws of capitalism in terms of class conflict; then, to change the social practices (e.g., the bourgeoisie's private ownership of the means of production or private property, state rule over the exchange controls) that had alienated and oppressed a wide sector of the population, the proletariat.

In *Capital* (1867)[1], Marx sought to unveil the precise mechanisms and laws of these oppressive practices of capitalism by devising a theory of value that treated the (capitalist) relations of production as unreal or fetishized. As he states, "the Class which has the means of material production at its disposal has control at the same time over the means of mental production."[1] Such control explains how exchange value reifies the actual use value of a commodity by allowing the power of money (appearance of value) to become the primary means of determining labour value and power. Here Marx employed the term surplus value or the unequal exchange between capital and labor to investigate the concrete effects of the reification of commodities.

Throughout the late 1800s and early 1900s, Marx's social theory of value provided a widely accepted, orthodox critique of capitalism. However, by the early to middle part of the twentieth century, tensions would begin to emerge within Marxism, which would give way to a new brand of Marxism. Western Marxism, as it would eventually come to be known, was a revisionist movement that sought to return to Hegel's holism in order to challenge the reductionism of Marxism.

Antonio Gramsci and Georg Lukács represent two of the most well-known theorists of Western Marxism. Lukács, for instance, argued that orthodox Marxism had relied on the inert immediacy of facts to validate its objectives. To rectify this problem, one had to relate these facts to a broader, more dynamic understanding of society as a whole. By comparison, Gramsci sought to articulate the ethical and cultural variants of Marxism by analyzing the interplay between the base (economic relations) and superstructure (cultural, political, and ethical factors). Here, Gramsci theorized that the scientific reductivism of orthodox Marxism ignored the consititutive tensions between the state and civil society. For Gramsci, historical materialism needed to take account of the dialectical interplay between the state and civil society, and explain the social forces of a counter-hegemonic civil society, in particular, the role of the organic intellectuals in educating the workers and peasants.

Endnote

1. Karl Marx, *Capital*, Vol. 1. (London: Penguin Books, 1990), Book I, p. 172.

Karl Marx, Selection from *Economic and Philosophic Manuscripts of 1844*

The outstanding thing in Hegel's *Phenomenology* and its final outcome—that is, the dialectic of negativity as the moving and generating principle—is thus first that Hegel conceives the self-genesis of man as a process, conceives objectification as loss of the object, as alienation and as transcendence of this alienation; that he thus grasps the essence of *labour* and comprehends objective man—true, because real man—as the outcome of man's *own labour*. The *real*, active orientation of man to himself as a species being, or his manifestation as a real species being (i.e., as a human being), is only possible by his really bringing out of himself all the *powers* that are his as the *species* man—something which in turn is only possible through the totality of man's actions, as the result of history—is only possible by man's treating these generic powers as objects: and this, to begin with, is again only possible in the form of estrangement.

We shall now demonstrate in detail Hegel's one-sidedness and limitations as they are displayed in the final chapter of the *Phenomenology*, "Absolute Knowledge"—a chapter which contains the concentrated spirit of the *Phenomenology*, the relationship of the *Phenomenology* to speculative dialectic, and also Hegel's *consciousness* concerning both and their relationship to one another.

Let us provisionally say just this much in advance: Hegel's standpoint is that of modern political economy. He grasps *labour* as the *essence* of man—as man's essence in the act of proving itself: he sees only the positive, not the negative side of labour. Labour is man's *coming-to-be for himself* within *alienation*, or as *alienated* man. The only labour which Hegel knows and recognizes is *abstractly mental* labour. Therefore, that which constitutes the *essence* of philosophy—the *alienation of man in his knowing of himself, or alienated* science *thinking itself*—Hegel grasps as its essence; and he is therefore able *vis-à-vis* preceding philosophy to gather together its separate elements and phases, and to present his philosophy as the philosophy. What the other philosophers did—that they grasped separate phases of nature and of human life as phases of self-consciousness, and indeed of abstract self-consciousness—is *known* to Hegel as the *doings* of philosophy. Hence his science is absolute.

Let us now turn to our subject.

Absolute Knowledge. The last chapter of the "Phenomenology."

The main point is that the *object of consciousness* is nothing else but *self-consciousness*, or that the object is only *objectified self-consciousness*—self-consciousness as object.

(Positing of man = self-consciousness.)

The issue, therefore, is to surmount the *object of consciousness*. *Objectivity* as such is regarded as an *estranged* human relationship which does not correspond to the *essence of man*, to self-consciousness. The *re-appropriation* of the objective essence of man, begotten in the form of estrangement as something alien, has the meaning therefore not only to annul *estrangement*, but *objectivity* as well. Man, that is to say, is regarded as a *non-objective, spiritual* being.

The movement of *surmounting the object of consciousness* is now described by Hegel in the following way:

The *object* reveals itself not merely as *returning into the self*—for Hegel that is the *one-sided* way of apprehending this movement, the grasping of only one side. Man is posited as equivalent to self. The self, however, is only the *abstractly* conceived man—man begotten by abstraction. Man is egotistic. His eye, his ear, etc., are *egotistic*. In him every one of his essential powers has the quality of *selfhood*. But it is quite false to say on that account "*Self-consciousness* has eyes, ears, essential powers." Self-consciousness is rather a quality of human nature, of the human eye, etc.; it is not human nature that is a quality of *self-consciousness*.

The self-abstracted and fixed for itself is man as *abstract egoist*—*egoism* raised in its pure abstraction to the level of thought. (We shall return to this point later.)

For Hegel the *essence of man—man*—equals *self-consciousness*. All estrangement of the human essence is therefore *nothing but estrangement of self-consciousness*. The estrangement of self-consciousness is not regarded as an *expression* of the *real* estrangement of the human being—its expression reflected in the realm of knowledge and thought. Instead, the *real* estrangement—that which appears real—is from *its innermost*, hidden nature (a nature only brought to light by philosophy) nothing but the *manifestation* of the estrangement of the real essence of man, of *self-consciousness*. The science which comprehends this is therefore called *Phenomenology*. All re-appropriation of the estranged objective essence appears, therefore, as a process of incorporation into self-consciousness: The man who takes hold of his essential being is *merely* the self-consciousness which takes hold of objective essences. Return of the object into the self is therefore the re-appropriation of the object.

The *surmounting of the object of consciousness, comprehensively* expressed, means:

1. That the object as such presents itself to consciousness as something vanishing.
2. That it is the alienation of self-consciousness which establishes thinghood.
3. That this externalization of self-consciousness has not merely a *negative* but a *positive* significance.
4. That it has this meaning not merely *for us* or *intrinsically*, but *for self-consciousness itself*.
5. *For self-consciousness, the negative of the object, its annulling of itself, has positive* significance—self-consciousness *knows* this nullity of the object—because self-consciousness itself alienates itself; for in this alienation it establishes *itself* as object, or, for the sake of the indivisible unity of *being-for-self*, establishes the object as itself.
6. On the other hand, there is also this other moment in the process, that self-consciousness has also just as much annulled and superseded this alienation and objectivity and resumed them into itself, being thus at home with *itself* in *its* other-being *as such*.

7. This is the movement of *consciousness* and in this movement consciousness is the totality of its moments.
8. Consciousness must similarly have taken up a relation to the object in all its aspects and phases, and have comprehended it from the point of view of each of them.

This totality of its determinate characteristics makes the object *intrinsically a spiritual being*; and it becomes so in truth for consciousness through the apprehending of each single one of them as *self* or through what was called above the *spiritual* attitude to them.

As to (1): That the object as such presents itself to consciousness as something vanishing—this is the above-mentioned *return of the object into the self*.

As to (2): *The alienation of self-consciousness* establishes *thinghood*. Because man equals self-consciousness, his alienated, objective essence, or *thinghood, equals alienated self-consciousness*, and *thinghood* is thus established through this alienation (thinghood being *that* which is an *object for man* and an object for him is really only that which is to him an essential object, therefore his *objective essence*. And since it is not *real Man*, nor therefore *Nature*—Man being *human Nature*—who as such is made the subject, but only the abstraction of man—self-consciousness—thinghood cannot be anything but alienated self-conciousness). It is only to be expected that a living, natural being equipped and endowed with objective (i.e., material) essential powers should have *real natural objects* of his essence; as is the fact that his self-alienation should lead to the establishing of a *real*, objective world—but a world in the form of *externality*—a world, therefore, not belonging to his own essential being, and an overpowering world. There is nothing incomprehensible or mysterious in this. It would be mysterious, rather, if it were otherwise. But it is equally clear that a *self-consciousness* can only establish *thinghood* through its alienation—i.e., establish something which itself is only an abstract thing, a thing of abstraction and not a *real* thing. It is clear, further, that thinghood is therefore utterly without any *independence*, any *essentiality vis-à-vis* self-consciousness; that on the contrary, it is a mere creature—something *posited* by self-consciousness. And what is posited, instead of confirming itself, is but a confirmation of the act of positing in which is concentrated for a moment the energy of the act as its product, *seeming* to give the de-posit—but only for a moment—the character of an independent, real substance.

Whenever real, corporeal *man*, man with his feet firmly on the solid ground, man exhaling and inhaling all the forces of nature, *establishes* his real, objective *essential powers* as alien objects by his externalization, it is not the *act of positing* which is the subject in this process: it is the subjectivity of *objective* essential powers, whose action, therefore, must also be something *objective*. A being who is objective acts objectively, and he would not act objectively if the objective did not reside in the very nature of his being. He creates or establishes only *objects, because* he is established by objects—because at bottom he is *nature*. In the act of establishing, therefore, this objective being does not fall from his state of "pure activity" into a *creating of the object*; on the contrary, his *objective* product only confirms his *objective* activity, establishing his activity as the activity of an objective, natural being.

Here we see how consistent naturalism or humanism distinguishes itself both from idealism and materialism, constituting at the same time the unifying truth of both. We see also how only naturalism is capable of comprehending the act of world history.

Man is directly a *natural being*. As a natural being and as a living natural being he is on the one hand furnished with *natural powers of life*—he is an *active* natural being. These forces exist in him as tendencies and abilities—as *impulses*. On the other hand, as a natural, corporeal, sensuous, objective being he is a *suffering*, conditioned and limited creature, like animals and plants. That is to say, the *objects* of his impulses exist outside him, as *objects* independent of him, yet these objects are *objects* of his *need*—essential *objects*, indispensable to the manifestation and confirmation of his essential powers. To say that man is a *corporeal*, living, real, sensuous, objective being full of natural vigour is to say that he has *real, sensuous, objects* as the objects of his being or of his life, or that he can only *express* his life in real, sensuous objects. To be objective, natural, and sensuous, and at the same time to have object, nature and sense outside oneself, or oneself to be object, nature and sense for a third party, is one and the same thing. *Hunger* is a natural *need*; it therefore needs a *nature* outside itself, an *object* outside itself, in order to satisfy itself, to be stilled. Hunger is an acknowledged need of my body for an *object* existing outside it, indispensable to its integration and to the expression of its essential being. The sun is the *object* of the plant—an indispensable object to it, confirming its life—just as the plant is an object of the sun, being an *expression* of the life-awakening power of the sun, of the sun's *objective* essential power.

A being which does not have its nature outside itself is not a *natural* being, and plays no part in the system of nature. A being which has no object outside itself is not an objective being. A being which is not itself an object for some third being has no being for its *object*; i.e., it is not objectively related. Its being is not objective.

An unobjective being is a *nullity*—an *un-being*.

Suppose a being which is neither an object itself, nor has an object. Such a being, in the first place, would be the *unique* being: there would exist no being outside it—it would exist solitary and alone. For as soon as there are objects outside me, as soon as I am not *alone*, I am *another*—another *reality* than the object outside me. For this third object I am thus an *other reality* than it; that is, I am its object. Thus, to suppose a being which is not the object of another being is to presuppose that *no* objective being exists. As soon as I have an object, this object has me for an object. But a *nonobjective* being is an unreal, nonsensical thing—something merely thought of (merely imagined, that is)—a creature of abstraction. To be *sensuous*, that is, to be an object of sense, to be a *sensuous* object, and thus to have sensuous objects outside oneself—objects of one's sensuousness. To be sensuous is to *suffer*.

Man as an objective, sensuous being is therefore a *suffering* being—and because he feels what he suffers, a *passionate* being. Passion is the essential force of man energetically bent on its object.

But man is not merely a natural being: he is a *human* natural being. That is to say, he is a being for himself. Therefore he is a *species being*, and has to confirm and manifest himself as such both in his being and in his knowing. Therefore, *human* objects are not natural objects as they immediately present themselves, and neither is *human sense* as it immediately *is*—as it is objectively—*human* sensibility, human objectivity. Neither nature objectively nor nature subjectively is directly given in a form adequate to the *human* being. And as everything natural has to have its *beginning*, *man* too has his act of coming-to-be—*history*—which, however, is for him a known history, and hence as an act of coming-to-be it is a conscious self-transcending act of coming-to-be. History is the true natural history of man (on which more later).

Thirdly, because this establishing of thinghood is itself only sham, an act contradicting the nature of pure activity, it has to be cancelled again and thinghood denied.

Re. 3, 4, 5 and 6. (3) This externalization of consciousness has not merely a *negative* but a *positive* significance, and (4) it has this meaning not merely *for us* or intrinsically, but for consciousness itself. (5) *For consciousness* the negative of the object, its annulling of itself, has *positive* significance—consciousness *knows* this nullity of the object because it alienates *itself*; for in this alienation it *knows* itself as object, or, for the sake of the indivisible unity of *being-for-itself*, the object as itself. (6) On the other hand, there is also this other moment in the process, that consciousness has also just as much annulled and superseded this alienation and objectivity and resumed them into itself, being thus *at home with itself* in its *other-being as such*.

As we have already seen: the appropriation of what is estranged and objective, or the annulling of objectivity in the form of *estrangement* (which has to advance from indifferent foreignness to real, antagonistic estrangement) means equally or even primarily for Hegel that it is *objectivity* which is to be annulled, because it is not the *determinate* character of the object, but rather its *objective* character that is offensive and constitutes estrangement for self-consciousness. The object is therefore something negative, self-annulling—a *nullity*. This nullity of the object has not only a negative but a *positive* meaning for consciousness, for such a *nullity* of the object is precisely the *self-confirmation* of the non-objectivity, of the *abstraction* of itself. For *consciousness itself* this nullity of the object has a positive meaning because it *knows* this nullity, the objective being, as *its self-alienation*; because it knows that it exists only as a result of its own *self-alienation*. ...

The way in which consciousness is, and in which something is for it, is *knowing*. Knowing is its sole act. Something therefore comes to be for consciousness in so far as the latter *knows* this *something*. Knowing is its sole objective relation. Consciousness, then, knows the nullity of the object (i.e., knows the non-existence of the distinction between the object and itself, the non-existence of the object for it) because it knows the object as its *self-alienation*; that is, it knows itself—knows knowing as the object—because the object is only the *semblance* of an object, a piece of mystification, which in its essence, however, is nothing else but knowing itself; which has confronted itself with itself and in so doing has confronted itself with a *nullity*—a something which has *no* objectivity outside the knowing. Or: knowing knows that in relating itself to an object it is only *outside itself*—that it only externalizes itself; that *it itself* appears to itself only *as an object*—or that that which appears to it as an object is only it itself.

On the other hand, says Hegel, there is at the same time this other moment in this process, that consciousness has just as much annulled and superseded this externalization and objectivity and resumed them into itself, being thus *at home* in its *other-being as such*.

In this discussion are brought together all the illusions of speculation.

First of all: consciousness—self-consciousness—is *at home with itself in its other-being as such*. It is therefore—or if we here abstract from the Hegelian abstraction and put the self-consciousness of man instead of Self-consciousness—*it is at home with itself in its other-being, as such*. This implies, for one thing, that consciousness (knowing as knowing, thinking as thinking) pretends to be directly the *other* of itself—to be the world of sense, the real world, life—thought over-reaching itself in thought (Feuerbach). This aspect is contained herein, inasmuch as consciousness as mere consciousness takes offence not at estranged objectivity, but at *objectivity as such*.

Secondly, this implies that self-conscious man, in so far as he has recognized and annulled and superseded the spiritual world (or his world's spiritual, general mode of being) as self-alienation, nevertheless again confirms this in its alienated shape and passes it off as his true mode of being—re-establishes it, and pretends to be *at home in his other-being as such*. Thus, for instance, after annulling and superseding religion, after recognizing religion to be a product of self-alienation, he yet finds confirmation of himself in *religion as religion*. Here is the root of Hegel's *false* positivism, or of his merely *apparent* criticism: this is what Feuerbach designated as the positing, negating and re-establishing of religion or theology—but it has to be grasped in more general terms. Thus reason is at home in unreason as unreason. The man who has recognized that he is leading an alienated life in politics, law, etc., is leading his true human life in this alienated life as such. Self-affirmation, *in contradiction* with itself—in contradiction both with the knowledge of and with the essential being of the object—is thus true *knowledge* and *life*.

There can therefore no longer be any question about an act of accommodation on Hegel's part *vis-à-vis* religion, the state, etc., since this lie is *the* lie of his principle.

If I *know* religion as *alienated* human, self-consciousness, then what I know in it as religion is not my self-consciousness, but my alienated self-consciousness confirmed in it. I therefore know my own self, the self-consciousness that belongs to its very nature, confirmed not in *religion* but rather in *annihilated* and *superseded* religion.

In Hegel, therefore, the negation of the negation is not the confirmation of the true essence, effected precisely through negation of the pseudo-essence. With him the negation of the negation is the confirmation of the pseudo-essence, or of the self-estranged essence in its denial; or it is the denial of this pseudo-essence as an objective being dwelling outside man and independent of him, and its transformation into the subject.

A peculiar role, therefore, is played by the act of *superseding* in which denial and preservation—denial and affirmation—are bound together.

Thus, for example, in Hegel's *Philosophy of Right*, *Private Right* superseded equals *Morality*, Morality superseded equals the *Family*, the Family superseded equals *Civil Society*, Civil Society superseded equals the *State*, the State superseded equals *World History*. In the *actual world* private right, morality, the family, civil society, the state, etc., remain in existence, only they have become moments of man—state of his existence and being—which have no validity in isolation, but dissolve and engender one another, etc. They have become *moments of motion*.

In their actual existence this *mobile* nature of theirs is hidden. It first appears and is made manifest in thought, in philosophy. Hence my true religious existence is my existence in the *philosophy of religion*; my true political existence is my existence within the *philosophy of right*; my true natural existence, existence in the *philosophy of nature*; my true artistic existence, existence in the *philosophy of art*; my true *human* existence, my existence in *philosophy*. Likewise the true existence of religion, the state, nature, art is the *philosophy* of religion, of nature, of the state and of art. If, however, the philosophy of religion, etc., is for me the sole true existence of religion, then, too, it is only as a *philosopher of religion* that I am truly religious, and so I deny *real* religious sentiment and the really *religious* man. But at the same time I *assert* them, in part within my own existence or within the alien existence which I oppose to them—for this *is* only their *philosophic* expression—and in part I assert them in their own original shape, for they have validity for me as merely the *apparent* other-being, as allegories, forms of their own true existence (i.e., of my *philosophical* existence) hidden under sensuous disguises.

In just the same way, *Quality* superseded equals *Quantity*, Quantity superseded equals *Measure*, Measure superseded equals *Essence*, Essence superseded equals *Appearance*, Appearance superseded equals *Actuality*, Actuality superseded equals the *Concept*, the Concept superseded equals *Objectivity*, Objectivity superseded equals the *Absolute Idea*, the Absolute Idea superseded equals *Nature*, Nature superseded equals *Ethical* Objective Mind, Ethical Mind superseded equals *Art*, Art superseded equals *Religion*, Religion superseded equals *Absolute Knowledge*.

On the one hand, this act of superseding is a transcending of the thought entity; thus, Private Property *as* a thought is transcended in the *thought* of morality. And because thought imagines itself to be directly the other of itself, to be *sensuous reality*—and therefore takes its own action for *sensuous, real action*—this superseding in thought, which leaves its object standing in the real world, believes that it has really overcome it. On the other hand, because the object has now become for it a moment of thought, thought takes it in its reality too to be self-confirmation of itself—of self-consciousness, of abstraction.

From the one point of view the existent which Hegel *supersedes* in philosophy is therefore not *real* religion, the *real* state, or *real* nature, but religion itself already become an object of knowledge, i.e., *Dogmatics*; the same with *Jurisprudence*, *Political Science* and *Natural Science*. From the one point of view, therefore, he stands in opposition both to the *real* thing and to immediate, unphilosophic *science* or the unphilosophic *conceptions* of this thing. He therefore contradicts their conventional conceptions.

On the other hand, the religious man, etc., can find in Hegel his final confirmation.

It is now time to lay hold of the *positive* aspects of the Hegelian dialectic within the realm of estrangement.

(a) *Annulling* as an objective movement of *retracting* the alienation *into self*. This is the insight, expressed within the estrangement, concerning the *appropriation* of the objective essence through the annulment of its estrangement; it is the estranged insight into the *real objectification* of man, into the real appropriation of his objective essence through the annihilation of the *estranged* character of the objective world, through the annulment of the objective world in its estranged mode of being—just as atheism, being the annulment of God, is the advent of theoretic humanism, and communism, as the annulment of private property, is the justification of real human life as man's possession and thus the advent of practical humanism (or just as atheism is humanism mediated with itself through the annulment of religion, whilst communism is humanism mediated with itself through the annulment of private property). Only through the annulment of this mediation—which is itself, however, a necessary premise—does positively self-deriving humanism, *positive humanism*, come into being.

But atheism and communism are no flight, no abstraction; they are not a losing of the objective world begotten by man—of man's essential powers given over to the realm of objectivity; they are not a returning in poverty to unnatural, primitive simplicity. On the contrary, they are but the first real coming-to-be, the realization become real for man, of man's essence—of the essence of man as something real.

Thus, by grasping the *positive* meaning of self-referred negation (if even again in estranged fashion) Hegel grasps man's self-estrangement, the alienation of man's essence, man's loss of objectivity and his loss of realness as finding of self, change of his nature, his objectification and realization. In short, within the sphere of abstraction, Hegel conceives labour as man's act of *self-genesis*—conceives man's relation to himself as an alien being and the manifesting of himself as an alien being to be the coming-to-be of *species-consciousness* and *species-life*.

(b) However, apart from, or rather in consequence of, the perverseness already described, this act appears in Hegel:

First of all as a *merely formal*, because abstract, act, because the human essence itself is taken to be only an *abstract, thinking essence*, conceived merely as self-consciousness.

Secondly, because the Conception is *formal* and *abstract*, the annulment of the alienation becomes a confirmation of the alienation; or again, for Hegel this movement of *self-genesis* and *self-objectification* in the form of *self-alienation* and *self-estrangement* is the *absolute*, and hence final, *expression of human life*—of life with itself as its aim, of life at rest in itself, of life that has attained oneness with its essence.

This movement, in its abstract form as dialectic, is therefore regarded as *truly human life*, and because it is nevertheless an abstraction—an estrangement of human life—it is regarded as a *divine process*, but as the divine process of man, a process traversed by man's abstract, pure, absolute essence that is distinct from him.

Thirdly, this process must have a bearer, a subject. But the subject first emerges as a result. This result—the subject knowing itself as absolute self-consciousness—is therefore *God*—absolute Spirit—*the self-knowing and self-manifesting Idea*. Real man and real nature become mere predicates—symbols of this esoteric, unreal man and of this unreal nature. Subject and predicate are therefore related to each other in absolute inversion—a *mystical subject-object* or a *subjectivity reaching beyond* the *object*—the *absolute subject* as a *process*, as *subject alienating* itself and returning from alienation into itself, but at the same time retracting this alienation into itself, and the subject as this process; a pure, *restless* revolving within itself.

Karl Marx, Selection from *Capital*

The Dual Character of the Labour Embodied In Commodities

Initially the commodity appeared to us as an object with a dual character, possessing both use-value and exchange-value. Later on it was seen that labour, too, has a dual character: in so far as it finds its expression in value, it no longer possesses the same characteristics as when it is the creator of use-values. I was the first to point out and examine critically this twofold nature of the labour contained in commodities. As this point is crucial to an understanding of political economy, it requires further elucidation.

Let us take two commodities, such as a coat and 10 yards of linen, and let the value of the first be twice the value of the second, so that, if 10 yards of linen = W, the coat = $2W$.

The coat is a use-value that satisfies a particular need. A specific kind of productive activity is required to bring it into existence. This activity is determined by its aim, mode of operation, object, means and result. We use the abbreviated expression 'useful labour' for labour whose utility is represented by the use-value of its product, or by the fact that its product is a use-value. In this connection we consider only its useful effect.

As the coat and the linen are qualitatively different use-values, so also are the forms of labour through which their existence is mediated—tailoring and weaving. If the use-values were not qualitatively different, hence not the products of qualitatively different forms of useful labour, they would be absolutely incapable of confronting each other as commodities. Coats cannot be exchanged for coats, one use-value cannot be exchanged for another of the same kind.

The totality of heterogeneous use-values or physical commodities reflects a totality of similarly heterogeneous forms of useful labour, which differ in order, genus, species and variety: in short, a social division of labour. This division of labour is a necessary condition for commodity production, although the converse does not hold; commodity production is not a necessary condition for the social division of labour. Labour is socially divided in the primitive Indian community, although the products do not thereby become commodities. Or, to take an example nearer home, labour is systematically divided in every factory, but the workers do not bring about this division by exchanging their individual products. Only the products of mutually independent acts of labour, performed in isolation, can confront each other as commodities.

To sum up, then: the use-value of every commodity contains useful labour, i.e., productive activity of a definite kind, carried on with a definite aim. Use-values cannot confront each other as commodities unless the useful labour contained in them is qualitatively different in each case. In a society whose products generally assume the form of commodities, i.e., in a society of commodity producers, this qualitative difference between the useful forms of labour which are carried on independently and privately by individual producers develops into a complex system, a social division of labour.

It is moreover a matter of indifference whether the coat is worn by the tailor or by his customer. In both cases it acts as a use-value. So, too, the relation between the coat and the labour that produced it is not in itself altered when tailoring becomes a special trade, an independent branch of the social division of labour. Men made clothes for thousands of years, under the compulsion of the need for clothing, without a single man ever becoming a tailor. But the existence of coats, of linen, of every element of material wealth not provided in advance by nature, had always to be mediated through a specific, productive activity appropriate to its purpose, a productive activity that assimilated particular natural materials to particular human requirements. Labour, then, as the creator of use-values, as useful labour, is a condition of human existence which is independent of all forms of society; it is an eternal natural necessity which mediates the metabolism between man and nature, and therefore human life itself.

Use-values like, coats, linen, etc., in short, the physical bodies of commodities, are combinations of turn elements, the material provided by nature, and labour. If we subtract the total amount of useful labour of different kinds which is contained in the coat, the linen, etc., a material substratum is always left. This substratum is furnished by nature without human intervention. When man engages in production, he can only proceed as nature does herself, i.e., he can only change the form of the materials. Furthermore, even in this work of modification he is constantly helped by natural forces. Labour is therefore not the only source of material wealth, i.e., of the use-values it produces. As William Petty says, labour is the father of material wealth, the earth is its mother.

Let us now pass from the commodity as an object of utility to the value of commodities.

We have assumed that the coat is worth twice as much as the linen. But this is merely a quantitative difference, and does not concern us at the moment. We shall therefore simply bear in mind that if the value of a coat is twice that of 10 yards of linen, 20 yards of linen will have the same value as a coat. As values, the coat and the linen have the same substance, they are the objective expressions of homogeneous labour. But tailoring and weaving are qualitatively different forms of labour. There are, however, states of society in which the same man alternately makes clothes and weaves. In this case, these two different modes of labour are only modifications of the labour of the same individual and not yet fixed functions peculiar to different individuals, just as the coat our tailor makes today, and the pair of trousers he makes tomorrow, require him only to vary his own individual labour. Moreover, we can see at a glance that in our capitalist society a given portion of labour is supplied alternately in the form of tailoring and in the form of weaving, in accordance with changes in the direction of the demand for labour. This change in the form of labour may well not take place without friction, but it must take place.

If we leave aside the determinate quality of productive activity, and therefore the useful character of the labour, what remains is its quality of being an expenditure of human labour-power. Tailoring and weaving, although they are qualitatively different productive activities, are both a productive expenditure of human brains, muscles, nerves, handsetc., and in this sense both human labour. They are merely two different forms of the expenditure of human labour-power. Of course, human labour-power must itself have attained a certain level of development before it can be expended in this or that form. But the value of a commodity represents human labour pure and simple, the expenditure of human labour in general. And just as, in civil society, a general or a banker plays a great part but man as such plays a very mean part, so, here too, the same is true of human labour. It is the expenditure of simple labour-power, i.e., of the labour-power possessed in his bodily organism by every ordinary man, on the average, without being developed in any special way. *Simple average labour*, it is true, varies in character in different countries and at different cultural epochs, but in a particular society it is given. More complex labour counts only as *intensified*, or rather *multiplied* simple labour, so that a smaller quantity of complex labour is considered equal to a larger quantity of simple labour. Experience shows that this reduction is constantly being made. A commodity may be the outcome of the most complicated labour, but through its *value* it is posited as equal to the product of simple labour, hence it represents only a specific quantity of simple labour. The various proportions in which different kinds of labour are reduced to simple labour as their unit of measurement are established by a social process that goes on behind the backs of the producers; these proportions therefore appear to the producers to have been handed down by tradition. In the interests of simplification, we shall henceforth view every form of labour-power directly as simple labour-power; by this we shall simply be saving ourselves the trouble of making the reduction.

Just as, in viewing the coat and the linen as values, we abstract from their different use-values, so, in the case of the labour represented by those values, do we disregard the difference between its useful forms, tailoring and weaving. The use-values coat and linen are combinations of, on the one hand, productive activity with a definite purpose, and, on the other, cloth and yarn; the values coat and linen, however, are merely congealed quantities of homogeneous labour. In the same way, the labour contained in these values does not count by virtue of its productive relation to cloth and yarn, but only as being an expenditure of human labour-power. Tailoring and weaving are the formative elements in the use-values coat and linen, precisely because these two kinds of labour are of different qualities; but only in so far as abstraction is made from their particular qualities, only in so far as both possess the same quality of being human labour, do tailoring and weaving form the substance of the values of the two articles mentioned.

Coats and linen, however, are not merely values in general, but values of definite magnitude, and, following our assumption, the coat is worth twice as much as the 10 yards of linen. Why is there this difference in value? Because the linen contains only half as much labour as the coat, so that labour-power had to be expended twice as long to produce the second as to produce the first.

While, therefore, with reference to use-value, the labour contained in a commodity counts only qualitatively, with reference to value it counts only quantitatively, once it has been reduced to human labour pure and simple. In the former case it was a matter of the 'how' and the 'what' of labour, in the latter of the 'how much', of the temporal duration of labour. Since the magnitude of the value of a commodity represents nothing but the quantity of labour embodied in it, it follows that all commodities, when taken in certain proportions, must be equal in value.

If the productivity of all the different sorts of useful labour required, let us say, for the production of a coat remains unchanged, the total value of the coats produced will increase along with their quantity. If one coat represents x days' labour, two coats will represent $2x$ days' labour, and so on. But now assume that the duration of the labour necessary for the production of a coat is doubled or halved. In the first case, one coat is worth as much as two coats were before; in the second case two coats are only worth as much as one was before, although in both cases one coat performs the same service, and the useful labour contained in it remains of the same quality. One change has taken place, however: a change in the quantity of labour expended to produce the article.

In itself, an increase in the quantity of use-values constitutes an increase in material wealth. Two coats will clothe two men, one coat will only clothe one man, etc. Nevertheless, an increase in the amount of material wealth may correspond to a simultaneous fall in the magnitude of its value. This contradictory movement arises out of the twofold character of labour. By 'productivity' of course, we always mean the productivity of concrete useful labour; in reality this determines only the degree of effectiveness of productive activity directed towards a given purpose within a given period of time. Useful labour becomes, therefore, a more or less abundant source of products in direct proportion as its productivity rises or falls. As against this, however, variations in productivity have no impact whatever on the labour itself represented in value. As productivity is an attribute of labour in its concrete useful form, it naturally ceases to have any bearing on that labour as soon as we abstract from its concrete useful form. The same labour, therefore, performed for the same length of time, always yields the same amount of value, independently of any variations in productivity. But it provides different quantities of use-values during equal periods of time; more, if productivity rises; fewer, if it falls. For this reason, the same change in productivity which increases the fruitfulness of labour, and therefore the amount of use-values produced by it, also brings about a reduction in the value of this increased total amount, if it cuts down the total amount of labour-time necessary to produce the use-values. The converse also holds.

On the one hand, all labour is an expenditure of human labour-power, in the physiological sense, and it is in this quality of being equal, or abstract, human labour forms the value of commodities. On the other hand, all labour is an expenditure of human labour-power in a particular form and with a definite aim, and it is in this quality of being concrete useful labour that it produces use-values.

The Value-Form, or Exchange-Value

Commodities come into the world in the form of use-values or material goods, such as iron, linen, corn, etc. This is their plain, homely, natural form. However, they are only commodities because they have a dual nature, because they are at the same time objects of utility and bearers of value. Therefore they only appear as commodities, or have the form of commodities, in so far as they possess a double form, i.e., natural form and value form.

The objectivity of commodities as values differs from Dame Quickly in the sense that 'a man knows not where to have it'. Not an atom of matter enters into the objectivity of commodities as values; in this it is the direct opposite of the coarsely sensuous objectivity of commodities as physical objects. We may twist and turn a single commodity as we wish; it remains impossible to grasp it as a thing possessing value. However, let us remember that commodities possess an objective character as values only in so far as they are all expressions of an identical social substance, human labour, that their objective character as values is therefore purely social. From this it follows self-evidently that it can only appear in the social relation between commodity and commodity. In fact we started from exchange-value, or the exchange relation of commodities, in order to track down the value that lay hidden within it. We must now return to this form of appearance of value.

Everyone knows, if nothing else, that commodities have a common value-form which contrasts in the most striking manner with the motley natural forms of their use-values. I refer to the money-form. Now, however, we have to perform a task never even attempted by bourgeois economics. That is, we have to show the origin of this money-form, we have to trace the development of the expression of value contained in the value-relation of com-modifies from its simplest, almost imperceptible outline to the dazzling money-form. When this has been done, the mystery of money will immediately disappear.

The simplest value-relation is evidently that of one commodity to another commodity of a different kind (it does not matter which one). Hence the relation between the values of two commodities supplies us with the simplest expression of the value of a single commodity.

(a) The Simple, Isolated, or Accidental Form of Value

x commodity A = y commodity B or: x commodity A is worth y commodity B.
(20 yards of linen = 1 coat, or: 20 yards of linen are worth 1 coat)

(1) The two poles of the expression of value: the relative form of value and the equivalent form

The whole mystery of the form of value lies hidden in this simple form. Our real difficulty, therefore, is to analyse it.

Here two different kinds of commodities (in our example the linen and the coat) evidently play two different parts. The linen expresses its value in the coat; the coat serves as the material in which that value is expressed. The first commodity plays an active role, the second a passive one. The value of the first commodity is represented as relative value, in other words the commodity is in the relative form of value. The second commodity fulfils the function of equivalent, in other words it is in the equivalent form.

The relative form of value and the equivalent form are two inseparable moments, which belong to and mutually condition each other; but, at the same time, they are mutually exclusive or opposed extremes, i.e., poles of the expression of value. They are always divided up between the different commodities brought into relation with each other by that expression. I cannot, for example, express the value of linen in linen. 20 yards of linen = 20 yards of linen is not an expression of value. The equation states rather the contrary: 20 yards of linen are nothing but 20 yards of linen, a definite quantity of linen considered as an object of utility. The value of the linen can therefore only be expressed relatively, i.e., in another commodity. The relative form of the value of the linen therefore presupposes that some other commodity confronts it in the equivalent form. On the other hand, this other commodity, which figures as the equivalent, cannot simultaneously be in the relative form of value. It is not the latter commodity whose value is being expressed. It only provides the material in which the value of the first commodity is expressed.

Of course, the expression 20 yards of linen = 1 coat, or 20 yards of linen are worth 1 coat, also includes its converse: 1 coat = 20 yards of linen, or 1 coat is worth 20 yards of linen. But in this case I must reverse the equation, in order to express the value of the coat relatively; and, if I do that, the linen becomes the equivalent instead of the coat. The same commodity cannot, therefore, simultaneously appear in both forms in the same expression of value. These forms rather exclude each other as polar opposites.

Whether a commodity is in the relative form or in its opposite, the equivalent form, entirely depends on its actual position in the expression of value. That is, it depends on whether it is the commodity whose value is being expressed, or the commodity in which value is being expressed.

(2) The relative form of value
(i) *The content of the relative form of value*
In order to find out how the simple expression of the value of a commodity lies hidden in the value-relation between two commodities, we must, first of all, consider the value-relation quite independently of its quantitative aspect. The usual mode of procedure is the precise opposite of this: nothing is seen in the value-relation but the proportion in which definite quantities of two sorts of commodity count as equal to each other. It is overlooked that the magnitudes of different things only become comparable in quantitative terms when they have been reduced to the same unit. Only as expressions of the same unit do they have a common denominator, and are therefore commensurable magnitudes.

Whether 20 yards of linen = 1 coat or = 20 coats or = x coats, i.e., whether a given quantity of linen is worth few or many coats, it is always implied, whatever the proportion, that the linen and the coat, as magnitudes of value, are expressions of the same unit, things of the same nature. Linen = coat is the basis of the equation.

But these two qualitatively equated commodities do not play the same part. It is only the value of the linen that is expressed. And how? By being related to the coat as its 'equivalent', or 'the thing exchangeable' with it. In this relation the coat counts as the form of existence of value, as the material embodiment of value, for only as such is it the same as the linen. On the other hand, the linen's own existence as value comes into view or receives an independent expression, for it is only as value that it can be related to the coat as being equal in value to it, or exchangeable with it. In the same way, butyric acid is a different substance from propyl formate. Yet both are made up of the same chemical substances, carbon (C), hydrogen (H) and oxygen (O). Moreover, these substances are combined together in the same proportions in each case, namely $C_4H_8O_2$. If now butyric acid were to be equated with propyl formate, then, in the first place, propyl formate would count in this relation only as a form of existence of $C_4H_8O_2$; and in the second place, it would thereby be asserted that butyric acid also consists of $C_4H_8O_2$. Thus by equating propyl formate with butyric add one would be expressing their chemical composition as opposed to their physical formation.

If we say that, as values, commodities are simply congealed quantities of human labour, our analysis reduces them, it is true, to the level of abstract value, but does not give them a form of value distinct from their natural forms. It is otherwise in the value relation of one commodity to another. The first commodity's value character emerges here through its own relation to the second commodity.

By equating, for example, the coat as a thing of value to the linen, we equate the labour embedded in the coat with the labour embedded in the linen. Now it is true that the tailoring which makes the coat is concrete labour of a different sort from the weaving which makes the linen. But the act of equating tailoring with weaving reduces the former in fact to what is really equal in the two kinds of labour, to the characteristic they have in common of being human labour. This is a roundabout way of saying that weaving too, in so far as it weaves value, has nothing to distinguish it from tailoring, and, consequently, is abstract human labour. It is only the expression of equivalence between different sorts of commodities which brings to view the specific character of value-creating labour, by actually reducing the different kinds of labour embedded in the different kinds of commodity to their common quality of being human labour in general.

However, it is not enough to express the specific character of the labour which goes to make up the value of the linen. Human labour-power in its fluid state, or human labour, creates value but is not itself value. It becomes value in its coagulated state, in objective form. The value of the linen as a congealed mass of human labour can be expressed only as an 'objectivity' [*Gegenständlichkeit*], a thing which is materially different from the linen itself and yet common to the linen and all other commodities. The problem is already solved.

When it is in the value-relation with the linen, the coat counts qualitatively as the equal of the linen, it counts as a thing of the same nature, because it is a value. Here it is therefore a thing in which value is manifested, or which represents value in its tangible natural form. Yet the coat itself, the physical aspect of the coat-commodity, is purely a use-value. A coat as such no more expresses value than does the first piece of linen we come across. This proves only that, within its value-relation to the linen, the coat signifies more than it does outside it, just as some men count for more when inside a gold-braided uniform than they do otherwise.

In the production of the coat, human labour-power, in the shape of tailoring, has in actual fact been expended. Human labour has therefore been accumulated in the coat. From this point of view, the coat is a 'bearer of value', although this property never shows through, even when the coat is at its most threadbare. In its value-relation with the linen, the coat counts only under this aspect, counts therefore as embodied value, as the body of value [*Wertkörper*]. Despite its buttoned-up appearance, the linen recognizes in it a splendid kindred soul, the soul of value. Nevertheless, the coat cannot represent value towards the linen unless value, for the latter, simultaneously assumes the form of a coat. An individual, A, for instance, cannot be 'your majesty' to another individual, B, unless majesty in B's eyes assumes the physical shape of A, and, moreover, changes facial features, hair and many other things, with every new 'father of his people'.

Hence, in the value-relation, in which the coat is the equivalent of the linen, the form of the coat counts as the form of value. The value of the commodity linen is therefore expressed by the physical body of the commodity coat, the value of one by the use-value of the other. As a use-value, the linen is something palpably different from the coat; as value, it is identical with the coat, and therefore looks like the coat. Thus the linen acquires a value-form different from its natural form. Its existence as value is manifested in its equality with the coat, just as the sheep-like nature of the Christian is shown in his resemblance to the Lamb of God.

We see, then, that everything our analysis of the value of commodities previously told us is repeated by the linen itself, as soon as it enters into association with another commodity, the coat. Only it reveals its thoughts in a language with which it alone is familiar, the language of commodities. In order to tell us that labour creates its own value in its abstract quality of being human labour, it says that the coat, in so far as it counts as its equal, i.e., is value, consists of the same labour as it does itself. In order to inform us that its sublime objectivity as a value differs from its stiff and starchy existence as a body, it says that value has the appearance of a coat, and therefore that in so far as the linen itself is an object of value [*Wertding*], it and the coat are as like as two peas. Let us note, incidentally, that the language of commodities also has, apart from Hebrew, plenty of other more or less correct dialects. The German word 'Wertsein' (to be worth), for instance, brings out less strikingly than the Romance verb '*valere*', '*valer*', '*valoir*' that the equating of commodity B with commodity A is the expression of value proper to commodity A. *Paris vaut bien une messe*!

By means of the value-relation, therefore, the natural form of commodity B becomes the value-form of commodity A, in other words the physical body of commodity B becomes a mirror for the value of commodity A. Commodity A, then, in entering into a relation with commodity B as an object of value [*Wertkörper*], as a materialization of human labour, makes the use-value B into the material through which its own value is expressed. The value of commodity A, thus expressed in the use-value of commodity B, has the form of relative value.

The Fetishism of the Commodity and Its Secret

A commodity appears at first sight an extremely obvious, trivial thing. But its analysis brings out that it is a very strange thing, abounding in metaphysical subtleties and theological niceties. So far as it is a use-value, there is nothing mysterious about it, whether we consider it from the point of view that by its properties it satisfies human needs, or that it first takes on these properties as the product of human labour. It is absolutely clear that, by his activity, man changes the forms of the materials of nature in such a way as to make them useful to him. The form of wood, for instance, is altered if a table is made out of it. Nevertheless the table continues to be wood, an ordinary, sensuous thing. But as soon as it emerges as a commodity, it changes into a thing which transcends sensuousness. It not only stands with its feet on the ground, but, in relation to all other commodities, it stands on its head, and evolves out of its wooden brain grotesque ideas, far more wonderful than if it were to begin dancing of its own free will.

The mystical character of the commodity does not therefore arise from its use-value. Just as little does it proceed from the nature of the determinants of value. For in the first place, however varied the useful kinds of labour, or productive activities, it is a physiological fact that they are functions of the human organism, and that each such function, whatever may be its nature or its form, is essentially the expenditure of human brain, nerves, muscles and sense organs. Secondly, with regard to the foundation of the quantitative determination of value, namely the duration of that expenditure or the quantity of labour, this is quite palpably different from its quality. In all situations, the labour-time it costs to produce the means of subsistence must necessarily concern mankind, although not to the same degree at different stages of development. And finally, as soon as men start to work for each other in any way, their labour also assumes a social form.

Whence, then, arises the enigmatic character of the product of labour, as soon as it assumes the form of a commodity? Clearly, it arises from this form itself. The equality of the kinds of human labour takes on a physical form in the equal objectivity of the products of labour as values; the measure of the expenditure of human labour-power by its duration takes on the form of the magnitude of the value of the products of labour; and finally the relationships between the producers, within which the social characteristics of their labours are manifested, take on the form of a social relation between the products of labour.

The mysterious character of the commodity-form consists therefore simply in the fact that the commodity reflects the social characteristics of men's own labour as objective characteristics of the products of labour themselves, as the socio-natural properties of these things. Hence it also reflects the social relation of the producers to the sum total of labour as a social relation between objects, a relation which exists apart from and outside the producers. Through this substitution, the products of labour become commodities, sensuous things which are at the same time supra-sensible or social. In the same way, the impression made by a thing on the optic nerve is perceived not as a subjective excitation of that nerve but as the objective form of a thing outside the eye. In the act of seeing, of course, light is really transmitted from one thing, the external object, to another thing, the eye. It is a physical relation between physical things. As against this, the commodity-form, and the value-relation of the products of labour within which it appears, have absolutely no connection with the physical nature of the commodity and the material [*dinglich*] relations arising out of this. It is nothing but the definite social relation between men themselves which assumes here, for them, the fantastic form of a relation between things. In order, therefore, to find an analogy we must take flight into the misty realm of religion. There the products of the human brain appear as autonomous figures endowed with a life of their own, which enter into relations both with each other and with the human race. So it is in the world of commodities with the products of men's hands. I call this the fetishism which attaches itself to the products of labour as soon as they are produced as commodities, and is therefore inseparable from the production of commodities.

As the foregoing analysis has already demonstrated, this fetishism of the world of commodities arises from the peculiar social character of the labour which produces them.

Objects of utility become commodities only because they are the products of the labour of private individuals who work independently of each other. The sum total of the labour of all these private individuals forms the aggregate labour of society. Since the producers do not come into social contact until they exchange the products of their labour, the specific social characteristics of their private labours appear only within this exchange. In other words, the labour or the private individual manifests itself as an element of the total labour of society only through the relations which the act of exchange establishes between the products, and, through their mediation, between the producers. To the producers, therefore, the social relations between their private labours appear as what they are, i.e., they do not appear as direct social relations between persons in their work, but rather as material [*dinglich*] relations between persons and social relations between things.

It is only by being exchanged that the products of labour acquire a socially uniform objectivity as values, which is distinct from their sensuously varied objectivity as articles of utility. This division of the product of labour into a useful thing and a thing possessing value appears in practice only when exchange has already acquired a sufficient extension and importance to allow useful things to be produced for the purpose of being exchanged, so that their character as values has already to be taken into consideration during production. From this moment on, the labour of the individual producer acquires a twofold social character. On the one hand, it must, as a definite useful kind of labour, satisfy a definite social need, and thus maintain its position as an element of the total labour, as a branch of the social division of labour, which originally sprang up spontaneously. On the other hand, it can satisfy the manifold needs of the individual producer himself only in so far as every particular kind of useful private labour can be exchanged with, i.e., counts as the equal of, every other kind of useful private labour. Equality in the full sense between different kinds of labour can be arrived at only if we abstract from their real inequality, if we reduce them to the characteristic they have in common, that of being the expenditure of human labour-power, of human labour in the abstract. The private producer's brain reflects this twofold social character of his labour only in the forms which appear in practical intercourse, in the exchange of products. Hence the socially useful character of his private labour is reflected in the form that the product of labour has to be useful to others, and the social character of the equality of the various kinds of labour is reflected in the form of the common character, as values, possessed by these materially different things, the products of labour.

Men do not therefore bring the products of their labour into relation with each other as values because they see these objects merely as the material integuments of homogeneous human labour. The reverse is true: by equating their different products to each other in exchange as values, they equate their different kinds of labour as human labour. They do this without being aware of it. Value, therefore, does not have its description branded on its forehead; it rather transforms every product of labour into a social hieroglyphic. Later on, men try to decipher the hieroglyphic, to get behind the secret of their own social product: for the characteristic which objects of utility have of being values is as much men's social product as is their language. The belated scientific discovery that the products of labour, in so far as they are values, are merely the material expressions of the human labour expended to produce them, marks an epoch in the history of mankind's development, but by no means banishes the semblance of objectivity possessed by the social characteristics of labour. Something which is only valid for this particular form of production, the production of commodities, namely the fact that the specific social character of private labours carried on independently of each other consists in their equality as human labour, and, in the product, assumes the form of the existence of value, appears to those caught up in the relations of commodity production (and this is true both before and after the above-mentioned scientific discovery) to be just as ultimately valid as the fact that the scientific dissection of the air into its component parts left the atmosphere itself unaltered in its physical configuration.

What initially concerns producers in practice when they make an exchange is how much of some other product they get for their own; in what proportions can the products be exchanged? As soon as these proportions have attained a certain customary stability, they appear to result from the nature of the products, so that, for instance, one ton of iron and two ounces of gold appear to be equal in value, in the same way as a pound of gold and a pound of iron are equal in weight, despite their different physical and chemical properties. The value character of the products of labour becomes firmly established only when they act as magnitudes of value. These magnitudes vary continually, independently of the will, foreknowledge and actions of the exchangers. Their own movement within society has for them the form of a movement made by things, and these things, far from being under their control, in fact control them. The production of commodities must be fully developed before the scientific conviction emerges, from experience itself, that all the different kinds of private labour (which are carried on independently of each other, and yet, as spontaneously developed branches of the social division of labour, are in a situation of all-round dependence on each other) are continually being reduced to the quantitative proportions in which society requires them. The reason for this reduction is that in the midst of the accidental and ever-fluctuating exchange relations between the products, the labour-time socially necessary to produce them asserts itself as a regulative law of nature. In the same way, the law of gravity asserts itself when a person's house collapses on top of him. The determination of the magnitude of value by labour-time is therefore a secret hidden under the apparent movements in the relative values of commodities. Its discovery destroys the semblance of the merely accidental determination of the magnitude of the value of the products of labour, but by no means abolishes that determination's material form.

Reflection on the forms of human life, hence also scientific analysis of those forms, takes a course directly opposite to their real development. Reflection begins *post festum*, and therefore with the results of the process of development ready to hand. The forms which stamp products as commodities and which are therefore the preliminary requirements for the circulation of commodities, already possess the fixed quality of natural forms of social life before man seeks to give an account, not of their historical character, for in his eyes they are immutable, but of their content and meaning. Consequently, it was solely the analysis of the prices of commodities which led to the determination of the magnitude of value, and solely the common expression of all commodities in money which led to the establishment of their character as values. It is however precisely this finished form of the world of commodities—the money form—which conceals the social character of private labour and the social relations between the individual workers, by making those relations appear as relations between material objects, instead of revealing them plainly. If I state that coats or boots stand in a relation to linen because the latter is the universal incarnation of abstract human labour, the absurdity of the statement is self-evident. Nevertheless, when the producers of coats and boots bring these commodities into a relation with linen, or with gold or silver (and this makes no difference here), as the universal equivalent, the relation between their own private labour and the collective labour of society appears to them in exactly this absurd form.

The categories of bourgeois economics consist precisely of forms of this kind. They are forms of thought which are socially valid, and therefore objective, for the relations of production belonging to this historically determined mode of social production, i.e., commodity production. The whole mystery of commodities, all the magic and necromancy that surrounds the products of labour on the basis of commodity production, vanishes therefore as soon as we come to other forms of production.

Antonio Gramsci, Selection from *Prison Notebooks*

The State

In the new "juridical" tendencies represented by the *Nuovi Studi* of Volpicelli and Spirito, the confusion between the concept of class-State and the concept of regulated society should be noted, as a critical point of departure. This confusion is especially noteworthy in the paper on *Economic Freedom* presented by Spirito at the Nineteenth Congress of the Society for Scientific Progress held at Bolzano in September 1930, and published in *Nuovi Studi* in the 1930 September–October issue.

As long as the class-State exists the regulated society cannot exist, other than metaphorically—i.e., only in the sense that the class-State too is a regulated society. The utopians, in as much as they expressed a critique of the society that existed in their day, very well understood that the class-State could not be the regulated society. So much is this true that in the types of society which the various utopias represented, economic equality was introduced as a necessary basis for the projected reform. Clearly in this the utopians were not utopians, but concrete political scientists and consistent critics. The utopian character of some of them was due to the fact that they believed that economic equality could be introduced by arbitrary laws, by an act of will, etc. But the idea that complete and perfect political equality cannot exist without economic equality (an idea to be found in other political writers, too, even right-wing ones—i.e., among the critics of democracy, in so far as the latter makes use of the Swiss or Danish model to claim that the system is a reasonable one for all countries) nevertheless remains correct. This idea can be found in the writers of the seventeenth century too, for example in Ludovico Zuccolo and in his book *Il Belluzzi*, and I think in Machiavelli as well. Maurras believes that in Switzerland that particular form of democracy is possible precisely because there is a certain common averageness of economic fortunes, etc.

The confusion of class-State and regulated society is peculiar to the middle classes and petty intellectuals, who would be glad of any regularisation that would prevent sharp struggles and upheavals. It is a typically reactionary and regressive conception. [1930–32]

In my opinion, the most reasonable and concrete thing that can be said about the ethical State, the cultural State, is this: every State is ethical in as much as one of its most important functions is to raise the great mass of the population to a particular cultural and moral level, a level (or type) which corresponds to the needs of the productive forces for development, and hence to the interests of the ruling classes. The school as a positive educative function, and the courts as a repressive and negative educative function, are the most important State activities in this sense: but, in reality, a multitude of other so-called private initiatives and activities tend to the same end—initiatives and activities which form the apparatus of the political and cultural hegemony of the ruling classes. Hegel's conception belongs to a period in which the spreading development of the bourgeoisie could seem limitless, so that its ethicity or universality could be asserted: all mankind will be bourgeois. But, in reality, only the social group that poses the end of the State and its own end as the target to be achieved can create an ethical State—i.e., one which tends to put an end to the internal divisions of the ruled, etc., and to create a technically and morally unitary social organism. [1931–32]

Hegel's doctrine of parties and associations as the "private" woof of the State. This derived historically from the political experiences of the French Revolution, and was to serve to give a more concrete character to constitutionalism. Government with the consent of the governed—but with this consent organised, and not generic and vague as it is expressed in the instant of elections. The State does have and request consent, but it also "educates" this consent, by means of the political and syndical associations; these, however, are private organisms, left to the private initiative of the ruling class. Hegel, in a certain sense, thus already transcended pure constitutionalism and theorised the parliamentary State with its party system. But his conception of association could not help still being vague, and primitive, halfway between the political and the economic; it was in accordance with the historical experience of the time, which was very limited and offered only one perfected example of organisation—the "corporative" (a politics grafted directly on to the economy). Marx was not able to have historical experiences superior (or at least much superior) to those of Hegel; but, as a result of his journalistic and agitational activities, he had a sense for the masses. Marx's concept of organisation remains entangled amid the following elements: craft organisation; Jacobin clubs; secret conspiracies by small groups; journalistic organisation.

The French Revolution offered two prevalent types. There were the "clubs"—loose organisations of the "popular assembly" type, centralised around individual political figures. Each had its newspaper, by means of which it kept alive the attention and interest of a particular clientele that had no fixed boundaries. This clientele then upheld the theses of the paper in the club's meetings. Certainly, among those who frequented the clubs, there must have existed tight, select groupings of people who knew each other, who met separately and prepared the climate of the meetings, in order to support one tendency or another—depending on the circumstances and also on the concrete interests in play.

The secret conspiracies, which subsequently spread so widely in Italy prior to 1848, must have developed in France after Thermidor among the second-rank followers of Jacobinism: with great difficulty in the Napoleonic period on account of the vigilant control of the police; with greater facility from 1815 to 1830 under the Restoration, which was fairly liberal at the base and was free from certain preoccupations. In this period, from 1815 to 1830, the differentiation of the popular political camp was to occur. This already seemed considerable during the "glorious days" of 1830, when the formations which had been crystallising during the preceding fifteen years now came to the surface. After 1830 and up to 1848, this process of differentiation became perfected, and produced some quite highly-developed specimens in Blanqui and Filippo Buonarroti.

It is unlikely that Hegel could have had first-hand knowledge of these historical experiences, which are, however, more vivid in Marx.

The revolution which the bourgeois class has brought into the conception of law, and hence into the function of the State, consists especially in the will to conform (hence ethicity of the law and of the State). The previous ruling classes were essentially conservative in the sense that they did not tend to construct an organic passage from the other classes into their own, i.e., to enlarge their class sphere "technically" and ideologically: their conception was that of a closed caste. The bourgeois class poses itself as an organism in continuous movement, capable of absorbing the entire society, assimilating it to its own cultural and economic level. The entire function of the State has been transformed; the State has become an "educator", etc.

How this process comes to a halt, and the conception of the State as pure force is returned to, etc. The bourgeois class is "saturated": it not only does not expand—it starts to disintegrate; it not only does not assimilate new elements, it loses part of itself (or at least its losses are enormously more numerous than its assimilations). A class claiming to be capable of assimilating the whole of society, and which was at the same time really able to express such a process, would perfect this conception of the State and of law, so as to conceive the end of the State and of law—rendered useless since they will have exhausted their function and will have been absorbed by civil society. [1931–32]

That the everyday concept of State is unilateral and leads to grotesque errors can be demonstrated with reference to Danièl Halévy's recent book *Décadence de la liberté*, of which I have read a review in *Nouvelles Littéraires*. For Halévy, "State" is the representative apparatus; and he discovers that the most important events of French history from 1870 until the present day have not been due to initiatives by political organisms deriving from universal suffrage, but to those either of private organisms (capitalist firms, General Staffs, etc.) or of great civil servants unknown to the country at large, etc. But what does that signify if not that by "State" should be understood not only the apparatus of government, but also the "private" apparatus of "hegemony" or civil society? It should be noted how from this critique of the State which does not intervene, which trails behind events, etc., there is born the dictatorial ideological current of the Right, with its reinforcement of the executive, etc. However, Halévy's book should be read to see whether he too has taken this path: it is not unlikely in principle, given his antecedents (sympathies for Sorel, for Maurras, etc.). [1930-32]

Curzio Malaparte, in the introduction to his little volume on the *Technique of the Coup d'Etat,* seems to assert the equivalence of the formula: "Everything within the State, nothing outside the State, nothing against the State" with the proposition: "Where there is freedom, there is no State". In the latter proposition, the term "freedom" cannot be taken in its ordinary meaning of "political freedom, freedom of the press, etc.", but as counterposed to "necessity"; it is related to Engels' proposition on the passage from the rule of necessity to the rule of freedom. Malaparte has not caught even the faintest whiff of the significance of the proposition. [1931–32]

In the (anyway superficial) polemic over the functions of the State (which here means the State as a politico-juridical organisation in the narrow sense), the expression "the State as *veilleur de nuit*" corresponds to the Italian expression "the State as policeman" and means a State whose functions are limited to the safeguarding of public order and of respect for the laws. The fact is glossed over that in this form of regime (which anyway has never existed except on paper, as a limiting hypothesis) hegemony over its historical development belongs to private forces, to civil society— which is "State" too, indeed is the State itself.

It seems that the expression *veilleur de nuit,* which should have a more sarcastic ring than "the State as policeman", comes from Lassalle. Its opposite should be "ethical State" or "interventionist State" in general, but there are differences between the two expressions. The concept of ethical State is of philosophical and intellectual origin (belonging to the intellectuals: Hegel), and in fact could be brought into conjunction with the concept of State-*veilleur de nuit*; for it refers rather to the autonomous, educative and moral activity of the secular State, by contrast with the cosmopolitanism and the interference of the religious-ecclesiastical organisation as a mediaeval residue. The concept of interventionist State is of economic origin, and is connected on the one hand with tendencies supporting protection and economic nationalism, and on the other with the attempt to force a particular State personnel, of landowning and feudal origin, to take on the "protection" of the working classes against the excesses of capitalism (policy of Bismarck and of Disraeli).

These diverse tendencies may combine in various ways, and in fact have so combined. Naturally liberals ("economists") are for the "State as *veilleur de nuit*", and would like the historical initiative to be left to civil society and to the various forces which spring up there—with the "State" as guardian of "fair play" and of the rules of the game. Intellectuals draw very significant distinctions as to when they are liberals and when they are interventionists (they may be liberals in the economic field and interventionists in the cultural field, etc.). The catholics would like the State to be interventionist one hundred per cent in their favour; failing that, or where they are in a minority, they call for a "neutral" State, so that it should not support their adversaries. [1935: 1st version 1930]

The following argument is worth reflecting upon: is the conception of the *gendarme*nightwatchman State (leaving aside the polemical designation: *gendarme,* nightwatchman, etc.) not in fact the only conception of the State to transcend the purely "economic-corporate" stages?

We are still on the terrain of the identification of State and government—an identification which is precisely a representation of the economic-corporate form, in other words of the confusion between civil society and political society. For it should be remarked that the general notion of State includes elements which need to be referred back to the notion of civil society (in the sense that one might say that State = political society + civil society, in other words hegemony protected by the armour of coercion). In a doctrine of the State which conceives the latter as tendentially capable of withering away and of being subsumed into regulated society, the argument is a fundamental one. It is possible to imagine the coercive element of the State withering away by degrees, as ever-more conspicuous elements of regulated society (or ethical State or civil society) make their appearance.

The expressions "ethical State" or "civil society" would thus mean that this "image" of a State without a State was present to the greatest political and legal thinkers, in so far as they placed themselves on the terrain of pure science (pure utopia, since based on the premise that all men are really equal and hence equally rational and moral, i.e., capable of accepting the law spontaneously, freely, and not through coercion, as imposed by another class, as something external to consciousness).

It must be remembered that the expression "nightwatchman" for the liberal State comes from Lassalle, i.e., from a dogmatic and non-dialectical statalist (look closely at Lassalle's doctrines on this point and on the State in general, in contrast with Marxism). In the doctrine of the State as regulated society, one will have to pass from a phase in which "State" will be equal to "government", and "State" will be identified with "civil society", to a phase of the State as nightwatchman—i.e., of a coercive organisation which will safeguard the development of the continually proliferating elements of regulated society, and which will therefore progressively reduce its own authoritarian and forcible interventions. Nor can this conjure up the idea of a new "liberalism", even though the beginning of an era of organic liberty be imminent. [1930–32]

If it is true that no type of State can avoid passing through a phase of economic-corporate primitivism, it may be deduced that the content of the political hegemony of the new social group which has founded the new type of State must be predominantly of an economic order: what is involved is the reorganisation of the structure and the real relations between men on the one hand and the world of the economy or of production on the other. The superstructural elements will inevitably be few in number, and have a character of foresight and of struggle, but as yet few "planned" elements. Cultural policy will above all be negative, a critique of the past; it will be aimed at erasing from the memory and at destroying. The lines of construction will as yet be "broad lines", sketches, which might (and should) be changed at all times, so as to be consistent with the new structure as it is formed. This precisely did not happen in the period of the mediaeval communes; for culture, which remained a function of the Church, was precisely anti-economic in character (i.e., against the nascent capitalist economy); it was not directed towards giving hegemony to the new class, but rather to preventing the latter from acquiring it. Hence Humanism and the Renaissance were reactionary, because they signalled the defeat of the new class, the negation of the economic world which was proper to it, etc. [1931–32]

Another element to examine is that of the organic relations between the domestic and foreign policies of a State. Is it domestic policies which determine foreign policy, or vice versa? In this case too, it will be necessary to distinguish: between great powers, with relative international autonomy, and other powers; also, between different forms of government (a government like that of Napoleon III had two policies, apparently—reactionary internally, and liberal abroad).

Conditions in a State before and after a war. It is obvious that, in an alliance, what counts are the conditions in which a State finds itself at the moment of peace. Therefore it may happen that whoever has exercised hegemony during the war ends up by losing it as a result of the enfeeblement suffered in the course of the struggle, and is forced to see a "subordinate" who has been more skilful or "luckier" become hegemonic. This occurs in "world wars" when the geographic situation compels a State to throw all its resources into the crucible: it wins through its alliances, but victory finds it prostrate, etc. This is why in the concept of "great power" it is necessary to take many elements into account, and especially those which are "permanent"—i.e., especially "economic and financial potential" and population. [1932–32]

Moral Science and Historical Materialism

The scientific base for a morality of historical materialism is to be looked for, in my opinion, in the affirmation that "society does not pose for itself tasks the conditions for whose resolution do not already exist". Where these conditions exist "the solution of the tasks *becomes* 'duty', 'will' *becomes* free". Morality would then become a search for the conditions necessary for the freedom of the will in a certain sense, aimed at a certain end, and the demonstration that these conditions exist. It should be a question also not of a hierarchy of ends but of a gradation of the ends to be attained, granted that what one wants to "moralise" is not just each individual taken singly but also a whole society of individuals.

Regularity and Necessity

How did the founder of the philosophy of praxis arrive at the concept of regularity and necessity in historical development? I do not think that it can be thought of as a derivation from natural science but rather as an elaboration of concepts born on the terrain of political economy, particularly in the form and with the methodology that economic science acquired from David Ricardo. Concept and fact of determined market: i.e., the scientific discovery that specific decisive and permanent forces have risen historically and that the operation of these forces presents itself with a certain "automatism" which allows a measure of "predictability" and certainty for the future of those individual initiatives which accept these forces after having discerned and scientifically established their nature. "Determined market" is therefore equivalent to "determined relation of social forces in a determined structure of the productive apparatus", this relationship being guaranteed (that is, rendered permanent) by a determined political, moral and juridical superstructure. After having established the character of these decisive and permanent forces and their spontaneous automatism (i.e., their relative independence from individual choices and from arbitrary government interventions), the scientist has, by way of hypothesis, rendered the automatism absolute; he has isolated the merely economic facts from the combinations of varying importance in which they present themselves in reality; he has established relations of cause and effect, of premises and conclusions; and he has thus produced an abstract scheme of a determined economic society. (On this realistic and concrete scientific construct there has subsequently been imposed a new, more generalised abstraction of "man" as such, "historical" and generic, and it is this abstraction that has come to be seen as "true" economic science.)

Given these conditions in which classical economics was born, in order to be able to talk about a new science or a new conception of economic science (which is the same thing), it would be necessary to have demonstrated that new relations of forces, new conditions, new premises, have been establishing themselves, in other words that a new market has been "determined" with a new "automatism" and phenomenism of its own, which present themselves as something "objective", comparable to the automatism of natural phenomena. Classical economics has given rise to a "critique of political economy" but it does not seem to me that a new science or a new conception of the scientific problem has yet been possible. The "critique" of political economy starts from the concept of the historical character of the "determined market" and of its "automatism", whereas pure economists conceive of these elements as "eternal" and "natural"; the critique analyses in a realistic way the relations of forces determing the market, it analyses in depth their contradictions, evaluates the possibilities of modification connected with the appearance and strengthening of new elements and puts forward the "transitory" and "replaceable" nature of the science being criticised; it studies it as life but also as death and finds at its heart the elements that will dissolve it and supersede it without fail, and it puts forward the "inheritor", the heir presumptive who must yet give manifest proof of his vitality (etc.).

It is true that in modern economic life the "arbitrary" element, whether at individual, consortium or State level, has acquired an importance it previously did not have and has profoundly disturbed the traditional automatism: but this fact is not sufficient in itself to justify the conception of new scientific problems, precisely because these interventions are arbitrary, vary in scale, and are unpredictable. It could justify the affirmation that economic life has been modified, that there is a "crisis", but this is obvious. Besides, it is not claimed that the old "automatism" has disappeared; it only asserts itself on a scale larger than before, at the level of major economic phenomena, while individual facts have "gone wild".

It is from these considerations that one must start in order to establish what is meant by "regularity", "law", "automatism" in historical facts. It is not a question of "discovering" a metaphysical law of "determinism", or even of establishing a "general" law of causality. It is a question of bringing out how in historical evolution relatively permanent forces are constituted which operate with a certain regularity and automatism. Even the law of large numbers, although very useful as a model of comparison, cannot be assumed as the "law" of historical events. In order to establish the historical origin of the philosophy of praxis (an element which is nothing less than its particular way of conceiving "immanence"), it will be necessary to study the conception of economic laws put forward by David Ricardo. It is a matter of realising that Ricardo was important in the foundation of the philosophy of praxis not only for the concept of "value" in economics, but was also "philosophically" important and has suggested a way of thinking and intuiting history and life. The method of "supposing that …", of the premiss that gives a certain conclusion, should it seems to me, be identified as one of the starting points (one of the intellectual stimuli) of the philosophical experience of the founders of the philosophy of praxis. It is worth finding out if Ricardo has ever been studied from this point of view.

It would appear that the concept of "necessity" in history is closely connected to that of "regularity" and "rationality". "Necessity" in the "speculative-abstract" and in the "historical-concrete" sense: necessity exists when there exists an efficient and active *premiss,* consciousness of which in people's minds has become operative, proposing concrete goals to the collective consciousness and constituting a complex of convictions and beliefs which acts powerfully in the form of "popular beliefs". In the *premiss* must be contained, already developed or in the process of development, the necessary and sufficient material conditions for the realisation of the impulse of collective will; but it is also clear that one cannot separate from this "material" premiss, which can be quantified, a certain level of culture, by which we mean a complex of intellectual acts and, as a product and consequence of these, a certain complex of overriding passions and feelings, overriding in the sense that they have the power to lead men on to action "at any price".

As we have said, this is the only way through which one can reach a historicist and not speculative-abstract conception of "rationality" (and therefore irrationality) in history.

Concepts of "providence" and "fortune", in the sense in which they are employed (speculatively) by Italian idealist philosophers and particularly Croce: one should look at Croce's book on Giambattista Vico, in which the concept of "providence" is translated into speculative terms and in which is to be found the beginnings of the idealist interpretation of Vico's philosophy. For the meaning of "fortune" in Machiavelli, one should look at Luigi Russo's writings. According to Russo, "fortune" has a double meaning for Machiavelli, objective and subjective. "Fortune" is the natural force of circumstances (i.e., the causal nexus) the chance concurrence of events, what providence is in the works of Vico; it can also be that transcendent power (i.e., God) mythologised in old mediaeval doctrine, but for Machiavelli this is then nothing other than individual "*virtù*" itself and its power is rooted in man's will. Machiavelli's "*virtù*", as Russo puts it, is no longer the *virtus* of the scholastics, which has an ethical character and takes its power from heaven, nor that of Livy, which generally means military valour, but it is the *virtù* of Renaissance man, which is capacity, ability, industriousness, individual strength, sensibility, intuition of opportunity and a measure of one's own possibilities.

After this Russo vacillates in his analysis. For him the concept of *fortune,* as force of circumstances, which in Machiavelli as in the Renaissance humanists still retains a *naturalistic and mechanical character,* will become *truth* and deepened historical perception only in the *rational providence* of Vico and Hegel. But it is important to point out that such concepts in Machiavelli never have a metaphysical character, as they do in the philosophers proper of humanism, but are simple and profound intuitions (and therefore philosophy!) of life, and are to be understood and explained as symbols of sentiments.

Georg Lukács, "What is Orthodox Marxism?" from *History and Class Consciousness*

2

We are now faced with the question of the methodological implications of these so-called facts that are idolised throughout the whole of Revisionist literature. To what extent may we look to them to provide guide-lines for the actions of the revolutionary proletariat? It goes without saying that all knowledge starts from the facts. The only question is: which of the data of life are relevant to knowledge and in the context of which method?

The blinkered empiricist will of course deny that facts can only become facts within the framework of a system—which will vary with the knowledge desired. He believes that every piece of data from economic life, every statistic, every raw event already constitutes an important fact. In so doing he forgets that however simple an enumeration of 'facts' may be, however lacking in commentary, it already implies an 'interpretation'. Already at this stage the facts have been comprehended by a theory, a method; they have been wrenched from their living context and fitted into a theory.

More sophisticated opportunists would readily grant this despite their profound and instinctive dislike of all theory. They seek refuge in the methods of natural science, in the way in which science distills 'pure' facts and places them in the relevant contexts by means of observation, abstraction and experiment. They then oppose this ideal model of knowledge to the forced constructions of the dialectical method.

If such methods seem plausible at first this is because capitalism tends to produce a social structure, that in great measure encourages such views. But for that very reason we need the dialectical method to puncture the social illusion so produced and help us to glimpse the reality underlying it. The 'pure' facts of the natural sciences arise when a phenomenon of the real world is placed (in thought or in reality) into an environment where its laws can be inspected without outside interference. This process is reinforced by reducing the phenomena to their purely quantitative essence, to their expression in numbers and numerical relations. Opportunists always fail to recognise that it is in the nature of capitalism to process phenomena in this way. Marx gives an incisive account of such a 'process of abstraction' in the case of labour, but he does not omit to point out with equal vigour that he is dealing with a *historical* peculiarity of capitalist society. "Thus the most general abstractions commonly appear where there is the highest concrete development, where one feature appears to be shared by many, and to be common to all. Then it cannot be thought of any longer in one particular form."

But this tendency in capitalism goes even further. The fetishistic character of economic forms, the reification of all human relations, the constant expansion and extension of the division of labour which subjects the process of production to an abstract, rational analysis, without regard to the human potentialities and abilities of the immediate producers, all these things transform the phenomena of society and with them the way in which they are perceived. In this way arise the 'isolated' facts, 'isolated' complexes of facts, separate, specialist disciplines (economics, law, etc.) whose very appearance seems to have done much to pave the way for such scientific methods. It thus appears extraordinarily 'scientific' to think out the tendencies implicit in the facts themselves and to promote this activity to the status of science.

By contrast, in the teeth of all these isolated and isolating facts and partial systems, dialectics insists on the concrete unity of the whole. Yet although it exposes these appearances for the illusions they are—albeit illusions necessarily engendered by capitalism—in this 'scientific' atmosphere it still gives the impression of being an arbitrary construction.

The unscientific nature of this seemingly so scientific method consists, then, in its failure to see and take account of the *historical character* of the facts on which it is based. This is the source of more than one error (constantly overlooked by the practitioners of the method) to which Engels has explicitly drawn attention. The nature of this source of error is that statistics and the 'exact' economic theory based upon them always lag behind actual developments. "For this reason, it is only too often necessary in current history, to treat this, the most decisive factor, as constant, and the economic situation existing at the beginning of the period concerned as given and unalterable for the whole period, or else to take notice of only those changes in the situation as arise out of the patently manifest events themselves and are therefore, likewise, patently manifest."

Thus we perceive that there is something highly problematic in the fact that capitalist society is predisposed to harmonise with scientific method, to constitute indeed the social premises of its exactness. If the internal structure of the 'facts' of their interconnections is essentially historical, if, that is to say, they are caught up in a process of continuous transformation, then we may indeed question when the greater scientific inaccuracy occurs. It is when I conceive of the 'facts' as existing in a form and as subject to laws concerning which I have a methodological certainty (or at least probability) that they no longer apply to these facts ? Or is it when I consciously take this situation into account, cast a critical eye at the 'exactitude' attainable by such a method and concentrate instead on those points where this *historical* aspect, this decisive fact of change really manifests itself?

The historical character of the 'facts' which science seems to have grasped with such 'purity' makes itself felt in an even more devastating manner. As the products of historical evolution they are involved in continuous change. But in addition they are also *precisely in their objective structure the products of a definite historical epoch, namely capitalism.* Thus when 'science' maintains that the manner in which data immediately present themselves is an adequate foundation of scientific conceptualisation and that the actual form of these data is the appropriate starting point for the formation of scientific concepts, it thereby takes its stand simply and dogmatically on the basis of capitalist society. It uncritically accepts the nature of the object as it is given and the laws of that society as the unalterable foundation of 'science'.

In order to progress from these 'facts' to facts in the true meaning of the word it is necessary to perceive their historical conditioning as such and to abandon the point of view that would see them as immediately given: they must themselves be subjected to a historical and dialectical examination. For as Marx says: "The finished pattern of economic relations as seen on the surface in their real existence and consequently in the ideas with which the agents and bearers of these relations seek to understand them, is very different from, and indeed quite the reverse of and antagonistic to their inner, essential but concealed core and the concepts corresponding to it."

If the facts are to be understood, this distinction between their real existence and their inner core must be grasped clearly and precisely. This distinction is the first premise of a truly scientific study which in Marx's words, "would be superfluous if the outward appearance, of things coincided with their essence". Thus we must detach the phenomena from the form in which they are immediately given and discover the intervening links which connect them to their core, their essence. In so doing, we shall arrive at an understanding of their apparent form and see it as the form in which the inner core necessarily appears. It is necessary because of the historical character of the facts, because they have grown in the soil of capitalist society. This twofold character, the simultaneous recognition and transcendence, of immediate appearances is precisely the dialectical nexus.

In this respect, superficial readers imprisoned in the modes of thought created by capitalism, experienced the gravest difficulties in comprehending the structure of thought in *Capital*. For on the one hand, Marx's account pushes the capitalist nature of all economic forms to their furthest limits, he creates an intellectual milieu where they can exist in their purest form by positing a society 'corresponding to the theory', i.e., capitalist through and through, consisting of none but capitalists and proletarians. But conversely, no sooner does this strategy produce results, no sooner does this world of phenomena seem to be on the point of crystallising out into theory than it dissolves into a mere illusion, a distorted situation appears as in a distorting mirror which is, however, "only the conscious expression of an imaginary movement."

Only in this context which sees the isolated facts of social life as aspects of the historical process and integrates them in a *totality*, can knowledge of the facts hope to become knowledge of *reality*. This knowledge starts from the simple (and to the capitalist world), pure, immediate, natural determinants described above. It progresses from them to the knowledge of the concrete totality, i.e., to the conceptual reproduction of reality. This concrete totality is by no means an unmediated datum for thought. "The concrete is concrete," Marx says, "because it is a synthesis of many particular determinants, i.e., a unity of diverse elements." Idealism succumbs here to the delusion of confusing the intellectual reproduction of reality with the actual structure of reality itself. For "in thought, reality appears as the process of synthesis, not as starting-point, but as outcome, although it is the real starting-point and hence the starting-point for perception and ideas."

Conversely, the vulgar materialists, even in the modern guise donned by Bernstein and others, do not go beyond the reproduction of the immediate, simple determinants of social life. They imagine that they are being quite extraordinarily 'exact' when they simply take over these determinants without either analysing them further or welding them into a concrete totality. They take the facts in abstract isolation, explaining them only in terms of abstract laws unrelated to the concrete totality. As Marx observes: "Crudeness and conceptual nullity consist in the tendency to forge arbitrary unmediated connections between things that belong together in an organic union."

The crudeness and conceptual nullity of such thought lies primarily in the fact that it obscures the historical, transitory nature of capitalist society. Its determinants take on the appearance of timeless, eternal categories valid for all social formations. This could be seen at its crassest in the vulgar bourgeois economists, but the vulgar Marxists soon followed in their footsteps. The dialectical method was overthrown and with it the methodological supremacy of the totality over the individual aspects; the parts were prevented from finding their definition within the whole and, instead, the whole was dismissed as unscientific or else it degenerated into the mere 'idea' or 'sum' of the parts. With the totality out of the way, the fetishistic relations of the isolated parts appeared as a timeless law valid for every human society.

Marx's dictum: "The relations of production of every society form a whole" is the methodological point of departure and the key to the *historical* understanding of social relations. All the isolated partial categories can be thought of and treated—in isolation—as something that is always present in every society. (If it cannot be found in a given society this is put down to 'chance' as the exception that proves the rule.) But the changes to which these individual aspects are subject give no clear and unambiguous picture of the real differences in the various stages of the evolution of society. These can really only be discerned in the context of the total historical process of their relation to society as a whole.

3

This dialectical conception of totality seems to have put a great distance between itself and reality, it appears to construct reality very 'unscientifically'. But it is the only method capable of understanding and reproducing reality. Concrete totality is, therefore, the category that governs reality. The rightness of this view only emerges with complete clarity when we direct our attention to the real, material substratum of our method, viz. capitalist society with its internal antagonism between the forces and the relations of production. The methodology of the natural sciences which forms the methodological ideal of every fetishistic science and every kind of Revisionism rejects the idea of contradiction and antagonism in its subject matter. If, despite this, contradictions do spring up between particular theories, this only proves that our knowledge is as yet imperfect. Contradictions between theories show that these theories have reached their natural limits; they must therefore be transformed and subsumed under even wider theories in which the contradictions finally disappear.

But we maintain that in the case of social reality these contradictions are not a sign of the imperfect understanding of society; on the contrary, they belong to *the nature of reality itself and to the nature of capitalism.* When the totality is known they will not be transcended and *cease* to be contradictions. Quite the reverse, they will be seen to be necessary contradictions arising out of the antagonisms of this system of production. When theory (as the knowledge of the whole) opens up the way to resolving these contradictions it does so by revealing the *real tendencies* of social evolution. For these are destined to effect a *real* resolution of the contradictions that have emerged in the course of history.

From this angle we see that the conflict between the dialectical method and that of 'criticism' (or vulgar materialism, Machism, etc.) is a social problem. When the ideal of scientific knowledge is applied to nature it simply furthers the progress of science. But when it is applied to society it turns out to be an ideological weapon of the bourgeoisie. For the latter it is a matter of life and death to understand its own system of production in terms of eternally valid categories: it must think of capitalism as being predestined to eternal survival by the eternal laws of nature and reason. Conversely, contradictions that cannot be ignored must be shown to be purely surface phenomena, unrelated to this mode of production.

The method of classical economics was a product of this ideological need. But also its limitations as a science are a consequence of the structure of capitalist reality and the antagonistic character of capitalist production. When, for example, a thinker of Ricardo's stature can deny the "necessity of expanding the market along with the expansion of production and the growth of capital", he does so (unconsciously of course), to avoid the necessity of admitting that crises are inevitable. For crises are the most striking illustration of the antagonisms in capitalist production and it is evident that "the bourgeois mode of production implies a limitation to the free development of the forces of production."

What was good faith in Ricardo became a consciously misleading apologia of bourgeois society in the writings of the vulgar economists. The vulgar Marxists arrived at the same results by seeking either the thorough-going elimination of dialectics from proletarian science, or at best its 'critical' refinement.

To give a grotesque illustration, Max Adler wished to make a critical distinction between dialectics as method, as the movement of thought on the one hand and the dialectics of being, as metaphysics on the other. His 'criticism' culminates in the sharp separation of dialectics from both and he describes it as a "piece of positive science" which "is what is chiefly meant by talk of real dialectics in Marxism". This dialectic might more aptly be called 'antagonism', for it simply "asserts that an opposition exists between the self-interest of an individual and the social forms in which he is confined". By this stroke the objective economic antagonism as expressed in the *class struggle* evaporates, leaving only a conflict between the *individual and society*. This means that neither the emergence of internal problems, nor the collapse of capitalist society, can be seen to be necessary. The end-product, whether he likes it or not, is a Kantian philosophy of history. Moreover, the structure of bourgeois society is established as the universal form of society in general. For the central problem Max Adler tackles, of the real "dialectics or, better, antagonism" is nothing but one of the typical ideological forms of the capitalist social order. But whether capitalism is rendered immortal on economic or on ideological grounds, whether with naive nonchalance, or with critical refinement is of little importance.

Thus with the rejection or blurring of the dialectical method history becomes unknowable. This does not imply that a more or less exact account of particular people or epochs cannot be given without the aid of dialectics. But it does put paid to attempts to understand history *as a unified process*. (This can be seen in the sociologically abstract, historical constructs of the type of Spencer and Comte whose inner contradictions have been convincingly exposed by modern bourgeois historians, most incisively by Rickert. But it also shows itself in the demand for a 'philosophy of history' which then turns out to have a quite inscrutable relationship to historical reality.) The opposition between the description of an aspect of history and the description of history as a unified process is not just a problem of scope, as in the distinction between particular and universal history. It is rather a conflict of method, of approach. Whatever the epoch or special topic of study, the question of a unified approach to the process of history is inescapable. It is here that the crucial importance of the dialectical view of totality reveals itself. For it is perfectly possible for someone to describe the essentials of an historical event and yet be in the dark about the real nature of that event and of its function in the historical totality, i.e., without understanding it as part of a unified historical process.

A typical example of this can be seen in Sismondi's treatment of the question of crisis. He understood the immanent tendencies in the processes of production and distribution. But ultimately, he failed because, for all his incisive criticism of capitalism, he remained imprisoned in capitalist notions of the objective and so necessarily thought of production and distribution as two independent processes, "not realising that the relations of distribution are only the relations of production *sub alia specia*". He thus succumbs to the same fate that overtook Proudhon's false dialectics; "he converts the various limbs of society into so many independent societies."

We repeat: the category of totality does not reduce its various elements to an undifferentiated uniformity, to identity. The apparent independence and autonomy which they possess in the capitalist system of production is an illusion only in so far as they are involved in a dynamic dialectical relationship with one another and can be thought of as the dynamic dialectical aspects of an equally dynamic and dialectical whole. "The result we arrive at," says Marx, "is not that production, distribution, exchange and consumption are identical, but that they are all members of one totality, different aspects of a unit.... Thus a definite form of production determines definite forms of consumption, distribution and exchange as well as *definite relations between these different elements....* A mutual interaction takes place between these various elements. This is the case with every organic body."

But even the category of interaction requires inspection. If by interaction we mean just the reciprocal causal impact of two otherwise unchangeable objects on each other, we shall not have come an inch nearer to an understanding of society. This is the case with the vulgar materialists with their one-way causal sequences (or the Machists with their functional relations). After all, there is, e.g., an interaction when a stationary billiard ball is struck by a moving one: the first one moves, the second one is deflected from its original path. The interaction we have in mind must be more than the interaction of *otherwise unchanging objects*. It must go further in its relation to the whole: for this relation determines the objective form of every object of cognition. Every substantial change that is of concern to knowledge manifests itself as a change in relation to the whole and through this as a change in the form of objectivity itself. Marx has formulated this idea in countless places. I shall cite only one of the best-known passages: "A negro is a negro. He only becomes a slave in certain circumstances. A cotton-spinning jenny is a machine for spinning cotton. Only in certain circumstances does it become capital. Torn from those circumstances it is no more capital than gold is money or sugar the price of sugar."

Thus the objective forms of all social phenomena change constantly in the course of their ceaseless dialectical interactions with each other. The intelligibility of objects develops in proportion as we grasp their function in the totality to which they belong. This is why only the dialectical conception of totality can enable us to understand *reality as a social process.* For only this conception dissolves the fetishistic forms necessarily produced by the capitalist mode of production and enables us to see them as mere illusions which are not less illusory for being seen to be necessary. These unmediated concepts, these 'laws' sprout just as inevitably from the soil of capitalism and veil the real relations between objects. They can all be seen as ideas necessarily held by the agents of the capitalist system of production. They are, therefore, objects of knowledge, but the object which is known through them is not the capitalist system of production itself, but the ideology of its ruling class.

Only when this veil is torn aside does historical knowledge become possible. For the function of these unmediated concepts that have been derived from the fetishistic forms of objectivity is to make the phenomena of capitalist society appear as suprahistorical essences. The knowledge of the real, objective nature of a phenomenon, the knowledge of its historical character and the knowledge of its actual function in the totality of society form, therefore, a single, undivided act of cognition. This unity is shattered by the pseudo-scientific method. Thus only through the dialectical method could the distinction between constant and variable capital, crucial to economics, be understood. Classical economics was unable to go beyond the distinction between fixed and circulating capital. This was not accidental. For "variable capital is only a particular historical manifestation of the fund for providing the necessaries of life, or the labour-fund which the labourer requires for the maintenance of himself and his family, and which whatever be the system of social production, he must himself produce and reproduce. If the labour-fund constantly flows to him in the form of money that pays for his labour, it is because the product he has created moves constantly away from him in the form of capital…. The transaction is veiled by the fact that the product appears as a commodity and the commodity as money."

The fetishistic illusions enveloping all phenomena in capitalist society succeed in concealing reality, but more is concealed than the historical, i.e., transitory, ephemeral nature of phenomena. *This* concealment is made possible by the fact that in capitalist society man's environment, and especially the categories of economics, appear to him immediately and necessarily in forms of objectivity which conceal the fact that they are the categories of the *relations of men with each other*. Instead they appear as things and the relations of things with each other. Therefore, when the dialectical method destroys the fiction of the immortality of the categories it also destroys their reified character and clears the way to a knowledge of reality. According to Engels in his discussion of Marx's *Critique of Political Economy*, "economics does not treat of things, but of the relations between persons and, in the last analysis, between classes; however, these relations are always *bound to things* and *appear as things*."

It is by virtue of this insight that the dialectical method and its concept of totality can be seen to provide real knowledge of what goes on in society. It might appear as if the dialectic relations between parts and whole were no more than a construct of thought as remote from the true categories of social reality as the unmediated formulae of bourgeois economics. If so, the superiority of dialectics would be purely methodological. The real difference, however, is deeper and more fundamental.

At every stage of social evolution each economic category reveals a definite relation between men. This relation becomes conscious and is conceptualised. Because of this the inner logic of the movement of human society can be understood at once as the product of men themselves and of forces that arise from their relations with each other and which have escaped their control. Thus the economic categories become dynamic and dialectical in a double sense. As 'pure' economic categories they are involved in constant interaction with each other, and that enables us to understand any given historical cross-section through the evolution of society. But since they have arisen out of human relations and since they function in the process of the transformation of human relations, the actual process of social evolution becomes visible in their reciprocal relationship with the reality underlying their activity. That is to say, the production and reproduction of a particular *economic* totality, which science hopes to understand, is necessarily transformed into the process of production and reproduction of a particular *social* totality; in the course of this transformation, 'pure' economics are naturally transcended, though this does not mean that we must appeal to any transcendental forces. Marx often insisted upon this aspect of dialectics. For instance: "Capitalist production, therefore, under its aspect of a continuous connected process or as a process of reproduction produces not only commodities, not only surplus value, but it also produces and reproduces the capitalist relation itself, on the one hand the capitalist and on the other, the labourer."

4

To posit oneself, to produce and reproduce oneself—that is *reality*. Hegel clearly perceived this and expressed it in a way closely similar to that of Marx, albeit cloaked in abstraction and misunderstanding itself and thus opening the way to further misunderstanding. "What is actual is necessary in itself," he says in the *Philosophy of Right*. "Necessity consists in this that the whole is sundered into the different concepts and that this divided whole yields a fixed and permanent determinacy. However, this is not a fossilised determinacy but one which permanently recreates itself in its dissolution." The deep affinities between historical materialism and Hegel's philosophy are clearly manifested here, for both conceive of theory as the *self-knowledge of reality*. Nevertheless, we must briefly point to the crucial difference between them. This is likewise located in the problem of reality and of the unity of the historical process.

Marx reproached Hegel (and, in even stronger terms, Hegel's successors who had reverted to Kant and Fichte) with his failure to overcome the duality of thought and being, of theory and practice, of subject and object. He maintained that Hegel's dialectic, which purported to be an inner, real dialectic of the historical process, was a mere illusion: in the crucial point he failed to go beyond Kant. His knowledge is no more than knowledge *about* an essentially alien material. It was not the case that this material, human society, came to know itself. As he remarks in the decisive sentences of his critique, "Already with Hegel, the absolute spirit of history has its material in the masses, but only finds adequate expression in philosophy. But the philosopher appears merely as the instrument by which absolute spirit, which makes history, arrives at self-consciousness after the historical movement has been completed. The philosopher's role in history is thus limited to this subsequent consciousness, for the real movement is executed unconsciously by the absolute spirit. Thus the philosopher arrives *post festum*." Hegel, then, permits "absolute spirit qua absolute spirit to make history only in appearance... (For, as absolute spirit does not appear in the mind of the philosopher in the shape of the creative world-spirit until after the event, it follows that it makes history only in the consciousness, the opinions and the ideas of the philosophers, only in the speculative imagination." Hegel's conceptual mythology has been definitively eliminated by the critical activity of the young Marx.

It is, however, not accidental that Marx achieved 'self-understanding' in the course of opposing a reactionary Hegelian movement reverting back to Kant. This movement exploited Hegel's obscurities and inner uncertainties in order to eradicate the revolutionary elements from his method. It strove to harmonise the reactionary content, the reactionary conceptual mythology, the vestiges of the contemplative dualism of thought and existence with the consistently reactionary philosophy which prevailed in the Germany of the day.

By adopting the progressive part of the Hegelian method, namely the dialectic, Marx not only cut himself off from Hegel's successors; he also split Hegel's philosophy in two. He took the historical tendency in Hegel to its logical extreme: he radically transformed all the phenomena both of society and of socialised man into historical problems: he concretely revealed the real substratum of historical evolution and developed a seminal method in the process. He measured Hegel's philosophy by the yardstick he had himself discovered and systematically elaborated, and he found it wanting. The mythologising remnants of the 'eternal values' which Marx eliminated from the dialectic belong basically on the same level as the philosophy of reflection which Hegel had fought his whole life long with such energy and bitterness and against which he had pitted his entire philosophical method), with its ideas of process and concrete totality, dialectics and history. In this sense Marx's critique of Hegel is the direct continuation and extension of the criticism that Hegel himself levelled at Kant and Fichte. So it came about that Marx's dialectical method continued what Hegel had striven for but had failed to achieve in a concrete form. And, on the other hand, the corpse of the written system remained for the scavenging philologists and system-makers to feast upon.

It is at reality itself that Hegel and Marx part company. Hegel was unable to penetrate to the real driving forces of history. Partly because these forces were not yet fully visible when he created his system. In consequence he was forced to regard the peoples and their consciousness as the true bearers of historical evolution. (But he did not discern their real nature because of the heterogeneous composition of that consciousness. So he mythologised it into the 'spirit of the people'.) But in part he remained imprisoned in the Platonic and Kantian outlook, in the duality of thought and being, of form and matter, notwithstanding his very energetic efforts to break out. Even though he was the first to discover the meaning of concrete totality, and even though his thought was constantly bent upon overcoming every kind of abstraction, matter still remained tainted for him with the '*stain* of the specific' (and here he was very much the Platonist). These contradictory and conflicting tendencies could not be clarified within his system. They are often juxtaposed, unmediated, contradictory and unreconciled. In consequence, the ultimate (apparent) synthesis had perforce to turn to the past rather than the future. It is no wonder that from very early on bourgeois science chose to dwell on these aspects of Hegel. As a result the revolutionary core of his thought became almost totally obscure even for Marxists.

A conceptual mythology always points to the failure to understand a fundamental condition of human existence, one whose effects cannot be warded off. This failure to penetrate the object is expressed intellectually in terms of transcendental forces which construct and shape reality, the relations between objects, our relations with them and their transformations in the course of history in a mythological fashion. By recognising that "the production and reproduction of real life (is) in the last resort the decisive factor in history", Marx and Engels gained a vantage point from which they could settle accounts with all mythologies. Hegel's absolute spirit was the last of these grandiose mythological schemes. It already contained the totality and its movement, even though it was unaware of its real character. Thus in historical materialism reason "which has always existed though not always in a rational form", achieved that 'rational' form by discovering its real substratum, the basis from which human life will really be able to become conscious of itself. This completed the programme of Hegel's philosophy of history, even though at the cost of the destruction of his system. In contrast to nature in which, as Hegel emphasises,[31] "change goes in a circle, repeating the same thing", change in history takes place "in the concept as well as on the surface. It is the concept itself which is corrected."

5

The premise of dialectical materialism is, we recall: "It is not men's consciousness that determines their existence, but on the contrary, their social existence that determines their consciousness." Only in the context sketched above can this premise point beyond mere theory and become a question of praxis. Only when the core of existence stands revealed as a social process can existence be seen as the product, albeit the hitherto unconscious product, of human activity. This activity will be seen in its turn as the element crucial for the transformation of existence. Man finds himself confronted by purely natural relations or social forms mystified into natural relations. They appear to be fixed, complete and immutable entities which can be manipulated and even comprehended, but never overthrown. But also this situation creates the possibility of praxis in the individual consciousness. Praxis becomes the form of action appropriate to the isolated individual, it becomes his ethics. Feuerbach's attempt to supersede Hegel foundered on this reef: like the German idealists, and to a much greater extent than Hegel, he stopped short at the isolated individual of 'civil society'.

Marx urged us to understand 'the sensuous world', the object, reality, as human sensuous activity. This means that man must become conscious of himself as a social being, as simultaneously the subject and object of the socio-historical process. In feudal society man "could not yet see himself as a social being because his social relations were still mainly natural. Society was far too unorganised and had far too little control over the totality of relations between men for it to appear to consciousness as *the* reality of man. (The question of the structure and unity of feudal society cannot be considered in any detail here.) Bourgeois society carried out the process of socialising society. Capitalism destroyed both the spatio-temporal barriers between different lands and territories and also the legal partitions between the different 'estates'

(Stände). In its universe there is a formal equality for all men; the economic relations that directly determined the metabolic exchange between men and nature progressively disappear. Man becomes, in the true sense of the word, a social being. Society becomes *the* reality for man.

Thus the recognition that society is reality becomes possible only under capitalism, in bourgeois society. But the class which carried out this revolution did so without consciousness of its function; the social forces it unleashed, the very forces that carried it to supremacy seemed to be opposed to it like a second nature, but a more soulless, impenetrable nature than feudalism ever was. It was necessary for the proletariat to be born for social reality to become fully conscious. The reason for this is that the discovery of the class-outlook of the proletariat provided a vantage point from which to survey the whole of society. With the emergence of historical materialism there arose the theory of the "conditions for the liberation of the proletariat" and the doctrine of reality understood as the total process of social evolution. This was only possible because for the proletariat the total knowledge of its class-situation was a vital necessity, a matter of life and death; because its class situation becomes comprehensible only if the whole of society can be understood; and because this understanding is the inescapable precondition of its actions. Thus the unity of theory and practice is only the reverse side of the social and historical position of the proletariat. From its own point of view self-knowledge coincides with knowledge of the whole so that the proletariat is at one and the same time the subject and object of its own knowledge.

The mission of raising humanity to a higher level is based, as Hegel rightly observed (although he was still concerned with nations), on the fact that these "stages of evolution exist as *immediate, natural principles*" and it devolves upon every nation (i.e., class) "endowed with such a *natural* principle to put it into practice". Marx concretises this idea with great clarity by applying it to social development: "If socialist writers attribute this world-historical role to the proletariat it is not because they believe…that the proletariat are gods. Far from it. The proletariat can and must liberate itself because when the proletariat is fully developed, its humanity and even the appearance of its humanity has become totally abstract; because in the conditions of its life all the conditions of life of contemporary society find their most inhuman consummation; because in the proletariat man is lost to himself but at the same time he has acquired a theoretical consciousness of this loss, and is driven by the absolutely imperious dictates of his misery—the practical expression of this necessity—which can no longer be ignored or whitewashed, to rebel against this inhumanity. However, the proletariat cannot liberate itself without destroying the conditions of its own life. But it cannot do that without destroying *all* the inhuman conditions of life in contemporary society which exist in the proletariat in a concentrated form."

Thus the essence of the method of historical materialism is inseparable from the 'practical and critical' activity of the proletariat: both are aspects of the same process of social evolution. So too, the knowledge of reality provided by the dialectical method is likewise inseparable from the class standpoint of the proletariat. The question raised by the Austrian Marxists of the methodological separation of the 'pure' science of Marxism from socialism is a pseudo-problem. For, the Marxist method, the dialectical materialist knowledge of reality, can arise only from the point of view of a class, from the point of view of the struggle of the proletariat. To abandon this point of view is to move away from historical materialism, just as to adopt it leads directly into the thick of the struggle of the proleteriat.

Historical materialism grows out of the "immediate, natural" life-principle of the proletariat; it means the acquisition of total knowledge of reality from this one point of view. But it does not follow from this that this knowledge or this methodological attitude is the inherent or natural possession of the proletariat as a class (let alone of proletarian individuals). On the contrary. It is true that the proletariat is the conscious subject of total social reality. But the conscious subject is not defined here as in Kant, where 'subject' is defined as that which can never be an object. The 'subject' here is not a detached spectator of the process. The proletariat is more than just the active and passive part of this process: the rise and evolution of its knowledge and its actual rise and evolution in the course of history are just the two different sides of the same real process. It is not simply the case that the working class arose in the course of spontaneous, unconscious actions born of immediate, direct despair (the Luddite destruction of machines can serve as a primitive illustration of this), and then advanced gradually through incessant social struggle to the point where it "formed itself into a class". But it is no less true that proletarian consciousness of social reality, of its own class situation, of its own historical vocation and the materialist view of history are all products of this self-same process of evolution which historical materialism understands adequately and for what it really is for the first time in history.

Thus the Marxist method is equally as much the product of class warfare as any other political or economic product. In the same way, the evolution of the proletariat reflects the inner structure of the society which it was the first to understand. "Its result, therefore, appears just as constantly presupposed by it as its presuppositions appear as its results." The idea of totality which we have come to recognise as the presupposition necessary to comprehend reality is the product of history in a double sense.

First, historical materialism became a formal, objective possibility only because economic factors created the proletariat, because the proletariat did emerge (i.e., at a particular stage of historical development), and because the subject and object of the knowledge of social reality were transformed. Second, this formal possibility became a real one only in the course of the evolution of the proletariat. If the meaning of history is to be found in the process of history itself and not, as formerly, in a transcendental, mythological or ethical meaning foisted on to recalcitrant material, this presupposes a proletariat with a relatively advanced awareness of its own position, i.e., a relatively advanced proletariat, and, therefore, a long preceding period of evolution. The path taken by this evolution leads from utopia to the knowledge of reality; from transcendental goals fixed by the first great leaders of the workers' movement to the clear perception by the Commune of 1871 that the working-class has "no ideals to realise", but wishes only "to liberate the elements of the new society." It is the path leading from the "class opposed to capitalism" to the class "for itself."

Seen in this light the revisionist separation of movement and ultimate goal represents a regression to the most primitive stage of the working-class movement. For the ultimate goal is not a 'state of the future' awaiting the proletariat somewhere independent of the movement and the path leading up to it. It is not a condition which can be happily forgotten in the stress of daily life and recalled only in Sunday sermons as a stirring contrast to workaday cares. Nor is it a 'duty', an 'idea' designed to regulate the 'real' process. The ultimate goal is rather that *relation to the totality* (to the whole of society seen as a process), through which every aspect of the struggle acquires its revolutionary significance. This relation informs every aspect in its simple and sober ordinariness, but only consciousness makes it real and so confers reality on the day-to-day struggle by manifesting its relation to the whole. Thus it elevates mere existence to reality. Do not let us forget either that every attempt to rescue the 'ultimate-goal' or the 'essence' of the proletariat from every impure contact with—capitalist—existence leads ultimately to the same remoteness from reality, from 'practical, critical activity' and to the same relapse into the utopian dualism of subject and object, of theory and practice to which Revisionism has succumbed.

The practical danger of every such dualism shows itself in the loss of any directive for *action*. As soon as you abandon the ground of reality that has been conquered and reconquered by dialectical materialism, as soon as you decide to remain on the 'natural' ground of existence, of the empirical in its stark, naked brutality, you create a gulf between the subject of an action and the milieux of the 'facts' in which the action unfolds so that they stand opposed to each other as harsh, irreconcilable principles. It then becomes impossible to impose the subjective will, wish or decision upon the facts or to discover in them any directive for action. A situation in which the 'facts' speak out unmistakably for or against a definite course of action has never existed, and neither can or will exist. The more conscientiously the facts are explored—in their isolation, i.e., in their unmediated relations—the less compellingly will they point in any one direction. It is self-evident that a merely subjective decision will be shattered by the pressure of uncomprehended facts acting automatically 'according to laws'.

Thus dialectical materialism is seen to offer the only approach to reality which can give action a direction. The self-knowledge, both subjective and objective, of the pro-letariat at a given point in its evolution is at the same time knowledge of the stage of development achieved by the whole society. The facts no longer appear strange when they are comprehended in their coherent reality, in the relation of all partial aspects to their inherent, but hitherto unelucidated roots in the whole: we then perceive the tendencies which strive towards the centre of reality, to what we are wont to call the ultimate goal. This ultimate goal is not an abstract ideal opposed to the process, but an aspect of truth and reality. It is the concrete meaning of each stage reached and an integral part of the concrete moment. Because of this, to comprehend it is to recognise the direction taken (unconsciously) by events and tendencies towards the totality. It is to know the direction that determines concretely the correct course of action at any given moment—in terms of the interest of the total process, viz. the emancipation of the proletariat.

However, the evolution of society constantly heightens the tension between the partial aspects and the whole. Just because the inherent meaning of reality shines forth with an ever more resplendent light, the meaning of the process is embedded ever more deeply in day-to-day events, and totality permeates the spatio-temporal character of phenomena. The path to consciousness throughout the course of history does not become smoother but on the contrary ever more arduous and exacting. For this reason the task of orthodox Marxism, its victory over Revisionism and utopianism can never mean the defeat, once and for all, of false tendencies. It is an ever-renewed struggle against the insidious effects of bourgeois ideology on the thought of the proletariat Marxist orthodoxy is no guardian of traditions, it is the eternally vigilant prophet proclaiming the relation between the tasks of the immediate present and the totality of the historical process. Hence the words of the *Communist Manifesto* on the tasks of orthodoxy and of its representatives, the Communists, have lost neither their relevance nor their value: "The Communists are distinguished from the other working-class parties *by this only*: 1. In the national struggles of the proletarians of the different countries, they point out and bring to the front the common interests of the *entire* proletariat, independent of nationality. 2. In the various stages of development which the struggle of the working class against the bourgeoisie has to pass through, they always and everywhere represent the interests of *the movement as a whole*."

3

Psychological Repression and the Perils of Modernity

Introduction

During the latter part of the nineteenth century, a second form of critical thought arose in conjunction with historical materialism: the critique of modern civilization and industrialized society. In this chapter, I have included selections from Nietzsche's *The Genealogy of Morals*, Freud's *Civilization and its Discontents*, and Weber's *Economy and Society* in order to show the ideational link between the internal mechanisms of the individual consciousness (repression) and modern society. In *Civilization and its Discontents* (1930), Freud conceives this link in terms of the antithesis between modern civilization and sexuality, or how civilization inhibits the instincts of the libido (an instinct derived from Eros). Freud's inquiry into this antithesis between aggression and civilization leads him to posit the existence of the death instinct (*Thanatos*). The juxtaposition of this instinct with Eros explains how the ego receives pleasure in moderating this instinct; hence, the return of the repressed ego.

Freud's scientific analysis reflects, and, in many ways validates Nietzsche's earlier philosophical insights into the paradoxical relationship between debtor and creditor, or the repressive nature of ethics and morality (religion). In Nietzsche's view, the progress of modern democratic society is premised upon the false idea that society had advanced beyond the barbarism of earlier periods. As he shows in his essay *The Genealogy of Morals* (1887), modern civil society represses the very noble feelings, instincts and spontaneity that invigorate its creativity, the will to power. In this way, the metaphysical and philosophical pursuit of truth evolves out of the contradictory relationship between debtor and creditor, that is, the creditor's self-induced pleasure in inflicting cruelty (bad conscience). Nietzsche's perspectivism, then, serves to expose the modern pathologies of democratic society (the loss of individual creativity and freedom).

Weber's sociological analyses focus on the effects of these pathologies or the ethical restrictions that modern bureaucracy, juridical authority place on social action and freedom. In the first part of *Economy and Society* (1922), Weber conceives these effects in terms of purposive rational action (action derived from the pursuit of moral and ethical values). In distinguishing between value and instrumental rationality, he shows how the scientific and formal rationality associated with bourgeois materialism (modern capitalism) detaches us from the very values that had previously directed our actions towards a final goal or religious worldview. Thus, it is this disenchantment with modern capitalist society that would drive his analysis of the dominant forms of authority and the erosion of freedom.

Together, then, Freud, Weber, and Nietzsche reveal a crucial set of social tensions between the individual and state/society. It would be these tensions, combined with the internal tensions within Marxism, that would encourage the Frankfurt School to formulate a reflexive or self-conscious theory that could bring together critical elements of Marxism, Hegelianism, Freudianism and Modernism.

Sigmund Freud, Selection from
Civilization and its Discontents

The manifestations of Eros were conspicuous and noisy enough. It might be assumed that the death instinct operated silently within the organism towards its dissolution, but that, of course, was no proof. A more fruitful idea was that a portion of the instinct is diverted towards the external world and comes to light as an instinct of aggressiveness and destructiveness. In this way the instinct itself could be pressed into the service of Eros, in that the organism was destroying some other thing, whether animate or inanimate, instead of destroying its own self. Conversely, any restriction of this aggressiveness directed outwards would be bound to increase the self-destruction, which is in any case proceeding. At the same time one can suspect from this example that the two kinds of instinct seldom—perhaps never—appear in isolation from each other, but are alloyed with each other in varying and very different proportions and so become unrecognizable to our judgement. In sadism, long since known to us as a component instinct of sexuality, we should have before us a particularly strong alloy of this kind between trends of love and the destructive instinct; while its counterpart, masochism, would be a union between destructiveness directed inwards and sexuality—a union which makes what is otherwise an imperceptible trend into a conspicuous and tangible one. The assumption of the existence of an instinct of death or destruction has met with resistance even in analytic circles; I am aware that there is a frequent inclination rather to ascribe whatever is dangerous and hostile in love to an original bipolarity in its own nature. To begin with it was only tentatively that I put forward the views I have developed here, but in the course of time they have gained such a hold upon me that I can no longer think in any other way. To my mind, they are far more serviceable from a theoretical standpoint that any other possible ones; they provide that simplification, without either ignoring or doing violence to the facts, for which we strive in scientific work. I know that in sadism and masochism we have always seen before us manifestations of the destructive instinct (directed outwards and inwards), strongly alloyed with erotism; but I can no longer understand how we can have overlooked the ubiquity of non-erotic aggressivity and destructiveness and can have failed to give it its due place in our interpretation of life. (The desire for destruction when it is directed *inwards* mostly eludes our perception, of course, unless it is tinged with erotism.) I remember my own defensive attitude when the idea of an instinct of destruction first emerged in psychoanalytic literature, and how long it took before I became receptive to it. That others should have shown, and still show, the same attitude of rejection surprises me less. For 'little children do not like it when there is talk of the inborn human inclination to 'badness', to aggressiveness and destructiveness, and so to cruelty as well. God has made them in the image of His own perfection; nobody wants to be reminded how hard it is to reconcile the undeniable existence of evil—despite the protestations of Christian Science—with His all-powerfulness or His all-goodness. The Devil would be the best way out as an excuse for God; in that way he would be playing the same part as an agent of economic discharge as the Jew does in the world of the Aryan ideal. But even so, one can hold God responsible for the existence of the Devil just as well as for the existence of the wickedness which the Devil embodies. In view of these difficulties, each of us will be well advised, on some suitable occasion, to make a low bow to the deeply moral nature of mankind; it will help us to be generally popular and much will be forgiven us for it.

The name 'libido' can once more be used to denote the manifestations of the power of Eros in order to distinguish them from the energy of the death instinct. It must be confessed that we have much greater difficulty in grasping that instinct; we can only suspect it, as it were, as something in the background behind Eros, and it escapes detection unless its presence is betrayed by its being alloyed with Eros. It is in sadism, where the death instinct twists the erotic aim in its own sense and yet at the same time fully satisfies the erotic urge, that we succeed in obtaining the clearest insight into its nature and its relation to Eros. But even where it emerges without any sexual purpose, in the blindest fury of destructiveness, we cannot fail to recognize that the satisfaction of the instinct is accompanied by an extraordinarily high degree of narcissistic enjoyment, owing to its presenting the ego with a fulfillment of the latter's old wishes for omnipotence. The instinct of destruction, moderated and tamed, and as it were, inhibited in its aim, must, when it is directed towards objects, provide the ego with the satisfaction of its vital needs and with control over nature. Since the assumption of the existence of the instinct is mainly based on theoretical grounds, we must also admit that is not entirely proof against theoretical objections. But this is how things appear to us now, in the present state of our knowledge; future research and reflection will no doubt bring further light which will decide the matter.

In all that follows I adopt the standpoint, therefore, that the inclination to aggression is an original, self-subsisting instinctual disposition in man, and I return to my view I was led to the idea that civilization was a special process which mankind undergoes, and I am still under the influence of that idea. I may now add that civilization is a process in the service of Eros, whose purpose is to combine single human individuals, and after that families, then races, peoples and nations, into one great unity, the unity of mankind. Why this has to happen, we do not know; the work of Eros is precisely this. These collections of men are to be libidinally bound to one another. Necessity alone, the advantages of work in common, will not hold them together. But man's natural aggressive instinct, the hostility of each against all and of all against each, opposes this programme of civilization. This aggressive instinct is the derivative and the main representative of the death instinct which we have found alongside of Eros and which shares world-dominion with it. And now, I think, the meaning of the evolution of civilization is no longer obscure to us. It must present the struggle between Eros and Death, between the instinct of life and the instinct of destruction, as it works itself out in the human species. This struggle is what all life essentially consists of, and evolution of civilization may therefore be simply described as the struggle for life of the human species. And it is this battle of the giants that our nurse-maids try to appease with their lullaby about Heaven.

VII

What means does civilization employ in order to inhibit the aggressiveness which opposes it, to make it harmless, to get rid of it, perhaps? We have already become acquainted with a few of these methods, but not yet with the one that appears to be the most important. This we can study in the history of the development of the individual. What happens in him to render his desire for aggression innocuous? Something very remarkable, which we should never have guessed and which is nevertheless quite obvious. His aggressiveness is introjected, internalized; it is, in point of fact, sent back to where it came from—that is, it is directed towards his own ego. There it is taken over by a portion of the ego, which sets itself, over against the rest of the ego as super-ego, and which now, in the form of 'conscience', is ready to put into action against ego the same harsh aggressiveness that the ego would have liked to satisfy upon other, extraneous individuals. The tensions between the harsh super-ego and the ego that is subjected to', is called by us the sense of guilt; it expresses itself as a need for punishment. Civilization, therefore, obtains mastery over the individual's dangerous desire for aggression by weakening and disarming it and by setting up an agency within him to watch over it, like a garrison in a conquered city.

As to the origin of the sense of guilt, the analyst has different views from other psychologists; but even he does not find it easy to give an account of it. To begin with, if we ask how a person comes to have a sense of guilt, we arrive at an answer which he knows to be 'bad'. But then we notice how little this answer tells us. Perhaps, after some hesitation, we shall add that even when a person has not actually *done* the bad thing but has only recognized in himself an *intention* to do it, he may regard himself as guilty; and the question then arises of why the intention is regarded as equal to the deed. Both cases, however, presuppose that one had already recognized the what is bad is reprehensible, is something that must not be carried out. How is this judgement arrived at? We may reject the existence of an original, as it were natural, capacity to distinguish good from bad. What is bad is often not at all what is injurious or dangerous to the ego; on the contrary, it may be something which is desirable and enjoyable to the ego. Here, therefore, there is an extraneous influence at work, and it is this that decides what is to be called good or bad. Since a person's own feelings would not have led him along this path, he must have had a motive for submitting to this extraneous influence. Such a motive is easily discovered in his helplessness and his dependence on other people, and it can best be designated as fear of loss of love. If he loses the love of another person upon whom he is dependent, he also ceases to be protected from a variety of dangers. Above all, he is exposed to the danger that this stronger person will show his superiority in the form of punishment. At the beginning, therefore, what is bad is whatever causes óne to be threatened with loss of love. For fear of that loss, one must avoid it. This, too, is the reason why it makes little difference whether one has already done the bad thing or only intends to do it. In either case the danger only sets in if and when the authority discovers it, and in either case the authority would behave in the same way.

This state of mind is called a 'bad conscience'; but actually it does not deserve this name, for at this state the sense of guilt is clearly only a fear of loss of love, 'social' anxiety. In small children it can never be anything else, but in many adults, too, it has only changed to the extent that the place of the father or the two parents is taken by the larger human community. Consequently, such people habitually allow themselves to do any bad thing which promises them enjoyment, so long as they are sure that the authority will not know anything about it or cannot blame them for it; they are afraid only of being found out. Present-day society has to reckon in general with this state of mind.

A great change takes place only when the authority is internalized through the establishment of super-ego. The phenomena of conscience then reach a higher stage. Actually it is not until now that we should speak of conscience or a sense of guilt. At this point, too, the fear of being found out comes to an end; the distinction, moreover, between doing something bad and wishing to do it disappears entirely, since nothing can be hidden from the super-ego, not even thoughts. It is true that the seriousness of the situation from a real point of view has passed away, for the new authority, the super-ego, has no motive that we know of for ill-treating the ego, with which it is intimately bound up; but genetic influence, which leads to the survival of what is past and has been surmounted, makes itself felt in the fact that fundamentally things remain as they were at the beginning. The super-ego torments the sinful ego with the same feeling of anxiety and is on the watch for opportunities of getting it punished by the external world.

At this second stage of development, the conscience exhibits a peculiarity which was absent from the first stage and which is no longer easy to account for. For the more virtuous a man is, the more severe and distrustful is its behaviour, so that ultimately it is precisely those people who have carried sinfliriess furthest who reproach themselves with the worst sinfulness. This means that virtue forfeits some part of its promised reward; the docile and continent ego does not enjoy the trust of its mentor, and strives in vain, it would seem, to acquire it. The objection will at once be made that these difficulties are artificial ones, and it will be said that a stricter and more vigilant conscience is precisely the hallmark of a moral man. Moreover, when saints call themselves sinners, they are not so wrong, considering the temptations to instinctual satisfaction to which they are exposed in a specially high degree—since, as is well known, temptations are merely increased by constant frustration, whereas an occasional satisfaction of them causes them to diminish, at least for the time being. The field of ethics, which is so full of problems, presents us with another fact: namely that ill-luck—that is, external frustration—so greatly enhances the power of the conscience in the super-ego. As long as things go well with a man, his conscience is lenient and lets the ego do all sorts of things; but when misfortune befalls him, he searches his soul, acknowledges his sinfulness, heightens the demands of his conscience, imposes abstinences on himself and punishes himself with penances.

Thus we know of two origins of the sense of guilt: one arising from fear of an authority, and the other, later on, arising from fear of the super-ego. The first insists upon a renunciation of instinctual satisfactions; the second, as well as doing this, presses for punishment, since the continuance of the forbidden wishes cannot be concealed from the super-ego. We have also learned how the severity of the-super-ego—the demands of conscience—is to be understood. It is simply a continuation of the severity of the external authority, to which it has succeeded and which it has in part replaced. We now see in what relationship the renunciation of instinct stands to the sense of guilt. Originally, renunciation of instinct was the result of fear of an external authority: one renounced one's satisfactions in order not to lose its love. If one has carried out this renunciation, one is, as it were, quits with the authority and no sense of guilt should remain. But with fear of the super-ego the case is different. Here, instinctual renunciation is not enough, for the wish persists and cannot be concealed from the super-ego. Thus, in spite of the renunciation that has been made, a sense of guilt comes about. This constitutes a great economic disadvantage in the erection of a super-ego, or, as we may put it, in the formation of a conscience. Instinctual renunciation now no longer has a completely liberating effect; virtuous continence is no longer rewarded with the assurance of love. A threatened external unhappiness—loss of love and punishment on the part of the external authority—has been exchanged for a permanent internal unhappiness, for the tension of the sense of guilt.

These interrelations are so complicated and at the same time so important that, at the risk of repeating myself, I shall approach them from yet another angle. The chronological sequence, then, would be as follows. First comes renunciation of instinct owing to fear of aggression by the *external* authority. (This is, of course, what fear of the loss of love amounts to, for love is a protection against this punitive aggression.) After that comes the erection of an *internal* authority, and renunciation of instinct owing to fear of it—owing to fear of conscience. In this second situation bad intentions are equated with bad actions, and hence come a sense of guilt and a need for punishment. The aggressiveness of conscience keeps up the aggressiveness of the authority. So far things have no doubt been made clear; but where does this leave room for the reinforcing influence of misfortune; (of renunciation imposed from without), and for the extraordinary severity of conscience in the best and most tractable people? We have already explained both these peculiarities of conscience, but we probably still have an impression that those explanations do not go to the bottom of the matter, and leave a residue still unexplained. And here at last an idea comes in which belongs entirely to psycho-analysis and which is foreign to people's ordinary way of thinking. This idea is of a sort which enables us to understand why the subject-matter was bound to seem so confused and obscure to us. For it tells us that conscience (or more correctly, the anxiety which later becomes conscience) is indeed the cause of instinctual renunciation to begin with, but that later the relationship is relented. Every renunciation of instinct now becomes a dynamic source of conscience and every fresh renunciation increases the latter's severity and intolerance. If we could only bring it better into harmony with what we already know about the history of the origin of conscience, we should be tempted to defend the paradoxical statement that conscience is the result of instinctual renunciation, or that instinctual renunciation (imposed on us from without) creates conscience, which then demands further instinctual renunciation.

Friedrich Nietzsche, Selection from *The Genealogy of Morals*

"Guilt," "Bad Conscience," and Related Matters

I

To breed an animal with the right to make promises—is not this the paradoxical problem nature has set itself with regard to man? And is it not man's true problem? That the problem has in fact been solved to a remarkable degree will seem all the more surprising if we do full justice to the strong opposing force, the faculty of oblivion. Oblivion is not merely a *vis inertiae*, as is often claimed, but an active screening device, responsible for the fact that what we experience and digest psychologically does not, in the stage of digestion, emerge into consciousness any more than what we ingest physically does. The role of this active oblivion is that of a concierge: to shut temporarily the doors and windows of consciousness; to protect us from the noise and agitation with which our lower organs work for or against one another; to introduce a little quiet into our consciousness so as to make room for the nobler functions and functionaries of our organism which do the governing and planning. This concierge maintains order and etiquette in the household of the psyche; which immediately suggests that there can be no happiness, no serenity, no hope, no pride, no *present*, without oblivion. A man in whom this screen is damaged and inoperative is like a dyspeptic (and not merely *like* one): he can't be done with anything.... Now this naturally forgetful animal, for whom oblivion represents a power, a form of strong health, has created for itself an opposite power, that of remembering, by whose aid, in certain cases, oblivion may be suspended specifically in cases where it is a question of promises. By this I do not mean a purely passive succumbing to past impressions, the indigestion of being unable to be done with a pledge once made, but rather an active not wishing to be done with it, a continuing will what has once been willed, a veritable "memory of the will"; so that, between the original determination and performance of the thing willed, a whole world of new things, conditions, even volitional acts, can be interposed without asking the long chain of the will. But how much all this presupposes! A man who wishes to dispose of his future of this manner must first have learned to separate necessary from accidental acts; to think causally; to see distant things as though they were near at hand; to distinguish means from ends. In short, he must have become not only calculating but himself calculable, regular even to his own perception, if he is to stand pledge for his own future as a guarantor does.

II

This brings us to the long story of the origin or genesis of responsibility. The task of breeding an animal entitled to make promises, involves, as we have already seen, the preparatory task of rendering man up to a certain point regular, uniform, equal among equals, calculable. The tremendous achievement which I have referred to in *Day break* as "the custom character of morals," that labor man accomplished upon himself over a vast period of time, receives its meaning and justification here even despite the brutality, tyranny, and stupidity associated with the process. With the help of custom and the social strait-jacket, man was, in fact, made calculable. However, if we place ourselves at the terminal point of this great process, where society and custom finally reveal their true aim, we shall find the ripest fruit of that tree to be the sovereign individual, equal only to himself, all moral custom left far behind. This autonomous, more than moral individual (the terms *autonomous* and *moral* are mutually exclusive) has developed his own, independent, long-range will, which dares to make promises; he has a proud and vigorous consciousness of what he has achieved, a sense of power and freedom, of absolute accomplishment. This fully emancipated man, master of his will, who dares make promises how should he not be aware of his superiority over those who are unable to stand security for themselves? Think how much trust, fear, reverence he inspires (all three fully *deserved*), and how, having that sovereign rule over himself, he has mastery too over all weaker-willed and less reliable creatures! Being truly free and possessor of a long range, pertinacious will, he also possesses a scale of values. Viewing others from the center of his own being, he either honors or disdains them. It is natural to him to honor his strong and reliable peers, all those who promise like sovereigns: rarely and reluctantly; who are chary of their trust; whose trust is a mark of distinction; whose promises are binding because they know that they will make them good in spite of all accidents, in spite of destiny itself. Yet he will inevitably reserve a kick for those paltry windbags who promise irresponsibly and a rod for those liars who break their word even in uttering it. His proud awareness of the extraordinary privilege responsibility confers has penetrated deeply and become a dominant instinct. What shall he call that dominant instinct, provided he ever feels impelled to give it a name? Surely he will call it his *conscience*.

IV

But how about the origin of that other somber phenomenon, the consciousness of guilt, "bad conscience"? Would you turn to our genealogists of morals for illumination? Let me say once again, they are worthless. Completely absorbed in "modern" experience, with no real knowledge of the past, no desire even to understand it, no historical instinct whatever, they presume, all the same, to write the history of ethics! Such an undertaking must produce results which bear not the slightest relation to truth. Have these historians shown any awareness of the fact that the basic moral term *Schuld* (guilt) has its origin in the very material term *Schulden* (to be indebted)? Of the fact that punishment, being a *compensation*, has developed quite independently of any ideas about freedom of the will indeed, that a very high level of humanization was necessary before even the much more primitive distinctions "with intent," "through negligence," "by accident," *compos mentis*, and their opposites could be made and allowed to weigh in the judgments of cases? The pat and seemingly natural notion (so natural that it has often been used to account for the origin of the notion of justice itself) that the criminal deserves to be punished *because* he could have acted otherwise, is in fact a very late and refined form of human reasoning; whoever thinks it can be found in archaic law grossly misconstrues the psychology of uncivilized man. For an unconscionably long time culprits were not punished because they were felt to be responsible for their actions; not, that is, on the assumption that only the guilty were to be punished; rather, they were punished the way parents still punish their children, out of rage at some damage suffered, which the doer must pay for. Yet this rage was both moderated and modified by the notion that for every damage there could somehow be found an equivalent, by which that damage might be compensated if necessary in the pain of the doer. To the question how did that ancient, deep-rooted, still firmly established notion of an equivalency between damage and pain arise, the answer is, briefly: it arose in the contractual relation between creditor and debtor, which is as old as the notion of "legal subjects" itself and which in its turn points back to the basic practices of purchase, sale, barter, and trade.

V

As we contemplate these contractual relationships we may readily feel both suspicion and repugnance toward the older civilizations which either created or permitted them. Since it was here that promises were made, since it was here that a memory had to be fashioned for the promiser, we must not be surprised to encounter every evidence of brutality, cruelty, pain. In order to inspire the creditor with confidence in his promise to repay, to give a guarantee for the stringency of his promise, but also to enjoin on his own conscience the duty of repayment, the debtor pledged by contract in case of non-payment he would offer another of this possessions, such as his body, or his wife, or his freedom, or even his life (or, in certain theologically oriented cultures, even his salvation or the sanctity of his tomb; as in Egypt, where the debtor's corpse was not immune from his creditor even in the grave). The creditor, moreover, had the right to inflict all manner of indignity and pain on the body of the debtor. For example, he could cut out an amount of flesh proportionate to the amount of the debt, and we find, very early, quite detailed legal assessments of the value of individual parts of the body. I consider it already a progress, "proof of a freer, more generous, more *Roman* conception of law, when the Twelve Tables decreed that it made no difference how much or little, in such a case, the creditor cut out *si plus minusve secuerunt, ne fraude esto*. Let us try to understand the logic of this entire method of compensations; it is strange enough. An equivalence is provided by the creditor's receiving, in place of material compensation such as money, land, or other possessions, a kind of *pleasure*. That pleasure is induced by his being able to exercise his power freely upon one who is powerless, by the pleasure of *faire le mal pour le plaisir de le faire*, the pleasure of rape. That pleasure will be increased in proportion to the lowliness of the creditor's own station; it will appear to him as a delicious morsel, a foretaste of a higher rank. In "punishing" the debtor, the creditor shares a seignorial right. For once he is given a chance to bask in the glorious feeling of treating another human being as lower than himself or, in case the actual punitive power has passed on to a legal "authority," of seeing him despised and mistreated. Thus compensation consists in a legal warrant entitling one man to exercise his cruelty on another.

VI

It is in the sphere of contracts and legal obligations that the moral universe of guilt, conscience, and duty, ("sacred" duty) took its inception. Those beginnings were liber-ally sprinkled with blood, as are the beginnings of everything great on earth. (And may we not say that ethics has never lost its reek of blood and to sure not even in Kant, whose categorical imperative smacks of cruelty?) It was then that the sinister knitting together of the two ideas *guilt* and *pain* first occurred, which by now have become quiet inextricable. Let us ask once more: in what sense could pain constitute repayment of a debt? In the sense that to make someone suffer was a supreme pleasure. In exchange for the damage he had incurred, including his displeasure, the creditor received an extraordinary amount of pleasure; something which he prized the more highly the more it disaccorded with his social rank. I am merely throwing this out as a suggestion, for it is difficult, and embarrassing as well, to get to the bottom of such underground developments. To introduce crudely the concept of vengeance at this point would obscure matters rather than clarify them, since the idea of vengeance leads us straight back to our original problem: how can the infliction of pain provide satisfaction? The delicacy—even more, the *tartufferie*—of (domestic animals like ourselves shrinks from imagining clearly to what extent cruelty constituted the collective delight of older mankind, how much it was an ingredient of all their joys, or how naively they manifested their cruelty, how they considered disinterested malevolence (Spinoza's *sympathia malevolens*) a normal trait, something to which one's conscience could assent heartily. Close observation will spot numerous survivals of this oldest and most thorough human delight in our own culture. In both *Daybreak* and *Beyond Good and Evil* I have pointed to that progressive sublimation and apotheosis of cruelty which not only characterizes the whole history of higher culture, but in a sense constitutes it. Not so very long ago, a royal wedding or great public celebration would have been incomplete without executions, tortures, or *autos da fé*; a noble household without some person whose office it was to serve as a butt for everyone's malice and cruel teasing. (Perhaps the reader will recall Don Quixote's sojourn at the court of the Duchess. *Don Quixote* leaves a bitter taste in our mouths today; we almost quail in reading it. This would have seemed very strange to Cervantes and to his contemporaries, who read the work with the clearest conscience in the world, thought it the funniest of books, and almost died laughing over it.) To behold suffering gives pleasure, but to cause another to suffer affords an even greater pleasure. This severe statement expresses an old, powerful, human, all too human sentiment though the monkeys too might endorse it, for it is reported that they heralded and preluded man in the devising of bizarre cruelties. There is no feast without cruelty, as man's entire history attests. Punishment, too, has its festive features.

VII

These ideas, by the way, are not intended to add grist to the pessimist's mill of *taedium vitae*. On the contrary, it should be clearly understood that in the days when people were unashamed of their cruelty life was a great deal more enjoyable than it is now in the heyday of pessimism. The sky overhead has always grown darker in proportion as man has grown ashamed of his fellows. The tired, pessimistic look, discouragement in face of life's riddle, the icy *no* of the man who loathes life are none of them characteristic of mankind's evilest eras. These phenomena are like marsh plants; they presuppose a bog—the bog of morbid finickiness and moralistic drivel which has alienated man from his natural instincts. On his way to becoming an "angel" man has acquired that chronic indigestion and coated tongue which makes not only *the naïve joy and innocence of the animal distasteful to him, but even life itself; so that* at times he stops his nose against himself and recites with Pope Innocent III the catalogue of his unsavorinesses ("impure conception, loathsome feeding in the mother womb, wretchedness of physical substance, vile stench, discharge of spittle, urine, and faeces"). Nowadays, when suffering is invariably quoted as the chief argument against existence, it might be well to recall the days when matters were judged from the opposite point of view; when people would not have missed for anything the pleasure of inflicting suffering, in which they saw a powerful agent, the principal inducement to living. By way of comfort to the milksops, I would also venture the suggestion that in those days pain did not hurt as much as it does today; at all events, such is the opinion of a doctor who has treated Negroes for complicated internal inflammations which would have driven the most stoical European to distraction—the assumption here being that the negro represents an earlier phase of human development. (It appears, in fact, that the curve of human susceptibility to pain drops abruptly the moment we go below the top layer of culture comprising ten thousand or ten million individuals. For my part, I am convinced that, compared with one night's pain endured by a hysterical bluestocking, all the suffering of all the animals that have been used to date for scientific experiments is as nothing. Perhaps it is even legitimate to allow the possibility that pleasure in cruelty is not really extinct today; only, given our greater delicacy, that pleasure has had to undergo a certain sublimation and subtilization, to be translated into imaginative and psychological terms in order to pass muster before even the tenderest hypocritical conscience. ("Tragic empathy" is one such term; another is *les nostalgies de la croix*.) What makes people rebel against suffering is not really suffering itself but the senselessness of suffering; and yet neither the Christian, who projected a whole secret machinery salvation into suffering, nor the naive primitive, who interpreted all suffering, from the standpoint of the spectator or the dispenser of suffering, would have conceived of it as senseless. In order to negate and dispose of the possibility of any secret, unwitnessed suffering, early man had to invent gods and a whole apparatus of intermediate spirits, invisible beings who could also see in the dark, and who would not readily let pass unseen any interesting spectacle of suffering. Such were the inventions with which life, in those days, performed its perennial trick of justifying itself, its "evil"; nowadays a different set of inventions would be needed, e.g., life as a riddle or a epistemological problem. According to primitive logic of feeling (but is our own so very different?) any evil was justified whose spectacle proved edifying to the gods. We need only study Calvin and Luther to realize how far the ancient conception of the gods as frequenters of cruel spectacles has penetrated into our European humanism. But one thing is certain: the Greeks could offer their gods no more pleasant condiment than the joys of cruelty. With what eyes did Homer's gods regard the destinies of men? What, in the last analysis, was the meaning of the Trojan War and similar tragic atrocities? There can be no doubt that they were intended as festivals for the gods, and, insofar as poets in this respect are more "divine" than other men, as festivals for the poets. In much the same manner the moral philosophers of Greece, at a later date, let the eyes of God dwell on the mortal struggles, the heroism, and the self-mortification of the virtuous man. The "Heracles" of stern virtue was on stage and was fully aware of it; to that nation of actors, unwitnessed virtue was inconceivable. Might not the audacious invention, by philosophers of that era, of man's free will, his absolute spontaneity in the doing of good or ill, have been made for the express purpose of insuring that the interest of the gods in the spectacle of human virtue could never be exhausted? This earthly stage must never be bare of truly novel, truly unprecedented suspense, complications, catastrophes. A truly deterministic world, whose movements the gods might readily foresee, must soon pall on them: reason enough why those friends of the gods, the philosophers, would not foist such a world on them. Ancient humanity, an essentially public and visual world, unable to conceive of happiness without spectacles and feasts, was full of tender regard for the "spectator." And, as we have said before, punishment too has its festive features.

VIII

We have observed that the feeling of guilt and personal obligation had its inception in the oldest and most primitive relationship between human beings, that of buyer and seller, creditor and debtor. Here, for the first time, individual stood and measured himself against individual. No phase of civilization, no matter how primitive, has been discovered in which that relation did not to some extent exist. The mind of early man was preoccupied to such an extent with price making, assessment of values, the devising and exchange of equivalents, that, in a certain sense, this may be said to have constituted his thinking. Here we find the oldest variety of human acuteness, as well as the first indication of human pride, of superiority over other animals. Perhaps our word *man* (*mantis*) still expresses something of that pride: man saw himself as the being that measures values, the "assaying" animal. Purchase and sale, together with their psychological trappings, antedate even the rudiments of social organization and covenants. From its rudimentary manifestation in interpersonal law, the incipient sense of barter, contract, guilt, right, obligation, compensation was projected into the crudest communal complexes (and their relations to other such complexes) together with the habit of measuring power against power. The eye had been entirely conditioned to that mode of vision; and with the awkward consistency of primitive thought, which moves with difficulty but, when it does move inexorably in one direction, early mankind soon reached the grand generalization that everything has its price, everything can be paid for. Here we have the oldest and naïvest moral canon of justice, of all "fair play," "good will," and "objectivity". Justice, at this level, is good will operating among men of roughly equal power, their readiness to come to terms with one another, to strike a compromise or, in the case of others less powerful, to force them to accept such a compromise.

XII

One word should be added here about the *origin* and the *purpose* of punishment, two considerations radically distinct and yet too frequently confounded. How have our genealogists of morals treated these questions? Naïvely, as always. They would discover some kind of "purpose" in punishment, such as to avenge, or to deter, and would then naïvely place this purpose at the origin of punishment as its *causa fiendi*. And this is all. Yet the criterion of purpose is the last that should ever be applied to a study of legal evolution. There is no set of maxims more important for an historian than this: that the actual causes of a thing's origin and its eventual uses, the manner of its incorporation into a system of purposes, are worlds apart; that everything that exists, no matter what its origin, is periodically reinterpreted by those in power in terms of fresh intentions; that all processes in the organic world are processes of outstripping and overcoming, and that, in turn, all outstripping and overcoming means reinterpretation, rearrangement, in the course of which the earlier meaning and purpose are necessarily either obscured or lost. No matter how well we understand the utility of a certain physiological organ (or of a legal institution, a custom, a political convention, an artistic genre, a cultic trait) we do not thereby understand anything of its origin. I realize that this truth must distress the traditionalist, for, from time immemorial, the demonstrable purpose of a thing has been considered its *causa fiendi*—the eye is made for seeing, the hand for grasping. So likewise, punishment has been viewed as an invention for the purpose of punishing. But all pragmatic purposes are simply symbols of the fact that a will to power has implanted its own sense of function in those less powerful. Thus the whole history of a thing, an organ, a custom, becomes a continuous *chain* of reinterpretations and rearrangements, which need not be causally connected among themselves, which may simply follow one another. The "evolution" of a thing a custom, an organ is not *progressus* towards a goal, let alone the most logical and shortest *progressus*, requiring the least energy and expenditure. Rather, it is a sequence of more or less profound, more or less independent processes of appropriation, including the resistances used in each instance, the attempted transformations for purposes of defense or reaction, as well as the results of successful counterattacks. While forms are fluid, their "meaning" is even more so. The same process takes place in every individual organism. As the whole organism develops in essential ways, the meaning of the individual organs too is altered. In some cases their partial atrophy or numerical diminution spells the increased strength and perfection of the whole. This amounts to saying that partial desuetude, atrophy and degeneration, the loss of meaning and purpose—in short, death—must be numbered among the conditions of any true *progressus*, which latter appears always in the form of the will and means to greater power and is achieved at the expense of numerous lesser powers. The scope of any "progress" is measured by all that must be sacrificed for its sake. To sacrifice humanity as mass to the welfare of a single stronger human species would indeed constitute progress....

I have emphasized this point of historical method all the more strongly because it runs counter to our current instincts and fashions, which would rather come to terms with the absolute hazardness or the mechanistic meaninglessness of event than with the theory of a will to power mirrored in all process. The democratic bias against anything that dominates or wishes to dominate, our modern *misarchism* (to coin a bad word for a bad thing) has gradually so sublimated and disguised itself that nowadays it can invade the strictest, most objective sciences without anyone's raising a word of protest. In fact it seems to me that this prejudice now dominates all of physiology and the other life sciences, to their detriment, naturally, since it has conjured away one of their most fundamental concepts, that of activity, and put in its place the concept of *adaptation*—a kind of second-rate activity, mere reactivity. Quite in keeping with that bias, Herbert Spencer has defined life itself as an ever more purposeful inner adaptation to external circumstances. But such a view misjudges the very essence of life; it overlooks the intrinsic superiority of the spontaneous, aggressive, overreaching, reinterpreting and reestablishing forces, on whose action adaptation gradually supervenes. It denies, even in the organism itself, the dominant role of the higher functions in which the vital will appears active and shaping. The reader will recall that Huxley strongly objected to Spencer's "administrative nihilism." But here it is a question of much more than simply "administration."

Max Weber, Selection from *Economy and Society*

1. The Definition of Sociology and of Social Action

Sociology (in the sense in which this highly ambiguous word is used here) is a science concerning itself with the interpretive understanding of social action, and thereby with a causal explanation of its course and consequences. We shall speak of "action" insofar as the acting individual attaches a subjective meaning to his behavior—be it overt or covert, omission or acquiescence. Action is "social" insofar as its subjective meaning takes account of the behavior of others and is thereby oriented in its course.

a. Methodological Foundations

1. "Meaning" may be of two kinds. The term may refer first to the actual existing meaning in the given concrete case of a particular actor, or to the average or approximate meaning attributable to a given plurality of actors; or secondly to the theoretically conceived *pure type* of subjective meaning attributed to the hypothetical actor or actors in a given type of action. In no case does it refer to an objectively "correct" meaning or one which is "true" in some metaphysical sense. It is this which distinguishes the empirical sciences of action, such as sociology and history, from the dogmatic disciplines in that area, such as jurisprudence, logic, ethics, and esthetics, which seek to ascertain the "true" and "valid" meanings associated with the objects of their investigation.

2. The line between meaningful action and merely reactive behavior to which no subjective meaning is attached, cannot be sharply drawn empirically. A very considerable part of all sociologically relevant behavior, especially purely traditional behavior, is marginal between the two. In the case of some psychophysical processes, meaningful, i.e., subjectively understandable, action is not to be found at all; in others it is discernible only by the psychologist. Many mystical experiences which cannot be adequately communicated in words are, for a person who is not susceptible to such experiences, not fully understandable. At the same time the ability to perform a similar action is not a necessary prerequisite to understanding; "one need not have been Caesar in order to understand Caesar." "Recapturing an experience" is important for accurate understanding, but not an absolute precondition for its interpretation.

Understandable and non-understandable components of a process are often inter-mingled and bound up together.

3. All interpretation of meaning, like all scientific observations, strives for clar-ity and verifiable accuracy of insight and comprehension (*Evidenz*). The basis for certainty in understanding can be either rational, which can be further subdivided into logical and mathematical, or it can be of an emotionally empathic or artistically appreciative quality. Action is rationally evident chiefly when we attain a completely clear intellectual grasp of the action-elements in their intended context of mean-ing. Empathic or appreciative accuracy is attained when, through sympathetic par-ticipation, we can adequately grasp the emotional context in which the action took place. The highest degree of rational understanding is attained in cases involving the meanings of logically or mathematically related propositions; their meaning may be immediately and unambiguously intelligible. We have a perfectly clear understanding of what it means when somebody employs the proposition $2 \times 2 = 4$ or the Pythago-rean theorem in reasoning or argument, or when someone correctly carries out a logical train of reasoning according to our accepted modes of thinking. In the same way we also understand what a person is doing when he tries to achieve certain ends by choosing appropriate means on the basis of the facts of the situation, as experience has accustomed us to interpret them. The interpretation of such rationally purposeful action possesses, for the understanding of the choice of means, the highest degree of verifiable certainty. With a lower degree of certainty, which is, however, adequate for most purposes of explanation, we are able to understand errors, including confusion of problems of the sort that we ourselves are liable to, or the origin of which we can detect by sympathetic self-analysis.

On the other hand, many ultimate ends or values toward which experience shows that human action may be oriented, often cannot be understood completely, though sometimes we are able to grasp them intellectually. The more radically they differ from our own ultimate values, however, the more difficult it is for us to understand them empathically. Depending upon the circumstances of the particular case we must be content either with a purely intellectual understanding of such values or when even that fails, sometimes we must simply accept them as given data. Then we can try to understand the action motivated by them on the basis of whatever oppor-tunities for approximate emotional and intellectual interpretation seem to be avail-able at different points in its course. These difficulties confront, for instance, people not susceptible to unusual acts of religious and charitable zeal, or persons who abhor extreme rationalist fanaticism (such as the fanatic advocacy of the "rights of man").

The more we ourselves are susceptible to such emotional reactions as anxiety, anger, ambition, envy, jealousy, love, enthusiasm, pride, vengefulness, loyalty, devo-tion, and appetites of all sorts, and to the "irrational" conduct which grows out of them, the more readily can we empathize with them. Even when such emotions are found in a degree of intensity of which the observer himself is completely incapable, he can still have a significant degree of emotional understanding of their meaning and can interpret intellectually their influence on the course of action and the selec-tion of means.

For the purposes of a typological scientific analysis it is convenient to treat all irrational, affectually determined elements of behavior as factors of deviation from a conceptually pure type of rational action. For example a panic on the stock exchange can be most conveniently analysed by attempting to determine first what the course of action would have been if it had not been influenced by irrational affects; it is then possible to introduce the irrational components as accounting for the observed deviations from this hypothetical course. Similarly, in analysing a political or military campaign it is convenient to determine in the first place what would have been a rational course, given the ends of the participants and adequate knowledge of all the circumstances. Only in this way is it possible to assess the causal significance of irrational factors as accounting for the deviations from this type. The construction of a purely rational course of action in such cases serves the sociologist as a type (ideal type) which has the merit of clear understandability and lack of ambiguity. By comparison with this it is possible to understand the ways in which actual action is influenced by irrational factors of all sorts, such as affects and errors, in that they account for the deviation from the line of conduct which would be expected on the hypothesis that the action were purely rational.

Only in this respect and for these reasons of methodological convenience is the method of sociology "rationalistic." It is naturally not legitimate to interpret this procedure as involving a rationalistic bias of sociology, but only as a methodological device. It certainly does not involve a belief in the actual predominance of rational elements in human life, for on the question of how far this predominance does or does not exist, nothing whatever has been said. That there is, however, a danger of rationalistic interpretations where they are out of place cannot be denied. All experience unfortunately confirms the existence of this danger.

4. In all the sciences of human action, account must be taken of processes and phenomena which are devoid of subjective meaning, in the role of stimuli, results, favoring or hindering circumstances. To be devoid of meaning is not identical with being lifeless or non-human; every artifact, such as for example a machine, can be understood only in terms of the meaning which its production and use have had or were intended to have; a meaning which may derive from a relation to exceedingly various purposes. Without reference to this meaning such an object remains wholly unintelligible. That which is intelligible or understandable about it is thus its relation to human action in the role either of means or of end; a relation of which the actor or actors can be said to have been aware and to which their action has been oriented. Only in terms of such categories is it possible to "understand" objects of this kind. On the other hand processes or conditions, whether they are animate or inanimate, human or non-human, are in the present sense devoid of meaning in so far as they cannot be related to an intended purpose. That is to say they are devoid of meaning if they cannot be related to action in the role of means or ends but constitute only the stimulus, the favoring or hindering circumstances. It may be that the flooding of the Dollart [at the mouth of the Elms river near the Dutch-German border] in 1277 had historical significance as a stimulus to the beginning of certain migrations of considerable importance. Human mortality, indeed the organic life cycle from the

helplessness of infancy to that of old age, is naturally of the very greatest sociological importance through the various ways in which human action has been oriented to these facts. To still another category of facts devoid of meaning belong certain psychic or psychophysical phenomena such as fatigue, habituation, memory, etc.; also certain typical states of euphoria under some conditions of ascetic mortification; finally, typical variations in the reactions of individuals according to reaction-time, precision, and other modes. But in the last analysis the same principle applies to these as to other phenomena which are devoid of meaning. Both the actor and the sociologist must accept them as data to be taken into account.

It is possible that future research may be able to discover non-interpretable uniformities underlying what has appeared to be specifically meaningful action, though little has been accomplished in this direction thus far. Thus, for example, differences in hereditary biological constitution, as of "races," would have to be treated by sociology as given data in the same way as the physiological facts of the need of nutrition or the effect of senescence on action. This would be the case if, and insofar as, we had statistically conclusive proof of their influence on sociologically relevant behavior. The recognition of the causal significance of such factors would not in the least alter the specific task of sociological analysis or of that of the other sciences of action, which is the interpretation of action in terms of its subjective meaning. The effect would be only to introduce certain non-interpretable data of the same order as others which are already present, into the complex of subjectively understandable motivation at certain points. (Thus it may come to be known that there are typical relations between the frequency of certain types teleological orientation of action or of the degree of certain kinds rationality and the cephalic index or skin color or any other biologically inherited characteristic.)

5. Understanding may be of two kinds: the first is the direct observational understanding of the subjective meaning of a given act as such, including verbal utterances. We thus understand by direct observation, in this case, the meaning of the proposition $2 \times 2 = 4$ when we hear or read it. This is a case of the direct rational understanding of ideas. We also understand an outbreak of anger as manifested by facial expression, exclamations or irrational movements. This is direct observational understanding of irrational emotional reactions. We can understand in a similar observational way the action of a woodcutter or of somebody who reaches for the knob to shut a door or who aims a gun at an animal. This is rational observational understanding of actions.

Understanding may, however, be of another sort, namely explanatory understanding. Thus we understand in terms of *motive* the meaning an actor attaches to the proposition twice two equals four, when he states it or writes it down, in that we understand what makes him do this at precisely this moment and in these circumstances. Understanding in this sense is attained if we know that he is engaged in balancing a ledger or in making a scientific demonstration, or is engaged in some other task of which this particular act would be an appropriate part. This is rational understanding of motivation, "which consists in placing the act in an intelligible and more inclusive context of meaning. Thus we understand the chopping of wood or aiming of a gun in terms of motive in addition to direct observation if we know that the woodchopper is working for a wage or is chopping a supply of firewood for his own use or possibly is doing it for recreation. But he might also be working off a fit of rage, an irrational case. Similarly we understand the motive of a person aiming a gun if we know that he has been commanded to shoot as a member of a firing squad, that he is fighting against an enemy, or that he is doing it for revenge. The last is affectually determined and thus in a certain sense irrational. Finally we have a motivational understanding of the outburst of anger if we know that it has been provoked by jealousy, injured pride, or an insult. The last examples are all affectually determined and hence derived from irrational motives. In all the above cases the particular act has been placed in an understandable sequence of motivation, the understanding of which can be treated as an explanation of the actual course of behavior. Thus for a science which is concerned with the subjective meaning of action, explanation requires a grasp of the complex of meaning in which an actual course of understandable action thus interpreted belongs. In all such cases, even where the processes are largely affectual, the subjective meaning of the action, including that also of the relevant meaning complexes, will be called the intended meaning. (This involves a departure from ordinary usage, which speaks of intention in this sense only in the case of rationally purposive action.)

6. In all these cases understanding involves the interpretive grasp of the meaning present in one of the following contexts: (a) as in the historical approach, the actually intended meaning for concrete individual action; or (b) as in cases of sociological mass phenomena, the average of, or an approximation to, the actually intended meaning; or (c) the meaning appropriate to a scientifically formulated pure type (an ideal type) of a common phenomenon. The concepts and "laws" of pure economic theory are examples of this kind of ideal type. They state what course a given type of human action would take if it were strictly rational, unaffected by errors or emotional factors and if, furthermore, it were completely and unequivocally directed to a single end, the maximization of economic advantage. In reality, action takes exactly this course only in unusual cases, as sometimes on the stock exchange; and even then there is usually only an approximation to the ideal type.

Every interpretation attempts to attain clarity and certainty, but no matter how clear an interpretation as such appears to be from the point of view of meaning, it cannot on this account claim to be the causally valid interpretation. On this level it must remain only a peculiarly plausible hypothesis. In the first place the "conscious motives" may well, even to the actor himself, conceal the various "motives" and "repressions" which constitute the real driving force of his action. Thus in such cases even subjectively honest self-analysis has only a relative value. Then it is the task of the sociologist to be aware of this motivational situation and to describe and analyse it, even though it has not actually been concretely part of the conscious intention of the actor, possibly not at all, at least not fully. This is a borderline case of the interpretation of meaning. Secondly, processes of action which seem to an observer to be the same or similar may fit into exceedingly various complexes of motive in the case of the actual actor. Then even though the situations appear superficially to be very similar we must actually understand them or interpret them as very different, perhaps, in terms of meaning, directly opposed. (Simmel, in his *Probleme der Geschichtsphilosophie*, gives a number of examples.) Third, the actors in any given situation are often subject to opposing and conflicting impulses, all of which we are able to understand. In a large number of cases we know from experience it is not possible to arrive at even an approximate estimate of the relative strength of conflicting motives and very often we cannot be certain of our interpretation. Only the actual outcome of the conflict gives a solid basis of judgment.

More generally, verification of subjective interpretation by comparison with the concrete course of events is, as in the case of all hypotheses, indispensable. Unfortunately this type of verification is feasible with relative accuracy only in the few very special cases susceptible of psychological experimentation. In very different degrees of approximation, such verification is also feasible in the limited number of cases of mass phenomena which can be statistically described and unambiguously interpreted. For the rest there remains only the possibility of comparing the largest possible number of historical or contemporary processes which, while otherwise similar, differ in the one decisive point of their relation to the particular motive or factor the role of which is being investigated. This is a fundamental task of comparative sociology. Often, unfortunately, there is available only the uncertain procedure of the "imaginary experiment" which consists in thinking away certain elements of a chain of motivation and working out the course of action which would then probably ensue, thus arriving at a causal judgment.

For example, the generalization called Gresham's Law is a rationally clear interpretation of human action under certain conditions and under the assumption that it will follow a purely rational course. How far any actual course of action corresponds to this can be verified only by the available statistical evidence for the actual disappearance of under-valued monetary units from circulation. In this case our information serves to demonstrate a high degree of accuracy. The facts of experience were known before the generalization, which was formulated afterwards; but without this successful interpretation our need for causal understanding would evidently be left unsatisfied. On the other hand, without the demonstration that what can here be assumed to be a theoretically adequate interpretation also is in some degree relevant to an actual course of action, a "law," no matter how fully demonstrated theoretically, would be worthless for the understanding of action in the real world. In this case the correspondence between the theoretical interpretation of motivation and its empirical verification is entirely satisfactory and the cases are numerous enough so that verification can be considered established. But to take another example, Eduard Meyer has advanced an ingenious theory of the causal significance of the battles of Marathon, Salamis, and Platea for the development of the cultural peculiarities of Greek, and hence, more generally, Western, civilization. This is derived from a meaningful interpretation of certain symptomatic facts having to do with the attitudes of the Greek oracles and prophets towards the Persians. It can only be directly verified by reference to the examples of the conduct of the Persians in cases where they were victorious, as in Jerusalem, Egypt, and Asia Minor, and even this verification must necessarily remain unsatisfactory in certain respects. The striking rational plausibility of the hypothesis must here necessarily be relied on as a support. In very many cases of historical interpretation which seem highly plausible, however, there is not even a possibility of the order of verification which was feasible in this case. Where this is true the interpretation must necessarily remain a hypothesis.

7. A motive is a complex of subjective meaning which seems to the actor himself or to the observer an adequate ground for the conduct in question. The interpretation of a coherent course of conduct is "subjectively adequate" (or "adequate on the level of meaning"), insofar as, according to our habitual modes of thought and feeling, its component parts taken in their mutual relation are recognized to constitute a "typical" complex of meaning. It is more common to say "correct." The interpretation of a sequence of events will on the other hand be called *causally* adequate insofar as, according to established generalizations from experience, there is a probability that it will always actually occur in the same way. An example of adequacy on the level of meaning of in this sense is what is, according to our current norms or calculation or thinking, the correct solution of an arithmetical problem. On the other hand, a causally adequate interpretation of the same phenomenon would concern the statistical probability that, according to verified generalizations from experience, there would be a correct or an erroneous solution of the same problem. This also refers to currently accepted norms but includes taking account of typical errors or of typical confusions. Thus causal explanation depends on being able to determine that there is a probability, which in the rare ideal case can be numerically stated, but is always in some sense calculable, that a given observable event (overt or subjective) will be followed or accompanied by another event.

A correct causal interpretation of a concrete course of action is arrived at when the overt action and the motives have both been correctly apprehended and at the same time their relation has become meaningfully comprehensible. A correct causal interpretation of typical action means that the process which is claimed to be typical is shown to be both adequately grasped on the level of meaning and at the same time the interpretation is to some degree causally adequate. If adequacy in respect to meaning is lacking, then no matter how high the degree of uniformity and how precisely its probability can be numerically determined, it is still an incomprehensible statistical probability, whether we deal with overt or subjective processes. On the other hand, even the most perfect adequacy on the level of meaning has causal significance from a sociological point of view only insofar as there is some kind of proof for the existence of a probability that action in fact normally takes the course which has been held to be meaningful. For this there must be some degree of determinable frequency of approximation to an average or a pure type.

11. We have taken for granted that sociology seeks to formulate type concepts and generalized uniformities of empirical process. This distinguishes it from history, which is oriented to the causal analysis and explanation of individual actions, structures, and personalities possessing cultural significance. The empirical material which underlies the concepts of sociology consists to a very large extent, though by no means exclusively, of the same concrete processes of action which are dealt with by historians. An important consideration in the formulation of sociological concepts and generalizations is the contribution that sociology can make toward the causal

explanation of some historically important phenomenon. As in the case of every generalizing science the abstract character of the concepts of sociology is responsible for the fact that, compared with actual historical reality, they are relatively lacking in fullness of concrete content. To compensate for this disadvantage, sociological analysis can offer a greater precision of concepts. This precision is obtained by striving for the highest possible degree of adequacy on the level of meaning. It has already been repeatedly stressed that this aim can be realized in a particularly high degree in the case of concepts and generalizations which formulate rational processes. But sociological investigation attempts to include in its scope various irrational phenomena, such as prophetic, mystic, and affectual modes of action, formulated in terms of theoretical concepts which are adequate on the level of meaning. In *all* cases, rational or irrational, sociological analysis both abstracts from reality and at the same time helps us to understand it, in that it shows with what degree of approximation a concrete historical phenomenon can be subsumed under one or more of these concepts. For example, the same historical phenomenon may be in one aspect feudal, in another patrimonial, in another bureaucratic, and in still another charismatic. In order to give a precise meaning to these terms, it is necessary for the sociologist to formulate pure ideal types of the corresponding forms of action which in each case involve the highest possible degree of logical integration by virtue of their complete adequacy on the level of meaning. But precisely because this is true, it is probably seldom if ever that a real phenomenon can be found which corresponds exactly to one of these ideally constructed pure types. The case is similar to a physical reaction which has been calculated on the assumption of an absolute vacuum. Theoretical differentiation (*Kasuistik*) is possible in sociology only in terms of ideal or pure types. It goes without saying that in addition it is convenient for the sociologist from time to time to employ average types of an empirical statistical character, concepts which do not require methodological discussion. But when reference is made to "typical" cases, the term should always be understood, unless otherwise stated, as meaning *ideal types*, which may in turn be rational or irrational as the case may be (thus in economic theory they are always rational), but in any case are always constructed with a view to adequacy on the level of meaning.

It is important to realize that in the sociological field as elsewhere, averages, and hence average types, can be formulated with a relative degree of precision only where they are concerned with differences of degree in respect to action which remains qualitatively the same. Such cases do occur, but in the majority of cases of action important to history or sociology the motives which determine it are qualitatively heterogeneous. Then it is quite impossible to speak of an "average" in the true sense. The ideal types of social action which for instance are used in economic theory are thus unrealistic or abstract in that they always ask what course of action would take place if it were purely rational and oriented to economic ends alone. This construction can be used to aid in the understanding of action not purely economically determined but which involves deviations arising from traditional restraints, affects, errors, and the intrusion of other than economic purposes or considerations. This can take place in two ways. First, in analysing the extent to which in the concrete case, or on the average for a class of cases, the action was in part economically determined along with the other factors. Secondly, by throwing the discrepancy between the actual course of events and the ideal type into relief, the analysis of the non-economic motives actually involved is facilitated. The procedure would be very similar in employing an ideal type of mystical orientation, with its appropriate attitude of indifference to worldly things, as a tool for analysing its consequences for the actor's relation to ordinary life—for instance, to political or economic affairs. The more sharply and precisely the ideal type has been constructed, thus the more abstract and unrealistic in this sense it is, the better it is able to perform its functions in formulating terminology, classifications, and hypotheses. In working out a concrete causal explanation of individual events, the procedure of the historian is essentially the same. Thus in attempting to explain the campaign of 1866, it is indispensable both in the case of Moltke and of Benedek to attempt to construct imaginatively how each, given fully adequate knowledge both of his own situation and of that of his opponent, would have acted. Then it is possible to compare with this the actual course of action and to arrive at a causal explanation of the observed deviations, which will be attributed to such factors as misinformation, strategical errors, logical fallacies, personal temperament, or considerations outside the realm of strategy. Here, too, an ideal-typical construction of rational action is actually employed even though it is not made explicit.

The theoretical concepts of sociology are ideal types not only from the objective point of view, but also in their application to subjective processes. In the great majority of cases actual action goes on in a state of inarticulate half-consciousness or actual unconsciousness of its subjective meaning. The actor is more likely to "be aware" of it in a vague sense than he is to "know" what he is doing or be explicitly self-conscious about it. In most cases his action is governed by impulse or habit. Only occasionally and, in the uniform action of large numbers, often only in the case of a few individuals, is the subjective meaning of the action, whether rational or irrational, brought clearly into consciousness. The ideal type of meaningful action where the meaning is fully conscious and explicit is a marginal case. Every sociological or historical investigation, in applying its analysis to the empirical facts, must take this fact into account. But the difficulty need not prevent the sociologist from systematizing his concepts by the classification of possible types of subjective meaning. That is, he may reason as if action actually proceeded on the basis of clearly self-conscious meaning. The resulting deviation from the concrete facts must continually be kept in mind whenever it is a question of this level of concreteness, and must be carefully studied with reference both to degree and kind. It is often necessary to choose between terms which are either clear or unclear. Those which are clear will, to be sure, have the abstractness of ideal types, but they are none the less preferable for scientific purposes. (On all these questions see "'Objectivity' in Social Science and Social Policy.")

B. Social Action

1. Social action, which includes both failure to act and passive acquiescence, may be oriented to the past, present, or expected future behavior of others. Thus it may be motivated by revenge for a past attack, defence against present, or measures of

defence against future aggression. The "others" may be individual persons, and may be known to the actor as such, or may constitute an indefinite plurality and may be entirely unknown as individuals. (Thus, money is a means of exchange which the actor accepts in payment because he orients his action to the expectation that a large but unknown number of individuals he is personally unacquainted with will be ready to accept it in exchange on some future occasion.)

2. Not every kind of action, even of overt action, is "social" in the sense of the present discussion. Overt action is non-social if it is oriented solely to the behavior of inanimate objects. Subjective attitudes constitute social action only so far as they are oriented to the behavior of others. For example, religious behavior is not social if it is simply a matter of contemplation or of solitary prayer. The economic activity of an individual is social only if it takes account of the behavior of someone else. Thus very generally it becomes social insofar as the actor assumes that others will respect his actual control over economic goods. Concretely it is social, for instance, if in relation to the actor's own consumption the future wants of others are taken into account and this becomes one consideration affecting the actor's own saving. Or, in another connection, production may be oriented to the future wants of other people.

3. Not every type of contact of human beings has a social character; this is rather confined to cases where the actor's behavior is meaningfully oriented to that of others. For example, a mere collision of two cyclists may be compared to a natural event. On the other hand, their attempt to avoid hitting each other, or whatever insults, blows, or friendly discussion might follow the collision, would constitute "social action."

4. Social action is not identical either with the similar actions of many persons or with every action influenced by other persons. Thus, if at the beginning of a shower a number of people on the street put up their umbrellas at the same time, this would not ordinarily be a case of action mutually oriented to that of each other, but rather of all reacting in the same way to the like need of protection from the rain. It is well known that the actions of the individual are strongly influenced by the mere fact that he is a member of a crowd confined within a limited space. Thus, the subject matter of studies of "crowd psychology," such as those of Le Bon, will be called "action conditioned by crowds." It is also possible for large numbers, though dispersed, to be influenced simultaneously or successively by a source of influence operating similarly on all the individuals, as by means of the press. Here also the behavior of an individual is influenced by his membership in a "mass" and by the fact that he is aware of being a member. Some types of reaction are only made possible by the mere fact that the individual acts as part of a crowd. Others become more difficult under these conditions. Hence it is possible that a particular event or mode of human behavior can give rise to the most diverse kinds of feeling—gaiety, anger, enthusiasm, despair, and passions of all sorts—in a crowd situation which would not occur at all or not nearly so readily if the individual were alone. But for this to happen there need not, at least in many cases, be any meaningful relation between the behavior of the individual and the fact that he is a member of a crowd. It is not proposed in the present sense to call action "social" when it is merely a result of the effect on the individual of the existence of a crowd as such and the action is not oriented to that fact on the level of meaning. At

the same time the borderline is naturally highly indefinite. In such cases as that of the influence of the demagogue, there may be a wide variation in the extent to which his mass clientele is affected by a meaningful reaction to the fact of its large numbers; and whatever this relation may be, it is open to varying interpretations.

But furthermore, mere "imitation" of the action of others, such as that on which Tarde has rightly laid emphasis, will not be considered a case of specifically social action if it is purely reactive so that there is no meaningful orientation to the actor imitated. The borderline is, however, so indefinite that it is often hardly possible to discriminate. The mere fact that a person is found to employ some apparently useful procedure which he learned from someone else does not, however, constitute, in the present sense, social action. Action such as this is not oriented to the action of the other person, but the actor has, through observing the other, become acquainted with certain objective facts; and it is these to which his action is oriented. His action is then *causally* determined by the action of others, but not meaningfully. On the other hand, if the action of others is imitated because it is fashionable or traditional or exemplary, or lends social distinction, or on similar grounds, it is meaningfully oriented either to the behavior of the source of imitation or of third persons or of both. There are of course all manner of transitional cases between the two types of imitation. Both the phenomena discussed above, the behavior of crowds and imitation, stand on the indefinite borderline of social action. The same is true, as will often appear, of traditionalism and charisma. The reason for the indefiniteness of the line in these and other cases lies in the fact that both the orientation to the behavior of others and the meaning which can be imputed by the actor himself, are by no means always capable of clear determination and are often altogether unconscious and seldom fully self-conscious. Mere "influence" and meaningful orientation cannot therefore always be clearly differentiated on the empirical level. But conceptually it is essential to distinguish them, even though merely reactive imitation may well have a degree of sociological importance at least equal to that of the type which can be called social action in the strict sense. Sociology, it goes without saying, is by no means confined to the study of social action; this is only, at least for the kind of sociology being developed here, its central subject matter, that which may be said to be decisive for its status as a science. But this does not imply any judgment on the comparative importance of this and other factors.

2. Types of Social Action

Social action, like all action, may be oriented in four ways. It may be:

1. *Instrumentally rational (zweckrational)*, that is, determined by expectations as to the behavior of objects in the environment and of other human beings; these expectations are used as "conditions" or "means" for the attainment of the actor's own rationally pursued and calculated ends;
2. *Value-rational (wertrational)*, that is, determined by a conscious belief in the value for its own sake of some ethical, aesthetic, religious, or other form of behavior, independently of its prospects of success;

3. *Affectual* (especially emotional), that is, determined by the actor's specific affects and feeling states;

4. *Traditional*, that is, determined by ingrained habituation.

1. Strictly traditional behavior, like the reactive type of imitation discussed above, lies very close to the borderline of what can justifiably be called meaningfully oriented action, and indeed often on the other side. For it is very often a matter of almost automatic reaction to habitual stimuli which guide behavior in a course which has been repeatedly followed. The great bulk of all everyday action to which people have become habitually accustomed approaches this type. Hence, its place in a systematic classification is not merely that of a limiting case because, as will be shown later, attachment to habitual forms can be upheld with varying degrees of self-consciousness and in a variety of senses. In this case the type may shade over into value rationality (*Wertrationalität*).

2. Purely affectual behavior also stands on the borderline of what can be considered "meaningfully" oriented, and often it, too, goes over the line. It may, for instance, consist in an uncontrolled reaction to some exceptional stimulus. It is a case of sublimation when affectually determined action occurs in the form of conscious release of emotional tension. When this happens it is usually well on the road to rationalization in one or the other or both of the above senses.

3. The orientation of value-rational action is distinguished from the affectual type by its clearly self-conscious formulation of the ultimate values governing the action and the consistently planned orientation of its detailed course to these values. At the same time the two types have a common element, namely that the meaning of the action does not lie in the achievement of a result ulterior to it, but in carrying out the specific type of action for its own sake. Action is affectual if it satisfies a need for revenge, sensual gratification, devotion, contemplative bliss, or for working off emotional tensions (irrespective of the level of sublimation).

Examples of pure value-rational orientation would be the actions of persons who, regardless of possible cost to themselves, act to put into practice their convictions of what seems to them to be required by duty, honor, the pursuit of beauty, a religious call, personal loyalty, or the importance of some "cause" no matter in what it consists. In our terminology, value-rational action always involves "commands" or "demands" which, in the actor's opinion, are binding on him. It is only in cases where human action is motivated by the fulfillment of such unconditional demands that it will be called value-rational. This is the case in widely varying degrees, but for the most part only to a relatively slight extent. Nevertheless, it will be shown that the occurrence of this mode of action is important enough to justify its formulation as a distinct type; though it may be remarked that there is no intention here of attempting to formulate in any sense an exhaustive classification of types of action.

4. Action is instrumentally rational (*zweckrational*) when the end, the means, and the secondary results are all rationally taken into account and weighed. This involves rational consideration of alternative means to the end, of the relations of the end to

the secondary consequences, and finally of the relative importance of different possible ends. Determination of action either in affectual or in traditional terms is thus incompatible with this type. Choice between alternative and conflicting ends and results may well be determined in a value-rational manner. In that case, action is instrumentally rational only in respect to the choice of means. On the other hand, the actor may, instead of deciding between alternative and conflicting ends in terms of a rational orientation to a system of values, simply take them as given subjective wants and arrange them in a scale of consciously assessed relative urgency. He may then orient his action to this scale in such a way that they are satisfied as far as possible in order of urgency, as formulated in the principle of "marginal utility." Value-rational action may thus have various different relations to the instrumentally rational action. From the latter point of view, however, value-rationality is always irrational. Indeed, the more the value to which action is oriented is elevated to the status of an absolute value, the more "irrational" in this sense the corresponding action is. For, the more unconditionally the actor devotes himself to this value for its own sake, to pure sentiment or beauty, to absolute goodness or devotion to duty, the less is he influenced by considerations of the consequences of his action. The orientation of action wholly to the rational achievement of ends without relation to fundamental values is, to be sure, essentially only a limiting case.

5. It would be very unusual to find concrete cases of action, especially of social action, which were oriented *only* in one or another of these ways. Furthermore, this classification of the modes of orientation of action is in no sense meant to exhaust the possibilities of the field, but only to formulate in conceptually pure form certain sociologically important types to which actual action is more or less closely approximated or, in much the more common case, which constitute its elements. The usefulness of the classification for the purposes of this investigation can only be judged in terms of its results.

Part III

Critical Synthesis

4

The Critique of Instrumental Reason
The Reification of Society

Introduction

The writings of the Frankfurt Institute of Social Research represent an important synthesis in critical social thought, which occurred between 1923 and 1965. As noted earlier, it was at this time that the term "critical theory" was formally adopted, albeit not officially until 1937. Below I have selected excerpts from Max Horkheimer's essay "Critical and Traditional Theory" (1937), which conceives critical theory as a self-reflexive theory of social change that is concerned with exposing the ideological content of social facts and scientific knowledge. For Horkheimer, the goal of critical theory is to free the individual and society from these ideological controls. By comparison, traditional theory, according to Horkheimer, focuses on the testability of truths and social facts and is rooted in postivist theory, which seeks to validate the objectivity of social facts. For Horkheimer, such objectivity fails to take stock of the social tensions between the individual and the changing social circumstances of society. By seeking to neutralize these tensions through experimentation and hypotheses, traditional theorists overlook the ways in which societal tensions shape our political consciousness.

I have also included a selection from Horkheimer and Adorno's *Dialectic of Enlightenment* (1946), which discusses the dark side of the Enlightenment or rather the emergence of an instrumental or technical logic that had stripped reason of its capacity to resist authoritarianism (for example, the culture industry: the network of corporate advertisers, marketing entertainment firms, and the media and their ability to manipulate the masses through advertisement). Such authoritarianism was not simply the result of the fetish of the commodity, in which the exchange/money value concealed the real value or content of labor. Rather, it reflected the total reification of the political consciousness: the deceptive symbols and inauthentic artefacts used by the culture industry to colonize the political consciousness or what Adorno referred to as the "totally administered society."

Nevertheless, the central reason why I have selected the *Dialectic of Enlightenment* is that it addresses one of the central political issues underlying the Frankfurt School's aesthetic critique of society: whether the power to manipulate the cultural tastes and democratic sentiments of the masses (what Walter Benjamin referred to as "the work of art in the age of mechanical reproduction") arose from humankind's domination over nature, which Nietzsche, as we saw earlier, had discussed in terms of slave ethics.

In *Negative Dialectics* (1966), Adorno would build on this critical idea of an oppressive and dark social totality by theorizing about the incommensurability between reason and being and knowledge and ontology. From this standpoint, the Hegelian absolute spirit or reconciliation between the consciousness and self-consciousness contradicts the very essence of dialectic, its negativity. In other words, reconciliation in this case mistakes the content of morality and/or rational design for appearance; it disguises the hidden reality of unbecoming which ultimately opposes the rationalistic and false pretensions of the process of becoming (realizing the emancipatory content of one's actions and ideas). It is this primordial resistance to the transcendence of the negation of the negation that presupposes the anti-progressive, false trajectory of enlightenment ideals. It is essential to stress here that Adorno's non-identity is neither an abandonment, nor a subversion of Hegel's dialectic. Rather, it constitutes an "exit" from Hegel's system, while retaining some of Hegel's insights into the false dichotomies of subject and object, and concept and being.

Marcuse would address this idea in the *One Dimensional Man*, by conceiving the subtle controls imposed by the technological elite (the media, advertising companies and military authorities) in terms of the erosion of the oppositions between the ego and externalized forms of authority (father figures, i.e., the Nazi leaders). In this manner, societal conformism signifies the ability of the technological elite to assimilate the radical energies of the libido; it demonstrates, in other words, how consumerism (identification with false TV heroes) has eclipsed the radical desire/action (praxis) for social change. Accordingly, by synthesizing Freudianism and Marxism, Marcuse was able to expose what he referred to as the 'flattening of the dialectic' or the dissolution of oppositions in society.

Endnotes

1. Walter Benjamin, *Illuminations*, edited and with an introduction by Hannah Arendt (New York: Shocken Books, 1968), p. 217.

Max Horkheimer, "Traditional and Critical Theory," from *Critical Theory: Selected Essays*

The traditional idea of theory is based on scientific activity as carried on within the division of labor at a particular stage in the latter's development. It corresponds to the activity of the scholar which takes place alongside all the other activities of a society but in no immediately clear connection with them. In this view of theory, therefore, the real social function of science is not made manifest; it speaks not of what theory means in human life, but only of what it means in the isolate sphere in which for historical reasons it comes into existence. Yet as a matter of fact the life of society is the result of all the work done in the various sectors of production. Even if therefore the division of labor in the capitalist system functions but poorly, its branches, including science, do not become for that reason self-sufficient and independent. They are particular instances of the way in which society comes to grips with nature and maintains its own inherited form. They are moments in the social process of production, even if they be almost or entirely unproductive in the narrower sense. Neither the structures of industrial and agrarian production nor the separation of the so-called guiding and executory functions, services, and works, of intellectual and manual operations are eternal or natural states practiced in particular forms of society. The seeming self-sufficiency enjoyed by work processes whose course is supposedly determined by the very nature of the object corresponds to the seeming freedom of the economic subject in bourgeois society. The latter believe they are acting according to personal determinations, whereas in fact even in their most complicated calculations they but exemplify the working of an incalculable social mechanism.

The false consciousness of the bourgeois savant in the liberal era comes to light in very diverse philosophical systems. It found an especially significant expression at the turn of the century in the Neo-Kantianism of the Marburg school. Particular traits in the theoretical activity of the specialist are here elevated to the rank of universal categories, of instances of the word mind, the eternal "Logos". More accurately, decisive elements in social life are reduced to the theoretical activity of the savant. Thus "the power of knowledge" is called "the power of creative origination". "Production" means the "creative sovereignty of thought". For any datum it must be possible to deduce all its determinations from theoretical systems and ultimately from mathematics; thus all finite magnitudes may be derived from the concept of the infinitely small by way of the infinitesimal calculus, and this process is precisely their "production". The ideal to be striven for is a unitary system of science which, in the sense just described, will be all-powerful. Since everything about the object is reduced to conceptual determinations, the end-result of such theoretical work is that nothing is to be regarded as material and stable. The determinative, ordering, unifying function is the sole foundation for all else, and towards it all human effort is directed. Production is production of unity, and production is itself the product. Progress in awareness of freedom really means, according to this logic, that the paltry snippet of reality which the savant encounters finds evermore adequate expression in the form of differential quotients In reality, the scientific calling is only one, nonindependent, element in the work or historical activity of man, but in such a philosophy the former replaces the latter. To the extent that it conceives of reason as actually determining the course of events in a future society, such a hypostatization of Logos as reality is also a camouflaged utopia. In fact, however, the self-knowledge of present-day man is not a mathematical knowledge of nature which claims to be the eternal Logos, but a critical theory of society as it is, a theory dominated at every turn by a concern for reasonable conditions of life.

The isolated consideration of particular activities and branches of activity, along with their contents and objects, requires for its validity an accompanying concrete awareness of its own limitations. A conception is needed which overcomes the one-sidedness that necessarily arises when limited intellectual processes are detached from their matrix in the total activity of society. In the idea of theory which the scholar inevitably reaches between working purely within his own discipline, the relation between fact and conceptual ordering of fact offers a point of departure for such a corrective conception. The prevailing theory of knowledge has, of course, recognized the problem which this relation raises. The point is constantly stressed that identical objects provide for one discipline problems to be resolved only in some distant future, while in another discipline they are accepted as simple facts. Connections which provide physics with research problems are taken for granted in biology. Within biology, physiological processes raise problems while psychological processes do not. The social sciences take human and nonhuman nature in its entirety as given and are concerned only with how relationships are established between man and nature and between man and man. However, an awareness of this relativity, immanent in bourgeois science, in the relationship between man and man. However an awareness of this relativity, immanent in bourgeois science, in the relationship between theoretical thought and facts, is not enough to bring the concept of theory to a new stage of development. What is needed is a radical reconsideration, not of the scientist alone, but of the knowing individual as such.

The whole perceptible world as present to a member of bourgeois society and as interpreted within a traditional world-view which is in continuous interaction with that given world, is seen by the perceiver as a sum-total of facts; it is there and must be accepted. The classificatory thinking of each individual is one of those social reactions by which men try to adapt to reality in a way that best meets their needs. But there is at this point an essential difference between the individual and society. The world which is given to the individual and which he must accept and take into account is, in its present and continuing form, a product of the activity of society as a whole. The objects we perceive in our surroundings—cities, villages, fields, and woods—bear the mark of having been worked on by man. It is not only in clothing and appearance, in outward form and emotional make-up that men are the product of history. Even the way they see and hear is inseparable from the social life-process as it has evolved over the millennia. The facts which our senses present to us are socially preformed in two ways: through the historical character of the object perceived and through the historical character of the perceiving organ. Both are not simply natural; they are shaped by human activity, and yet the individual perceives himself as receptive and passive in the act of perception. The opposition of passivity and activity, which appears in knowledge theory as a dualism of sense-perception and understanding, does not hold for society, however, in the same measure as for the individual. The individual sees himself as passive and dependent, but society, though made up of individuals, is an active subject, even if a nonconscious one and, to that extent, a subject only in an improper sense. This difference in the existence of man and society is an expression of the cleavage which has up to now affected the historical forms of social life. The existence of society has either been founded directly on oppression or been the blind outcome of conflicting forces, but in any event not the result of conscious spontaneity on the part of individuals. Therefore the meaning of "activity" and "passivity" changes according as these concepts are applied to society or to individual. In the bourgeois economic mode the activity of society is blind and concrete, that of individuals abstract and conscious.

Human production also always has an element of planning to it. To the extent then that the facts which the individual and his theory encounter are socially produced, there must be rationality in them, even if in a restricted sense. But social action always involves, in addition, available knowledge and its application. The perceived fact is therefore co-determined by human ideas and concepts, even before its conscious theoretical elaboration by the knowing individual. Nor are we to think here only of experiments in natural science. The so-called purity of objective event to be achieved by the experimental procedure is, of course, obviously connected with technological conditions, and the connection of these in turn with the material process of production is evident. But it is easy here to confuse two questions: the question of the mediation of the factual through the activity of society as a whole, and the question of the influence of the measuring instrument, that is, of a particular action, upon the object being observed. The latter problem, which continually plagues physics, is no more closely connected with the problem that concerns us here than is the problem of perception generally, including perception in everyday life. Man's physiological apparatus for sensation itself largely anticipates the order followed in physical experiment. As man reflectively records reality, he separates and rejoins pieces of it, and concentrates on some particulars while failing to notice others. This process is just as much a result of the modern mode of production, as the perception of a man in a tribe of primitive hunters and fishers is the result of the conditions of his existence (as well, of course, as of the object of perception).

We must go on now to add that there is a human activity which has society itself for its object. The aim of this activity is not simply to eliminate one or other abuse, for it regards such abuses as necessarily connected with the way in which the social structure is organized. Although it itself emerges from the social structure, is purpose is not, either in its conscious intention or in its objective significance, the better functioning of any element in the structure. On the contrary, it is suspicious of the very categories of better, useful appropriate, productive, and valuable, as these are understood in the present order, and refuses to take them as nonscientific presuppositions about which one can do nothing. The individual as a rule must simply accept the basic conditions of his existence as given and strive to fulfill them; he finds his satisfaction and praise in accomplishing as well as he can the tasks connected with his place in society and in courageously doing his duty despite all the sharp criticism he may choose to exercise in particular matters. But the critical attitude of which we are speaking is wholly distrustful of the rules of conduct with which society as presently constituted provides each of its members. The separation between individual and society in virtue of which the individual accepts as natural the limits prescribed for his activity is relativized in critical theory. The latter considers the overall framework which is conditioned by the blind interaction of individual activities (that is, the existent division of labor and the class distinctions) to be a function which originates in human action and therefore is a possible object of planful decision and rational determination of goals.

The two-sided character of the social totality in its present form becomes, for men who adopt the critical attitude, a conscious opposition. In recognizing the present form of economy and the whole culture which it generates to be the product of human work as well as the organization which mankind was capable of and has provided for itself in the present era, these men identify themselves with this totality and conceive it as will and reason. It is their own world. At the same time, however, they experience the fact that society is comparable to nonhuman natural processes, to pure mechanisms, because cultural forms which are supported by war and oppression are not the creations of a unified, self-conscious will. That world is not their own but the world of capital.

In traditional theoretical thinking, the genesis of particular objective facts, the practical application of the conceptual systems by which it grasps the facts, and the role of such systems in action, are all taken to be external to the theoretical thinking itself. This alienation, which finds expression in philosophical terminology as the separation of value and research, knowledge and action, and other polarities, protects the savant from the tensions we have indicated and provides an assured framework for his activity. Yet a kind of thinking which does not accept this framework seems to have the ground taken out from under it. If a theoretical procedure does not take the form of determining objective facts with the help of the simplest and most differentiated conceptual systems available, what can it be but an aimless intellectual game, half conceptual poetry, half impotent expression of states of mind? The investigation into the social conditioning of facts and theories may indeed be a research problem, perhaps even a whole field for theoretical work, but how can such studies be radically different from other specialized efforts? Research into ideologies, or sociology of knowledge, which has been taken over from the critical theory of society and established as a special discipline, is not opposed either in its aim or in its other ambitions to the usual activities that go on within classificatory science.

In this reaction to critical theory, the self-awareness of thought as such is reduced to the discovery of the relationship that exists between intellectual positions and their social location. Yet the structure of the critical attitude, inasmuch as its intentions go beyond prevailing social ways of acting, is no more closely related to social disciplines thus conceived than it is to natural science. Its opposition to the traditional concept of theory springs in general from a difference not so much of objects as of subjects. For men of the critical mind, the facts, as they emerge from the work of society, are not extrinsic in the same degree as they are for the savant or for members of other professions who all think like little savants. The latter look towards a new kind of organization of work. But in so far as the objective realities given in perception are conceived as products which in principle should be under human control and, in the future at least, will in fact come under it, these realities lose the character of pure factuality.

The scholarly specialist "as" scientist regards social reality and its products as extrinsic to him, and "as" citizen exercises his interest in them through political articles, membership in political parties or social service organizations, and participation in elections. But he does not unify these two activities, and his other activities as well, except, at best, by psychological interpretation. Critical thinking, on the contrary, is motivated today by the effort really to transcend the tension and to abolish the opposition between the individual's purposefulness, spontaneity, and rationality, and those work-process relationships on which society is built. Critical thought has a concept of man as in conflict with himself until this opposition is removed. If activity governed by reason is proper to man, then existent social practice, which forms the individual's life down to its least details, is inhuman, and this inhumanity affects everything that goes on in the society. There will always be something that is extrinsic to man's intellectual and material activity, namely nature as the totality of as yet unmastered elements with which society must deal. But when situations which really depend on man alone, the relationships of men in their work, and the course of man's own history are also accounted part of "nature," the resultant extrinsicality is not only not a suprahistorical eternal category (even pure nature in the sense described is not that), but it is a sign of contemptible weakness. To surrender to such weakness is nonhuman and irrational.

Bourgeois thought is so constituted that in reflection on the subject which exercises such thought a logical necessity forces it to recognize an ego which imagines itself to be autonomous. Bourgeois thought is essentially abstract, and its principle is an individuality which inflatedly believes itself to be the ground of the world or even to be the world without qualification, an individuality separated off from events. The direct contrary of such an outlook is the attitude which holds the individual to be the unproblematic expression of an already constituted society; an example would be a nationalist ideology. Here the rhetorical "we" is taken seriously; speech is accepted as the organ of the community. In the internally rent society of our day, such thinking, except in social questions, sees nonexistent unanimities and is illusory.

Critical thought and its theory are opposed to both the types of thinking just described. Critical thinking is the function neither of the isolated individual nor of a sum-total of individuals. Its subject is rather a definite individual in his real relation to other individuals and groups, in his conflict with a particular class, and, finally, in the resultant web of relationships with the social totality and with nature. The subject is no mathematical point like the ego of bourgeois philosophy; his activity is the construction of the social present. Furthermore, the thinking subject is not the place where knowledge and object coincide, nor consequently the starting-point for attaining absolute knowledge. Such an illusion about the thinking subject, under which idealism has lived since Descartes, is ideology in the strict sense, for in the limited freedom of the bourgeois individual puts on the illusory form of perfect freedom and autonomy. As a matter of fact, however, in a society which is untransparent and without self-awareness the ego, whether active simply as thinker or active in other ways as well, is unsure of itself too. In reflection on man, subject and object are sundered; their identity lies in the future, not in the present. The method leading to such an identification may be called explanation in Cartesian language, but in genuinely critical thought explanation signifies not only a logical process but a concrete historical one as well. In the course of it both the social structure as a whole and the relation of the theoretician to society are altered, that is both the subject and the role of thought are changed. The acceptance of an essential unchangeableness between subject, theory, and object thus distinguishes the Cartesian conception from every kind of dialectical logic.

How is critical thought related to experience? One might maintain that if such thought were not simply to classify but also to determine for itself the goals which classification serves, in other words its own fundamental direction, it would remain locked up within itself, as happened to idealist philosophy. If it did not take refuge in utopian fantasy, it would be reduced to the formalistic fighting of sham battles. The attempt legitimately to determine practical goals by thinking must always fail. If thought were not content with the role given to it in existent society, if it were not to engage in theory in the traditional sense of the word, it would necessarily have to return to illusions long since laid bare.

Yet, as far as the role of experience is concerned, there is a difference between traditional and critical theory. The viewpoints which the latter derives from historical analysis as the goals of human activity, especially the idea of a reasonable organization of society that will meet the needs of the whole community, are immanent in human work but are not correctly grasped by individuals or by the common mind. A certain concern is also required if these tendencies are to be perceived and expressed. According to Marx and Engels such a concern is necessarily generated in the proletariat. Because of its situation in modern society the proletariat experiences the connection between work which puts ever more powerful instruments into men's hands in their struggle with nature, and the continuous renewal of an outmoded social organization. Unemployment, economic crises, militarization, terrorist regimes—in a word, the whole condition of the masses—are not due, for example, to limited technological possibilities, as might have been the case in earlier periods, but to the circumstances of production which are no longer suitable to our time. The application of all intellectual and physical means for the mastery of nature is hindered because in the prevailing circumstances these means are entrusted to special, mutually opposed interests. Production is not geared to the life of the whole community while heeding also the claims of individuals; it is geared to the power-backed claims of individuals while being concerned hardly at all with the life of the community. This is the inevitable result, in the present property system, of the principle that it is enough for individuals to look out for themselves.

But it must be added that even the situation of the proletariat is, in this society, no guarantee of correct knowledge. The proletariat may indeed have experience of meaninglessness in the form of continuing and increasing wretchedness and injustice in its own life. Yet this awareness is prevented from becoming a social force by the differentiation of social structure which is still imposed on the proletariat from above and by the opposition between personal class interests which is transcended only at very special moments. Even to the proletariat the world superficially seems quite different than it really is. Even an outlook which could grasp that no opposition really exists between the proletariat's own true interests and those of society as a whole, and would therefore derive its principles of action from the thoughts and feelings of the masses, would fall into slavish dependence on the status quo. The intellectual is satisfied to proclaim with reverent admiration the creative strength of the proletariat and finds satisfaction in adapting himself to it and in canonizing it. He fails to see that such an evasion of theoretical effort (which the passivity of his own thinking spares him) and of temporary opposition to the masses (which active theoretical effort on his part might force upon him) only makes the masses blinder and weaker than they need be. His own thinking should in fact be a critical, promotive factor in the development of the masses. When he wholly accepts the present psychological state of that class which, objectively considered embodies the power to change society, he has the happy feeling of being linked with an immense force and enjoys a professional optimism. When the optimism is shattered in periods of crushing defeat, many intellectuals risk falling into a pessimism about society and a nihilism which are just as ungrounded as their exaggerated optimism had been. They cannot bear the thought that the kind of thinking which is most topical, which has the deepest grasp of the historical situation, and is most pregnant with the future, must at certain times isolate its subject and throw him back upon himself.

If critical theory consisted essentially in formulations of the feelings and ideas of one class at any given moment, it would not be structurally different from the special branches of science. It would be engaged in describing the psychological contents typical of certain social groups; it would be social psychology. The relation of being to consciousness is different in different classes of society. If we take seriously the ideas by which the bourgeoisie explains its own order—free exchange, free competition, harmony of interests, and so on—and if we follow them to their logical conclusion, they manifest their inner contradiction and therewith their real opposition to the bourgeois order. The simple description of bourgeois self-awareness thus does not give us the truth about this class of men. Similarly, a systematic presentation of the contents of proletarian consciousness cannot provide a true picture of proletarian existence and interests. It would yield only an application of traditional theory to a specific problem, and not the intellectual side of the historical process, of proletarian emancipation. The same would be true if one were to limit oneself to appraising and making known the ideas not of the proletariat in general but of some more advanced sector of the proletariat, for example a party or its leadership. The real task set here would be the registering and classifying of facts with the help of the most suitable conceptual apparatus, and the theoretician's ultimate goal would be the prediction of future socio-psychological phenomena. Thought and the formation of theory would be one thing and its object, the proletariat, another.

If, however, the theoretician and his specific object are seen as forming a dynamic unity with the oppressed class, so that his presentation of societal contradictions is not merely an expression of the concrete historical situation but also a force within it to stimulate change, then his real function emerges. The course of the conflict between the advanced sectors of the class and the individuals who speak out the truth concerning it, as well as of the conflict between the most advanced sectors with their theoreticians and the rest of the class, is to be understood as a process of interactions in which awareness comes to flower along with its liberating but also its aggressive forces which incite while also requiring discipline. The sharpness of the conflict shows in the ever present possibility of tension between the theoretician and the class which his thinking is to serve. The unity of the social forces which promise liberation is at the same time their distinction (in Hegel's sense); it exists only as a conflict which continually threatens the subjects caught up in it. This truth becomes clearly evident in the person of the theoretician; he exercises an aggressive critique not only against the conscious defenders of the status quo but also against distracting, conformist, or utopian tendencies within his own household.

The traditional type of theory, one side of which finds expression in formal logic, is in its present form part of the production process with its division of labor. Since society must come to grips with nature in future ages as well, this intellectual technology will not become irrelevant but on the contrary is to be developed as fully as possible. But the kind of theory which is an element in action leading to new social forms is not a cog in an already existent mechanism. Even if victory or defeat provides a vague analogy to the confirmation or failure of scientific hypotheses, the theoretician who sets himself up in opposition to society as it is does not have the consolation that such hypotheses are part of his professional work. He cannot sing for himself the hymn of praise which Poincaré sang to the enrichment deriving even from hypotheses that must be rejected. His profession is the struggle of which his own thinking is a part and not something self-sufficient and separable from the struggle. Of course, many elements of theory in the usual sense enter into his work: the knowledge and prognosis of relatively isolated facts, scientific judgments, the elaboration of problems which differ from those of other theoreticians because of his specific interests but nonetheless manifest the same logical form.

Traditional theory may take a number of things for granted: its positive role in a functioning society, an admittedly indirect and obscure relation to the satisfaction of general needs, and participation in the self-renewing life process. But all these exigencies about which science need not trouble itself because their fulfillment is rewarded and confirmed by the social position of the scientist, are called into question in critical thought. The goal at which the latter aims, namely the rational state of society, is forced upon him by present distress. The theory which projects such a solution to the distress does not labor in the service of an existing reality but only gives voice to the mystery of that reality. However cogently absurdities and errors may be uncovered at any given moment, however much every error may be shown to be taking its revenge, yet the overall tendency of the critical theoretical undertaking receives no sanction from so-called healthy human understanding; it has no custom on its side, even when it promises success. Theories, on the contrary, which are confirmed or disproved in the building of machines, military organizations, even successful motion pictures, look to a clearly distinguishable consumer group, even when like theoretical physics they are pursued independently of any application or consist only in a joyous and virtuous playing with mathematical symbols; society proves its humaneness by rewarding such activity.

It is the task of the critical theoretician to reduce the tension between his own insight and oppressed humanity in whose service he thinks. But in the sociological concept of which we speak detachment from all classes is an essential mark of the intelligentsia, a sort of sign of superiority of which it is proud. Such a neutral category corresponds to the abstract self-awareness typical of the savant. To the bourgeois consumer under liberalism knowledge meant knowledge that was useful in some circumstances or other, no matter what kind of knowledge might be in question; the sociology we speak of approaches knowledge in the same way at the theoretical level. Marx and Mises, Lenin and Liefmann, Jaurès and Jevons all come under the same sociological heading, unless the politicians are left out of the list and put down as potential students of the political scientists, sociologists, and philosophers who are the real men of knowledge. From them the politician is to learn to use "such and such a means" when he takes "such and such a stand"; he must learn whether the practical position he adopts can be implemented with logical consistency. A division of labor is established between men who in social conflicts affect the course of history and the social theoreticians who assign them their standpoint.

Critical theory is in contradiction to the formalistic concept of mind which underlies such an idea of the intelligentsia. According to this concept there is only one truth, and the positive attributes of honesty, internal consistency, reasonableness, and striving for peace, freedom, and happiness may not be attributed in the same sense to any other theory and practice. There is likewise no theory of society, even that of the sociologists concerned with general laws, that does not contain political motivations, and the truth of these must be decided not in supposedly neutral reflection but in personal thought and action, in concrete historical activity. Now, it is disconcerting that the intellectual should represent himself in this way, as though a difficult labor of thought, which he alone could accomplish, were the prime requirement if men were accurately to choose between revolutionary, liberal and fascist ends and means. The situation has not been like that for many decades. The avant-garde in the political struggle need prudence, but not academic instruction on their so-called standpoint. Especially at a time when the forces of freedom in Europe are themselves disoriented and seeking to regroup themselves anew, when everything depends on nuances of position within their own movement, when indifference to substantive content, created by defeat, despair, and corrupt bureaucracy, threatens to overwhelm all the spontaneity, experience, and knowledge of the masses despite the heroic efforts of a few, a conception of the intelligentsia which claims to transcend party lines and is therefore abstract represents a view of problems that only hides the decisive questions.

Mind is liberal. It tolerates no external coercion, no revamping of its results to suit the will of one or other power. But on the other hand it is not cut loose from the life of society; it does not hang suspended over it. In so far as mind seeks autonomy or man's control over his own life no less than over nature, it is able to recognize this same tendency as a force operative in history. Considered in isolation, the recognition of such a tendency seems neutral; but just as mind is unable to recognize it without having first been stimulated and become concerned, neither can it make such recognition a generally accepted fact without a struggle. To that extent, mind is not liberal. Intellectual efforts which arise here and there without any conscious connection with a particular practical commitment but vary according to different academic or other tasks that promise success, intellectual efforts which take now this, now that for their field of concentration, may be useful in the service of one or other historical tendency. But for all their formal correctness (and what theoretical structure, however radically faulted, cannot fulfill the requirements of formal correctness?), they can also hinder and lead astray the development of the mind. The abstract sociological concept of an intelligentsia which is to have missionary functions is, by its structure, an hypostatization of specialized science. Critical theory is neither "deeply rooted" like totalitarian propaganda nor "detached" like the liberalist intelligentsia.

Our consideration of the various functions of traditional and critical theory brings to light the difference in their logical structure. The primary propositions of traditional theory define universal concepts under which all facts in the field in question are to be subsumed; for example, the concept of a physical process in physics or an organic process in biology. In between primary propositions and facts there is the hierarchy of genera and species with their relations of subordination. Facts are individual cases, examples, or embodiments of classes. There are no differences due to time between the unities in the system. Electricity does not exist prior to an electrical field, nor a field prior to electricity, any more than wolf as such exists before or after particular wolves. As far as an individual knower is concerned there may be one or other temporal sequence among such relationships, but no such sequence exists in the objects themselves.

The critical theory of society also begins with abstract determinations; in dealing with the present era it begins with the characterization of an economy based on exchange. The concepts Marx uses, such as commodity, value, and money, can function as genera when, for example, concrete social relations are judged to be relations of exchange and when there is question of the commodity character of goods. But the theory is not satisfied to relate concepts of reality by way of hypotheses. The theory begins with an outline of the mechanism by which bourgeois society, after dismantling feudal regulations, the guild system, and vassalage, did not immediately fall apart under the pressure of its own anarchic principle but managed to survive. The regulatory effects of exchange are brought out on which bourgeois economy is founded. The conception of the interaction of society and nature, which is already exercising its influence here, as well as the idea of a unified period of society, of its self-preservation, and so on, spring from a radical analysis, guided by concern for the future, of the historical process. The relation of the primary conceptual interconnections to the world of facts is not essentially a relation of classes to instances. It is because of its inner dynamism that the exchange relationship, which the theory outlines, dominates social reality, as, for example, the assimilation of food largely dominates the organic life of plant and brute beast.

In critical theory, as in traditional theory, more specific elements must be introduced in order to move from fundamental structure to concrete reality. But such an intercalation of more detailed factors—for example the existence of large money reserves, the diffusion of these in sectors of society that are still precapitalist, foreign trade—is not accomplished by simple deduction as in theory that has been simplified for specialized use. Instead, every step rests on knowledge of man and nature which is stored up in the sciences and in historical experience. This is obvious, of course, for the theory of industrial technology. But in other areas too a detailed knowledge of how men react is applied throughout the doctrinal developments to which we have been referring. For example, the statement that under certain conditions the lowest strata of society have the most children plays an important role in explaining how the bourgeois society built on exchange necessarily leads to capitalism with its army of industrial reserves and its crises. To give the psychological reasons behind the observed fact about the lower classes is left to traditional science.

Thus the critical theory of society begins with the idea of the simple exchange of commodities and defines the idea with the help of relatively universal concepts. It then moves further, using all knowledge available and taking suitable material from the research of others as well as from specialized research. Without denying its own principles as established by the special discipline of political economy, the theory shows how an exchange economy, given the condition of men (which, of course, changes under the very influence of such an economy), must necessarily lead to a heightening of those social tensions which in the present historical era lead in turn to wars and revolutions.

The necessity just mentioned, as well as the abstractness of the concepts, are both like and unlike the same phenomena in traditional theory. In both types of theory there is a strict deduction if the claim of validity for general definitions is shown to include a claim that certain factual relations will occur. For example, if you are dealing with electricity, such and such an event must occur because such and such characteristics belong to the very concept of electricity. To the extent that the critical theory of society deduces present conditions from the concept of simple exchange, it includes this kind of necessity, although it is relatively unimportant that the hypothetical form of statement be used. That is, the stress is not on the idea that wherever a society based on simple exchange prevails, capitalism must develop—although this is true. The stress is rather on the fact that the existent capitalist society, which has spread all over the world from Europe and for which the theory is declared valid, derives from the basic relation of exchange. Even the classificatory judgments of specialized science have a fundamentally hypothetical character, and existential judgments are allowed, if at all, only in certain areas, namely the descriptive and practical parts of the discipline. But the critical theory of society is, in its totality, the unfolding of a single existential judgment. To put it in broad terms, the theory says that the basic form of the historically given commodity economy on which modern history rests contains in itself the internal and external tensions of the modern era; it generates these tensions over and over again in an increasingly heightened form; and after a period of progress, development of human powers, and emancipation for the individual, after an enormous extension of human control over nature, it finally hinders further development and drives humanity into a new barbarism.

Max Horkheimer and Theodor Adorno, Selection from *Dialectic of Enlightenment*

The mythic terror feared by the Enlightenment accords with myth. Enlightenment discerns it not merely in unclarified concepts and words, as demonstrated by semantic language-criticism, but in any human assertion that has no place in the ultimate context of self-preservation. Spinoza's "*Conatus sese conservandi primum et unicum virtutis est fundamentum*" contains the true maxim of all Western civilization, in which the religious and philosophical differences of the middle class are reconciled. The self (which, according to the methodical extirpation of all natural residues because they are mythological, must no longer be either body or blood, or soul, or even the natural I), once sublimated into the transcendental or logical subject, would form the reference point of reason, of the determinative instance of action. Whoever resigns himself to life without any rational reference to self-preservation would, according to the Enlightenment—and Protestantism—regress to prehistory. Impulse as such is as mythic as superstition; to serve the god not postulated by the self is as idiotic as drunkenness. Progress has prepared the same fate for both adoration and descent into a state of directly natural being, and has anathematized both the self-abandonment of thought and that of pleasure. The social work of every individual in bourgeois society is mediated through the principle of self; for one, labor will bring an increased return on capital; for others, the energy for extra labor. But the more the process of self-preservation is effected by the bourgeois division of labor, the more it requires the self-alienation of the individuals who must model their body and soul according to the technical apparatus. This again is taken into account by enlightened thought: in the end the transcendental subject of cognition is apparently abandoned as the last reminiscence of subjectivity and replaced by the much smoother work of automatic control mechanisms. Subjectivity has given way to the logic of the allegedly indifferent rules of the game, in order to dictate all the more unrestrainedly. Positivism, which finally did not spare thought itself, the chimera in a cerebral form, has removed the very last insulating instance between individual behavior and the social norm. The technical process, into which the subject has objectified itself after being removed from the consciousness, is free of the ambiguity of mythic thought as of all meaning altogether, because reason itself has become the mere instrument of the all-inclusive economic apparatus. It serves as a general tool, useful for the manufacture of all other tools, firmly directed toward its end, as fateful as the precisely calculated movement of material production, whose result for mankind is beyond all calculation. At last its old ambition, to be a pure organ of ends, has been realized. The exclusiveness of logical laws originates in this unique functional significance, and ultimately in the compulsive nature of self-preservation. And self-preservation repeatedly culminates in the choice between survival and destruction, apparent again in the principle that of two contradictory propositions only one can be true and only one false. The formalism of this principle, and of the entire logic in which form it is established, derives from the opacity and complexity of interests in a society in which the maintenance of forms and the preservation of individuals coincide only by chance. The derivation of thought from logic ratifies in the lecture room the reification of man in the factory and the office. In this way the taboo encroaches upon the anathematizing power, and enlightenment upon the spirit which itself comprises. Then, however, nature as true self-preservation is released by the very process which promised to extirpate it, in the individual as in the collective destiny of crisis and armed conflict. If the only norm that remains for theory is the ideal of unified science, practice must be subjected to the irrepressible process of world history. The self that is wholly comprehended by civilization resolves itself in an element of the inhumanity which from the beginning has aspired to evade civilization. The primordial fear of losing one's own name is realized. For civilization, pure natural existence, animal and vegetative, was the absolute danger. One after the other, mimetic, mythic and meta-physical modes of behavior were taken as superseded eras, any reversion to which was to be feared as implying a reversion of the self to that mere state of nature from which it had estranged itself with so huge an effort, and which therefore struck such terror into the self. In every century, any living reminiscence of olden times, not only of nomadic antiquity but all the more of the pre-patriarchal stages, was most rigorously punished and extirpated from human consciousness. The spirit of enlightenment replaced the fire and the rack by the stigma it attached to all irrationality, because it led to corruption. Hedonism was moderate, finding the extreme no less odious than did Aristotle. The bourgeois ideal of naturalness intends not amorphous nature, but the virtuous mean. Promiscuity and asceticism, excess and hunger, are directly identical, despite the antagonism, as powers of disintegration. By subjecting the whole of life to the demands of its maintenance, the dictatorial minority guarantees, together with its own security, the persistence of the whole. From Homer to modern times, the dominant spirit wishes to steer between the Scylla of a return to mere reproduction and the Charybdis of unfettered fulfillment; it has always mistrusted any star other than that of the lesser evil. The new German pagans and warmongers want to set pleasure free once more. But under the pressure of labor, through the centuries, pleasure has learned self-hatred, and therefore in the state of totalitarian emancipation remains mean and disabled by self-contempt. It remains in the grip of the self-preservation to which it once trained reason—deposed in the meantime. At the turning points of Western civilization, from the transition to Olympian religion up to the Renaissance, Reformation, and bourgeois atheism, whenever new nations and classes more firmly repressed myth, the fear of uncomprehended, threatening nature, the consequence of its very materialization and objectification, was reduced to animistic superstition, and the subjugation of nature was made the absolute purpose of life within and without. If in the end self-preservation has been automated, so reason has been abandoned by those who, as administrators of production, entered upon its inheritance and now fear it in the persons of the disinherited. The essence of enlightenment is the alternative whose ineradicability is that of domination. Men have always had to choose between their subjection to nature or the subjection of nature to the Self. With the extension of the bourgeois commodity economy, the dark horizon of myth is illumined by the sun of calculating reason, beneath whose cold rays the seed of the new barbarism grows to fruition. Under the pressure of domination human labor has always led away from myth—but under domination always returns to the jurisdiction of myth.

The entanglement of myth, domination, and labor is preserved in one of the Homeric narratives. Book XII of the Odyssey tells of the encounter with the Sirens. Their allurement is that of losing oneself in the past. But the hero to whom the temptation is offered has reached maturity through suffering. Throughout the many mortal perils he has had do endure, the unity of his own life, the identity of the individual, has been confirmed for him. The regions of time part for him as do water, earth, and air. For him, the flood of that-which-was has retreated from the rock of the present, and the future lies cloudy on the horizon. What Odysseus left behind him entered into the nether world; for the self is still so close to prehistoric myth, from whose womb it tore itself, that its very own experienced past becomes mythic prehistory. And it seeks to encounter that myth through the fixed order of time. The threefold schema is intended to free the present moment from the power of the past by referring that power behind the absolute barrier of the unrepeatable and placing it at the disposal of the present as practicable knowledge. The compulsion to rescue what is gone as what is living instead of using it as the material of progress was appeased only in art, to which history itself appertains as a presentation of past life. So long as art declines to pass as cognition and is thus separated from practice, social practice tolerates it as it tolerates pleasure. But the Sirens' song has not yet been rendered powerless by reduction to the condition of art. They know "everything that ever happened on this so fruitful earth," including the events in which Odysseus himself took part, " all those things that Argos' sons and the Trojans suffered by the will of goods on the plains of Troy." While they directly evoke the recent past, with the irresistible promise of pleasure as which their song is heard, they threaten the patriarchal order which renders to each man his life only in return for his full measure of time. Whoever falls for their trickery must perish, whereas only perpetual presence of mind forces an existence from nature. Even though the Sirens know all that has happened, they demand the future as the price of that knowledge, and the promise of the happy return is the deception with which the past ensnares the one who longs for it. Odysseus is warned by Circe, that divinity of reversion to the animal whom he resisted and who therefore gives him strength to resist other powers of disintegration. But the allurement of the Sirens remains superior; no one who hears their song can escape. Men had to do fearful things to themselves before the self, the identical, purposive, and virile nature of man, was formed, and something of that recurs in every childhood. The strain of holding the I together adheres to the I in all stages; and the temptation to lose it has always been there with the blind determination to maintain it. The narcotic intoxication which permits the atonement of deathlike sleep for the euphoria in which the self is suspended, is one of the oldest social arrangements which mediate between self-preservation and self-destruction—an attempt of the self to survive itself. The dread of losing the self and of abrogating together with the self the barrier between oneself and other life, the fear of death and destruction, is intimately associated with a promise of happiness which threatened civilization in every moment. Its road was that of obedience and labor, over which fulfillment shines forth perpetually—but only as illusive appearance, as devitalized beauty. The mind of Odysseus, inimical both to his own death and to his own happiness, is aware of this. He knows only two possible ways to escape. One of them he prescribes for his men. He plugs their ears with wax, and they must row with all their strength. Whoever would survive must not hear the temptation of that which is unrepeatable, and he is able to survive only by being unable to hear it. Society has always made provision for that. The laborers must be fresh and concentrate as they look ahead, and must ignore whatever lies to one side. They must doggedly sublimate in additional effort the drive that impels to diversion. And so they become practical.—The other possibility Odysseus, the seigneur who allows the others to labor for themselves, reserves to himself. He listens, but while bound impotently to the mast; the greater the temptation the more he has his bonds tightened—just as later the burghers would deny themselves happiness all the more doggedly as it drew closer to them with the growth of their own power. What Odysseus hears is without consequence for him; he is able only to nod his head as a sign to be set free from his bonds; but it is too late; his men, who do not listen, know only the song's danger but nothing of its beauty, and leave him at the mast in order to save him and themselves. They reproduce the oppressor's life together with their own, and the oppressor is no longer able to escape his social role. The bonds with which he has irremediably tied himself to practice, also keep the Sirens away from practice: their temptation is neutralized and becomes a mere object of contemplation—becomes art. The prisoner is present at a concert, an inactive eavesdropper like later concertgoers, and his spirited call for liberation fades like applause. Thus the enjoyment of art and manual labor break apart as the world of prehistory is left behind. The epic already contains the appropriate theory. The cultural material is in exact correlation to work done according to command; and both are grounded in the inescapable compulsion to social domination of nature.

Measures such as those taken on Odysseus' ship in regard to the Sirens form pre-sentient allegory of the dialectic of enlightenment. Just as the capacity of representation is the measure of domination, and domination is the most powerful thing that can be represented in most performances, so the capacity of representation is the vehicle of progress and regression at one and the same time. Under the given conditions, exemption from work—not only among the unemployed but even at the other end of the social scale—also means disablement. The rulers experience exis-tence, with which they need no longer concern themselves, only as a substratum, and hence wholly ossify into the condition of the commanding self. Primitive man experienced the natural thing merely as the evasive object of desire. "But the master, who has interposed the servant between it and himself, in this way relates himself only to the dependence of the thing and enjoys it pure; however, he leaves the aspect of [its] independence to the servant, who works upon it." Odysseus is represented in labor. Just as he cannot yield to the temptation to self-abandonment, so, as proprietor, he finally renounces even participation in labor, and ultimately even its management, whereas his men—despite their closeness to things—cannot enjoy their labor because it is performed under pressure, in desperation, with senses stopped by force. The ser-vant remains enslaved in body and soul; the master regresses. No authority has yet been able to escape paying this price, and the apparent cyclical nature of the advance of history is partly explained by this debilitation, the equivalent of power. Mankind, whose versatility and knowledge become differentiated with the division of labor, is at the same time forced back to anthropologically more primitive stages, for with the technical easing of life the persistence of domination brings about a fixation of the instincts by means of heavier repression. Imagination atrophies. The disaster is not merely that individuals might remain behind society or its material production. Where the evolution of the machine has already turned into that of the machinery of domination (so that technical and social tendencies, always interwoven, converge in the total schematization of men), untruth is not represented merely by the outdis-tanced. As against that, adaptation to the power of progress involves the progress of power, and each time anew brings about those degenerations which show not unsuc-cessful but successful progress to be its contrary. The curse of irresistible progress is irresistible regression.

This regression is not restricted to the experience of the sensuous world bound up with the circumambient animate, but at the same time affects the self-dominant intel-lect, which separates from sensuous experience in order to subjugate it. The unification of intellectual functions by means of which domination over the senses is achieved, the resignation of thought to the rise of unanimity, means the impoverishment of thought and of experience: the separation of both areas leaves both impaired. The restriction of thought to organization and administration, practiced by rulers from the cunning Odysseus to the naive managing directors of today, necessarily implies the restriction which comes upon the great as soon as it is no longer merely a question of manipulating the small. Hence the spirit becomes the very apparatus of domination and self-domination which bourgeois thought has always mistakenly supposed it to be. The stopped ears which the pliable proletarians have retained ever since the time of myth have no advantage over the immobility of the master. The over-maturity of society lives by the immaturity of the dominated. The more complicated and precise the social, economic, and scientific apparatus with whose service the production system has long harmonized the body, the more impoverished the experiences which it can offer. The elimination of qualities, their conversion into functions, is translated from science by means of rationalized modes of labor to the experiential world of nations, and tends to approximate it once more to that of the amphibians. The regression of the masses today is their inability to hear the unheard-of with their own ears, to touch the unapprehended with their own hands—the new form of delusion which deposes every conquered mythic form. Through the mediation of the total society which embraces all relations and emotions, men are once again made to be that against which the evolutionary law of society, the principle of self, had turned: mere species beings, exactly like one another through isolation in the forcibly united collectivity. The oarsmen, who cannot speak to one another, are each of them yoked in the same rhythm as the modern worker in the factory, movie theater, and collective. The actual working conditions in society compel conformism—not the conscious influences which also made the suppressed men dumb and separated them from truth. The impotence of the worker is not merely a stratagem of the rulers, but the logical consequence of the industrial society into which the ancient Fate—in the very course of the effort to escape it—has finally changed.

But this logical necessity is not conclusive. It remains tied to domination, as both its reflection and its tool. Therefore its truth is no less questionable than its evidence is irrefutable. Of course thought has always sufficed concretely to characterize its own equivocation. It is the servant that the master cannot check as he wishes. Domination, ever since men settled down, and later in the commodity society, has become objectified as law and organization and must therefore restrict itself. The instrument achieves independence: the mediating instance of the spirit, independently of the will of the master, modifies the directness of economic injustice. The instruments of domination, which would encompass all—language, weapons, and finally machines—must allow themselves to be encompassed by all. Hence in domination the aspect of rationality prevails as one that is also different from it. The "objectivity" of the means, which makes it universally available, already implies the criticism of that domination as whose means thought arose. On the way from mythology to logistics, thought has lost the element of self-reflection, and today machinery disables men even as it nurtures them. But in the form of machines the alienated *ratio* moves toward a society which reconciles thought in its fixed form as a material and intellectual apparatus with free, live, thought, and refers to society itself as the real subject of thought. The specific origin of thought and its universal perspective have always been inseparable. Today, with the transformation of the world into industry, the perspective of universality, the social realization of thought, extends so far that in its behalf the rulers themselves disavow thought as mere ideology. The bad conscience of cliques which ultimately embody economic necessity is betrayed in that its revelations, from the intuitions of the Leader to the dynamic *Weltanschauung,* no longer recognize (in marked contrast to earlier bourgeois apologetics) their own misdeeds as necessary consequences of statutory contexts. The mythological lies of mission and destiny which they use as substitutes never declare the whole truth: gone are the objective laws of the market which ruled in the actions of the entrepreneurs and tended toward catastrophe. Instead the conscious decision of the managing directors executes as results (which are more obligatory than the blindest price-mechanisms) the old law of value and hence the destiny of capitalism. The rulers themselves do not believe in any objective necessity, even though they sometimes describe their concoctions thus. They declare themselves to be the engineers of world history. Only the ruled accept as unquestionable necessity the course of development that with every decreed rise in the standard of living makes them so much more powerless. When the standard of living of those who are still employed to service the machines can be assured with a minimal part of the working time available to the rulers of society, the superfluous reminder, the vast mass of the population, is drilled as yet another battalion—additional material to serve the present and future great plans of the system. The masses are fed and quartered as the army of the unemployed. In their eyes, their reduction to mere objects of the administered life, which preforms every sector of modern existence including language and perception, represents objective necessity, against which they believe there is nothing they can do. Misery as the antithesis of power and powerlessness grows immeasurably, together with the capacity to remove all misery permanently. Each individual is unable to penetrate the forest of cliques and institutions which, from the highest levels of command to the last professional rackets, ensure the boundless persistence of status. For the union boss, let alone the director, the proletarian (should he ever come face to face with him) is nothing but a supernumerary example of the mass while the boss in his turn has to tremble at the thought of his own liquidation.

The absurdity of a state of affairs in which the enforced power of the system over men grows with every step that takes it out of the power of nature, denounces the rationality of the rational society as obsolete. Its necessity is illusive, no less than the freedom of the entrepreneurs who ultimately reveal their compulsive nature in their inevitable wars and contracts. This illusion, in which a wholly enlightened mankind has lost itself, cannot be dissolved by a philosophy which, as the organ of domination, has to choose between command and obedience. Without being able to escape the confusion which still ensnares it in prehistory, it is nevertheless able to recognize the logic of either-or, of consequence and antimony, with which it radically emancipated itself from nature, as this very nature, unredeemed and self-alienated. Thinking, in whose mechanism of compulsion nature is reflected and persists, inescapably reflects its very own self as its own forgotten nature—as a mechanism of compulsion.

Ideation is only an instrument. In thought, men distance themselves from nature in order thus imaginatively to present it to themselves—but only in order to determine how it is to be dominated. Like the thing, the material tool, which is held on to in different situations as the same thing, and hence divides the world as the chaotic, many sided, and disparate from the known, one, and identical, the concept is the ideal tool, fit to do service for everything, wherever it can be applied. And so thought becomes illusionary whenever it seeks to deny the divisive function, distancing and objectification. All mystic unification remains deception, the impotently inward trace of the absolved revolution. But while enlightenment maintains its justness against any hypostatization of utopia and unfailingly proclaims domination to be disunion, the dichotomy between subject and object that it will not allow to be obscured becomes the index of the untruth of that dichotomy and of truth. The proscription of superstition has always signified not only the progress of domination but its compromise. Enlightenment is more than enlightenment—the distinct representation of nature in its alienation. In the self-cognition of the spirit as nature in disunion with itself, as in prehistory, nature calls itself to account; no longer directly, as *mana*—that is, with the alias that signifies omnipotence—but as blind and lame. The decline, the forfeiture, of nature consists in the subjugation of nature without which spirit does not exist. Through the decision in which spirit acknowledges itself to be domination and retreats into nature, it abandons the claim to domination which makes it a vassal of nature. Even though in the flight from necessity, in progress and civilization, mankind cannot hold the course without abandoning knowledge itself, at least it no longer mistakes the ramparts that it erects against necessity (the institutions and practices of subjection that have always redounded on society from the subjection of nature) for guarantees of the freedom to come. Every progress made by civilization has renewed together with domination that prospect of its removal. Whereas, however, real history is woven out of a real suffering that is not lessened in proportion to the growth of means for its abrogation, the realization of the prospect is referred to the notion, the concept. For it does not merely, as science, distance men from nature, but, as the self-consideration of thought that in the form of science remains tied to blind economic tendency, allows the distance perpetuating injustice to be measured. By virtue of this remembrance of nature in the subject, in whose fulfillment the unacknowledged truth of all culture lies hidden, enlightenment is universally opposed to domination; and the call to check enlightenment resounded even in the time of Vanini less out of fear of exact science than out of that hatred of undisciplined ideas which emerges from the jurisdiction of nature even as it acknowledges itself to be nature's very dread of its own self. The priests always avenged *mana* on the prophet of enlightenment, who propitiated *mana* by a terror-stricken attitude to what went by the name of terror, and the augurs of the Enlightenment were one with the priests in their hybris. In its bourgeois form, the Enlightenment had lost itself in its positivistic aspect long before Turgot and d'Alembert. It was never immune to the exchange of freedom for the pursuit of self-preservation. The suspension of the concept, whether in the name of progress or of culture—which had already long before tacitly leagued themselves against the truth—opened the way for falsehood. And this in a world that verified only evidential propositions, and preserved thought—degraded to the achievement of great thinkers—as a kind of stock of superannuated clichés, no longer to be distinguished from truth neutralized as a cultural commodity.

But to recognize domination, even in thought itself, as unreconciled nature, would mean a slackening of the necessity whose perpetuity socialism itself prematurely confirmed as a concession to reactionary common sense. By elevating necessity to the status of the basis for all time to come, and by idealistically degrading the spirit forever to the very apex, socialism held on all too surely to the legacy of bourgeois philosophy. Hence the relation of necessity to the realm of freedom would remain merely quantitative and mechanical, and nature, posited as wholly alien—just as in the earliest mythology—would become totalitarian and absorb freedom together with socialism. With the abandonment of thought, which in its reified form of mathematics, machine, and organization avenges itself on the men who have forgotten it, enlightenment has relinquished its own realization. By taking everything unique and individual under its tutelage, it left the uncomprehended whole the freedom, as domination, to strike back at human existence and consciousness by way of things. But true revolutionary practice depends on the intransigence of theory in the face of the insensibility with which society allows thought to ossify. It is not the material prerequisites of fulfillment—liberated technology as such—which jeopardize fulfillment. That is asserted by those sociologists who are again searching for an antidote, and—should it be a collectivist measure—to master the antidote. Guilt is a context of social delusion. The mythic scientific respect of the peoples of the earth for the *status quo* that they themselves unceasingly produce, itself finally becomes positive fact: the oppressor's fortress in regard to which even revolutionary imagination despises itself as utopianism and decays to the condition of pliable trust in the objective tendency of history. As the organ of this kind of adaptation, as a mere construction of means, the Enlightenment is as destructive as its romantic enemies accuse it of being. It comes into its own only when it surrenders the last remaining concordance with the latter and dares to transcend the false absolute, the principle of blind domination. The spirit of this kind of unrelenting theory would turn even the mind of relentless progress to its end. Its herald Bacon dreamed of the many things "which kings with their treasure cannot buy, nor with their force command," of which "their spials and intelligencers can give no news." As he wished, they fell to the burghers, the enlightened heirs of those kings. While bourgeois economy multiplied power through the mediation of the market, it also multiplied its objects and powers to such an extent that for their administration not just the kings, not even the middle classes are no longer necessary, but all men. They learn from the power of things to dispense at last with power. Enlightenment is realized and reaches its term when the nearest practical ends reveal themselves as the most distant goal now attained, and the lands of which "their spials and intelligencers can give no news," that is, those of the nature despised by dominant science, are recognized as the lands of origin. Today, when Bacon's utopian vision that we should "command nature by action"—that is, in practice—has been realized on a tellurian scale, the nature of the thralldom that he ascribed to unsubjected nature is clear. It was domination itself. And knowledge, in which Bacon was certain the "sovereignty of man lieth hid," can now become the dissolution of domination. But in the face of such a possibility, and in the service of the present age, enlightenment becomes wholesale deception of the masses.

Theodor Adorno, Selection from *Negative Dialectics*

The Possibility of Philosophy

Philosophy, which once seemed obsolete, lives on because the moment to realize it was missed. The summary judgment that it had merely interpreted the world, that resignation in the face of reality had crippled it in itself, becomes a defeatism of reason after the attempt to change the world miscarried. Philosophy offers no place from which theory as such might be concretely convicted of the anachronisms it is suspected of, now as before. Perhaps it was an inadequate interpretation which promised that it would be put into practice. Theory cannot prolong the moment its critique depended on. A practice indefinitely delayed is no longer the forum for appeals against self-satisfied speculation; it is mostly the pretext used by executive authorities to choke, as vain, whatever critical thoughts the practical change would require.

Having broken its pledge to be as one with reality or at the point of realization, philosophy is obliged ruthlessly to criticize itself. Once upon a time, compared with sense perception and every kind of external experience, it was felt to be the very opposite of naïveté; now it has objectively grown as naïve in its turn as the seedy scholars feasting on subjective speculation seemed to Goethe, one hundred and fifty years ago. The introverted thought architect dwells behind the moon that is taken over by extroverted technicians. The conceptual shells that were to house the whole, according to philosophical custom, have in view of the immense expansion of society and of the strides made by positive natural science come to seem like relics of a simple barter economy amidst the late stage of industrial capitalism. The discrepancy (since decayed into a commonplace) between power and any sort of spirit has grown so vast as to foil whatever attempts to understand the preponderance might be inspired by the spirit's own concept. The will to this understanding bespeaks a power claim denied by that which is to be understood.

The most patent expression of philosophy's historical fate is the way the special sciences compelled it to turn back into a special science. If Kant had, as he put it, "freed himself from the school concept of philosophy for its world concept," it has now, perforce, regressed to its school concept. Whenever philosophers mistake that for the world concept, their pretensions grow ridiculous. Hegel, despite his doctrine of the absolute spirit in which he included philosophy, knew philosophy as a mere element of reality, an activity in the division of labor, and thus restricted it. This has since led to the narrowness of philosophy, to a disproportionateness to reality that became the more marked the more thoroughly philosophers forgot about the restriction—the more they disdained, as alien, any thought of their position in a whole which they monopolized as their object, instead of recognizing how much they depended on it all the way to the internal composition of their philosophy, to its immanent truth.

To be worth another thought, philosophy must rid itself of such naïveté. But its critical self-reflection must not halt before the highest peaks of its history. Its task would be to inquire whether and how there can still be a philosophy at all, now that Hegel's has fallen, just as Kant inquired into the possibility of metaphysics after the critique of rationalism. If Hegel's dialectics constituted the unsuccessful attempt to use philosophical concepts for coping with all that is heterogeneous to those concepts, the relationship to dialectics is due for an accounting insofar as his attempt failed.

Dialectics Not A Standpoint

No theory today escapes the marketplace. Each one is offered as a possibility among competing opinions; all are put up for choice; all are swallowed. There are no blinders for thought to don against this, and the self-righteous conviction that my own theory is spared that fate will surely deteriorate into self-advertising. But neither need dialectics be muted by such rebuke, or by the concomitant charge of its superfluity, of being a method slapped on outwardly, at random. The name of dialectics says no more, to begin with, than that objects do not go into their concepts without leaving a remainder, that they come to contradict the traditional norm of adequacy. Contradiction is not what Hegel's absolute idealism was bound to transfigure it into: it is not of the essence in a Heraclitean sense. It indicates the untruth of identity, the fact that the concept does not exhaust the thing conceived.

Yet the appearance of identity is inherent in thought itself, in its pure form. To think is to identify. Conceptual order is content to screen what thinking seeks to comprehend. The semblance and the truth of thought entwine. The semblance cannot be decreed away, as by avowal of a being-in-itself outside the totality of cogitative definitions. It is a thesis secretly implied by Kant—and mobilized against him by Hegel—that the transconceptual "in itself" is void, being wholly indefinite. Aware that the conceptual totality is mere appearance, I have no way but to break immanently, in its own measure, through the appearance of total identity. Since that totality is structured to accord with logic, however, whose core is the principle of the excluded middle, whatever will not fit this principle, whatever differs in quality, comes to be designated as a contradiction. Contradiction is nonidentity under the aspect of identity; the dialectical primary of the principle of contradiction makes the thought of unity the measure of heterogeneity. As the heterogeneous collides with its limit it exceeds itself.

Dialectics is the consistent sense of nonidentity. It does not begin by taking a standpoint. My thought is driven to it by its own inevitable insufficiency, by my guilt of what I am thinking. We are blaming the method for the fault of the matter when we object to dialectics on the ground (repeated from Hegel's Aristotelian critics on) that whatever happens to come into the dialectical mill will be reduced to the merely logical form of contradiction, and that (an argument still advanced by Croce) the full diversity of the noncontradictory, of that which is imply differentiated, will be ignored. What we differentiate will appear divergent, dissonant, negative for just as long as the structure of our consciousness obliges it to strive for unity: as long as its demand for totality will be its measure for whatever is not identical with it. This is what dialectics holds up to our consciousness as a contradiction. Because of the immanent nature of consciousness, contradictoriness itself has an inescapably and fatefully legal character. Identity and contradiction of thought are welded together. Total contradiction is nothing but the manifested untruth of total identification. Contradiction is nonidentity under the rule of a law that affects the nonidentical as well.

Reality and Dialectics

This law is not a cogitative law, however. It is real. Unquestionably, one who submits to the dialectical discipline has to pay dearly in the qualitative variety of experience. Still, in the administered world the impoverishment of experience by dialectics, which outrages healthy opinion, proves appropriate to the abstract monotony of that world. Its agony is the world's agony raised to a concept. Cognition must bow to it, unless concretion is once more to be debased into the ideology it starts becoming in fact.

Another version of dialectics contented itself with a debilitated renascence: with its intellectual-historical derivation from Kant's *aporias* and from that which the systems of his successors projected but failed to achieve. It can be achieved only negatively. Dialectics unfolds the difference between the particular and the universal, dictated by the universal. As the subject-object dichotomy is brought to mind it becomes inescapable for the subject, furrowing whatever the subject thinks, even objectively—but it would come to an end in reconcilement. Reconcilement would release the nonidentical, would rid it of coercion, including spiritualized coercion; it would open the road to the multiplicity of different things and strip dialectics of its power over them. Reconcilement would be the thought of the many as no longer inimical, a thought that is anathema to subjective reason.

Dialectics serves the end of reconcilement. It dismantles the coercive logical character of its own course; that is why it is denounced as "panlogism." As idealistic dialectics, it was bracketed with the absolute subject's predominance as the negative impulse of each single move of the concept and of its course as a whole. Historically, such primacy of the subject has been condemned even in the Hegelian conception that eclipsed the individual human consciousness as well as the transcendental one of Kant and Fichte. Subjective primacy was not only supplanted by the impotence of the weakening thought, which the world's overpowering course deters from construing it, but none of the reconcilements claimed by absolute idealism—and no other kind remained consistent—has stood up, whether in logic or in politics and history. The inability of consistent idealism to constitute itself as anything but the epitome of contradiction is as much the logical consequence of its truth as it is the punishment incurred by its logicity *qua* logicity; it is appearance as much as necessity.

Yet reopening the case of dialectics, whose non-idealistic form has since degenerated into a dogma as its idealistic one did into a cultural asset, will not decide solely about the actuality of a traditional mode of philosophizing, nor about the actuality of the philosophical structure of cognitive objects. Through Hegel, philosophy had regained the right and the capacity to think substantively instead of being put off with the analysis of cognitive forms that were empty and, in an emphatic sense, null and void. Where present philosophy deals with anything substantive at all, it lapses either into the randomness of a weltanschauung or into that formalism, that "matter of indifference," against which Hegel had risen. There is historical evidence of this in the evolution of phenomenology, which once was animated by the need for contents and became an invocation of being, a repudiation of any content as unclean.

The fundamental result of Hegel's substantive philosophizing was the primacy of the subject, or—in the famous phrase from the Introduction to his *Logic*—the "identity of identity and nonidentity." He held the definite particular to be definable by the mind because its immanent definition was to be nothing but the mind. Without this supposition, according to Hegel, philosophy would be incapable of knowing anything substantive or essential. Unless the idealistically acquired concept of dialectics harbors experiences contrary to the Hegelian emphasis, experiences independent of the idealistic machinery, philosophy must inevitably do without substantive insight, confine itself to the methodology of science, call that philosophy, and virtually cross itself out.

The Antagonistic Entirety

Such a concept of dialectics makes us doubt its possibility. However varied, the anticipation of moving in contradictions throughout seems to teach a mental totality—the very identity thesis we have just rendered inoperative. The mind which ceaselessly reflects on contradiction in the thing itself, we hear, must be the thing itself if it is to be organized in the form of contradiction; the truth which in idealistic dialectics drives beyond every particular, as onesided and wrong, is the truth of the whole, and if that were not preconceived, the dialectical steps would lack motivation and direction. We have to answer that the object of a mental experience is an antagonistic system in itself—antagonistic in reality, not just in its conveyance to the knowing subject that rediscovers itself therein. The coercive state of reality, which idealism had projected into the region of the subject and the mind, must be retranslated from that region. What remains of idealism is that society, the objective determinant of the mind, is as much an epitome of subjects as it is their negation. In society the subjects are unknowable and incapacitated; hence its desperate objectivity and conceptuality, which idealism mistakes for something positive.

The system is not one of the absolute spirit; it is one of the most conditioned spirit of those who have it and cannot even know how much it is their own. The subjective preconception of the material production process in society—basically different from its theoretical constitution—is the unresolved part, the part unreconciled with the subjects. Their own reason, unconscious like the transcendental subject and establishing identity by barter, remains incommensurable with the subjects it reduces to the same denominator: the subject as the subject's foe. The preceding generality is both true and untrue: true, because it forms that "ether" which Hegel calls spirit; untrue, because its reason is no reason yet, because its universality is the product of particular interests. This is why a philosophical critique of identity transcends philosophy. But the ineffable part of the utopia is that what defies subsumption under identity—the "use value," in Marxist terminology—is necessary anyway if life is to go on at all, even under the prevailing circumstances of production. The utopia extends to the sworn enemies of its realization. Regarding the concrete utopian possibility, dialectics is the ontology of the wrong state of things. The right state of things would be free of it: neither a system nor a contradiction.

Disenchantment of the Concept

Philosophy, Hegel's included, invites the general objection that by inevitably having concepts for its material it anticipates an idealistic decision. In fact no philosophy, not even extreme empiricism, can drag in the *facta bruta* and present them like cases in anatomy or experiments in physics; no philosophy can paste the particulars into the text, as seductive paintings would hoodwink it into believing. But the argument in its formality and generality takes as fetishistic a view of the concept as the concept does in interpreting itself naively in its own domain: in either case it is regarded as a self-sufficient totality over which philosophical thought has no power. In truth, all concepts, even the philosophical ones, refer to nonconceptualities, because concepts on their part are moments of the reality that requires their formation, primarily for the control of nature. What conceptualization appears to be from within, to one engaged in it—the predominance of its sphere, without which nothing is known—must not be mistaken for what it is in itself. Such a semblance of being-in-itself is conferred upon it by the motion that exempts it from reality, to which it is harnessed in turn.

Necessity compels philosophy to operate with concepts, but this necessity must not be turned into the virtue of their priority—no more than, conversely, criticism of that virtue can be turned into a summary verdict against philosophy. On the other hand, the insight that philosophy's conceptual knowledge is not the absolute of philosophy—this insight, for all its inescapability, is again due to the nature of the concept. It is not a dogmatic thesis, much less a naively realistic one. Initially, such concepts as that of "being" at the start of Hegel's *Logic* emphatically mean nonconceptualities. Dissatisfaction with their own conceptuality is part of their meaning, although the inclusion of nonconceptuality in their meaning makes it tendentially their equal and thus keeps them trapped within themselves. The substance of concepts is to them both immanent, as far as the mind is concerned, and transcendent as far as being is concerned. To be aware of this is to be able to get rid of concept fetishism. Philosophical reflection makes sure of the nonconceptual in the concept. It would be empty otherwise, according to Kant's dictum; in the end, having ceased to be a concept of anything at all, it would be nothing.

A philosophy that lets us know this, that extinguishes the autarky of the concept, strips the blindfold from our eyes. That the concept is a concept even when dealing with things in being does not change the fact that on its part it is entwined with a nonconceptual whole. Its only insulation from that whole is its reification—that which establishes it as a concept. The concept is an element in dialectical logic, like any other. What survives in it is the fact that nonconceptuality has conveyed it by way of its meaning, which in turn establishes its conceptuality. To refer to nonconceptualities—as ultimately, according to traditional epistemology, every definition of concepts requires nonconceptual, deictic elements—is characteristic of the concept, and so is the contrary: that as the abstract unit of the noumena subsumed thereunder it will depart from the noumenal. To change this direction of conceptuality, to give it a turn toward nonidentity, is the hinge of negative dialectics. Insight into the constitutive character of the nonconceptual in the concept would end the compulsive identification which the concept brings unless halted by such reflection. Reflection upon its own meaning is the way out of the concept's seeming being-in-itself as a unit of meaning.

Constellation

The unifying moment survives without a negation of negation, but also without delivering itself to abstraction as a supreme principle. It survives because there is no step-by-step progression from the concepts to a more general cover concept. Instead, the concepts enter into a constellation. The constellation illuminates the specific side of the object, the side which to a classifying procedure is either a matter of indifference or a burden.

The model for this is the conduct of language. Language offers no mere system of signs for cognitive functions. Where it appears essentially as a language, where it becomes a form of representation, it will not define its concepts. It lends objectivity to them by the relation into which it puts the concepts, centered about a thing. Language thus serves the intention of the concept to express completely what it means. By themselves, constellations represent from without what the concept has cut away within: the "more" which the concept is equally desirous and incapable of being. By gathering around the object of cognition, the concepts potentially determine the object's interior. They attain, in thinking, what was necessarily excised from thinking.

The Hegelian usage of the term "concrete"—according to which the thing itself is its context, not its pure selfhood—takes note on this; and yet, for all the criticism of discursive logic, that logic is not ignored. But Hegelian dialectics was a dialectics without language, while the most literal sense of the word "dialectics" postulates language; to this extent, Hegel remained an adept of current science. He did not need language in an emphatic sense, since everything, even the speechless and opaque, was to him to be spirit, and the spirit would be the context. That supposition is past salvaging. Instead, what is indissoluble in any previous thought context transcends its seclusion in its own, as nonidentical. It communicates with that from which it was separated by the concept. It is opaque only for identity's claim to be total; it resists the pressure of that claim. But as such it seeks to be audible. Whatever part of nonidentity defies definition in its concept goes beyond its individual existence; it is only in polarity with the concept, in staring at the concept, that it will contract into that existence. The inside of nonidentity is its relation to that which it is not, and which its managed, frozen self-identity withholds from it. It only comes to in relinquishing itself, not in hardening—this we can still learn from Hegel, without conceding anything to the repressive moments of his relinquishment doctrine.

The object opens itself to a monadological insistence, to a sense of the constellation in which it stands; the possibility of internal immersion requires that externality. But such an immanent generality of something individual is objective as sedimented history. This history is in the individual thing and outside it; it is something encompassing in which the individual has its place. Becoming aware of the constellation in which a thing stands is tantamount to deciphering the constellation which, having come to be, it bears within it. The *chorismos* of without and within is historically qualified in turn. The history locked in the object can only be delivered by a knowledge mindful of the historic positional value of the object in its relation to other objects—by the actualization and concentration of something which is already known and is transformed by that knowledge. Cognition of the object in its constellation is cognition of the process stored in the object. As a constellation, theoretical thought circles the concept it would like to unseal, hoping that it may fly open like the lock of a well-guarded safe-deposit box: in response, not to a single key or a single number, but to a combination of numbers.

Constellation in Science

How objects can be unlocked by their constellation is to be learned not so much from philosophy, which took no interest in the matter, as from important scientific investigations. The scientific accomplishment often ran ahead of its philosophical comprehension, ahead of scientivism. And we certainly need not start out from a work's own content, in line with such metaphysical inquiries as Benjamin's "Origin of German Tragedy" which take the very concept of truth for a constellation. We must go back to a scholar of so positivistic a bent as Max Weber, who did—quite in the sense of subjectivist epistemology—understand "ideal types" as aids in approaching the object, devoid of any inherent substantiality and capable of being reliquefied at will. But as in all nominalism, however insignificant it may consider its concepts, some of the nature of the thing will come through and extend beyond the benefit to our thinking practice—not the least of our motivations for criticizing an unreflected nominalism!—so are Weber's material works far more object-directed than the South-West German methodology would lead us to expect.

Actually the concept is sufficient reason for the thing insofar as the exploration of a social object, at least, is falsified if confined to dependencies within its domain, to dependencies that have established the object, and if its determination by the totality is ignored. Without the supraordinated concept, those dependencies conceal the most real among them, the dependence on society; and this dependence is not to be adequately compensated by the individual *res* which the concept covers. Yet it appears through the individual alone, and thus the concept in turn is transformed in specific cognition. When Weber, in his treatise on Protestant ethics and the spirit of capitalism, raised the question of defining capitalism, he—in contrast with current scientific practice—was as well aware of the difficulty of defining historical concepts as previously only philosophers had been: Kant, Hegel, Nietzsche. He explicitly rejected the delimiting procedure of definition, the adherence to the schema *genus proximum, differentia specifica*, and asked instead that sociological concepts be "gradually composed" from "individual parts to be taken from historic reality. The place of definitive conceptual comprehension cannot, therefore, be the beginning of the inquiry, only the end."

Whether such a definition is always necessary at the end—or whether, even without a formal definitory result, what Weber calls "composing" can be equal to his epistemological goal—remains unsettled. Definitions are not the be-all and end-all of cognition, as popular scientivism holds; but neither are they to be banished. A thinking whose course made us incapable of definition, unable even for moments to have a succinct language represent the thing, would be as sterile, probably, as a thinking gorged with verbal definitions. More essential, however, is that to which Weber gives the name of "composing," a name which orthodox scientists would find unacceptable. He is indeed looking only at the subjective side, at cognitive procedure; but the "compositions" in question are apt to follow similar rules as their analogue, the musical compositions. These are subjectively produced, but they work only where the subjective production is submerged in them. The subjectively created context—the "constellation"—becomes readable as sign of an objectivity: of the spiritual substance.

What resembles writing in such constellations is the conversion into objectivity, by way of language, of what has been subjectively thought and assembled. This element is not one of Max Weber's themes, but even a procedure as indebted as his to the traditional ideal and theory of science does not lack it. The most mature of his works seem at times to suffer from a glut of verbal definitions borrowed from jurisprudence, but a close look will show that these are more than definitions. They are not mere conceptual fixations. Rather, by gathering concepts round the central one that is sought, they attempt to express what that concept aims at, not to circumscribe it to operative ends. The concept of capitalism, for instance, which is so crucial in every respect is emphatically set off by Weber from such isolated and subjective categories as acquisitiveness or the profit motive—in a manner similar to Marx's, by the way. In capitalism, says Weber, the oft-cited profit motive must take its bearings from the principle of lucrativity and from the market chances; it must utilize the calculation of capital and interest; organized in the form of free labor, with household and business expenses separated, capitalism necessitates bookkeeping and a rationalistic legal system in line with its pervasive governing principle of rationality at large.

The completeness of this list remains in doubt. We have to ask, in particular, whether Weber's stress on rationality, his disregarding of the class relation that reproduces itself by way of the barter of equivalents, will not as a mere method equate capitalism too much with its "spirit"—although that barter and its problematics would certainly be unthinkable without rationality. But the capitalist system's increasingly integrative trend, the fact that its elements entwine into a more and more total context of functions, is precisely what makes the old question about the cause—as opposed to the constellation—more and more precarious. We need no epistemological critique to make us pursue constellations; the search for them is forced upon us by the real course of history. In Weber's case the constellations take the place of systematics, which one liked to tax him with lacking, and this is what proves his thinking to be a third possibility beyond the alternative of positivism and idealism.

Indirectness By Objectivity

In negative dialectics not even the transmission of essence and phenomenality, of concept and thing, will remain what it was: the subjective moment in the object. What transmits the facts is not so much the subjective mechanism of their pre-formation and comprehension as it is the objectivity heteronomous to the subject, the objectivity behind that which the subject can experience. This objectivity is denied to the primary realm of subjective experience. It is preordinated to that realm. Wherever, in the current manner of speaking, judgment is too subjective at the present historical stage, the subject, as a rule, will automatically parrot the *consensus omnium*. To give the object its due instead of being content with the false copy, the subject would have to resist the average value of such objectivity and to free itself as a subject. It is on this emancipation, not on the subject's insatiable repression, that objectivity depends today. The superiority of objectification in the subjects not only keeps them from becoming subjects; it equally prevents a cognition of objectivity. This is what became of what used to be called "the subjective factor." It is now subjectivity rather than objectivity that is indirect, and this sort of mediation is more in need of analysis than the traditional one.

The subjective mechanisms of mediation serve to lengthen the objective ones to which each subject, including the transcendental one, is harnessed. The pre-subjective order (which in turn essentially constitutes the subjectivity that is constitutive for epistemology) sees to it that data are apperceived in this way and in no other, according to their claim. What in the Kantian deduction of categories remains ultimately "given" and, by Kant's own admission, accidental—that reason can have these and no other basic concepts at its disposal—is attributed to what the categories, according to Kant, have yet to establish. But the fact that indirectness is universal does not entitle us to reduce all things between heaven and earth to its level, as if transmitting an immediacy were the same as transmitting a concept. To concepts, mediation is essential; the concept itself is immediately, by nature, its own transmission; but the indirectness of something direct is a reflexive determination that makes sense only in regard to its opposite, the direct thing. There is nothing that is not transmitted, and yet, as Hegel emphasized, indirectness must always refer to some transmitted thing, without which there would be no indirectness. That there is no transmitted thing without indirectness, on the other hand, is a purely privative and epistemological fact, the expression of our inability to define "something" without mediation, and little more than the tautology that to think something is to think.

Conversely, there would be no mediation without "something." Directness does not involve being transmitted in the same sense in which indirectness involves something direct that would be transmitted. Hegel neglected this difference. The transmission of something direct refers to its mode: to knowledge of it, and to the bounds of such knowledge. Immediacy is no modality, no mere definition of the "how" for a consciousness. It is objective: its concept, the concept of immediacy, points to that which can not be removed by its own concept. Mediation makes no claim whatever to exhaust all things; it postulates, rather, that what it transmits is not thereby exhausted. Directness itself, on the other hand, stands for a moment that does not require cognition—or mediation in the same sense in which cognition necessitates immediacy.

As long as philosophers employ the concepts "direct" and "indirect"—concepts they cannot forgo for the time being—the language will bear witness to the facts denied by the idealist version of dialectics. That this version ignores the seemingly minimal difference serves to make it plausible. The triumphant finding that immediacy is wholly indirect rides roughshod over indirectness and blithely ends up with the totality of the concept, which nothing nonconceptual can stop any more. It ends up with the absolute rule of the subject.

In dialectics, however, it is not total identification that has the last word, because dialectics lets us recognize the difference that has been spirited away. Dialectics can break the spell of identification without dogmatically, from without, contrasting it with an allegedly realistic thesis. The circle of identification—which in the end always identifies itself alone—was drawn by a thinking that tolerates nothing outside it; its imprisonment is its own handiwork. Such totalitarian and therefore particular rationality was historically dictated by the threat of nature. That is its limitation. In fear, bondage to nature is perpetuated by a thinking that identifies, that equalizes everything unequal. Thoughtless rationality is blinded to the point of madness by the sight of whatsoever will elude its rule. For the present, reason is pathic; nothing but to cure ourselves of it would be rational. Even the theory of alienation, the ferment of dialectics, confuses the need to approach the heteronomous and thus irrational world—with the archaic barbarism that the longing subject cannot love what is alien and different, with the craving for incorporation and persecution. If the alien were no longer ostracized, there hardly would be any more alienation.

Herbert Marcuse, Selection from *One Dimensional Man*

The New Forms of Control

To the degree to which freedom from want, the concrete substance of all freedom, is becoming a real possibility, the liberties which pertain to a state of lower productivity are losing their former content. Independence of thought, autonomy, and the right to political opposition are being deprived of their basic critical function in a society which seems increasingly capable of satisfying the needs of the individuals through the way in which it is organized. Such a society may justly demand acceptance of its principles and institutions, and reduce the opposition to the discussion and promotion of alternative policies *within* the status quo. In this respect, it seems to make little difference whether the increasing satisfaction of needs is accomplished by an authoritarian or a non-authoritarian system. Under the conditions of a rising standard of living, non-conformity with the system itself appears to be socially useless, and the more so when it entails tangible economic and political disadvantages and threatens the smooth operation of the whole. Indeed, at least in so far as the necessities of life are involved, there seems to be no reason why the production and distribution of goods and services should proceed through the competitive concurrence of individual liberties.

Freedom of enterprise was from the beginning not altogether a blessing. As the liberty to work or to starve, it spelled toil, insecurity, and fear for the vast majority of the population. If the individual were no longer compelled to prove himself on the market, as a free economic subject, the disappearance of this kind of freedom would be one of the greatest achievements of civilization. The technological processes of mechanization and standardization might release individual energy into a yet uncharted realm of freedom beyond necessity. The very structure of human existence would be altered; the individual would be liberated from the work world's imposing upon him alien needs and alien possibilities. The individual would be free to exert autonomy over a life that would be his own. If the productive apparatus could be organized and directed toward the satisfaction of the vital needs, its control might well be centralized such control would not prevent individual autonomy, but render it possible.

This is a goal within the capabilities of advanced industrial civilization, the "end" of technological rationality. In actual fact, however, the contrary trend operates: the apparatus imposes its economic and political requirements for defense and expansion on labor time and free time, on the material and intellectual culture. By virtue of the way it has organized its technological base, contemporary industrial society tends to be totalitarian. For "totalitarian" is not only a terroristic political coordination of society, but also a non-terroristic economic-technical coordination which operates through the manipulation of needs by vested interests. It thus precludes the emergence of an effective opposition against the whole. Not only a specific form of government or party rule makes for totalitarianism, but also a specific system of production and distribution which may well be compatible with a "pluralism" of parties, newspapers, "countervailing powers," etc.

Today political power asserts itself through its power over the machine process and over the technical organization of the apparatus. The government of advanced and advancing industrial societies can maintain and secure itself only when it succeeds in mobilizing, organizing, and exploiting the technical, scientific, and mechanical productivity available to industrial civilization. And this productivity mobilizes society as a whole, above and beyond any particular individual or group interests. The brute fact that the machine's physical power surpasses that of the individual, and of any particular group of individuals, makes the machine the most effective political instrument in any society whose basic organization is that of the machine process. But the political trend may be reversed; essentially the power of the machine is only the stored-up and projected power of man. To the extent to which the work world is conceived of as a machine and mechanized accordingly, it becomes the *potential* basis of a new freedom for man.

Contemporary industrial civilization demonstrates that it has reached the state at which "the free society" can no longer be adequately defined in the traditional terms of economic, political, and intellectual liberties, not because these liberties have become insignificant, but because they are too significant to be confined within the traditional forms. New modes of realization are needed, corresponding to the new capabilities of society.

Such new modes can be indicated only in negative terms because they would amount to the negation of the prevailing modes. Thus economic freedom would mean freedom *from* the economy—from being controlled by economic forces and relationships; freedom from the daily struggle for existence, from earning a living. Political freedom would mean liberation of the individuals *from* politics over which they have no effective control. Similarly, intellectual freedom would mean the restoration of individual thought now absorbed by mass communication and indoctrination, abolition of "public opinion" together with its makers. The unrealistic sound of these propositions is indicative, not of their utopian character, but of the strength of the forces which prevent their realization, The most effective and enduring form of warfare against liberation is the implanting of material and intellectual needs that perpetuate obsolete forms of the struggle for existence.

The intensity, the satisfaction and even the character of human needs, beyond the biological level, have always been preconditioned. Whether or not the possibility of doing or leaving, enjoying or destroying, possessing or rejecting something is seized as a *need* depends on whether or not it can be seen as desirable and necessary for the prevailing societal institutions and interests. In this sense, human needs are historical needs and, to the extent to which the society demands the repressive development of the individual, his needs themselves and their claim for satisfaction are subject to overriding critical standards.

We may distinguish both true and false needs. "False" are those which are superimposed upon the individual by particular social interests in his repression: the needs which perpetuate toil, aggressiveness, misery, and injustice. Their satisfaction might be most gratifying to the individual, but this happiness is not a condition which has to be maintained and protected if it serves to arrest the development of the ability (his own and others) to recognize the disease of the whole and grasp the chances of curing the disease. The result then is euphoria in unhappiness. Most of the prevailing needs to relax, to have fun, to behave and consume in accordance with the advertisements, to love and hate what other love and hate, belong to this category of false needs.

Such needs have a societal content and function which are determined by external powers over which the individual has no control; the development and satisfaction of these needs is heteronomous. No matter how much such needs may have become the individual's own, reproduced and fortified by the conditions of his existence; no matter how much he identifies himself with them and finds himself in their satisfaction, they continue to be what they were from the beginning—products of a society whose dominant interest demands repression.

The prevalence of repressive needs is an accomplished fact, accepted in ignorance and defeat, but a fact that must be undone in the interest of the happy individual as well as all those whose misery is the price of his satisfaction. The only needs that have an unqualified claim for satisfaction are the vital ones—nourishment, clothing, lodging at the attainable level of culture. The satisfaction of these needs is the prerequisite for the realization of *all* needs, of the unsublimated as well as the sublimated ones.

For any consciousness and conscience, for any experience which does not accept the prevailing societal interest as the supreme law of thought and behavior, the established universe of needs and satisfactions is a fact to be questioned—questioned in terms of truth and falsehood. These terms are historical throughout, and their objectivity is historical. The judgment of needs and their satisfaction, under the given conditions, involves standards or *priority*—standards which refer to the optimal development of the individual, of all individuals, under the optimal utilization of the material and intellectual resources available to man. The resources are calculable. "Truth" and "falsehood" of needs designate objective conditions to the extent to which the universal satisfaction of vital needs, and beyond it, the progressive alleviation of toil and poverty, are universally valid standards. But as historical standards, they do not only vary according to area and stage of development, they also can be defined only in (greater or lesser) *contradiction* to the prevailing ones. What tribunal can possibly claim the authority of decision?

In the last analysis, the question of what are true and false needs must be answered by the individuals themselves, but only in the last analysis; that is, if and when they are free to give their own answer. As long as they are kept incapable of being autonomous, as long as they are indoctrinated and manipulated (down to their very instincts), their answer to this question cannot be taken as their own. By the same token, however, no tribunal can justly arrogate to itself the right to decide which needs should be developed and satisfied. Any such tribunal is reprehensible, although our revulsion does not do away with the question: how can the people who have been the object of effective and productive domination by themselves create the conditions of freedom?

The more rational, productive, technical, and total the repressive administration of society becomes, the more unimaginable the means and ways by which the administered individuals might break their servitude and seize their own liberation. To be sure, to impose Reason upon an entire society is a paradoxical and scandalous idea—although one might dispute the righteousness of a society which ridicules this idea while making its own population into objects of total administration. All liberation depends on the consciousness of servitude, and the emergence of this consciousness is always hampered by the predominance of needs and satisfactions which, to a great extent, have become the individual's own. The process always replaces one system of preconditioning by another; the optimal goal is the replacement of false needs by true ones, the abandonment of repressive satisfaction.

The distinguishing features of advanced industrial society is its effective suffocation of those needs which demand liberation—liberation also from that which is tolerable and rewarding and comfortable—while it sustains and absolves the destructive power and repressive function of the affluent society. Here, the social controls exact the overwhelming need for the production and consumption of waste; the need for stupefying work where it is no longer a real necessity; the need for modes of relaxation which soothe and prolong this stupefication; the need for maintaining such deceptive liberties as free competition at administered prices, a free press which censors itself, free choice between brands and gadgets.

Under the rule of a repressive whole, liberty can be made into a powerful instrument of domination. The range of choice open to the individual is not the decisive factor in determining the degree of human freedom, but *what* can be chosen and what *is* chosen by the individual. The criterion for free choice can never be an absolute one, but neither is it entirely relative. Free election of masters does not abolish the masters or the slaves. Free choice among a wide variety of goods and services does not signify freedom if these goods and services sustain social controls over a life of toil and fear—that is, if they sustain alienation. And the spontaneous reproduction of superimposed needs by the individual does not establish autonomy; it only testifies to the efficacy of the controls.

Our insistence on the depth and efficacy of these controls is open to the objection that we overrate greatly the indoctrinating power of the "media", and that by themselves the people would feel and satisfy the needs which are now imposed upon them. The objection misses the point. The preconditioning does not start with the mass production of radio and television and with the centralization of their control. The people enter this stage as preconditioned receptacles of long standing; the decisive difference is in the flattening out of the contrast (or conflict) between the given and the possible, between the satisfied and the unsatisfied needs. Here, the so-called equalization of class distinctions reveals its ideological function. If the worker and his boss enjoy the same television program and visit the same resort places, if the typist is as attractively made up as the daughter of her employer, if the Negro owns a Cadillac, if they all read the same newspaper, then this assimilation indicates not the disappearance of classes, but the extent to which the needs and satisfactions that serve the preservation of the Establishment are shared by the underlying population.

Indeed, in the most highly developed areas of contemporary society, the transplantation of social into individual needs is so effective that the difference between them seems to be purely theoretical. Can one really distinguish between the mass media as instruments of information and entertainment, and as agents of manipulation and indoctrination? Between the automobile as nuisance and as convenience? Between the horrors and the comforts of functional architecture? Between the work for national defense and the work for corporate gain? Between the private pleasure and the commercial and political utility involved in increasing the birth rate?

We are again confronted with one of the most vexing aspects of advanced industrial civilization: the rational character of its irrationality. Its productivity and efficiency, its capacity to increase and spread comforts, to turn waste into need, and destruction into construction, the extent to which this civilization transforms the object world into an extension of man's mind and body makes the very notion of alienation questionable. The people recognize themselves in their commodities; they find their soul in their automobile, hi-fi set, split-level home, kitchen equipment. The very mechanism which the individual to his society has changed, and social control is anchored in the new needs which it has produced.

The prevailing forms of social control are technological in a new sense. To be sure, the technical structure and efficacy of the productive and destructive apparatus has been a major instrumentality for subjecting the population to the established social division of labor throughout the modern period. Moreover, such integration has always been accompanied by more obvious forms of compulsion: loss of livelihood, the administration of justice, the police, the armed forces. It still is. But in the contemporary period, the technological controls appear to be the very embodiment of Reason for the benefit of all social groups and interests—to such an extent that all contradiction seems irrational and all counteraction impossible.

No wonder then that, in the most advanced areas of this civilization, the social controls have been introjected to the point where even individual protest is affected at its roots. The intellectual and emotional refusal "to go along" appears neurotic and impotent. This is the socio-psychological aspect of the political event that marks the contemporary period: the passing of the historical forces which, at the preceding stage of industrial society, seemed to represent the possibility of new forms of existence.

But the term "introjection" perhaps no longer describes the way in which the individual by himself reproduces and perpetuates the external controls exercised by his society. Introjection suggests a variety of relatively spontaneous processes by which a Self (Ego) transposes the "outer" into the "inner". Thus introjection implies the existence of an inner dimension distinguished from and even antagonistic to the external exigencies—an individual consciousness and an individual unconscious *apart from* public opinion and behavior. The idea of "inner freedom" here has its reality: it designates the private space in which man may become and remain "himself".

Today this private space has been invaded and whittled down by technological reality. Mass production and mass distribution claim the *entire* individual, and industrial psychology has long since ceased to be confined to the factory. The manifold processes of introjection seem to be ossified in almost mechanical reactions. The result is, not adjustment but *mimesis:* an immediate identification of the individual with *his* society and, through it, with the society as a whole.

This immediate, automatic identification (which may have been characteristic of primitive forms of association) reappears in high industrial civilization; its new "immediacy", however, is the product of a sophisticated, scientific management and organization. In this process, the "inner" dimension of the mind in which opposition to the status quo can take root is whittled down. The loss of this dimension, in which the power of negative thinking—the critical power of Reason—is at home, is the ideological counterpart to the very material process in which advanced industrial society silences and reconciles the opposition. The impact of progress turns Reason into submission to the facts of life, and to the dynamic capability of producing more and bigger facts of the same sort of life. The efficiency of the system blunts the individuals' recognition that it contains no facts which do not communicate the repressive power of the whole. If the individuals find themselves in the things which shape their life, they do so, not by giving, but by accepting the law of things—not the law of physics but the law of their society.

I have just suggested that the concept of alienation seems to become questionable when the individuals identify themselves with the existence which is imposed upon them and have in it their own development and satisfaction. This identification is not illusion but reality. However, the reality constitutes a more progressive stage of alienation. The latter has become entirely objective; the subject which is alienated is swallowed up by its alienated existence. There is only one dimension, and it is everywhere and in all forms. The achievements of progress defy ideological indictment as well as justification; before their tribunal, the "false consciousness" of their rationality becomes the true consciousness.

This absorption of ideology into reality does not, however, signify the "end of ideology". On the contrary, in a specific sense advanced industrial culture is *more* ideological than its predecessor, inasmuch as today the ideology is in the process of production itself. In a provocative form, this proposition reveals the political aspects of the prevailing technological rationality. The productive apparatus and the goods and services which it produces "sell" or impose the social system as a whole. The means of mass transportation and communication, the commodities of lodging, food, and clothing, the irresistible output of the entertainment and information industry carry with them prescribed attitudes and habits, certain intellectual and emotional reactions which bind the consumers more or less pleasantly to the producers and, through the latter, to the whole. The products indoctrinate and manipulate; they promote a false consciousness which is immune against its falsehood. And as these beneficial products become available to more individuals in more social classes, the indoctrination they carry ceases to be publicity; it becomes a way of life. It is a good way of life—much better than before—and as a good way of life, it militates against qualitative change. Thus emerges a pattern of *one-dimensional thought and behavior* in which ideas, aspirations, and objectives that, by their content, transcend the established universe of discourse and action are either repelled or reduced to terms of this universe. They are redefined by the rationality of the given system and of its quantitative extension.

The trend may be related to a development in scientific method: operationalism in the physical, behaviorism in the social sciences. The common feature is a total empiricism in the treatment of concepts; their meaning is restricted to the representation of particular operations and behavior. The operational point of view is well illustrated by P.W. Bridgeman's analysis of the concept of length:

> We evidently know what we mean by length if we can tell what the length of any and every object is, and for the physicist nothing more is required. To find the length of an object, we have to perform certain physical operations. The concept of length is therefore fixed when the operations by which length is measured are fixed: that is, the concept of length involves as much and nothing more than the set of operations by which length is determined. In general, we mean by any concept nothing more than a set of operations; *the concept is synonymous with the corresponding set of operations.*

Bridgman has seen the wide implications of this mode of thought for the society at large:

> To adopt the operational point of view involves much more than a mere restriction of the sense in which we understand 'concept', but means a far-reaching change in all our habits of thought, in that we shall no longer permit ourselves to use as tools in our thinking concepts of which we cannot give an adequate account in terms of operation.

Bridgman's prediction has come true. The new mode of thought is today the predominant tendency in philosophy, psychology, sociology, and other fields. Many of the most seriously troublesome concepts are being "eliminated" by showing that no adequate account of them in terms of operations or behavior can be given. The radical empiricist onslaught (I shall subsequently, in chapter VII and VIII, examine its claim to be empiricist) thus provides the methodological justification for the debunking of the mind by the intellectuals—a positivism which, in its denial of the transcending elements of Reason, forms the academic counterpart of the socially required behavior.

Outside the academic establishment, the "far-reaching change in all our habits of thought" is more serious. It serves to coordinate ideas and goals with those exacted by the prevailing system, to enclose them in the system, and to repel those which are irreconcilable with the system. The reign of such a one-dimensional reality does not mean that materialism rules, and that the spiritual, metaphysical, and bohemian occupations are petering out. On the contrary, there is a great deal of "Worship together this week," "Why not try God," Zen, existentialism, and beat ways of life, etc. But such modes of protest and transcendence are no longer contradictory to the status quo and no longer negative. They are rather the ceremonial part of practical behaviorism, its harmless negation, and are quickly digested by the status quo of its healthy diet.

One-dimensional thought is systematically promoted by the makers of politics and their purveyors of mass information. Their universe of discourse is populated by self-validating hypotheses which, incessantly and monopolistically repeated, become hypnotic definitions or dictations. For example, "free" are the institutions which operate (and are operated on) in the countries of the Free World; other transcending modes of freedom are by definition either anarchism, communism, or propaganda. "Socialistic" are all encroachments on private enterprises not undertaken by private enterprises itself (or by government contracts), such as universal and comprehensive health insurance, or the protection of nature from all too sweeping commercialization, or the establishment of public services which may hurt private profit. This totalitarian logic of accomplished facts has its Eastern counterpart. There, freedom is the way of life instituted by a communist regime, and all other transcending modes of freedom are either capitalistic, or revisionist, or leftist sectarianism. In both camps, non-operational ideas are non-behavioral and subversive. The movement of thought is stopped at barriers which appear as the limits of Reason itself.

Such limitation of thought is certainly not new. Ascending modern rationalism, in its speculative as well as empirical form, shows a striking contrast between extreme critical radicalism in scientific and philosophic method on the one hand, and an uncritical quietism in the attitude towards established and functioning social institutions. Thus Descartes' *ego cogitans* was to leave the "great public bodes" untouched, and Hobbes held that "the present ought always to be preferred, maintained, and accounted best." Kant agreed with Locke in justifying revolution *if and when* it has succeeded in organizing the whole and in preventing subversion.

However, these accommodating concepts of Reason were always contradicted by the evident misery and injustice of the "great public bodies" and the effective, more or less conscious rebellion against them. Societal conditions existed which provoked and permitted real dissociation from the established state of affairs; a private as well as political dimension was present in which dissociation could develop into effective opposition, testing its strength and the validity of its objectives.

With the gradual closing of this dimension by the society, the self-limitation of thought assumes a larger significance. The interrelation between scientific-philosophical and societal processes, between theoretical and practical Reason, asserts itself "behind the back" of the scientists and philosophers. The society bars a whole type of oppositional operations and behavior; consequently, the concepts pertaining to them are rendered illusory or meaningless. Historical transcendence appears as metaphysical transcendence, not acceptable to science and scientific thought. The operational and behavioral point of view, practiced as a "habit of thought" at large, becomes the view of the established universe of discourse and action, needs and aspirations. The "cunning of Reason" works, as it so often did, in the interest of the powers that be. The insistence on operational and behavioral concepts turn against the efforts to free thought and behavior *from* the given reality and *for* the suppressed alternatives. Theoretical and practical Reason, academic and social behaviorism meet on common ground: that of an advanced society which makes scientific and technical progress into an instrument of domination.

"Progress" is not a neutral term; it moves toward specific ends, and these ends are defined by the possibilities of ameliorating the human condition. Advanced industrial society is approaching the stage where continued progress would demand the radical subversion of the prevailing direction and organization of progress. This stage would be reached when material production (including the necessary services) becomes automated to the extent that all vital needs can be satisfied while necessary labor time is reduced to marginal time. From this point on, technical progress would transcend the realm of necessity, where it served as the instrument of domination and exploitation which thereby limited its rationality; technology would become subject to the free play of faculties in the struggle for the pacification of nature and of society.

Such a state is envisioned in Marx's notion of the "abolition of labor." The term "pacification of existence" seems better suited to designate the historical alternative of a world which—through an international conflict which transforms and suspends the contradictions within the established societies—advances on the brink of a global war. "Pacification of existence" means the development of man's struggle with man and with nature, under conditions where the competing needs, desires, and aspirations are no longer organized by vested interests in domination and scarcity—an organization which perpetuates the destructive forms of this struggle.

Today's fight against this historical alternative finds a firm basis in the underlying population, and finds its ideology in the rigid orientation of thought and behavior to the given universe of facts. Validated by the accomplishments of science and technology, justified by its growing productivity, the status quo defies all transcendence. Faced with the possibility of pacification on the grounds of its technical and intellectual achievements, the mature industrial society closes itself against this alternative. Operationalism, in theory and practice, becomes the theory and practice of *containment*. Underneath its obvious dynamics, this society is a thoroughly static system of life: self-propelling in its oppressive productivity and in its beneficial coordination. Containment of technical progress goes hand in hand with its growth in the established direction. In spite of the political fetters imposed by the status quo, the more technology appears capable of creating the conditions for pacification, the more are the minds and bodies of man organized against this alternative.

The most advanced areas of industrial society exhibit throughout these two features: a trend toward consummation of technological rationality, and intensive efforts to contain this trend within the established institutions. Here is the internal contradiction of this civilization: the irrational element in its rationality. It is the token of its achievements. The industrial society which makes technology and science its own is organized for the ever-more-effective domination man and nature, for the ever-more-effective utilization of its resources. It becomes irrational when the success of these efforts opens new dimensions of human realization. Organization for peace is different from organization for war; the institutions which served the struggle for existence cannot serve the pacification of existence. Life as an end is qualitatively different from life as a means.

Such a qualitatively new mode of existence can never be envisaged as the mere by-product of economic and political changes, as the more or less spontaneous effect of the new institutions which constitute the necessary prerequisite. Qualitative change also involves a change in the *technical* basis on which this society rests—one which sustains the economic and political institutions through which the "second nature" of man as an aggressive object of administration is stabilized. The techniques of industrialization are political techniques; as such, they prejudge the possibilities of Reason and Freedom.

To be sure, labor must precede the reduction of labor, and industrialization must precede the development of human needs and satisfactions. But as all freedom depends on the conquest of alien necessity, the realization of freedom depends on the *techniques* of this conquest. The highest productivity of labor can be used for the perpetuation of labor, and the most efficient industrialization can serve the restriction and manipulation of needs.

When this point is reached, domination—in the guise of affluence and liberty—extends to all spheres of private and public existence, integrates all authentic opposition, absorbs all alternatives. Technological rationality reveals its political character as it becomes the great vehicle of better domination, creating a truly totalitarian universe in which society and nature, mind and body are kept in a state of permanent mobilization for the defense of this universe.

5

State Capitalism
Its Limitations and Possibilities

Introduction

The political economists of the Frankfurt School (Franz Newmann, Otto Kirkheimer, and Friedrich Pollock) argued that totalitarianism constituted a new ideological form of state-run capitalism. A postcapitalist social formation, in this sense, represented the state's advanced political capacity to organize the distribution and flow of market goods. Along with this social formation came different formulations of full employment and domestic and foreign investment of an intrusion of state politics into the market place that displaced the liberal features of the economy, including individual enterprise and the free flow of manufactured goods and services.

In his essay "State Capitalism: Possibilities and Limitations" (1941) Pollock argued that the Nazi regime disrupted competition and the exchange of goods, and individual property rights that had formerly safeguarded the individual against the effects of excessive state intervention into the market. In this way, Pollock distinguished between democratic and totalitarian state capitalism in order to show the unfolding internal tensions within capitalism.

While the political economists of the Frankfurt School held slightly different views of state capitalism, there remained the issue of how the School regarded the political economy of the Soviet state. In fact, the Frankfurt School had, by and large, focused much, if not all of its attention on the Nazi and fascist states, while remaining silent on this issue of the Soviet state. Marcuse, who was not regarded as an economist per se, finally addressed this issue in his essay "The Dialectic of the Soviet State" (1958). In the essay, he argues that the Soviet state bureaucracy, while providing a system in which the proletariat had become the subject and object of coercion, remained inhibited by its own bureaucratic special interests. Perhaps more importantly, according to Marcuse, the Soviet state faced international challenges of economic competition and trade, which, in turn, limited its capacity to promote the people's objective social needs.

Whether or not one agrees with Marcuse's rather sobering assessment of the Soviet state, it does call attention to the social and economic obstacles to freedom and justice. Yet, the question that arises here is whether Marcuse's one-dimensional man and Adorno's and Horkheimer's critique of instrumental reason had outstripped the capacity of critical theory to actively resist and overcome these social obstacles. Did they, in other words, abandon the need for a critical theory of social action that could articulate the limits and possibilities of resisting authoritarianism? Moreover, is it possible to see their rejection of the progressive aspects of reason as undermining the social task of critical theory that they had formulated in the early years: namely, to develop a self-reflexive theory rooted in historical materialism? Such questions, as we shall see, would serve as the basis of Habermas's hermeneutical conception of dialectical reason, or his theory of communicative action.

Friedrich Pollock, "State Capitalism: Its Possibilities and Limitations"

A New Set of Rules

State capitalism replaces the methods of the market by a new set of rules based upon a combination of old and new means.

1. A general plan gives the direction for production, consumption, saving, and investment. The introduction of the principle of planning into the economic process means that a plan is to be constructed for achieving on a national scale certain chosen ends with all available resources. It does not necessarily imply that all details are planned in advance or that no freedom of choice at all is given to the consumer. But it contrasts sharply with the market system inasmuch as the final word on what needs shall be satisfied, and how, is not left to the anonymous and unreliable poll of the market, carried through *post festum*, but to a conscious decision on ends and means at least in a broad outline and before production starts. The discussion of planning has come to a point where it seems as if the arguments raised against the technical workability of such a general plan can be refuted. The genuine problem of a planned society does not lie in the economic but in the political sphere, in the principles to be applied in deciding what needs shall have preference, how much time shall be spent for work, how much of the social product shall be consumed and how much used for expansion, etc. Obviously, such decisions cannot be completely arbitrary but are to a wide degree dependent upon the available resources.

2. Prices are no longer allowed to behave as masters of the economic process but are administered in all important sections of it. This follows from the principle of planning and means that in favor of a planned economy the market is deprived of its main function. It does not mean that prices cannot exist any longer, but that if they do they have thoroughly changed their character. Nothing may seem on the surface to have changed, prices are quoted and goods and services paid for in money; the rise and fall of single prices may be quite common. But the relations between prices and cost of production on the one side, and demand and supply on the other, while strictly interconnected in their totality, become disconnected in those cases where they tend to interfere with the general plan. What remains of the market system behaves like its predecessor, but its function has changed from that of a general manager of the economic process into that of a closely controlled tool. In the last decades administered prices have contributed much toward destroying the market automatism without creating new devices for taking over its "necessary" functions. They served to secure monopoly profits at the expense of the nonmonopolistic market prices. Under state capitalism they are used as a supplementary device for incorporating production and consumption into the general plan.

3. The profit interests of both individuals and groups, as well as all other special interests, are to be strictly subordinated to the general plan or whatever stands in

its place. To understand the consequences of this principle leads far towards under-standing totalitarian striking power. There are two conflicting interpretations of the role of profit interests in Nazi Germany. The one claims that the profit motive still plays the same role as before; the other states that the capitalists have been deprived of their social position and that profit in the old meaning does not exist any longer. We think that both tend to overlook the transformation of such a category as "profit" in modern society. Profit interests may still be very significant in the totalitarian forms of state capitalistic society. But even the most powerful profit interests gradually become subordinate to the general "plan." No state capitalistic government can or will dispense with the profit motive, for two reasons. First, elimination of the profit motive would destroy the character of the entire system, and, second, in many respects the profit motive remains as an efficient incentive. In every case, however, where the interest of single groups or individuals conflicts with the general plan or whatever serves as its substitute, the individual interest must give way. This is the real meaning of the ideology *Gemeinnutz geht vor Eigennutz*. The interest of the ruling group as a whole is decisive, not the individual interests of those who form the group. The significance of this state capitalist principle can be fully grasped when it is contrasted with recent experiences in countries where private capitalism still prevails and where strong group interests prevent the execution of many urgent tasks necessary for the "common good." This needs no bad will or exceptional greed to explain it. In a system based upon the self-interest of every person, this principle can sometimes be expected to come to the fore in a form that contradicts the optimism of its underlying philosophy. If ever the statement was true that "private vices are public benefits," it could only have been under conditions where the typical economic unit was comparatively small and the free market functioned.

State capitalist policy, which opposed liberalism, has understood that there are narrow limits beyond which the pursuit of private interests cannot be reconciled with efficient general planning, and it has drawn the consequences.

4. In all spheres of state activity (and under state capitalism, that means in all spheres of social life as a whole), guesswork and improvisation give place to the principles of scientific management. This rule is in conformity with state capitalism's basic conception of society as an integrated unit comparable to one of the modern giants in steel, chemical, or motorcar production. Large-scale production requires not only careful general planning but systematic elaboration of all single processes. Every waste or error in preparing materials and machinery and in drafting the elements of production is multiplied numerous times and may endanger the productive process as a whole. The same holds true for society as soon as the previous differentiation between private cost (e.g., wages) and social cost (e.g., unemployment) is replaced by a measurement of the single process in terms of its ability to obtain what the planner considers the most desirable social product. But once this principle of "rationalization" has become mandatory for all public activities, it will be applied in spheres which previously were the sanctuary of guesswork, routine, and muddling through: military preparedness, the conduct of war, behavior towards public opinion, application of the coercive power of the state, foreign trade and foreign policy, etc.

5. Performance of the plan is enforced by state power so that nothing essential is left to the functioning of laws of the market or other economic "laws." This may be interpreted as a supplementary rule which states the principle of treating all economic problems as in the last analysis political ones. Creation of an economic sphere into which the state should not intrude, essential for the era of private capitalism, is radically repudiated. Replacement of the mechanics of laissez-faire by governmental command does not imply the end of private initiative and personal responsibility, which might even be put on a broader basis but will be integrated within the framework of the general plan. During the nonmonopolistic phase of private capitalism, the capitalist (whether an individual or a group of shareholders represented by its manager) had power over his property within the limits of the market laws. Under state capitalism, this power has been transferred to the government which, though still limited by certain "natural" restrictions, is free from the tyranny of an uncontrolled market. The replacement of the economic means by political means as the last guarantee for the reproduction of economic life, changes the character of the whole historic period. It signifies the transition from a predominantly economic to an essentially political era.

Under private capitalism, all social relations are mediated by the market; men meet each other as agents of the exchange process, as buyers or sellers. The source of one's income, the size of one's property are decisive for one's social position. The profit motive keeps the economic mechanism of society moving. Under state capitalism men meet each other as commander or commanded; the extent to which one can command or has to obey depends in the first place upon one's position in the political set-up and only in a secondary way upon the extent of one's property. Labor is appropriated directly instead of by the "roundabout" way of the market. Another aspect of the changed situation under state capitalism is that the profit motive is superseded by the power motive. Obviously, the profit motive is a specific form of the power motive. Under private capitalism, greater profits signify greater power and less dependence upon the commands of others. The difference, however, is not only that the profit motive is a mediated form of the power motive, but that the latter is essentially bound up with the power position of the ruling group while the former pertains to the individual only.

Control of Production

A discussion of the means by which state capitalism could fulfill its program must hew closely to the technical and organizational possibilities available today in all highly industrialized countries. We refer not to any future developments but to the use which could be made here and now of the available resources. If, however, it can be shown that a state capitalist system can carry out more successfully than the market does the "necessary" functions required by the division of labor, it seems reasonable to expect that much greater resources could be made available within a short period. State capitalism must solve the following problems in the sphere of production if a rising social product is to result: create full employment based upon coordination of all productive units; reproduce the existing resources of plant, raw materials, management, and labor on a level adequate to technical progress; and expand the existing plant. All these tasks must be embodied in the general plan. Given this plan, the execution hinges upon the solution of merely technical and administrative tasks instead of on the economic task of producing for an unknown and largely unforeseeable market. Production is for a clearly defined use, not "commodity" production in the meaning of a market system. The experiences piled up by modern giant enterprises and associations of enterprises in carrying through enormous plans make total production control technically possible. Specific means of control include modern statistical and accounting methods, regular reporting of all changes in plant and supply, systematic training of workers for future requirements, rationalization of all technical and administrative processes, and all the other devices developed in the huge modern enterprises and cartels. In addition to these traditional methods which have superseded the occult entrepreneurial art of guessing correctly what the future market demand will be, the state acquires the controlling power implied in complete command over money and credit. The banks are transformed into mere government agencies. Every investment, whether it serves replacement or expansion, is subject to plan, and neither oversaving nor overexpansion, neither an "investment strike" nor *Fehlinvestitionen* can create large-scale disturbances. Errors which are bound to occur can be traced with comparative ease owing to the central position on the planning board. While they may amount to sheer waste, their damaging effects may be minimized by charging them off to the economy as a whole instead of to a single enterprise. Besides the banks, many of the organizations developed by business interests (trade associations, cartels, chambers of commerce, etc.) serve as, or are transformed into, government agencies for the control of production. The rigid control of capital, whether in its monetary form or as plant, machinery, and commodities, fundamentally transforms the quality of private property in the means of production and its owner, the "capitalist." While a good many of the risks (not all of them) borne by the owner under private capitalism might have been eliminated, only so much profit is left to him as the government sees fit to allow. Regulation of prices, limitation of distributed profits, compulsory investment of surplus profits in government bonds or in ventures which the capitalist would not have chosen voluntarily, and, finally, drastic taxation—all these measures converge to the same end, namely, to transform the capitalist into a mere rentier whose income is fixed by government decree as long as his investments are successful but who has no claim to withdraw his capital if no "interests" are paid.

The trend toward the situation described in our model has been widely discussed during recent years. An extreme statement is that of E. F. M. Durbin: "Property in industrial capital has wholly lost the social functions supposed to be grounded in it. It has ceased to be the reward for management, and it has largely ceased to serve as a reward for personal saving. Property in capital has become the functionless claim to a share in the product of industry. The institution is worse than indefensible—it is useless." The same phenomenon is criticized in the following comment: "Emphasis of management today is not upon venture, upon chancetaking as capitalism requires, but is upon price control, market division, avoidance of risk. This may be good short-range policy. But: if business isn't willing to take chances, somebody soon is going to ask why it should enjoy profits, why the management cannot be hired by Government, which is called on to do all the chancetaking, and might want to direct industry."

This trend toward losing his social function as the private owner of capital has found its expression in the stockholder's loss of control over the management. It has culminated so far in the new German legislation on joint-stock companies in which the stockholders are deprived by law of any right to interfere with management.

To sum up, under state capitalism the status of the private capitalist is changed in a threefold way.

1. The entrepreneurial and the capitalist functions, i.e., direction of production and discretion in the investment of one's capital, are separated from each other. Management becomes virtually independent of "capital" without necessarily having an important share in corporate property.
2. The entrepreneurial and capitalist functions are interfered with or taken over by the government.
3. The capitalist (insofar as he is not accepted as entrepreneur on the merits of his managerial qualifications) is reduced to a mere rentier.

Here the question of incentive arises. In private capitalism, the decisive incentives for the capitalist to maintain, expand, and improve production are the profit interest and the permanent threat of economic collapse if the efforts should slacken. The noncapitalists are driven to cooperate efficiently by hunger and their desire for a better life and security. Under state capitalism, both groups lose essential parts of their incentive. What new devices will take over their most "necessary" functions? What will prevent stagnation and even regression in all spheres of state capitalistic society? In relation to the majority of the population, those who neither own nor command the means of production, the answer is simple. The whip of unemployment is replaced by political terror, and the promise of material and ideological rewards continues to incite to the utmost personal effort. The profit motive still plays an important role for capitalists and the managerial bureaucracy, since large compensation is granted for efficient investment and management. Personal initiative is freed from obstructing property interests and systematically encouraged. Within the controlling group, however, the will to political power becomes the center of motivation. Every decision is at bottom oriented to the goal of maintaining and expanding the power of the group as a whole and of each of its members. New industrial empires are being built and old ones expanded with this goal in mind. But we also have here the source of the principle that individual interests must always be subordinated to the common (group) interest. This principle in turn contributes decisively to strengthening governmental control, since only a strong government can integrate conflicting interests while serving the power interests of the whole group.

Control of Distribution

"We have learned how to produce everything in practically unlimited quantities, but we don't know how to distribute the goods." This is the popular formulation to describe the riddle of private capitalism in its latest phase. Given a general plan and the political power to enforce it, state capitalism finds ample technical means for distributing everything that can be produced with the available resources. The main difficulty of private capitalism is eliminated by the fact that under such capitalism the success of production does not necessarily depend upon finding buyers for the product at profitable prices in an unstable market, but is consciously directed towards satisfying public and private wants which are to a large extent defined in advance. Adjustments which must be made as a result of technical errors in the general plan or unexpected behavior in consumer demands need not lead to losses for the individual producer and even less to economic disaster for him. Losses easily can be pooled by the administration. The means which are available for carrying over the "necessary" distributive function of a competitive market may be conveniently classified into direct allocation (priorities, quotas, etc.) and administered prices. The former applies above all to the distribution of goods to producers, the latter refers mainly to the sphere of consumption. There is, however, no sharp dividing line between the fields of application of the two means. Labor is the outstanding example in which a combination of both methods is applied.

In constructing a rough model of the distributive mechanism under state capitalism, we always have to keep in mind that production and producers' consumption are two aspects of the same process. Since under modern conditions producer and consumer are, as a rule, not the same person, distribution serves as a means of integrating them. The production plan is based on a comparatively arbitrary decision as to how much of the social product is to be available for consumption and how much is to be used for expansion.

All major problems of distribution under state capitalism have been discussed thoroughly in the literature on socialist planning published within the last decade. While all writers in favor of a planned society agree that the tyranny of the market must be abolished, differences of opinion exist on the question of where to draw the limits for the use of a pseudo-market. Some writers recommend that the managers of the socialized industry should "behave as if under competitive capitalism." They should "play at competition." A model partly constructed on the results of this discussion may be used to illustrate how distribution works under state capitalism. The distribution of goods to producers starts from the following situation:

1. Most productive facilities are privately owned but controlled by the government;
2. Each industry is organized in cartels;
3. Prices react to changes in supply and demand as well as to changes in the cost of structure within the limits permitted by the plan authority and the monopolies;
4. A general plan for the structure of the social product is in existence.

Under these circumstances a system of priorities and quotas will guarantee the execution of the plan in its broad lines. These allocations cover reproduction of existing resources, expansion (including defense), and the total output of consumers goods, which every industry shall produce. Within each industry a quota system will provide for the distribution according to a more detailed plan or according to expressions of consumer choice. Not much room is left in this set-up for flexible prices. The partial survival of the profit motive will induce manufacturers who are offered higher prices for their products to bid up in turn the prices of their "factors." But the "office of price control" will not permit prices to go higher than is compatible with the general plan. Since all major units of production are under the control of cartels, the propensity to keep prices flexible should not be overestimated. Governmental control will be immensely facilitated by the enormous role of public works necessary to maintain full employment under all circumstances.

Full employment in the strict sense of the word can be achieved in regard to labor only. Due to technological facts, it is not possible in the case of plant and equipment. New plant and new machinery constructed according to the latest technical development require a minimum size of plant, which as a rule leads to temporary overcapacity at the moment of completion. If no ways for using this overcapacity can be found speedily, some idleness of capital will arise. This might happen with entire durable goods industries (e.g., machine tools) if the need for their product is temporarily saturated. Neither this nor other "maladjustments" can produce the cumulative effects so vicious under the free market system, for the capital owner might be compensated for his loss out of pooled profits or public sources, and provision for a constant reserve in planning the labor supply will take care of the displaced workers. Technological unemployment will be handled in a similar way. It has been shown that the opposite case, periodical shortage of capital, can be avoided in a planned society.

Labor under state capitalism is allocated to the different sections of production like other resources. This does not prevent the planning authorities from differentiating wages. On the contrary, premiums in the form of higher real wages can be granted wherever extra efforts are demanded. The slave driver's whip is no workable means for extracting quality products from highly skilled workers who use expensive machinery. This differentiation in wage schedules, however, is not the outcome of market conditions but of the wage administrator's decision. No entrepreneur is allowed to pay higher wages than those fixed by this agency.

With absolute control of wages, the government is in a position to handle the distribution of consumers goods with comparative ease. In cases of severe scarcity, as in wartime, direct allocation of consumers goods might be the only adequate means for their distribution. In such a case consumer choice is very limited but not entirely ruled out. If, however, a somewhat more adequate supply of consumer goods is available, the consumer may be as free or, with the greater purchasing power created by full employment, even more free in his choice under state capitalism than he is now. In order to achieve this goal with the means now at hand, a pseudo-market for consumer goods will be established. The starting point for its operation is a clearly defined relation between purchasing power which will be spent for consumption and the sum of prices of all available consumer goods. Both sums must be equal. In other words, the total income paid out to consumers, minus taxes, compulsory, and voluntary savings, must be the same as the total price of all consumer goods which are for sale. If the "net" consumer income should be higher, a scramble for goods and a bidding up of prices would result (under our definition that net income excludes savings). If it should be lower, only part of the products could be distributed. The first step toward distributing the consumer goods is therefore to make the net income of all consumers in a given period equivalent to the sum of consumer goods output as decided by the general plan and the available inventory. This first step will prove insufficient for two reasons:

1. The consumers' voluntary savings may deviate from the plan—they may save either more or less than was expected in calculating the equilibrium. Both cases may be remedied by the use of the market laws of demand and supply, which will create inflationary or deflationary price movements to "clear the market"—if the price controlling agencies permit it.

2. The consumers' choices may deviate from the calculations of the planners—they may prefer some products and reject others. Here again the old market mechanism may be allowed to come into play to enforce higher prices for goods in greater demand and to lower prices where and as long as an oversupply exists. A system of subsidies and surtaxes will eliminate serious losses as well as surplus profits which could disturb the functioning of the plan. The distributive agency may completely "overrule" the consumers' choice for all practical purposes by fixing prices either extremely high or disproportionately low. So far the price mechanism obeys the same laws as in the free market system. The difference becomes manifest in the effects which changing prices exercise on production. The price signals influence production only insofar as is compatible with the general plan and the established public policy on consumption. Price movements serve as a most valuable instrument for announcing differences between consumers' preferences and the production plan. They cannot, however, compel the planning authority to follow these manifestations of consumers' will in the same way they compel every nonmonopolistic producer in a free market. Under private capitalism, the monopolist, in resisting the market signals, disrupts the whole market system at the expense of all nonmonopolistic market parties. Under state capitalism the disconnection between price and production can do no harm because the function of coordinating production and consumption has been transferred from the market to the plan authority. Much attention has been given to the question of how consumers' choice can be calculated in advance. No "God-like" qualities are required for the planning board. It has been shown that freedom of consumers' choice actually exists only to a very limited degree. In studying large numbers of consumers, it becomes evident that size of income, tradition, and propaganda are considerably leveling down all individual preference schedules. The experiences of large manufacturing and distributing concerns as well as of cartels contribute a most valuable supplement to the special literature on planning.

Economic Limitations of State Capitalism

In raising the question of economic limitations, we point to those which may restrict the arbitrariness of the decisions in state capitalism as contrasted with other social structures in which they may not appear. We are not concerned with limitations that apply to every social set-up, e.g., those which result from the necessity to reproduce the given resources and to maintain full employment and optimum efficiency. The first and most frequent objection against the economic workability of a state capitalistic system is that it is good only in a scarcity economy, especially for periods of war preparedness and war. For a scarcity economy, so runs the argument, most of the economic difficulties against which private capitalism struggles do not exist. Over-production and overinvestment need not be feared, and all products, however ineffi-ciently produced, and however bad their quality, find a ready demand. As soon as the temporary emergency has passed, however, and a greater supply becomes available in all fields, state capitalism will prove utterly inadequate for securing the best use of available resources, for avoiding bottlenecks in one product and overproduction in others, and for providing the consumers with what they may demand at the lowest possible cost. Even if all means of production are under governmental control, efficient planning is possible only under conditions of emergency. The argument advanced for this view can be boiled down to the following: In a planned economy costs cannot be accounted for, the free choice of the consumers must be disregarded, the motives for efficient production and distribution disappear, and as a result a planned economy must under modern conditions be much less productive than a market economy.

We think that anyone who seriously studies the modern literature on planning must come to the conclusion that, whatever his objections to the social consequences of planning, these arguments against its economic efficiency no longer hold. All technical means for efficient planning, including the expansion of production in accordance with consumer wants and the most advanced technical possibilities, and taking into account the cost in public health, personal risks, unemployment (never adequately calculated in the cost sheet of private enterprise)—all these technical means are available today.

Another counterargument holds that as soon as state capitalism turns from concen-trating upon armaments to a genuine peace economy, its only alternative, if it wants to avoid unemployment, is to spend a very substantial part of the national income for the construction of modern "pyramids," or to raise considerably the standard of living. No economic causes exist which could prevent a state capitalistic government from doing so. The obstacles are of a political nature and will be dealt with later.

A third argument points in the opposite direction. It objects that state capitalism necessarily leads to a standstill in technics or even a regress. Investments will slow down and technical progress cease if the market laws are put out of operation. As long as competitive armament continues, the contrary will probably be true. Besides the profit motive, the vital interests of the controlling group will stimulate both investment and technical progress. In the effort to maintain and extend its power, the controlling group will come into conflict with foreign interests, and its success will depend upon its military force. This, however, will be a function of the technical efficiency. Any slackening in the speed of technical progress might lead to military inferiority and to destruction. Only after all possible enemies have disappeared, because the whole world will be controlled by one totalitarian state, will the problem of technological progress and capital expansion come to the fore.

Are there, one may ask, no economic limitations at all to the existence and expan-sion of state capitalism? With its rise, will a utopia emerge in which all economic wants can easily be fulfilled if political factors don't interfere? Did not the liberal the-ory also believe it had proved that the market system will guarantee its constituents the full use of all resources if not interfered with? And did it not become apparent later that inherent forces prevented the market system from functioning and ushered in growing interference by private monopolies and the government? Forewarned as we are, we are unable to discover any inherent economic forces, "economic laws" of the old or a new type, which could prevent the functioning of state capitalism. Government control of production and distribution furnishes the means for eliminating the economic causes of depressions, cumulative destructive processes, and unemployment of capital and labor. We may even say that under state capitalism economics as a social science has lost its object. Economic problems in the old sense no longer exist when the coordination of all economic activities is effected by conscious plan instead of by the natural laws of the market. Where the economist formerly racked his brain to solve the puzzle of the exchange process, he meets, under state capitalism, with mere problems of administration. There are indeed limitations to state capitalism, but they derive from natural conditions as well as from the very structure of the society which state capitalism seeks to perpetuate.

Natural and Other Noneconomic Limitations

1. To be fully workable, state capitalism needs an adequate supply of raw material, plans, and labor of all kinds (technicians, administrators, skilled and unskilled labor) characteristic for a highly industrialized country. Without a plentiful supply of raw materials and the outfit in machinery and skill of a modern industrial society, great waste must accompany state capitalistic intervention, possibly greater than under a market economy. For the first limitation, inadequate supply of raw materials, a typical example is offered by Nazi Germany. The enormous machinery which had to be built to compensate for the insufficiency of the raw material basis—too small to cope with the armament program—and the difficulties for the producer in obtaining raw materials and, in consequence, new machinery, cannot be attributed to the system itself, but to the fact that one of its main prerequisites was lacking from the very beginning.

On the other hand, many of the Soviet Russian economic failures may be traced back to the lack of both raw materials and adequate development of the productive forces. Lack of trained technicians, skilled workers, and the qualities known as work discipline, all of which are plentiful only in highly industrialized countries, goes a long way in explaining the slow progress of rearming, reorganizing the transportation system, and raising or even maintaining the standard of living in Soviet Russia. But even here a government-controlled economic system has shown the power to survive under conditions where a system of free enterprise would have collapsed completely. Government-controlled foreign trade and the development of an industry for ersatz materials may overcome the limitations of a too narrow basis of raw materials. Filling the gap between a fully industrialized and a chiefly agricultural economy is a much more painful and drawn-out process.

2. Differences in vital interests will crop up in the group or groups controlling the state. They can stem from different positions within the administration, different programs for maintaining or expanding power, or the struggle for the monopoly of

control. Unless adequate provisions are made for overcoming these differences, bad compromises and continuous struggle will arise.

3. Conflicting interests within the ruling class might thwart the construction of a general plan embodying the optimum of all available resources for achieving consistent chosen ends. The choice of the ends itself represents a major problem as long as no common will has been established. In our discussion we started always from the assumption "given a general plan." This means a plan for certain ends which must be chosen from among a variety of possible ones.

Once the minimum requirements for consumption, replacement, and expansion are fulfilled, the planners have a great deal of leeway. If their decisions do not converge into a consistent program, no general plan for the optimum use and development of the given productive forces can be drafted.

4. Conflicting interests, however, do not operate in the ruling group only. Since totalitarian state capitalism is the expression of an antagonistic society at its worst, the will to dominate from above and the counterpressure from below cut deeply into the pseudo-liberty of the state capitalised planners. The planning board, while vested with all the technical means for directing the whole economic process, is itself an arena of struggle among social forces beyond its control. It will be seen that planning in an antagonistic society is only in a technical sense the same tool as that used by a society in which harmony of interests has been established. Political considerations interfere at every step with the construction and execution of an optimum plan. The following paragraphs will offer some examples.

How will expansion of production and technical progress be motivated and fear of aggression or objects for new conquest have vanished? Will not the dreaded technological standstill make its appearance under such conditions, thus spoiling all chances of reducing the drudgery of labor while raising the standard of living? A case could be made out for the view that a new set of motivations will arise under totalitarian state capitalism which will combine the drive for power over men with the will to power over nature and counteract the development toward a static economy. But this is such a distant perspective that we may leave the question open, the more so since under totalitarian capitalism there are serious reasons to keep the productive forces static.

Under a state capitalistic set-up, will the general standard of living rise beyond narrow limits if the expansion program permits? This question can be answered in the affirmative for the democratic form of state capitalism only. For its authoritarian counterpart, however, the problem is different. The ruling minority in a totalitarian state maintains its power not only by terror and atomization but by controlling the means of production and keeping the dominated majority in complete spiritual dependence. The masses have no chance of questioning the durability and justification of the existing order; the virtues of war are developed and all "effeminacy," all longing for individual happiness, is rooted out. A rise in the standard of living might dangerously counteract such a policy. It would imply more leisure time, more professional skill, more opportunity for critical thinking, out of which a revolutionary spirit might develop. It is a wide spread error that the most dangerous revolutions are instigated by the most miserable strata of society. The revolutionary craving for liberty and justice found its most fertile breeding ground not among the paupers but among individuals and groups who were themselves in a relatively better position. The ruling group in totalitarian state capitalism might therefore decide that from the point of view of its own security a low general standard of living and long, drudging working hours are desirable. An armament race and the excitement over threat of foreign "aggression" seem to be appropriate means for keeping the standard of living low and the war virtues high while maintaining full employment and promoting technical progress. Such a constellation, however, would furnish a striking example for a political limitation of productivity.

The highly speculative question might be permitted: What would happen if totalitarian state capitalism were embodied in a unified world state in which the threat of aggression had disappeared for good? Even public works of undreamed scope could not prevent the general standard of living from rising under conditions of full employment. In such a case the most clever devices of ideological mass domination and the grimmest terror are unlikely to uphold for a long period a minority dictatorship which can no longer claim itself to be necessary to maintain production and to protect the people from foreign aggression. If our assumption is correct that totalitarian state capitalism will not tolerate a high standard of living for the masses and cannot survive mass unemployment, the consequence seems to be that it cannot endure in a peace economy. As long as one national state capitalism has not conquered the whole earth, however, there will always be ample opportunities to spend most of the productive excess capacity (excess over the requirements for a minimum standard of living) for ever-increasing and technically more perfect armaments.

Why can the policy of aggression not come to a standstill before one state has conquered the entire world? Even after a totalitarian state has acquired full autarchy within its own territory, "preparedness" and foreign wars must be on at a rapid pace in order to protect against aggression from outside and revolution from within. A democratic state capitalism, while safe from within, is menaced by totalitarian aggression and must arm to the teeth and be ready to fight until all totalitarian states have been transformed into democracies. In the last century it became evident that a society based on slave labor could not exist side by side with one organized on the principle of free labor. The same holds true in our day for democratic and totalitarian societies.

Control of the State under State Capitalism

If state capitalism is a workable system, superior in terms of productivity to private capitalism under conditions of monopolistic market disruption, what are the political implications? If the state becomes the omnipotent comptroller of all human activities, the question "who controls the comptroller" embraces the problem of whether state capitalism opens a new way to freedom or leads to the complete loss of it as far as the overwhelming majority is concerned. Between the two extreme forms of state capitalism, the totalitarian and the democratic, numerous others are thinkable. Everything depends upon which social groups in the last analysis direct the decisions of a government whose power has in all matters—"economic" well as "non-economic"—never been surpassed in modern history. The following is intended as a rough sketch of the social structure under totalitarian state capitalism.

1. The government is controlled by, and composed of, a new ruling class. We have defined this new class as an amalgamation of the key bureaucrats in business, state, and party, allied with the remaining vested interests. We have already mentioned that inherited or acquired wealth may still play a role in opening a way to this ruling group, but that it is not essential for participating in the group. One's position in the economic and administrative set-up, together with party affiliations and personal qualification, is decisive for one's political power. The new ruling class, by its grip on the state, controls everything it wants to, the general economic plan, foreign policy, rights and duties, life and death of the individual. Its decisions are not restrained by any constitutional guarantees but by a set of rules only, designed for maintaining and expanding its own power. We have seen what control over the general economic plan involves: all the basic decisions on how to distribute the "factors of production" among producer and consumer goods, on the working day, labor condition, on wages and prices. To sum up, control of the general economic plan means control over the standard of living. Antagonisms of interests among the groups within the ruling class might lead to serious difficulties. The class interest of maintaining the new status, however, will probably be strong enough for a long time to overcome these antagonisms before they can turn into a menace to the system. The persons who form the ruling class have been prepared for their task by their position in, or their cooperation with, the monopolistic institutions of private capitalism. There, a rapidly growing number of decisive functions had become invested in a comparatively small group of bureaucrats. The leader-and-follower principle flourished long before it was promulgated as the basic principle of society, since more and more responsibility had been centralized in the top offices of government, business, trade unions, and political parties.

2. Those owners of capital who are "capitalists" without being managers and who could exercise great political influence during the whole era of private capitalism no longer have any necessary social functions. They receive interest on their investments for as long a time and in the measure that the new ruling class may be willing to grant. From the point of view of their social utility, they constitute a surplus population. Under the impact of heavy inheritance taxes, controlled stock markets, and the generally hostile attitude of the new ruling class against the *raffende Kapital*, these "capitalists" will probably disappear. The widespread hatred against them could develop only because the economic laws of capitalism had transformed their social role into that of parasites.

3. A semi-independent group, not belonging to the ruling class but enjoying more privileges than the *Gefolgschaften*, are the free professions and the middle-sized and small businesses under governmental control. Both will disappear wherever a fully developed state capitalism corresponding to our model is reached. The process of concentration which gains unprecedented momentum under state capitalism absorbs

the independent small and medium-sized enterprise. The trend towards socialization of medicine, of journalism and other free professions, transforms their members into government employees.

4. The great majority of the people fall into the category of salaried employees of all types. They are subject to the leader principle of command and obedience. All their political rights have been destroyed, and carefully planned atomization has simplified the task of keeping them under strict control. Labor's right to bargain collectively, to strike, to change jobs and residence at will (if its market position permits) is abolished. Work becomes compulsory, wages are fixed by government agencies, the leisure time of the worker and his family is organized from above. In some respects, this is antithetical to the position of labor under private capitalism and revives many traits of feudal conditions.

5. The new state openly appears as an institution in which all earthly power is embodied and which serves the new ruling class as a tool for its power politics. Seemingly independent institutions like party, army, and business form its specialized arms. A complicated relation exists, however, between the means and those who apply them, resulting in some genuine independence for these institutions. Political domination is achieved by organized terror and overwhelming propaganda on the one side, on the other by full employment and adequate standard living for all key groups, the promise of security and a life of greater abundance for every subject who submits voluntarily and completely. This system is far from being based upon rude force alone. In that it provides many "real" satisfactions for its subjects, it exists partly with the consent of the governed, but this consent cannot change the antagonistic character of a state capitalistic society in which the power interests of the ruling class prevent the people from fully using the productive forces for their own welfare and from having control over the organization and activities of society.

We have referred here and there to what we think are particular traits of the democratic form of state capitalism. Since no approaches to it have so far been made in practice, and since the discussion of its structure is still in a formative stage, no attempt will be made here to construct a model for it.

The trend toward state capitalism is growing, however, in the nontotalitarian states. An increasing number of observers admit, very often reluctantly, that private capitalism is no longer able to handle the new tasks. "All plans for internal post-war reconstruction start with the assumption that more or less permanent government controls will have replaced *laissez-faire* methods both in the national and the international sphere. Thus the choice is not between totalitarian controls and return to 'free enterprise'; the choice is between totalitarian controls and controls voluntarily accepted by the people of each country for the benefit of society as a whole." It is the lesson of all large-scale measures of government interference that they will contribute to the disruption of the market mechanism if they are not coordinated into a general plan. If government is to provide for all the items recognized as mandatory in the more serious postwar reconstruction programs, it must be vested with adequate powers, and these might not stop short of state capitalism.

It is of vital importance for everybody who believes in the values of democracy that an investigation be made as to whether state capitalism can be brought under democratic control. The social as well as the moral problem with which the democracies are confronted has been formulated as follows "How can we get effective use of our resources, yet at the same time preserve the underlying values in our tradition of liberty and democracy? How can we employ our unemployed, how can we use our plant and equipment to the full, how can we take advantage of the best modern technology, yet, in all this make the individual source of value and individual fulfillment in society the basic objective? How can we obtain effective organization of resources, yet at the same time retain the maximum freedom of individual action?" Totalitarian state capitalism offers the solution of economic problems at the price of totalitarian oppression. What measures are necessary to guarantee control of the state by the majority of its people instead of by a small minority? What ways and means can be devised to prevent the abuse of the enormous power vested in state, industrial, and party bureaucracy under state capitalism? How can the loss of economic liberty be rendered compatible with the maintenance of political liberty? How can the disintegrative motive forces of today be replaced by integrative ones? How will the roots from which insurmountable social antagonisms develop be eliminated so that there will not arise a political alliance between dissentient partial interests and the bureaucracy aiming to dominate the majority? Can democratic state capitalism be more than a transitory phase leading either to total oppression or to doing away with the remnants of the capitalistic system?

The main obstacles to the democratic form of state capitalism are of a political nature and can be overcome by political means only. If our thesis proves to be correct, society on its present level can overcome the handicaps of the market system by economic planning. Some of the best brains of this country are studying the problem of how such planning can be done in a democratic way, but a great amount of theoretical work will have to be performed before answers to every question will be forthcoming.

Herbert Marcuse, "The Dialectic of the Soviet State," from *Soviet Marxism*

A brief summary suffices to recall the chief elements in Stalin's theory of the retention and growth of the socialist state. In contrast to Engels's formula of the "withering away" of the state, which is valid for the victory of socialism in all or in a majority of countries, the socialist state must assume new decisive functions under the conditions of "socialism in one country" and "capitalist encirclement." These functions change in accordance with the internal development and the international situation. In the first phase of the development (from the October revolution to the "elimination of the exploiting classes"), the functions of the state were: (a) "to suppress the overthrown classes inside the country," (b) "to defend the country from foreign attack," and (c) "economic organization and cultural education." In the second phase (from the "elimination of the capitalist elements in town and country" to the "complete victory of the socialist system and the adoption of the new constitution") function

(a) ceased and was supplanted by that of "protecting socialist property"; functions (b) and (c) "fully remained." Moreover, the state is to continue also in the period of communism "unless the capitalist encirclement" is liquidated, and "unless the danger of foreign military attack has disappeared"—only then will it "atrophy." As early as 1930, Stalin had condensed the dialectic of the socialist state to the formula: "The highest possible development of the power of the State with the object of preparing the conditions for the dying away of the State—that is the Marxist formula." Later on, emphasis was placed on the strengthening of the state power prior to and during the transition to communism.

The continuation of the state in the first period of socialism is implied in the original Marxian conception. Marx assumed that the "enslaving subordination of the individuals to the division of labor" would continue during the First Phase of socialism. Consequently, the state would continue; its "withering away would be gradual and preceded by a period of transformation" of the political institutions. Thus was the development outlined by Engels as early as 1847, and it was again emphasized in the eighties in his polemic against the anarchists:

> The anarchists ... declare that the proletarian revolution must begin with the abolition of the political organization of the state. But the only organization which the proletariat finds available (*fertig*) after its victory is the state. This state may have to undergo considerable changes before it can fulfil its new functions. But to destroy it in one moment would mean to destroy the only organization with which the victorious proletariat would exercise the power which it has just conquered—to subdue its capitalist enemies and to carry through that economic revolution of society without which the victory would of necessity end in a new defeat.

The Marx quotations around which Lenin built his refutation of Kautsky in *State and Revolution* do not contradict this conception. The "state machinery" which is to be shattered, the "bureaucratic and military machinery" which cannot be transferred from one hand to the other but must be "broken up," is the machinery of the bourgeois class state. To be sure, according to Marx, all historical forms of the state were forms of the class state—but in so far as the first phase of socialism still is "affected" with its capitalist heritage, so is its state. However, while the socialist state continues to exercise coercive functions, its substance has undergone a fundamental change: the socialist state is the proletariat, constituted as the ruling class. Consequently, in terms of class position and class interests, the subject and the object of coercion are identical. In this sense, the state of the first phase is a "non-state," the state "broken up" and "shattered." Since political power is, "properly" speaking, "merely the organized power of one class for oppressing another," the class identity between the subject and object of the state now tends to transform coercion into rational administration. Marx and Engels summarized the changes in the function of the state as this very transformation: "The public functions will lose their political character and be transformed into the simple administrative function of watching over the true interest of society."

In contrast to this conception, the Soviet state exercises throughout political and governmental functions against the proletariat itself; domination remains a specialized function in the division of labor and is as such the monopoly of a political, economic, and military bureaucracy. This function is perpetuated by the centralized authoritarian organization of the productive process, directed by groups which determine the needs of society (the social product and its distribution) independent of the collective control of the ruled population. Whether or not these groups constitute a "class" in the Marxian sense is a problem of Marxist exegesis. The fact is that Soviet Marxism itself stresses the "directing" function of the state as distinguished from the underlying institutions, and that this state retains the separation of the "immediate producers" from collective control over the process of production. Soviet Marxism justifies this "anomaly" by the anomalous circumstances of socialism in a "capitalist environment." These circumstances are supposed to require the continuation and even the growth of the state as a system of *political* institutions, and the exercise by the state of oppressive economic, military, police, and educational functions over and against society. The Soviet state thus takes shape exactly as that structure which Engels described as characteristic of class society: the "common societal functions" become a "new branch of the division of labor" and thereby constitute *particular* interests separate from those of the population. The state is again a reified, hypostatized power.

As such a power, the state, according to Soviet Marxism, becomes the Archimedean point from which the world is moved into socialism, the "basic instrument" for the establishment of socialism and communism. Soviet Marxism links the perpetuated hypostatization of the state to the very-progress of socialist construction. The argument runs as follows: With the overthrow of capitalism and the nationalization of the economy, the Bolshevik Revolution laid the foundation for a state which represents the interests of the urban and rural proletariat. The state is their state, and, consequently, the further development of the revolution takes place "from above" rather than "from below." The liquidation of the "old bourgeois economic order in rural areas" and the creation of a "socialist collective farm order" was such a revolution from above, "on the initiative of the existing regime with the support of the basic masses of the peasantry." The firm institutionalization of the state in the revolution from above took shape under the first Five-Year Plan, which revolutionized the economic order of the country not only over and above and against the "immediate interests" of workers and peasants, but also by subjecting them to the bureaucratic-authoritarian organization of production. According to Stalinism, transition to the subsequent stages of socialism will likewise be made by strengthening the institutionalized state rather than by dissolving it. But the hypostatization of the regime implied in these formulations might boomerang against alterations in the political structure necessitated by international and internal developments. The power of the state has its objective limits. In the later period of Stalinism, Soviet Marxism emphasized that the state itself is subject to general socioeconomic laws, that its forms "are changing and will continue to change in line with the development of our country and with the changes in the international situation." In Soviet Marxist evaluation, such internal and international developments were asserting themselves on the ground of the achievements of Stalinism and were calling for a corresponding change in Soviet theory and strategy.

Before outlining the trend in the development of the state envisaged by Soviet Marxism, the question must be asked: Who or what is that Soviet state? Neither the rise of the Soviet intelligentsia as a new ruling group, nor its composition and its privileges are any longer disputed facts—least so in the USSR. The recruitment and training of highly qualified specialists, technicians, managers, etc., is continually emphasized and their privileges are advertised. Moreover the uninterrupted growth of this group is considered one of the essential preconditions for the transition to communism. Decisive in the problem of the development of the state are not merely the privileges of the governmental bureaucracy, its numerical strength, and its caste character, but the basis and scope of its power. Obviously the bureaucracy has a vital interest in maintaining and enhancing its privileged position. Obviously, there are conflicts among various groups within the bureaucracy. In order to evaluate their significance for the tendential development of Soviet society, an attempt must be made to determine whether or not there is a political and economic basis for using the special position of the bureaucracy (or special positions within the bureaucracy) for exploding and changing the structure of Soviet society. The following paragraphs suggest only some of the general aspects pertaining to such an attempt.

We have emphasized that Soviet Marxism admits the existence of contradictory interests in Soviet society and derives them from the existence of different forms of Socialist property and labor. As specific sources of contradictions are mentioned: the coexistence of state, collective, and private property in the means of production; the difference between mental and physical labor; the stratification into intelligentsia, workers, and peasants; the uneven development of the two main divisions of social production. As long as the bureaucracy is a special branch in the division of labor, engendering a special position in society, it has a separate, special interest. According to Soviet Marxism, these "internal" contradictions, and with them the separate position of the bureaucracy, will "flatten out" with the gradual equalization of mental and physical labor, which in turn will result from the gradual elimination of the lag of production relations behind the growth of the productive forces. The elimination of the class position of the bureaucracy (but not of the bureaucracy itself) thus will appear as a "by-product" of the transition from socialism to communism. At that stage, the bureaucracy would still exercise special functions but no longer within an institutionalized, hierarchical division of functions; the bureaucracy would be "open" and lose its "political" content to the degree to which, with the wealth of the material and intellectual productive forces, the general societal functions would become exchangeable among the individuals. Is the Soviet Marxist assumption of such a trend even theoretically consistent with the actual structure of the Soviet state?

Bureaucracy by itself, no matter how huge it is, does not generate self-perpetuating power unless it has an economic base of its own from which its position is derived, or unless it is allied with other social groups which possess such a power base. Naturally, the traditional sources of economic power are not available to the Soviet bureaucracy; it does not own the nationalized means of production. But obviously "the people," who constitutionally own the means of production, do not control them. Control, therefore, and not ownership must be the decisive factor. But unless further defined, "control" is an insufficient index for the real locus of power. Is it exercised simply by particular interests independent enough to assert themselves against others, or are these interests themselves subject to overriding laws and forces? With respect to the Soviet system and its organization of production, distinction must be made between technical-administrative and social control. The two levels of control would coincide if those which manage the industrial and agricultural key establishments determine by and for themselves and as a special group entrepreneurial and labor policies, thereby wielding decisive influence over the social need and its satisfaction. Such a coincidence cannot be taken for granted. In Soviet doctrine, it is the Party which exercises the social control overriding all technical-administrative control, and since the Party is fused with the state, social control assumes the form of centralized and planned political control. But the same question as to the ultimate superseding control must be asked with respect to the Party—even its top leadership comprises various groups and interests, including managerial ones. Obviously, the "people" can be excluded: there is no effective social control "from below." Thus, two possibilities are left: either (1) a specific group within the bureaucracy exercises control over all the rest of the bureaucracy (in which case this group would be the autonomous subject of social control); or (2) the bureaucracy as a "class" is truly sovereign, i.e., the ruling group (in which case social and technical-administrative controls would coincide). This alternative will be discussed presently.

Personal power, even if effectively institutionalized, does not define social control. Stalin's dictatorship may well have overridden all divergent interests by virtue of his factual power. However, this personal power was itself subject to the requirements of the social system on whose continued functioning it depended, and over and above the subsistence minimum, these requirements were codetermined by the interests controlling the industrial and agricultural basis, and by those of the police and the army. The same holds true, to a much greater extent, for the post-Stalinist leadership. The search for the locus of social control thus leads back from personal dictatorship to the alter native formulated above. But there seems to be no separate homogeneous group to which social control could be meaningfully attributed. The top ruling group is itself changing and comprises "representatives" of various bureaucracies and branches of the bureaucracies, economic as well as political: management, army, party. Each of them has a special interest and aspires for social control. But the monopolization of power is counteracted by two forces: on the one side, the Central Plan, in spite of its vagaries, loopholes, and corrections, ultimately supersedes and integrates the special interests; on the other side, the entire bureaucracy, up to the highest level, is subject to the competitive terror, or, after the relaxation of the terror, to the highly incalculable application of political or punitive measures, leading to the loss of power. To be sure, the Central Plan is itself the work of the bureaucracy in the main branches of the system: government, party, armed forces, management; but it is the result of their combined and adjusted interests and negotiations, ensuing in a sort of general interest which in turn depends on the internal growth of Soviet society. This relation also played an important role in the development of the terror.

Terror is the centralized, methodical application of incalculable violence (incalculable for the objects of the terror, and also for the top groups and even the practitioners of the terror)—not only in an emergency situation, but in a normal state of affairs. As long as the Soviet state relied on such incalculable application, it relied on terroristic force—although the terror would approximate a normal competitive social system to the degree to which the punitive measures (such as removal from office, demotion) would be nonviolent. In its historical function, terror may be progressive or regressive, depending upon whether it actually promotes, through the destruction of repressive institutions, the growth of liberal ones, and the rational utilization of the productive forces. In the Soviet state, the terror is of a twofold nature: technological and political. Inefficiency and poor performance at the technical and business level are punished; so is any kind of nonconformity: politically and dangerously suspect attitudes, opinions, behavior. The two forms are interconnected, and efficiency is certainly often judged on political grounds. However, with the elimination of all organized opposition, and with the continued success of the totalitarian administration, the terror tends to become predominantly technological, and, in the USSR itself, strictly political terror seems to be the exception rather than the rule. The completely standardized clichés of the political charges, which no longer even pretend to be rational, plausible, and consistent, may well serve to conceal the real reason for the indictment: differences in the timing and implementation of administrative measures on whose substance the conflicting parties agree.

The technological terror is omnipresent—but this very omnipresence implies a high degree of indifference toward special privilege and position. An action started on a low level may involve the highest level if the circumstances are "favorable." The chiefs themselves are not immune—they are not the absolute masters of oppression. The circumstances which set the machine in motion against a specific target seem to be the end-constellation of numerous cross currents in the areas of the respective bureaucracies. The ultimate decision in prominent cases is also likely to be the result of negotiations and compromises among the top groups—each representing its own "apparatus," but each apparatus again subject to competitive controls within the framework of the Central Plan and the then prevailing principles of foreign and domestic policy. This framework leaves much room for personal and clique influences and interests, corruption, and profiteering; it also permits one group (and one individual of the group) to come out on top—but it also sets the limits beyond which the monopolization of power cannot go without upsetting the structure on which Soviet power rests establishment of complete socialist property on the land, total mechanization, and assimilation of urban and rural life and labor. In foreign policy, through "hard" and "soft" periods, through local wars and "peace offensives," Lenin's guidance stands supreme: to preserve the "respite" for the building of socialism and communism in coexistence with the capitalist world. Here, too, the interpretation of the governing principles, and the decision on the timing and scope of the measures which they stipulate, remain ultimately the monopoly of a top group of leaders. But no matter how its composition and number may change, nor how the extent of consultation and compromise with the lower strata of the bureaucracy may vary, the governing principles seem to be rigid enough to define the limits of special powers and to preclude their institutionalization within a system governed by these principles.

The Soviet bureaucracy thus does not seem to possess a basis for the effective perpetuation of special interests against the overriding general requirements of the social system on which it lives. The bureaucracy constitutes a separate class which controls the underlying population through control of the economic, political, and military establishments, and exercise of this control engenders a variety of special interests which assert themselves in the control; however, they must compromise and ultimately succumb to the general policy which none of the special interests can change by virtue of its special power. Does this mean that the bureaucracy represents the common interest of society as a whole?

In a society composed of competing groups with different economic, occupational, and administrative interests, "common interest" is not per se a meaningful term. Even if one assumes that the general rise in the material and cultural living conditions with a maximum of individual liberty and security defines the common interest of every civilized society, it appears that in any nonhomogeneous society the realization of this interest will proceed in conflict with the interests of some of the (privileged) groups in society. The common interest would not be identical with the interest of all and each; it would remain an "ideological" concept. This antagonistic situation prevails not only in the relationship between the bureaucracy and the underlying population, but also in that between the urban and rural groups, and even between different subgroups within these groups, such as between male and female, skilled and unskilled workers. Even in a highly advanced industrial society with abundant resources, the rise in the general standard of living and of general freedom could take place only as a most unequal development, overriding the immediate interests of large parts of the population. Just as the social need is not identical with the individual needs, so is the realization of "universal" liberty and justice at one and the same time also injustice and unfreedom in individual cases (and even in the case of whole social groups). The very universality of right and law—the guarantor of freedom and justice—demands such negation and limitation by virtue of the fact that it must necessarily abstract from "particularities."

The inequality implied in the common interest would be much greater in a backward society; neither nationalization nor central planning per se would eliminate it. The common interest would retain a high degree of "abstractness" as against the immediate interest (although this abstractness may be gradually reduced as society develops). In other words, the traditional distinction between the general (common) interest and the sum-total of particular interests would hold true, and the former would have to be defined in terms of its own—as a separate entity, as the social interest over and above individual interests. Soviet Marxism defines the former in relation to the productive forces and their organization; the social interest is said to be represented by those groups and interests which promote the development of the productive forces. This relation is itself a historical factor, to be defined in terms of the political and economic situation of the respective society.

In the case of Soviet society the accelerated development of its productive forces is considered a prerequisite for the survival and competitive strength of the Soviet state in the circumstances of "coexistence." The position of the bureaucracy thus depends on the expansion of the productive apparatus, and the specific and conflicting interests within the bureaucracy are superseded, through the mechanisms of technology and force, diplomacy and power politics, by this common social interest. The Soviet bureaucracy therefore represents the social interest in a hypostatized form, in which the individual interests are separated from the individuals and arrogated by the state.

The Soviet state emerges as the institutionalized collective in which the Marxian distinction between the immediate and the real (objective historical) interest is made the rationale for the building of the political structure. The state is the manifestation of the real (the social) interest, but as such the state is "not yet" identical with the interests of the people whom it rules: their immediate interests do "not yet" coincide with the objective social interest. For example, the people want less work, more free-dom, more consumer goods—but, according to the official theory, the still prevailing backwardness and scarcity necessitate the continued subordination of these interests to the social interest of armament and industrialization. This is the old discrepancy between the individual and society, represented by the state; however, in Soviet the-ory, it occurs at a new stage of the historical process. Formerly, the state represented not the interest of society as a whole but that of the ruling class. To be sure, in a sense, the class state too represented the collective interest in so far as it organized and sustained the orderly reproduction of society as a whole and the development of the productive forces. However, the conflict between their rational development in the common interest and their private-profit utilization was, within the framework of the class state, insoluble and vitiated the identity of interests. As this conflict ripened, the class state would become of necessity ever more regressive and a fetter to the development of society. In contrast, the Soviet state is supposed to run the opposite course, capable of resolving the conflict and of establishing the harmony between individual and social need on the basis of an all-out development of productivity.

Part IV

Global Society

6

Communicative Action Theory
Hermeneutics and Recognition

Introduction

The period between 1966 to the present-day brings us into the age of globalization. Here we begin with a selection from Habermas's *The Theory of Communicative Action* (Volume 1), and parts of his article "Citizenship and National Identity" (1990). The former includes his critique of Adorno's and Horkheimer's critique of instrumental reason and Weber's theory of societal rationalization. Habermas argues that Weber's thesis lacks the cognitive components to provide a steering mechanism for understanding social evolution and societal rationalization. In his view, money and power, rather than eroding democratic freedom, engendered social and functional differentiation in society. Understanding the progressive elements of this process required a hermeneutical and pragmatic understanding of social action: a discursive and inter-subjective framework rooted in the distinction between communicative and strategic action and the cognitive struggle to reach mutual understanding on issues.

Thus, for Habermas, fallible reason constitutes an important feature of the discursive struggle to reach consensus; for it shows how rational consensus formation is achieved through the force of the better argument. As such, there is no telos or final purpose to guide and regulate human conduct; only the progressive and open-ended formation of law, rules, and cultural norms whose legitimacy is rooted in rational deliberation.

By the 1990s, Habermas began to focus increasingly on the dynamics of EU integration, including the effects of immigration and economic globalization. In his essay "Citizenship and National Identity" he theorizes that globalization has eroded many of the traditional democratic features of the constitutional (nation) state. For Habermas, the lawmaking process of the constitutional state consists of argumentation, deliberation and bargaining, which link the force of the better argument with the legitimization of norms. Thus, when state lawmakers and leaders of the constitutional state debate and pass a bill, they also legitimize the rules of procedure by linking the enactment of this bill with the democratic will of the people. It is this legitimizing source of power associated with the legal process that raises the central question of whether such a process can be realized in the form of an EU state.

The other normative question that Habermas's theory of the constitutional state raises is whether the focus on legitimacy and procedural will formation obscures the limits our empirical understanding of the (and emotive) struggle for recognition. For Axel Honneth, Habermas's failure in this sense requires further consideration of Hegel's identity logic. In the *Struggle for Recognition* (1995), Honneth argues that the struggle for moral recognition reflects the deeply embedded moral and social conflict between the individual and society: where moral injury or insult fuels the desire for love, solidarity, respect, and social mobility.

The normative thrust of his book, however, constitutes the main point of departure in Nancy Fraser's essay on the dilemmas of recognition. Here Fraser challenges the normative and hermeneutical basis of Honneth's theory, arguing that social inequality gives rise to demands for social redistribution that cannot be fully reconciled to normative-based claims, or objective patterns of solidarity and love. Accordingly, the tensions between normative/ethical claims (the common good and self-standing moral commitments) and structuralist arguments cannot be downplayed. Indeed, such tensions, as we shall see, underscore the conflict between structuralist-based interpretations and normative ethics in critical IR theory.

Jürgen Habermas, Selection from
The Theory of Communicative Action

In terms of Hegel's own concepts, the dialectical reconciliation of the universal and the particular remains metaphysical because it does not give its due to what is "nonidentical" in the particular. The structure of reified consciousness continues on in the very dialectic that is offered as a means of overcoming it, because everything that is of the nature of a thing counts for it as radically evil: "Whoever wants to 'dynamize' everything that is into pure activity tends to be hostile toward the other, the alien, whose name we are reminded of, and not without good reason, in alienation, the nonidentity for which not only consciousness but a reconciled humanity is to be made free."

But if negative dialectics presents itself as the only possible path of reconstruction—a path that cannot be traversed discursively—how then can we explicate the idea of reconciliation in the light of which alone Adorno is able to make the shortcomings of the idealist dialectic visible? From the beginning, critical theory labored over the problem of giving an account of its own normative foundations; since Horkheimer and Adorno made their turn to the critique of instrumental reason early in the 1940s, this problem has become drastically apparent. Horkheimer first takes up two positions that react in opposite ways to the replacement of objective reason by subjective reason, to the disintegration of religion and metaphysics. In the chapter of the *Eclipse of Reason* entitled "Conflicting Panaceas," he develops a position with two fronts: one against approaches in contemporary philosophy that are oriented to the tradition and the other against scientism; these fronts have remained decisive for the intraphilosophical arguments of critical theory until the positivism debate. The actual situation to which Horkheimer refers is a controversy between representatives of logical positivism and certain currents of neo-Thomism. Neo-Thomism stands here for any attempt to link up with Plato or Aristotle so as to renew the ontological claim of philosophy to comprehend the world as a whole, whether precritically or under the banner of objective idealism, and to put back together again metaphysically the moments of reason that separated out in the modern development of the spirit—the different aspects of validity: the true, the good, and the beautiful.

Thus the appeal to critical reflection cannot be understood as a disguised call to retreat to a Marxistically restored Hegel; it can only be understood as a first step toward a self-reflection of the sciences—which has since actually been carried out. For one thing, the self-criticism developed within the framework of the analytic theory of science has, with admirable consistency led to the—ambiguous—positions of so-called postempiricism (Lakatos, Toulmin, Kuhn, Hesse, Feyerabend). For another in the debate concerning the methodological foundations of the social sciences, the program of a unified science has been abandoned under the influence of phenomenology, hermeneutics ethnomethodology, linguistic philosophy—and critical theory as well—without any clear alternative coming into view. It is by no means the case that these two lines of argument have led to an unambiguous resumption of the rationality problematic; they have left room for sceptical and, above all, relativistic conclusions (Feyerabend, Elkana). Viewed retrospectively, therefore, it does not look as if Horkheimer could safely have left critical reflection to the "cunning" of scientific development. Besides, this perspective was quite alien to him. Nevertheless, Horkheimer and Adorno did not consider their task to be a substantive critique of science; they did not take it upon themselves to start from the situation of the disintegration of objective reason, to follow the thread of a subjective reason externalized in its objects as it displayed itself in the practice of the most advanced sciences, to develop a "phenomenological" concept of knowledge expanded through self-reflection, in order thereby to open up one not the only) avenue of access to a differentiated but encompassing concept of rationality. Instead, they submitted subjective reason to an unrelenting critique from the ironically distanced perspective of an objective reason that had fallen irreparably into ruin.

This paradoxical step was motivated, on the one hand, by the conviction that "great" philosophy, of which Hegel was the culmination and endpoint, could no longer of itself systematically develop and ground the idea of reason, the idea of a universal reconciliation of spirit and nature, and that in this respect it had perished together with metaphysical-religious world views. On the other hand, however, the time had passed for the realization of philosophy that was once possible, as Marx had proclaimed; as a result, philosophy remained, so to speak, the only memorial to the promise of a humane social life. In this respect, under the ruins of philosophy there lay buried the only truth from which thought could draw its negating, reification-transcending power.

Horkheimer and Adorno face the following problem. On the one hand, they do not agree with Lukács' view that the seemingly complete rationalization of the world has its limit in the formal character of its own rationality; they criticize this thesis empirically, by reference to the forms of manifestation of a penetrating rectification of culture and inner nature, and theoretically, by showing that even the objective idealism developed in Hegelian Marxism simply carries on the line of identity thinking and reproduces in itself the structures of reified consciousness. On the other hand, Horkheimer and Adorno radicalize Lukács' critique of reification. They do not consider the rationalization of the world to be only "seemingly complete"; and thus they need a conceptual apparatus that will allow them nothing less than to denounce the whole as the untrue. They cannot achieve this aim by way of an immanent critique of science, because a conceptual apparatus that could satisfy their desiderata would still share the pretensions of the great philosophical tradition. But this tradition—and this is the Weberian thorn still in critical theory—cannot be simply renewed with its systematic pretensions; it has "outlived" its own claims; in any case, it cannot be renewed in the form of philosophy. I shall try to make clear how the authors of the *Dialectic of Enlightenment* attempt to resolve this difficulty—and at what cost.

First of all, Horkheimer and Adorno generalize the category of reification. This can be laid out in three steps, if we keep in view their implicit starting point, namely the theory of reification developed by Lukács in *History and Class Consciousness*.

a) Lukács derived the form of objectivity specific to capitalist society from an analysis of the wage-labor relation, which is characterized by the commodity form of labor power; he further derived from this the structures of reified consciousness as these are expressed in the *Verstandesdenken* of the modern sciences, particularly in Kant's philosophical interpretation of them. By contrast, Horkheimer and Adorno regard these structures of consciousness—what they refer to as subjective reason and identifying thought—as fundamental. The abstraction of exchange as only the historical form in which identifying thought develops its world-historical influence and determines the forms of intercourse of capitalist society. The occasional references to real abstractions that have become objective in exchange relations cannot conceal the fact that Horkheimer and Adorno do not like Lukács (and Sohn Rethel)—derive the form of thought from the commodity form. Identifying thought, whose force Adorno sees at work rather in first philosophy than in science, lies deeper historically than the formal rationality of the exchange relation although it does first gain its universal significance through the differentiation of the medium of exchange value.

b) After this, if you will, "idealist" retranslation of the concept of reification into the context of the philosophy of consciousness, Horkheimer and Adorno give such an abstract interpretation of the structures of reified consciousness that it covers not only the theoretical form of identifying thought but even the confrontation of goal-oriented acting subjects with external nature. This confrontation comes under the idea of the self-preservation of the subject; thought is in the service of technical mastery over, and informed adaptation to, an external nature that is objectivated in the behavioral circuit of instrumental action. It is "instrumental reason" that is at the basis of the structures of reified consciousness. In this way, Horkheimer and Adorno anchor the mechanism that produces the reification of consciousness in the anthropological foundations of the history of the species, in the form of existence of a species that has to reproduce itself through labor. With this they take back in part the abstraction they made at first, namely the detachment of thought from the context of reproduction. Instrumental reason is set out in concepts of subject-object relations. The interpersonal relation between subject and subject, which is decisive for the model of exchange, has no constitutive significance for instrumental reason.

c) This abstraction from the dimension of society is rescinded in a last step, but in a curious way. Horkheimer and Adorno do not understand "the mastery of nature" as a metaphor; they reduce the control of external nature, the command over human beings, and the repression of one's own internal nature, to a common denominator, under the name of "domination." Identifying thought, first expanded into instrumental reason, is now further expanded into a logic of domination over things *and* human beings.

Lukács used the concept of reification to describe that peculiar compulsion to assimilate interhuman relations (and subjectivity) to the world of things, which comes about when social actions are no longer coordinated through values, norms, or linguistic understanding, but through the medium of exchange value. Horkheimer and Adorno detach the concept not only from the special historical context of the rise of the capitalist economic system but from the dimension of interhuman relations altogether; and they generalize it temporally (over the entire history of the species) and substantively (the same logic of domination and imputed to both cognition in the service of self-preservation and the repression of instinctual nature). This double generalization of the concept of reification leads to a concept of instrumental reason that shifts the primordial history of subjectivity and the self-formative process of ego identity into an encompassing historico-philosophical perspective.

It is the task of critique to recognize domination as unreconciled nature even within thought itself. But even if thought had mastered the idea of reconciliation, even if it were not in the position of having to let this idea come to it from without, how could it transform mimetic impulses into insights, discursively in its own element, and not merely intuitively, in speechless "mindfulness"? How could it do so if thought is always identifying thought, tied to operations that have no specifiable meaning outside the bounds of instrumental reason—all the more so today when, with the triumphal procession of instrumental reason, the reification of consciousness seems to have become universal?

Unlike Marcuse, Adorno no longer wanted to get out of his aporia—and in this he was more consistent than Horkheimer. "Negative Dialectics" is both an attempt to circumscribe what cannot be said discursively and an admonition to seek refuge nonetheless in Hegel in this situation. It is the "Aesthetic Theory" that first seals the surrender of all cognitive competence to art in which the mimetic capacity gains objective shape. Adorno withdraws the theoretical claim: Negative dialectics and aesthetic theory can now only "helplessly refer to one another."

Adorno had already seen in the early thirties that philosophy had to learn "to renounce the question of totality" and "to get along without the symbolic function in which up to now, at least in idealism, the particular seemed to represent the universal." At that time, referring to Benjamin's concept of the allegorical, he had already methodically appropriated the motif of "awakening the enciphered, the petrified" in a history that had become a second nature, and he had proposed a program of "interpreting what is without intention" through "assembling the most minute and insignificant details," a program that forswore the self-certainty of "autonomous ratio."

Later, as he is attempting to break away from the dialectic of enlightenment, Adorno returns to these tentative attempts to avoid the shadow of identifying thought, with the aim of radicalizing them. Negative dialectics is now to be understood only as an exercise, a drill. In reflecting dialectical thought once more, it exhibits what we can only catch sight of in this way: the aporetic nature of the concept of the nonidentical. It is by no means the case that "aesthetics is one step further removed from the truth content of its objects than negative dialectics, which already has to do with concepts." Rather, because it has to do with concepts, critique can only show why the truth that escapes theory finds a refuge in the most advanced works of modern art—out of which we surely could not coax it without an aesthetic theory.

If one looks back from Adorno's late writings to the intentions that critical theory initially pursued, one can weigh the price that the critique of instrumental reason had to pay for the aporias it consistently owns up to. A philosophy that withdraws behind the lines of discursive thought to the "mindfulness of nature" pays for the wakening powers of its exercises by renouncing the goal of theoretical knowledge, and thus by renouncing that program of "interdisciplinary materialism" in whose name the critical theory of society was once launched in the early thirties. Horkheimer and Adorno had already given up this goal by the beginning of the forties, without, however, acknowledging the practical consequences of relinquishing a connection to the social sciences; otherwise they would not have been in a position to rebuild the Institute for Social Research after the War. Nevertheless, as the foreword to *Dialectic of Enlightenment* clearly explains, they had given up the hope of being able to redeem the promise of early critical theory.

Against this, I want to maintain that the program of early critical theory foundered not on this or that contingent circuit stance, but from the exhaustion of the paradigm of the philosophy of consciousness. I shall argue that a change of paradigm to the theory of communication makes it possible to return to the undertaking that was *interrupted* with the critique of instrumental reason; and this will permit us to take up once again the since-neglected tasks of a critical theory of society.

The societal subject behaves in relation to nature just as the individual subject does in relation to objects: Nature is objectivated and dominated for the sake of reproducing the life of society. The resistance of the law-governed nexus of nature, on which the societal subject toils in knowing and acting, thereby continues on in the formation of society and of its individual members. The relations between subject and object regulated by instrumental reason determine not only the relationship between society and external nature that is expressed historically in the state of productive forces, particularly of scientific-technical progress. The structure of exploiting an objectivated nature that is placed at our disposal repeats itself within society, both in interpersonal relations marked by the suppression of social classes and in intrapsychic relations marked by the repression of our instinctual nature.

But the conceptual apparatus of instrumental reason is set up to make it possible for subjects to exercise control over nature and *not* to tell an objectivated nature what is to be done to it. Instrumental reason is also "subjective" in the sense that it expresses the relations between subject and object from the advantage point of the knowing and acting subject and not from that of the perceived and manipulated object. For this reason, it does *not* provide the explicative tools needed to explain what the instrumentalization of social and intrapsychic relations means from the perspective of the violated and deformed contexts of life. (Lukács wanted to glean this aspect from societal rationalization by means of the concept of reification.) Thus the appeal to social solidarity can merely indicate *that* the instrumentalization of society and its members destroys something; but it cannot say explicitly *wherein* this destruction consists.

The critique of instrumental reason, which remains bound to the conditions of the philosophy of the subject, denounces as a defect something that it cannot explain in its defectiveness because it lacks a conceptual framework sufficiently flexible to capture the integrity of what is destroyed through instrumental reason. To be sure, Horkheimer and Adorno do have a name for it: *mimesis*. And even though they cannot provide a theory of mimesis, the very name calls forth associations—and they are intended: Imitation designates a relation between persons in which the one accommodates to the other, identifies with the other, empathizes with the other. There is an allusion here to a relation in which the surrender of the one to the example of the other does not mean a loss of self but a gain and an enrichment. Because the mimetic capacity escapes the conceptual framework of cognitive-instrumentally determined subject-object relations, it counts as the sheer opposite of reason, an impulse Adorno does not simply deny to the latter any cognitive function. In his aesthetics he attempts to show what the work of art owes to the power of mimesis to unlock, to open up. But the rational core of mimetic achievements can be laid open only if we give up the paradigm of the philosophy of consciousness—namely, a subject that represents objects and toils with them—in favor of the paradigm of linguistic philosophy—namely, that of intersubjective understanding or communication—and puts the cognitive instrumental aspect of reason in its proper place as part of a more encompassing *communicative rationality.*

This change of paradigm lies near at hand in the few passages in which Adorno does decide to provide some explication of the complementary ideas of reconciliation and freedom; but he does not carry it through. At one point he illustrates the idea of reconciliation with a reference to Eichendorff's saying about the "beautiful alien": "The state of reconciliation would not annex" what is unfamiliar or alien with philosophical imperialism; instead, it would find its happiness in the fact that the latter, in the closeness allowed, remains something distant and different something that is beyond being either heterogeneous or proper." Adorno describes reconciliation in terms of an intact intersubjectivity that is only established and maintained in the reciprocity of mutual understanding based on free recognition. George Herbert Mead had already elevated symbolically mediated interaction to the new paradigm of reason and had based reason on the communicative relation between subjects, which is rooted in the mimetic act of role-taking—that is, in ego's making his own the expectations that alter directs to him. I shall be coming back to Mead's basic ideas below.

Adorno cannot elucidate the mimetic capacity by means of an abstract opposition to instrumental reason. The structures of reason to which Adorno merely alludes first become accessible to analysis when the ideas of reconciliation and freedom are deciphered as codes for a form of intersubjectivity, however utopian it may be, that makes possible a mutual and constraint-free understanding among individuals in their dealings with one another, as well as the identity of individuals who come to a compulsion-free understanding with themselves—sociation without repression. This means, on the one hand, a change of paradigm within action theory: from goal-directed to communicative action, and, on the other hand, a change of strategy in an effort to reconstruct the modern concept of rationality that became possible with the decentration of our understanding of the world. The phenomena in need of explication are no longer, in and of themselves, the knowledge and mastery of an objective nature, but the intersubjectivity of possible understanding and agreement—at both the interpersonal and intrapsychic levels. The focus of investigation thereby shifts from cognitive-instrumental rationality to communicative rationality. And what is paradigmatic for the latter is not the relation of a solitary subject to something in the objective world that can be represented and manipulated, but the intersubjective relation that speaking and acting subjects take up when they come to an understanding with one another about something. In doing so, communicative actors move in the medium of a natural language, draw upon culturally transmitted interpretations, and relate simultaneously to something in the one objective world, something in their common social world, and something in each's own subjective world.

In contrast to *representation* or *cognition, coming to an understanding* requires the rider *uncoerced,* because the expression is meant to be used here as a normative concept. From the perspective of the participants, coming to an understanding is not an empirical event that causes de facto agreement; it is a process of mutually convincing one another in which the actions of participants are coordinated on the basis of motivation by reasons. "Coming to an understanding" refers to communication aimed at achieving a valid agreement. It is only for this reason that we may hope to obtain a concept of rationality by clarifying the formal properties of action oriented to reaching understanding—a concept expressing the interconnection of those moments of reason that became separated in the modern period, no matter whether we look for these moments in cultural value spheres, in differentiated forms of argumentation, or in the communicative practice of everyday life, however distorted that may be.

The transition from the philosophy of consciousness to language analysis that was accomplished by formal semantics in the wake of Frege and Wittgenstein is, to be sure, only a first step. This becomes clear precisely in connection with the phenomenon of self-consciousness. Experiential sentences in the first-person singular do provide a methodologically reliable starting point for analyzing the concept of the "I" as the experience of self-knowledge that is accessible only intuitively. Ernst Tugendhat has also shown that the above-mentioned problem with ego-logical theories of consciousness dissolves if we reformulate its initial question in semantic terms. At the same time, however, a language analysis restricted to the semantic point of view loses sight of the full meaning of the relation-to-self that is present the performative use of the expression "I"; for this type of analysis replaces the relation between subject and object or system and environment with *another two-term relation*—that between sentence and state of affairs—and thus remains within the relation-to-self in an epistemic way. Once again the *experiences* that the ego affirms of itself in experimental sentences are represented as *states of affairs* or inner episodes to which it has privileged access, and are thereby assimilated to entities of the world. One only gets hold of that relation-to-self that has traditionally been thematized—and distorted—as self-consciousness if one extends the semantic line of inquiry in a pragmatic direction. Thus it is analysis of the meaning of the performative—and not of the referential—use of the expression "I" within the system of personal pronouns that offers a promising approach to the problematic of self-consciousness.

If we assume that the human species maintains itself through the socially coordinated activities of its members and that this coordination has to be established through communication—and in certain central spheres through communication aimed at reaching agreement—then the reproduction of the species *also* requires satisfying the conditions of a rationality that is inherent in communicative action. These conditions have become perceptible in the modern period with the decentration of our understanding of the world and the differentiation of various universal validity claims. To the extent that religious-metaphysical world-views lose their credibility, the concept of self-preservation changes, but not only in the respect emphasized by Blumenberg. It does, as he argues, lose its teleological alignment with objective ends, so that a self-preservation that has become absolute can move up to the rank of an ultimate end for cognition and success-oriented action. At the same time, to the degree that the normative integration of everyday life is loosened up, the concept of self-preservation takes a direction that is at once universalistic and individualistic. A process of self-preservation that has to satisfy the rationality conditions of communicative action becomes dependent on the integrative accomplishments of subjects who coordinate their action via criticizable validity claims. Thus, what is characteristic of the position of modern consciousness is less the unity of self-preservation and self-consciousness than the relation expressed in bourgeois philosophy of history and society: The social-life context reproduces itself *both* through the media-controlled purposive-rational actions of its members *and* through the common will anchored in the communicative practice of all individuals.

A subjectivity that is characterized by communicative reason resists the denaturing of the self for the sake of self-preservation. Unlike instrumental reason, communicative reason cannot be subsumed without resistance under a blind self-preservation. It refers neither to a subject that preserves itself in relating to objects via representation and action, nor to a self-maintaining system that demarcates itself from an environment, but to a symbolically structured lifeworld that is constituted in the interpretive accomplishments of its members and only reproduced through communication. Thus communicative reason does not simply encounter ready-made subjects and systems; rather, it takes part in structuring what is to be preserved. The utopian perspective of reconciliation and freedom is ingrained in the conditions for the communicative sociation of individuals; it is built into the linguistic mechanism of the reproduction of the species.

On the other hand, societal imperatives of self-preservation establish themselves not only in the teleology of individual members' actions but also in the functional interconnection of the aggregated effects of action. The integration of members of society that takes place via processes of reaching understanding is limited not only by the force of competing interests but also by the weight of systemic imperatives of self-preservation that develop their force objectively in operating through the action orientations of the actors involved. The problem of reification arises less from a purposive rationality that has been absolutized in the service of self-preservation, from an instrumental reason that has gone wild, than from the circumstance that an unleashed functionalist reason of system maintenance disregards and overrides the claim to reason ingrained in communicative sociation and lets the rationalization of the lifeworld run idle.

Jürgen Habermas, "Citizenship and National Identity"

Until the mid-eighties, history seemed to be entering that crystalline state known as *posthistoire*. This was Arnold Gehlen's term for the strange feeling that the more things change, the more they remain the same. *Rien ne va plus*—nothing really surprising can happen anymore. Locked in by systemic constraints, all the possibilities seemed to have been exhausted, all the alternatives frozen, and any remaining options drained of meaning. Since then this mood has completely changed. History is once again on the move, accelerating, even overheating. New problems are shifting the old perspectives. What is more important, new perspectives are opening up for the future, points of view that restore our ability to perceive alternative courses of action.

Three historical movements of our contemporary period, once again in flux, affect the relation between citizenship and national identity: (1) In the wake of German unification, the liberation of the East Central European states from Soviet tutelage, and the nationality conflicts breaking out across Eastern Europe, the question concerning the future of the nation-state has taken on an unexpected topicality. (2) The fact that the states of the European Community are gradually growing together, especially with the caesura that will be created when a common market is introduced in 1993, sheds light on the relation between the nation-state and democracy: the democratic processes constituted at the level of the nation-state lag hopelessly behind the economic integration taking place at a supranational level. (3) The tremendous tide of immigration from the poor regions of the East and South, with which Europe will be increasingly confronted in the coming years, lends the problem of asylum a new significance and urgency. This process exacerbates the conflict between the universalistic principles of constitutional democracy, on the one hand, and the particularistic claims to preserve the integrity of established forms of life, on the other.

These three topics offer an occasion for the conceptual clarification of some normative perspectives from which we can gain a better understanding of the complex relation between citizenship and national identity.

1   The Past and Future of the Nation-State

The events in Germany and the Eastern European states have given a new twist to a long-standing discussion in the Federal Republic about the path to a "postnational society." Many German intellectuals have complained, for example, about the democratic deficits of a unification process that is implemented at the administrative and economic levels without the participation of citizens; they now find themselves accused of "postnational arrogance." This controversy over the form and tempo of political unification is fueled not only by the contrary feelings of the disputing parties but also by conceptual unclarities. One side sees the accession of the five new Länder to the Federal Republic as restoring the unity of a nation-state torn apart four decades ago. From this viewpoint, the nation represents the prepolitical unity of a community with a shared historical destiny (*Schicksalsgemeinschaft*). The other side sees political unification as restoring democracy and the rule of law in a territory where civil rights have been suspended in one form or another since 1933. From this viewpoint, what used to be West Germany was no less a nation of enfranchised citizens than is the new Federal Republic. This republican usage strips the term "nation-state" of precisely those prepolitical and ethnic-cultural connotations that have accompanied the expression in modern Europe. Dissolving the semantic connections between state citizenship and national identity honors the fact that today the classic (form of the nation-state is, with the transition of the European Community to a political union, disintegrating. This is confirmed by a glance back at its genesis in early modernity.

In modern Europe, the premodern form of *empire* that used to unite numerous peoples remained rather unstable, as shown in the cases of the Holy Roman Empire or the Russian and Ottoman empires. A second, federal form of state emerged from the belt of Central European cities. It was above all in Switzerland that a *federation* developed that was strong enough to balance the ethnic tensions within a multicultural association of citizens. But it was only the third form, the centrally administered *territorial state,* that came to have a lasting formative effect on the structure of the

European system of states. It first emerged—as in Portugal, Spain, France, England, and Sweden—from kingdoms. Later, as democratization proceeded along the lines of the French example, it developed into the *nation-state*. This state formation secured the boundary conditions under which the capitalist economic system could develop worldwide. That is, the nation-state provided the infrastructure for an administration disciplined by the rule of law, and it guaranteed a realm of individual and collective action free of state interference. Moreover—and this is what primarily interests us here—it laid the foundation for the ethnic and cultural homogeneity that made it possible, beginning in the late eighteenth century, to forge ahead with the democratization of government, albeit at the cost of excluding and oppressing minorities. Nation-state and democracy are twins born of the French Revolution. From a cultural point of view, they both stand under the shadow of nationalism.

This national consciousness is a specifically modern manifestation of cultural integration. The political consciousness of national membership arises from a dynamic that first took hold of the population after processes of economic and social modernization had torn people from their places in the social hierarchy, simultaneously mobilizing and isolating them as individuals. Nationalism is a form of consciousness that presupposes an appropriation, filtered by historiography and reflection, of cultural traditions. Originating in an educated bourgeois public, it spreads through the channels of modern mass communication. Both elements, its literary mediation and its dissemination through public media, lend to nationalism its artificial features; its somewhat constructed character makes it naturally susceptible to manipulative misuse by political elites.

The history of the term "nation" reflects the historical genesis of the nation-state. For the Romans, *Natio* was the goddess of birth and origin. *Natio* refers, like *gens* and *populus* but unlike *civitas*, to peoples and tribes who were not yet organized in political associations; indeed, the Romans often used it to refer to "savage," "barbaric," or "pagan" peoples. In this classical usage, then, nations are communities of people of the same descent, who are integrated geographically, in the form of settlements or neighborhoods, and culturally by their common language, customs, and traditions, but who are not yet politically integrated through the organizational form of the state. This meaning of "nation" persisted through the Middle Ages and worked its way into the vernacular languages in the fifteenth century. Even Kant still wrote that "those inhabitants...which recognize themselves as being united into a civil whole through common descent, are called a nation (*gens*)." However, in the early-modern period a competing usage arose: the nation is the bearer of sovereignty. The estates represented the "nation" over against the "king." Since the middle of the eighteenth century, these two meanings of "nation"—community of descent and "people of a state"—have intertwined. With the French Revolution, the "nation" became the source of state sovereignty, for example, in the thought of Emmanuel Sieyès. Each nation is now supposed to be granted the right to political self-determination. The intentional democratic community (*Willensgemeinschaft*) takes the place of the ethnic complex.

With the French Revolution, then, the meaning of "nation" was transformed from a prepolitical quantity into a constitutive feature of the political identity of the citizens of a democratic polity. At the end of the nineteenth century, the conditional relation between ascribed national identity and acquired democratic citizenship could even be reversed. Thus the gist of Ernest Renan's famous saying, "the existence of a nation is…a daily plebiscite," was already directed *against* nationalism. After 1871, Renan could rebut Germany's claims to the Alsace by referring to the inhabitants' French nationality only because he thought of the "nation" as a nation of citizens, and not as a community of descent. The nation of citizens finds its identity not in ethnic and cultural commonalities but in the practice of citizens who actively exercise their rights to participation and communication. At this juncture, the republican strand of citizenship completely parts company with the idea of belonging to a prepolitical community integrated on the basis of descent, shared tradition, and common language. Viewed from this end, the initial fusion of national consciousness with republican conviction only functioned as a catalyst.

The nationalism mediated by the works of historians and romantic writers, hence by scholarship and literature, grounded a collective identity that played a *functional* role for the notion of citizenship that originated in the French Revolution. In the melting pot of national consciousness, the ascriptive features of one's origin were transformed into just so many results of a conscious appropriation of tradition. Ascribed nationality gave way to an achieved nationalism, that is, to a conscious product of one's own efforts. This nationalism was able to foster people's identification with a role that demanded a high degree of personal commitment, even to the point of self-sacrifice; in this respect, general conscription was simply the flip side of civil rights. National consciousness and republican conviction in a sense proved themselves in the willingness to fight and die for one's country. This explains the complementary relation that originally obtained between nationalism and republicanism: one became the vehicle for the emergence of the other.

However, this social-psychological connection does not mean that the two are linked at the conceptual level. National independence and collective self-assertion against foreign nations can be understood as a collective form of freedom. This national freedom does not coincide with the genuinely political freedom that citizens enjoy within a country. For this reason, the modern understanding of this republican freedom can, at a later point, cut its umbilical links to the womb of the national consciousness of freedom that originally gave it birth. The nation-state sustained a close connection between "demos" and "ethos" only briefly. Citizenship was never conceptually tied to national identity.

The concept of citizenship developed out of Rousseau's concept of self-determination. "Popular sovereignty" was initially understood as a delimitation or reversal of royal sovereignty and was judged to rest on a contract between a people and its government. Rousseau and Kant, by contrast, did not conceive of popular sovereignty as the transfer of ruling authority from above to below or as its distribution between two contracting parties. For them, popular sovereignty signified rather the transformation of authority into *self-legislation*. A historical pact, the civil contract, is replaced here by the social contract, which functions as an abstract model for the way in which an authority legitimated only through the implementation of democratic self-legislation is *constituted*. Political authority thereby loses its character of quasi-natural violence: the *auctoritas* of the state should be purged of the remaining elements of *violentia*.

According to this idea, "only the united and consenting Will of all—…by which each decides the same for all and all decide the same for each—can legislate."

This idea does not refer to the substantive generality of a popular will that would owe its unity to a prior homogeneity of descent or form of life. The consensus fought for and achieved in an association of free and equal persons ultimately rests only on the unity of a *procedure* to which all consent. This procedure of democratic opinion- and will-formation assumes a differentiated form in constitutions based on the rule of law. In a pluralistic society, the constitution expresses a formal consensus. The citizens want to regulate their living together according to principles that are in the equal interest of each and thus can meet with the justified assent of all. Such an association is structured by relations of mutual recognition in which each person can expect to be respected by all as free and equal. Each and every person should receive a three-fold recognition: they should receive equal protection and equal respect in their integrity as irreplaceable individuals, as members of ethnic or cultural groups, and as citizens, that is, as members of the political community. This idea of a self-determining political community has assumed a variety of concrete legal forms in the different constitutions and political systems of Western Europe and the United States.

In the language of law, though, "*Staatsbürgerschaft,*" "*citoyenneté,*" or "citizenship" referred for a long time only to nationality or membership in a state; only recently has the concept been enlarged to cover the status of citizens defined in terms of civil rights. *Membership in a state* assigns a particular person to a particular nation whose existence is recognized in terms of international law. Regardless of the internal organization of state authority, this definition of membership, together with the territorial demarcation of the country's borders, serves to delimit the state in social terms. In the democratic constitutional state, which understands itself as an association of free and equal persons, state membership depends on the principle of voluntariness. Here, the conventional ascriptive characteristics of domicile and birth (*jus soli* and *jus sanguinis*) by no means justify a person's being irrevocably subjected to that government's sovereign authority. These characteristics function merely as administrative criteria for attributing to citizens an assumed, implicit consent, to which the right to emigrate or to renounce one's citizenship corresponds.

Today, though, the expressions "*Staatsbürgerschaft*" or "citizenship" are used not only to denote organizational membership in a state but also for the status materially defined by civil rights and duties. The Basic Law of the Federal Republic has no explicit parallel to the Swiss notion of active citizenship. However, taking Article 33, section 1, of the Basic Law as its starting point, German legal thought has expanded the package of civil rights and duties, especially the basic rights, to generate an overall status of a similar kind. In the republican view, citizenship has its point of reference in the problem of the legal community's self-organization, whereas its core consists in the rights of political participation and communication. The status of citizen fixes in particular the democratic rights to which the individual can reflexively lay claim in order to *change* his material legal status.

In the philosophy of law, two contrary interpretations of this active citizenship vie with each other for pride of place. The role of the citizen is given an individualist and instrumentalist reading in the liberal tradition of natural law starting with John

Locke, whereas a communitarian and ethical understanding of this role has emerged in the republican tradition of political philosophy going back to Aristotle. In the first case, citizenship is conceived along the lines of an organizational membership that grounds a legal status. In the second case, it is modeled after a self-determining ethnic-cultural community. In the first interpretation, individuals remain outside the state. In exchange for organizational services and benefits, they make specific contributions, such as voting inputs and tax payments, to the reproduction of the state. In the second interpretation, citizens are integrated into the political community like the parts of a whole, in such a way that they can develop their personal and social identity only within the horizon of shared traditions and recognized political institutions. On the liberal reading, citizens do not differ essentially from private persons who bring their prepolitical interests to bear vis-à-vis the state apparatus. On the republican reading, citizenship is actualized solely in the collective practice of self-determination. Charles Taylor describes these two competing concepts of citizen as follows:

One [model] focuses mainly on individual rights and equal treatment, as well as a government performance which takes account of the citizen's preferences. This is what has to be secured. Citizen capacity consists mainly in the power to retrieve these rights and ensure equal treatment, as well as to influence the effective decisionmakers…. [T]hese institutions have an entirely instrumental significance…. [N]o value is put on participation in rule for its own sake….

The other model, by contrast, defines participation in self-rule as of the essence of freedom, as part of what must be secured. This is…an essential component of citizen capacity…. Full participation in self-rule is seen as being able, at least part of the time, to have some part in the forming of a ruling consensus, with which one can identify along with others. To rule and be ruled in turn means that at least some of the time the governors can be "us," and not always "them."

The holistic model of a community that incorporates its citizens in every aspect of their lives is in many respects inadequate for modern politics. Nevertheless, it has an advantage over the organizational model, in which isolated individuals confront a state apparatus to which they are only functionally connected by membership: the holistic model makes it clear that political autonomy is an end in itself that can be realized not by the single individual privately pursuing his own interests but only by all together in an intersubjectively shared practice. The citizen's legal status is constituted by a network of egalitarian relations of mutual recognition. It assumes that each person can adopt the participant perspective of the first-person plural—and not just the perspective of an observer or actor oriented to his own success.

Legally guaranteed relations of recognition do not, however, reproduce themselves of their own accord. Rather, they require the cooperative efforts of a civic practice that no one can be compelled to enter into by legal norms. It is for good reason that modern coercive law does not extend to the motives and basic attitudes of its addressees. A legal duty, say, to make active use of democratic rights has something totalitarian about it. Thus the legally constituted status of citizen depends on the *supportive spirit* of a consonant background of legally noncoercible motives and attitudes of a citizenry oriented toward the common good. The republican model of citizenship reminds us that constitutionally protected institutions of freedom are worth only what a population *accustomed* to political freedom and settled in the "we" perspective of active self-determination makes of them. The legally institutionalized role of citizen must be embedded in the context of a liberal political culture. This is why the communitarians insist that citizens must "patriotically" identify with their form of life. Taylor, too, postulates a shared consciousness that arises from the identification with the consciously accepted traditions of one's own political and cultural community: "The issue is, can our patriotism survive the marginalization of participatory self-rule? As we have seen, a patriotism is a common identification with an historical community founded on certain values.... But it must be one whose core values incorporate freedom."

With this, Taylor seems to contradict my thesis that there is only a historically contingent and not a conceptual connection between republicanism and nationalism. Studied more closely, however, Taylor's remarks boil down to the statement that the universalist principles of constitutional democracy need to be somehow anchored in the political culture of each country. Constitutional principles can neither take shape in social practices nor become the driving force for the dynamic project of creating an association of free and equal persons until they are situated in the historical context of a nation of citizens in such a way that they link up with those citizens' motives and attitudes.

Axel Honneth, "Disrespect and Resistance: The Moral Logic of Social Conflicts," from *The Struggle for Recognition*

At a pretheoretical level, Marx, Sorel, and Sartre—the three representatives of the tradition brought to light above—could always count on the fact that the self-understanding of the social movements of their day was shot through with the semantic potential of a vocabulary of recognition. For Marx, who followed the working class's attempts at organizing from the closest distance, it was beyond doubt that the overarching aspirations of the emerging movement could be brought together under the concept of 'dignity'. Sorel, a theoretical forerunner of French syndicalism, employed the conservative-sounding category of 'honour' to express the moral content of the political demands of the workers' movement. And the Sartre of the fifties encountered in Frantz Fanon's famous book an anti-colonialist manifesto that attempted to explicate the experience of oppressed Black Africa by drawing directly on Hegel's doctrine of recognition. However much the idea of tracing social conflicts to the violation of implicit rules of mutual recognition may have been an essential element of the everyday political observations of these three theorists, this experience was hardly reflected in the conceptual framework of the emerging social sciences: in the contexts in which the category of social struggle plays any constitutive role at all in revealing social reality, it quickly came to be defined, under the influence of Darwinian or utilitarian models, in terms of competition over material opportunities.

Although Emile Durkheim and Ferdinand Tönnies both approached the development of empirical sociology with the intention of critically diagnosing the moral crises of modern societies, neither of them give the phenomenon of social confrontation a systematic role in their basic concepts. However many insights they may have had into the moral preconditions for social integration, they drew few theoretical conclusions from this for the category of social conflict. Max Weber, on the other hand, who sees the process of socialization as virtually geared towards a conflict of social groups, excludes every aspect of moral motivation from his conceptual definition of 'struggle'. According to the famous formulations of his 'Basic Sociological Concepts', an action context involves a social relationship of struggle 'insofar as the action is oriented intentionally to carrying out the actor's own will against the resistance of the other party or parties' in order to increase the actor's power or chance of survival. And Georg Simmel, finally, who devotes a famous chapter of his *Sociology* to the socializing function of conflict, systematically considers a form of social 'sensitivity to difference' (along with 'hostility') as a source of conflict, but he does so little to trace this dimension of personal or collective identity back to inter-subjective preconditions associated with recognition that it is impossible for moral experiences of disrespect to come into view as the occasions for social conflicts. Once again, as in so many respects, the sociological work of the pragmatist 'Chicago School' constitutes a notable exception.

Thus, within academic sociology, the internal connection that often holds between the emergence of social movements and the moral experience of disrespect has, to a large extent, been theoretically severed at the start. The motives for rebellion, protest, and resistance have generally been transformed into categories of 'interest', and these interests are supposed to emerge from the objective inequalities in the distribution of material opportunities without ever being linked, in any way, to the everyday web of moral feelings. Relative to the predominance that the Hobbesian conceptual model acquired within modern social theory, the incomplete, even misguided, proposals of Marx, Sorel, and Sartre have remained mere fragments of an invisible, undeveloped theoretical tradition. Today, anyone who tries to reconnect with this disrupted effective history of Hegel's counter-model, in order to acquire the foundations for a normatively substantive social theory, will have to rely primarily on a concept of social struggle that takes as its starting-point moral feelings of indignation, rather than pre-given interests. In what follows, I want to reconstruct the essential features of an alternative—Hegelian and Meadian—paradigm of this sort, up to the point at which it begins to become apparent that recent trends within historiography can support the asserted connection between moral disrespect and social struggle.

Even just our effort to develop an empirically grounded phenomenology of forms of recognition made clear that none of the three fields of experience can be adequately described without reference to an inherent conflict: the experience of a particular form of recognition was shown to be bound up with the disclosing of new possibilities with regard to identity, which necessarily result in a struggle for the social recognition of those new forms of identity. Of course, the three spheres of recognition do not all contain the type of moral tension that can set social conflicts in motion, for a struggle can only be characterized as 'social' to the extent that its goals can be generalized beyond the horizon of individuals' intentions, to the point where they can become the basis for a collective movement. With regard to the distinctions made above, the initial implication of this is that love, as the most basic form of recognition, does not entail moral experiences that could lead, of their own accord, to the formation of social conflicts. Every love relationship does, to be sure, involve an existential dimension of struggle, insofar as the inter-subjective balance between fusion and ego-demarcation can only be maintained through the overcoming of resistance on both sides. But the goals and desires connected with this cannot be generalized beyond the circle of primary relationships, at least not in a way that would make them matters of public concern. The forms of recognition associated with rights and social esteem, by contrast, do represent a moral context for societal conflict, if only because they rely on socially generalized criteria in order to function. In light of norms of the sort constituted by the principle of moral responsibility or the values of society, personal experiences of disrespect can be interpreted and represented as something that can potentially affect other subjects. Whereas here, in the case of legal relations and communities of value, individual goals are, in principle, open to social universalization, in love relationships they are necessarily enclosed within the narrow boundaries of a primary relationship. This categorial restriction already gives us an initial, rough idea of how a social struggle must be understood within the context of our discussion. We are dealing here with a practical process in which individual experiences of disrespect are read as typical for an entire group, and in such a way that they can motivate collective demands for expanded relations of recognition.

What is striking about this provisional definition, to begin with, is the purely negative fact that it is neutral with regard to the usual distinctions within the sociology of conflict. If one interprets social struggle from the perspective of moral experiences in the manner mentioned, there is no theoretical pre-commitment in favour of either non-violent or violent resistance. Instead, at the level of description, it is left entirely open whether social groups employ material, symbolic, or passive force to publicly articulate and demand restitution for the disrespect and violation that they experience as being typical. The suggested conception is also neutral with respect to the traditional distinction between intentional and unintentional forms of social conflict, since it asserts nothing about the degree to which actors have to be aware of the driving moral motivation of their action. Here, one can easily imagine cases in which social movements intersubjectively misidentify, as it were, the moral core of their resistance by explicating it in the inappropriate terms of mere interest-categories. Finally, the idea that personal and impersonal goals represent exclusive alternatives does not entirely apply to a struggle understood in this way, since the struggle can, in principle, only be determined by those *universal* ideas and appeals in which individual actors see their particular experiences of disrespect eliminated in a positive manner. There must be a semantic bridge between the impersonal aspirations of a social movement and their participants' private experiences of injury, a bridge that is sturdy enough to enable the development of collective identity.

The descriptive openness that thus characterizes the suggested concept of social struggle stands in contrast to the fixed core of its explanatory content. Unlike all utilitarian models of explanation, it suggests the view that motives for social resistance and rebellion are formed in the context of moral experiences stemming from the violation of deeply rooted expectations regarding recognition. These expectations are internally linked to conditions for the formation of personal identity in that they indicate the social patterns of recognition that allow subjects to know themselves to be both autonomous and individuated beings within their socio-cultural environment.

If these normative expectations are disappointed by society, this generates precisely the type of moral experience expressed in cases where subjects feel disrespected. Hurt feelings of this sort can, however, become the motivational basis for collective resistance only if subjects are able to articulate them within an intersubjective framework of interpretation that they can show to be typical for an entire group. In this sense, the emergence of social movements hinges on the existence of a shared semantics that enables personal experiences of disappointment to be interpreted as something affecting not just the individual himself or herself but also a circle of many other subjects. As Mead saw, the need for such semantics is met by the moral doctrines or ideas that are able normatively to enrich our notions of social community. Along with the prospect of broadened recognition relations, these languages open up an interpretive perspective for identifying the social causes of individual injuries. Thus, as soon as ideas of this sort have gained influence within a society, they generate a subcultural horizon of interpretation within which experiences of disrespect that, previously, had been fragmented and had been coped with privately can then become the moral motives for a collective 'struggle for recognition'.

When we try to grasp, in this way, the process by which social struggles emerge, they turn out to involve the experience of recognition in more than just the regard mentioned. The collective resistance stemming from the socially critical interpretation of commonly shared feelings of being disrespected is not solely a practical instrument with which to assert a claim to the future expansion of patterns of recognition. For the victims of disrespect—as has been shown in philosophical discussions, in literature, and in social history—engaging in political action also has the direct function of tearing them out of the crippling situation of passively endured humiliation and helping them, in turn, on their way to a new, positive relation-to-self. The basis for this secondary motivation for struggle is connected to the structure of the experience of disrespect itself. As we have seen, social shame is a moral emotion that expresses the diminished self-respect typically accompanying the passive endurance of humiliation and degradation. If such inhibitions on action are overcome through involvement in collective resistance, individuals uncover a form of expression with which they can indirectly convince themselves of their moral or social worth. For, given the anticipation that a future communication-community will recognize them for their present abilities, they find themselves socially respected as the persons that they cannot, under present circumstances, be recognized for being. In this sense, because engaging in political struggle publicly demonstrates the ability that was hurtfully disrespected, this participation restores a bit of the individual's lost self-respect. This may, of course, be further strengthened by the recognition that the solidarity within the political groups offers by enabling participants to esteem each other.

The foregoing may seem to suggest that all social confrontations and forms of conflict follow the same pattern of a struggle for recognition. On this view, the emergence of every collective act of resistance and rebellion would be traceable to an invariant framework of moral experiences, within which social reality would be interpreted in terms of a historically changing grammar of recognition and disrespect. A thesis of this sort would lead, however, to the fatal consequence of requiring one to dispute, from the outset, the possibility of social struggles that obey a logic of the more-or-less conscious pursuit of collective interests. That this is not the case—that is, that not all forms of resistance have their roots in injury to moral claims—is clearly shown by the many historical cases in which it was purely the securing of economic survival that motivated massive protest and revolt. Interests are basic goal-directed orientations that accompany the economic and social circumstances of individuals, if only because individuals must try to obtain the conditions for their own reproduction. Such interests become collective attitudes to the extent to which various subjects become aware of the commonality of their social situation and, because of this, come to see themselves as confronting similar tasks of reproduction. Feelings of having been disrespected, on the other hand, form the core of moral experiences that are part of the structure of social interaction because human subjects encounter one another with expectations for recognition, expectations on which their psychological integrity turns. Feelings of having been unjustly treated can lead to collective actions to the extent to which they come to be experienced by an entire circle of subjects as typical for their social situation. The models of conflict that start from collective interests are those that trace the development and course of social struggles back to attempts on the part of social groups to obtain or enlarge control over certain opportunities for their reproduction. This same line is also taken by all those approaches that want to broaden the spectrum of these interest-guided struggles by including cultural and symbolic goods within the definition of group-specific opportunities for reproduction. By contrast, the models of conflict that start from collective feelings of having been unjustly treated are those that trace the emergence and the course of social struggles back to moral experiences of social groups who face having legal or social recognition withheld from them. In the first case, we are dealing with the analysis of competition for scarce goods, whereas in the second case, we are dealing with the analysis of a struggle over the intersubjective conditions for personal integrity.

It is important to stress, however, that this second model of conflict, based on a theory of recognition, should not try to replace the first, utilitarian model but only extend it. It will always be an empirical question as to the extent to which a social conflict follows the logic of the pursuit of interests or the logic of the formation of moral reactions.

That notwithstanding, social theory's fixation on the dimension of interests has so thoroughly obscured our view of the societal significance of moral feelings that today recognition-theoretic models of conflict have the duty not only to extend but possibly to correct. The collective interest behind a conflict does not have to be seen as something ultimate or original but may rather have been constituted within a horizon of moral experience that admits of normative claims to recognition and respect. This is the case, for example, wherever the social esteem for a person or group is so obviously correlated to the level of control over certain goods that only the acquisition of those goods can lead to the corresponding recognition. A number of historical studies point in the direction of just such a corrective interpretation of social conflicts by focusing on the everyday moral culture of the lower social classes. The results of these studies can help to lend empirical support to the model of conflict developed here and to defend it against obvious criticisms.

Not least under the influence of utilitarian currents of thought, historical research on political movements was, for a long time, so wedded to the standard model of the collective pursuit of interests that the moral grammar of social struggles had to remain hidden from it. This only changed in a lasting fashion after the methodological intersection of social anthropology and cultural sociology gave rise, two decades ago, to a form of historiography that was able to perceive more broadly and more accurately the normative presuppositions of the way lower social classes engaged in conflict. The advantage of this approach over conventional historiography lies in its heightened attention to the horizon of moral norms of action that are subtly involved in everyday life. Aided by the tools of anthropological field research, it became possible for historical studies to reveal the implicit rules of the normative consensus on which the political reactions of various subcultures depend. The impetus for this sort of reorientation, by which the utilitarian presuppositions of the earlier tradition could be replaced by normative premises, undoubtedly came from the English historian E. P. Thompson. His investigations of the everyday moral conceptions that motivated the English lower classes to resist the introduction of capitalist industrialization prepared the way for an entire line of research. Thompson took his lead from the idea that social rebellion can never be merely a direct expression of experiences of economic hardship and deprivation. Rather, what counts as an unbearable level of economic provision is to be measured in terms of the moral expectations that people consensually bring to the organization of the community. Hence, practical protest and resistance typically arise when a change in the economic situation is experienced as a violation of this tacit but effective consensus. In this sense, the investigation of social struggles presupposes an analysis of the moral consensus that unofficially governs, within a context of social cooperation, the distribution of rights and responsibilities between the dominators and the dominated.

To be sure, this shift of perspective was not yet enough to generate the results that, at a historical level, would support the thesis that social confrontations can in principle be understood in terms of the moral pattern of a struggle for recognition. For that, the further point needed to be demonstrated that every violation of an implicit consensus among those affected is experienced as something that denies them social recognition and, as a result, injures their feelings of self-worth. The first approach to explicating a motivational nexus of this sort has been developed in historical studies that have taken Thompson's approach and extended it along the dimension of individual or collective identity. Once the component of subjects' practical relation-to-self was taken into account, it quickly became apparent that, for participants, the existing consensus in each historical case amounts to a normative order that organizes relationships of mutual recognition. In this field, pioneering work has been done by Barrington Moore, and it is no coincidence that his concept of an 'implicit social contract' connects up with Thompson's idea of a 'moral economy'. His comparative studies of revolutionary uprisings in Germany between 1848 and 1920 concluded that the active and militant subgroups within the working class were primarily those that felt their previously recognized self-understanding to be massively threatened by sociopolitical changes. Moore treats the implicit social contract—that is, the normative consensus among the cooperating groups within a community—as a loosely organized system of rules that determine the conditions for mutual recognition. Hence, as soon as an implicit consensus of this sort is disrupted by politically imposed inno-vations, this leads almost inevitably to social disrespect for the inherited identity of individual subgroups. And, in Moore's view, it is only this jeopardizing of the pos-sibility for collective self-respect that generates broad-based political resistance and social revolts.

Today, Moore's position is strengthened by historical studies that locate the moti-vational impetus for political uprisings in the injury inflicted upon group-specific notions of honour. This research—well exemplified by Andreas Griessinger's study of eighteenth-century journeyman artisans—adds the further component of iden-tity to Thompson's approach by systematically connecting the political disappoint-ment of moral expectations with the overthrow of traditionally conceived relations of recognition.

Studies of this sort provide sufficient experiential detail to serve as initial empiri-cal support for the thesis that social confrontations follow the pattern of a struggle for recognition. A serious disadvantage arises, however, from the fact that the role these works ascribe to the internal logic of recognition relations is too limited to admit of anything but a historical account of particular lifeworlds. Whether they are sponta-neous revolts, organized strikes, or passive forms of resistance, the events depicted always retain something of the character of mere episodes, because their position within the moral development of society does not, as such, become clear. But this gap between individual processes and an overarching developmental process can only be bridged once the logic according to which recognition relationships are expanded itself becomes the referential system for historical accounts.

Posing the task in this way makes it necessary to conceive of the model of con-flict discussed so far no longer solely as an explanatory framework for the emer-gence of social struggles, but also as an interpretive framework for a process of moral formation. Even just the reference back to the logic of the expansion of recognition relationships allows for the systematic classification of what would otherwise remain an uncomprehended occurrence. Every unique, historical struggle or conflict only reveals its position within the development of society once its role in the establish-ment of moral progress, in terms of recognition, has been grasped. In addition, of course, the radical broadening of the perspective from which historical processes are to be observed demands a change in our view of the primary research material. The feeling of being unjustly treated and the experience of being disrespected, both of which are relevant for the explanation of social struggles, no longer appear only as motives for action but also come to be examined with regard to the moral role that must be attributed to each of them in the development [*Entfaltung*] of relations of recognition. As a consequence, moral feelings—until now, the emotional raw mate-rials of social conflicts—lose their apparent innocence and turn out to be retarding or accelerating moments within an overarching developmental process. Of course, this last formulation also makes unmistakably clear the challenges facing a theoreti-cal approach that is supposed to be able to model the struggle for recognition as a historical process of moral progress: in order to be able to distinguish between the progressive and the reactionary, there has to be a normative standard that, in light of a hypothetical anticipation of an approximate end-state, would make it possible to mark out a developmental direction.

Hence, the general framework of interpretation on which we must rely describes the process of moral development through which, in the course of an idealized sequence of struggles, the normative potential of mutual recognition has unfolded. A model of this sort finds its point of departure in the theoretical distinctions learned from Hegel and Mead. Taken together, the three forms of recognition—love, rights, and esteem—constitute the social conditions under which human subjects can develop a positive attitude towards themselves. For it is only due to the cumulative acquisition of basic self-confidence, of self-respect, and of self-esteem—provided, one after another, by the experience of those three forms of recognition—that a person can come to see himself or herself, unconditionally, as both an autonomous and an individuated being and to identify with his or her goals and desires. But even this tripartite division owes its existence to a theoretical projection of differentiations that are found only in modern societies back into a hypothetically supposed original situation. For, as we have seen in our analysis, legal relations are unable to dislodge themselves from a customarily ethical framework of social esteem until they have been subjected to the claims of post-conventional morality. Insofar as this is the case, it is natural to assume, as the original situation of the formative process to be described, a form of social interaction in which these three patterns of recognition are still intertwined in an undifferentiated manner. One thing that may speak in favour of this is the existence of an archaic group morality, in which aspects of care are not fully separated from either the rights of tribal members or their social esteem. Thus, the moral learning process that the envisioned interpretive framework is supposed to model has to accomplish two completely different tasks: it must both differentiate the various patterns of recognition and then, within the spheres of interaction thus established, unleash the inherent potential of each. If we distinguish, in this sense, between the establishment of new levels of recognition and the development of their own internal structures, then it is not difficult to see that only the second process directly provides the occasion for social struggles.

Although the differentiation of patterns of recognition stems from social struggles that involve demands for recognition only in the very broad sense of releasing potentials for subjectivity, the result of this process marks the attainment of a socio-cultural level at which each of these structures, with its own internal logic, can become effective. Once love for persons is separated, at least in principle, from legal recognition and social esteem, three forms of mutual recognition have emerged that are geared towards specific developmental potentials as well as distinct types of struggle. At this point, for the first time, we find normative structures built into legal relations (with the possibilities for universalization and de-formalization [*Materialisierung*] and into communities of value (with the possibilities for individualization and equalization)—normative structures that can become accessible via emotionally laden experiences of disrespect and that can be appealed to in the struggles resulting from these experiences. The breeding-ground for these collective forms of resistance is prepared by sub-cultural semantics in which a shared language is found for feelings of having been unjustly treated, a language that points—however indirectly—to possibilities for expanding relationships of recognition. It is the task of the envisioned interpretive framework to describe the idealized path along which these struggles have been able to unleash the normative potential of modern law and of esteem. This framework lets an objective-intentional context emerge, in which historical processes no longer appear as mere events but rather as stages in a conflictual process of formation, leading to a gradual expansion of relationships of recognition. Accordingly, the significance of each particular struggle is measured in terms of the positive or negative contribution that each has been able to make to the realization of undistorted forms of recognition. To be sure, such a standard cannot be obtained independently of a hypothetical anticipation of a communicative situation in which the intersubjective conditions for personal integrity appear to be fulfilled. Thus, ultimately, Hegel's account of a struggle for recognition can only be brought up to date again (albeit with less ambitious claims) if his conception of ethical life can also—in a modified, desubstantialized form—regain its plausibility.

Nancy Fraser, "Dilemmas of Justice in the Post-Socialist Age: From Redistribution to Recognition?" from *Justice Interruptus*

The Redistribution-Recognition Dilemma

I propose to distinguish two broadly conceived, analytically distinct understandings of injustice. The first is socioeconomic injustice, which is rooted in the political-economic structure of society. Examples include exploitation (having the fruits of one's labor appropriated for the benefit of others); economic marginalization (being confined to undesirable or poorly paid work or being denied access to income-generating labor altogether), and deprivation (being denied an adequate material standard of living).

Egalitarian theorists have long sought to conceptualize the nature of these socioeconomic injustices. Their accounts include Marx's theory of capitalist exploitation, John Rawls's account of justice as fairness in the choice of principles governing the distribution of "primary goods," Amartya Sen's view that justice requires ensuring that people have equal "capabilities to function," and Ronald Dworkin's view that it requires "equality of resources." For my purposes here, however, we need not commit ourselves to any one particular theoretical account. We need only subscribe to a rough and general understanding of socioeconomic injustice informed by a commitment to egalitarianism.

The second understanding of injustice is cultural or symbolic. Here injustice is rooted in social patterns of representation, interpretation, and communication. Examples include cultural domination (being subjected to patterns of interpretation and communication that are associated with another culture and are alien and/or hostile to one's own); nonrecognition (being rendered invisible by means of the authoritative representational, communicative, and interpretative practices of one's culture); and disrespect (being routinely maligned or disparaged in stereotypic public cultural representations and/or in everyday life interactions).

Some political theorists have recently sought to conceptualize the nature of these cultural or symbolic injustices. Charles Taylor, for example, has drawn on Hegelian notions to argue that nonrecognition or misrecognition...can be a form of oppression, imprisoning someone in a false, distorted, reduced mode of being. Beyond simple lack of respect, it can inflict a grievous wound, saddling people with crippling self-hatred. Due recognition is not just a courtesy but a vital human need.

Likewise, Axel Honneth has argued that

we owe our integrity...to the receipt of approval or recognition from other persons. [Negative concepts such as "insult" or "degradation"] are related to forms of disrespect, to the denial of recognition. [They] are used to characterize a form of behavior that does not represent an injustice solely because it constrains the subjects in their freedom for action or does them harm. Rather, such behavior is injurious because it impairs these persons in their positive understanding of self—an understanding acquired by intersubjective means.

Similar conceptions inform the work of many other critical theorists, including Iris Marion Young and Patricia J. Williams, who do not use the term 'recognition.' Once again, however, it is not necessary here to settle on a particular theoretical account. We need only subscribe to a general and rough understanding of cultural injustice, as distinct from socioeconomic injustice.

Despite the differences between them, both socioeconomic injustice and cultural injustice are pervasive in contemporary societies. Both are rooted in processes and practices that systematically disadvantage some groups of people vis-à-vis others. Both, consequently, should be remedied.

Of course, this distinction between economic injustice and cultural injustice is analytical. In practice, the two are intertwined. Even the most material economic institutions have a constitutive, irreducible cultural dimension; they are shot through with significations and norms. Conversely, even the most discursive cultural practices have a constitutive, irreducible political-economic dimension; they are underpinned by material supports. Thus, far from occupying two airtight separate spheres, economic injustice and cultural injustice are usually interimbricated so as to reinforce each other dialectically. Cultural norms that are unfairly biased against some are institutionalized in the state and the economy; meanwhile, economic disadvantage impedes equal participation in the making of culture, in public spheres and in everyday life. The result is often a vicious circle of cultural and economic subordination.

Despite these mutual entwinements, I shall continue to distinguish economic injustice and cultural injustice analytically. And I shall also distinguish two correspondingly distinct kinds of remedy. The remedy for economic injustice is political-economic restructuring of some sort. This might involve redistributing income, reorganizing the division of labor, subjecting investment to democratic decision making, or transforming other basic economic structures. Although these various remedies differ importantly from one another, I shall henceforth refer to the whole group of them by the generic term "redistribution." The remedy for cultural injustice, in contrast, is some sort of cultural or symbolic change. This could involve upwardly revaluing disrespected identities and the cultural products of maligned groups. It could also involve recognizing and positively valorizing cultural diversity. More radically still, it could involve the wholesale transformation of societal patterns of representation, interpretation, and communication in ways that would change *everybody's* sense of self. Although these remedies differ importantly from one another, I shall henceforth refer to the whole group of them by the generic term "recognition."

Once again, this distinction between redistributive remedies and recognition remedies is analytical. Redistributive remedies generally presuppose an underlying conception of recognition. For example, some proponents of egalitarian socioeconomic redistribution ground their claims on the "equal moral worth of persons"; thus, they treat economic redistribution as an expression of recognition." Conversely, recognition remedies sometimes presuppose an underlying conception of redistribution. For example, some proponents of multicultural recognition ground their claims on the imperative of a just distribution of the "primary good" of an "intact cultural structure"; they therefore treat cultural recognition as a species of redistribution. Such conceptual entwinements notwithstanding, however, I shall leave to one side questions such as, do redistribution and recognition constitute two distinct, irreducible, *sui generis* concepts of justice, or alternatively, can either one of them be reduced to the other? Rather, I shall assume that however we account for it metatheoretically, it will be useful to maintain a working, first-order distinction between socioeconomic injustices and their remedies, on the one hand, and cultural injustices and their remedies, on the other.

With these distinctions in place, I can now pose the following questions: What is the relation between claims for recognition, aimed at remedying cultural injustice, and claims for redistribution, aimed at redressing economic injustice? And what sorts of mutual interferences can arise when both kinds of claims are made simultaneously?

There are good reasons to worry about such mutual interferences. Recognition claims often take the form of calling attention to, if not performatively creating, the putative specificity of some group and then of affirming its value. Thus, they tend to promote group differentiation. Redistribution claims, in contrast, often call for abolishing economic arrangements that underpin group specificity. (An example would be feminist demands to abolish the gender division of labor.) Thus, they tend to promote group differentiation. The upshot is that the politics of recognition and the politics of redistribution often appear to have mutually contradictory aims. Whereas the first tends to promote group differentiation, the second tends to undermine it. Thus, the two kinds of claim stand in tension with each other; they can interfere with, or even work against, each other.

Here, then, is a difficult dilemma. I shall henceforth call it the redistribution-recognition dilemma. People who are subject to both cultural injustice and economic injustice need both recognition and redistribution. They need both to claim and to deny their specificity. How, if at all, is this possible? Before taking up this question, let us consider precisely who faces the recognition-redistribution dilemma.

Exploited Classes, Despised Sexualities, and Bivalent Collectivities

Imagine a conceptual spectrum of different kinds of social collectivities. At one extreme are modes of collectivity that fit the redistribution model of justice. At the other extreme are modes of collectivity that fit the recognition model. In between are cases that prove difficult because they fit both models of justice simultaneously.

Consider, first, the redistribution end of the spectrum. At this end let us posit an ideal-typical mode of collectivity whose existence is rooted wholly in the political economy. It will be differentiated as a collectivity, in other words, by virtue of the economic structure, as opposed to the cultural order, of society. Thus, any structural injustices its members suffer will be traceable ultimately to the political economy. The root of the injustice, as well as its core, will be socioeconomic maldistribution, and any attendant cultural injustices will derive ultimately from that economic root. At bottom, therefore, the remedy required to redress the injustice will be political-economic redistribution, as opposed to cultural recognition.

In the real world, to be sure, political economy and culture are mutually intertwined, as are injustices of distribution and recognition. Thus, we may question whether there exist any pure collectivities of this sort. For heuristic purposes, however, it is useful to examine their properties. To do so, let us consider a familiar example that can be interpreted as approximating the ideal type: the Marxian conception of the exploited class, understood in an orthodox way. And let us bracket the question of whether this view of class fits the actual historical collectivities that have struggled for justice in the real world in the name of the working class.

In the conception assumed here, class is a mode of social differentiation that is rooted in the political-economic structure of society. A class exists as a collectivity only by virtue of its position in that structure and of its relation to other classes. Thus, the Marxian working class is the body of persons in a capitalist society who must sell their labor power under arrangements that authorize the capitalist class to appropriate surplus productivity for its private benefit. The injustice of these arrangements, moreover, is quintessentially a matter of distribution. In the capitalist scheme of social reproduction, the proletariat receives an unjustly large share of the burdens and an unjustly small share of the rewards. To be sure, its members also suffer serious cultural injustices, the "hidden (and not so hidden) injuries of class." But far from being rooted directly in an autonomously unjust cultural structure, these derive from the political economy, as ideologies of class inferiority proliferate to justify exploitation. The remedy for the injustice, consequently, is redistribution, not recognition. Overcoming class exploitation requires restructuring the political economy so as to alter the class distribution of social burdens and social benefits. In the Marxian conception, such restructuring takes the radical form of abolishing the class structure as such. The task of the proletariat, therefore, is not simply to cut itself a better deal but "to abolish itself as a class." The last thing it needs is recognition of its difference. On the contrary, the only way to remedy the injustice is to put the proletariat out of business as a group.

Now consider the other end of the conceptual spectrum. At this end we may posit an ideal-typical mode of collectivity that fits the recognition model of justice. A collectivity of this type is rooted wholly in culture, as opposed to in political economy. It is differentiated as a collectivity by virtue of the reigning social patterns of interpretation and evaluation, not by virtue of the division of labor. Thus, any structural injustices its members suffer will be traceable ultimately to the cultural-valuational structure. The root of the injustice, as well as its core, will be cultural misrecognition, while any attendant economic injustices will derive ultimately from that cultural root.

At bottom, therefore, the remedy required to redress the injustice will be cultural recognition, as opposed to political-economic redistribution.

Once again, we may question whether there exist any pure collectivities of this sort, but it is useful to examine their properties for heuristic purposes. An example that can be interpreted as approximating the ideal type is the conception of a despised sexuality, understood in a specific way. Let us consider this conception, while leaving aside the question of whether this view of sexuality fits the actual historical homosexual collectivities that are struggling for justice in the real world.

Sexuality in this conception is a mode of social differentiation whose roots do not lie in the political economy because homosexuals are distributed throughout the entire class structure of capitalist society, occupy no distinctive position in the division of labor, and do not constitute an exploited class. Rather, their mode of collectivity is that of a despised sexuality, rooted in the cultural-valuational structure of society. From this perspective, the injustice they suffer is quintessentially a matter of recognition. Gays and lesbians suffer from heterosexism: the authoritative construction of norms that privilege heterosexuality. Along with this goes homophobia: the cultural devaluation of homosexuality. Their sexuality thus disparaged, homosexuals are subject to shaming, harassment, discrimination, and violence, while being denied legal rights and equal protections—all fundamentally denials of recognition. To be sure, gays and lesbians also suffer serious economic injustices; they can be summarily dismissed from paid work and are denied family-based social-welfare benefits. But far from being rooted directly in the economic structure, these derive instead from an unjust cultural-valuational structure. The remedy for the injustice, consequently, is recognition, not redistribution. Overcoming homophobia and heterosexism requires changing the cultural valuations (as well as their legal and practical expressions) that privilege heterosexuality, deny equal respect to gays and lesbians, and refuse to recognize homosexuality as a legitimate way of being sexual. It is to revalue a despised sexuality, to accord positive recognition to gay and lesbian sexual specificity.

Matters are thus fairly straightforward at the two extremes of our conceptual spectrum. When we deal with collectivities that approach the ideal type of the exploited working class, we face distributive injustices requiring redistributive remedies. When we deal with collectivities that approach the ideal type of the despised sexuality, in contrast, we face injustices of misrecognition requiring remedies of recognition. In the first case, the logic of the remedy is to put the group out of business as a group. In the second case, on the contrary, it is to valorize the group's "groupness" by recognizing its specificity.

Matters become murkier, however, once we move away from these extremes. When we consider collectivities located in the middle of the conceptual spectrum, we encounter hybrid modes that combine features of the exploited class with features of the despised sexuality. These collectivities are "bivalent." They are differentiated as collectivities by virtue *of both* the political-economic structure *and* the cultural-valuational structure of society. When oppressed or subordinated, therefore, they suffer injustices that are traceable to both political economy and culture simultaneously. Bivalent collectivities, in sum, may suffer both socioeconomic maldistribution and cultural misrecognition in forms where neither of these injustices is an indirect effect of the other, but where both are primary and co-original. In that case, neither redistributive remedies alone nor recognition remedies alone will suffice. Bivalent collectivities need both.

Both gender and "race" are paradigmatic bivalent collectivities. Although each has peculiarities not shared by the other, both encompass political-economic dimensions and cultural-valuational dimensions. Gender and "race," therefore, implicate both redistribution and recognition.

Gender, for example, has political-economic dimensions because it is a basic structuring principle of the political economy. On the one hand, gender structures the fundamental division between paid "productive" labor and unpaid "reproductive" and domestic labor, assigning women primary responsibility for the latter. On the other hand, gender also structures the division within paid labor between higher-paid, male-dominated, manufacturing and professional occupations and lower-paid, female-dominated "pink-collar" and domestic service occupations. The resul'. is a political-economic structure that generates gender-specific modes of exploitation, marginalization, and deprivation. This structure constitutes gender as a political-economic differentiation endowed with certain classlike characteristics. When viewed under this aspect, gender injustice appears as a species of distributive injustice that cries out for redistributive redress. Much like class, gender justice requires transforming the political economy so as to eliminate its gender structuring. Eliminating gender-specific exploitation, marginalization, and deprivation requires abolishing the gender division of labor—both the gendered division between paid and unpaid labor and the gender division within paid labor. The logic of the remedy is akin to the logic with respect to class: it is to put gender out of business as such. If gender were nothing but a political-economic differentiation, in sum, justice would require its abolition.

That, however, is only half the story. In fact, gender is not only a political-economic differentiation but a cultural-valuational differentiation as well. As such, it also encompasses elements that are more like sexuality than class and that bring it squarely within the problematic of recognition. Certainly, a major feature of gender injustice is androcentrism: the authoritative construction of norms that privilege traits associated with masculinity. Along with this goes cultural sexism: the pervasive devaluation and disparagement of things coded as "feminine," paradigmatically—but not only—women. This devaluation is expressed in a range of harms suffered by women, including sexual assault, sexual exploitation, and pervasive domestic violence; trivializing, objectifying, and demeaning stereotypical depictions in the media; harassment and disparagement in all spheres of everyday life; subjection to androcentric norms in relation to which women appear lesser or deviant and that work to disadvantage them, even in the absence of any intention to discriminate; attitudinal discrimination; exclusion or marginalization in public spheres and deliberative bodies; and denial of full legal rights and equal protections. These harms are injustices of recognition. They are relatively independent of political economy and are not merely "super-structural." Thus, they cannot be remedied by political-economic redistribution alone but require additional independent remedies of recognition. Overcoming androcentrism and sexism requires changing the cultural valuations (as well as their legal and practical expressions) that privilege masculinity and deny equal respect to women. It requires decentering androcentric norms and revaluing a despised gender. The logic of the remedy is akin to the logic with respect to sexuality: it is to accord positive recognition to a devalued group specificity.

Gender, in sum, is a bivalent mode of collectivity. It contains a political-economic face that brings it within the ambit of redistribution. Yet it also contains a cultural-valuational face that brings it simultaneously, within the ambit of recognition. Of course, the two faces are not neatly separated from each other. Rather, they intertwine to reinforce each other dialectically because sexist and androcentric cultural norms are institutionalized in the state and the economy, and women's economic disadvantage restricts women's "voice," impeding equal participation in the making of culture, in public spheres and in everyday life. The result is a vicious circle of cultural and economic subordination. Redressing gender injustice, therefore, requires changing both political economy and culture.

But the bivalent character of gender is the source of a dilemma. Insofar as women suffer at least two analytically distinct kinds of injustice, they necessarily require at least two analytically distinct kinds of remedy: both redistribution and recognition. The two remedies pull in opposite directions, however, and are not easily pursued simultaneously. Whereas the logic of redistribution is to put gender out of business as such, the logic of recognition is to valorize gender specificity.

7

Critical IR Theory
Dialogic Communities, Ethics, and Normativity

Introduction

This chapter features the seminal works of critical international theory. Here, I have selected four works that stress the normative dimension of IR theory, or the constitutive role of ethics and dialogue in international relations theory. As such, Mark Hoffman's essay, "Critical Theory and the Inter-paradigm Debate" (1987), represents one of the first attempts to situate critical theory in IR. His argument is that critical theory, while remaining limited in some respects, represents an emerging paradigm of IR theory. Following Hoffman, Andrew Linklater, in his essay "The Question of the Next Stage in International Relations Theory" (1992), would claim that the emancipatory project needed to be "positioned" within IR theory, or structured in terms of the immanent modes of exclusion and inclusion in international relations. Here, Linklater formulates three modes of critical IR theory: normative, praxeological, and sociological. The normative and sociological domains, for instance, refer to the individual's, state's, and group's shared moral commitments to international justice and freedom, and to the historical and social structures of the international system, respectively; while the praxeological domain refers to human governance and how actions of individuals are being directed toward the cosmopolitan ideals of justice, freedom, and equality. Central to these three modes is the idea that open-ended dialogue between and among citizens validates the opportunities for reasoned consensus at the global level. From this standpoint, Habermas's discursive ethics enables Linklater to demonstrate how the communicative struggles for global forms of citizenship and rights reflect our changing self-ethical understandings of society, or the expanding social and global contexts of justice.

In *The Restructuring of International Relations Theory* (1995), Mark Neufeld argues that formulating a critical IR theory requires a self-reflexive normative theory to move beyond positivism and postmodern relativism. As he points out "to see the third debate as marking a conclusive break with positivist legacy, an opening to theoretical reflexivity, would be a mistake." In this way, normative IR theory constitutes an immanent theory of social justice and universal morality.

Still, it is important not to overstress the commensurability between normative-ethical and structuralist-based critical theories of international relations. Not all of our moral and ethical commitments, in other words, can be reduced to the structural/material forces of society, such as social inequality. In his essay "The Role of Normative in IR Theory," Mervyn Frost, for instance, argues that our moral obligation to uphold human rights turns on the multiple ways of interpreting the importance of human rights. As he suggests, the complexity of our normative obligations and moral commitments requires us to analyze the context-specific meaning of these obligations.

Endnotes

1. See also Michael Banks, "The Inter-Paradigm Debate," in Margot Light and A.J.R. Groom (eds.) *International Relations: A Handbook of Current Theory* (London: Frances Pinter, 1985), pp. 7–26.
2. Mark Neufeld, *The Restructuring of International Relations Theory* (Cambridge: Cambridge University Press, 1995).

Mark Hoffman, "Critical Theory and the Inter-Paradigm Debate"[*]

Introduction

International Relations as an academic discipline is at a major crossroads. Since it was first constituted as an academic discipline in the immediate aftermath of the First World War, International Relations has moved through a series of 'debates' with the result that in the course of its development, and as a consequence of these debates, International Relations theory has been undergoing constant change and modification. After moving through the debate between Idealism and Realism in the inter-war period, between Realism and Behaviouralism in the Great Debate of the 1960s, through to the complementary impact of Kuhn's development of the idea of 'paradigms' and the post-behavioural revolution of the early 1970s and on to the rise of International Political Economy and neo-Marxist, structuralist dependency theory in the late 1970s and early 1980s, International Relations has arrived at a point that Banks has termed the 'inter-paradigm debate'. The effect of this evolutionary process is contradictory. On the one hand, it makes the discipline exciting and alive because of the diversity of approaches, issues and questions within it, creating opportunities for research which would previously have been deemed to be outside the boundaries of the discipline. On the other hand, the lack of an agreed core to the subject has led to confusion and a degree of intellectual insecurity. The problem the discipline faces is that, unlike the 1950s and 1960s when Realism reigned supreme, there is no longer any clear sense of what the discipline is about, what its core concepts are, what its methodology should be, what central issues and questions it should be addressing. In many ways, it is now easier to say what International Relations is not than what it is.

It is important to highlight two important aspects of the breakdown of the Realist consensus that has dominated International Relations. The first is that it has undermined the legitimacy of claims that International Relations is a discrete area of action and discourse, separate from social and political theory. The second is a similarity to the pattern of development which Bernstein pointed to in *The Restructuring of Social and Political Theory*. Bernstein characterised this restructuring as a 'dialectical movement' of thought from the positivistic, empirically-based social sciences which sought to develop knowledge in a fashion analogous to the natural sciences, through the tradition of phenomenology and hermeneutics and the recognition of the necessity to seek an interpretative understanding of the inter-subjective values which underlie and constitute the social world. The problem with Positivism and Empiricism is that they have the capacity to describe but not to understand or explain. The problem with interpretative social sciences is that they have the capacity to understand but not to critique the boundaries of understanding. It is this dialectical movement which gives rise to the need for critical theory to shift the bases of both empirical and interpretative knowledge. Critical theory, through the process of self-understanding

---

[*] *Millenium: Journal of International Studies.* This article first appeared in *Millenium*, Vol. 16, No. 2, 1987, and is reproduced with the permission of the publisher.

and self-reflection, is able to provide a critique of the existing social order and point to its immanent capacity for change and for the realisation of human potential. The movement that Bernstein describes as taking place in social and political theory has developed to the point that it is now possible to talk about the beginnings of a critical theory of international relations, both in terms of individuals working in and developing this area and in terms of a body of literature.

The development of critical theory within International Relations has had two sources—one internal, the other external—and revolves around a central core of authors, notably Robert Cox, John Maclean. Richard Ashley, Kubálková and Cruikshank, Sylviu Brucan, Ekhart Krippendorf, and Andrew Linklater. Internally, the development of critical theory was driven by a reaction to the rearticulation of Realism in Kenneth Waltz's *Theory of International Politics*, with Ashley being the best example. Externally, there was the development of critical theory perspectives independent of the theoretical developments within International Relations that was then used to critique Neorealism from a 'point already arrived at', with Cox being the best example. Both drew from the development of critical theory and saw this as providing the basis for an attack on the epistemological foundations of the discipline.

Perhaps the most important effort in this direction was the article published by Robert Cox in this Journal six years ago and recently reprinted in Robert Keohane's edited volume on Neorealism. In it, Cox argues that International Relations is premised on a set of categories derived from an understanding of the world in which states are the 'principle aggregation of political power' and where there is a clear separation between the state and civil society, with foreign policy as the 'pure expression of state interests'. Cox argues that this separation is no longer tenable: state and civil society are intrinsically related. The degree of interpenetration is such that International Relations must now account for the 'plurality of forms of state expressing different configurations of state/society complexes' as well as a broader understanding of domestic 'social forces' and their relationship to the development of state structures and world orders.

Cox draws implicitly on the links between interests and knowledge that are central to the Frankfurt School. As Cox puts it, theory is always for someone and for something. Theory always serves some purpose and never exists in a vacuum. It is inevitably the product of a certain historical period and circumstances, a reflection of a certain point in time, of a particular social and political order. But in addition to this, theory must reflect on the nature and circumstances of its origins and be able to identify and be aware of its limitations. It must also be aware of the possibilities within it for the transformation of a particular order. Theory must not only describe, explain and understand, but must also be capable of recognising and eliminating the distortions within it which serve to reproduce and reinforce a particular order as universalised and ahistorical. Therefore, in addition to theory being for someone and something, theory must also be able to give an account of itself.

Cox also discusses the nature of theory, which has important similarities with the work of the Frankfurt School. He distinguishes between theoretical perspectives on the basis of the purpose of theory: it can either be a guide solving problems *within* the terms of a particular perspective, or it can reflect on the process of theorising itself, which raises the possibility of choosing a different perspective—in which case the problematic becomes one of creating an alternative world order. The former perspective gives rise to problem-solving theory, the latter to critical theory. What is interesting is that Cox collapses Habermas's distinction between technical and practical interests into the idea of problem-solving and reverts back to Horkheimer's basic dichotomy between traditional theory and critical theory. It is also important to note that while Cox does draw on the ideas of the Frankfurt School, he also makes use of the writings of Vico and particularly of Gramsci. Indeed, his ideas may owe more to the latter two than to the former.

It can be seen that the development of a critical theory of international relations has drawn substantially from the development of critical theory within social and political theory, as outlined by Bernstein, as we as from other sources. It offers a perspective that entails an historical component, a normative component, a self-reflective critical component and that is related to the real world as a practical guide for action. The question arises, however, of how it relates to what has preceded it in International Relations theory. How does critical theory relate to Banks's three paradigms? Does either Realism, Pluralism or Structuralism measure up to the standards set out by Cox for a critical theory of international relations?

Critical Theory and Realism

Within the realist paradigm it is possible to identify a number of distinct and divergent strands. Although they share a set of basic assumptions, they are also characterised by a number of important distinctions in terms of the theory they put forward, the concepts they use and the factors they emphasise. Ashley makes use of Habermas's three cognitive knowledge interests to highlight some of these differences.

Technical cognitive interests manifest themselves in what Ashley terms 'technical realism' which he identifies with structural Realism and Neorealism. The prime exemplar of this approach is Waltz's *Theory of International Politics*. This form of realism is epistemologically based upon Empiricism and Positivism. Waltz argues that there is a remarkable similarity in the political behaviour of states. He takes this to indicate an international system in which there is a structure of constraints and conditions to which no state is immune. The structure of the system is such that it has the capacity to frustrate virtually all anti-systemic forces. This results in a uniformity in the nature of state behaviour. The diversity of state forms is of no consequence for Waltz's theory: a state is a state is a state. The only thing that distinguishes one state from another is its military and political power. The important aspect of international relations thus becomes the distribution of power within the system at any one time. Waltz's theory can therefore account for change *within* the system but not a change *of* the system. But Waltz would argue that the latter is a near impossibility in any case. The anarchic nature of the state system, and the fact that states are reliant on themselves for their security, means that a self-help system constantly reproduces itself. As a consequence the best we can hope for is an understanding of the structure which will provide the basis for the development of rational policies in the pursuit of stable balances of power.

To be fair to Waltz, he does not accept the possibility of a critical theory of international relations. Waltz could argue that a fundamental premise of critical theory is that the social, economic and political structure it is dealing with has to have the potential for change within it. But Waltz's argument is that when we come to the realm of the inter-state system, such a potential does not exist precisely because of the nature of the system. In 'A Response to My Critics', Waltz accepts that he has engaged in problem-solving theory (on Cox's criteria) but more or less says that, given the nature of the state system, nothing else can be done.

Practical cognitive interests manifest themselves in what Ashley terms 'practical realism'. Ashley identifies this form of realism with the work of Morgenthau. This is accurate to a point, but it is also possible to read Morgenthau in a manner which would place him in the realm of technical Realism. An example of practical realism that more clearly exemplifies this category is the 'English School' and in particular Hedley Bull's *Anarchical Society*. For the English School, the central starting point is the uniqueness of the system of states in displaying both order and elemental society in the absence of an overarching sovereign. It seeks to describe, explain and understand the nature of the consensus that provides the basis for stability and order in international society. Through the ideas of a 'diplomatic culture' and an 'international political culture' it outlines the norms, rules, values and language of discourse and action that are essential to the cohesion of the society of state and the maintenance of order within it. International order is not premised on a distribution of power, as it is for Waltz, but on the strength of the diplomatic and international political cultures. The reproduction of this order depends on the willing consent of the member-states and adherence to its basic norms regarding diplomacy, sovereignty and international law. Through an historical understanding of the nature of these norms, the approach provides the basis not only for their preservation but also their expansion: it provides an understanding of the society of states' origins, development, evolution and potential transformation (though Bull sees the possibilities of devolving into an international system as more likely than its evolution to a higher plane). Practical realism is an advance on technical realism in its incorporation of both an historical and normative dimension. However, it fails the test of critical theory by virtue of its failure to understand the ideological component of the approach, particularly the content of the norms, rules and values that underpin the society of states.

This problem is compounded by its relationship to technical realism. Technical realism constrains the potential for transformation within practical realism by identifying what Ashley terms the 'true tradition'. This defines what is worthy of interpretation and understanding by practical realism, but it cannot call into question the nature of realism itself. Thus, realism, defined in terms of this relationship between technical and practical realism, takes the world as given; it reifies a world order and as a consequence can only engage in problem-solving. It performs an ideological function in legitimising an order in which only certain interests are realised—the technical and practical interests of states and the state system. This leaves it void of emancipatory interests, of the humanist element that is central to critical theory.

The most notable effort at developing a critical realist theory of international relations is that of Ashley. Ashley's 'Dialectical Competence Model' argues for the need to preserve classical Realism's rich insights into international political practice, while at the same time exposing the conditions and limits on the potential for change in this tradition. The difficulty with Ashley's alternative model, as Waltz argues, is that it does not look very different from Waltz's approach, except that it is wrapped up in a capital-ist world economy blanket. Ashley, like Waltz, starts by asserting a structurally deter-mined system in which his balance of power regime produces sovereign states. It is not clear, however, how this structural dominance is to be overcome. Ashley seems to be pointing to the dynamics of the capitalist world economy, but, as Waltz asks, does this change lead away from the balance of power regime. If not, then Ashley has substituted one form of a structural system that is immune to anti-systemic forces for Waltz's, and the differences between the two become of little consequence in terms of their overall effect. Thus, while it is possible to point to a dialectical component in Ashley's model, it is open to question whether there is a critical or emancipatory component. Ashley's model is critical only if the criteria for critical theory are narrowed to mean simply a dialectical relationship: that within the existing order there exists the seed of its own destruction. But Ashley's model lacks Cox's criteria of critical theory being able to stand outside itself. It does not offer a different set of ordering principles, nor is there any component of self-realisation or emancipation of human potential. What we are offered is a determining principle, the balance of power, and an argument that the state sys-tem produced by this ordering principle is historically and economically contingent. But what Ashley does not indicate is whether it is this ordering principle that is open to transformation or merely the historically contingent form of social, political and economic organisation that arises from it. If it is only the latter, then we are left with a structural determinism that is in many ways anathema to critical theory.

The difficulty with trying to develop a critical realist theory of international rela-tions is that there is an inherent contradiction in this effort. Critical theory, which has as a central concern the enhancement of the self-realisation of human potential, runs up against the core assumptions, concepts and concerns of political realism. The central elements of Realism necessarily limit the potential for critical theory in that tradition. The limitations are so great as to make it almost impossible to conceive of the nature and content of a critical realist theory of international relations. If a theory of international relations moved in the direction that critical theory suggests, it would have moved so drastically from the core assumptions of political realism that it would be a misnomer to speak of it as a critical realist theory of international relations.

This is not to imply that there is not much of value in Ashley's work. Ashley has done a great deal of work in laying down the foundations for a critical theory of inter-national relations. It is particularly valuable in pointing to the limitations that exist within political Realism and its emphasis on technical cognitive interests. However, what Ashley doesn't seem to recognise is that the nature of his critiques of realism are so devastating as to leave little left to build on. Gilpin, Waltz and Herz all point in this direction in their replies: Gilpin by arguing that Ashley misunderstands the nature of political Realism; Waltz by accepting that he has engaged in problem-solving; Herz by moving away from Ashley's characterisation of his realism as 'emancipatory'. The process of breaking down the cognitive reinforcement of technical and practical Realism means that there will be little left of the central assumption of realism on which to build a critical theory of international relations.

Critical Theory and Pluralism

There has been little contact between critical theory and what Banks describes as the pluralist paradigm. What contact there has been has been for the most part disparaging of pluralist approaches. Cox, for example, lumps pluralist approaches into the category of problem-solving theory. This is odd given that the pluralist approaches developed in reaction to the very reification of an international order founded on realism, which Cox himself critiques. Rather than taking the world as given, pluralism was concerned with describing and developing an alternative conception of world order.

Nevertheless, within the diversity of pluralist approaches it is possible to identify some approaches which correspond to technical cognitive interests and which we may term, after Ashley, 'technical pluralism'. The study of issue-regime politics by Vasquez and Mansbach, of interdependence by Keohane and Nye, and the development of regime theory, are all examples of this form of pluralism. They manifest a technical cognitive interest in that they seek an understanding of these new phenomena in the international system in order to enhance the capability to cope with, control and manipulate them in the pursuit of the national interest. Others, such as transnationalism (and some work on interdependence), are epistemologically tied to technical cognitive interests via empiricism. However, the nature of the links between technical and practical interests also provides the empirical basis for the development of forms of pluralism which seek to go beyond the enhancement of state capabilities. In defining a new set of phenomena, largely related to the action of individuals, it expands the set of social relations which are open to understanding. Two efforts along these lines are worth mentioning: the World Order Models Project (WOMP) and Burton's world society approach.

WOMP starts with a rejection of political realism as the empirical basis for a theory of international relations. It attacks the Hobbesian notion of politics contained in Realism (which, as mentioned above, Habermas attacked as undermining the classical notion of politics) and Realism's historical understanding of an unchanging and transcendent structure of international relations. WOMP's analysis builds upon four central components: the belief that a fundamental transformation is occuring at the global level due to the actions of individuals and changes in technology; that a wide range of problems has been created by these transformations resulting in the internationalisation of social, economic and political issues; that the state is an inappropriate agency for dealing with these problems; and that there is a need to develop alternative future worlds, fundamentally concerned with values relating to the solution of these problems and the development of human beings. The problems it points to are not tied necessarily to the capitalist world economy but point to problems with the system of states itself. WOMP therefore does not point to change and radical restructuring of the system. It details a set of norms which provide the inter-subjective basis for the development of a new global culture and community. Importantly, this new global community will not be arrived at or develop organically but will be necessitated by external factors relating to the four major problems identified by WOMP, requiring a fundamental change in human values. It seeks to illustrate paths to alternative future worlds and to provide a guide to action. What is interesting to note is that WOMP starts with emancipatory cognitive interests and then develops alternative world orders incorporating technical and practical cognitive interests. In relation to Cox's outline of critical theory, WOMP lacks an historical understanding and may fall foul of Cox's point that a critical theory, in addition to having a normative content, must also be able to clarify the range of possible alternatives, and that its utopianism is constrained by an understanding of historical processes which limit the choice of alternative orders to those which are feasible transformations of the existing world.

Burton offers an eclectic approach to International Relations. He starts with a fundamentally different conception of the world, seeing it as a world society—a cobweb of relationships between a diverse range of actors. This approach moves beyond the analysis of relationships between similar units and focuses on relationships that criss-cross and transcend levels of analysis. Burton's world society approach manifests practical and emancipatory cognitive interests. Though there is a large element of description in Burton's approach it is almost completely lacking in technical cognitive interests relating to manipulation and control. Two components of Burton's very rich and varied tapestry are worth focusing on: his approach to conflict resolution and his ideas relating to human needs.

A large element of Burton's work has been concerned with the development of what Burton terms 'problem-solving techniques' for third-party mediation of conflicts. The first thing to note is that it is wrong to equate Burton's use of the term 'problem-solving' with Cox's. Burton's use of the idea of 'puzzle-solving' is more or less the same as Cox's notion of problem-solving theory. What Burton has attempted to do is develop a set of techniques that facilitate the process of understanding and reflection, by parties to a conflict, about the nature of conflict itself, the nature of their particular conflict and the possibilities of developing a shared consensus about the problem which allows for a self-sustaining resolution of the conflict. Though it does spell out a series of techniques for the mediators, these are not techniques for manipulation or control, but ones that provide a means of assisting the processes of self-realisation by the parties to the conflict. The mediators do not impose or even suggest a solution. To do so would run counter to everything Burton has tried to do in developing mediation techniques: it would result in settlement, not resolution; it would be an exercise in power or control. The premises of Burton's approach coincide very closely with Habermas's ideas about self-understanding and self-realisation and conform to the idea that the transformation of a situation has to be immanent. Burton is not seeking outcomes on a grandly utopian scale, but the development of universalised principles that provide a guide to action.

The second major feature of Burton's approach is the centrality he accords to the fulfilment of human needs, which can be seen as a manifestation of emancipatory cognitive interests despite Burton's effort to present them as scientifically and objectively knowable. For example, Burton points to a naturalistic, ontological craving for identity and security within a community or group, but he does not accept the idea of the state as the legitimate or natural embodiment of this need for identification. It is on the basis of the fulfillment of needs such as this that the legitimacy of relationships and institutions is based: the failure to meet human needs on the part of institutions, through the development of a gulf between human needs and institutional needs, is a primary source of conflict that can be avoided. There is, then, a strong affinity with critical theory in Burton's emphasis on human needs, on the notion of legitimacy and on the need for autonomy from the exercise of coercive power.

The component of Cox's critical theory that is lacking from Burton's approach is, as with WOMP, an understanding of historical contexts. This is particularly important in relation to the satisfaction of human needs. The understanding of the deprivation of human needs cannot take place without an analysis and understanding of the historical, social, economic and political contexts that give rise to them. It is also important in recognising that human needs and their content cannot be ahistorically defined or determined. In particular, their content may be historically contingent. Furthermore, since outcomes are a central concern in Burton's approach, it needs to develop an understanding of what types of institutions facilitate the fulfillment of human needs, other than those very broad defined as 'legitimate' institutions. Despite these problems, Burton's world society approach and WOMP may have stronger claims to critical theory credentials than might at first appear likely.

Critical Theory and Structuralism

The approaches that are incorporated within the structuralist paradigm have, in some senses, the closest affinity to critical theory. This is partly because they share common roots as developments of the Marxist tradition in social and political theory, and partly because they have a similar relationship to International Relations in that they developed outside of the discipline and there have only recently been attempts to incorporate them into the subject. Most of the approaches developed as a reaction to positivism and modernisation theories which took an historically contingent understanding of development and attempted to universalise it both in theory and in practice. One of the most widely known of these efforts at developing an alternative explanation of the development problem is the world system analysis approach.

Unlike realism, which posits a pattern of recurrence and repetition and sees the international system as a set of relations among relatively separate entities with the state as the basic unit of analysis, the world systems approach argues that there is a single integrated world system with a logic and structure of its own. The logic of the system is the logic of a world capitalist economy. It argues that the barriers to development are not internal but external, relating to the structural characteristics of the global economy which defines a core, semi-periphery and periphery. There is no real prospect for meaningful change in the status or position of the periphery without a system-wide transformation. Most importantly for International Relations, the state system is seen as the historically contingent political organisation of the capitalist world economy.

Some authors, such as Anderson, take the analysis a step further in combining an analysis of domestic society, state structures and the organisation of societies within an international economic and military order. The effect of such an approach is a complete breakdown of the boundaries between domestic and international politics and the centrality of political economy in the study of the world system.

The strengths of such an approach are its conceptual categories and its method of concrete analysis drawing on the tradition of historical materialism. It provides the potential for a unified theory of domestic and international politics which Waltz argues is the prerequisite for a critical theory of international relations. It provides an understanding of the complex arrangements of various social formations within the world system and an unprecedented level of sophistication in the analysis of the fundamental constraints on the possibilities for transformation of the system. This theoretical and descriptive knowledge of the system of states provides the basis for the development of practical knowledge geared towards change by distinguishing those elements which are central to world order, and those which are historically contingent.

Structuralist approaches, on the whole, tend to coincide with the first four elements of Cox's criteria for critical theory which point to the need to explain our position within historical processes as a basis for system transformation. As such they provide the theoretical and empirical foundation for a critical theory, as well as a mode of analysis. What the structuralist approaches lack is any substantive development of practical cognitive interests, an explicit normative element other than that which it implicitly draws from Marxism and a guide to action. They therefore constitute an important component of a critical theory of international relations but cannot constitute such a theory on their own.

Conclusions

Critical theory represents the next stage in the development of International Relations theory. However, as the preceding discussion has shown, critical theory will need to draw on several diverse components of current International Relations theory. In this sense it has the potential for creating a new focus within the discipline of International Relations that is post-realist and post-Marxist. It provides the basis for the reintegration of International Relations into the broader traditions and concerns of social and political theory, and it allows us to build on the distinctiveness of International Relations as a contribution to the development of critical social theory. This does not mean of course that International Relations as an area of study, or its subfields, are to be discarded. It does mean that they will have to be reformulated and restructured. Paraphrasing Sheldon Wolin, the point of International Relations theory is not simply to alter the way we look at the world, but to alter the world. It must offer more than mere description and an account of current affairs. It must also offer us a significant choice, and a critical analysis of the quality and direction of life.

Mark Neufeld, from *The Restructuring of International Relations Theory*

Defining Theoretical Reflexivity

...theoretical reflexivity can be defined in general terms as 'theoretical reflection on the process of theorizing itself'. It is important to recognize that within the parameters of this general definition, at least three core elements can be identified: (i) self-consciousness about underlying premises; (ii) the recognition of the inherently politico-normative dimension of paradigms and the normal science tradition they sustain; and (iii) the affirmation that reasoned judgments about the merits of contending paradigms are possible in the absence of a neutral observation language. These three elements will be treated in turn. Furthermore, in the effort to show the essential incompatibility of a fully reflexive orientation with positivism, each element will be related to the positivist conception of theory and knowledge.

Being aware of the underlying premises of one's theorizing is the first core element of theoretical reflexivity. That is, theoretical reflexivity is understood to involve attention to, and disclosure of, the too-often unstated presuppositions upon which theoretical edifices are erected.

If reflexivity were limited to this first element, then the positivist forms of theorizing which have dominated the discipline of International Relations would qualify with little difficulty as reflexive forms of theory; positivist notions of theory require that the sum total of generalizations be derived axiomatically from *clearly identified starting assumptions*. It is the presence of the two additional elements, however, which are incompatible with—and indeed, emerged from challenges to—positivist forms of theory that makes reflexivity a virtual antonym of positivism.

The second element of reflexivity is the recognition of the inherently politico-normative content of paradigms and the normal science traditions they generate. To understand the sense in which this element of reflexivity stands in opposition to positivist theorizing, it is important to recall the first tenet of the positivist tradition: that of 'truth as correspondence'.

As will be recalled from our discussion in the last chapter, 'truth as correspondence' is one of three core tenets of positivism. That is, positivism stipulates that theoretical explanations will be true to the extent that they accurately reflect empirical reality; to the extent that they correspond to the facts.

It will also be recalled that this tenet rests upon a particular assumption: that of the separation of subject and object, of observer and observed. In other words, the tenet of 'truth as correspondence' assumes that through the proper application of research design and techniques, the researcher(s) can be 'factored out', leaving behind a description of the world 'as it truly is'. In short, the tenet of 'truth as correspondence' is the expression of the goal of rendering science a 'process without a subject'.

The consequence of this tenet and of this assumption is that a number of problematic issues are swept aside. In making the separation of subject and object a defining condition of science, the positivist approach ignores the active and vital role played by the community of researchers in the production and validation of knowledge. It ignores the fact that the standards which define 'reliable knowledge' are dependent upon their acceptance and application by a research community.

As a result, a number of important questions not only go unanswered—they are never raised. They include questions of the historical origin and nature of the community-based standards which define what counts as reliable knowledge, as well as the question of the merits of those standards in the light of possible alternatives. These questions do not arise in positivist-inspired theorizing because the central standard of scientific truth—that of truth as correspondence—is seen to belong not to a time-bound human community of scientific investigators, but to an extra-historical natural realm. In short, the knowledge-defining standard of positivism is understood to be 'Nature's own'.

In contrast, a theoretically reflexive orientation is one whose starting point stands in radical opposition to that of positivism in that it rejects the notion of objective standards existing independently of human thought and practice. In this, reflexively oriented theorists draw philosophical sustenance from the efforts to develop a post-positivist philosophy of science associated with the work of Kuhn and Feyerabend, as well as the linguistic turn in social and political theory, manifest in the Wittgensteinian analysis of 'language games', neo-pragmatist renditions of Gadamerian 'philosophical hermeneutics', and Foucault's analysis of power-knowledge discourses. As different as these approaches are, all serve to undermine the assumption that it is ever possible to separate subject (the knower) and object (the known) in the manner postulated by positivism. Simply put, if the paradigm (language game/tradition/discourse) tells us not only how to interpret evidence, but determines what will count as valid evidence in the first place, the tenet of 'truth as correspondence' to 'the facts' can no longer be sustained.

Thus it is that the notion of reflexivity directs us beyond merely identifying the underlying assumptions of our theorizing. It directs us to recognize that the very existence of objective standards for assessing competing knowledge claims must be questioned. It moves us to understand that the standards which determine what is to count as reliable knowledge are not nature's, but rather always *human* standards—standards which are not given but made, not imposed by nature but adopted by convention by the members of a specific community.

In so doing, moreover, we are compelled to acknowledge the politico-normative content of scholarly investigation.

In short, 'ideas, words, and language are not mirrors which copy the "real" or "objective" world'—as positivist conceptions of theory and knowledge would have it—but rather tools with which we cope with "our" world'. Consequently, there is a fundamental link between epistemology—the question of what counts as 'reliable knowledge'—and politics: the problems, needs and interests deemed important and legitimate by a given community for which 'reliable knowledge' is being sought.

The inextricably politico-normative aspect of scholarship has an important consequence for the social sciences in terms of the incommensurability thesis (that contending paradigms are not only incompatible but actually have 'no common measure'). In the case of the natural sciences, one may reasonably contest the thesis that contending paradigms are incommensurable, given their shared politico-normative goal of instrumental control of nature. In the case of the social sciences, however, different paradigms have not only different terminologies, but are often constructed in terms of quite different values and oriented to serving quite different political projects. Consequently, the thesis of the radical incommensurability of contending paradigms in a social science such as International Relations is much more difficult to dispute.

We arrive now at the third element of a fully reflexive orientation: the affirmation of the possibility of reasoned judgments in the absence of objective standards. Once again, this element of reflexivity can best be understood in relation to positivism. As was noted above, positivism strives, by means of the separation of subject and object, to derive a 'neutral observation language' which will allow for a point by point comparison of rival paradigms. In this context, it is important to note the possibility of a reasoned assessment of empirical claims. Indeed, it is not going too far to assert that for positivists this assumption is at the core of reason itself.

The faith in the possibility of a neutral observation language and the accompanying conviction that such a language is a necessary condition for reasoned assessment explains much of the distress exhibited by positivists in the face of the assertions about incommensurability. To accept incommensurability is, for positivists, to promote what Popper termed the 'Myth of the Framework' according to which 'we are prisoners caught in the framework of our theories; our expectations; our past experiences; our language', and that as a consequence we cannot communicate with or judge those working in terms of a different paradigm.

In contrast, reflexive theorists accept incommensurability as the necessary consequence of the fact that paradigm-specific knowledge-defining standards are themselves intimately connected to and embedded in competing social and political agendas, the politico-normative contents of which are not amenable to any neutral observation language. At the same time, however, reflexive theorists do not accept that recognizing contending paradigms as incommensurable means reasoned assessments are impossible. Rather, a reflexive orientation sees how both the positivist insistence on 'truth as correspondence' and Popper's notion of the 'Myth of the Framework' are expressions of a common philosophical apprehension. They are both expressions of what Bernstein has termed the 'Cartesian anxiety'—the notion, central to identitarian thinking from Rene Descartes to the present, that should we prove unsuccessful in our search for the Archimedean point of indubitable knowledge which can serve as the foundation for human reason, then rationality must give way to irrationality, and reliable knowledge to madness.

As the driving force of modern philosophy, the Cartesian anxiety—which is reflected in positivism's insistence on the ahistorical, extra-social standard of 'truth as correspondence'—is bound up with the conception of knowledge that Aristotle called *episteme:* apodictic knowledge of the order and nature of the cosmos. Furthermore, the peculiarly modern fear that the undermining of the viability of *episteme* must lead inexorably to irrationality and chaos is the result of the limiting of the modem conception of knowledge and rationality to *episteme.*

It is this limiting of reason, moreover, which has resulted in the marginalization and impoverishment of normative discourse. Given the positivist emphasis on the centrality of a neutral observation language, the treatment of normative issues in mainstream social science has typically taken the form of descriptive accounts of individual value preferences. One might, of course, engage in crude utilitarian calculation to determine the course offering the most in terms of human happiness. Foreclosed, however, is the reasoned adjudication of the inherent value of competing normative claims. Indeed, in the realm of normative discourse the hold of the positivist model of social science has been so powerful that it has made us 'quite incapable of seeing how reason does and can really function in the domain'.

Consequently, the means of exorcising the Cartesian anxiety lies in elucidating a conception of reason which is not limited to *episteme,* and which does not depend on a fixed Archimedean point outside of history or on the existence of a neutral observation language. It is worth noting that just such an effort has been underway in contemporary social and political theory. It is evident in Charles Taylor's privileging of Hegel's 'interpretive or hermeneutical dialectics'—a form of reasoning which, in contrast to the claim of 'strict dialectics' (which makes claims to an undeniable starting point), posits no such foundation and yet still aims to convince us by means of reasoned arguments: by the overall plausibility of the interpretations [it] give[s]'.

It is evident in Hans-Georg Gadamer's linguistically based reappropriation of the Aristotelian notion of *phronesis* which, in contrast to *episteme,* is oriented to the exercise of reasoned judgment not in the context of the timeless and unchanging, but of the variable and contingent. It is evident in Jürgen Habermas' contribution to the theory of 'communicative action', in particular the discursive validation of truth claims. And perhaps most strikingly, given the predominance achieved by the notion of 'paradigm' in contemporary International Relations theory, it is evident in Richard Bernstein's re-evaluation of Kuhn, as someone whose work leads us not to the Myth of the Framework—as was charged by Popper—but rather evidences a movement toward a form of 'practical reason' having great affinity to Gadamer's reconceptualization of *phronesis.* In all of these efforts and more, the emphasis is upon the elucidation of a form of reason which refuses to limit our conception of human rationality to a mechanical application of an eternal, unchanging standard; which affirms that a broader and more subtle conception of reason is possible than that which underlies both the positivist tenet of 'truth as correspondence' and that of radical relativism as the logical consequence of incommensurability; which experiences no self-contradiction when employing a 'language of qualitative worth', and which is thus as suited to a consideration of normative claims as it is to empirical ones.

Expanding the conception of reason beyond positivistic *episteme* is vital to a reflexive orientation. For having reclaimed normative discourse as a domain in which reason can and does function, reflexive theorists argue that what makes paradigms incommensurable—the politico-normative content of the normal science they generate—also makes reasoned assessments of them possible. In short, judgments about contending paradigms are possible by means of reasoned assessments of the politico-normative content of the projects they serve, of the ways of life to which they correspond.

Having established what reflexivity is, perhaps it would be useful, by way of conclusion, to state briefly what it is not. Reflexivity is not a 'research programme' designed to provide cumulative knowledge about the world of empirical facts or about the world of theory. Nor can reflexivity be reduced to the idea that while agreement on facts is possible, value disagreements will continue to plague scholars in their quest for disciplinary consensus. Finally, reflexivity does not provide specific, *a priori* standards or criteria for assessing the merits of contending paradigms. Reflexivity is 'theoretical self-consciousness' involving (i) a recognition of the interrelationship of the conception of 'facts' and 'values' on the one hand, and a community-specific social and political agenda on the other, and (ii) an openness to engaging in reasoned dialogue to assess the merits of contending paradigms.

It may be useful to conclude by reflecting on some of the implications of a fully reflexive orientation for the members of the International Relations scholarly community on a personal, self-definitional level. As was noted, a reflexive orientation leads us to view rival paradigms as incommensurable 'coping vocabularies' linked to contending social agendas and political projects. It should also be noted that recognizing such a link greatly facilitates rationally comparing incommensurable paradigms. Simply put, once the link between 'coping vocabulary' and political project is recognized, the question of 'which paradigm is superior?' can be restated as 'which general social agenda/concrete political project is most appropriate to the global *polis*?'; the question of 'what is reliable knowledge?' can be reformulated as 'how should we live?'.

This recognition is imperative in the discipline of International Relations. Given that paradigms validate themselves in terms of both social actors and specific purposes, the question of social identity and political purpose can no longer be avoided by those who comprise the community of International Relations scholars. For if it is true that at the level of scholarship, '[paradigms] compete by virtue of the accounts they provide in explaining *what we as scholars...define as central to our purpose, enquiry, ideology*', then reflexivity directs us to a broader debate about which 'purposes', which 'enquiries' and which 'ideologies' merit the support and energy of International Relations scholars. If it is true that, to paraphrase Fichte, 'the sort of comprehensive theory one chooses depends on what sort of person one is', then the question of the kind of people International Relations scholars are cannot be avoided.

To adopt a fully reflexive stance is to recognize that participating in the 'normal science' tradition of any paradigm means—consciously or not—lending support to a specific political project; it is to accept that to engage in paradigm-directed puzzle-solving is—intentionally or not—to direct one's energies to the establishment and maintenance of a specific global order. As a consequence, it becomes vital to engage in a critical examination of the relative merits of rival political projects and of contending global orders. For once it is recognized that the knowledge-defining standards that we adopt are not neutral, but have an undeniable politico-normative content, then it becomes imperative that we make a reasoned assessment of that content a central component of our deliberations about international politics.

Of course, the notion that all scholarship has a politico-normative content may well provoke significant resistance in the members of a community who have laboured hard to achieve for the discipline the title of 'science'. Such a notion runs counter to the self-image of impartial, unbiased observer of international reality. Indeed, it may even prompt the charge that reflexivity is but a veiled attempt to 'politicize the discipline'. If it does so, this would indeed be ironic. The point of reflexivity is, after all, that the study of world politics always has been informed by political agendas, and that it is time that the content of those agendas be brought out into the open and critically assessed.

To conclude, it has been argued that the questions central to theoretical reflexivity have begun to make their appearance in contemporary theorizing about international politics, albeit at the margins of the discipline. This appearance, moveover, can be understood as signalling a potentially far-reaching restructuring of International Relations theory, consistent with title emancipation-oriented tradition of critique.

Andrew Linklater, "The Question of the Next Stage in International Relations Theory: A Critical-Theoretical Point of View"*

Following the major advances which have occurred over the past fifteen years, international relations theory has reached a turning point in its development. In the late

* *Millenium: Journal of International Studies.* This article first appeared in *Millenium*, Vol. 21, No. 1, 1992, and is reproduced with the permission of the publisher.

1970s, when traditional realism and rationalism were being developed in a more rigorous and sophisticated way, perspectives such as international political economy began to open up new possibilities in the field. Since then, many of these new approaches have been promoted into the ranks of the established perspectives, but a more profound challenge to orthodoxy has been posed by other approaches, including Marxism, critical theory, post-modernism and now feminism. The exponents of these perspectives have argued for a major restructuring of international relations theory, with the result that a far-reaching discussion is now under way on what the subject is, and ought to be, about. The question of the next stage in international relations theory which may succeed this debate is the theme addressed in this paper.

Many diverse and conflicting accounts of the next stage of the discipline currently exist. One example, alluded to in the title of this paper, is Mark Hoffman's controversial statement that Frankfurt School critical theory points towards the next stage in international relations theory, in which significant progress beyond the inter-paradigm debate can take place. In another approach, Richard Ashley and R.B.J. Walker, writing in a post-modern vein, have argued that the search for the resolution of major theoretical disputes within the field should be abandoned. By forsaking this ambition, they argue, students of international relations can explore the new intellectual possibilities emerging as realist hegemony comes to an end and the disciplinary crisis widens. Reflecting on these and other new accounts, Robert Keohane has observed that, challenging as they are, new theoretical departures will remain marginal in the field unless they develop concrete empirical research programmes which shed light on the central issues of world politics.

Although there is widespread recognition that recent theoretical developments have provided fresh impetus and new direction in the study of international relations, many complex questions about the next stage still have to be answered. The contrasting images of possible future directions just noted suggest quite different answers: one, that international theory modelled on Frankfurt School critical theory can lend cohesion to the field; two, that the next stage in international relations theory should be concerned with the subversion of orthodoxies, the deconstruction of disciplinary boundaries and the admission of previously marginal or dissident concerns; and three, that the danger of epistemological and methodological distraction should be acknowledged and greater effort should be spent on relating the new approaches to more conventional undertakings in the field. Overlapping with the first and last answers is the additional suggestion that the orthodox approaches of realism and strategic studies should, in the post-Cold War era, incorporate emancipatory method and aspirations of critical social theory.

Given these opposing viewpoints it seems safe to assume that the precise contribution of the newer approaches to the study of world politics will be vigorously debated in the years to come. When this debate has run its course, critical social theory, post-modernism and feminism will have left an indelible impression upon the field. It is extremely unlikely that the study of international relations will quickly relapse into the insularity which prevailed before these new directions began to be explored. Yet the future of the new approaches is not the only, or even the most important, aspect of contemporary debates. The larger issue lying behind all the discussions of whether the study of international relations should be governed by traditional themes, current intellectual considerations or by some unforeseen combination of both is the identity of the field as a whole in the years ahead.

This paper addresses these issues from the vantage point of Frankfurt School social theory. The central argument is, in one respect, at odds with Hoffman's claim that critical social theory is the next stage in the development of international relations theory. The lack of significant progress in developing a critical theory of international relations makes Hoffman's claim that critical theory can point the way appear premature. One purpose of this paper is to outline how the critical theory of international relations can be taken beyond the present impasse. As I will argue, questions of inclusion and exclusion are central to international relations, since states and the state system are, in themselves, systems of inclusion and exclusion. These questions have several dimensions: normative, concerning the philosophical justifications for excluding some persons from particular social arrangements while admitting others; sociological, concerning the workings and maintenance of systems of inclusion and exclusion; and praxeological, concerning the impact of systems of inclusion and exclusion on human action. By delving more deeply into these normative, sociological and praxeological dimensions of logics of inclusion and exclusion in world politics we can begin to map out a new way forward for the theory of international relations.

A second objective is to show that developments within critical international theory are significant for the field as a whole. This attempt to reunify international relations under the guidance of critical theory is based on the belief that the current sense of disciplinary crisis and uncertainty about future directions is not, in the long term, beneficial to the field. Recent warnings about the dangers of escaping the grip of one orthodoxy only to fall into the hands of another have to be taken seriously. No claim is made that critical theory is uniquely or lavishly endowed with the resources needed to flag the right course for the field. What is suggested is that critical theory possesses a vision of international relations which, when articulated more fully, can give direction to the field as a whole. While critical theory itself may not be the next stage, it can nevertheless shed light on what the ensuing phase should be. Critical theory can clarify the nature of the common scholarly enterprise to which different perspectives are related by setting out the particular strengths of different approaches and by showing how they can be drawn more closely together.

Inclusion and Exclusion: A Preliminary Inquiry

There is some consensus now that Marxism is no longer the principal expression of critical theory, but there is also much uncertainty about where critical, reflective analysis of society should head from here. Virtually every critique of historical materialism has taken issue with its assumption that production is the pre-eminent force in human development, and virtually every challenge has stressed Marxism's failure to consider various forms of domination which are not reducible to class. Military, national or ethnic, racial and gender domination are a most frequently cited in this regard.

With these problems in mind, Habermas has argued that Marx highlighted the evolution of the social conquest of nature and underestimated the role of independent evolutionary logics in the moral-cultural sphere. According to Habermas, the recon-struction of critical theory therefore requires a far greater understanding of the part that moral learning has played in the development of the human race. Following a Kantian theme, Habermas argued that human societies have evolved by learning how to use universal moral principles to resolve conflicting claims about the organisation of social and political life. Modern challenges to class, ethnic, gender and racial forms of exclusion, challenges which stress the principle of self-determination, illustrate this social evolution.

Various feminist and post-modern writers have taken issue with Habermas's account of moral progress, arguing that there are no grounds for supposing that a commitment to universalism reveals the superiority of the Western concept of the individual, European ethical codes or Western forms of life. Their central contention is that universal moralities have been as exclusionary as the particularistic loyalties and sentiments which they purport to leave behind. Ideas of linear historical prog-ress, for example, have been used to justify Western domination of non-European societies. The critics argue that notions of ethical progress and moral universality are wholly arbitrary, and that no attempt to reconstruct historical materialism, or to salvage critical social theory, can be established on these foundations.

These criticisms of moral universalism do not, however, lead to the conclusion that nothing can be said about questions of exclusion. Foucault, for one, attempted to understand and criticize modes of exclusion without making an appeal to uni-versal moral foundations. It is arguable, moreover, that the ideas which have been advanced by Habermas and Foucault can be incorporated within a single framework. Habermas's aim of bringing patterns of moral and cultural learning within a new critical theory can be strengthened by emulating Foucault's analysis of systems of exclusion.

There are two points to make here. First, to modify Habermas's claims about moral learning in light of Foucault's analysis, the ways in which human beings learn how to include and exclude each other should be central to social research—as central as, say, the way in which human societies interact with the natural environment. Second, the concern to resist various forms of exclusion—a concern which Habermas and Foucault share—privileges moral universals in the end. Some conception of tolerance or autonomy—some desired condition in which all individuals enjoy the same right to participate in open dialogue—features, in both accounts. Building on these points, it is important to understand the ways in which social actors learn how to include and exclude one another, and how they arrive at more rigorous tests of the legitimacy of inclusive and exclusive practices.

The importance of understanding inclusion and exclusion is illustrated by Hedley Bull's approach to the Third World's revolt against the West. In Bull's analysis, when the modern system of states developed, the Europeans denied membership to the non-European peoples on the grounds that they were morally and politically defi-cient. Yet Europeans had to find means of reconciling the lower status of the non-European peoples with the principles of human equality and universality intrinsic to the Christian world-view. Their efforts to overcome this tension resulted in various doctrines such as the Great Chain of Being in the eighteenth century and the specu-lative philosophies of history and evolutionary frameworks of the last two hundred years. None of these has been convincing. In fact, the West's universal morality was turned against it when the non-European states struggled to gain access to the economic and political resources from which they had been excluded. Western states were pressed to break down past structures of exclusion in response to Third World claims for justice. But the revolt against the West went further when non-Western cultures started to shake off the moral assumptions and cultural symbols of the West. The West was invited to create a more just world order, not relying entirely on Western values and not excluding cultural differences. Bull's account of the expansion of international society reveals how the original members of that society devised principles of inclusion and exclusion, and how the new membership sought to transform them. The sensitivity to exclusion in the international system during the last century, and in modern societies in the last two hundred years, invites the more general observation that social inclusion and exclusion is important in all societies, irrespective of place or time.

The universality of inclusion and exclusion is evident in many different ways. All societies have practices and procedures which define who does and does not belong, many of which are archaic forms of inclusion and exclusion which predate the formation of class-divided societies. Marx and Engels occasionally observed this, although critics such as Debray argued that they did not take the point seriously enough. The critics of cosmopolitanism frequently invoke these forms as evidence of a deep human desire to belong to societies clearly anchored in time and space, and committed to maintaining differences between members and aliens. Michael Walzer, and other defenders of bounded communities, have maintained that principles of inclusion and exclusion are fundamental to all societies, because all societies have to determine the rules governing 'the distribution of membership'" before all else. Whatever one's normative response to these communitarian arguments may be, there can be no doubt that practices of inclusion and exclusion are as primary, elementary and universal as, say, the goals of controlling violence, protecting property and upholding confidence and trust which Bull emphasised in *The Anarchical Society.*

At the micro-social level, such principles are constitutive of the immediate social institutions and relations, from kinship and face-to-face relationship to local and occupational groupings, which human beings encounter in their everyday lives. More broadly, as Martin Wight's discussion of cultural differentiation in *Systems of States* emphasised, principles of inclusion and exclusion are fundamental to belief systems that determine who does and does not belong to international societies and civilisations. At all levels a minimal criteria must be satisfied, and basic conditions met, before admission is allowed. Each level from the face-to-face upwards affects the others and is shaped by them in turn. Invariably, they are intermingled with other forms of exclusion revolving around differences of class, ethnicity, gender and race.

Elaborate and at times conflicting forms of inclusion and exclusion permeate all levels of society and politics, and all social actors know that their lives are interwoven with them. Because the former are constitutive not only of society in the abstract but of individual and collective identity, it can be assumed that social actors everywhere possess some account of why such arrangements exist, harbour opinions about their legitimacy and can offer evidence, when asked of how they impinge upon decisions about the conduct of everyday life. In all societies human beings learn how to deal with the normative, sociological and praxeological aspects of systems of inclusion and exclusion. In modem societies, moreover, the rationale of these systems is the subject of continuing scrutiny.

Social and political inquiry is generally undertaken on the assumption that it is possible to improve upon the explanations and understandings of everyday life. One implicit, if not explicit, purpose of normative inquiry is to ask if there are valid (even universally true) means of choosing between modes of inclusion and exclusion; one dimension of sociological analysis is to inquire into the origins and development of these modes; one element of praxeological exploration is to ask whether societies should preserve traditional arrangements and accompanying roles and responsibilities or modify or transform them. These questions arise for all social actors, albeit without the systematic, abstract and reflective procedures found in the human sciences.

It is also the case that social observers are as immersed in systems of inclusion and exclusion as those whose actions they examine and purport to explain. The renowned disputes about the quest for objectivity, neutrality and detachment in the social sciences have concerned the question of whether cultural and historical assumptions inevitably colour all social and political investigation. There is general agreement that there is no Archimedean viewpoint, since some culturally and historically specific values and perspectives are always privileged within, and others excluded from, a given mode of inquiry. Developing the point more recently, post-modernists have stressed the phenomenon of intellectual exclusion in different disciplines. In international relations, post-modernists have argued that the claim that the scientific method alone can provide objective knowledge, and the belief that the discipline is primarily concerned with strategic relations between states, are two hegemonic and exclusionary perspectives within an arbitrarily defined field.

The post-modern emphasis on intellectual exclusion is important for the present argument because it opposes attempts to create totalising perspectives of the kind which Marxism represented. For post-modernism, a critical theory which aims for a global account of exclusionary practices cannot avoid generating its own brand of intellectual and political exclusion. In one respect the argument is perfectly correct, since all theory is, to some extent, its 'own time apprehended in thought' and all perspectives require constant renewal. Many of these warnings have been heeded by Habermas, among others, in the course of reworking Frankfurt School critical theory. To take this further, one might note that Marx asked normative, sociological and praxeological questions about class-based exclusion in general and the capitalist form in particular. The issue for contemporary critical theory is how to free this mode of inquiry from the limitations of class analysis. Developing a critical theory of the varieties of social and political exclusion is the approach advocated here.

Inclusion and Exclusion in International Relations

It is now appropriate to ask whether critical theory has the capacity to integrate elements of different perspectives on international politics within a synoptic framework. The observation that systems of inclusion arid exclusion are an integral element of world politics has already been made in passing. The more specific point that sovereign states are immersed in different layers of inclusion and exclusion can be illustrated in at least three ways. The first and most obvious point is that the state is a system of inclusion and exclusion in its own right, with precise distinctions between citizens and aliens, and concepts of sovereignty and territoriality.

The second point is that exclusionary states participate in an exclusive society of states which is held together by international norms and moral principles. Societies of states, in turn, can be exclusionary by debarring those deemed unfit to belong, as in the last when European states invoked 'the standard of civilisation' to identify the societies which were too backward to join their ranks. Similar practices are evident in the international treatment of pariah states such as South Africa and Iraq in more recent times. As previously noted, the claim that the exclusion of non-Western societies could no longer be justified was one reason for Western states admitting previously excluded peoples to the society of states on the same terms as original member states.

The third point is that there exists a moral conviction that individuals belong not only to their sovereign states, but to a more inclusive community of humankind or at least, through the states, to a society of states. This idea has been central to arguments both for moving beyond exclusionary states to some unified world order, and for incorporating cosmopolitan values within the society of states. Critics and sceptics often argue that the advocates of a community of humankind privilege a limited range of culturally-specific powers or needs, usually those valued by the West, and devalue or denigrate those which are cherished elsewhere. The thesis that it is necessary to strike a balance between the search for transcultural values and respect for cultural differences in modem international relations tries to resolve these differing points of view.

Because societies belong to these distinctive realms which place different, even conflicting, demands upon them, they are forced to decide where their moral priorities belong. Self-regarding sovereign states are frequently pressed to defend the moral basis of their foreign policy to citizens and outsiders alike. They are often criticized when domestic practices favour dominant ethnic groups and exclude minorities, when foreign policy protects national security but ignores the rights of peoples elsewhere, and when the use of force places military victory ahead of responsibilities to minimise harm to non-combatants. These questions which combine matters of general principle and praxeology frequently arise in the conduct of foreign policy. Again from the angle of praxeology, states in modern times have had to decide whether or not technological innovation and change requires the modification of traditional diplomatic norms, such as the principle of sovereignty. The need to monitor these dimensions of world politics has never been greater than in the late twentieth century, especially in Europe where many are questioning traditional arguments for sovereignty.

Normative, sociological and praxeological questions have also been central to the different theories of international relations. Normative international theory has been concerned with the reasons for and against giving priority to the exclusionary state, as opposed to a more inclusive society of, states or cosmopolitan community of humankind. Various perspectives have addressed the sociological question of whether the sovereign state will remain unaffected by economic and technological change, or will transfer many of its powers to new regional and global bodies. As far as praxeology is concerned, many approaches have asked whether or not the conduct of foreign policy is based on a full appraisal of all the possibilities which exist. The question of what roles there are for the international protection of human rights, humanitarian intervention, and so forth exemplifies this last form of analysis.

Most approaches to international relations consider one or more of these questions about inclusion and exclusion in the system of states. Indeed, it is arguable that these enduring concerns provide the study of international relations with its distinctive identity, and it is plausible to ask if it is possible to bring different approaches (which deal with only one aspect of inclusion and exclusion, or with several levels but only partially) within a single perspective.

Some of the more wide-ranging approaches offer answers to all three questions: sociological, normative and praxeological. This is the case with the realist and rationalist traditions which, by virtue of their scope, provide a benchmark from which to judge other perspectives. Realism accounts for the preeminent role of the exclusionary state and the failure of visions of human unity by arguing that the struggle for power and security is paramount in any system of states. This empirical focus is linked with a critique of cosmopolitan designs and panaceas, and with a refusal to concede that those who argue for alternative world orders monopolise the moral high ground. At the praxeological level, realists argue that the conduct of foreign policy should be governed by the prudent search for national security, combined with the preparedness to maintain international order through the careful management of the balance of power.

In contrast, rationalists provide a vision of an anarchical society in which there are multiple communities: the sovereign state, the society of states and the nascent, but tangible, community of humankind. Their sociology of international relations has emphasised the way in which 'Western values' give each community its place, and suggest the order which should prevail among them. These considerations are reflected in the rationalists' philosophical and praxeological inquiries. Recognising that the identification with human society has been a powerful element in Western culture, rationalists have displayed sympathy with cosmopolitan aspirations while adding the cautionary note that often order must take priority over justice. Their defence of the principle of non-intervention, and their general scepticism about the prospects for promoting a wide range of human rights, have been enduring themes.

Some of these rationalist views were reworked in the 1980s. Rationalists saw an emerging cosmopolitan culture of modernity, reflected in the greater willingness of states to defend the causes of human rights and international distributive justice. The more fluid nature of world politics was accompanied by subtle changes in rationalism and by the assimilation of themes usually associated with revolutionism. Earlier arguments about the way in which both utopian excess and the crass pursuit of self-interest could jeopardise international order were reiterated. Nevertheless, rationalists suggested that states were moving beyond earlier practices of exclusion by learning the need for new transcultural values and institutions which respond to the aspirations of new states and non-Western cultures, and to the needs of individuals.

Although the idealist tradition is usually distinguished from realism by its belief that international relations should promote the realisation of universal values, some versions of realism have also defended breaking down spurious forms of global exclusion. In *Nationalism and After*, Carr argued that 'the exclusive solution' to political community was no longer relevant in the modern world. Within nation-states, the practice of restricting citizenship to the most powerful groups had been discredited in the nineteenth and twentieth centuries. During the same period, the supposition that the international community simply revolved around the great powers had also fallen out of favour. In world politics, as in the domestic realm, the modern question, for Carr, is how to create new forms of political community in which the ideals of freedom and equality would gain expression at both the sub-national and transnational levels.

It is encouraging, as far as a grand synthesis is concerned, that the three approaches of realism, rationalism and idealism either overlap or converge in major respects. But the grounds for optimism are more apparent than real, for there are many ways of challenging the synthesizing project of critical theory. A broader overview of rival perspectives of world politics would reveal just how little consensus there is about what the field is and ought to be. Developments in the discipline in recent years have certainly not built significant new bridges between the various 'islands of theory'. Many will therefore doubt that there are any grounds for supposing that critical theory can guide us beyond the inter-paradigm debate.

Some brief comments on the differences between critical theory and neorealism will indicate the kind of conflicts which would need to be resolved before such a movement could take place. Robert Cox and Kenneth Waltz, exponents of these rival perspectives, differ on at least the following four areas: the purpose of social and political inquiry; the appropriate methodology for the field; the object of analysis and the scope of the inquiry; and how international relations is distinct from, and related to, other areas of intellectual endeavour. From the vantage-point of critical social theory, the purpose of social inquiry is to promote emancipation by providing enlightenment about the constraints upon human autonomy. This goal is at odds with the alleged problem-solving aim of neorealism, which is to ensure that relations between states are managed as smoothly as possible, to minimise the potential for conflict.

These disparate aims require different methodological approaches. Waltz argues that a rigorous analysis of international politics must clarify the differences between reductionist and systemic approaches, and contrast anarchic and hierarchic political systems. While familiarity with methodological developments in the philosophy of science, economics and sociology is essential, according to Waltz, his central concern is to avoid the reductionist fallacy by means of a systemic approach which explains why states are compelled to reproduce the anarchic international system. With its emancipatory aims, on the other hand, Cox's critical-theoretical methodology belongs to what has been called the radical-dialectical approach. This method is used to identify forms of conflict and patterns of development which could lead to the transformation of world order.

For Waltz, the struggle for power and security is the propelling principle in the international system and the proper object of inquiry. For Cox, understanding the prospects for global change requires a much broader focus which takes into account the connections between modes of production, state structures and world order. Waltz argues that the international system can be conceived as a domain apart, although reality is, he admits, far more complex. Delimiting the scope of the analysis is the price which has to be paid for a sharpened intellectual focus. Waltz thinks the gains are great enough to warrant starting from the assumption that the study of world politics is an autonomous area of investigation. Cox, in contrast, argues that the practice of limiting the scope of the inquiry to strategic domain leads to a distorted and ideological account of international relations. Seeking a better understanding of world politics, Cox argues for a Gramscian version of historical materialism which reaches beyond classical international relations theory.

The differences between realism and critical theory form one small part of the total range of disputes within the field. A more sweeping analysis would indicate that no perspective, realism and critical theory included, commands a consensus about the nature and purpose of the field. There is little agreement on a general theoretical approach, and little agreement, to recall the four points at issue between critical theory and neorealism, about the ultimate purpose of social inquiry, the principal empirical realities of world politics, the methodology which is most appropriate, and the scope or range of the inquiry. Not only is there little consensus about these areas, but the proliferation of new approaches over the last few years makes agreement harder to attain. The quest for a synthesis faces scepticism from those who doubt that it is possible, and opposition from others, including post-modernists, who ask if it is worthwhile.

Post-Modernism: Disciplines as States

The central problem for post-modernists is the existence of 'sovereign' claims to shape human loyalties, construct linear histories and impose social and political boundaries, when truth and meaning are in doubt and forms of identity are in question. From this perspective, every attempt to reach final resolutions in these domains reveals no more than aesthetic preference or the display of arbitrary power. Post-modernism aims to bring all 'sovereign' solutions into question.

Post-modernists direct their criticisms not only at the sovereign power of the nation-state, but also at all efforts to clearly define and demarcate disciplines such as international relations; Ashley and Walker suggest that there are several important similarities between states and disciplines. Both have specific boundaries which define what is inside and what lies outside a settled domain. Both possess systems of surveillance and instruments of disciplinary power for regulating and policing the lives of citizens, and for identifying who does and does not belong. Both rely upon a specific conception of time, and instill memories of origins, discrete epochs and decisive watersheds to regulate collective identities. Similarities are evident in the way that both disciplinary boundaries and national frontiers are determined arbitrarily and maintained by force. In the post-modern view, these contrivances never eradicate the marginal, but tend to foster dissidence and encourage revolt.

Extending the parallels between states and disciplines, Ashley and Walker have argued that any attempt to restore order to the disciplinary crisis which presently pervades international relations reveals a sovereign male voice, similar to the Leviathan in the aftermath of the state of nature. The post-modernist does not seek to transcend diversity in a synthesising perspective but to heighten the perception of crisis so that arbitrary constraints on human improvisation are challenged and broken down.

From this point of view, there is no foundation for an agreement about the aim and purpose of the study of world politics: no secure method and no certain way of resolving differences of opinion about domain or scope. Post-modern writers oppose Holsti's view that the disciplinary crisis should provoke a concerted effort to re-establish the common intellectual enterprise and to bring order and harmony to its disparate parts. Rather than invent means of bringing different islands of theory together, post-modernists seek to 'impede, disrupt and delay' such an endeavour.

In the post-modernist view, the fact that, as Waltz puts it, nothing ever seems to accumulate in the study of international relations is no cause for alarm and no reason to lament. In one sense, too much accumulation is precisely the problem: too much accretion, at any rate, of allegedly final resolutions and too little sense of uncharted terrain. Post-modernism protests against intellectual dogmatism and disciplinary closure; it argues for forging new connections between diverse academic points of view, and between academic inquiry and movements of dissent on the margins of society and politics. As such, it is a powerful advocate of the need to explore new forms of community and different expressions of human identity. Parallels exist between these ideas and the argument that the study of international relations should shed both the hegemonic qualities which betray its Western origins, and its continuing preoccupation with Eurocentric concerns.

These arguments, however, are not prescriptive in the sense of submitting detailed plans of the future of the subject and the preferred destiny of society. What postmodernism opposes is relatively clear: intellectual and social closure. It displays scepticism towards present orthodoxies and putative resolutions on the grounds that they depend on exclusionary practices. Beyond that, what postmodernism stands for is more difficult to pin down, although for its advocates this is a sign of strength rather than a manifestation of poverty or weakness.

The contention that post-modernism should be more forthcoming in this regard is captured by Biersteker's remark that there is an obligation to proffer some means of choosing between competing perspectives. Concerned to rebut the supposition that post-modernism believes that 'everything is permitted' and 'anything goes', Ashley and Walker proclaim the ethic of freedom. Although they attempt to distinguish this ethic from all moralities which 'exclude those people who would transgress (their) limitations', there is no doubt that it creates its own limits. 'Where this ethics is rigorously practised', Ashley and Walker note, 'no voice can effectively claim to stand heroically upon some exclusionary ground'. To take it seriously, there must be a commitment to a dialogue which transcends 'the institutional limitations that separate nations, classes, occupational categories, genders, and races'.

There are some parallels here with Habermas's defence of open, unconstrained dialogue, which also, at times, found support from Foucault. That said, the post-modern ethic implicitly assumes that the greater universal is the tolerance of diversity, a supposition which prompts an old question about whether or not it is right for the liberal to tolerate the intolerant. Post-modernism seems to imply that it should not, but the larger issue is how far a more extensive range of disputes about the purpose, focus, method and scope of international relations can be settled by better argument, rather than by aesthetic judgment, fiat or force.

For post-modernism, there is nothing in the supposed history of the discipline which contains the key to reconciling intellectual differences, and there is nothing to signpost the path of development which should be explored in the future. No history of great debates, or of the proliferation of perspectives, reveals what should be cancelled or preserved. No dialectical development weaving the elements of different perspectives together in a tidier synthesis is possible.

The post-modernists are correct in noting that there is no meaning in the history of international relations, at least not in the Hegelian sense of an inevitable and unilinear development of ideas about world politics. Yet, an analysis of its recent history can reveal what is at stake in the major debates, and what gains and losses have occurred in attempts to develop a more adequate account of international relations. By considering what different perspectives claim to achieve and what others accuse them of overlooking, it may be easier to understand what should be preserved within a more encompassing approach. The exercise is dialectical, seeking to show how different perspectives can contribute to a larger whole, and revealing that it is possible 'to order and transcend diversity without substituting a new orthodoxy for the old'.

There has been some progress in the United States over the last twenty years in deciding how to order the principal areas of debate. The first phase began when the theorists of interdependence argued that realism is an incomplete perspective which confuses one part of world politics—the struggle for security and power—for the whole, which includes the added potential for international co-operation in the context of global interdependence.

Responding to this criticism, Waltz argued that although interdependence is a tangible phenomenon, it is not as novel or as important as liberal analysts suppose. The strength of neorealism, according to Waltz, is that it denies the need to explore the links between everything which might be salient to the study of world politics, and concentrates instead on the strategic forces which dominate international affairs. Recognising that all conceptual frameworks generate distorted images rather than mirror-like reflections of the world, the neorealist does not aim to explain everything, but isolates the forces which are absolutely decisive.

Realism, however, was vulnerable to attack on epistemological grounds. The argument that empiricism is untenable gained support in the 1970s and 1980s. The accent of social inquiry then fell on how any argument about primary forces in political life could be verified, if empirical inquiry could not supply an unambiguous answer and the facts did not speak for themselves. The main theme was acknowledged in Waltz's argument that the neorealist selection of primary forces was anchored in the desire to understand what could and could not be controlled. When Cox and Ashley struck the first blow for critical theory in the early 1980s, they challenged the contention that knowledge should be constituted solely by a 'technical interest' in control. They argued that the quest for knowledge should be grounded in an emancipatory interest in freeing human beings from unnecessary social constraints. Their argument, that the success of any empirical research programme cannot be established by showing that its findings correspond with an independent reality, pointed to other ways of identifying the adequacy of empirical projects, specifically, by means of an analysis of the cognitive interests which underlie them.

The details of the argument were set out by Habermas, who identified three modes of social inquiry with their related cognitive interests: positivism, which assumes that social and political knowledge is obtained by emulating the experimental procedures of the natural sciences, and which grounds inquiry in the human interest in control; hermeneutics, which grows out of the need for inter-subjective understanding, and maintains that the cultural sciences involve the different activity of analysing the meanings which human beings attach to their actions; and critical theory, which analyses social constraints and cultural understandings from a superior human interest in enlightenment and emancipation.

This line of argument invites all social analysts to reflect upon the cognitive interests and normative assumptions which underpin their research, without implying that from now on all research must be critical-theoretical. It further suggests a particular way of approaching disagreements about the purpose, object, method and scope of international relations. The first implication is that the normative purpose of social inquiry should be considered before all else. Clarifying the purpose of the inquiry precedes and facilitates the definition of the object of inquiry: once the object of inquiry is clear, the matter of method can be considered. Finally, when these issues are settled, various inferences about the scope of the inquiry and its relationship with other areas of the social sciences and humanities can be established. Starting with this logic of social inquiry, the discussion now turns to the promise and potential of critical international theory to illuminate the object of inquiry.

Critical Theory and the Next Stage

The object of analysis from a critical-theoretical point of view can best be identified by posing the normative, sociological and praxeological questions that arise from systems of inclusion and exclusion in world politics. Identifying and outlining possible answers to these questions is the first task. The second is to explain how some leading approaches to international relations can be clustered around this project, in order to add coherence to the field and to underline the common intellectual enterprise. What follows starts with the normative question of the state, proceeds to consider the sociological question of community, and ends with the question of praxeology and reform.

The Normative Question of the State

Since critical theory begins with a prima facie commitment to human equality, the first question to ask concerning the normative question of the state concerns the justification for excluding human being from any social arrangement. One answer is suggested in Habermas's claim that advanced moral codes are committed to granting every human being an equal right to participate in open dialogue about the configuration of society and politics. The crucial consequence that stems from this claim is that there are no valid grounds for excluding any human being from dialogue in advance. No system of exclusion passes this moral test unless its constitutive principles can command the consent of all, in particular those to be excluded from the social arrangement in question.

This conclusion has important implications for the normative theory of the state and international relations. In the seventeenth century, social contract theorists such as Pufendorf affirmed the rights of citizens to set up sovereign states of their own volition;

there was no prima facie obligation to win the consent of those who would not belong to a state which was being established. The cosmopolitan revision of this approach requires the consent of the excluded to legitimate the separateness of the state. Sovereign rights cannot be conferred unilaterally on the self, and while national boundaries are not without significance, they cannot be regarded as morally exhaustive.

This emphasis on the consent of the excluded recalls the seventeenth century contractarian approach, relayed to later social and political thought by Rousseau and Kant, and eventually to Rawls. Modern contractarians might argue that the next step in the argument should be to create a modified Rawlsian original condition, in which contractors are asked to select principles of inclusion and exclusion behind a veil of ignorance. Critics of this approach, however, rightly point to major difficulties such as defending the preferences imputed to contractors.

The contractarian position is of only heuristic value, since no contractor can enter a political dialogue, *ab initio*, without any prior understanding of the moral rights and duties which define their relations with co-nationals and the rest of humankind. The notion of answerability to others in the context of a universal dialogue has a history; it clearly emerges out of concrete, exclusionary moralities which, more importantly, it calls into question. In the modern state, the moral status of sovereignty has been questioned from perspectives which argue for realigning the rights of citizens and the rights of humanity.

This enterprise of questioning traditional sovereign rights in light of the moral claims of the wider human community resembles the method of immanent critique used by the Frankfurt School. Instead of appealing to an ethical standard which is external to the state, this approach turns the state's own universal moral discourse against its questionable particularistic practices. In modern times, it presses the anti-exclusionary dynamic in the evolution of modern citizenship further by considering its ramifications for the domain of world politics. The anti-exclusionary dynamic is the trend of lowering the barriers which prevent excluded groups, such as subordinate classes, racial and national minorities, and women from enjoying the social and political rights monopolised by more powerful groups. To press this further is to recognise that the nation-state is one of the few bastions of exclusion which has not had its rights and claims against the rest of the world seriously questioned.

The normative purpose of critical theory is to facilitate the extension of moral and political community in international affairs. Ethical universalism underpins the ideal that separate national communities should refer the question of sovereignty to the moral bench of international institutions. But it is not a form of universalism with an in-built hostility to cultural diversity and difference. The normative ideal of the extension of community does not simply involve bringing aliens or outsiders within one homogeneous, moral association. It also entails recognition of the rights of groups, such as indigenous peoples, which fall within the jurisdiction of the sovereign state, but which suffer exclusion from full participation in the national community. This vision of a world political community is similar to some that have arisen from consideration of the future of Europe: it is a vision which argues for greater power for sub-national and transnational loyalties, alongside older, but transformed, national identities and separate, but not sovereign, states.

The Sociological Question of Community

One important conclusion follows from the observation that national boundaries have greater significance than they morally ought to possess: critical theory needs to develop an empirical account of the constraints upon, and prospects for, the appearance of post-sovereign international relations. This will require a sociology of community, to ascertain whether political community is likely to expand or to contract, remain bound up with the sovereign state or change so that sub-national and transnational loyalties acquire greater importance.

The founders of regional integration theory made an impressive start in developing a sociology of community, although their approach was limited to an analysis of the social and political ramifications of economic unification. Any attempt to build upon these foundations will have to examine a larger range of issues and forces. No sociology of community will proceed very far if it neglects state-building, geopolitics and war. No account will succeed if it overlooks the effects of commerce or production at the domestic and international levels. No account will reach far enough if it neglects the cultural dimensions of international relations which shape domestic and international order and structure images of the self and the other.

Numerous perspectives can contribute to a sociology of community, although there is no single one which covers the entire range of salient processes. In this respect, the theories of regional integration in the 1950s and 1960s certainly warrant attention, as do subsequent analyses of interdependence and the more recent developments of neo-liberal institutionalism. Few will doubt the significance of realism, rationalism and international political economy, or the importance of the sociological literature on language, culture and communication, for the sociology of community. An analysis of the formation of the boundaries of community requires the integration of themes drawn from sociology and social theory as well as more familiar areas of international relations.

Integrating such material is another matter. One way of doing so can be found in the related discussions of social learning in sociology and international relations. The idea of social learning has been a recurrent theme in international relations since the end of the Second World War, most notably in the work of neo-functionalist writers such as Ernst Haas, in their analyses of the evolution of habits of co-operation in Western Europe. Joseph Nye and Robert Keohane have referred to social learning in their analysis of international regimes, complex interdependence and nuclear cooperation, and George Modelski, invoking Kant, has stressed the same theme with regard to evolutionary logics in the world system. Notwithstanding such references, there has been no attempt to develop a classification of forms of social learning within the field, and no analysis of the way in which their interaction shapes the inclusive and exclusionary arrangements present in different societies.

One of the more useful typologies of social learning, set out in Habermas's reconstruction of historical materialism, identifies the following three categories: technical-instrumental learning, which concerns how to best exploit nature; strategic social learning, which concerns the means of controlling actual or potential adversaries; and moral-practical learning, which concerns the creation of reproducible social relations and more reflective and universal ethical codes. Habermas's analysis of social learning sets out some of the fundamental ideas which can be incorporated within a sociology of logics of inclusion and exclusion in international relations. More specifically, it may be useful to ask if modes of inclusion and exclusion are the result of the interplay between the sorts of learning processes which Habermas identifies.

Many different perspectives within international relations contain insights into one or more of these forms of learning, and a focus on social learning is a promising way of bringing their respective themes together. Realism and strategic studies have been concerned with various aspects of learning how to control or outmanoeuvre adversaries. Rationalism has dealt with the ways in which states and civilisations learn how to establish international order, and how to regulate their affairs in accordance with cosmopolitan principles of justice. Various schools of international political economy comment on all of these processes in their analyses of power and production, which introduce the often-neglected sphere of interaction with nature. To develop this approach much more would have to be known about the way in which state-building, geopolitics, war, production and the moral-cultural sphere interact to give rise to the dominant systems of inclusion and exclusion in international relations. Given a focus on learning processes, the aim would be to understand shifts from learning how to promote self-interest in an anarchic system of states to learning how to maintain order between diverse states and civilisations and how to define and institutionalise cosmopolitan principles of morality. This last consideration brings us to the question of praxeology.

The Praxeological Question of Reform

Praxeological questions arise because new forms of political community will not develop without human intervention. In international relations, praxeological inquiry invariably begins by asking whether states in the context of anarchy have the freedom of choice to bring new social and political relations into being. Due to the dominance of the realist emphasis on international systemic constraints, on the tension between power and morality, and on the dangers of idealist praxeology, the question of how states and other social actors could create new political communities and identities has never been adequately addressed. Providing an adequate answer is a central requirement for the critical theory of international relations.

Perhaps ironically, Carr's political realism is a useful point of departure. It can best be developed by integrating some Kantian themes which also arise in rationalism. For Carr, reflections on political practice should be cognisant of systemic constraints, while recognising that an exclusive preoccupation with constraints will stifle initiative and promote sterility. The choice between realism and idealism can be avoided by focusing on the question of how states can transcend the divisive pursuit of national security by creating international order, and transform a minimal order between states into a cosmopolitan community of humankind or Kantian universal kingdom of ends.

Kant believed that an answer to this question was inherent in the character of the modern state and its emphasis on universal human rights. The idea of modern citizenship had profound internationalist implications, in Kant's view, as in the views of

Michael Doyle and Christopher Brewin in more recent times. In their view, liberal states are obliged to express their political principles in three related spheres of citizenship—national (*ius civile*), international (*ius gentium*) and cosmopolitan (*ius cosmopoliticum*). States which have contested various forms of exclusion within their boundaries are obliged to question exclusion in international affairs. Attempts to promote principles of social justice, and the rights of individuals and groups such as indigenous peoples, ethnic minorities and non-Western cultures, exemplify a growing concern for the victims of exclusion in the international system during the past century.

Very few governments or societies commit themselves to an ethical foreign policy in which the allegiance to a cosmopolitan morality rivals the quest for national power and international order in importance. A sociology of community, of the kind outlined earlier, could explain why some states are more sympathetic to internationalism than others. In this context, it would be intriguing to return to some earlier themes in foreign policy analysis, to examine the fate of specific internationalist ideas in the policy process. The focus on national images, operational codes, cognitive maps and structures of decision provides a useful starting-point for an analysis of different levels of tolerance for internationalist foreign policy. International institutions can be considered, in a similar light, as the arenas in which global themes are articulated, defended and implemented. Discussions of the evolution of international conventions dealing with human rights and basic needs, common heritage, common security, the rights of indigenous peoples and so forth, are especially important ways of forging connections between critical theory and the analysis of foreign policy. A critical approach to foreign policy analysis can explore the ways in which the potential for internationalism which exists in most modern states can be realised in international conventions which enshrine the moral principles of an alternative world order.

Conclusion

Critical theory can best contribute to the next stage of international relations theory by exploring normative, sociological and praxeological questions about systems of inclusion and exclusion in world politics. It outlines the common intellectual enterprise to which different perspectives belong, and suggests ways in which their themes could be assembled within a more comprehensive conceptual framework. In response to the criticism that such projects are in danger of building a restrictive new orthodoxy, the answer is that critical theory does not attempt to assign each perspective its rightful place. Moving back and forth between the critical-theoretical framework and individual perspectives is the next stage which needs to be undertaken to develop this project further. The research framework outlined above would then be modified as each perspective was considered in turn.

The specific contribution that critical theory can make to the next stage of international relations theory starts from the premise that the emancipatory project ought to be more central to the field. Critical theory presents the case for recovering the old idealist programme, modernised to take account of the various intellectual developments and debates which have shaped the field over the past sixty or seventy years. In this context, five considerations are especially important: whether the questions about inclusion and exclusion which have been raised in this discussion are as significant as the paper suggests; whether these questions provide some insight into the debates about purpose, object of inquiry, method and scope which traditionally have divided the field; whether different perspectives can be integrated in the ways outlined; whether a balance between intellectual coherence and diversity can be struck in the manner suggested; and, finally, whether it is the case that every perspective contributes important themes to the next stage, but none of them, critical theory included, maps out the field in its entirety. In the end, this is why is it is incumbent upon us all, no matter what our starting point maybe, to explain what our perspectives can bring to the next stage in international relations theory.

Mervyn Frost, "The Role of Normative Theory in IR"[*]

In his article 'The International Imagination: IR Theory and "Classical Social Analysis"' Justin Rosenberg once again criticises the realist paradigm which is so dominant in the discipline of international relations (IR). He points to criticisms of realism which have been made repeatedly over a long period of time. The central points are: that realist theory is unhistorical; that it is too general to be useful; that it is not holistic; and finally that it ignores the moral dimension of IR. He notes that in spite of repeated criticism realist theory remains dominant. No counter theory which 'combines *historical* understanding, *substantive* explanation, *totalizing* theory and a *moral* vocation of reason' has emerged. In order to remedy this, Rosenberg advocates the application of C. Wright Mills' classic social analysis (published as *The Sociological Imagination*) to the realm of international studies.

Mills' argument is directed specifically against two approaches to social science which he calls 'grand theory' and 'abstracted empiricism'. The former he portrays as too general to be of use and the latter as being overly concerned with facts extracted from their wider context. Both ignore the ethical dimensions of sociology. In place of these, Mills advocates the sociological imagination. The core of his proposed method is articulated in four overlapping themes: the grounding of social thought in substantive problems; the use of historical and comparative depth of field; the perception of the social world as a totality; and, finally, a commitment to the ideals of reason and freedom.

It seems hard not to agree with the suggestion that in IR we ought to take account of these broad themes. The discipline has been preoccupied with rather static social models that have often been unhistorical, and there is no doubt that overall insufficient attention has been paid to normative issues. Indeed, it is difficult to imagine who would not agree with the importance of these themes stated in these broad terms.

In this brief discussion I shall focus on what C. Wright Mills has to say about the place of normative theory in his proposed method. This narrow line of questioning, I believe, will show that Mills, in spite of his interest in freedom and reason (both normative concerns), is guilty of not engaging in normative theory in the fully fledged

* *Millenium: Journal of International Studies*. This article first appeared in *Millenium*, Vol. 23, No. 1, 1994, and is reproduced with the permission of the publisher.

way which is required of post-positivist social science. For this reason I argue, IR would be ill advised to appropriate C. Wright Mills' method as it stands.

Before getting into the details of my argument, two preliminary matters will be dealt with. First, I shall explain what I mean by 'engaging in normative theory' and, second, I shall briefly indicate the present place and standing of normative theory within the discipline.

We engage in normative theory when we attempt the complicated task of explaining the meaning of, setting out the relationships which hold between, and seeking to evaluate different comprehensive patterns of core normative concepts such as liberty, equality, justice, human rights, political obligation, sovereignty, group rights, self-determination, property rights, restitution, retribution, and so on. With regard to domestic politics there is a tradition of scholars who have engaged in normative theory. Great names include, Plato, Aristotle, Augustine, Aquinas, Machiavelli, Hobbes, Locke, Rousseau, Hegel, Bentham, Oakeshott, J.S. Mill, Rawls, and Walzer to mention but a few. Typical questions for normative theorists are: What is liberty? Is there a conflict between liberty and equality? To what political authorities (if any) do we owe obligations? In IR key questions are: Is state sovereignty an important value? Is sovereignty more or less important than individual human rights? How should we think about just distributions of resources in the international context? What wars (if any) are just? How ought wars to be fought? Do all nations have the right to self-determination? What duties do citizens of well-off states owe to economic refugees from poor states? There are no easy answers to these questions and engaging in normative theory is complicated, difficult and of great practical importance. The conclusions of normative arguments (which are quite often based on weak arguments) are the springboards from which individuals and nations have launched their historic, sometimes heroic, and often tragic deeds down the ages.

Contemporary IR has until recently neglected normative theory for a cluster of different reasons which include a commitment to the canons of positivist social science (which was based on a radical distinction between facts and values), scepticism about the epistemological status of value statements, and the dominance of the realist paradigm in IR which insists on the primacy of power over idealism. Over the past few decades, however, positivist social science has been subject to sustained criticism. It has been shown that the lives we live and the claims we make are incompatible with thoroughgoing moral scepticism. In addition, within IR realism has been severely questioned. The direction of the debate among scholars has conferred a certain legitimacy on normative theory. These meta-theoretical developments, which have paved the way for the emergence of normative theory within IR, have been given added backing by recent developments in world politics (the end of the Cold War and the emergence of new states) which have posed a series of practical questions which clearly require normative answers. For example, what should the international community do with the stream of claims for self-determination from groups within the ex-Soviet Union? What duties, if any, does the European Union owe economic refugees from the East?

In recent years normative theory has gone through a modest boom. Books and articles on the topic have appeared. But, in spite of this development, normative theory still remains at the margins of the discipline. A major reason for this is that there is still within the discipline a bias towards objective explanation which, it is believed, can be undertaken without engaging in normative theory.

Returning to Rosenberg's article, 'The International Imagination', I shall argue that although it acknowledges a moral vocation for social science, it does not correctly identify the ways in which normative theory is salient to social inquiry. Although both Mills and Rosenberg acknowledge that our ethical commitments help us identify the social problems to be investigated, they nonetheless maintain that the sociological investigation of the problem can be carried out in an objective way which does not engage in normative theory. It is this contention that I challenge.

Mills writes, '[t]he values that have been the thread of classic social analysis, I believe, are *freedom and reason*.' Indeed, he identifies a commitment to these two values as one of the four core elements of the sociological imagination. Yet, in spite of its centrality, he says very little about precisely what this commitment involves, other than indicating a link between these values and democracy. In his argument against grand theory and abstracted empiricism Mills' argues that these approaches involve the abdication of the vocation of social science and a surrender to the bureaucratisation of reason and the transformation of social science into a technical instrument.

In order to avoid this, the social scientist must start by asking what values 'are cherished yet threatened, and what values are cherished and supported, by the characterising trends of our period'. Expanding on this further on, he says, '[n]o problem can be adequately formulated unless the values involved and the apparent threat to them are stated. These values and their impediment constitute the terms of the problem itself'. In our time, Mills argues, people are often not aware of cherished values, but 'are aware of a threat. That is the experience of uneasiness, of anxiety'. What social scientists are called upon to do is 'to make clear the elements of contemporary uneasiness and indifference'. The people may not know what values are threatened, but Mills does; the values in question are freedom and reason. In explicitly declaring the centrality of these values, Mills says that he is revealing his biases and he hopes that those who disagree with him will do the same. Through this process then 'the moral problems of social study—the problem of social science as a public issue—will be recognised, and discussion will become possible'.

What the vocation requires, says Rosenberg, is 'tirelessly rendering visible and public the actual structures of power within a society in order to enlarge the possible realm of democratic self-government'. Toward the end of the article Rosenberg writes:

> Finally, the international imagination does not eschew ethical judgement; yet nor does it suppose that an intellectual method exists which can itself resolve moral dilemmas. Its principal contribution is the illumination of the objective, structural responsibility of individuals and groups for particular outcomes, whatever formal bonds of obligation are held to obtain. Its purpose is to educate moral choice by drawing out the real human relations involved—not to replace it with philosophical guarantees or technical formulae.

What does all this mean within the realm of international relations? What are structures? What is this 'structural responsibility' which may be illuminated by sociologists? In *The Sociological Imagination*, Mills gives several indications of what he means by structure. He refers to the distinction between the personal experience of war, on the one hand, and a structural understanding of it, on the other. From the personal point of view, an individual seeks to understand what is happening around him. He does this in order to secure his survival, to secure a safe position in the army, and so on. In contrast 'the structural issues of war have to do with its causes; with what types of men it throws up into command; with its effects upon economic and political, family and religious institutions, with the unorganised irresponsibility of a world of nation states'. He indicates that structural analysis has to do with power, which may well exist in situations within which there is no power consensus.

The social structure of society, says Mills, is 'the combination of institutions classified according to the functions each performs'. The most inclusive of these structures is the nation state, within which two important structures are the bureaucracy and the army. We can now summarise the sociologists task, according to Mills, as follows: people find themselves embedded in structures. The most important of these is the nation state within which the army and bureaucracy are important. Freedom, reason and democracy are in many ways threatened by these structures and it is the task of sociology to make clear the nature of this threat. Finally, he indicates that sociologists ought to identify the points of vulnerability within structures which, in turn, would allow for efforts at promoting social change.

We now have a rough idea of what Mills' 'structures' are. But what precisely is the 'structural responsibility' to which both Mills and Rosenberg refer? A reading of *The Sociological Imagination* suggests that Mills had in mind something akin to the following. In the modern army and bureaucracy the individuals at the micro levels behave with great rational sophistication. They know that in order to maximise their strategic short term advantages they need to behave in certain known ways. They also know what their formal obligations are within these institutions, *i.e.,* they behave rationally and, in terms of the rules of this institution, they act morally. But they have no conception of the meaning of the whole social edifice. This they experience as a brute given, a fact of nature, since they can see no reason in the sum of rational and moral actions of all the people involved. They thus feel alienated, but are unable to explain why they feel this way. Mills believes that by revealing to people the macro structure of society, people will come to understand what threatens their freedom and will have a chance to formulate freedom establishing alternatives. They will have an idea of how to act in order to bring these about. This structural revelation has been the task undertaken by all classical social theorists such as Marx, Engels, Simmel, Weber, Frohm and Freud.

We can now understand the tension which Rosenberg points to between formal obligation and structural responsibility. A soldier's formal obligation may be to fight the just war as directed by his government. However, in the light of a structural analysis he may decide that his 'structural obligation' is to oppose the system of states as a whole (because he believes that war is structurally 'built in'). In the Millsian view, then, the task of the theorist is to make apparent how structures are constraining freedom and democracy. There are several problems with this way of understanding the link between structural analysis and normative theory in International Relations (or, for that matter, in any of the other social sciences). First, it is simply not the case that the mere revealing of structures, of and by themselves, makes it clear to us what our moral responsibilities are. What these are is a matter for moral argument—for normative theory. The arguments involved may be very difficult indeed. Consider the example of a soldier to whom the overall structure of the system of states has been made apparent. Once it has been made known to him just how he fits into the war system it may still be far from clear to him what his responsibilities are. Here are few questions which may bother him:

- Were I simply to stay in the army would I be legitimizing the whole system which I now understand?
- How far back in time and over how wide an area does my responsibility stretch?
- If it can be shown that the state system has been responsible for many 'unjust' wars in the past, am I responsible for all of them?
- If it can be shown that the poor states of the world are in a structurally vulnerable position because of a prior act of colonisation by my state a century ago, am I to consider myself responsible for that state's present dependence?

Even if our soldier answers all these questions in the affirmative, other questions remain. The most important of these is: What should he do about his structural responsibility? Should he become a conscientious objector, a mutineer, or a revolutionary? Or ought he to confine himself to lobbying his government to attempt to change the war system by strengthening the role played by the United Nations?

Having posed these questions, others follow thick and fast. Would it be good if all soldiers became conscientious objectors, mutineers or revolutionaries? If this happened states would lose their coercive power and would be unable to impose their authority. Would this be a good outcome? What system of enforcement would people use to uphold their rights? If the structure of the present system was responsible for many conquests and expansionist campaigns in the past should our soldier advocate that these be unraveled? How far back should this unraveling be taken?

This long series of questions makes clear, I hope, how the straightforward revealing of structures does not simply illuminate our 'structural responsibility'. The point which I am making does not alter when thinking of the responsibility of groups rather than that of our single foot soldier. What our responsibilities are, and indeed whether there is such a thing as 'structural responsibility' at all, is a matter for normative theory proper. It would involve putting together a full normative theory which would deal with the value of the individual, the ethical links between the individual and the social arrangements in which he lives (family, civil society, church, state, international organisations, etc.), the links between these and notions of military duty, the meaning of war, the meaning of just war, and a study of the relationships between freedom, equality, justice, democracy and so on.

There is a second and more fundamental weakness to the method which Rosenberg advocates. Put boldly, the method suggests that social structure and normative concerns may be examined separately. Although Mills admits that norms are involved in identifying the problems to be investigated (*i.e.,* values under threat help us identify what structures to investigate) and that after our structural analysis values will help us identify what needs to be done, he still maintains that structures are examinable independently of normative considerations. Thus, it turns out that Mills, and thus, surprisingly, Rosenberg too, is an empiricist. Mills is explicit about this. He overtly acknowledges a strict acceptance of the fact/value distinction. What *is* can be studied quite independently from what *ought* to be.

In the light of developments in the philosophy of the social sciences over the past few decades this position is no longer tenable. Over the past few decades many social theorists have argued that in our attempts to explain and understand social reality normative concerns enter at every point, not merely after the empirical analysis has been completed. I cannot cover here the whole history of these developments in the philosophy of social science, but I can summarise the main findings which, taken together, form a widely accepted canon.

First, when the International Relations scholar (or any other social scientist) sets out to explain a set of phenomena in world politics his/her theory choice is not value neutral as positivist social science would have us believe. Realists show by their choice of theory a commitment to the value of the state and the system of states. Those who choose to explain world politics in terms of interdependence theory similarly display a commitment to pluralist values which takes note of and values a range of social groups beyond the state. Those who choose Marxist theories similarly indicate a value commitment to the liberation of the working class. Second, what theorists count as salient facts, which might verify or falsify their theories, are determined by the theory itself. Thus, to put the matter crudely, the scientist's values determine the theory she/he chooses and then beyond that, the theory in turn determines what are to count as facts. Following this line of thought, Martin Hollis and Steve Smith point to the difficulty of testing Realist, Pluralist and Structural theories of IR against one another.

> It is not simply that they have different views of the world, but that they each define what is the evidence in a different way. There is no body of evidence that we could use to compare their explanations. For example, those who adhere to Realism simply do not see the same world as those who adhere to Pluralism or Structuralism: they see different actors, different issues, and different pieces of evidence.

Third, social scientists face the added problem that what they are seeking to explain are the actions of people. Actions do not present themselves in a straightforward, objective way, but require interpretation by the social scientist. This requires the theorist to take seriously the self understandings of the actors being investigated; this includes taking account of their value systems (*e.g.*, in order to understand the conflict in Bosnia-Herzogovina, the community of states needs to understand the value systems of the nationalist movements operative there). Fourth, the social scientist has to be aware that she/he also is an actor interpreting the actions of others. Thus his/her act of interpretation itself needs interpreting and this requires taking into account the values which she/he herself holds.

It is this last turn which poses the most difficult problem for social scientists and it is here that normative questions enter most persistently. Imagine an IR scholar called JR who is committed to the 'international imagination'. What he seeks to explain are the recent events in the former Yugoslavia especially insofar as these have become an issue in International Relations. In terms of the canon of his own method (*i.e.*, the 'international imagination') his aim is to reveal the underlying structural determinants of these vents. Before JR can uncover these structures (so that he can reveal to people their structural responsibility) he must give some, superficial (*i.e.*, on the surface, non structural) account of what is happening in that region. Whatever is happening there does not present itself unambiguously to JR (or anyone else). There are a number of possible interpretations and what he chooses to regard as the valid one will have a profound effect on whatever it is that he later claims to find beneath the surface in the structural realm. Social systems are not like bridges which unambiguously stand there clearly defined with their structures attached underneath.

Consider the following possible interpretations (the structural question is posed in parenthesis after each):

1. What is happening in Bosnia may be understood as the liberation struggles of three historic primordial ethnic groups, each with its own history, language, religion and so on. (What are the structural determinants of this?)
2. What is happening in Bosnia is the breakdown of the old Yugoslav state apparatus, which is creating opportunities for war-lords to foster insecurity. Having done this these war-lords are then able to present themselves as Hotfoesian sovereigns who can deliver order. They seek to secure legitimacy for their activities by appeals to nationalism. (What are the structural determinants of this?)
3. What we perceive in Bosnia is the confrontation between pro-European, pro-Western, 'civilised' groups on the one hand and 'backward' groups on the other. (What structures determine this?)

Before tackling the structural questions, JR would have to decide which of these interpretations is the best. (He may not simply make an arbitrary choice, based on taste or the throw of dice). Making this decision will depend in part on JR having some insight into the self understandings of the parties involved. This will require a questioning of the parties involved including, the 'war-lords', the governments of Bosnia, the Croatian and Serbian governments and the conventional military leaders. This questioning will bring out the interpretations of each of these actors and each of their interpretations will be shot through with value judgements. JR will not simply be able to accept these interpretations (with the value judgements embedded in them), but will himself have to evaluate them in terms of his own normative commitments.

In order to demonstrate this, consider JR's interrogation of the testimony provided to him by a Croatian war-lord. This war-lord claims to be fighting for the liberation of the Croatian minority in Bosnia. JR establishes that the war-lord certainly presents himself in this way in private, at public rallies and through the media. But JR might in the light of evidence at hand, question this self interpretation. He may find that for forty years the people the warlord claims to speak for did not agitate for their own state. He may find that, on the contrary, they got on perfectly well with their Bosnian Serb and Bosnian Muslim neighbours, that they inter-married, worked happily together in the civil service (including the police force) and voted in national elections. He might find that a majority of the people feel bewildered and bemused at the fighting rather than fiercely nationalistic. Finally, he may find that this warlord started out by murdering people from his own nation who sought a compromise deal in the early stages of the dispute.

In light of this, JR decides that in spite of what the warlord says, he is in fact better understood as an opportunist who is running a protection racket 'dolled up' as a national liberation struggle, than as a nationalist leader. Making this judgement requires that JR have some idea about what counts as a genuine national liberation struggle. This in turn presupposes that JR has a rather full (and complex) normative theory which would have to include in it ideas about the link which ought to hold between nations and states, about when it is appropriate for a nation to secede from the state within which it finds itself, about what rights for minorities ought to be constitutionally protected within states, about the conflict between individual and group rights and about the ways in which these might be legitimately resolved.

Consider JR attempting to interpret the civilisation *versus* barbarism claim. The claim (which is made by some Croats) is that the dispute in Yugoslavia is the confrontation between the civilised West and the barbarous East. Can JR simply accept their self-descriptions (and reserve for himself his private evaluation of their acts)? He cannot plausibly do this because what the Croats are saying to him is not 'we think we are defending civilisation and we do not care what you think' rather they are asking JR to believe that what they are saying about the struggle in their country is true; they want JR (and everybody else who will listen to them) to believe this and to act in support of their cause. In other words JR is not simply called upon to listen to how they interpret their own actions. He is required to judge whether their claim is valid or not. Once again this requires JR's involvement in a rather sophisticated normative exercise. What is civilisation? What kinds of behaviour threaten it? What is the appropriate response of civilised people to threats to their civilisation? (and so on). These are profoundly normative tasks.

What I have argued here is that JR and other International Relations scholars have to take normative positions, not as Mills and Rosenberg would have it, on either side of an empirical structural analysis. Structural analysis (of whatever sort) has to be preceded by very sophisticated normative arguments. Normative theory proper (not vague references to freedom, reason and democracy) is called for before any structural analysis can take place.

My claim is that all social theorists start out with this rather thick normative engagement with the subject under investigation, but almost always the normative position is implicit; it does not get spelled out or rationally defended. This fact, of course, opens up the possibility that the normative stance implicit in the inquiry is often 'half baked', incoherent, full of internal contradictions and the like. It is high time that this state of affairs is remedied; that international relations theorists be required to spell out and defend their normative positions. They are not at present required to do so, because they all still live in the shadow of positivism according to which the facts of the matter can be determined in a value-free way.

8

Global Political Economy
Social Forces and Dialectic

Introduction

The selections from this chapter encompass a range of Marxian and Neo-Gramscian-based perspectives on the international political economy. Robert Cox's seminal article on the social forces of world order (1981) represents one of the first attempts to bring critical theory into the discourse of the international political economy. Cox is perhaps best-known for having distinguished between a "problem solving" and "critical theory" approach in IR. He conceives the former in terms of the use of scientific variables to explain and measure the causal impact of state behavior; the latter, as an open-ended reflexive theory of the social forces of the international political economy, which focuses on the transformation of social practices. In his view, the international order is anything but static, but rather is being continually reshaped by changing social and historical circumstances. In this way, Cox's article lays the groundwork for later critical theory perspectives on the international political economy, including Claire Cutler's analysis (1999) of the changing role of authority in the international political economy. Here, Cutler argues that the growing influence of private actors has blurred the boundaries between private and public authority in the global realm. Following Justin Rosenberg, she claims that sovereignty in the global political economy is anything but absolute or ontologically given (objective). Rather, it is a social construct that is rapidly changing in form and content. Indeed, as Rosenberg notes if "sovereignty is redefined as a social form, and hence is specific to a very distinctive kind of society, then the consolidation of sovereignty and its generalization into a global states-system must imply a concrete historical process of social upheaval and transformation."

In his essay, "Globalization, Market Civilization, and Disciplinary Neo-Liberalism (1995)," Stephen Gill draws on the work of Gramsci to theorize about the new constitutionalization of world order via the dialectical interplay of the base and superstructure forces, and consent and coercion. As he suggests, the importance of working toward a critical understanding of the legitimacy of political structures requires further analysis of the dialectical and social forces of the changing world order; more specifically, the interplay between global elites, who dictate the flows of capital, labor and information, and the counter-hegemonic blocs, notably, the transnational networks of dissident NGOs, womens, peace, environmental, and social movements.

Given these critical theory perspectives on the world economy, the question(s) that arises is how the political content of sovereignty has changed in relation to the social forces of the international political economy? How should we understand this change in relation to society (global) as a whole? And what social science methods will allow us to understand the open-ended and objective reality of this change in the global political economy? Christian Heine's and Benno Teschke's response to these questions is that we need to reconsider the methodological value of dialectic. More specifically, Heine and Teschke argue that the dialectic, because it focuses renewed attention on the open-ended nature of praxis, allows us to critically investigate the contradictory relations between subject and object and structure and agency. In this sense, the dialectic "denaturalizes the object domain," or cause and effect insofar as "social totality is comprehended though concepts and is not merely conceptual." Whether or not the dialectic resolves the above tensions between critical theory approaches to the international political economy and normative ethics, it does reveal the important challenges for working beyond these tensions.

Endnotes

1. Justin Rosenberg, *The Empire of Civil Society* (Cambridge: Polity Press, 1990), p. 135.
2. Christian Heine and Benno Teschke, "Sleeping Beauty and the Dialectical Awakening: On the Potential of Dialectic for International Relations", *Millennium: Journal of International Studies*, Vol. 24, No. 2 (1995), p. 418.

Robert Cox, "Social Forces, States and World Order"*

Social Forces, Hegemony and Imperialism

Represented as a fit between material power, ideology and institutions, hegemony may seem to lend itself to a cyclical theory of history; the three dimensions fitting together in certain times and places and coming apart in others. This is reminiscent of earlier notions of *virtū*, or of the *weltgeist* migrating from people to people. The analogy merely points to something which remains unexplained. What is missing is some theory as to how and why the fit comes about and comes apart. It is my contention that the explanation may be sought in the realm of social forces shaped by production relations.

Social forces are not to be thought of as existing exclusively within states. Particular social forces may overflow state boundaries, and world structures can be described in terms of social forces just as they can be described as configurations of state power. The world can be represented as a pattern of interacting social forces in which states play an intermediate though autonomous role between the global structure of social forces and local configurations of social forces within particular countries. This may be called a political economy perspective of the world: power is seen as *emerging* from social processes rather than taken as given in the form of accumulated material capabilities, that is as the result of these processes. (Paraphrasing Marx, one could describe the latter, neo-realist view as the "fetishism of power.") In reaching for a political economy perspective, we move from identifying the structural characteristics of world orders as configurations of material capabilities, ideas and institutions to explaining their origins, growth and demise in terms of the interrelationships of the three levels of structures.

It is, of course, no great discovery to find that, viewed in the political economy perspective, the *pax britannica* was based both on the ascendancy of manufacturing capitalism in the international exchange economy, of which Britain was the center, and on the social and ideological power, in Britain and other parts of northwest Europe, of the class which drew its wealth from manufacturing. The new bourgeoisie did not need to control states directly; its social power became the premise of state politics.

The demise of this hegemonic order can also be explained by the development of social forces. Capitalism mobilized an industrial labor force in the most advanced countries, and from the last quarter of the nineteenth century industrial workers had an impact on the structure of the state in these countries. The incorporation of the industrial workers, the new social force called into existence by manufacturing capitalism, into the nation involved an extension in the range of state action in the form of economic intervention and social policy. This in turn brought the factor of domestic welfare (i.e., the social minimum required to maintain the allegiance of the workers) into the realm of foreign policy. The claims of welfare competed with the exigencies of liberal internationalism within the management of states; as the former

---

* *Millenium: Journal of International Studies.* This article first appeared in *Millenium*, Vol. 10, No. 2, 1981, and is reproduced with the permission of the publisher.

gained ground, protectionism, the new imperialism and ultimately the end of the gold standard marked the long decline of liberal internationalism. The liberal form of state was slowly replaced by the welfare nationalist form of state.

The spread of industrialization, and mobilization of social classes it brought about, not only changed the nature of states but also altered the international configuration of state power as new rivals overtook Britain's lead. Protectionism, as the means of building economic power comparable to Britain's, was for these new industrial countries more convincing than the liberal theory of comparative advantage. The new imperialisms of the major industrial powers were a projection abroad of the welfare nationalist consensus among social forces sought or achieved within the nations. As both the material predominance of the British economy and the appeal of the hegemonic ideology weakened, the hegemonic world order of the mid-nineteenth century gave place to a non-hegemonic configuration of rival power blocs.

Imperialism is a rather loose concept which in practice has to be newly defined with reference to each historical period. There is little point in looking for any "essence" of imperialism beyond the forms which dominance and subordination take in different successive world order structures. The actual form, whether activated by states, by social forces (e.g., the managements of multinational corporations), or some combination of both, and whether domination is primarily political or economic, is to be determined by historical analysis, and not by deductive reasoning.

The expansive capitalism of the mid-nineteenth century brought most of the world into the exchange relations of an international economy centered in London. The liberal imperialism of this phase was largely indifferent as to whether or not peripheral countries were formally independent or under the political-administrative control of a colonial power, provided that the rules of the international economy were observed. Canada and Argentina, for example, had similar positions in real terms, though one had colonial and the other independent status. In the phase of liberal imperialism, local authorities, who were often precapitalist in their relationship to the production process (e.g., traditional agrarian-based rulers), kept their countries in the commercial system. During the second phase, that of the so-called new imperialism following the 1870s, direct state control began to supplant the less formal patterns of the commercial period. Capitalist production relations under this political aegis penetrated the periphery more thoroughly, notably in the extraction of raw materials and the building of the infrastructure (roads, railways, ports, and commercial and governmental administrations) required to link the colonies more closely with the metropole.

Capitalist production relations generated new social forces in the periphery. Outsiders came to play important roles in the local society, some as agents of the colonial administration and of big capital from the metropole, others in smaller business, filling the interstices between big capital and traditional local production (for example, Chinese in southeast Asia, the Indians in east Africa or the Lebanese in west Africa). A local workforce often numerically small and materially better off than the majority of the population, was drawn into capitalist production. This politically strategic group was opposed to capital on wage and labor issues but aligned with it as regards the development of the capitalist production sector. An indigenous petty bourgeoisie also grew up, occupying the subordinate positions in colonial administration and metropole-based enterprises, as well as in local small business. A local state apparatus emerged under colonial tutelage, encouraging the new production relations by methods ranging from the introduction of compulsory labor or a head tax as a means of generating a labor force, to reproducing, in the colonial context, some of the institutions and procedures of the industrial relations of the metropole.

The existence in the colonial territory of these new social forces, labor and the petty bourgeoisie, which could agree on a nationalist political program, together with the introduction by the colonial administration of the elements of a modern state apparatus (control of which could be the aim of this program) laid the basis for the anticolonial revolt which swept the colonial world after the Second World War. This movement reacted against administrative control from the metropole, but not continued involvement in capitalist production and exchange relations. The anti-imperialist label on the forces which replaced the structures created by the second phase or new imperialism obscured their role in ushering in yet a third phase of imperialism.

James Petras, in his use of the concept of an imperial state system, has posed a number of questions concerning the structural characteristics of states in the present world order. The dominant imperial state and subordinate collaborator states differ in structure and have complementary functions in the imperial system; they are not just more and less powerful units of the same kind, as might be represented in a simple neorealist model. A striking feature in his framework is that the imperial state he analyzes is not the whole U.S. government; it is "those executive bodies within the 'government' which are charged with promoting and protecting the expansion of capital across state boundaries." The imperial system is at once more than and less than the state. It is more than the state in that it is a transnational structure with a dominant core and dependent periphery. This part of the U.S. government is at the system's core, together (and here we may presume to enlarge upon Petras' indications) with interstate institutions such as the IMF and the World Bank symbiotically related to expansive capital, and with collaborator governments (or at any rate parts of them linked to the system) in the system's periphery. It is less than the state in the sense that nonimperial, or even anti-imperial, forces may be present in other parts of both core and periphery states. The unity of the state, posited by neorealism, is fragmented in this image, and the struggle for and against the imperial system may go on within the state structures at both core and periphery as well as among social forces ranged in support and opposition to the system. The state is thus a necessary but insufficient category to account for the imperial system. The imperial system itself becomes the starting point of inquiry.

The imperial system is a world order structure drawing support from a particular configuration of social forces, national and transnational, and of core and periphery states. One must beware of slipping into the language of reification when speaking of structures; they are constraints on action, not actors. The imperial system includes some formal and less formal organizations at the system level through which pressures on states can be exerted without these system-level organizations actually usurping state power. The behavior of particular states or of organized economic and social interests, however, finds its meaning in the larger totality of the imperial system. Actions are shaped either directly by pressures projected through the system or indirectly by the subjective awareness on the part of actors of the constraints imposed by the system. Thus one cannot hope to understand the imperial system by identifying imperialism with actors, be they states or multinationals; these are both dominant elements in the system, but the system as a structure is more than their sum. Furthermore, one must beware of ignoring the principle of dialectic by overemphasizing the power and coherence of a structure, even a very dominant one. Where a structure is manifestly dominant, critical theory leads one to look for a counterstructure, even a latent one by seeking out its possible bases of support and elements of cohesion. At this point, it is preferable to revert to the earlier terminology which referred to hegemonic and nonhegemonic world order structures. To introduce the term "imperial" with reference to the *pax americana* risks both obscuring the important difference between hegemonic and non-hegemonic world orders and confusing structurally different kinds of imperialism (e.g., liberal imperialism, the new or colonial imperialism, and the imperial system just outlined). The contention here is that the *pax americana* was hegemonic: it commanded a wide measure of consent among states outside the Soviet sphere and was able to provide sufficient benefits to the associated and subordinate elements in order to maintain their acquiescence. Of course, consent wore thin as one approached the periphery where the element of force was always apparent, and it was in the periphery that the challenge to the imperial system first became manifest.

It was suggested above how the particular fit between power, ideology, and institutions constituting the *pax americana* came into being. Since the practical issue at the present is whether or not the *pax americana* has irretrievably come apart and if so what may replace it, two specific questions deserving attention are: (1) what are the mechanisms for maintaining hegemony in this particular historical structure? and (2) what social forces and/or forms of state have been generated within it which could oppose and ultimately bring about a transformation of the structure?

The Internationalization of the State

A partial answer to the first question concerns the internationalization of the state. The basic principles of the *pax americana* were similar to those of the *pax britannica*—relatively free movement of goods, capital and technology and a reasonable degree of predictability in exchange rates. Cordell Hull's conviction that an open trading world was a necessary condition of peace could be taken as its ideological text, supplemented by confidence in economic growth and ever-rising productivity as the basis for moderating and controlling conflict. The postwar hegemony was, however, more fully institutionalized than the *pax britannica* and the main function of its institutions was to reconcile domestic social pressures with the requirements of a world economy. The International Monetary Fund was set up to provide loans to countries with balance of payments deficits in order to provide time in which they could make adjustments, and to avoid the sharp deflationary consequences of an automatic gold standard. The World Bank was to be a vehicle for longer term financial assistance. Economically weak countries were to be given assistance by the system itself, either directly through the system's institutions or by other states after the system's institutions had certified their conformity to the system's norms. These institutions incorporated mechanisms to supervise the application of the system's norms and to make financial assistance effectively conditional upon reasonable evidence of intent to live up to the norms.

This machinery of surveillance was, in the case of the western allies and subsequently of all industrialized capitalist countries, supplemented by elaborate machinery for the harmonization of national policies. Such procedures began with the mutual criticism of reconstruction plans in western European countries (the U.S. condition for Marshall aid funds), continued with the development of annual review procedure in NATO (which dealt with defense and defense support programs), and became an acquired habit of mutual consultation and mutual review of national policies (through the OECD and other agencies).

The notion of international obligation moved beyond a few basic commitments, such as observance of the most favored nation principle or maintenance of an agreed exchange rate, to a general recognition that measures of national economic policy affect other countries and that such consequences should be taken into account before national policies are adopted. Conversely, other countries should be sufficiently understanding of one country's difficulties to acquiesce in short-term exceptions. Adjustments are thus perceived as responding to the needs of the system as a whole and not to the will of dominant countries. External pressures upon national policies were accordingly internationalized.

Of course, such an internationalized policy process presupposed a power structure, one in which central agencies of the U.S. government were in a dominant position. But it was not necessarily an entirely hierarchical power structure with lines of force running exclusively from the top down, nor was it one in which the units of interaction were whole nation-states. It was a power structure seeking to maintain consensus through bargaining and one in which the bargaining units were fragments of states. The power behind the negotiation was tacitly taken into account by the parties.

The practice of policy harmonization became such a powerful habit that when the basic norms of international economic behavior no longer seemed valid, as became the case during the 1970s, procedures for mutual adjustment of national economic policies were, if anything, reinforced. In the absence of clear norms, the need for mutual adjustment appeared the greater.

State structures appropriate to this process of policy harmonization can be contrasted with those of the welfare nationalist state of the preceding period. Welfare nationalism took the form of economic planning at the national level and the attempt to control external economic impacts upon the national economy. To make national planning effective, corporative structures grew up in most industrially advanced countries for the purpose of bringing industry, and also organized labor, into consultation with the government in the formulation and implementation of policy. National and industrial corporative structures can raise protectionist or restrictive obstacles to the adjustments required for adaptation of national economies to the world economy in a hegemonic system. Corporatism at the national level was a response to the conditions of the interwar period; it became institutionally consolidated in western Europe just as the world structure was changing into something for which national corporatism was ill-suited.

The internationalization of the state gives precedence to certain state agencies—notably ministries of finance and prime ministers' offices—which are key points in the adjustment of domestic to international economic policy. Ministries of industries, labor ministries, planning offices, which had been built up in the context of national corporatism, tended to be subordinated to the central organs of internationalized public policy. As national economies became more integrated in the world economy it was the larger and more technologically advanced enterprises that adapted best to the new opportunities. A new axis of influence linked international policy networks with the key central agencies of government and with big business. This new informal corporative structure overshadowed the older more formalized national corporatism and reflected the dominance of the sector oriented to the world economy over the more nationally oriented sector of a country's economy.

The internationalization of the state is not, of course, limited to advanced capitalist core countries. It would not be difficult to make a catalogue of recent cases in peripheral countries where institutions of the world economy, usually as a condition for debt renewal, have dictated policies which could only be sustained by a coalition of conservative forces. Turkey, Peru, and Portugal are among those recently affected. As for Zaire, a conference of creditors laid down the condition that officials of the IMF be placed within the key ministries of the state to oversee the fulfillment of the conditions of debt renewal.

The Internationalization of Production

The internationalization of the state is associated with the expansion of international production. This signifies the integration of production processes on a transnational scale, with different phases of a single process being carried but in different countries. International production currently plays the formative role in relation to the structure of states and world order that national manufacturing and commercial capital played in the mid-nineteenth century.

International production expands through direct investment, whereas the rentier imperialism, of which Hobson and Lenin wrote, primarily took the form of portfolio investment. With portfolio investment, control over the productive resources financed by the transaction passed with ownership to the borrower. With direct investment, control is inherent in the production process itself and remains with the originator of the investment. The essential feature of direct investment is possession, not of money, but of knowledge—in the form of technology and especially in the capacity to continue to develop new technology. The financial arrangements for direct investment may vary greatly, but all are subordinated to this crucial factor of technical control. The arrangements may take the form of wholly owned subsidiaries, joint ventures with local capital sometimes put up by the state in host countries, management contracts with state-owned enterprises, or compensation agreements with socialist enterprises whereby, in return for the provision of technology, these enterprises become suppliers of elements to a globally organized production process planned and controlled by the source of the technology. Formal ownership is less important than the manner in which various elements are integrated into the production system.

Direct investment seems to suggest the dominance of industrial capital over finance capital. The big multinational corporations which expand by direct investment are, to some degree, self-financing and to the extent that they are not they seem capable of mobilizing money capital in a number of ways, such as through local capital markets (where their credit is better than that of national entrepreneurs), through the Euro-currency markets, through infusions of capital from other multinationals linked to technology and production agreements, through state subsidies, and so forth. And yet, particularly since the 1970s, finance capital seems to be returning to prominence through the operations of the multinational banks, not only in the old form of rentier imperialism administering loans to peripheral states, but also as a network of control and private planning for the world economy of international production. This network assesses and collectivizes investment risks and allocates investment opportunities among the participants in the expansion of international production, that is, it performs the function of Lenin's collective capitalist in the conditions of late-twentieth-century production relations.

International Production and Class Structure

International production is mobilizing social forces, and it is through these forces that its major political consequences vis-à-vis the nature of states and future world orders may be anticipated. Hitherto, social classes have been found to exist within nationally defined social formations, despite rhetorical appeals to the international solidarity of workers. Now, as a consequence of international production, it becomes increasingly pertinent to think in terms of a global class structure alongside or superimposed upon national class structures.

At the apex of an emerging global class structure is the transnational managerial class. Having its own ideology, strategy and institutions of collective action, it is a class both in itself and for itself. Its focal points of organization, the Trilateral Commission, World Bank, IMF and OECD, develop both a framework of thought and guidelines for policies. From these points, class action penetrates countries through the process of internationalization of the state. The members of this transnational class are not limited to those who carry out functions at the global level, such as executives of multinational corporations or as senior officials of international agencies, but include those who manage the internationally oriented sectors within countries, the finance ministry officials, local managers of enterprises linked into international production systems, and so on.

National capitalists are to be distinguished from the transnational class. The natural reflex of national capital faced with the challenge of international production is protectionism. It is torn between the desire to use the state as a bulwark of an independent national economy and the opportunity of filling niches left by international production in a subordinate symbiotic relationship with the latter.

Industrial workers have been doubly fragmented. One line of cleavage is between established and nonestablished labor. Established workers are those who have attained a status of relative security and stability in their jobs and have some prospects of career advancement. Generally they are relatively skilled, work for larger enterprises, and have effective trade unions. Nonestablished workers, by contrast, have insecure employment, have no prospect of career advancement, are relatively less skilled, and confront great obstacles in developing effective trade unions. Frequently, the nonestablished are disproportionately drawn from lower-status ethnic minorities, immigrants and women. The institutions of working class action have privileged established workers. Only when the ideology of class solidarity remains powerful, which usually means only in conditions of high ideological polarization and social and political conflict, do organizations controlled by established workers (unions and political parties) attempt to rally and act for nonestablished workers as well.

The second line of cleavage among industrial workers is brought about by the division between national and international capital (i.e., that engaged in international production). The established workers in the sector of international production are potential allies of international capital. This is not to say that those workers have no conflict with international capital, only that international capital has the resources to resolve these conflicts and to isolate them from conflicts involving other labor groups by creating an enterprise corporatism in which both parties perceive their interest as lying in the continuing expansion of international production.

Established workers in the sector of national capital are more susceptible to the appeal of protectionism and national (rather than enterprise) corporatism in which the defense of national capital, of jobs and of the workers' acquired status in industrial relations institutions, are perceived to be interconnected.

Nonestablished labor has become of particular importance in the expansion of international production. Production systems are being designed so as to make use of an increasing proportion of semi-skilled (and therefore frequently nonestablished) in relation to skilled (and established) labor. This tendency in production organization makes it possible for the center to decentralize the actual physical production of goods to peripheral locations in which an abundant supply of relatively cheap nonestablished labor is to be found, and to retain control of the process and of the research and development upon which its future depends.

As a nonestablished workforce is mobilized in Third-World countries by international production, governments in these countries have very frequently sought to preempt the possibility of this new social force developing its own class-conscious organizations by imposing upon it structures of state corporatism in the form of unions set up and controlled by the government or the dominant political party. This also gives local governments, through their control over local labor, additional leverage with international capital regarding the terms of direct investment. If industrial workers in Third-World countries have thus sometimes been reduced to political and social quiescence, state corporatism may prove to be a stage delaying, but in the long run not eliminating, a more articulate self-consciousness.

Even if industry were to move rapidly into the Third World and local governments were, by and large, able to keep control over their industrial workforces, most of the populations of these countries may see no improvement, but probably a deterioration, in their conditions. New industrial jobs lag far behind increases in the labor force, while changes in agriculture dispossess many in the rural population. No matter how fast international production spreads, a very large part of the world's population in the poorest areas remains marginal to the world economy, having no employment or income, or the purchasing power derived from it. A major problem for international capital in its aspiration for hegemony is how to neutralize the effect of this marginalization of perhaps one-third of the world's population so as to prevent its poverty from fueling revolt.

Social Forces, State Structures, and Future World Order Prospects

It would, of course, be logically inadmissible, as well as imprudent, to base predictions of future world order upon the foregoing considerations. Their utility is rather in drawing attention to factors which could incline an emerging world order in one direction or another. The social forces generated by changing production processes are the starting point for thinking about possible futures. These forces may combine in different configurations, and as an exercise one could consider the hypothetical configurations most likely to lead to three different outcomes as to the future of the system. The focus on these three outcomes is not, of course, to imply that other outcomes or configurations of social forces are possible.

First, is the prospect for a new hegemony being based upon the global structure of social power generated by the internationalizing of production. This would require a consolidation of two presently powerful and related tendencies: the countries, and the continuing internationalization of the state. Implicit in such an outcome is a continuance of monetarism as the orthodoxy of economic policy, emphasizing the stabilization of the world economy (anti-inflationary policies and stable exchange rates) over the fulfillment of domestic sociopolitical demands (the reduction of unemployment and the maintenance of real-wage levels). The interstate power configuration which could maintain such a world order, provided its member states conformed to this model, is a coalition centering upon the United States, the Federal Republic of Germany, and Japan, with the support of other OECD states, the co-optation of a few of the more industrialized Third-World countries, such as Brazil, and of leading conservative OPEC countries, and the possibility of revived détente allowing for a greater linkage of the Soviet sphere into the world economy of international production. The new international division of labor, brought about through the progressive decentralization of manufacturing into the Third World by international capital, would satisfy demands for industrialization from those countries. Social conflict in the core countries would be combated through enterprise corporatism, though many would be left unprotected by this method, particularly the nonestablished workers. In the peripheral countries, social conflict would be contained through a combination of state corporatism and repression.

The social forces opposed to this configuration have been noted above. National capital, those sections of established labor linked to national capital, newly mobilized nonestablished workers in the Third World, and social marginals in the poor countries are all in some way or another potentially opposed to international capital, and to the state and world order structures most congenial to international capital. These forces do not, however, have any natural cohesion, and might be dealt with separately, or neutralized, by an effective hegemony. If they did come together under particular circumstances in a particular country, precipitating a change of regime, then that country might be dealt with in isolation through the world structure. In other words, where hegemony failed within a particular country, it could reassert itself through the world structure.

A second possible outcome is a nonhegemonic world structure of conflicting power centers. Perhaps the most likely way for this to evolve would be through the ascendancy in several core countries of neo-mercantilist coalitions which linked national capital and established labor, and were determined to opt out of arrangements designed to promote international capital and to organize their own power and welfare on a national or sphere-of-influence basis. The continuing pursuit of monetarist policies may be the single most likely cause of neomercantilist reaction. Legitimated as anti-inflationary, monetarist policies have been perceived as hindering national capital (because of high interest rates), generating unemployment (through planned recession), and adversely affecting relatively deprived social groups and regions dependent upon government services and transfer payments (because of budget-balancing cuts in state expenditures). An opposing coalition would attack monetarism for subordinating national welfare to external forces, and for showing an illusory faith in the markets (which are perceived to be manipulated by corporate-administered pricing). The likely structural form of neomercantilism within core-states would be industry-level and national-level corporatism, bringing national capital and organized labor into a relationship with the government for the purpose of making and implementing of state policy. Peripheral states would have much the same structure as in the first outcome, but would be more closely linked to one or another of the core-country economies.

A third and more remotely possible outcome would be the development of a counter-hegemony based on a Third-World coalition against core-country dominance and aiming toward the autonomous development of peripheral countries and the termination of the core-periphery relationship. A counterhegemony would consist of a coherent view of an alternative world order, backed by a concentration of power sufficient to maintain a challenge to core countries. While this outcome is foreshadowed by the demand for a New International Economic Order, the prevailing consensus behind this demand lacks a sufficiently clear view of an alternative world political economy to constitute counterhegemony. The prospects of counterhegemony lies very largely in the future development of state structures in the Third World.

The controlling social force in these countries is, typically, what has been called a "state class," a combination of party, bureaucratic and military personnel and union leaders, mostly petty-bourgeois in origin, which controls the state apparatus and through it attempts to gain greater control over the productive apparatus in the country. The state class can be understood as a local response to the forces generated by the internationalizing of production, and an attempt to gain some local control over these forces. The orientation of the state class is indeterminate. It can be either conservative or radical. It may either bargain for a better deal within the world economy of international production, or it may seek to overcome the unequal internal development generated by international capital.

State classes of the first orientation are susceptible to incorporation into a new hegemonic world economy, and to the maintenance of state corporatist structures as the domestic counterpart to international capital. The second orientation could provide the backing for counterhegemony. However, a state class is only likely to maintain the second and more radical orientation if it is supported from below in the form of a genuine populism (and not just a populism manipulated by political leaders). One *may* speculate that this could come about through the unfolding social consequences of international production, such as the mobilization of a new nonestablished labor force coupled with the marginalization of an increasing part of the urban population. The radical alternative could be the form of response to international capital in Third-World countries, just as neomercantilism could be the response in richer countries. Each projects a particular state structure and vision of world order.

Justin Rosenberg, Selection from
The Empire of Civil Society

Sovereignty as a Capitalist Political Form

These observations may turn out to be of considerable relevance to IR. For what is the political form under discussion here if not the conceptual building-block of the discipline, namely the sovereign state? This is a category in need of some clarification. Most commentators accept that the primacy denoted by the term 'sovereignty' cannot be defined straightforwardly as the ability of the state to control activities within its borders or resist external constraint on its freedom of action. Apart from anything else, there are just too many small, weak states in the world for this to be empirically plausible. For this reason, we all learn that its absolute properties refer to its juridical status. A sovereign state does not share jurisdiction with Church and nobility as under feudalism, or suffer systematic subordination to a party organization as under Soviet communism. Yet sovereignty is not just the legal paramountcy of the state—and even if it were, it is not easy to see how this could be sustained without exercising a preponderance of power. Much IR theorizing on the subject seems to waver uncertainly between these two definitions, substantive and formal, switching back and forth depending on the particular issues being discussed. Excited claims that the latest wave of military or communications technology, or the latest round of 'globalization' in the world economy, are rendering the concept of sovereignty obsolete alternate with firm denials of any diminution in the political, legal and military monopolies commanded by the state. As a result, students often find the whole issue of sovereignty deeply enigmatical: an absolute form of rule which seems never to be absolute in practice even though, for some reason, the formal constitution of the international system rests on the assumption that it is so.

What are we to do with what Waltz has called this 'bothersome concept'? Perhaps a first step might be to cease thinking about sovereignty as a self-evident starting point—which is what we do if we accept its own legal or political self-definition. Perhaps instead we should think of it as a form of political rule historically specific to the distinctive configuration of social relations which define capitalism as a kind of society. For sovereignty also, crucially, involves the idea of the state being outside, over against civil society, autonomous, 'purely political'. What do these phrases mean?

In part, they mean that 'the primacy of geopolitics' gives the state executive a warrant to override internal interest groups in the conduct of foreign policy. However, something like this could apply in any hierarchical society incorporated into a geopolitical system, and it is therefore not specific to sovereignty, the form of rule held to distinguish the modern state. Nor do they mean that the state is not involved in regulating civil society. It is, after all, the state which frames laws, upholds contracts, raises taxes and implements policies designed to promote the development of the sphere of production.

None of these, however, need involve the state moving into that other realm of political command, namely the privatized sphere of production, by taking over the process of surplus extraction itself. Where it does do this, for example by extending its direct ownership through nationalization, it can find that the *sovereign* character of its rule diminishes. It no longer stands over against civil society. Industrial disputes are immediately political disputes. The appropriation of the surplus becomes an object of public 'political' struggle within the state rather than private political struggle within the productive corporations of civil society. The private despotism of the workplace becomes the public despotism of the state. A process such as this seemed to be a factor in the British 'Winter of Discontent' of 1978–79: the sovereignty of the state was eroded because the day-to-day separation between politics and economics was blurred, and the government therefore found itself dragged into one industrial dispute after another.

Conversely, however, the restoration of the sovereignty of the state in such circumstances is also the restoration of the private political sphere and of the class power of capital in this sphere of production. In fact, is this not what happened next in the British case? The Labour government fell, and was replaced by Margaret Thatcher's Conservative administration, which came into office with a commitment to 'roll back the frontiers of the state'. On the face of it, this commitment seemed to be contradicted by the evidence, namely the failure to reduce public spending levels, the reinforcement of the coercive arm of the state, and the transparent use of state legislative authority to intervene in industry by reducing the legal power of organized labour. But if we understand the capitalist separation of politics and economics in the manner suggested by Ellen Wood, then a real underlying consistency emerges which concerns the *sovereignty* of the state.

For the sovereignty of the state does depend on both a kind of abstraction from production and the reconstitution of the state-political sphere as external to civil society. But this is not an abstraction which means that the sovereignty of the state is neutral. On the contrary, its very form is a dimension of class power because it entails the parallel consolidation of private political power in production. An illustration of what this can mean in practice was the British miners' strike of 1984–85. Since it is known that the government gave the Coal Board every possible assistance behind the scenes, its insistence that the strike was an industrial dispute and not the business of the state can be made sense of only in terms of a determination to redefine 'the political' as outside and separate from surplus extraction, a re-definition whose other half was necessarily the restoration of private political power in production. Perhaps the two most oft-repeated goals of the government during the dispute were that an impersonal rule of law should be upheld, and that 'management should be allowed to manage'. In other words, the state was neither withdrawing from civil society nor necessarily encroaching further upon it. It was reimposing the separation of political functions between public and private spheres which is the *form* of both class power and state power under capitalism.

All this suggests that we should define sovereignty primarily not in terms of the practical ability of the state to command the behaviour of its citizens, nor yet as a kind of residual legal paramountcy. To be sure, without these there would be no sovereign states. But these descriptive attributes, enormous though their practical significance is, do not comprise an explanation of why the modern state assumes its distinctive 'purely political' form. By contrast, if we define sovereignty as the social form of the state in a society where political power is divided between public and private spheres, it becomes apparent that at least some of the confusion over whether modern state power is strong or weak, autonomous or determined, sovereign or constrained has been unnecessary. For under capitalism, these are not necessarily dichotomies.

The Sovereign States-System

The Structural Implications of Sovereignty

The historical rise of the sovereign state is thus one aspect of a comprehensive reorganization of the forms of social power. The change that it works in the form and content of the international system is no less startling. For under this new arrangement, while relations of citizenship and jurisdiction define state borders, any aspects of social life which are mediated by relations of exchange in principle no longer receive a political definition (though they are still overseen by the state in various ways) and hence may extend across these borders. And if political functions which used to be in state hands are now assigned to a private political sphere fronted by a set of exchange relations, then these political functions will travel.

This is indeed what has occurred. It is now possible, in a way that would have been unthinkable under feudalism, to command and exploit productive labour (and natural resources) located under the jurisdiction of another state. This is because capitalist relations of surplus extraction are organized through a contract of exchange which is defined as 'non-political'. It must be reiterated that it simply will not do to call this 'economics' and think we have explained anything unless we *either* say that this is the first time there has been such a phenomenon as 'economics' *or* define it more closely as capitalist economics. And either way, we have to include in our definition the peculiar state-form which is its other half, because these functions can be regarded as non-political only on the assumption that politics has been redefined to restrict it to general communal functions.

Historically, this transformation seems to have been accomplished in Europe in two broad, overlapping phases. The first phase comprised the processes of state-building, that is, the centralizing of political authority by absolutist monarchs, the suppression of rival centres of power and the construction of a bureaucratic machinery of government This made it possible for monarchs to exercise a much more absolute and exclusive jurisdiction, so that states became much more sharply defined territorially. The modern political map of the world is a perfectly fitting jigsaw in which all the separate, interlocking pieces are clearly marked in different colours. For much of orthodox IR, the modern world begins here, where the impossible patchwork of medieval Christendom is replaced by territorially unified jurisdictions. However, lagging some way behind this process of state-building there followed the liberal transformation of the state discussed above—which eventually overthrew absolutism. And as a result of *this* process, it actually becomes less and less realistic to try to theorize the international system in terms of relations between states alone. Moreover, if we take the two processes together over the whole period, we must say that what looks to the naked eye like an unprecedented concentrating of power in the hands of the state apparatus (as certain functions are centralized as never before) is simultaneously a dramatic *disaggregation* of social functions and social power, between public and private spheres.

Clearly, the trick here, as this overall shift takes place, is to keep our eye on *both* political spheres which emerge (that is, public and private), otherwise we will assume that what we are seeing is simply a shift from empire to states-system, which could safely be treated purely in its external aspect. In the public political sphere this is indeed the form of the shift. And if we watch only that external, public sphere, it would then seem that we could theorize the international system by listing the *differentia specifica* of a states-system as compared with an empire, and understand its properties *sui generis* as those of anarchy. This is the path of realism. But it ignores the changing structural definition and content of 'the political'. And its effect is precisely to occlude the distinctive character of modern international power.

For it is this formal disjunctive (between public and private political realms) which explains part of the paradox of sovereignty: why it is both more absolute in its 'purely political' prerogatives than other historical forms of rule, and yet highly ambiguous as a measure of actual power. It explains how we can see simultaneously an enhanced territorial differentiation between states together with an unprecedented porousness and interdependence.

Viewed in this way, it becomes increasingly apparent that in realism reality is standing on its head. Realists tell us that the modern international political system is different because it is a states-system organized by anarchy rather than an empire organized by centralized command. However, if the above discussion is sound, then, to be true, this statement needs to be turned right way up. It is not so much that modern international politics is different because it is a states-system; rather, we can have a global states-system only because modern 'politics' is different. And the surest way to misunderstanding here is precisely the attempt to theorize this difference in abstraction from the historically specific kind of society which produces this form of politics. For the form itself is not inert or neutral, but rather suffused with determinations deriving from its capitalist character.

Once this point is seen, we can (and will) go on to explore the distinctive properties of this social form of geopolitics—including the character of anarchy. But if empire is taken to mean the expansion of political command beyond the territory of the originating community in order to accumulate resources from outside, then the last thing this portends is the end of empire. Rather it means that the exercise of imperial power, like domestic social power, will have two linked aspects: a public political aspect which concerns the management of the states-system, and a private political aspect which effects the extraction and relaying of surpluses. It means the rise of a new kind of empire: the empire of civil society.

Political Implications of Sovereignty

It has just been suggested that what we witness in the emergence of the modern states-system is actually the development of a new form of imperial power characteristic of a fundamentally new kind of (capitalist) social structure. It was also implied that a theoretical understanding of contemporary international relations would therefore have to encompass both the public political and the private political aspects of international power which emerge in the modern period. This may seem to invite the charge that we have done no more than reinvent the wheel. For each of these aspects, public political and private political, has its own specificities: military, legal and territorial for the one; and civil, profit-seeking and transnational for the other. Moreover, they are largely carrid out by identifiably distinct actors: states and private corporations. And therefore has not the work of international political economy already produced the necessary reformulation by posing the discipline in terms of the interaction of states and markets?

The answer must be negative. For assuming the separation of politics and economics as a starting point in this way is not a theoretically innocent assumption. It is to assume the automatic reproduction of the particular human social relations which bring about and sustain this institutional separation. And we cannot assume this, partly because these relations have not obtained for most of history, perhaps more importantly because there are still large areas of humanity where they do not obtain; but mainly because even where they do obtain, they are continually being contested. Much of the content of international relations, past and present, is the outcome of continuous struggle over the reproduction of these capitalist social relations. If we assume their reproduction, then we exclude from our account the very human agency and historical *process* we are trying to recover as the basis of the social world. We see that world not as the daily outcome of definite social relations between real living individuals, but as the timeless clash of disembodied social forms: the remorseless grinding of the balance of power, the ghostly motions of the invisible hand.

But this is to imply that, in some way parallel to the earlier example of the miners' strike, the sovereign form of the states-*system* is itself the object and outcome of struggle and contestation. What could this mean?

Consider the fate of the New International Economic Order (NIEO). From the mid 1970s, emboldened by the example of OPEC, a large group of Third World governments (organized as the Group of 77) used their numerical majority in the General Assembly of the United Nations to press through demands for a reform of the international economy. In 1974 the General Assembly adopted a 'Charter of Economic Rights and Duties of States' which included provisions for linking commodity prices to prices of manufacture, the expropriation of foreign invesments, increased controls on the activities of multinationals, and so on. Here, then, was an attempt to challenge the separation of politics and economics, the separation which enabled the private dimension of the relationship between Western and Third World societies to count as non-political. Of course, majority votes in the General Assembly have no binding force, and the campaign for the NIEO failed for a number of reasons, including dis-unity among the southern states pressing for it. The point, however, is the form that this failure took.

By the mid 1980s, the UN was in financial difficulties due to the reduction or delay of funding by disenchanted Western governments. Moreover, a number of the Group of 77 were now submitting themselves to International Monetary Fund (IMF) restruc-turing packages in exchange for debt-rescheduling agreements. Now, the negotiation of economic terms by indebted countries with the IMF does not count as a political process; none the less, it did embody a dramatic reversal of the very programme which these countries had been attempting to advance by political means. For a prominent feature of these packages was a withdrawal of the state from direct control of prices through subsidy and tariff—a withdrawal which effected, in principle at least, a new separation of politics and economics, and thereby opened these societ-ies further to the world market. The geographical progress of this outcome among the countries involved could be followed throughout the 1980s in the spread of what became known as 'IMF riots'—mass demonstrations against price increases imple-mented by governments as part of IMF restructuring packages. By January 1989, these had occurred in twenty-three countries.

It would be hazardous to draw any substantive conclusions from these events. But the overall pattern of this episode is surely too suggestive to pass without comment. The Group of 77 pressed for further public political regulation through the UN; their defeat was registered in a fuller than ever subordination to private economic mecha-nisms through the IMF. By reimposing the separation of the world economy from the formal political institutions of the states-system, the West was able to restore simultaneously the private freedom of capital and the purely political sovereignty of the states-system, both of which were challenged by the NIEO.

Significantly, this denouement of the 1980s coincided historically with a vigor-ous revival of both neo-liberal economic theory (and deregulation) and neorealist state theory (and flexing of the coercive military arm of the state). These supplanted the 1970s vogue for 'complex interdependence' and fears of international ungovern-ability, replacing them with a revived definition of the sovereign individuality of the state.

The NIEO, however, was a comparatively minor episode. What *was* the entire Soviet experience and the Cold War which dominated world politics for the last four decades, if not an enormous geopolitical challenge to the social form of the modern states-system? The Soviet Union was precisely not a sovereign state, in the sense that we have been discussing sovereignty. It did not stand outside a distinct private sphere of surplus extraction. It moved in and took it over. And it supported other govern-ments who did the same—who, by overthrowing the separation of politics and eco-nomics, withdrew their societies from the world market, and hence from the reach of private Western power. This was ultimately the political content of the Cold War.

With the best will in the world, it would be impossible to understand the Soviet presence in the international system in terms of states and markets. It was precisely an attempt to abolish both of them.

Marx would have us go even further. For him, the increasingly global, continuously fought-over separation of politics and economics—meaning the actual construction of the world market and the linked emergence of a sovereign states-system—was the central unfinished theme of modern world history. In fact, for Marx it is what has 'produced world history for the first time'.

By this stage we had already noted the descriptive affinities between the political institutions of the society in question and the theoretical ambiguities of the treatment of sovereignty in IR. These affinities led us to merge the two in a redefinition of sovereignty as the abstracted social form of the state specific to (and partly constitutive of) capitalist social relations. Once this connection was made, we sought to develop its implications for theorizing the sovereign states-system. These implications were of two kinds. First, the differentiation of spheres provided the structural precondition for a simultaneous enhancement of territorial definition of polities and yet deepening of material integration of social reproduction across borders. This was seen to give rise to a wholly new idiom of geopolitical power which we named 'the empire of civil society'. But second, our attention to the underlying structural interdependence of the public and private spheres led us to identify sovereignty itself as a contested social form because of its profound imbrication in the reproduction of these new forms of (private) power. Searching for manifestations of this within contemporary international history, we found first the NIEO, then the Cold War, and finally, pursuing a hint from Marx, the emergence of the modern international system itself.

Now, if sovereignty is redefined as a social form, and hence is specific to a very distinctive kind of society, then the consolidation of sovereignty and its generalization into a global states-system must imply a concrete *historical process* of social upheaval and transformation. And since this process is what produces the states-system in its modern form, then arguably it is here—rather than strictly in the diplomatic interchange between preconstituted states—that we shall find the real and continuing history of the international system. With this move, we have finally broken out of the realist framework for thinking about the origins of the sovereign states-system, and have instead linked up our account with the broader historical processes of social transformation involved in the making of the modern world.

Claire Cutler, "Locating Authority in the Global Political Economy"

The Law Merchant, Capitalism, and State Authority

Today the law merchant provides a crucial link between local and global political legal orders. It provides the mechanism for the extraterritorial application of national commercial law, thus establishing rules governing the interface of different national legal and political orders. It also provides a normative framework generated by a transnational elite, a mercatocracy, that comprises corporate and government actors whose interests are associated more generally with the transnational expansion of capitalism. However, this has not always been the case. In its earliest development, the law merchant operated outside the general social and economic conditions of the day, quite independent of local political authorities. This was to change with the emergence of the state system, the development of centralized state authority, and the move from the feudal to a capitalist political economy. These developments produced different authority structures, which in turn rested upon different social conditions. As Anderson shows, the nature of social unity changed in the context of transformations in the mode of production. The feudal mode of production was "characterized by a complex unity...a juridical amalgamation of economic exploitation with political authority". Political sovereignty was "never focussed in a single centre. The functions of the state were disintegrated in a vertical allocation downwards, at each level of which political and economic relations were...integrated. This parcelization of sovereignty was constitutive of the whole feudal mode of production". Although Anderson describes the feudal mode of production as "an organic unity of economy and polity", it was neither territorially centralized nor fixed. In addition, fractures in the social foundation were evident in resistance from those at the interstices of society, the tensions between town and manor, and the search for public authority resulting from ambiguity as regards political authority. In feudal society the right to rule was neither territorialized nor centralized, but diffuse and ambiguous. There was no distinction between public and private to provide the foundation for social unity or political authority. As a result, the feudal mode of production gave rise to "a constant struggle to establish a 'public' authority outside the compact web of private jurisdictions". Anderson shows how the public/private distinction developed with the growth of centralized and absolutist state authority and with evolving conceptions of property. The reception of Roman law with its notions of unconditional and absolute ownership was an important development in Western Europe, replacing medieval conceptions of conditional and contingent property rights and facilitating the centralization of political control. The development was significant because it signaled "the spread of commodity relations in the countryside that was to define the long transition from feudalism to capitalism in the West". Roman law differentiated between civil law (*jus*), regulating private and economic relations among citizens, and public law (*lex*), regulating relations between the state and its subjects. The recognition of the two spheres facilitated "commodity exchange in the transitional economies of the epoch," while at the same time enhancing the consolidation and "concentration of aristocratic power in a centralized state apparatus". This Anderson describes as a "double social movement": the "juridically unconditional character of private property consecrated by the one found its contradictory counterpart in the formally absolute nature of the imperial sovereignty exercised by the other."

The historical specificity of political authority begins to appear with moves from feudalism to absolutism, to mercantilism, and to capitalism. These moves involved definitions of authority resting upon distinct modes of production, which generated historically specific social and political relations. To the extent that there was a social unity or normative solidarity or a constituency to produce a civic consensus in medieval Europe, the instrumentalities were Christendom and the generally recognized norms of property rights and free exchange generated by the merchant communities. Christianity, however, achieved only a "minimal normative solidarity across state, ethnic, class and gender boundaries," uniting the Mediterranean and northwestern countries of Europe, but not eastern Byzantium. The law merchant provided a normative framework for merchants engaged in long-distance trade and for those residing in the special towns and city-states where merchants were accorded significant freedom and autonomy. The authority structure with regard to production and exchange was thus dualistic: local transactions were heavily regulated by religious and a diversity of political authorities, while long-distance and overseas exchange was conducted privately by merchants, under their own system of law, procedure, and institutions.

The erosion of this fusion and its transformation into separate spheres of civil society and political jurisdiction came with the growing territorialization, localization, and centralization of political authority in the absolutist state. The right to rule came to be located in centralized states. This gradually worked an erosion and eventually the disappearance of the law merchant as an autonomous legal order. The recognition of separate private and public realms translated, in international law, into the distinction between public and private international law. Public international law applied to states and their international relations, while private international law applied to private individual and corporate actors. The law merchant and its courts were incorporated into domestic legal systems where they were reconfigured as private international trade law.

Under the capitalist mode of production, as distinct from the feudal or mercantilist modes of production, the relationship between owners and producers—between capital and labor—"assumes a purely economic form," distinct from feudal tribute or mercantilist domination. It is crucial to note that the separation of economic exchange relations from political relations under capitalism is not simply a separation of different and independent spheres. As Justin Rosenberg notes, it is a distinction that is "internal to the mode of production", which has not effected an "evacuation of relations of domination from the realm of production". Rather, as Giddens observes, the distinction has "insulated" economic relations from political control. The capitalist mode of production transformed political powers into economic powers and defined the latter as a separate "apolitical" sphere.

Significantly, as part of this transformation, the law merchant was privatized and neutralized of political content as it became a component of *private* international trade law. As such it was regarded as a body of commercial law and practice, operating neutrally amongst market participants, deemed to be of equal bargaining power. This facilitated the consolidation of nationally based capitalism by providing the legal framework for the emergence of market society.

The nature and locus of political authority has thus changed and shifted with changes in the mode of production. As states consolidated their power into territorially fixed units, commercial relations were subjected to national regulatory controls and the merchant class disappeared as an autonomous group. At this time, the law merchant was incorporated into national legal commercial systems and became an integral part of the national commercial law of states. It became part of the process of state-building and an integral component of emerging nationally based capitalism.

With the transformation in political authority that attended the territorialization of political authority and the privatization of economic exchange, political authorities became more involved in regulating international commercial transactions. By the late nineteenth century, national commercial regulation eroded the uniformity of the law merchant and generated a movement in favor of harmonizing and unifying international commercial law. Initially, this movement was private and European in origin and nature. However, states became involved around the turn of the century and the movement expanded to include non-European states. With the creation of the United Nations and institutions charged with the unification of law, the movement attained global dimensions. The influence of the United States in generating legal rules and decision-making procedures has been crucial to emergence of the New Law Merchant, of which the unification movement is an integral aspect. The unification movement provides the institutional and ideological context for globalizing merchant laws and practices. It is driven by transnational insurance, transport, and financial corporations, national chambers of commerce, and cooperative government officials engaged in competitive deregulation and the creation of a permissive and voluntary regulatory framework. The movement is generating model laws, voluntary codes, and "soft laws" that are not legally binding, but rely on consent of commercial actors. For example, the *Principles of International Commercial Contracts* reflect the emphasis given to the private ordering of commercial relations and have been enthusiastically adopted by the international business community. They are generally consistent with moves to create a permissive environment for commercial and corporate activities. In addition, contemporary unification efforts reflect corporate and state concerns about intensifying international commercial competition and seek to secure and protect corporate interests in a manner consistent with "neoliberal discipline" and the "new constitutionalism." Stephen Gill observes that the contemporary restructuring of production and finance in the context of "disciplinary neoliberalism" and a "new constitutionalism," which render states accountable to international capital and market forces, exercises a powerful disciplinary influence and is reconfiguring the state and state-society relations.

The modern law merchant is an integral aspect of this politico-legal framework. Globalized productive relations are articulated through and embodied within property rights. The law merchant links local and global political economies together through a system of rules and procedures that protect and advance global property rights. Moreover, global corporate property relations are advanced by a *mercatocracy*: a transnational business class that includes private commercial actors whose work is facilitated by cooperative governments and international institutions committed to consolidating and advancing the global accumulation of capital. The *mercatocracy* forms an "historic bloc," united through material and ideological commitments to neoliberalism. The overwhelming value placed by this historic bloc on disembedding productive relations from both state and society through privatization is refiguring the boundary between private and public authority structures. The modern unification movement is facilitating the denationalization of capital and the disembedding of commercial activities from governmental and social controls by expanding the powers of transnational corporations. Indeed, as a significant step forward in the "globalization" of legal thinking, the unification movement is providing a crucial ideological service. It legitimizes the private, corporate ordering of transnational productive relations, functioning very much as an integral aspect of transnational capitalism. Critics of the unification movement note the unrepresentative nature of private unification efforts and the marginalization of the commercial interests of less-developed states. In creating a privileged sphere for first-world corporate activity, the movement forms an essential element in the reconfiguration of political authority resulting from the contemporary globalization of productive relations.

The material and ideological hegemony exercised by the contemporary historic bloc raises crucial problems for locating and identifying "authority" globally. The challenge lies in depicting authority in a late-capitalist and post-modern world where "political" authority ostensibly stops at the territorial borders of the state, while "economic" relations do not. Liberalism masks the "political" nature of these economic exchanges and obscures the extent to which the territorial state has ceased to run coextensively with the "right to rule" or is definitive of and constitutive of political authority. The discussion will turn to consider how Gramscian notions of hegemony assist in meeting this challenge.

Authority and Hegemony

...Liberalism renders *private* authority an impossibility by creating the distinction between public and private activities and locating the "right to rule" or authority squarely in the public sphere. This plays out in a number of ways of direct relevance to the analysis of global authority. First, when combined with state-centric analysis, the public/private distinction renders the political significance of transnational and multinational corporations invisible. The political significance of transnational corporations, which are major agents of private power and key players in the creation of the New Law Merchant, is filtered through the lenses of state power, or corporations are denied status as full subjects of the law under conventional theoretical approaches. Second, the association of authority with the public sphere limits the discourse of authority and its "subjects" to the state and its territorial boundaries. The assumption of a rigid separation of matters "inside" the state and matters "outside" the state is of particular importance to the blindness of realist and liberal theories to interactions between global and local political and economic developments and the roles played by transnational corporations and the law merchant in structuring these interactions. Rosenberg addresses this separation and states that "ignoring domestic non-state processes renders their actual transnational extension invisible. This in turn makes it impossible (or irrelevant) to conceive other global structures of power apart from the political—because the only visible agents are other states". This is a daunting task given the conditioning influence of the distinction on international theory and state practice. But it is a particularly important task because it is here, at the meeting place of the local and the global and the domestic and the foreign, that the authority of law merchant is located. Moreover, and of equal significance, transnational corporations as central agents in the development and globalization of merchant laws and institutions are actively engaged in ruling themselves and others through the institutions and rules that constitute private authority.

Charges that conventional approaches to the study of international relations and law are unable to capture the spatial and temporal conditions that configure post-modern political, economic, and social space have generated calls for "a new conception of historical agency as a dispersed property of human societies which state organizations will always attempt to mobilize, but which is never reducible to state policy." Considerable discontent stems from the analytical deficiencies of statist theorizing that derives from an ontology that reifies the state and a positivist epistemology that objectifies this condition and results in "a determinate construction of political reality which entails a series of hidden propositions and symptomatic silences." Concern that the concept of the territorial state-society is ideologically motivated and deeply flawed, analytically and historically, has contributed to efforts to reformulate our understanding of global authority.

The depiction of private authority and the generation of a "new conception of historical agency" require reconsideration of the dualisms and distinctions we have here just discussed, including economics/politics; private/public; local/global; domestic/international. They also require further analysis of the consensual/coercive nature of authority. Gramscian notions of hegemony provide a useful way of capturing the nature of the relationship between consent and coercion in the construction of authority. In Gramsci's formulation, hegemony involves a delicate and changing balance between relations of consent and coercion. However, hegemony based upon consent still retains a coercive element, which is ever-present and becomes dominant when consensus breaks down. This is evident in Gramsci's distinction between "civil society" and "political society." According to Gramsci, "civil society" is the ensemble of organisms commonly called "private," while "political society" is the state: "they correspond on the one hand to the function of 'hegemony' which the dominant group exercises throughout society and on the other hand to the 'direct domination' or command exercised through the state and 'juridical' government." Ethical hegemony is based upon consent, which is attributable to the intellectual and moral leadership of what Gramsci referred to as organic intellectuals. However, consent can deteriorate producing a "crisis of authority" when the intellectuals cease to exercise influence over society, at which time pure force and the coercive arm of the state and political society come to dominate.

Hegemony, in this sense, operates as part of the dialectical movement between relations of coercion and consent. Moreover, hegemony functions in a broader context of material, institutional, and ideological conditions constituting an historic bloc in which intellectuals play a crucial role in generating consensual social relations. What makes these intellectuals "organic" is their nature as expressions and embodiments of the dominant ideology and mode of production. As Robert Cox observes, hegemony in international relations is "not merely an order among states. It is an order within a world economy with a dominant mode of production which penetrates into all countries and links into other subordinate modes of production." Significantly, world hegemony "is expressed in universal norms, institutions and mechanisms which lay down general rules of behaviour for states and for those forces of civil society that cut across national boundaries—rules which support the dominant mode of production". This is an apt description of international law, in general, which "rests on values, or at least interests, genuinely shared by narrow or specialized transnational subcultures or communities of diplomats, bureaucrats, and elites". It is also a very appropriate description of the law merchant. The law merchant is the embodiment of hegemonic corporate knowledge and values and it operates as a knowledge structure that "determines what knowledge is discovered, how it is stored, and who communicates it by what means to whom and on what terms". Trade lawyers, government officials, and corporate officers form a mercatocracy of organic intellectuals articulate and organize hegemony by defining and redefining the world in terms that secure and maintain the authority of the dominant class. Liberal-inspired contract law provides the ideological foundation for a knowledge structure that presents "freedom of contract" and the private regulation of international commercial relations as the "best of all possible worlds." This is a world consistent with justice, freedom, equality, efficiency, and nature. Indeed, the law merchant reinscribes the dialectical relationship between consent and coercion in the very fabric of commercial practice through principles of contract, property, and corporate law that rationalize and objectify the free and consensual nature of private exchange and subordinate its coercive aspects. Duncan Kennedy, in writing about the role that law played in the construction of capitalism, refers to this as "coercion in the service of freedom," for although the principles of freedom of contract (and the alienability of property) characterized the economic system as "free," "state coercion was omnipresent" in the general enforcement powers of the state. However, since these powers are not invoked unless the parties to the agreements refuse to comply, the coercive aspect of the exchange relationship is obscured and is subordinated to the consensual aspect, giving the impression of contractual freedom. Moreover, presumptions of equality are built right into the law and into commercial agreements. Legal presumptions of the equal bargaining power of competent commercial actors create a formalistic appearance of equality in instances where the commercial arrangements are highly asymmetrical and uneven as a reflection of the underlying asymmetry of power between labor and capital.

It is noteworthy that the most ardent critics of the justice, equality, neutrality, and consensuality of private international trade relations are less-developed states which perceive themselves on the periphery of the global political economy and states which, while developed, have limited abilities to bargain equally with transnational shipping, insurance, and financial corporations. These states have attempted to create a more equitable playing field and a fairer distribution of benefits through changes in legal rules, documents, and terms governing contracting.

Corporate legal elites imbued with neoliberal ideology regulate their ranks by limiting entry to other lawyers trained to believe in the superiority of private law. They form a core of "organic intellectuals" whose role is to generalize societal and governmental support for the private regulation of international commerce. They are facilitating the expansion of private corporate power, which is increasingly isolated from public international law doctrinally, substantively, and ideologically. They are also isolated from public scrutiny and review by their designation as practitioners of private and, hence, apolitical law.

Corporate global power thus operates ideologically by removing private international law from the domain of politics and, hence, from scrutiny and review. In this way, private international law has been unable to generate a critical voice. Unlike public international law where critical theory is considerably well developed, private international law remains isolated and is rendered resistant to criticism by an ideology that permits little challenge. The silencing of counterhegemonic voices is achieved by a knowledge structure that privileges expert knowledge and by ideologically driven notions of political authority that rest upon assumptions of social unity that are problematic historically, analytically, and normatively. However, it is important to avoid overstating the "totalizing" nature of this hegemony and underestimating fractures in national and transnational social unity. Indeed, the balance between consent and coercion in international commercial relations is not static, but is variable. It is possible to contemplate the sort of analysis that has the potential of generating critical and counterhegemonic voices. The law merchant constitutes the juridical conditions of modern capitalism, but this is obscured by its invisibility. The first step is to render it visible by examining the normative foundations of transnational merchant law and by studying the processes and agents involved in generating and enforcing its norms and in linking local and global political economies. The approach must, however, be historical in order to capture the complex nature of the material, ideational, and institutional conditions that have constituted and reconstituted the law merchant as the juridical conditions of capitalism and, thus, as a central component of changing patterns of global authority. Moreover, the approach is inescapably normative. While critical theory is associated with enhanced theoretical reflexivity, it is also associated with the concern of creating an alternate world.

Stephen Gill, "Globalisation, Market Civilisation, and Disciplinary Neoliberalism"*

The present world order involves a more 'liberalised' and commodified set of historical structures, driven by the restructuring of capital and apolitical shift to the right. This process involves the spatial expansion and social deepening of economic liberal definitions of social purpose and possessively individualist patterns of action and politics. Current transformations can be related to Braudels' concept of *'longue durée'*, insofar as the structure and language of social relations is now more conditioned by the long-term commodity logic of capital. Capitalist norms and practices pervade the *géstes répétés* of everyday life in a more systematic way than in the era of welfare-nationalism and state capitalism (from the 1930s to the 1960s), so that it may be apposite to speak of the emergence of what I call a 'market civilisation'. Below I will sketch some fundamental aspects of neoliberal market civilisation, and show how they constitute a temporary politics of supremacy in the emerging world order.

---

* *Millenium: Journal of International Studies.* This article first appeared in *Millenium*, Vol. 24, No. 2, 1995, and is reproduced with the permission of the publisher.

By market civilisation, I mean a contradictory movement or set of transformative practices. The concept entails, on the one hand, cultural, ideological, and mythic forms understood broadly as an ideology or myth of capitalist progress. These representations are associated with the cumulative aspects of market integration and the increasingly expansive structures of accumulation, legitimation, consumption, and work. They are largely configured by the power of transnational capital. On the other hand, market civilisation involves patterns of social disintegration and exclusionary and hierarchical patterns of social relations. Indeed, whilst the concept of the *longue durée* suggests the lineage and depth of market practices, it can be argued that a disturbing feature of market civilisation is that it tends to generate a perspective on the world that is ahistorical, economistic, materialistic, 'me-oriented', short-termist, and ecologically myopic. Although the governance of this market civilisation is framed by the discourse of globalising neoliberalism and expressed through the interaction of free enterprise and the state, its coordination is achieved through a combination of market discipline and the direct application of political power. In this sense, there has been a 'globalisation of liberalism', involving the emergence of market civilisation: neoliberal globalisation is the latest phase in a process that originated before the dawning of the Enlightenment in Europe, and accelerated in the nineteenth century with the onset of industrial capitalism and the consolidation of the integral nation-state.

The purpose of this essay is to probe aspects of this situation which, following Antonio Gramsci, we call one of 'organic crisis'. This crisis involves a restructuring of prevailing ideas, institutions, and material capacities that constitute historical structures of world order. 'In every country the process is different, although the content is the same. And the content is the crisis of the ruling class's hegemony.... A "crisis of authority" is spoken of...this is precisely...a general crisis of the state'. When we introduce the issues of power and justice into our examination of neoliberal forms of globalisation, what is emerging is a politics of supremacy, rather than a politics of justice or hegemony. For example, a situation of bourgeois hegemony implies the construction of an historical bloc that transcends social classes and channels their direction into an active and largely legitimate system of rule. This implies a fusion of economic, political, and cultural elements of society (state and civil society) into a political alliance or coalition that combines coercion and consent. That is, the creation of such a bloc presupposes opposition and a means for incorporating or defeating it in a process of struggle. Whilst there is no compromise by the leading class fraction on the fundamentals of the mode of production, there is nevertheless an inclusion, politically, of a significant range of interests. Subordinate classes thus carry weight within the formulation of state policy. By a situation of supremacy, I mean rule by a non-hegemonic bloc of forces that exercises dominance for a period over apparently fragmented populations, until a coherent form of opposition emerges.

In the present era, this supremacist bloc can be conceptualised as commensurate with the emergence of a market-based transnational free enterprise system, which is dependent for its conditions of existence on a range of state-civil society complexes. It is both 'outside' and 'inside' the state: it forms part of the 'local' political structures as well as serving to constitute a 'global' political and civil society. Thus, in my sketch of the power structures of contemporary global politics, with significant local variations, a transnational historical bloc is outlined, with its nucleus largely comprising elements of the G-7 state apparatuses and transnational capital (in manufacturing, finance, and services), and associated privileged workers and smaller firms (*e.g.*, small and middle-sized businesses linked as contractors or suppliers, import-export businesses, and service companies, such as stockbrokers, accountants, consultancies, lobbyists, educational entrepreneurs, architects, and designers).

One vehicle for the emergence of this situation has been policies that tend to subject the majority to market forces whilst preserving social protection for the strong (*e.g.*, highly skilled workers, corporate capital, or those with inherited wealth). These policies are cast within a neoliberal discourse of governance that stresses the efficiency, welfare, and freedom of the market, and self-actualisation through the process of consumption. However, the effects of these policies are hierarchical and contradictory, so that it is also possible to say that the neoliberal turn can itself be interpreted as partly a manifestation of a crisis of governmental authority and credibility, indeed of governability, within and across a range of societies. It represents what Gramsci called 'a rift between popular masses and ruling ideologies' expressed in widespread 'scepticism with regard to all theories and general formulae…and to a form of politics which is not simply realistic in fact…but which is cynical in its immediate manifestation'.

Indeed, partly because aspects of this political-civilisational pattern provoke resistance and political counter-movements, many associated political forms are 'illiberal', authoritarian, and anti-democratic in nature. Here, prevailing class forces of transnational capital seek to stabilise their dominance in a global situation that approximates 'passive revolution'. Passive revolution refers politically to a situation characterised by 'dominance without leadership', or 'dictatorship without hegemony'. Where necessary, this may entail limited formal democratisation, in a strategy that involves either *transformism* (the 'formation of an ever-more extensive ruling class' through incorporation and absorption of rival elites, often leading to their 'annihilation or decapitation', *e.g.*, Salinas' Mexico), or *Caesarism* (*e.g.*, 'where the forces in conflict balance each other in a catastrophic manner' so that a dictatorial tendency prevails, perhaps as in Yeltsin's Russia). Thus, the statement that we are in a situation of organic crisis suggests that, whilst there has been a growth in the structural power of capital, its contradictory consequences mean that neoliberalism has failed to gain more than temporary dominance over our societies.

Analysing Power and Knowledge in the Global Political Economy

The dominant forces of contemporary globalisation are constituted by a neoliberal historical bloc that practices a politics of supremacy within and across nations. The idea of an historical bloc—a concept which is one of the most fundamental innovations of Gramsci's political theory—is consistent in some ways with what Michel Foucault called a 'discursive formation': a set of ideas and practices with particular conditions of existence, which are more or less institutionalised, but which may be only partially understood by those that they encompass. Both concepts allow us to make sense of the way that practices and understandings come to pervade many areas of social and political life, in complex, perhaps unpredictable and contested, ways.

Karl Marx' concept of 'commodity fetishism' (the ways in which the exchange of commodities in the money form masks the conditions and struggles associated with the production of commodities) can also be related to the content of the prevailing cultural discourse, insofar as it enables us to identify the basic social form that it presupposes: the way in which capitalist commercialisation shapes outlooks, identities, time-horizons, and conceptions of social space. The increasingly widespread commodification of social relations is partly reflected in the growing cultural preoccupation with surface textures and symbols rather than historical depth, and with architectural collage and immediacy, that characterises some forms of post-modernism. David Harvey notes (perhaps forgetting the potential impact of new technologies) that, for Foucault, the only irreducible element is the human body, which is the particular 'site' at which discursive repression is ultimately experienced and localised. For Foucault, nevertheless, this very individualised and localised 'moment' is also where 'resistance' to repressive discourse can occur.

Foucault's approach is useful in the way that it highlights the constitution and constraints of various discursive forms, and for its emphasis on the way in which certain forms of power and knowledge serve to constitute particular aspects of civilisation. However, despite its preoccupation with localised, capillary forms of power/ knowledge, the Foucauldian view often lacks a convincing way of linking these forms of power to macro-structures. Foucault identifies a 'great transformation' at the start of the nineteenth century that produced a new 'historical, comparative grammar'. This was an 'archaeological rupture' in modes of thought so general that it came to bear on 'the general rules of one or several discursive formations', including, as he notes, both Ricardian and Marxian Political Economy. Yet, how does Foucault explain this transformation? He speaks elusively of multiple determinations, but strangely missing from his explanation of this epistemological revolution is any sustained analysis of the rise of capital as a social relation, or indeed any attempt to speak of capital's power, either specifically or in general. A discussion of historical struggle over the modalities of power and knowledge is also missing.

Thus, despite the Foucauldian preoccupation with the problematic of power/ knowledge as localised and institutionalised by discourse, with localised resistance through interventions in the systems of power/knowledge, there is little by way of an emancipatory dimension to this perspective and no adequate link between macro and micro-structures of power in the approach. Even in a world where we might accept the postulate of multiple identities and a radical sense of discontinuity in forms of representation and human consciousness, unless our social perspective is one of the ostrich, it seems difficult to ignore the overwhelming evidence of a tremendous growth of inequality over the past two decades: income has been radically redistributed between labour and capital in an era of stagnating growth in most of the OECD nations. Indeed, the concentration of capital has proceeded very much along the lines anticipated by Marx, and thus must be central to any explanation of the present global transformation; just as the incipient forms of capitalist industrialisation were central to the epistemological changes in the nineteenth century, and to the new representations of political economy, that were revealed by Foucault's archaeological excavations.

My approach, then, uses certain Foucauldian ideas, but repositions them within an historical materialist framework to sketch a model of power that is able to account for those who are included and those who are excluded or marginalised in the global political economy. Whereas Foucault tends to depict power relations in an all-encompassing way, perhaps the usefulness of his concepts of discursive formation and panopticism is more specific. They apply to some members of what John Kenneth Galbraith calls the 'culture of contentment': people who are exemplars of the commodified and normalised society par *excellence*. These people are Foucault's willing victims, who hold credit cards and provide or call for the wider provision of personal information that can be manipulated in data bases.

By contrast, the marginalised are both within the societies of the culture of consumption and elsewhere in the world. They may have forms of knowledge that are not amenable to rationalisation and discipline in the sense implied by Foucault, and they may not necessarily cooperate with normalising practices. They may actively seek to develop counter-hegemonic forms of power/knowledge. South Africa, the archetypal 'panoptic' society is an example of the exercise of this kind of power. Here, state violence and surveillance could not prevent change. Thus, Foucault represents a cry of outrage at the taming of the individual, and he inaugurates a purely defensive strategy of localised resistance. However, historical materialism goes much further in an attempt to theorise and to promote collective action to create an alternative form of society: even from within a prison, as Gramsci's notebooks show so clearly. This is why it is necessary to theorise the problem of change in local and global dimensions, and to look beyond the currently fragmented forms of opposition to neoliberal supremacy.

'Disciplinary' Neoliberalism

In social theory, the term 'discipline' is used in a number of slightly different ways. Max Weber defined the concept of discipline as follows: '[t]hose who obey are not necessarily obedient or an especially large mass, nor are they necessarily united in a specific locality. What is decisive for discipline is that obedience of a plurality of men is rationally uniform'. 'Rational uniformity' can be observed in classes, status groups, and political parties, which are all phenomena of the distribution of power in society: 'discipline' is, therefore, a form of the exercise of power within social organisations. For Emile Durkheim, (self) discipline, or the restraint of one's inclinations, is a means to develop reasoned behaviour and thus foster the moral growth of the healthy personality: unregulated emotions can produce *anomie*. For Foucault, 'discipline' is sometimes used in ways that approximate Weber and Durkheim, but generally the term is used to indicate both a modernist framework of understanding that underpins a terrain of knowledge, and a system of social and individual control: '[t]he Enlightenment, which discovered the liberties, also invented the disciplines'.

The concept of discipline advanced here combines macro- and micro-dimensions of power: the structural power of capital; the ability to promote uniformity and obedience within parties, cadres, organisations, and especially in class formations associated with transnational capital (perhaps involving self-discipline in the Durkheimian sense); and particular instances of disciplinary power in a Foucauldian sense. Thus, 'disciplinary neoliberalism' is a concrete form of structural and behavioural power; it combines the structural power of capital with 'capillary power' and 'panopticism'. In other words, neoliberal forms of discipline are not necessarily universal nor consistent, but they are bureaucratised and institutionalised, and they operate with different degrees of intensity across a range of 'public' and 'private' spheres. In this sense, discipline is both a transnational and a local dimension of power, and these dimensions of discipline are one dimension of the supremacist transnational historical bloc that I have sketched in the previous section.

New Constitutionalism and Global Governance

Disciplinary neoliberalism is institutionalised at the macro-level of power in the quasi-legal restructuring of state and international political forms: the 'new constitutionalism'. This discourse of global economic governance is reflected in the conditionality policies of the Bretton Woods organisations, quasi-constitutional regional arrangements such as NAFTA or Maastricht, and the multilateral regulatory framework of the new World Trade Organisation. It is reflected in the global trend towards independent central banks, with macroeconomic policy prioritising the 'fight against inflation'.

New constitutionalism is a macro-political dimension of the process whereby the nature and purpose of the public sphere in the OECD has been redefined in a more privatised and commodified way, with its economic criteria defined in a more globalised and abstract frame of reference. The accountability of governments to 'markets' is mainly to material forces and the sentiments of investment managers in the bond markets, as well as to the conditionality of the Bretton Woods organisations. It has grown in a period of fiscal crisis and in accordance with the growing salience of 'new constitutionalist' discourses of global governance. The new constitutionalism can be defined as the political project of attempting to make transnational liberalism, and if possible liberal democratic capitalism, the sole model for future development. It is therefore intimately related to the rise of market civilisation.

New constitutionalist proposals are often implicit rather than explicit. Nevertheless, they emphasise market efficiency, discipline, and confidence; economic policy credibility and consistency; and limitations on democratic decision-making processes. Proposals imply or mandate the insulation of key aspects of the economy from the influence of politicians or the mass of citizens by imposing, internally and externally, 'binding constraints' on the conduct of fiscal, monetary, trade, and investment policies. Ideology and market power are not enough to ensure the adequacy of neoliberal restructuring. It is worth noting that the United States is the least likely of any country to submit to such constraints—although its leaders insist that they be applied systematically to other states. Nonetheless, even the autonomy of the United States, Japan, and the European Union is constrained in matters of macroeconomic policy by the globalisation of finance and production. Smaller and less self-sufficient states tend to be correspondingly more sensitive and vulnerable to global financial pressures.

In effect, new constitutionalism confers privileged rights of citizenship and representation on corporate capital, whilst constraining the democratisation process that has involved struggles for representation for hundreds of years. Central, therefore, to new constitutionalism is the imposition of discipline on public institutions, partly to prevent national interference with the property rights and entry and exit options of holders of mobile capital with regard to particular political jurisdictions. These initiatives are also linked to efforts to define appropriate policy, partly by strengthening surveillance mechanisms of international organisations and private agencies, such as the bond raters. Governments in need of external financing are forced to provide data. One reason for this is to make domestic economic and political agents and trends more transparent to global supervisors in the IMF or Bank for International Settlements (BIS), as well as to the increasingly influential private bond-rating agencies such as Moody's and Standards and Poor. Indeed, initiatives based on new constitutionalist surveillance assumptions were launched at the G-7 Summit in Halifax, Nova Scotia, in June 1995. The G-7 leaders opted to strengthen surveillance mechanisms under the *aegis* of the IMF, World Bank, and BIS, after the failure of existing methods of surveillance was revealed by the Mexican financial crisis of 1994–95.

By contrast, traditional notions of constitutionalism are associated with political rights, obligations, and freedoms, and procedures that give institutional form to the state. Constitutions define, describe, and outline the rights and obligations of citizens; common policy-making institutions with authority over the entire polity; the limits to the scope of action of these institutions; and, of course, enforcement mechanisms and ratification and amendment procedures.

Turning to recent examples of neoliberal forms of regionalisation, there is a difference in kind between North America and Western Europe. Here, I represent both examples more as projects rather than as exemplars of the final crystallisation of neoliberal dominance. For example, questions of European unification have been made more complex not only by German unification, but also by the accession of new Nordic members and the prospect of further enlargement to encompass former communist-ruled nations. NAFTA is also undergoing considerable turbulence and contestation, not only within each member nation, but also more broadly in Latin America.

The European Union has citizenship for individuals from member countries, and has partly accountable mechanisms for negotiation, ratification, amendment, and enforcement, and for incorporating and weighting the interests of the smaller European nations. However, although social and welfare policy and regulation have been institutionalised in the EU since the Treaty of Rome, for example with respect to migrant workers (Article 51), equal treatment of men and women (Article 119), protection of workers (Article 118), and the health and safety of workers (Article 118 and 118a of the Single European Act), implementation has been patchy despite the influence of trades unions, some political parties, and, in some cases, the European Court for Human Rights. In large part, this inconsistency has been the result of employer opposition. A further reason is the development of unaccountable intergovernmental agencies. Nevertheless, the political centre of gravity of European political economy has recently tilted towards definitions which reflect a financial and free trade conception: that is, a neoliberal view of Europe, as opposed to the more social democratic idea of 'social Europe'. This is reflected in many of the Maastricht provisions, especially the proposals for a largely unaccountable European central banking system, and fiscal/public debt provisions intended to be binding on all future governments in the EU.

North American arrangements are more hierarchical and asymmetrical, understood both in inter-state terms and in terms of the class structures of each nation. NAFTA is premised upon a low level of political institutionalisation and a hub-and-spoke configuration of power, with the United States at the centre of a continentalised political economy. This is even more the case with the Caribbean Basin Initiative, which can be terminated unilaterally by the United States. The United States has negotiated the implicit right to monitor and control large areas of Canadian political life in the US-Canada Free Trade Agreement. The US-Canada Agreement specifies that each side has to notify the other 'party' by advanced warning, of *intended* federal or provincial government policy that *might* affect the other side's interests, as defined by the agreement.

Because of Canada's extensive economic integration with the United States, this situation necessarily affects the vast majority of Canadian economic activity, but not *vice versa*. Thus, Canadian governments no longer can contemplate an independent or interventionist economic strategy. In both NAFTA and the US-Canada Agreement there are no transnational citizenship rights other than those accorded to capital, and these are defined to favour US-registered companies. Finally, NAFTA can only be amended by agreement of all signatories. Whilst these arrangements place binding constraints on the policies of Canada and Mexico, to a certain degree, the United States retains constitutional autonomy and important prerogatives: its trade law is allowed to override treaty provisions, notwithstanding the rights of redress that are available to participants through the dispute settlement mechanisms.

In other words, the US government is using access to its vast market as a lever of power, linked to a reshaping of the international business climate, by subjecting other nations to the disciplines of the new constitutionalism, whilst largely refusing to submit to them itself, partly for strategic reasons. Indeed, one of the arguments expressed by former European Union President Jacques Delors in favour of comprehensive West European economic and monetary union was strategic: to offset economic unilateralism from the United States, in matters of money and trade.

Thus, an American-centred global neoliberalism mandates a separation of politics and economics in ways that may narrow political representation and constrain democratic social choice in many parts of the world. New constitutionalism, which ratifies this separation, may have become the *de facto* discourse of governance for most of the global political economy. This discourse involves a hierarchy of pressures and constraints on government autonomy that vary according to the size, economic strength, form of state and civil society, and prevailing national and regional institutional capabilities, as well as the degree of integration into global capital and money markets.

Neoliberal Contradictions and the Movement of History

Neoliberal forms of rationality are largely instrumental and are concerned with finding the best means to achieve calculated ends. For neoliberals, primary motivations are understood in a possessively individualistic framework. Motivation is provided by fear and greed, and is reflected in the drive to acquire more security and more goods. Yet, any significant attempt to widen this pattern of motivation would entail an intensification of existing accumulation and consumption patterns, tending to deplete or to destroy the eco-structures of the planet, making everyone less secure and perhaps more vulnerable to disease (even the powerful). Thus, if North American patterns of accumulation and consumption were to be significantly extended, for example to China, the despoliation of the global eco-structure would be virtually assured. Even so, the central ideological message and social myth of neoliberalism is that such a possibility is both desirable and attainable for all: insofar as limitations are recognised, this is at best through a redefinition of the concept of 'sustainable development' so as to make it consistent with the continuation of existing patterns of accumulation and consumption.

Whilst existing patterns of consumption have a more-or-less exclusive quality, depending on the form and place of consumption, their very existence requires that public goods be provided locally and globally so as to underpin production, consumption, and exchange processes. Governments throughout the world are required to regulate and to compensate for the social, economic, and ecological problems attendant upon existing patterns of consumption and production. This means that the state must find ways to sustain the tax base and to police and regulate the market society. This may prove difficult when prevailing economic ideology and the organisation of the world economy validate, on the one hand, cuts in public expenditure and reducing the scope of state action, and, on the other, a burgeoning black or informal economy and a tendency for organised criminal syndicates to grow in strength. Nevertheless, as new constitutionalist arrangements suggest, to extract surplus globally, capital depends on national and global public goods provision.

Therefore, the logic of neoliberalism is contradictory: it promotes global economic integration (and hence the need for global public goods), but also generates depletion of resources and the environment, as well as undermining the traditional tax base and the capacity to provide public goods. Indeed, neoclassical economic thinking, which lies at the heart of neoliberal discourse, tends to ignore, with impunity, ecological constraints such as the laws of thermodynamics. Moreover, neoliberal macroeconomic policies, aligned to the ideology of the competition state, may generate a more conflictual inter-state dynamic that may prolong economic stagnation for the vast majority of the world's population, through, for example, competitive austerity and beggar-thy-neighbour currency depreciation.

According to Walter Benjamin, within myth the passage of time takes the form of predestination, such that human control is denied. Thus, the operation of the neoliberal myth of progress in market civilisation is intended implicitly to engender a fatalism that denies the construction of alternatives to the prevailing order, and thus, negates the idea that history is made by collective human action. Whilst it might be argued that the generation of such a myth is central to the hegemony of capital, we might recast it in Polanyian terms: neoliberalism holds out the reified prospect of a 'stark utopia'. As Adam Smith intimated in *The Theory of Moral Sentiments,* and as Polanyi pointed out, a pure market system is a utopian abstraction and any attempt to construct it fully would require an immensely authoritarian application of political power through the state. One reason for this is the recent tendency for exploitation to intensify, in part because of the apparent domination of production and the state by finance. This would raise doubts about the viability of a minimal or 'night-watchman' state, as portrayed in liberal ideology. Indeed, it can be shown that many of the neoliberal forms of state have been authoritarian. In some cases, this has involved considerable coercive power to destroy opposition or eliminate the possibility of a third way: such as in Chile in 1973, or in post-communist Eastern Europe.

Restructuring along market-driven lines tends to generate a deepening of social inequality, a rise in the rate and intensity of the exploitation of labour, growth in social polarisation, gender inequality, a widespread sense of social and economic insecurity, and, not least, pervasive disenchantment with conventional political practice. Such a situation may also open the door to the appeals of extremist political movements, whilst more broadly giving rise to resistance and counter-mobilisation. Indeed, in the context of the growing salience of biological discourses concerning social life, one might suggest that there may be a social Darwinist dimension to the neoliberal world order. This proposition is supported by evidence of the renaissance of fascism and atavistic forms of nationalism.

Thus, whilst the restructuring of forms of state along neoliberal lines has apparently accelerated in recent years there are indications that remaking state and society along these lines lacks moral credibility, authority, and legitimacy. This is partly because the rule and the burdens of market forces are most frequently imposed hierarchically on the weaker states and social actors, whilst the more powerful receive tax write-offs, state subsidies, and other prerogatives. However, one should be careful not to overstate the degree to which this represents the universalisation of a new form of world order. In fact, the very existence of the neoliberal structural adjustment programmes of the World Bank, and of IMF stabilisation measures, shows that economic liberalisation has a very long way to go before it can be considered the new development paradigm for the majority of the world's population.

Indeed, such policies are contested even within the ranks of the G-7, and the conflicts between the different models of capitalist development this entails can be expected to continue. One reason for G-7 conflicts is that the socio-economic systems of Germany and Japan are less attuned to pure market forces. For example, in Japan, important political forces seem to have adopted the Hirschian view that the very operation of capitalist market forces depends upon their restraint, and on the maintenance of traditional systems of obligations and institutions that cause people to behave *as if* they respect the law, and accept not only the contractual but also the customary nature of market transactions.

Thus, we should not conflate propaganda with history. History has not 'ended' and alternatives are created politically. In *The Great Transformation,* Polanyi argued that a 'double movement' of free economic and self-protecting social and political forces operated to configure global politics in the 1930s. The New Deal, fascism, Nazism, and populist movements of left and right reflected opposition to global *laissez faire* and the power of financial capital. For Gramsci, the 1930s involved the death throes of the old order, and the struggle of a new order to be born. By analogy, one can suggest that today we may be in, or entering into, a period of a new 'double movement': one that certainly manifests many morbid symptoms. The coming years will probably involve a substantial intensification of political conflict. It seems likely that this will incorporate the contradictory political tendencies associated with, on the one hand, democratic and progressive forces, and, on the other, the growing forces of reaction, such as the resurgence of fascism and certain forms of fundamentalist politics or criminal elements in world politics. Indeed, a new double movement would be different in character from that of the 1930s, not least because its concerns would be more global and wide-ranging in nature, and might include nuclearism, the proliferation of conventional weapons, ecology, gender questions, the globalisation of organised crime, and the re-regulation of new global information and financial grids.

Put differently, there is a growing contradiction between the tendency towards the globality and universality of capital in the neoliberal form and the particularity of the legitimation and enforcement of its key exploitative relations by the state. Whereas capital tends towards universality, it cannot operate outside of or beyond the political context, and involves planning, legitimation, and the use of coercive capacities by the state. This forms the key substantive problem for a theory of international relations, at least as seen from an historical materialist perspective. In this context, one of the main tasks of political economy today is to understand and theorise the possibilities for the transformation of these dimensions of world order, in the context of consciousness, culture, and material life.

Christian Heine and Benno Teschke, "Sleeping Beauty and the Dialectical Awakening: On the Potential of Dialectic for International Relations"*

Epistemology, Incommensurability, and the Inter-Paradigm Debate in IR

Before we deal in detail with the dialectic of concrete totality, we would like to address a central problem in the inter-paradigm debate in IR. For a debate to succeed, the standards of communication for critique must first be spelled out. Without such 'second-order' clarification, participants keep talking past each other. We shall argue the case for a second-order discourse as the ultimate arena for critical inter-paradigm communication in IR. We retain from the debates in the philosophy of the social sciences that empirical as well as immanent modes of critique are insufficient for multi-paradigmatic discourses. Yet, that approach which vehemently demands second-order critique—dialectic—has consistently been relegated to the sidelines of IR.

It is clear that a part of the deadlock in the IR inter-paradigm debate stems from an underthematisation of the epistemological presuppositions upon which theoretical statements are predicated. Paradigms—usually loosely viewed as clusters of theoretical assumptions inter-subjectively introduced through the discourse of scholars—are incommensurable. They are incommensurable with regard to the problems they pose and the solutions they offer. Since, as Thomas Kuhn expounds, methodologies/epistemologies are internal to paradigms, and usually not separately articulated, the basis for any meaningful inter-paradigm debate is lacking.

For example, the marginalisation of epistemological expositions has arguably contributed to the fact that a central category of IR, like the 'state' and the 'autonomy of

---

* *Millenium: Journal of International Studies.* This article first appeared in *Millenium*, Vol. 25, No. 2, 1996, and is reproduced with the permission of the publisher.

the political', was not seriously questioned for decades. The sole-unitary-rational-actor approach was common wisdom. Yet, such a conceptualisation rests on certain *a priori* assumptions and yields specific implications for research results. With the juxtaposition of Realism against various other approaches in the 1970s and 1980s in particular, concepts of the state proliferated on the basis of different meta-theoretical assumptions (*e.g.,* Pluralism, World-Systems Theory). They range from seeing the state as a 'free-floating power-network' to just another actor in the international arena competing with nongovernmental organisations, international organisations, quangos, and transnational actors for power abroad and legitimacy at home. The multiplicity of conceptualisations of the state often leaves the IR student perplexed.

In trying to find secure ground, the occurrence that one and the same social phenomenon (fact) is differently conceptualised can usually not be conclusively decided by pointing to the 'empirical evidence' as the final authority. This is due to the value-infusion each scholar brings to bear on his/her research. Arguably, the dispute can only be brought to a conclusion, if not agreement, if the respective preconditions for each empirical statement are spelled out. As long as those assumptions are not openly stated, we may remain forever stuck at the level of plausibility-judgements (that which Hegel termed 'opinions about this and that'), or indeed at the level of criteria like elegance, parsimony, fruitfulness, or cultural conformity. Therefore, it is not only a question of intellectual honesty to explicate the premises upon which social science is conducted, but a question of necessity for every form of meaningful debate, critique, and possibly refutation.

Critique as a Mode of Inter-Paradigm Communication

Expanding the last point, *critique,* as the mode of inter-paradigm communication, has three possible avenues of engagement: either as (1) empirical critique, (2) immanent critique, or (3) fundamental critique on the epistemological level. Of these, only the last form of critique has survived in recent debates in the philosophy of social sciences.

Empirical critique is the testing ground for deductive-nomological research (especially Karl Popper's Critical Rationalism). It implies that a theory comprises laws and/or theoretical generalisations. Empirical statements logically deduced from these theories (conjectures) are hypothetically advanced and applied to the empirical material. If the empirical data do not comply with the conjecture, then the theory is refuted, and needs to be reformulated or abandoned. If the data confirm the statement, the theory stands as not (yet) falsified, *i.e.,* preliminarily valid.

Kuhn has convincingly challenged the Popperian logic of science. Against a Popperian notion of cumulative progress in science, in which gradual approximation to knowledge replaced questions of truth, Kuhn could show historically the dialectical and revolutionary development of science. He defended the prosaic thesis that in periods of 'normal science', 'anomalies' accumulate and trigger 'scientific revolutions' which, after a period of crisis, lead to the adoption of new paradigms. Kuhn concluded that theories tend to remain unfalsified; they are merely displaced or repressed for reasons which have more to do with a sociology of science or a psychology of research, than with a logic of discovery. However, Kuhn's logic of paradigm shifts remains confined to an inner-scientific dynamic, disembedded from wider socio-historical forces. Curiously, Popper and Kuhn converge, in the final analysis, in accepting the inter-subjectively agreed nature of paradigms and their irrational shifts. In other words, what makes critique conclusive is not the 'empirical evidence' itself, but the consent of a community of researchers on what may qualify as such. Thus, the whole exercise remains self-referential and immune from, so to speak, external critical intervention.

Immanent critique seeks to find out whether theoretical conclusions follow with *logical necessity* from those epistemological or pre-scientific assumptions which the scholar has made. This entails the application of the laws of formal logic (internal consistency, the principle of non-contradiction *etc.*) and the disclosure of the consequences and implications of the assumptions made. Hans Morgenthau's substantial work, for example, constantly swerves between, on the one hand, a scientific assertion of the 'objective laws of politics' which a rational inquiry into the historical evidence could establish, and, on the other, a moral point of reference reflecting a deep-seated conviction/value-judgement on man's nature as a power-maximiser. The former 'objective laws' aver that, because states act under the competitive conditions of international anarchy, they do and should seek power as a means for self-preservation. The latter position—a type of 'political ontology' as the philosophical basis for Realism—is deeply imbued with normative assumptions: man's *animus dominandi* as an end in itself. Immanent critique would uncover the contradictions between the two. Immanent critique, however, would not reopen the inter-paradigm debate; it would simply trade off one possible avenue at the expense of another, or call for a reworking of parts of their theory in line with the parameters set.

Therefore, a third form of critique as a mode of inter-paradigm debate is called for: fundamental critique as a second-order discourse. Paul Feyerabend, following Kuhn, proffered the thesis that paradigms are incommensurable. Moreover, he argued that slavish adherence to a prescribed and canonised logic of research proves deleterious to innovative thinking, against the background of the richness of human experience and spontaneity. Therefore, to cut short his argument, science dissolves into a sea of relativism: *anything goes*. This 'dadaist' position is untenable, if we do not want to play out 'anti-human' science against a gut-commitment to human freedom *à la* Feyerabend. Science is socio-historically mediated and, by feeding back into society, is of general social concern. Consequently, as Roy Bhaskar claims, 'justifications within science are a social matter—but they require and are given ontological grounds'. Ontology, and, concomitantly, epistemology and methodology, thus circumscribe the ultimate arena of critical contestation. Maximally, a meta-theoretical display of thoughts is required; minimally, science has to explicate its modes of conceptualisations. Thus, social scientists must, in an act of self-reflexivity, spell out how reality is apprehended in thought, how he/she conducts his/her concept-formation, and what is more, how concept-formation helps to critically explain social life, and ultimately history. In other words, we need an articulated standard of rationality which is open and accessible to critique. This is the *sine qua non* of all scientific endeavours. We suggest that dialectic is an articulated standard for fundamental scientific critique.

The Marginalisation of Dialectic in IR

Dialectic has not yet been sufficiently explicated in IR. It occupies a special place in the canon of social scientific methods and, although the rhythms of intellectual demand and supply have generated a short resurgence of dialectic in the social sciences in the 1960s and 1970s, in IR, the 'dialectical sleeping beauty' is still hibernating in the impassable mazes of 'metaphysics'. Usually, it simply falls between the conventional standard-bearers of empirical-analytical approaches revolving around the cognitive ideal of causal explanation, on the one hand, and of hermeneutical approaches revolving around understanding, meaning, and intersubjectivity, on the other. It does not even lead a fringe existence comparable to normative, anti-foundationalist (post-modernist), or to what in the Anglo-Saxon world is understood by critical-theoretical perspectives. A nuanced book explicitly concerned with meta-theoretical questions like Martin Hollis and Steve Smith's *Explaining and Understanding International Relations* denies dialectic a place in the index. A brilliant synopsis on the development of the philosophy of the social sciences like Richard Bernstein's *The Restructuring of Social and Political Theory* mentions the term only fleetingly. Dialectic is equally absent from what is perhaps the most comprehensive and thorough IR textbook on theory and approaches, J.E. Dougherty and R.L. Pfaltzgraff's *Contending Theories of International Relations*. The list could be extended *ad infmitum*. Yet, you may find a very limited number of studies in IR which implicitly or explicitly use the dialectical method or call for its popularisation.

In stark contrast to such neglect, a glance at the last five decades in the field of philosophy of science shows that its primary concern took the form of a continuous, sometimes open, sometimes subterranean engagement with the tenets of dialectical logic (Popper, Kuhn, Imre Lakatos, Feyerabend, Wolfgang Stegmüller). Therefore, there is some irony in the fact that a dispute like that involved in the agency-structure debate flared up in the late 1980s without taking cognisance of, for example, the German Positivist dispute. In this dispute, scholars like Popper and Ralf Dahrendorf on the one side, and Theodor Adorno and Jürgen Habermas on the other, clashed about questions of how agents shape and are shaped by society, and how we may adequately formulate scientific statements about a socially-produced and symbolically-structured reality of which the social scientist is *both* the subject and the object.

Thus, there is a widespread, but often unarticulated consensus that the social sciences in general, and IR in particular, are concerned with the following: on the one hand, either finding nomothetical patterns (usually defensively formulated in the form of correlations of the kind if A, then B, without asking why A in the first place), or generalisations inferred from repeatedly observed regularities; or, on the other hand, building up a casuistry of ideal types *à la* Max Weber under which any particular historical instance can be conveniently subsumed and stored away (as, most notably, in Martin Wight, Hedley Bull, and Adam Watson), or, alternatively, that IR historiography inquires idiographically into the uniqueness and contingency of particular events by proceeding hermeneutically or by plain narration. This state of affairs does not, of course, exclude those 'trespassers' who try to find laws of a middle range, correlations, cycles, or long waves in history; or those partisans of the

Verstehen tradition who venture into sociological territory, if, for example, they are to explore decision-making processes.

We do not claim to be able to reconcile these two traditions—analytic-causal and hermeneutic-understanding—within the scope of this paper. We do claim, however, that this paper sketches the rough draft for an epistemological and methodological alternative. On this point, we constructively engage with what is currently conducted as the third, or, depending on one's mode of counting, fourth debate in the discipline of IR, namely the question of the next post-positivist/dissident stage in IR theory. Its main theme is precisely that, today, IR theory cannot dispense with a self-reflexive inquiry into its cognitive foundations.

The customary derision *vis-à-vis* epistemology and methodology—banished to the antechamber of 'real science'—forgets that in order to arrive at the chamber of science, the curious intruder has to pass through the former.

After much paradigm-profusion and inter-paradigm confusion, it is about time that our Sleeping International Beauty receives the awakening dialectical kiss.

The Dialectic of the Concrete Totality

So far we have argued the case for meta-theoretical inter-paradigm communication. However, a mere argumentative confrontation of meta-theories will repeat, on the theoretical level, the inconclusiveness of exchanging substantive statements. In this last part, we attempt to substantiate the alternative metatheoretical framework of dialectic relating to its specific logical structure, its meaning of praxis and reason, its resolution of the problem of ontology, the status of totality, its relation between theory and praxis, and its mode of concept formation. Having done this, we may be in a position to offset the aforementioned shortcomings of IR scholarship: its artificially restricted object-domain, its reliance on instrumental rationality, the absence of theorising about systemic transformation, and its neglect of collective agency. What privileges dialectic are three irrefragable premises. First, if the aim of thinking is to comprehend reality, and if it is accepted that reality is itself contradictory, then the mode of thinking must reflect these social contradictions. 'The dialectical contradiction expresses the real antagonisms which do not become visible within the logical-scientistic system of thought'. Thus, as against the cognitive ideal of 'non-contradiction' as upheld by orthodox science based on formal logic, dialectical logic operates precisely on the opposite principle—the principle of contradiction. Contradictions are not logical blunders, but capture the real historically- and socially-constituted antagonisms in the world. As such, they do not face each other as absolute opposites (in orthodox thought as antinomies), but are capable of solution (transcendence). Transcendence, however, is a practical, not a logical problem.

Second, dialectic is tied to praxis as the most encompassing term for the entire spectrum of human activities. Whereas most traditions prioritise one form of action as against all others (for example, the rational-actor model or the communicative-interaction model), so that history is read through the lenses of merely one form of action, dialectic retains a sense of the diversity of past, present, and future expressions of human agency. Production (purposive rationality), cognition (reflexivity), and communication (inter-subjectivity) are logically coeval or co-primordial. All of these forms of praxis flow into and arise out of humanity's social metabolism with nature.

Third, in the Enlightenment, praxis was governed by an emphatic notion of Reason as the underlying principle for a philosophy of history. Within this tradition, Reason split subsequently into three diverging strands. For Immanuel Kant, Reason was relegated to a metaphysical regulative idea, leaving us with a diminished notion of understanding (*Verstand*). G.W.F. Hegel then retrieved Kant's transcendental idea of Reason, and maintained that Reason unfolds dynamically in the course of history as mediated through consciousness. As against these classical idealist stances, Karl Marx reinstated the necessity of practical Reason and secularised history as unfolding social praxis with no predetermined fixed terminus. The conflicts of history, as Marx insinuated, have prepared humanity in consciousness and materiality to reconcile social life and its relation to nature in a socially non-exploitative and ecologically aware manner.

Ontology Sublated: Praxis—Totality

The open dialectic of the concrete totality proffers one simple yet decisive claim: human praxis is the linchpin of history. 'The first premise of all human history is, of course, the existence of living human individuals'. Marx specifies this seemingly trivial statement by arguing that *praxis* denotes the appropriation and transformation of nature through cognition, interaction, and labour, in and through time and space. This is always an inter-subjective and reciprocally enriching and modifying process out of which spring immediately manifold social relations. The collective cultivation of nature, as it develops spontaneously in history, entails nevertheless a certain patterned organisation through which society reproduces itself: social relations of production. The historically specific mode by which surplus is extracted from the direct producer, and by which the non-producing class feeds off the producing class, informs the division of labour, the co-ordination of social and gendered roles, the exchange of goods, the ideational forms of consciousness, and the configurations of authority and subordination. We can speak, in short, of a rich and many-sided totality in never-ending motion.

'Ontological essences', understood as timeless structures, are fundamentally opposed to the very nature of history as becoming. In the sixth thesis on Feuerbach, Marx emphasises that 'the human essence is no abstraction inherent in each single individual. In its reality it is the ensemble of human relations'. As these ensembles are ever-changing, the conceptual comprehension of this flux—in order to fend off the danger of conceptual abstractions and concomitant reifications—has to come to terms with this flux 'fluently'. Three conclusions follow: (1) science (thinking) is on the wrong track if it sees its primary purpose as the pursuit of positive and universal social laws, or in once-and-for-all definitions; (2) concepts have to remain malleable and open for new concretisations; (3) the process of conceptual thinking can therefore never be terminated.

What this may entail shall be shown by means of the concept 'praxis'. In a specific historical context, it takes on a 'closed' and 'objectified' connotation: praxis as the everyday routine under heteronomous social relations. The concept changes its content when the objective conditions for the comprehension of its full possibilities develop. Then, potentiality becomes actuality. Praxis turns into an open category underlying the politics of possibility. In other words, the concrete content of praxis, or human agency, cannot be defined in the abstract. We can only grasp its meaning as a determinate moment in respective concrete historical situations.

Hegel admonished that it is much more difficult to liquefy fixed thoughts than to liquefy sensuous existence, meaning that whilst social reality is constantly changing, our definitions tend to remain fixed. Therefore, scientific propositions on reality aspiring to the status of truth-claims can only grasp relative, not absolute knowledge of reality. Dialectic can illuminate the arduous path to truth. However, in dialectic, knowledge and truth are not to be confounded. In the context of our discipline, this means that we are trying to develop a theory *of* international relations, not a static international relations theory claiming transhistorical validity. The criteria for the former type of theory are necessarily time-bound and relate themselves to subject/object relations in their concretion. Accordingly, thinking has its truth not *in itself,* but only in conscious praxis *in and for itself.* In the second thesis on Feuerbach, Marx wrote that

> the question whether objective truth can be attributed to human thinking is not a question of theory but is a *practical question.* Man must prove the truth, *i.e.,* the reality and power, the this-worldliness of his thinking in praxis. The dispute over the reality or non-reality of thinking that is isolated from praxis is a purely *scholastic* question.

The historicity of truth itself leads to the question of what constitutes enlightened praxis. Provided that the last criterion for truth lies in praxis, the open dialectic of concrete totality, to take the early Habermas on board, entails that its validity-claims lie ultimately in successful processes of enlightenment. In history, enlightened praxis emerges negatively, each time anew, over and above concrete forms of unreason in historical contexts.

Against the ontological abstraction of praxis *per se* as an absolute statement—as, for example in the fictions of *homo oeconomicus, homo politicus, homo faber, homo ludens,* and *homo communicans* dialectic necessarily contextualises human praxis in concrete totalities. For, in the present, man is always already confronted with the objectifications of previous subjects. In other words, man's praxis is, each time respectively, mediated by and to its surrounding social totality as the product of the past. In history, there is never human praxis as such (therefore there should be no abstract ontological claim), but only human praxes (plural) in concrete respective contexts.

Subjects are confronted by their objectified externalisations. History is the process of the contradictory subject-object dialectic.

The only way to resolve the sham problem of ontology in philosophy in its search for essentialisms is to dynamise ontology itself: man in his concrete becoming. In fact, ontology is sublated in praxis, and yet, man remains nature-bound. This means that humanity is always and everywhere obliged to labour nature for its reproduction, yet the forms of this engagement are infinite.

Subject—Object: Concrete Totality

Subject and object make up the dialectical totality. There are three dimensions to the *concrete* totality: (1) it is a methodological postulate; (2) it is an epistemological principle for the cognition of reality; and (3) it is the materialist concept which captures the relationship between man/woman, society and nature. The subject's emanations—manual and intellectual labour—are praxis. The subjectivity of thinking expresses the historicity of its own time. This conception of thinking rebels against Cartesian absolute and transhistorical thinking. In its respective subjectivity it turns critical. Critical thinking reflects about the object-world, which is nothing but the produce of humanity's own labouring. In interaction (manual and intellectual activity), humanity reproduces the moments of totality each time anew.

This should not be read as if the totality-postulate implies the analysis of the sum-total of facts. Totality is not the mere additive aggregation of facts, which is impossible to achieve in face of the infinity of facts and phenomena and of their developing character. In this respect, the precept of totality is far removed from a 'totalising/dogmatic' discourse. What the totality-postulate insinuates is precisely not a 'totalising theory', but the epistemological possibility of the cognisability of the parts in relation to the social totality. In other words, totality in terms of the object-domain, can only be grasped as a relative totality, not as absolute totality. 'Totality signifies reality as a structured dialectical whole, within which and from which any particular fact (or any group or set of facts) can be rationally comprehended'. These facts (or parts/moments) have their truth only in relation to the whole. Yet, this whole does not exist over and above the parts of which it is composed. Totality produces and reproduces itself only through its moments.

This dialectic thought avoids two traps: on the one hand, parts are not isolated from their social genesis and reified in the process (blank empiricism); on the other hand, the whole, emptied of its components, is not abstracted as a petrified 'system' or an anaemic configuration of 'structures'. Dialectic transcends the artificial prioritisation of either the atom or the system, the agent or the structure. To this extent, Anthony Giddens' structuration theory revamps the old philosophical bone of contention concerning free will and determination in a non-dialectical diction, conflating the fundamental difference between formal and dialectical logic.

Epistemology: Theory and Praxis

Epistemologically, theory and praxis are not to be severed from each other. The dialectic of the concrete totality understands theory to be a form of praxis. The mental activity of appropriating and comprehending reality is nothing else but a moment of man's metabolic struggle with nature. Praxis encompasses thus both labour as the material form, and thinking as the mental form of appropriating and thereby transforming nature and, *uno actu,* our social relations. Praxis, and more concretely, needs and interests, thus provide the epistemological ground for cognition. Inversely, insight into the product-character of all things social—constitutes the possibility for their cognisability. This thought goes right back to Giambattista Vico: '[v]erum et factum convertuntur', translated as 'the true' and 'the made' are convertible.

Praxis sets two forms of dialectic in motion. Objective dialectic covers the motion of things in their totality *in* themselves; subjective dialectic grasps the objective dialectic in thought and comprehends thus things in their totality *for* themselves. In other words, objective dialectic denotes the relationship of the genesis and the dynamic of the social totality as it unfolds in history driven through social antagonisms (contradictions); subjective dialectic comprehends the objective dialectic as the dialectic of appearance and essence, of form and content. The 'heuristic' distinction between objective and subjective dialectic does not imply that there are two independent processes at work. Being the moment of consciousness, subjective dialectic feeds back into objective dialectic. Marx understood his own theoretical efforts in this dialectical way: subjective dialectic as theoretically expressed in Marx's critique of political economy constitutes a necessary contradictory moment in the transformation of the objective dialectic. The real world does not remain untouched by its conceptualisation. Yet, the social totality is comprehended in thought through concepts, but it is not merely conceptual.

Thinking is never a vain exercise. Even the most lofty contemplation is governed by three characteristics: (1) we are thinking about something: an object; (2) our thinking is sparked by an interest, what Habermas termed a 'knowledge-guiding interest'; and (3) the interest struggles for the practical implementation of thinking.

By being object-related and interest-motivated, thinking is always practically consequential, even if it only leads to the conclusion to desist from action. It is in itself transformative and potentially subversive. Surely, this does not mean that 'structures of power can be dissolved simply through a cognitive re-appropriation of alienated social forms'. However, it does mean, as Marx understood his own theoretical endeavours, that insight into power relations formulated as critique is a necessary moment for the dynamics of history. This form of science does not debouch into positivist explanation, although its explanatory power is superior to a reductionist analytical tradition, but appeals as critique to the practical Reason of those involved in and subjected to asymmetrical relations of social power. Therefore, science, as a collective and systematic exercise, is not a paranoid and hypostatised pastime, but a moment of the mastering (*Bewältigung*) of the natural and social world. It is the means which humanity has developed in order to alleviate its life-processes.

From the Abstract to the Concrete

Certainly, dialectic cannot be reduced to one operationalisable method. However, the movement from the abstract to the concrete as a mode of concept-formation is central to Marx's dialectic. Dialectic distinguishes between the representation (*Vorstellung*) of a thing and the concept (*Begriff*) of the thing. The method of thinking, the way in which reality is comprehended, is a movement from observation and representation to the concept, which is another way of coming to terms with appearance and essence. In other words, the intellectual journey rises from the abstract to the concrete.

It proceeds as follows: sense-perceptions present to us social phenomena (data) in their immediate appearances, their immediacy. The sensually perceived phenomena are objective in their materiality as understood by common sense, for nothing reveals to the naked eye the social forces which went into their making. At the same time, they are abstract for being as yet uncomprehended. At this stage, these social phenomena are still unspecified and empty in content. The mere reflection of these abstractions in mind amounts to nothing more th[a]n their abstracted doubling (empiricism). In contrast, dialectical thinking claims that the facticity of the facts is not synonymous with their cognition (*Erkenntnis*). The step from perception to cognition, however, lies in retrieving what generates social phenomena, that is, human praxis, which via various mediations objectifies itself in even the remotest social appearances. For example, whilst common sense would define the state abstractly in terms of its attributes and functions (as, for example, in Max Weber's classical ideal-typical definition), dialectic would resist abstractions. It would comprehend a particular state objectively in terms of the social praxes necessary for its formation and for the reproduction of the social totality, and subjectively in terms of the inter-subjective uses to which the state is harnessed.

To summarise the argument, from the thing in its abstraction, dialectical thinking descends to the most simple determinations of the phenomena. From there, thinking ascends to the concept as the concretised phenomenon: concrete now also in thought as synthesised knowledge, a conceptualised 'unity of the diverse'. Concept formation is thus the constructive reproduction of the 'real-abstract' as a 'concrete-in-thought'. Ideally, these consolidated concepts would eventually enter into a comprehensive picture of society writ large.

Conclusion

Dialectic entails the following advantages for social science. First, it is self-reflective and understands itself to be a form of praxis. Objective and subjective dialectic are a contradictory unit (theory as praxis). Second, it accounts for the process-character of society as a developing and forming totality (historicity). Third, it specifies the dynamic of this process-character, which it pinpoints in social antagonisms (contradictions). Fourth, the relation of all things social to their source, human praxis, denaturalises the object-domain by exposing its product-character (appearance/ social content). Fifth, such product-character permits the cognisability of social phenomena (non-agnosticism). The impulse for cognition (theory) derives from human interest fuelled—via various mediations—by man's necessary and constant exchange with nature. Sixth, it is critical *vis-à-vis* both 'naturalising' social sciences and the alienated forms of modernity themselves (thinking as critique). Seventh, it rejects closed accounts of history and maintains the open dialectic as necessity and contingency, ultimately dependent on human action (open history). Finally, it operates with a dialectical concept of reason-in-praxis, not with an abstract vocation of a Cartesian *cogito* (practical Reason).

With such a programme at hand, we can overcome the conventional distinction between the 'political' and the 'economic', the state and the market, IR and

International Political Economy (IPE), rationality and reason, and dissolve such reifications by relating them to human praxis. The intellectual division of labour arises historically in tandem with the emergence of capitalist modernity and the differentiation of society into apparently discrete spheres of social action. Dialectic does not reify these spheres into levels or structures, to be theorised in abstraction from the overall reproduction of society, but tries to retrace the social content expressed in these differentiated spheres within one theoretical framework. In capitalist societies, the separating out of the 'economic' from the 'political' is rooted in the historical commodification of labour-power allowing surplus appropriation to take place by non-political means. The capitalist market appears as the 'invisible hand' which exerts this peculiar non-coercive coercion—celebrated by liberalism as choice—driving the dispossessed worker into the private labour contract. Although this appears to be a purely economic exercise based upon mutual agreement, the state remains vital in upholding, if need be by force, private property, and in enforcing private contracts through law. Only if we can think in terms of totality can this constitutive nexus between the 'economic' and the 'political' be unearthed. Once this separation is historically accomplished, and universalised in a crisis-ridden process of capital-driven geopolitical competition, it remains the state's foremost task to articulate and mediate capitalist strategies of reproduction among states. Modern capitalist international relations are then based on a welter of political mechanisms (praxes) ranging from sheer violence to consensus-building measures. This, in a condensed form, translates our four dialectical dimensions (social totality, context of justification, historicity, and praxis/practical reason) into a viable research programme of modern international relations. We suggest that the epistemological requirements of dialectic offset the four disciplinary shortcomings *in abstracto* and offer their explanatory power in empirically-controlled critical research.

Dialectical IR theory cannot live without posing critically the *cui bono* question: who gains from IR orthodoxy and all its capricious variations, and how does this penetrate our all-too-familiar world order? Also, the individual in its life-project—in questions of life and death, wealth and poverty, and the human capacity of self-fulfillment—concretely depends on global relations of domination and subordination. The critique of the objectification of the subject remains the central vocation of IR as a social science. With all sympathy for the "excluded," the "victimised," the "disempowered," and the "gendered," our attention should not be deflected from the social sources of power and production. If we want to open up "space for thinking," we should investigate how this space became closed in the first place.

We submit that the open and critical dialectic of concrete totality is an alternative way of comprehending international social phenomena in an epistemologically exhaustive and methodologically coherent manner.

Part V

*A New Critical Phase?
Normative Critical
Theory and its Critics*

9

Postmodern Thought
Genealogy, Power/Knowledge, and Deconstruction

Introduction

This chapter introduces the reader to the works of three essential thinkers whose ideas and critiques constitute the core of postmodernist thought and the sources of postmodernism in IR. Michel Foucault's essay, "Power/Knowledge" critically analyzes the problematic features of sovereignty, or its destabilizing and arbitrary meaning as a governing societal norm. As Foucault shows, the legitimization of power disguises the effects of sovereign power: namely, the repression and the subjugation of other discourses. In this sense, knowledge is power insofar as the dominant knowledge of sovereign power masks the operations of dissident power. It is this process of the legitimization of knowledge that Lyotard addresses in *The Postmodern Condition* (1984). Lyotard argues that the meta-narrative represents a particular form of legitimization, in which one referent serves to legitimize all other practices, norms, and conventions of society. It is this process of linking one chosen form of knowledge with legitimization that presupposes the coercive tactics of the meta-narrative.

Resisting hegemonic power, then, implies not only the affirmation of a plurality of truths, but also the living elements of militant ideologies. This is one of the main reasons why Derrida returns to Marxism, with the aim of showing how Marxism remains an undying form of resistance. For, as he insists, the specter of Marx's revolution (systematic resistance to oppressive authoritative structures) lives on "since ghosts never die... '[they] remain always to come and to come back'."[1] It is this challenge of recognizing what Derrida refers to as the "undeconstructible" otherness (or justice as being irreducible to law or right) that makes deconstruction a seemingly immanent (albeit thorny) feature of social critical theory. On the other hand, it is precisely this relativization of the idea of justice that also problematizes the dialectic as a method of immanent critique.

To recall, Heine and Teschke argued that dialectic could provide a self-reflexive method for working beyond the limitations of postmodernism. But here it could also be argued that dialect as immanent critique remains, at least for now, far too unwieldy or conceptual to steer us beyond the challenges posed by postmodernism. In fact, the reason why postmodernism is significant in this sense is that it reveals the immanence of exclusion.

Endnotes

1. Jacques Derrida, *Specters of Marx* (New York: Routledge, 1994), p. 99.

Michel Foucault, "Two Lectures" from *Power/Knowledge*

A certain fragility been discovered in the very bedrock of existence—even, and perhaps above all, in those aspects of it that are most familiar, most solid and most intimately related to our bodies and to our everyday behaviour. But together with this sense of instability and this amazing efficacy, of discontinuous, particular and local criticism, one in fact also discovers something that perhaps was not initially foreseen, something one might describe as precisely the inhibiting effect of global, *totalitarian theories*. It is not that these global theories have not provided nor continue to provide in a fairly consistent fashion useful tools for local research: Marxism and psychoanalysis are proofs of this. But I believe these tools have only been provided on the condition that the theoretical unity of these discourses was in some sense put in abeyance, or at least curtailed, divided, overthrown, caricatured, the atricalised, or what you will. In each case, the attempt to think in terms of a totality has in fact proved a hindrance to research.

So, the main point to be gleaned from these events of the last fifteen years, their predominant feature, is the *local* character of criticism. That should not, I believe, be taken to mean that its qualities are those of an obtuse, naive or primitive empiricism; nor is it a soggy eclecticism, an opportunism that laps up any and every kind of theoretical approach nor does it mean a self-imposed ascetism which taken by itself would reduce to the worst kind of theoretical impoverishment. I believe that what this essentially local character of criticism indicates in reality is an autonomous, non-centralised kind of theoretical production, one that is to say whose validity is not dependent on the approval of the established regimes of thought.

It is here that we touch upon another feature of these events that has been manifest for some time now: it seems to me that this local criticism has proceeded by means of what one might term 'a return of knowledge'. What I mean by that phrase is this: it is a fact that we have repeatedly encountered, at least at a superficial level, in the course of most recent times, an entire thematic to the effect that it is not theory but life that matters, not knowledge but reality, not books but money etc.; but it also seems to me that over and above, and arising out of this thematic, there is something else to which we are witness, and which we might describe as an *insurrection of subjugated knowledges*.

By subjugated knowledges I mean two things: on the one hand, I am referring to the historical contents that have been buried and disguised in a functionalist coherence or formal systemisation. Concretely, it is not a semiology of the life of the asylum, it is not even a sociology of delinquency, that has made it possible to produce an effective criticism of the asylum and likewise of the prison, but rather the immediate emergence of historical contents. And this is simply because only the historical contents allow us to rediscover the ruptural effects of conflict and struggle that the order imposed by functionalist or systematising thought is designed to mask. Subjugated knowledges are thus those blocs of historical knowledge which were present but disguised within the body of functionalist and systematising theory and which criticism—which obviously draws upon scholarship—has been able to reveal.

On the other hand, I believe that by subjugated knowledges one should under-stand something else, something which in a sense is altogether different, namely, a whole set of knowledges that have been disqualified as inadequate to their task or insufficiently elaborated: naive knowledges, located low down on the hierarchy, beneath the required level of cognition or scientificity. I also believe that it is through the re-emergence of these low-ranking knowledges, these unqualified, even directly disqualified knowledges (such as that of the psychiatric patient, of the ill person, of the nurse, of the doctor—parallel and marginal as they are to the knowledge of medi-cine—that of the delinquent etc.), and which involve what I would call a popular knowledge (*le savoir des gens*) though it is far from being a general commonsense knowledge, but is on the contrary a particular, local, regional knowledge, a differen-tial knowledge incapable of unanimity and which owes its force only to the harshness with which it is opposed by everything surrounding it—that it is through the re-appearance of this knowledge, of these local popular knowledges, these disqualified knowledges, that criticism performs its work.

However, there is a strange kind of paradox in the desire to assign to this same cat-egory of subjugated knowledges what are on the one hand the products of meticulous, erudite, exact historical knowledge, and on the other hand local and specific knowl-edges which have no common meaning and which are in some fashion allowed to fall into disuse whenever they are not effectively and explicitly maintained in themselves. Well, it seems to me that our critical discourses of the last fifteen years have in effect discovered their essential force in this association between the buried knowledges of erudition and those disqualified from the hierarchy of knowledges and sciences.

In the two cases—in the case of the erudite as in that of the disqualified knowledges—with what in fact were these buried, subjugated knowledges really concerned? They were concerned with a *historical knowledge of struggles.* In the specialised areas of erudition as in the disqualified, popular knowledge there, lay the memory of hostile encounters which even up to this day have been confined to the margins of knowledge.

What emerges out of this is something one might call a genealogy, or rather a mul-tiplicity of genealogical researches, a painstaking rediscovery of struggles together with the rude memory of their conflicts. And these genealogies, that are the com-bined product of an erudite knowledge and a popular knowledge, were not possible and could not even have been attempted except on one condition, namely that the tyranny of globalising discourses with their hierarchy and all their privileges of a theoretical *avant-garde* was eliminated.

Let us give the term *genealogy* to the union of erudite knowledge and local memo-ries which allows us to establish a historical knowledge of struggles and to make use of this knowledge tactically today. This then will be a provisional definition of the genealogies which I have attempted to compile with you over the last few years.

You are well aware that this research activity, which one can thus call genealogi-cal, has nothing at all to do with an opposition between the abstract unity of theory and the concrete multiplicity of facts. It has nothing at all to do with a disqualifica-tion of the speculative dimension which opposes to it, in the name of some kind of scientism, the rigour of well established knowledges. It is not therefore via an empiri-cism that the genealogical project unfolds, nor even via a positivism in the ordinary sense of that term. What it really does is to entertain the claims to attention of local, discontinuous, disqualified, illegitimate knowledges against the claims of a unitary body of theory which would filter, hierarchise and order them in the name of some true knowledge and some arbitrary idea of what constitutes a science and its objects. Genealogies are therefore not positivistic returns to a more careful or exact form of science. They are precisely anti-sciences. Not that they vindicate a lyrical right to ignorance or non-knowledge: it is not that they are concerned to deny knowledge or that they esteem the virtues of direct cognition and base their practice upon an immediate experience that escapes encapsulation in knowledge. It is not that with which we are concerned. We are concerned, rather, with the insurrection of knowledges that are opposed primarily not to the contents, methods or concepts of a science, but to the effects of the centralising powers which are linked to the institution and functioning of an organised scientific discourse within a society such as ours. Nor does it basically matter all that much that this institutionalisation of scientific discourse is embodied in a university, or, more generally, in an educational apparatus, in a theoretical-commercial institution such as psychoanalysis or within the framework of reference that is provided by a political system such as Marxism; for it is really against the effects of the power of a discourse that is considered to be scientific that the genealogy must wage its struggle.

To be more precise, I would remind you how numerous have been those who for many years now, probably for more than half a century, have questioned whether Marxism was, or was not, a. science. One might say that the same issue has been posed, and continues to be posed, in the case of psychoanalysis, or even worse, in that of the semiology of literary texts. But to all these demands of: 'Is it or is it not a science?', the genealogies or the genealogists would reply: 'If you really want to know, the fault lies in your very determination to make a science out of Marxism or psychoanalysis or this or that study'. If we have any objection against Marxism, it lies in the fact that it could effectively be a science. In more detailed terms, I would say that even before we can know the extent to which something such as Marxism or psychoanalysis can be compared to a scientific practice in its everyday functioning, its rules of construction, its working concepts, that even before we can pose the question of a formal and structural analogy between Marxist or psychoanalytic discourse, it is surely necessary to question ourselves about our aspirations to the kind of power that is presumed to accompany such a science. It is surely the following kinds of question that would need to be posed: What types of knowledge do you want to disqualify in the very instant of your demand: 'Is it a science'? Which speaking, discoursing subjects—which subjects of experience and knowledge—do you then want to 'diminish' when you say: 'I who conduct this discourse am conducting a scientific discourse, and I am a scientist'? Which theoretical-political *avant garde* do you want to enthrone in order to isolate it from all the discontinuous forms of knowledge that circulate about it? When I see you straining to establish the scientificity of Marxism I do not really think that you are demonstrating once and for all that Marxism has a rational structure and that therefore its propositions are the outcome of verifiable procedures; for me you are doing something altogether different, you are investing Marxist discourses and those who uphold them with the effects of, a power which the West since Medieval times has attributed to science and has reserved for those engaged in scientific discourse.

By comparison, then, and in contrast to the various projects which aim to inscribe knowledges in the hierarchical order of power associated with science, a genealogy should be seen as a kind of attempt to emancipate historical knowledges from that subjection, to render them, that is, capable of opposition and of struggle against the coercion of a theoretical, unitary, formal and scientific discourse. It is based on a reactivation of local knowledges—of minor knowledges, as Deleuze might call them—in opposition to the scientific hierarchisation of knowledges and the effects intrinsic to their power: this, then, is the project of these disordered and fragmentary genealogies. If we were to characterise it in two terms, then 'archaeology' would be the appropriate methodology of this analysis of local discursivities, and 'genealogy' would be the tactics whereby, on the basis of the descriptions of these local discursivities, the subjected knowledges which were thus released would he brought into play.

So, it is the rules of right, the mechanisms of power, the effects of truth or if you like, the rules of power and the powers of true discourses, that can be said more or less to have formed the general terrain of my concern, even if, as I know full well, I have traversed it only partially and in a very zig-zag fashion. I should like to speak briefly about this course of research, about what I have considered as being its guiding principle and about the methodological imperatives and precautions which I have sought to adopt. As regards the general principle involved in a study of the relations between right and power, it seems to me that in Western societies since Medieval times it has been royal power that has provided the essential focus around which legal thought has been elaborated. It is in response to the demands of royal power, for its profit and to serve as its instrument or justification, that the juridical edifice of our own society has been developed. Right in the West is the King's right. Naturally everyone is familiar with the famous, celebrated, repeatedly emphasised role of the jurists in the organisation of royal power. We must not forget that the re-vitalisation of Roman Law in the twelfth century was the major event around which, and on whose basis, the juridical edifice which had collapsed after the fall of the Roman Empire was reconstructed. This resurrection of Roman Law had in effect a technical and constitutive role to play in the establishment of the authoritarian, administrative, and, in the final analysis, absolute power of the monarchy. And when this legal edifice escapes in later centuries from the control of the monarch, when, more accurately, it is turned against that control, it is always the limits of this sovereign power that are put in question, its prerogatives that are challenged. In other words, I believe that the King remains the central personage in the whole legal edifice of the West. When it comes to the general organisation of the legal system in the West, it is essentially with the King, his rights, his power and its eventual limitations, that one is dealing. Whether the jurists were the King's henchmen or his adversaries, it is of royal power that we are speaking in every case when we speak of these grandiose edifices of legal thought and knowledge.

There are two ways in which we do so speak. Either we do so in order to show the nature of the juridical armoury that invested royal power, to reveal the monarch as the effective embodiment of sovereignty, to demonstrate that his power, for all that it was absolute, was exactly that which befitted his fundamental right. Or, by contrast, we do so in order to show the necessity of imposing limits upon this sovereign power, of submitting it to certain rules of right, within whose confines it had to be exercised in order for it to remain legitimate. The essential role of the theory of right, from medieval times onwards, was to fix the legitimacy of power; that is the major problem ground which the whole theory of right and sovereignty is organised.

When we say that sovereignty is the central problem of right in Western societies, what we mean basically is that the essential function of the discourse and techniques of right has been to efface the domination intrinsic to power in order to present the latter at the level of appearance under two different aspects: on the one hand, as the legitimate rights of sovereignty, and on the other, as the legal obligation to obey it. The system of right is centred entirely upon the King, and it is therefore designed to eliminate the fact of domination and its consequences.

My general project over the past few years has been, in essence, to reverse the mode of analysis followed by the entire discourse of right from the time of the Middle Ages. My aim, therefore, was to invert it, to give due weight, that is, to the fact of domination, to expose both its latent nature and its brutality. I then wanted to show not only how right is, in a general way, the instrument of this domination—which scarcely needs saying—but also to show the extent to which, and the forms in which right (not simply the laws but the whole complex of apparatuses, institutions and regulations responsible for their application) transmits and puts in motion relations that are not relations of sovereignty, but of domination. Moreover, in speaking of domination I do not have in mind that solid and global kind of domination that one person exercises over others, or one group over another, but the manifold forms of domination that can be exercised within society. Not the domination of the King in his central position, therefore, but that of his subjects in their mutual relations: not the uniform edifice of sovereignty, but the multiple forms of subjugation that have a place and function within the social organism.

The system of right, the domain of the law, are permanent agents of these relations of domination, these polymorphous techniques of subjugation. Right should be viewed, I believe, not in terms of a legitimacy to be established, but in terms of the methods of subjugation that it instigates.

The problem for me is how to avoid this question, central to the theme of right, regarding sovereignty and the obedience of individual subjects in order that I may substitute the problem of domination and subjugation for that of sovereignty and obedience. Given that this was to be the general line of my analysis, there were a certain number of methodological precautions that seemed requisite to its pursuit. In the very first place, it seemed important to accept that the analysis in question should not concern itself with the regulated and legitimate forms of power in their central locations, with the general mechanisms through which they operate, and the continual effects of these. On the contrary, it should be concerned with power at its extremities, in its ultimate destinations, with those points where it becomes capillary, that is, in its more regional and local forms and institutions. Its paramount concern, in fact, should be with the point where power surmounts the rules of right which organise and delimit it and extends itself beyond them, invests itself in institutions, becomes embodied in techniques, and equips itself with instruments and eventually even violent means of material intervention. To give an example: rather than try to discover where and how the right of punishment is founded on sovereignty, how it is presented in the theory of monarchical right or in that of democratic right, I have tried to see in what ways punishment and the power of punishment are effectively embodied in a certain number of local, regional, material institutions, which are concerned with torture or imprisonment, and to place these in the climate—at once institutional and physical, regulated and violent—of the effective apparatuses of punishment. In other words, one should try to locate power at the extreme points of its exercise, where it is always less legal in character.

A second methodological precaution urged that the analysis should not concern itself with power at the level of conscious intention or decision; that it should not attempt to consider power from its internal point of view and that it should refrain from posing the labyrinthine and unanswerable question: 'Who then has power and what has he in mind? What is the aim of someone who possesses power?' Instead, it is a case of studying power at the point where its intention, if it has one, is completely invested in its real and effective practices. What is needed is a study of power in its external visage, at the point where it is in direct and immediate relationship with that which we can provisionally call its object, its target, its field of application, there— that is to say—where it installs itself and produces its real effects.

Let us not, therefore, ask why certain people want to dominate, what they seek, what is their overall strategy. Let us ask, instead, how things work at the level of on-going subjugation, at the level of those continuous and uninterrupted processes which subject our bodies, govern our gestures, dictate our behaviours etc. In other words, rather than ask ourselves how the sovereign appears to us in his lofty isola- tion, we should try to discover how it is that subjects are gradually, progressively, really and materially constituted through a multiplicity of organisms, forces, ener- gies, materials, desires, thoughts etc. We should try to grasp subjection in its material instance as a constitution of subjects.

A third methodological precaution relates to the fact that power is not to be taken to be a phenomenon of one individual's consolidated and homogeneous domina- tion over others, or that of one group or class over others. What, by contrast, should always be kept in mind is that power, if we do not take too distant a view of it, is not that which makes the difference between those who exclusively possess and retain it, and those who do not have it and submit to it. Power must by analysed as something which circulates, or rather as something which only functions in the form of a chain. It is never localised here or there, never in anybody's hands, never appropriated as a commodity or piece of wealth. Power is employed and exercised through a net- like organisation. And not only do individuals circulate between its threads; they are always in the position of simultaneously undergoing and exercising this power. They are not only its inert or consenting target; they are always also the elements of its articulation. In other words, individuals are the vehicles of power, not its points of application.

The individual is not to be conceived as a sort of elementary nucleus, a primitive atom, a multiple and inert material on which power comes to fasten or against which it happens to strike, and in so doing subdues or crushes individuals. In fact, it is already one of the prime effects of power that certain bodies, certain gestures, certain discourses, certain desires, come to be identified and constituted as individuals. The individual, that is, is not the *vis-à-vis* of power; it is, I believe, one of its prime effects. The individual is an effect of power, and at the same time, or precisely to the extent to which it is that effect, it is the element of its articulation. The individual which power has constituted is at the same time its vehicle.

There is a fourth methodological precaution that follows from this: when I say that power establishes a network through which it freely circulates, this is true only up to a certain point. In much the same fashion we could say that therefore we all have a fascism in our heads, or, more profoundly, that we all have a power in our bodies. But I do not believe that one should conclude from that that power is the best distributed thing in the world, although in some sense that is indeed so. We are not dealing with a sort of democratic or anarchic distribution of power through bodies. That is to say, it seems to me—and this then would be the fourth methodological precaution—that the important thing is not to attempt some kind of deduction of power starting from its centre and aimed at the discovery of the extent to which it permeates into the base, of the degree to which it reproduces itself down to and including the most molecular elements of society. One must rather conduct an *ascending* analysis of power, starting, that is, from its infinitesimal mechanisms, which each have their own history, their own trajectory, their own techniques and tactics, and then see how these mechanisms of power have been—and continue to be—invested, colonised, utilised, involuted, transformed, displaced, extended etc., by ever more general mechanisms and by forms of global domination. It is not that this global domination extends itself right to the base in a plurality of repercussions: I believe that the manner in which the phenomena, the techniques and the procedures of power enter into play at the most basic levels must be analysed, that the way in which these procedures are displaced, extended and altered must certainly be demonstrated; but above all what must be shown is the manner in which they are invested and annexed by more global phenomena and the subtle fashion in which more general powers or economic interests are able to engage with these technologies that are at once both relatively autonomous of power and act as its infinitesimal elements. In order to make this clearer, one might cite the example of madness. The descending type of analysis, the one of which I believe one ought to be wary, will say that the bourgeoisie has, since the sixteenth or seventeenth century, been the dominant class; from this premise, it will then set out to deduce the internment of the insane. One can always make this deduction, it is always easily done and that is precisely what I would hold against it. It is in fact a simple matter to show that since lunatics are precisely those persons who are useless to industrial production, one is obliged to dispense with them. One could argue similarly in regard to infantile sexuality—and several thinkers, including Wilhelm Reich have indeed sought to do so up to a certain point. Given the domination of the bourgeois class, how can one understand the repression of infantile sexuality? Well, very simply—given that the human body had become essentially a force of production from the time of the seventeenth and eighteenth century, all the forms of its expenditure which did not lend themselves to the constitution of the productive forces—and were therefore exposed as redundant—were banned, excluded and repressed. These kinds of deduction are always possible. They are simultaneously correct and false. Above all they are too glib, because one can always do exactly the opposite and show, precisely by appeal to the principle of the dominance of the bourgeois class, that the forms of control of infantile sexuality could in no way have been predicted. On the contrary, it is equally plausible to suggest that what was needed was sexual training, the encouragement of a sexual precociousness, given that what was fundamentally at stake was the constitution of a labour force whose optimal state, as we well know, at least at the beginning of the nineteenth century, was to be infinite: the greater the labour force, the better able would the system of capitalist production have been to fulfil and improve its functions.

I believe that anything can be deduced from the general phenomenon of the domination of the bourgeois class. What needs to be done is something quite different. One needs to investigate historically, and beginning from the lowest level, how mechanisms of power have been able to function. In regard to the confinement of the insane, for example, or the repression and interdiction of sexuality, we need to see the manner in which, at the effective level of the family, of the immediate environment, of the cells and most basic units of society, these phenomena of repression or exclusion possessed their instruments and their logic, in response to a certain number of needs. We need to identify the agents responsible for them, their real agents (those which constituted the immediate social *entourage*, the family, parents, doctors etc.), and not be content to lump them under the formula of a generalised bourgeoisie. We need to see how these mechanisms of power, at a given moment, in a precise conjuncture and by means of a certain number of transformations, have begun to become economically advantageous and politically useful. I think that in this way one could easily manage to demonstrate that what the bourgeoisie needed, or that in which its system discovered its real interests, was not the exclusion of the mad or the surveillance and prohibition of infantile masturbation (for, to repeat, such a system can perfectly well tolerate quite opposite practices), but rather, the techniques and procedures themselves of such an exclusion. It is the mechanisms of that exclusion that are necessary, the apparatuses of surveillance, the medicalisation of sexuality, of madness, of delinquency, all the micro-mechanisms of power, that came, from a certain moment in time, to represent the interests of the bourgeoisie.

As for our fifth methodological precaution: it is quite possible that the major mechanisms of power have been accompanied by ideological productions. There has, for example, probably been an ideology of education, an ideology of the monarchy, an ideology of parliamentary democracy etc.; but basically I do not believe that what has taken place can be said to be ideological. It is both much more and much less than ideology. It is the production of effective instruments for the formation and accumulation of knowledge—methods of observation, techniques of registration, procedures for investigation and research, apparatuses of control. All this means that power, when it is exercised through these subtle mechanisms, cannot but evolve, organise and put into circulation a knowledge, or rather apparatuses of knowledge, which are not ideological constructs.

By way of summarising these five methodological precautions, I would say that we should direct our researches on the nature of power not towards the juridical edifice of sovereignty, the State apparatuses and the ideologies which accompany them, but towards domination and the material operators of power, towards forms of subjection and the inflections and utilisations of their localised systems, and towards strategic apparatuses. We must eschew the model of Leviathan in the study of power. We must escape from the limited field of juridical sovereignty and State institutions, and instead base our analysis of power on the study of the techniques and tactics of domination.

In short, what I have wanted to demonstrate in the course of the last few years is not the manner in which at the advance front of the exact sciences the uncertain, recalcitrant, confused dominion of human behaviour has little by little been annexed to science: it is not through some advancement in the rationality of the exact sciences that the human sciences are gradually constituted. I believe that the process which has really rendered the discourse of the human sciences possible is the juxtaposition, the encounter between two lines of approach, two mechanisms, two absolutely heterogeneous types of discourse: on the one hand there is the re-organisation of right that invests sovereignty, and on the other, the mechanics of the coercive forces whose exercise takes a disciplinary form. And I believe that in our own times power is exercised simultaneously through this right and these techniques and that these techniques and these discourses, to which the disciplines give rise invade the area of right so that the procedures of normalisation come to be ever more constantly engaged in the colonisation of those of law. I believe that all this can explain the global functioning of what I would call a *society of normalisation*. I mean, more precisely, that disciplinary normalisations come into ever greater conflict with the juridical systems of sovereignty: their incompatibility with each other is ever more acutely felt and apparent; some kind of arbitrating discourse is made ever more necessary, a type of power and of knowledge that the sanctity of science would render neutral. It is precisely in the extension of medicine that we see, in some sense, not so much the linking as the perpetual exchange or encounter of mechanisms of discipline with the principle of right. The developments of medicine, the general medicalisation of behaviours, conducts, discourses, desires etc., take place at the point of intersection between the two heterogeneous levels of discipline and sovereignty. For this reason, against these usurpations by the disciplinary mechanisms, against this ascent of a power that is tied to scientific knowledge, we find that there is no solid recourse available to us today, such being our situation, except that which lies precisely in the return to a theory of right organised around sovereignty and articulated upon its ancient principle. When today one wants to object in some way to the disciplines and all the effects of power and knowledge that are linked to them, what is it that one does, concretely, in real life, what do the Magistrates Union or other similar institutions do, if not precisely appeal to this canon of right, this famous, formal right, that is said to be bourgeois, and which in reality is the right of sovereignty? But I believe that we find ourselves here in a kind of blind alley: it is not through recourse to sovereignty against discipline that the effects of disciplinary power can be limited, because sovereignty and disciplinary mechanisms are two absolutely integral constituents of the general mechanism of power in our society.

If one wants to look for a non-disciplinary form of power, or rather, to struggle against disciplines and disciplinary power, it is not towards the ancient right of sovereignty that one should turn, but towards the possibility of a new form of right, one which must indeed be anti-disciplinarian, but at the same time liberated from the principle of sovereignty. It is at this point that we once more come up against the notion of repression, whose use in this context I believe to be doubly unfortunate. On the one hand, it contains an obscure reference to a certain theory of sovereignty, the sovereignty of the sovereign rights of the individual, and on the other hand, its usage introduces a system of psychological reference points borrowed from the human sciences, that is to say, from discourses and practices that belong to the disciplinary realm. I believe that the notion of repression remains a juridical-disciplinary notion whatever the critical use one would make of it. To this extent the critical application of the notion of repression is found to be vitiated and nullified from the outset by the two-fold juridical and disciplinary reference it contains to sovereignty on the one hand and to normalisation on the other.

Jacques Derrida, "Conjuring Marxism," from *Specters of Marx*

Today, in these times, a new "world order" seeks to stabilize a new, necessarily new disturbance [*dérèglement*] by installing an unprecedented form of hegemony. It is a matter, then, but as always, of a novel form of war. It at least resembles a great "conjuration" against Marxism, a "conjurement" of Marxism: once again, another attempt, a new, always new mobilization to struggle against it, against that which and those whom it represents and will continue to represent (the idea of a new International), and to combat an International by exorcising it.

Very novel and so ancient, the conjuration appears both powerful and, as always, worried, fragile, anxious. The enemy to be conjured away, for those sworn to the conjuration, is, to be sure, called Marxism. But people are now afraid that they will no longer recognize it. They quake at the hypothesis that, by virtue of one of those metamorphoses that Marx talked about so much ("metamorphosis" was one of his favorite words throughout his life), a new "Marxism" will no longer have the face by which one was accustomed to identify it and put it down. Perhaps people are no longer afraid of Marxists, but they are still afraid of certain non-Marxists who have not renounced Marx's inheritance, crypto-Marxists, pseudo- or para-"Marxists" who would be standing by to change the guard, but behind features or quotation marks that the anxious experts of anti-communism are not trained to unmask.

Besides the reasons just given, we will privilege this figure of conjuration for still other reasons. They have already begun to make their appearance. In its two concepts (conjuration and conjurement, *Verschwörung* and *Beschwörung*), we must take into account another essential meaning: the act that consists in swearing, taking an oath, therefore promising, deciding, taking a *responsibility*, in short, committing oneself in a performative fashion—as well as in a more or less secret fashion, and thus more or less public, there where this frontier between the public and the private is constantly being displaced, remaining less assured than ever, as the limit that would permit one to identify the political. And if this important frontier is being displaced, it is because the medium in which it is instituted, namely, the medium of the media themselves (news, the press, tele-communications, techno-tele-discursivity, techno-tele-iconicity, that which in general assures and determines the *spacing* of public space, the very possibility of the *res publica* and the phenomenality of the political), this element itself is neither living nor dead, present nor absent: it spectralizes. It does not belong to ontology, to the discourse on the Being of beings, or to the essence of life or death. It requires, then, what we call, to save time and space rather than just to make up a word, *hauntology*. We will take this category to be irreducible, and first of all to everything it makes possible: ontology, theology, positive or negative onto-theology.

This dimension of performative interpretation, that is, of an interpretation that transforms the very thing it interprets, will play an indispensable role in what I would like to say this evening. "An interpretation that transforms what it interprets" is a definition of the performative as unorthodox with regard to speech act theory as it is with regard to the 11th Thesis on Feuerbach ("The philosophers have only *interpreted* the world in various ways; the point, however, is to *change it* [*Die Philosophen haben die Welt nur verschieden interpretiert; es kömmt aber drauf an, sie zu verändern*]").

If I take the floor at the opening of such an impressive, ambitious, necessary or risky, others might say historic colloquium; if, after hesitating for a long time and despite the obvious limits of my competence, I nevertheless accepted the invitation with which Bernd Magnus has honored me, it is not in the first place in order to propose a scholarly, philosophical discourse. It is first of all so as not to flee from a responsibility. More precisely, it is in order to submit for your discussion several hypotheses on the nature of such a responsibility. What is ours? In what way is it historical? And what does it have to do with so many specters?

No one, it seems to me, can *contest* the fact that a dogmatics is attempting to install its worldwide hegemony in paradoxical and suspect conditions. There is today in the world a *dominant* discourse, or rather one that is on the way to becoming dominant, on the subject of Marx's work and thought, on the subject of Marxism (which is perhaps not the same thing), on the subject of the socialist International and the universal revolution, on the subject of the more or less slow destruction of the revolutionary model in its Marxist inspiration, on the subject of the rapid, precipitous, recent collapse of societies that attempted to put it into effect at least in what we will call for the moment, citing once again the *Manifesto*, "old Europe," and so forth. This dominating discourse often has the manic, jubilatory, and incantatory form that Freud assigned to the so-called triumphant phase of mourning work. The incantation repeats and ritualizes itself, it holds forth and holds to formulas, like any animistic magic. To the rhythm of a cadenced march, it proclaims: Marx is dead, communism is dead, very dead, and along with it its hopes, its discourse, its theories, and its practices. It says: long live capitalism, long live the market, here's to the survival of economic and political liberalism!

If this hegemony is attempting to install its dogmatic orchestration in suspect and paradoxical conditions, it is first of all because this triumphant conjuration is striving in truth to disavow, and therefore to hide from, the fact that never, never in history, has the horizon of the thing whose survival is being celebrated (namely, all the old models of the capitalist and liberal world) been as dark, threatening, and threatened. And never more "historic," by which we mean inscribed in an absolutely novel moment of a process that is nonetheless subject to a law of iterability.

What are we doing by speaking, with these first words, of a *dominant* discourse and of an *incontestable* self-evidence regarding it?

At least *two things*. We are obviously having recourse to received concepts: (1) that of hegemony ("dominant discourse") and (2) that of testimony ("*incontestable* self-evidence"). We will have to account for these and justify them.

1. We have implicitly referred (particularly so as to speak of what no one, I presume, would dream of contesting) to that which everywhere organizes and commands public manifestation or testimony in the public space. In question here is a set constituted by *three* indissociable places or apparatuses of our culture:

a. There is first of all the culture called more or less properly political (the official discourses of parties and politicians in power in the world, virtually everywhere Western models prevail, the speech or the rhetoric of what in France is called the "classe politique").

b. There is also what is rather confusedly qualified as mass-media culture: "communications" and interpretations, selective and hierarchized production of "information" through channels whose power has grown in an absolutely unheard-of fashion at a rhythm that coincides precisely, no doubt not fortuitously, with that of the fall of regimes on the Marxist model, a fall to which it contributed mightily but—and this is not the least important point—in forms and modes of appropriation, and at a speed that also affect in an essential fashion the very concept of public space in so-called liberal democracies; and at the center of this colloquium the question of media teletechnology, economy, and power, in their irreducibly spectral dimension, should cut across all our discussions. What can one do with the Marxist schemas in order to deal with this today—theoretically and practically—and thus in order to change it? To put it in a word that would sum up the *position* I am going to defend (and what I am putting forward here, pardon me for saying this again, corresponds more to a *position-taking* than to the work such a position calls for, presupposes, or prefigures), these schemas appear both indispensable and insufficient in their present form. Marx is one of the rare thinkers of the past to have taken seriously, at least in its principle, the originary indissociability of technics and language, and thus of tele-technics (for every language is a tele-technics). But it is not at all to denigrate him, it is even to speak in what we will still dare to call the *spirit of Marx*, it is almost to quote word for word his own predictions, it is to *register* [prendre acte] and to *confirm* to say: as regards tele-technics, and thus also as regards science, he could not accede to the experience and to the anticipations on this subject that are ours today.

c. There is finally scholarly or academic culture, notably that of historians, sociologists and politologists, theoreticians of literature, anthropologists, philosophers, in particular political philosophers, whose discourse is itself relayed by the academic and commercial press, but also by the media in general. For no one will have failed to notice that the three places, forms, and powers of culture that I have just identified (the expressly political discourse of the "political class," media discourse, and intellectual, scholarly, or academic discourse) are more than ever welded together by the same apparatuses or by ones that are indissociable from them. These apparatuses are doubtless complex, differential, conflictual, and overdetermined. But whatever may be the conflicts, inequalities, or overdeterminations among them, they communicate and cooperate at every moment toward producing the greatest force with which to assure the hegemony or the imperialism in question. They do so thanks to the mediation of what is called precisely the media in the broadest, most mobile, and, considering the acceleration of technical advances, most technologically invasive sense of this term. As it has never done before, either to such a degree or in these forms, the politico-economic hegemony, like the intellectual or discursive domination, passes by way of techno-mediatic power—that is, by a power that at the same time, in a differentiated and contradictory fashion, *conditions and endangers* any democracy. Now, this power, this differentiated set of powers cannot be analyzed or potentially combatted, supported here, attacked there, without taking into account so many *spectral* effects, the new speed of *apparition* (we understand this word in its ghostly sense) of the simulacrum, the synthetic or prosthetic image, and the virtual event, cyberspace and surveillance, the control, appropriations, and speculations that today deploy unheard-of powers. Have Marx and his heirs helped us to think and to treat this phenomenon? If we say that the answer to this question is at once *yes* and *no, yes* in one respect, *no* in another, and that one must filter, select, differentiate, restructure the questions, it is only in order to announce, in too preliminary a fashion, the tone and the general form of our conclusions: namely, that one *must assume the inheritance* of Marxism, assume its most "living" part, which is to say, paradoxically, that which continues to put back on the drawing board the question of life, spirit, or the spectral, of life-death beyond the opposition between life and death. This inheritance must be reaffirmed by transforming it as radically as will be necessary. Such a reaffirmation would be both faithful to something that resonates in Marx's appeal—let us say once again in the spirit of his injunction—and in conformity with the concept of inheritance in general. Inheritance is never a *given*, it is always a task. It remains before us just as unquestionably as we are heirs of Marxism, even before wanting or refusing to be, and, like all inheritors, we are in mourning. In mourning in particular for what is called Marxism. *To be*, this word in which we earlier saw the word of the spirit, means, for the same reason, to inherit. All the questions on the subject of being or of what is to be (or not to be) are questions of inheritance. There is no backward-looking fervor in this reminder, no traditionalist flavor. Reaction, reactionary, or reactive are but interpretations of the structure of inheritance. That we *are* heirs does not mean that we *have* or that we *receive* this or that, some inheritance that enriches us one day with this or that, but that the *being* of what we are *is* first of all inheritance, whether we like it or know it or not. And that, as Hölderlin said so well, we can only *bear witness* to it. To bear witness would be to bear witness to what we *are* insofar as we *inherit*, and that—here is the circle, here is the chance, or the finitude—we inherit the very thing that allows us to bear witness to it. As for Hölderlin, he calls this language, "the most dangerous of goods," given to man "so that he bears witness to having inherited what he is [*damit er zeuge, was er sei/ geerbt zu haben*]."

2. When we advance at least the hypothesis that the dogma on the subject of the end of Marxism and of Marxist societies is today, tendentially, a "dominant discourse," we are still speaking, of course, in the Marxist code. We must not deny or dissimulate the problematic character of this gesture. Those who would accuse it of being circular or begging the question would not be altogether wrong. At least provisionally, we are placing our trust, in fact, in this form of critical analysis we have inherited from Marxism: In a given situation, provided that it is determinable and determined

as being that of a socio-political antagonism, a hegemonic force always seems to be represented by a dominant rhetoric and ideology, whatever may be the conflicts between forces, the principal contradiction or the secondary contradictions, the over-determinations and the relays that may later complicate this schema—and therefore lead us to be suspicious of the simple opposition of *dominant* and *dominated*, or even of the final determination of the forces in conflict, or even, more radically, of the idea that force is always stronger than weakness (Nietzsche and Benjamin have encouraged us to have doubts on this score, each in his own way, and especially the latter when he associated "historical materialism" with the inheritance, precisely, of some "weak messianic force"). Critical inheritance: one may thus, for example, speak of a dominant discourse or of dominant representations and ideas, and refer in this way to a hierarchized and conflictual field without necessarily subscribing to the concept of social class by means of which Marx so often determined, particularly in *The German Ideology*, the forces that are fighting for control of the hegemony. And even quite simply of the State. When, for example, in evoking the history of ideas, the *Manifesto* declares that the "ruling ideas [*die herrschenden Idem*] of each age have ever been the ideas of its ruling class [*der herrschenden Klasse*]", it is not out of the question for a selective critique to filter the inheritance of this utterance so as to keep this rather than that. One may continue to speak of domination in a field of forces not only while suspending the reference to this ultimate support that would be the identity and the self-identity of a social class, but even while suspending the credit extended to what Marx calls the idea, the determination of the superstructure as idea, ideal or ideological representation, indeed even the discursive form of this representation. All the more so since the concept of idea implies this irreducible genesis of the spectral that we are planning to re-examine here.

But let us retain provisionally, for this very preliminary moment of our introduction, the schema of the dominant discourse. If such a discourse tends today to be getting the upper hand on the new stage of geopolitics (in the rhetoric of the politician, in the consensus of the media, over the most visible and resonant part of intellectual or academic space), it is the one that diagnoses, in all sorts of tones and with an unshakeable assurance, not only the end of societies constructed on the Marxist model but the end of the whole Marxist tradition, even of the reference to the works of Marx, not to say the end of history, period. All of this would have finally come to term in the euphoria of liberal democracy and of the market economy. This triumphant discourse seems relatively homogeneous, most often dogmatic, sometimes politically equivocal and, like dogmatisms, like all conjurations, secretly worried and manifestly worrisome. The protocol of our conference evokes the example of the book by Francis Fukuyama, *The End of History and the Last Man*. Is not what we have here a new gospel, the noisiest, the most mediatized [*médiatique*], the most "successful" one on the subject of the death of Marxism as the end of history? This work frequently resembles, it is true, the disconcerting and tardy by-product of a "footnote": *nota bene* for a certain Kojève who deserved better. Yet the book is not as bad or as naive as one might be led to think by the frenzied exploitation that exhibits it as the finest ideological showcase of victorious capitalism in a liberal democracy which has finally arrived at the plenitude of its ideal, if not of its reality. In fact, although it remains essentially, in the tradition of Leo Strauss relayed by Allan Bloom, the grammar school exercise of a young, industrious, but come-lately reader of Kojève (and a few others), one must recognize that here or there this book goes beyond nuance and is sometimes suspensive to the point of indecision. To the questions elaborated in its own fashion, it on occasion ingenuously adds, so as to cover all the bases, what it calls "two broad responses, from the Left and the Right, respectively". It would thus merit a very close analysis. This evening we will have to limit ourselves to what concerns the *general structure* of a thesis indispensable, precisely in the very structure of its logic, in the formulation of its formula, to the anti-Marxist conjuration.

It is by design, of course, that we called it a moment ago a "gospel."

Why a gospel? Why would the formula here be neo-testamentary? This book claims to bring a "positive response" to a question whose formation and formulation are never interrogated in themselves. It is the question of whether a "coherent and directional History of mankind" will eventually lead "the greater part of humanity," as Fukuyama calmly, enigmatically, and in a fashion at once modest and impudent calls it, toward "liberal democracy". Of course, while answering "yes" to this question in this form, Fukuyama admits, on the same page, to an awareness of everything that allows one to have one's doubts: the two world wars, the horrors of totalitarianism—Nazi, fascist, Stalinist—the massacres of Pol Pot, and so forth. One can assume that he would have agreed to extend this disastrous list. He does not do so, one wonders why and whether this limitation is contingent or insignificant. But according to a schema that organizes the argumentation of this strange plea from one end to the other, all these cataclysms (terror, oppression, repression, extermination, genocide, and so on), these "events" or these "facts" would belong to *empiricity* to the "empirical flow of events in the second half of the century", they would remain "empirical" phenomena accredited by "empirical evidence". Their accumulation would in no way refute the ideal orientation of the greater part of humanity toward liberal democracy. As *such*, as *telos* of a progress, this orientation would have the form of an ideal finality. Everything that appears to contradict it would belong to historical empiricity, however massive and catastrophic and global and multiple and recurrent it might be. Even if one admitted the simplicity of this summary distinction between empirical reality and ideal finality, one would still not know how this absolute orientation, this anhistoric *telos* of history gives rise, very precisely *in our day*, in these days, *in our time*, to an event which Fukuyama speaks of as "good news" and that he dates very explicitly from "The most remarkable evolution of the last quarter of the twentieth century". To be sure, he recognizes that what he describes as the collapse of the worldwide dictatorships of the right or the left has not always "given way…to stable liberal democracies". But he believes he can assert that, as of this date, and this is the good news, a dated news, "liberal democracy remains the only coherent political aspiration that spans different regions and cultures around the globe." This "move toward political freedom around the globe," according to Fukuyama, would have been everywhere accompanied, "sometimes followed, sometimes preceded," he writes, by "a liberal revolution in economic thought." The alliance of liberal democracy and of the "free market," there's the "good news" of this last quarter century. This evangelistic figure is remarkably insistent. Since it prevails or claims to prevail on a geopolitical scale, it deserves to be at least underscored.

(We are thus going to underscore it, as well as the figure of the Promised Land, which is at once close to it and dissociated from it for two reasons that we can only indicate here in parentheses. *On the one hand*, these biblical figures play a role that seems to exceed the simple rhetorical cliché they appear to be. *On the other hand*, they demand attention all the more so in that, in a fashion that is not fortuitous, the greatest symptomatic or metonymic concentration of what remains irreducible in the worldwide conjuncture in which the question of "whither Marxism" is inscribed today has its place, its figure, or the figure of its place in the Middle East: three other messianic eschatologies mobilize there all the forces of the world and the whole "world order" in the ruthless war they are waging against each other, directly or indirectly; they mobilize simultaneously, in order to put them to work or to the test, the old concepts of State and nation-State, of international law, of tele-techno-medio-economic and scientifico-military forces, in other words, the most archaic and the most modern spectral forces. One would have to analyze, in the limitless breadth of their worldwide historical stakes, since the end of the Second World War, in particular since the founding of the State of Israel, the violence that preceded, constituted, accompanied, and followed it on every side, *at the same time* in conformity with *and* in disregard of an international law that therefore appears today to be *at the same time* more contradictory, imperfect, and thus more perfectible and necessary than ever. Such an analysis can no longer avoid granting a determining role to this war of messianic eschatologies in what we will sum up with an ellipsis in the expression "appropriation of Jerusalem." The war for the "appropriation of Jerusalem" is today the world war. It is happening everywhere, it is the world, it is today the singular figure of its being "out of joint." Now, still in too elliptical a fashion, let us say that in order to determine in its radical premises Middle-Eastern violence as an unleashing of messianic eschatologies and as infinite combinatory possibilities of holy alliances [a word that must be put in the plural to account for what makes the triangle of the three religions said to be religions of the Book turn in these alliances], Marxism remains at once indispensable and structurally insufficient: it is still necessary *but* provided it be transformed and adapted to new conditions and to a new thinking of the ideological, provided it be made to analyze the new articulation of techno-economic causalities and of religious ghosts, the dependent condition of the juridical at the service of socio-economic powers or States that are themselves never totally independent with regard to capital [but there is no longer, there never was just capital, nor capitalism in the singular, but capitalisms plural—whether State or private, real or symbolic, always linked to spectral forces—or rather *capitalizations* whose antagonisms are irreducible].

This transformation and this opening up of Marxism are in conformity with what we were calling a moment ago the *spirit of Marxism*. If analysis of the Marxist type remains, then, indispensable, it appears to be radically insufficient there where the Marxist ontology grounding the project of Marxist science or critique *also itself carries with it and must carry with it, necessarily*, despite so many modern or postmodern denials, a messianic eschatology. On this score at least, paradoxically and despite the fact that it necessarily participates in them, it cannot be *simply* classified among the ideologems or theologems whose critique or demystification it calls for. In saying that, we will not claim that this messianic eschatology common both to the religions it criticizes and to the Marxist critique must be simply deconstructed. While it is common to both of them, with the exception of the content [but none of them can accept, of course, this *epokhē* of the content, whereas we hold it here to be essential to the messianic in general, as thinking of the other and of the event to come, it is also the case that its formal structure of promise exceeds them or precedes them. Well, what remains irreducible to any deconstruction, what remains as unde-constructible as the possibility itself of deconstruction is, perhaps, a certain experi-ence of the emancipatory promise; it is perhaps even the formality of a structural messianism, a messianism without religion, even a messianic without messianism, an idea of justice—which we distinguish from law or right and even from human rights—and an idea of democracy—which we distinguish from its current concept and from its determined predicates today [permit me to refer here to "Force of Law" and *The Other Heading*]. But this is perhaps what must now be thought and thought otherwise in order to ask oneself where Marxism is going, which is also to say, where Marxism is leading and where is it to be led [*où conduire le Marxisme*]: where to lead it by interpreting it, which cannot happen without transformation, and not where can it lead us such as it is or such as it will have been.

We return to the *neo-evangelistic* rhetoric of Fukuyama: "we have become so accus-tomed by now to expect that the future will contain bad news with respect to the health and security of decent, democratic political practices that we have problems recognizing *good news* when it comes. And yet, the *good news* has come." The neo-evangelistic insistence is significant for more reasons than one. A little further on, this Christian figure crosses the Jewish prefiguration of the Promised Land. But in order to take its distance from it right away. If the development of modern physics is not for nothing in the advent of the good news, notably, Fukuyama tells us, inasmuch as it is linked to a technology that permits "the limitless accumulation of wealth" and "an increasing homogenization of all human societies," it is "in the first place" because this "technology confers decisive military advantages on those countries that possess it". Now, although it is essential and indispensable to the advent or the "good news" proclaimed by Fukuyama, this physico-tech-no-military given only leads us as far, he says, as the gates of this "Promised Land": "But while modern natural science guides us to the gates of the Promised Land of liberal democrary, it does not deliver us to the Promised Land itself, for there is no economically necessary reason why advanced industrialization should produce political liberty."

But at a certain point promise and decision, which is to say responsibility, owe their possibility to the ordeal of undecidability which will always remain their condition. And all the grave stakes we have just named in a few words would come down to the question of what one understands, with Marx and after Marx, by effectivity, effect, operativity, work, labor [*Wirklichkeit, Wirkung*, work, operation], living work in their supposed opposition to the spectral logic that also governs the effects of virtuality, of simulacrum, of "mourning work," of ghost, *revenant*, and so forth. And of the justice that is their due. To put it in a few words, deconstructive thinking of the trace, of iterability, of prosthetic synthesis, of supplementarity, and so forth, goes beyond this opposition, beyond the ontology it presumes. Inscribing the possibility of the reference to the other, and thus of radical alterity and heterogeneity, of differance, of technicity, and of ideality in the very event of presence, in the presence of the present that it dis-joins *a priori in* order to make it possible [thus impossible in its identity or its contemporaneity with itself], it does not deprive itself of the means with which to take into account, or to render an account of, the effects of ghosts, of simulacra, of "synthetic images," or even, to put it in terms of the Marxist code, of ideologems, even if these take the novel forms to which modern technology will have given rise. That is why such a deconstruction has never been Marxist, no more than it has ever been non-Marxist, although it has remained faithful to a certain spirit of Marxism, to at least one of its spirits for, and this can never be repeated too often, there is *more than one* of them and they are heterogeneous.)

J.F. Lyotard, Selection from *The Postmodern Condition*

8. The Narrative Function and the Legitimation of Knowledge

Today the problem of legitimation is no longer considered a failing of the language game of science. It would be more accurate to say that it has itself been legitimated as a problem, that is, as a heuristic driving force. But this way of dealing with it by reversing the situation is of recent date. Before it came to this point (what some call positivism), scientific knowledge sought other solutions. It is remarkable that for a long time it could not help resorting for its solutions to procedures that, overtly or not, belong to narrative knowledge.

This return of the narrative in the non-narrative, in one form or another, should not be thought of as having been superseded once and for all. A crude proof of this: what do scientists do when they appear on television or are interviewed in the newspapers after making a "discovery"? They recount an epic of knowledge that is in fact wholly unepic. They play by the rules of the narrative game; its influence remains considerable not only on the users of the media, but also on the scientist's sentiments. This fact is neither trivial nor accessory: it concerns the relationship of scientific knowledge to "popular" knowledge, or what is left of it. The state spends large amounts of money to enable science to pass itself off as an epic: the State's own credibility is based on that epic, which it uses to obtain the public consent its decision makers need.

It is not inconceivable that the recourse to narrative is inevitable, at least to the extent that the language game of science desires its statements to be true but does not have the resources to legitimate their truth on its own. If this is the case, it is necessary to admit an irreducible need for history understood, as outlined above—not as a need to remember or to project (a need for historicity, for accent), but on the contrary as a need to forget (a need for *metrum*).

We are anticipating ourselves. But as we proceed we should keep in mind that the apparently obsolete solutions that have been found for the problem of legitimation are not obsolete in principle, but only in their expression; we should not be surprised if we find that they have persisted to this day in other forms. Do not we ourselves, at this moment, feel obliged to mount a narrative of scientific knowledge in the West in order to clarify its status?

The new language game of science posed the problem of its own legitimation at the very beginning—in Plato. This is not the proper place for an exegesis of the passages in the *Dialogues* in which the pragmatics of science is set in motion, either explicitly as a theme or implicitly as a presupposition. The game of dialogue, with its specific requirements, encapsulates that pragmatics, enveloping within itself its two functions of research and teaching. We encounter some of the same rules previously enumerated: argumentation with a view only to consensus (*homologia*); the unicity of the referent as a guarantee for the possibility of agreement; parity between partners; and even an indirect recognition that it is a question of a game and not a destiny, since those who refuse to accept the rules, out of weakness or crudeness, are excluded.

There remains the fact that, given the scientific nature of the game, the question of its own legitimacy must be among those raised in the dialogues. A well-known example of this, which is all the more important since it links this question to that of sociopolitical authority from the start, is to be found in books 6 and 7 of *The Republic*. As we know, the answer, at least part of it, comes in the form of a narrative—the allegory of the cave, which recounts how and why men yearn for narratives and fail to recognize knowledge. Knowledge is thus founded on the narrative of its own martyrdom.

With modern science, two new features appear in the problematic of legitimation. To being with, it leaves behind the metaphysical search for a first proof or transcendental authority as a response to the question: "How do you prove the proof?" or, more generally, "Who decides the conditions of truth?" It is recognized that the conditions of truth, in other words, the rules of the game of science, are immanent in that game, that they can only be established within the bonds of a debate that is already scientific in nature, and that there is no other proof that the rules are good than the consensus extended to them by the experts.

Accompanying the modern proclivity to define the conditions of a discourse in a discourse on those conditions is a renewed dignity for narrative (popular) cultures, already noticeable in Renaissance Humanism and variously present in the Enlightenment, the *Sturm und Drang*, German idealist philosophy, and the historical school in France. Narration is no longer an involuntary lapse in the legitimation process. The explicit appeal to narrative in the problematic of knowledge is concomitant with the liberation of the bourgeois classes from the traditional authorities. Narrative knowledge makes a resurgence in the West as a way of solving the problem of legitimating the new authorities. It is natural in a narrative problematic for such a question to solicit the name of a hero as its response: *Who* has the right to decide for society? Who is the subject whose prescriptions are norms for those they obligate?

This way of inquiring into sociopolitical legitimacy combines with the new scientific attitude: the name of the hero is the people, the sign of legitimacy is the people's consensus, and their mode of creating norms is deliberation. The notion of progress is a necessary outgrowth of this. It represents nothing other than the movement by which knowledge is presumed to accumulate—but this movement is extended to the new sociopolitical subject. The people debate among themselves about what is just or unjust in the same way that the scientific community debates about what is true or false; they accumulate civil laws just as scientists accumulate scientific laws; they perfect their rules of consensus just as the scientists produce new "paradigms" to revise their rules in light of what they have learned.

It is clear that what is meant here by "the people" is entirely different from what is implied by traditional narrative knowledge, which, as we have seen, requires to instituting deliberation, no cumulative progression, no pretension to universality; these are the operators of scientific knowledge. It is therefore not at all surprising that the representatives of the new process of legitimation by "the people" should be at the same time actively involved in destroying the traditional knowledge of peoples, perceived from that point forward as minorities or potential separatist movements destined only to spread obscurantism.

We can see too that the real existence of this necessarily abstract subject (it is abstract because it is uniquely modeled on the paradigm of the subject of knowledge—that is, one who sends-receives denotative statements with truth-value to the exclusion of other language games) depends on the institutions within which that subject is supposed to deliberate and decide, and which comprise all or part of the State. The question of the State becomes intimately entwined with that of scientific knowledge.

But it is also clear that this interlocking is many sided. The "people" (the nation, or even humanity), and especially their political institutions, are not content to know—they legislate. That is, they formulate prescriptions that have the status of norms. They therefore exercise their competence not only with respect to denotative utterances concerning what is true, but also prescriptive utterances with pretentions to justice. As already said, what characterizes narrative knowledge, what forms the basis of our conception of it, precisely that it combines both of these kinds of competence, not to mention all the others.

The mode of legitimation we are discussing, which reintroduces narrative as the validity of knowledge, can thus take two routes, depending on whether it represents the subject of the narrative as cognitive or practical, as a hero of knowledge or a hero of liberty. Because of this alternative, not only does the meaning of legitimation vary, but it is already apparent that narrative itself is incapable of describing that meaning adequately.

9. Narratives of the Legitimation of Knowledge

We shall examine two major versions of the narrative of legitimation. One is more political, the other more philosophical; both are of great importance in modern history, in particular in the history of knowledge and its institutions.

The subject of the first of these versions is humanity as the hero of liberty. All peoples have a right to science. If the social subject is not already the subject of scientific knowledge, it is because that has been forbidden by priests and tyrants. The right to science must be reconquered. It is understandable that this narrative would be directed more toward a politics of primary education, rather than of universities and high schools. The educational policy of the French Third Republic powerfully illustrates these presuppositions.

It seems that this narrative finds it necessary to de-emphasize higher education. Accordingly, the measures adopted by Napoleon regarding higher education are generally considered to have been motivated by the desire to produce the administrative and professional skills necessary for the stability of the State. This overlooks the fact that in the context of the narrative of freedom, the State receives its legitimacy not from itself but from the people. So even if imperial politics designated the institutions of higher education as a breeding ground for the officers of the State and secondarily, for the managers of civil society, it did so because the nation as a whole was supposed to win its freedom through the spread of new domains of knowledge to the population, a process to be effected through agencies and professions within which those cadres would fulfill their functions. The same reasoning is a fortiori valid for the foundation of properly scientific institutions. The State resorts to the narrative of freedom every time it assumes direct control over the training of the "people," under the name of the "nation," in order to point them down the path of progress.

With the second narrative of legitimation, the relation between science, the nation, and the State develops quite differently. It first appears with the founding, between 1807 and 1810, of the University of Berlin, whose influence on the organization of higher education in the young countries of the world was to be considerable in the nineteenth and twentieth centuries.

At the time of the University's creation, the Prussian ministry had before it a project conceived by Fichte and counterproposals by Schleiermacher. Wilhelm von Humboldt had to decide the matter and came down on the side of Schleiermacher's more "liberal" option.

Reading Humboldt's report, one may be tempted to reduce his entire approach to the politics of the scientific institution to the famous dictum: "Science for its own sake." But this would be to misunderstood the ultimate aim of his policies, which is guided by the principle of legitimation we are discussing and is very close to the one Schleiermacher elucidates in a more thorough fashion.

Humboldt does indeed declare that science obeys its own rules, that the scientific institution "lives and continually renews itself on its own, with no constraint or determined goal whatsoever." But he adds that the University should orient its constituent element, science, to "the spiritual and moral training of the nation." How can this *Bildung*-effect result from the disinterested pursuit of learning? Are not the State, the nation, the whole of humanity indifferent to knowledge for its own sake? What interests them, as Humboldt admits, is not learning, but "character and action."

The minister's adviser thus faces a major conflict, in some ways reminiscent of the split introduced by the Kantian critique between knowing and willing: it is a conflict between a language game made of denotations answerable only to the criterion of truth, and a language game governing ethical, social, and political practice that necessarily involves decisions and obligations, in other words, utterances expected to be just rather than true and which in the final analysis lie outside the realm of scientific knowledge.

However, the unification of these two sets of discourse is indispensable to the *Bildung* aimed for by Humboldt's project, which consists not only in the acquisition of learning by individuals, but also in the training of a fully legitimated subject of knowledge and society. Humboldt therefore invokes a Spirit (what Fichte calls Life), animated by three ambitions, or better, by a single, threefold aspiration: "that of deriving everything from an original principle" (corresponding to scientific activity), "that of relating everything to an ideal" (governing ethical and social practice), and "that of unifying this principle and this ideal in a single Idea" (ensuring that the scientific search for true causes always coincides with the pursuit of just ends in moral and political life). This ultimate synthesis constitutes the legitimate subject.

Humboldt adds in passing that this triple aspiration naturally inheres in the "intellectual character of the German nation." This is a concession, but a discreet one, to the other narrative, to the idea that the subject of knowledge is the people. But in truth this idea is quite distant from the narrative of the legitimation of knowledge advanced by German idealism. The suspicion that men like Schleiermacher, Humboldt, and even Hegel harbor towards the State is an indication of this. If Schleiermacher fears the narrow nationalism, protectionism, utilitarianism, and positivism that guide the public authorities in matters of science, it is because the principle of science does not reside in those authorities, even indirectly. The subject of knowledge is not the people, but the speculative spirit. It is not embodied, as in France after the Revolution, in a State, but in a System. The language game of legitimation is not state-political, but philosophical.

The great function to be fulfilled by the universities is to "lay open the whole body of learning and expound both the principles and the foundations of all knowledge." For "there is no creative scientific capacity without the speculative spirit." "Speculation" is here the name given the discourse on the legitimation of scientific discourse. Schools are functional; the University is speculative, that is to say, philosophical. Philosophy must restore unity to learning, which has been scattered into separate sciences in laboratories and in pre-university education; it can only achieve this in a language game that links the sciences together as moments in the becoming of spirit, in other words, which links them in a rational narration, or rather meta-narration. Hegel's *Encyclopedia* (1817–27) attempts to realize this project of totalization, which was already present in Fichte and Schelling in the form of the idea of the System.

It is here, in the mechanism of developing a Life that is simultaneously Subject, that we see a return of narrative knowledge. There is a universal "history" of spirit, spirit is "life," and "life" is its own self-presentation and formulation in the ordered knowledge of all of its forms contained in the empirical sciences. The encyclopedia of German idealism is the narration of the "(hi)story" of this life-subject. But what it produces is a metanarrative, for the story's narrator must not be a people mired in the particular positivity of its traditional knowledge, nor even scientists taken as a whole, since they are sequestered in professional frameworks corresponding to their respective specialities.

The narrator must be a metasubject in the process of formulating both the legitimacy of the discourses of the empirical sciences and that of the direct institutions of popular cultures. This metasubject, in giving voice to their common grounding, realizes their implicit goal. It inhabits the speculative University. Positive science and the people are only crude versions of it. The only valid way for the nation-state itself to bring the people to expression is through the mediation of speculative knowledge.

It has been necessary to elucidate the philosophy that legitimated the foundation of the University of Berlin and was meant to be the motor both of its development and the development of contemporary knowledge. As I have said, many countries in the nineteenth and twentieth centuries adopted this university organization as a model for the foundation or reform of their own system of higher education, beginning with the United States. But above all, this philosophy—which is far from dead, especially in university circles—offers a particularly vivid representation of one solution to the problem of the legitimacy of knowledge.

Research and the spread of learning are not justified by invoking a principle of usefulness. The idea is not at all that science should serve the interests of the State and/or civil society. The humanist principle that humanity rises up in dignity and freedom through knowledge is left by the wayside. German idealism has recourse to a metaprinciple that simultaneously grounds the development of learning, of society, and of the State in the realization of the "life" of a Subject, called "divine Life" by Fichte and "Life of the spirit" by Hegel. In this perspective, knowledge first finds legitimacy within itself, and it is knowledge that is entitled to say what the State and what Society are. But it can only play this role by changing levels, by ceasing to be simply the positive knowledge of its referent (nature, society, the State, etc.), becoming in addition to that the knowledge of the knowledge of the referent—that is, by becoming speculative. In the names "Life" and "Spirit," knowledge names itself.

A noteworthy result of the speculative apparatus is that all of the discourses of learning about every possible referent are taken up not from the point of view of their immediate truth-value, but in terms of the value they acquire by virtue of occupying a certain place in the itinerary of Spirit or Life—or, if preferred, a certain position in the Encyclopedia recounted by speculative discourse. That discourse cites them in the process of expounding for itself what it knows, that is, in the process of self-exposition. True knowledge, in this perspective, is always indirect knowledge; it is composed of reported statements that are incorporated into the metanarrative of a subject that guarantees their legitimacy.

The same thing applies for every variety of discourse, even if it is not a discourse of learning; examples are the discourse of law and that of the State. Contemporary hermeneutic discourse is born of this presupposition, which guarantees that there is meaning to know and thus confers legitimacy upon history (and especially the history of learning). Statements are treated as their own autonyms and set in motion in a way that is supposed to render them mutually engendering: these are the rules of speculative language. The University, as its name indicates, is its exclusive institution.

But, as I have said, the problem of legitimacy can be solved using the other procedures as well. The difference between them should be kept in mind: today, with the status of knowledge unbalanced and its speculative unity broken, the first version of legitimacy is gaining new vigor.

According to this version, knowledge finds its validity not within itself, not in a subject that develops by actualizing its learning possibilities, but in a practical subject—humanity. The principle of the movement animating the people is not the self-legitimation of knowledge, but the self-grounding of freedom or, if preferred, its self-management. The subject is concrete, or supposedly so, and its epic is the story of its emancipation from everything that prevents it from governing itself. It is assumed that the laws it makes for itself are just, not because they conform to some outside nature, but because the legislators are, constitutionally, the very citizens who are subject to the laws. As a result, the legislator's will—the desire that the laws be just—will always coincide with the will of the citizen, who desires the law and will therefore obey it.

Clearly, this mode of legitimation through the autonomy of the will gives priority to a totally different language game, which Kant called imperative and is known today as prescriptive. The important thing is not, or not only, to legitimate denotative utterances pertaining to the truth, such as "The earth revolves around the sun," but rather to legitimate prescriptive utterances pertaining to justice, such as "Carthage must be destroyed" or "The minimum wage must be set at x dollars." In this context, the only role positive knowledge can play is to inform the practical subject about the reality within which the execution of the prescription is to be inscribed. It allows the subject to circumscribe the executable, or what it is possible to do. But the executory, what should be done, is not within the purview of positive knowledge. It is one thing for an undertaking to be possible and another for it to be just. Knowledge is no longer the subject, but in the service of the subject: its only legitimacy (though it is formidable) is the fact that it allows morality to become reality.

This introduces a relation of knowledge to society and the State which is in principle a relation of the means to the end. But scientists must cooperate only if they judge that the politics of the State, in other words the sum of its prescriptions, is just. If they feel that the civil society of which they are members is badly represented by the State, they may reject its prescriptions. This type of legitimation grants them the authority, as practical human beings, to refuse their scholarly support to a political power they judge to be unjust, in other words, not grounded in a real autonomy. They can even go so far as to use their expertise to demonstrate that such autonomy is not in fact realized in society and the State. This reintroduces the critical function of knowledge. But the fact remains that knowledge has no final legitimacy outside of serving the goals envisioned by the practical subject, the autonomous collectivity.

This distribution of roles in the enterprise of legitimation is interesting from our point of view because it assumes, as against the system-subject theory, that there is no possibility that language games can be unified or totalized in any metadiscourse. Quite to the contrary, here the priority accorded prescriptive statements—uttered by the practical subject—renders them independent in principle from the statements of science, whose only remaining function is to supply this subject with information.

10

Postmodernism and Feminism in IR

Introduction

As the selected essays of Chapter 9 showed, resistance exposes the effects of the politics of exclusion. This of course does not mean that we should all become postmodern strategists. Rather, it merely affirms the fluid and viable position of postmodernism in critical IR theory debates. In turning, then, to postmodernism in IR, it is important to realize the intellectual thrust of postmodernism I mentioned earlier: that postmodernism is a self-critical form of intellectual inquiry that challenges the legitimacy of power at the international and local levels. In doing so, it problematizes the content and legitimacy of sovereignty or any theory or interpretation that, as Richard Ashley and R.B.J. Walker note, "represents an attempt to impose exclusionary boundaries."

More importantly, it also calls attention to what Ashley and Walker refer to as a "disciplinary crisis," in which dissidence exposes the privileged, preconceived boundaries within and between disciplines and groups. In this fashion, dissidence reflects "a crisis that folds out beyond a discipline's imagined boundaries, connecting to a crisis of the human sciences, a crisis of patriarchy, a crisis of governability, a crisis of late industrial society, a generalized crisis of modernity."

But if dissidence is fundamental to understanding the ongoing crisis in the production of knowledge, how do we explain the relationship between resistance and the historical emergence of state sovereignty? This is the question taken up in Jens Bartelson's *A Genealogy of Sovereignty* (1995). Here, Bartelson draws on Foucault to explain the differing historical phases of the legitimization of knowledge and the social practices that have come to legitimize the exercise of sovereign power. Sovereignty, according to him, is a privileged social construct; but one that exposes the link between the normalizing function of rules—or how rules come to be accepted as given norms and social practices—and the exercise of power.

In addition to postmodernism, feminism offers an equally important alternative critique of sovereignty. Drawing on both postmodernist and Marxist thought, feminists in IR seek to expose the biases and exclusionary practices associated with the patriarchical structure of international relations. For the most part, feminists have sought to link the rigid focus on the conventions of war among states with the exclusion of women's voices on the issue of peace. As such, IR's focus on war and conflict reflects a disengagement from the long-term prospects of peace. Not only is this true of international society, but also of IR as a discipline (the lack of women in IR departments, for instance). In this manner, Christine Sylvester's formulation of a method of empathy seeks to investigate the distinction between the emotions related to war and violence, and the emotive sources associated with peace.

Accordingly, the problematic issue that postmodernism and feminism raises for critical IR theory is whether the emancipatory project can offer the framework for a cohesive fourth debate; or alternatively, if there is common conceptual terrain upon which to formulate a cohesive, empirically relevant critical IR theory.

Endnotes

1. Richard Ashley and R.B.J. Walker, "Reading Dissidence/Writing the Discipline: Crisis and the Question of Sovereignty in International Studies," *International Studies Quarterly*, Vol. 34, No. 3 (1990), 387.
2. Ibid., 387.

Richard Ashley and R.B.J. Walker, "Reading Dissidence/Writing the Discipline: Crisis and the Question of Sovereignty in International Studies"*

We need to know what it is about dissident works that prompts attention to them. Why, put simply, should critical readers even care? The answer cannot be that dissident works of thought promise to provide a better method, a superior framework, a more powerful way of producing more convincing answers and more certain solutions to questions and problems, that a discipline readily poses. These works eschew heroic promises such as these, and as we have seen, their critics often indict them for the eschewal. There must be another answer.

Our answer can be baldly stated: dissident works of thought elicit attention and prompt critical readings because these works accentuate and make more evident a sense of crisis, what one might call a crisis of the discipline of international studies. They put the discipline's institutional boundaries in question and put its familiar modes of subjectivity, objectivity, and conduct in doubt; they render its once seemingly self-evident notions of space, time, and progress uncertain; and they thereby make it possible to traverse institutional limitations, expose questions and difficulties, and explore political and theoretical possibilities hitherto forgotten or deferred. In short, dissident works of thought help to accentuate a disciplinary crisis whose single most pronounced symptom is that the very idea of "the discipline" enters thought as a question, a problem, a matter of uncertainty.

Disciplinary Crisis/Cultural Crisis

...Any rendering of disciplinary crisis will immediately be seen by some or many not a representation that is adequate to a referent reality but as an arbitrary contrivance, a groundless fiction, and perhaps even a work of rhetoric that does violence to contending interpretations in the service of a political will. The point can be put quite simply: in this situation, words fail.

If, however, one can agree that words somehow fail to do justice to the disciplinary crisis occasioning critical readings of works of dissidence, then, ironically, one can also agree with our interpretation of that crisis. For at bottom we are saying no more than this: However one might interpret the role of dissident works of thought in the accentuation of disciplinary crisis, the crisis itself involves the discipline's opening out into a region of intrinsically ambiguous, intrinsically indeterminate activity that knows no necessary bounds and unsettles every attempt to produce an enclosing representation of what the discipline is and does. Whether one speaks of the "discipline of international studies," the "discipline of international relations," the "discipline of international politics," or the "discipline of world [or maybe 'global'] politics," the words manifestly fail, even as they promise, to discipline meaning. The words but broadly connote (they cannot denote) a boundless nontime and nonplace—a

---

* From *International Studies Quarterly*, Vol. 34, No. 3, 1990.

deterritorialized, extraterritorial zone of discourse—where the work of producing the subjects, the objects, and the interpretations of an institutional order and its limits visibly eludes the certain control of that order's supposedly reigning categories.

Of course, understanding a disciplinary crisis in this way makes it hard to confine the notion of crisis to a discipline alone. One cannot say that it is just a crisis of the discipline of international studies, because the crisis, so understood, puts in doubt any imaginable boundaries that would separate the discipline of international studies from other disciplines and, indeed, from all other contested sites of modern global life. To think of disciplinary crisis in this way is thus to understand a crisis that folds out beyond a discipline's imagined boundaries, connecting to a crisis of the human sciences, a crisis of patriarchy, a crisis of governability, a crisis of late industrial society, a generalized crisis of modernity.

More specifically, to think of a disciplinary crisis in this way is to understand that the crisis-prompting effect of dissidence in the discipline of international studies resonates with the effects of marginal and dissident movements in all sorts of other localities. It resonates with the effects of feminist movements questioning the modes of social and political discipline engendered as "masculine," ecological movements questioning the disciplines of "industrial society," peace movements questioning the disciplines of "national security" estates, worker movements questioning the disciplines of "managerial order," and cultural movements questioning the disciplines of "information." "International studies," "masculinity," "industrial society," "national security," "managerial order," "information"—these and countless other words must now be written in quotation marks because the modes of disciplining domains of human conduct they would designate are now openly in question, in doubt, in crisis. The boundaries that would separate one domain from another and one dissident struggle from another are put, as it were, under erasure. The attempt to impose boundaries—to exclude the concerns of cultural and ecological movements from the political programs of worker movements, say, or to exclude feminist scholarship from international studies—becomes distinctly visible. It becomes immediately recognizable as an attempt to *impose* exclusionary boundaries. And the attempt itself is thereby politicized, coming to be seen as an arbitrary act of power whose very undertaking incites resistance and the transgression of any boundaries that might be marked.

This, though, is not all there is to say about this crisis. If we are to prepare the way for an understanding of the practices of dissident movements—especially the role of dissident works of thought in the crisis of international studies—then we must carefully examine several aspects of this crisis. We believe that at least eight points need to be made

First, it would be wrong to say that the sort of crisis experienced by the discipline or by modern culture more generally is in any sense a contemporary or recent event. It is as old as modernity itself. As historians would remind us, the cultural crisis of modernity that today's dissidents take seriously has occurred not just recently but very often in the history that modern culture claims as its own. Examples would include the breakdown of the traditional virtues in Athens at the time of Socrates and Aristophanes, the decline of the Hellenistic world, and the recession of the Church as an effective center of temporal authority that marked the opening of the Renaissance. Other examples would be the end of metaphysics at the time of Kant and, much more recently, the de(Euro)centering of geopolitical thought occasioned by movements of decolonization.

Second, although crisis so understood cannot be traced to any determinate origin or cause, one can, in a way reminiscent of Durkheim's notion of dynamic density, offer a very general proposition: the emergence of crisis can be attributed to an agitation and acceleration of social activity such that it strains, ruptures, overflows. or otherwise *transgresses* the institutional limitations of a social order. Crisis can be attributed, in other words, to a proliferation of transgressions of the institutional boundaries that would differentiate, mark off, and fix time, space, and identity within a social order, including the identities of subjects as agents of knowing and the objects that they would know. Such instances of transgression might of course occur in the small, as it were. They might occur, for instance, in the discordant moments of the plantation or factory as much as the conservatory or studio, in the dreams and unspeakable frustrations of the journeyman or clerk as much as the inspirations of the poet or scientific genius. They might also occur in wider scope, as when the overwhelming growth of demands upon the institution of the parish dole in the countryside of an England in the throes of feudal crisis contributed to the acceleration of people's movement from country to town. More contemporary examples of pervasive transgressions can be found in a variety of ambiguous happenings of interest to scholars of international relations, especially those often broadly alluded to (but not really designated) under the heading "interdependence." When transgressions are pervasive, highly visible, and not easily contained in specific institutional sites—when institutional boundaries blur into openly traversable margins and the margins widen relative to the institutional spaces the boundaries would supposedly contain—they produce a generalized social crisis of the sort we have in mind.

Third, the effect of such transgressions is not only to put institutional boundaries in doubt but also to deprive an institutional order of stable oppositions. In a crisis of this sort, there is no clear and indubitable sense of inside versus outside, domestic versus international, particular versus universal, developed versus underdeveloped, reality versus ideology, paradigm versus counterparadigm, fact versus fiction, political theory versus political practice, identity versus difference, progress versus regress, continuity versus change, father versus mother, rationality versus irrationality, system of communication and circulating exchange value versus nature, positivity versus negativity, maturity versus immaturity, seriousness versus play, sense versus nonsense. These and other oppositions are openly contested. Accordingly, any attempt to invoke some privileged interpretation of, say, reason in order to control events cast as irrational—or to invoke some privileged interpretation of domestic order to fend off the dangers of international anarchy—is immediately susceptible to question. The privileged notion of reason invoked can be shown to contain and depend upon traces of the irrationality it opposes. The privileged notion of domestic order can be shown to be grounded in nothing more than an anarchic struggle of contesting interpretations that traverses any imaginable domestic bounds. In sum, the discourse of an institutional order can no longer reliably respond to ambiguous and uncertain events by recurring to contradictions, to dialectic, to the promise of resolution through determinate negation.

Fourth, a crisis of this sort may be called a *crisis of representation*. Just "now," just "here," in the institutional order in crisis, there is no possibility of a well-delim-ited, identical presence of a subject whose interior meanings might be re-presented in words, for it is impossible to exclude the contesting interpretations of subjective being that must be absent if this presence is simply to be. There is, likewise, no fixed and indubitable presence of an external object to which words, as re-presentations, might be referred, because the active subjectivity that must be absent if an object is to be purely objective cannot be excluded. Without the absolute presence of an institutionalized subject whose meanings words might represent and without the absolute presence of an institutionalized object to which words, as representations, might refer, the word breaks off. Words can no longer *do justice* because they no longer bear a promise of certain, literal judgment on behalf of a social order, a com-munity, a discipline, a culture.

As a result, the very possibility of truth is put in doubt. Every representation appears not as a copy or recovery of something really present in some other time or place but as a representation of other representations—none original, each equally arbitrary, and none able to exclude other representations in order to be a pure presence, an absolute origin of truth and meaning in itself. On trial is the self-evident reality of objects which might be unambiguously represented, assigned a definite social value, and entered into circulation in a system of communication or exchange. On trial, too, is the very life of the institutionalized subject of the social order. In crisis, subjects and objects appear not as sources of meanings that might be signified or represented in words but as open texts that are ever in the process of being inscribed through a hazardous contest of representations. The subject is deprived of a sense of self-evident identity. What does it mean for this subject to speak sincerely, truthfully, in a way that projects its inner being? What is the inner being of the subject that must be nur-tured and protected in an order that would be just or true to its subjects? In a crisis of representation, these questions become unanswerable. Every answer is immediately received as but one more groundless representation, no more and no less sincere or legitimate than any other.

Fifth, several attitudes emerge in response to the unfolding of such a crisis, but two especially are worthy of note. With Anthony Giddens, Yosef Lapid, and Jim George and David Campbell, we might call one of these attitudes *celebratory*:

> A celebratory attitude greets the event of crisis in a posture of joyous affirmation, a posture that privileges the estrangement, paradox, ambiguity, and opportunities for creativity, on the one hand, over the supposed need to cast every word and deed as a familiar representation of stable metaphysical certitudes, on the other. The celebratory attitude does not aspire to return to some comforting, securely bounded domicile of self-evident being. It instead exhibits a readi-ness to explore the new cultural connections and resulting new modes of thinking and doing that become possible when boundaries are traversed and hitherto separated cultural texts meet, contradict, combine in ambivalent relations, and relativize one another.

Another attitude, which would include Giddens's "despairing" and "dogmatic" responses as well as the posture of "systematic reconstruction" that Giddens and Lapid call for, might be called *religious*:

A religious attitude reverses the priorities of the celebratory. The proliferation of cultural possibilities is not welcomed but received as an irruption of unnameable dangers, and the event of crisis is greeted with a sadness, a sense of nostalgia, a kind of homesickness for an institutional order that can impose stable boundaries and bring an ambiguous and indeterminate reality under control. As in the thought, writings, and practices of today's neoconservatives and other "liberals disillusioned by reality," the religious response casts the event negatively, in terms of the absence of a center, a collapse of foundations, a loss of a self-evident origin of meaning and authority, a destruction of a domicile of pure identity, a descent into an abyss of hopelessness. It sees in crisis a dangerous moment in which the institutionalized subject is made witness to the possibility of its own dissolution and death.

It should not be thought that these two attitudes amount to alternative positions, perspectives, or modes of subjective being that are or could be dialectically opposed, as if the religious attitude might repress the celebratory and the celebratory might seek emancipation from the religious. These are practical attitudes or postures working in time, and they are keenly sensitive to the temporality of their real situation and to the contingency of every imaginable position. They are not coherent and totalizing (mis)representations of reality offered as if projecting a fixed and timeless voice from which truth and power reliably originate as one. As attitudes, they share and mutually call forth a sense of the crisis to which they reply, a crisis in which a paradoxical reality seems to undo every position and resist enclosure in any totalizing representation. If the one relates to the crisis optimistically—joyfully affirming the unfolding of unnameable possibilities emerging with the transgression of limitations once taken for granted—and the other relates to it anxiously—lamenting the passing of a time in which identity was secured by limitations not doubted—both start from the recognition that in the crisis of the present all limitations are in fact in question and all positions or perspectives are undone. Both understand that here and now no stable position might be appealed to as a source of truth and power capable of fixing limitations anew. And both, therefore, are deprived of any timeless and universal basis for self-affirmation—for the proof of the rightness, truth, or ethical standing of the attitudes themselves.

Where the two attitudes differ—and it is surely a very important difference—is in their practical orientations connecting the immediacy of an uncertain location to the wider world and linking memories through the ambiguous present to imaginations of possible futures. They differ, in other words, in their dispositions to action amidst the undecidable ambiguities of space, time, and identity encountered here and now. It is a difference of register, if you will:

The celebratory reception to crisis proceeds in a register *of freedom*, a freedom that is prior to all abstract and universalizing notions of necessary limitations, of interior or exterior necessity, of need, even of intrinsically needful subjects whose needs might now be repressed or distorted in denial of their freedom. Affirming the reality of the crisis, a celebratory attitude does not deny that people live hazardous lives and confront serious perils. It does not deny that people's labors, even their procreative and cognitive labors of self-making, are channeled and bent to tasks that they do not originate in the localities of their work. Yet a celebratory posture, in facing up to these conditions, also gives pride of place to the reality of a crisis in which there is no stable position or perspective that can determine for one and all what these local struggles mean, what their stakes must be, what universal needs are repressed or negated. It does not try to hold on to some imagined totalizing standpoint—in crisis but a rarefied ideal—that would regulate discourse regarding what must be done. Instead, as the name implies, it celebrates a space of freedom—freedom for thought, for political action in reply to hazards and dangers, for the exploration of new modes of ethical conduct detached from the presumption of a transcendental standpoint—that opens up when, in crisis, this ideal is deprived of practical force.

The religious reception, by contrast, proceeds in a register of *desire*. Even in crisis, it refuses to turn loose of the ideal, now grown abstract, of a self-identical institutional subject contentedly at home with an institutional order whose limitations are self-evidently given and at one with the word. It holds fast, that is, to the ideal of inhabiting a securely bounded territory of truth and literal meaning beyond doubt, a place given as if by some author beyond time, a place where the unruly can be reliably named and tamed and the man of unquestioning faith can be secure. Privileging this abstract ideal as a pure positivity, the religious posture then understands the crisis of the present not in a way open to its opportunities as well as its dangers, but as a pure negativity—a loss, a lack, a repression or corruption of something necessary and intrinsically valuable. It receives the present crisis, therefore, as something to fear. And it turns this fear into a desire, a desire to fill the void, to compensate for the lack, to impose a center of universal judgment capable of effecting limitations and fixing a space, a time, an identity beyond question.

Sixth, where thought and conversation are dominated by religious attitudes and animated by this desire, they take on the cast of what would be familiar to us as political discourse, for they are preoccupied with the paradoxical political problem *of sovereignty*. It is a problem posed amidst a crisis of representation: an unmappable region of ambiguity, uncertainty, indeterminacy, and multiplying cultural possibilities where time knows no certain measure, space knows no certain bounds, and human conduct reliably obeys no law—not laws of nature, not laws of language, and not laws of father, king, or state. It is a problem of enclosing this boundless region, defining what is alien to it, making it a territory in space and time, giving it a temporal metric, and imposing thereupon a center of judgment beyond doubt that can effectively police the boundaries, fend off the alien, preside over all questions of difference and change within, and decide for one and all what every disputed happening must mean. Four propositions regarding discourses of sovereignty merit notice:

1. Discourses of sovereignty cannot relate to their object, sovereignty, as other than a problem or question. This is so because sovereignty enters discourse not as a matter of describing something that is thought to be real, already present, and perhaps distinguishable from other equally real and present things, but precisely as a reflection on a lack, on a loss, on something that might have been but is no longer. In a crisis of representation where the word breaks off, there is no taken-for-granted understanding of reality that goes without saying and that reliably functions as a shared background in terms of which people can stabilize meanings and orient and justify what they say and do.

To speak of sovereignty, therefore, is never to name something that already is. It can never be to refer to some source of truth and power that is self-identical, that simply exists on its own, that goes without saying. "[S]overeignty has no identity, is not *self, for itself, toward itself, near itself*" (Derrida, 1978:265). Even when one asserts, for example, that "God," "king," "man," "nation," or "social scientific discipline" is sovereign beyond doubt—even when one says that such a figure, to the exclusion of all others, can decide all questions of time, space, and identity within an institutional order—the very need to still doubts by pronouncing the assertion belies the assertion itself. Always a work of imagination, the assertion announces a question that is tinged with desire: How to fill the void. How to compensate for the lack.

2. The problem of sovereignty is profoundly paradoxical. Accenting the root, we may say that it is pro*found* in the sense that it is preoccupied with the problem of foundation: a fundamental principle, a supporting structure, a base on which society rests, a fund of authority capable of endowing possibilities, accrediting action, and fixing limitations. Accenting the prefix, we may say that it is *pro*found in the sense that that it proceeds from a situation ahead of all foundation,

in favor or support of foundation, to produce or bring forth foundation, that will count as or substitute for the foundation now lacking. When one adds something about the nature of the desired foundation—that to be effective it must be regarded as infinitely deep, self-founding, dependent upon no activity that proceeds without foundations, and hence a foundation beyond doubt—one sees the paradox.

To come to terms with the problem, formalize it as a problem, affirm its centrality to a discourse, and deliberate it in the search for solutions is to guarantee that the problem cannot be solved. It is to announce to one and all that any "resolution" proffered in the circumstances of a crisis of representation is but one more groundless representation—no less legitimate than any other perhaps, but also no more. And it is thereby to insure that that which is offered as the foundation capable of imposing limitations and stilling all doubts will itself be received as an object of doubt.

3. It follows that texts or discourses that would produce a semblance of a resolution to the problem of sovereignty must engage in a kind of duplicity. While necessarily opening up and responding to the crisis of representation that occasions them, they must also move by various devices to accomplish two things. On the one hand, they must make it possible to stigmatize and exclude from the domain of serious discourse those happenings, postures, and interpretations whose serious consideration would put the proposed resolution in doubt. This, of course, is a work of stigmatization and exclusion that, in the absence of the sovereign foundation to be established by the resolution, can only be arbitrary and subject to dispute. On the other hand, and in the same stroke, they must make it possible to understand that this work of stigmatization and exclusion, far from groundless, is itself undertaken in the service of a sovereign foundation *already* beyond question, a resolution *already* finished and given.

Clearly, such moves are as paradoxical as the problem they undertake to resolve. Clearly, too, such moves cannot call attention to themselves, as if they deserve to be formalized and announced as central to the enterprise undertaken by a text or discourse. Such moves must be offered not as theory inviting critical deliberation but in the manner of performative postures emerging in reply to instantly apprehensible difficulties and dangers and promising to show how these difficulties and dangers might be arrested or resolved. They must be offered not as part of the central and ostensibly timeless logic of resolution, but in an exigent mood belonging to the margins of the text or discourse and summoning the central logic of resolution into being.

4. The "resolutions" to the problem of sovereignty proffered by texts or discourses can only be unstable and tentative. They are *unstable* because the texts or discourses that would enact such "resolutions" cannot really be rid of the paradoxes of space, time, and identity that become visible in crisis and that the texts or discourses purport to solve. The margins of these texts or discourses always involve the arbitrary deployment of cultural resources in the performance of the paradoxical moves just mentioned—moves which, were they taken seriously, would undo the supposedly, central logic by which a "resolution" is made to seem certain and final.

Such "resolutions" are *tentative* because texts or discourses are able to postpone serious and unsettling attention to their marginal performance of these moves only so long as the moves themselves are received in an attitude of immediate and unquestioning familiarity, as that which goes without saying. With the unfolding of a crisis of representation—with time, change, the acceleration of activity, and the transgression of institutional limitations hitherto unquestioned—the themes, postures, words, and images that might once have elicited such a spontaneous and unquestioning reception are no longer able to do so. No longer self-evident, they become strange, of dubious validity, and subject to dispute in terms of their pretensions to truth. As this is so, the arbitrary marginal moves that a text or discourse undertakes through the development of these cultural resources take on a certain transparency, becoming immediately visible as the paradoxical moves they are. And when this happens, the supposed "resolution" at the supposed center of a text—always dependent upon the paradoxical moves at its margins—comes to be seen as no resolution at all. Paradox displaces the paradigmatic "resolution." Crisis surfaces. And wherever religious desire moves, the paradoxical problem of sovereignty announces itself anew.

These four propositions, taken together, suggest another, more general than the rest. When spoken in a religious register of desire, the word "sovereignty" is often used ideologically, as if it represented some source of meaning, some effective organizational principle, some mode of being already in place, some simply and self-evidently given resolution of paradoxes of space, time, and identity. Yet this word is only spoken amid and in reply to a crisis of representation where paradoxes of space, time, and identity displace all certain referents and put all origins of truth and meaning in doubt. As this is so, sovereignty cannot really represent any of these things. The word can but connote a boundless region of ambiguous activity that a vagabond desire—itself rootless, powerless, and empty of content save a rarefied ideal of an exclusionary order born of metaphysical grace—would mark off, fill, and claim as a territory of its own. It can but connote a boundless region of freedom that desire, ever in search of an elusive finality, might struggle to exclude and forget but can never finally erase from its memory.

Seventh, what we know to be the great texts of modern political discourse—among them the texts that the discipline of international studies memorializes as the cultural inheritance fixing its identity—are intimately engaged in a crisis of just the sort we have been discussing. Machiavelli, Hobbes, Rousseau, Bentham, Marx, Kant, Weber—the texts signed by these and many other names emerge and work in specific sites and circumstances where transgressions of institutional limitations proliferate. They emerge and reply to historical circumstances where margins widen, ambiguity and chance seem to undermine every certain referent, temporality seems to displace every extratemporal standpoint, forgotten pasts and deferred futures intrude upon the present, words lose their capacity to still violence and come to seem violent themselves, the play of power eludes the controlling word of truth, the very idea of truth is shaken, what it means to speak meaningfully and seriously is in doubt, and a crisis of representation unfolds. In various ways, these texts engage that crisis. They affirm it. They celebrate and exploit the rich variety of cultural resources—the paradoxes, the ironies, the opportunities for parody and figurative play—that become possible precisely when institutional limitations on thought and discourse are put in question, forgotten texts can be reopened, and alien themes can be examined anew. Exploiting these resources, they provide exciting accounts of the crisis they engage—accounts that seem somehow to speak to other uncertain times, including our own. Yet these texts can also be read to do something else as well. They can be read for the ways in which they seem to speak in answer to a religious desire or, more exactly, to provide a semblance of a resolution to a paradoxical problem of sovereignty to which, in crisis, this desire gives form. These are, then, highly ambiguous texts. They are paradoxically open to different ways of reading.

Eighth, with the emergence of the question of sovereignty in crisis, texts such as these become part of the openly contested cultural terrain. Contested themselves, they offer resources by which contest is waged. In general, these texts might be read and put to work in a crisis of representation in two ways, each projecting one of the two attitudes to which crisis gives rise. One is a way of reading undertaken in a religious register of desire. According to what it actively labors to do to a text, we might call it a *memorializing* reading. The other is a way of reading undertaken in a celebratory register of freedom. We might call it *countermemorializing* reading. Both take their texts quite seriously, although the two differ greatly in their understanding of seriousness.

For a memorializing reading, to take a text seriously is to try to retrace, reaffirm, and be at one with the workings of desire within it:

> Coming to an ambiguous and paradoxical text, a memorializing reading posits and privileges the abstract ideal of a unique and unequivocal sovereign figure who would control the authentic meaning of the text, and it aspires to arrive at an interpretation that would be at one with the intentions and will of this figure. It therefore proceeds from that moment in a text when uncertainties and paradoxes of a crisis of representation are actively encountered as threats to this sovereign figure, and hence take on colorations of fear, to that moment when this posited sovereign is redeemed and secured through the text's production of an ostensibly coherent and final resolution to paradoxes of space, time, and identity. For a memorializing reading, this heroic resolution in the face of utter uncertainty is what the text must be remembered for all time and from all perspectives to mean.

> One result is to attribute to a text a high degree of coherence. The text can be easily summed up and even shamelessly caricatured, often in a short list of supposedly basic assumptions or principles, because all the text's encounters with paradox, ambiguity, and indeterminacy are read over into the domain of difficulties and dangers that the text, in its culminating moment, shows us how to resolve. Paradox, ambiguity, and indeterminacy are not allowed to disturb the ostensibly central logic of resolution that redeems the sovereign presence posited at the start.

> Another result is to turn the text into a uniquely interpretable paradigm in which a discipline, a tradition, a culture might anchor an identity. Memorialized as paradigm, the text is not principally remembered as a static representation of a referent reality (which might, after all, be quite unlike the reality of the present). It is remembered as an iterable exemplar of how men and women of religious desire might fear, think, act, and resolve paradoxes of space, time, and identity even in our own unrepresentable times. It is remembered as that most strange sort of foundation: an exemplary way in which a sovereign mode of being iterably founds itself in reply to chance events, uncertainties, and unsettling paradoxes of space and time.

For a countermemorializing reading, to take a text seriously is not to retrace and reaffirm the workings of desire. It is not to posit and give priority to a religious ideal of a sovereign center that supposedly rules a text and might show us how to rule ourselves and our own difficult times. It is decidedly not to try to enclose a discipline's discourse within a heroic narrative of paradox resolved and paradigm redeemed—a narrative whose limitations we, in honoring the memory of the text, must endlessly recite in our own contemporary labors. On the contrary, for a countermemorializing reading, to take a text seriously is to give serious attention to the unfinalized celebration of freedom and paradox that goes on within it, a celebration that the text can never really still or exclude. It is therefore to refuse to forget what a memorializing reading must forget in order to claim to retrieve a unique meaning from a text: that these classical texts are already intimately and actively caught up in a crisis of representation, much like our own, in which any supposed sovereign resolution of paradoxes of space, time, and identity can never be more than a question, a problem, a paradox in its own right.

> Refusing to repeat this willful amnesia, countermemorializing readings analyze afresh the ways in which classic texts contend with ambiguity, uncertainty, and resistant counterinterpretations of all sorts; avail themselves of all manner of disparate cultural resources; and struggle at the same time to impose a sovereign perspective capable of resolving paradoxes of space, time, and identity *and* to marginalize those paradoxes, already alive, that would unsettle any sovereign perspective they might try to impose. Affirming the very real crisis-emergent paradoxes that occasion a text and that the text would marginalize, a countermemorializing reading shows

how they threaten to render radically unstable the pretenses of sovereign resolution dutifully recorded in memorializing readings.

> The result on the whole is to enrich, not diminish, the cultural resources of a discipline, community, or culture. The discipline that pays its respects to a textual inheritance so read is not limited to the ritual rehearsal of the "resolutions" to the problem of sovereignty given pride of place in memorializing readings. Nor is it surprised to find that the "resolutions" promised by its texts prove to be unstable in the present time. It is drawn instead to appreciate the intrinsic ambiguity, uncertainty, irony, and recombinatorial possibilities of its own textual inheritance. It is able to see that contemporary encounters with paradoxes of time, space, and political identity do not mark the "end of the discipline" or "the end of modernity." They are already there in the discipline's and the culture's textual "beginnings."

It's not difficult to find instances of these two modes of reading in the literature of international relations. Consider, for example, contesting interpretations of Machiavelli's *The Prince*. Waltz's reading memorializes *The Prince*. In it, Machiavelli is cast as a paradigmatic figure—at once a foundation and origin—of the realist tradition in which Waltz would locate his own theorization of balance of power. In Waltz's reading, too, what is affirmed is the *resolution* to the paradoxical problem of sovereignty toward which *The Prince*, in projecting a religious desire, no doubt wants to move in its closing "Exhortation": the production of a state that is unitary, bounded and distinct from its external environment, and decisively controlled by a unique center of governance. Thus, for Waltz, Machiavelli exemplifies a kind of timeless *raison d'etat* among unitary territorial states wanting to survive and bending every means to this end. And Waltz himself, working from a "foundation" memorialized in this way, can then proceed to assume that the problem of sovereignty is always already solved. He can start from an assumption that permits him to theorize an "anarchic" domain of "international politics" among sovereign territorial states that is already differentiated from the "hierarchical, orders" within sovereign territorial states.

Walker's reading of *The Prince* is a countermemorializing reading. Here it becomes clear that Machiavelli's text can hardly provide a foundation or origin of the sort of realist tradition Waltz would like to invoke. The most unsettling of paradoxical problems resides at the very center of Machiavelli's concerns: how to *found* a state. In Walker's reading, precisely because *The Prince* is referring to the special problems of new states whose unity and boundaries certainly *cannot* be assumed under conditions of cultural crisis in which Machiavelli writes, the text that Waltz and so many others would treat "as the unproblematic origin of tradition is itself obsessed with the highly problematic nature of origins, of foundations, of the establishment and subsequent politics of traditions". Once Machiavelli is read this way, *The Prince* is no longer caricatured as a paradigm capable of founding and limiting the thought of a tradition or discipline that would religiously affirm the solution to the problem of sovereignty it so desparately desires to reiterate in its own uncertain times. The enclosure of Machiavelli-as-paradigm folds open, and the *The Prince* connects to *The Discourses on Livy*, *The History of Florence*, *The Art of War*, and beyond even these texts to the wide-ranging Renaissance struggles of Machiavelli, Guicciardini, Savanarola, and others to make sense of paradoxical problems of time, space, and political community by calling upon, questioning, turning, and introducing once forgotten terms to the shaken categories of Christian universalist thought.

Crisis and the Role of Dissidence

We have come far enough in our consideration of crisis—a crisis of a discipline, a crisis of modernity—to enable us to take up the second of our two concerns. We can now see *why* it has been possible for dissident works of thought to activate a sense of disciplinary crisis. We can also understand *how* dissident works of thought, given this possibility, have proceeded to exploit it, thereby prompting critical readings of the sort that concern us here. Let us first take up the "why," the question of the conditions of possibility.

Why is disciplinary crisis possible? Dissident works of thought, we can say at the outset, have not incited a sense of crisis by approaching a naive and insular discipline, paradigm, or tradition from beyond its boundaries, as if bearing news from far-off lands or, as detractors might say, from the foreign capitols of contemporary fashion. Nor have they hurled their literary wits and intellectual devices at the ramparts of a coherent tradition, thereby to puncture holes and let light in. And certainly they have not fomented crisis by laying siege to a discipline, tradition, or paradigm, hoping that the attrition of a discipline's intellectual resources will lead its adherents not only to give up faith in Machiavelli, Hobbes, Kant, Grotius, Bull, Deutsch, Hoffmann, Waltz, and others, but also to fling open gates to a parading army bearing the promised sustenance of Derrida, Foucault, Baudrillard, Bakhtin, Todorov, Kristeva, Barthes, and more. All of these images involve imagining territories, borders, walls already in place. All thereby impose two limitations on the way in which we think about the condition of the discipline prior to the onset of crisis and about the location of dissidents in relation to the discipline:

> 1. On a spatial dimension, they require us to imagine an initial situation of dichotomously opposed positions for any work of thought: with regard to the discipline, the images suggest, one must be inside or outside, for or against. The images reserve the oppositional space of the outside as the dissidents' *point d'appui.*

> 2. On a temporal dimension, the images require us to understand crisis as a moment of discontinuity that opens up when the discipline's continuous time, homogeneous place, and coherent and well-bounded textual inheritance breaks up or gives way. The images imply that works of dissidence, beginning on the outside, must somehow disturb a prior stable continuity in order to produce the discontinuity of crisis.

In both of these respects, these images miscast the situation. This can be seen with the benefit of hindsight, that is to say, from the "point of view" of the crisis that we have come to sense so keenly today. Whether one speaks in a celebratory register of freedom or a religious register of desire, one cannot fail to notice that remembrances of a supposed "pre-crisis past" are very much a part of the disputed terrain in the crisis of today. If, in crisis, "we" must refer to "ourselves" in quotation marks—thus to signal doubts as to who, doing what kind of work and saying what kinds of things, really belongs in "our" conversation—"we" must also allow that this is in large measure due to emerging uncertainties and ambiguities regarding the inheritance to which "we" are indebted. Members of a discipline, a paradigm, or a tradition "we" might claim to be. But "we" cannot say for sure who "we" are because "we" cannot decide what must be the exclusionary boundaries of the remembered inheritance to which "we" in "our" work must pay respects. Every attempt to fix the territoriality of a discipline, paradigm, or tradition today by offering one or another memorializing reading of a supposedly pure and incontrovertible inheritance (for example, the attempts to fix the supposed continuity of "the tradition" in Keohane's and Gilpin's readings of Thucydides) is immediately exposed as an arbitrary construction in countermemorializing readings of the same cultural inheritance. What *is* the inheritance to which we owe a debt? What *must* it mean for us? What limitations inscribed in "our" textual history *must* be obeyed by those who would claim that their work honors and continues this history? In the crisis of today, these questions have become undecidable.

How could this have happened? Answering this question, we see the point: If, in crisis, we are today unable to decide how to limit, read, and remember the textual history in which to anchor a discipline or paradigm, this can only be because the textual history to which we refer has *never* been a territory of unequivocal and continuous meaning. It has never been fixed through time, well-bounded, and closed to contesting interpretations. The discipline's textual history has always been paradoxically open to a proliferation of mutually destabilizing readings. It has always contained tensions and paradoxes that not only threaten to undo the supposed certitude of any position from which interpretation proceeds but also threaten to make way for other readings that a supposedly correct reading, to be thought correct, must exclude.

One simply cannot say, then, that there once was a time prior to the present crisis in which the discipline proudly stood before dissident scholars as a continuous, well-bounded territory. *No such territory ever existed. No exclusionary boundaries ever separated the discipline from other supposedly alien and incommensurable elements of a culture beyond—not in todays disciplinary crisis and not before.* Even if it is possible to romanticize a past in which the discourse of international studies managed to sustain some semblance of an unequivocal voice at one with a continuous disciplinary heritage and occupying a definite territorial domain, this could not have been because this voice and the supposed boundaries demarcating its place really were fixed, sure, and undisputed. It could only have been because it was possible for a time (and by means analyzable) actively to marginalize, forget, and defer encounters with paradoxes, contesting themes, and resistant interpretations that are always part of the disciplinary inheritance, that transgress all imaginable boundaries, and that render radically unstable all renditions of an unequivocal voice. It could only have been because it was possible for a time to marginalize the very paradoxes, themes, and interpretations whose increasing visibility at the supposed core of the discipline have produced the sense of disciplinary crisis today.

To understand this is to see why dissident works of thought issuing from the margins have been able to incite a sense of crisis in international studies. In a discipline or in modern culture more generally, we have suggested, a crisis of representation is occasioned by the proliferation of transgressions of institutional limitations, and if this is so, then a condition of crisis is that institutional boundaries be transgressable. This condition, we can now say, has always been satisfied by the discipline of international studies. The "boundaries" of the discipline, never more than contingent and ambiguous effects of active and arbitrary labors of marginalization, have always been susceptible to transgression.

How have dissident works of thought incited disciplinary crisis? In addressing this second question it makes sense to begin where dissident works of thought begin, with that most paradoxical of "beginnings": marginality. In contrast to scholarly works that would speak in unison with the supposed "core" of a discipline, tradition, or paradigm, works of thought that issue from the margins cannot seriously entertain a religious attitude. For them, the contingency, ambiguity, and transgressability of "boundaries" has always been the immediate reality of life to be celebrated. Why is this so? The answer lies in the visibility of paradox at the margins. How, given this celebratory attitude, are marginal works of thought oriented to conduct themselves? The answer lies in what we might call the *ethics* of marginal conduct.

Marginality: the visibility of paradox. What constitutes the so-called sovereign "core" of a discipline or paradigm is not, as we have seen, a territory, position, or homogeneous point of view anchored and defined by reference to a coherent, continuous, and well-bounded textual inheritance. What constitutes a "core" is the ability, in whatever location, actively to sustain for some time a semblance of a commanding sovereign presence by adopting a certain blindness to the paradoxical labors by which, even now, memorializing readings of a textual inheritance are undertaken and unsettling encounters with paradoxes of space, time, and identity are marginalized. Here, where the work of marginalization can be forgotten, it can make sense to speak in a religious register of desire and affirm memorialized foundations. Here, where it is possible to forget the dependence of a discipline or paradigm and its supposed foundations on this active and arbitrary labor of marginalization, one can profess a sovereign right to fill an exclusionary space and to speak and act in a way that represents and defends a coherent, well-bounded territory. One can speak in a register of desire, play the hero's part, and say, "This work speaks for the discipline, the tradition, the paradigm, and it speaks in answer to those alien happenings and difficulties that would pose a challenge, a puzzlement, or a danger." One can do this and *get away with it*, if only for a time.

What constitutes marginality is precisely the manifest inability to speak and labor in a register of desire and get away with it, even for a moment. Like the notion of a "core," the notion of a "margin" cannot really designate a time, a space, a code, a canon, a point of view, a future Utopian order, an order nostalgically recalled, a personifiable state of mind, or a *point d'appui* of any sort. What distinguishes a "margin" of a discipline or paradigm from its so-called "core," accordingly, cannot be some real positions that might be marked on a social or intellectual map. What distinguishes the "margin" is that "here" and "now" it is impossible to do what must be done if, in answer to a religious desire, some semblance of a well-bounded and coherent territory is to be sustained: it is impossible to be blind to the active labor of marginalizing paradoxes of space, time, and identity that threaten to undo every pretense that one might speak a sovereign voice of a discipline, a paradigm, a community, or a culture.

Where are the "margins?" In the paradoxical instant when the peace researcher discovers that her dynamic arms race models in the Richardson tradition—her attempts to think us out of processes that occur when decision makers "don't stop to think"—impose fixed parameters that suppose and affirm the necessary stoppage of thought. In the reading of Weber that takes seriously Weber's engagement with Nietzsche as well as Marx. In the moment where the analyst comes to see that representations of voluntaristic agency disrupt representations of the autonomous determinations of generative social structures and vice versa—and that "structuration" can mean for her no more than a desire to affirm and occupy some scientific standpoint prior to all representations that can surely resolve the paradoxes of agency and structure. In the instant when a theorization of an international anarchy/domestic hierarchy dichotomy is disrupted by the dissolution of one of two poles of a supposedly bipolar world. In the work of a theorist who wants to make sense of Third World sovereignty, where anarchy seems to be on the "inside" and the center of authority seems to be on the "outside." In the work of positivistic regime theorists who discover, as Kratochwil and Ruggie show, that an objectivist epistemology cannot sustain a study of regimes when the ontology of regimes is subjective through and through. In the frustrations of feminist theorists whose efforts to gain a hearing for their insidious questions are greeted by a discipline's condescending guidance regarding the "influences" one must not fall prey to, the questions one must not ask. In the work of scholars studying social movements whose practices, strangely, seem little concerned with the problem of seizing, toppling, or controlling the "actor" that international theory declares to be central.

Where, again, are the margins? They are all those boundless, unnameable regions of activity where an itinerate religious desire immediately struggles to marginalize paradoxes of time, space, and identity; where this active and arbitrary work of marginalization is highly visible and cannot be forgotten; where, thanks to the visibility of the struggle, desire necessarily fails; and where, as a result, the sovereignty of a discipline or paradigm becomes a strange and rarefied ideal, a question never finally answerable, a paradoxical task that cannot be one's own. This is what "marginality" means. It can mean no more.

For works of thought that issue from the margins, therefore, only a celebratory posture can take seriously life's real possibilities and limitations. In the marginal site, only the register of freedom—a register that affirms and exploits ambiguity, uncertainty, and the transgressability of institutional boundaries—can effectively speak to the paradoxes, dangers, and opportunities immediately unfolding.

It is thus quite clear why works of thought issuing from the margins are *disposed* to celebrate and take advantage of the transgressability of boundaries, itself the condition of crisis. But if we are to answer the "how" question posed, we need to understand something about the practical orientation—one might say the *diplomatic ethos*—implicit in works of thought that would proceed in a celebratory register of freedom. In terms of ethical discipline at least, dissident works of thought issuing from the margins are already doing very well on their own.

Marginality: the ethics of conduct. It is often noted, as we have noted, that speaking and acting in a celebratory register of freedom involves a readiness to question supposedly fixed standards of sovereign judgment and to transgress institutional limitations, and from this it is often inferred that conduct in this register amounts to a sort of licentious activity whose credo might be "Anything goes!" It is inferred that when words and deeds proceed in this register of freedom every notion of criticizing and disciplining conduct is out the window because, given the refusal to refer conduct to some presumably fixed and universal standard of judgment, every word and deed must be presumed to be as good, as ethical, or as effective as the next.

This, surely, is an important understanding of ethical discipline. No doubt it has prevailed for some time in modern culture, spanning at least from Hobbes's moral philosophy through Kant's categorical imperative to Habermas's universal pragmatics of the ideal speech situation. And certainly a readiness positively to value this understanding articulates well with the workings of a nomadic and abstract desire, a religious desire to effect a territorial domicile where men of unquestioning faith can innocently and securely dwell. Even so, it is not the only understanding imaginable, and it is not immune to criticism. Consider just two criticisms.

First, this territorializing understanding of ethics is intrinsically paradoxical. In the discipline of international studies and in general, to be practically effective any semblance of a sovereign center to which ethical discourse might be referred depends upon the *forgetting* of the ongoing labor of marginalizing those ambiguities, uncertainties, and contesting interpretations that would even now undo or disrupt the pretense of sovereign certitude. As this is so, any understanding of disciplined, ethical conduct that would aspire to cast all activities in the clarifying light of a sovereign center of universal judgment—in the light of some given consensus, for example, or some canon for the production of consensus—ironically depends upon the exemption of certain activities from the critical, juridical light to which it would refer. It depends upon the undertaking of an active labor of marginalization that must be forgotten, that must elude this light, that cannot be justified or licensed by reference to a center of critical judgment, and that cannot be disciplined in this way. A universalistic ethical system, so understood, always depends upon a reach of activity that exceeds the system's ethical grasp.

Second, as noted, to speak in a register of desire and value the abstract ideal of a territorial and sovereign-centered ethical discipline as a pure positivity—to value it as at once the necessary precondition and telos of human beings' ethical discourse—is also to value work conducted in a celebratory register as purely negative, as work that negates ethical considerations and leaves people unable to distinguish good conduct from bad or better events from worse. This valuation, though, is an instance of conduct in its own right, and so we might ask of it some ethical questions. Why is this valuation good, right, or better than others? Why should *we* embrace it to the exclusion of attempts to explore other ways of thinking questions of ethics, of social discipline, or self-discipline? Why, especially, if any attempt to intone a universal "we" today must include those multiplying marginal sites where religious desire is visibly untenable in the sense that it visibly fails to resolve paradoxes of space, time, and identity and to produce for people any secure and practicable territorial tenancy? In all the widening margins of a discipline and a culture, the question echoes: why?

If those who profess to be comfortably at home and at one with the ostensibly sovereign centers of a discipline or a culture feign deafness to the question, those who labor in the margins do not sit idly awaiting answers that can never come. There are more important things to do. After all, there are dangers to be avoided and dealt with. There are resources of life to be produced. There are conditions of scarcity—limitations on the social resources that one can access and put to use in the locality of one's labors. Encroaching from every direction there is a variety of disparate narratives, each projected as if from some sovereign center, but no one more true to one's paradoxical situation than the next. These narratives visibly vie to project themselves into one's uncertain location, to claim one's time, to control one's space, to impose representations of what one necessarily is and does, to summon justifications of oneself and one's conduct in terms of some distant norm against which one might always be seen to fail, and to impose some penalties of deprivation or exclusion in instances of failure. And yet there is no prospect that one can, with the resources locally available, resolve the paradoxes of one's immediate situation, exclude ambiguities and contesting interpretations, and make of oneself and one's locality an extension of any of the territories of sovereign being projected by these narratives. With none of these territories can one be innocently, contentedly, and safely at home.

It is easy to see how persons in such a situation would refuse a religious orientation whose ideal of sovereign being can be deployed to impose limitations and sanction punishments while speaking not at all to the practical hazards and difficulties of making life go on in these uncertain marginal circumstances. It is easy to see how persons would be given to speak and act in a register of freedom, to exploit the ambiguities before them, to question those limitations institutionalized as necessary, and to expand the resources available to them. But it is also easy to see something more. If conduct in the margins proceeds in a celebratory register of freedom, it certainly will not announce that "Anything goes!" Precisely because freedom is valued under circumstances like these, no maxim could be considered less efficacious. Here especially, one must always be prepared to understand that some ways of acting, speaking, and writing are better or worse, more or less effective, and more or less dangerous. Here especially, questions of ethical discipline, even diplomacy, are paramount....

There are uncertainties and risks involved in any attempt to test institutional limitations and open up cultural possibilities in concrete historical situations. To question, test, and expose the arbitrariness of institutional limitations that traverse one's immediate locality is *in principle* to open up one's space of freedom by exposing cultural resources hitherto forgotten or closed off. Were it possible to treat one's immediate locality in *isolation* from others, one might say that that is all there is to it. Viewing the immediate site as an enclosed world unto itself, a paradigm in and for itself, one could make an unrestrained questioning of limitations one's principle of conduct. One could unhesitatingly judge good all conduct conforming to this principle. But it is plain that this notion of isolation itself involves a limitation, a boundary that separates the locality from sites beyond. And it is plain, too, that in questioning this limitation, one becomes sensitive to the possibility that there are other sites beyond one's own where one's questioning and testing of limitations might constitute a danger. There are, after all, other people who are trying to get on with their lives in ambiguous and hazardous circumstances, and these people might try to inscribe their identities and demarcate their ambiguous locations by appeal to institutional categories that at once presuppose and affirm the necessity and impermeability of the very limitations one might question in one's own local site. For them, the institutional categories might be practical resources of life—resources that empower. And for them, the questioning of limitations supposedly fixed in these categories might threaten to deprive them of these resources, depleting their power and leaving them in a highly vulnerable condition of scarcity.

True, one's questioning of these limitations presupposes the possibility that the institutional categories are contingent and in the process of being imposed, not necessary and already given; that the boundaries inscribed in these categories are transgressable in all directions; that, in fact, the people who would locate themselves in terms of these boundaries are not really *other* to oneself; and that the opening of these boundaries would expand spaces and cultural resources of freedom that are "theirs" as much as one's own. But to presuppose this is also to presuppose the possibility that the people who would locate themselves in terms of the boundaries one questions are in circumstances no less paradoxical, no less uncertain than one's own: they share one's own problem of freedom even if, in their specific concrete circumstances, they rely on different resources and contend with a different constellation of immediate limitations on what can be thought, said, and done. In other words, one must allow that "their" immediate and very real strategic situations in the struggle for freedom are not behind one's own or inferior to one's own but simply *differing* from one's own. That is why there are risks.

If, in the process of testing limitations, one assumes that one's local strategic situation is a *paradigm* for the struggle for freedom wherever it unfolds, then one is all too likely to be impatient with others' labors in others' strategic situations. In one's impatience, one is all too likely to be insensitive to the ways in which one's own conduct—one's way of questioning limitations—might ramify beyond one's locality and threaten to deprive others of the cultural resources by which they reply to the problem of freedom in other equally difficult strategic settings. In turn, this threat, so real to others, is likely to generate most unfortunate results. Wanting to sustain the cultural resources that empower them in their own local strategic situations, those who are threatened are likely to participate in those arbitrary practices by which institutional boundaries are affirmed.

For them, the result is to consecrate some semblance of a sovereign territorial ground they might call their own, even at a cost of freedom. No longer are they so able as they might once have been to exploit those cultural resources that must be marginalized and forgotten if these boundaries, and just these, are to define the domain they defend as their own. For the one who would question these boundaries, the result is disastrous. With the hardening of boundaries, one's own domain of freedom is now more limited. What is worse, one must now contend with some semblance of a sovereign "they" who are likely to know one as an alien Other. Given what "they" know to be the scarcity of "their" resources, "they" might be given to claim one's own resources and practical space as "their" own and to judge one's conduct and find it wanting by "their" standards. Such an outcome is *dangerous*. It is *bad*, far *worse* than others that might have been produced.

Jens Bartelson, "The Problem: Deconstructing Sovereignty," from *A Genealogy of Sovereignty*

Making Sense of Sovereignty: Centrality and Ambiguity

Passing through the hands of politicians and philosophers during centuries, the concept of sovereignty has been not only constitutive of what modern politics *is*, and what modern political science is all *about*, but also a perennial source of theoretical confusion. Despite the wide agreement about its central place in our political vocabulary and understanding, the concept has eluded almost every attempt of rigorous definition and conceptual analysis. To take two influential remarks on the concept of sovereignty:

> It [sovereignty] was never more than a convenient label; and when distinctions began to be made between political, legal and economic sovereignty or between internal and external sovereignty, it was clear that the label had ceased to perform its proper function as a distinguishing mark for a single category of phenomena.... The concept of sovereignty is likely to become in the future even more blurred and indistinct man it is at present.

> In the light of this analysis it would appear a mistake to treat 'sovereignty' as denoting a genus of which the species can be distinguished by suitable adjectives, and there would seem to be a strong case for giving up so protean a word.

It is interesting to note that these death blows to the scientific usage of the concept of sovereignty were written before and after the most violent manifestation of sovereign statehood in modernity, and as such they are typical of the standard operating procedure for handling conceptual ambiguity and opacity in empirical political science. Whenever the semantic analysis fails, the recalcitrant concept is banished from empirical discourse, as if the empiricist quest for clarity itself were sovereign. As Nietzsche once noted, only that which has no history can be defined; to start a history of sovereignty with a definition of the term sovereignty would be to subject its historicity to the sovereignty of the present, and hence to narrow the scope of investigation. Instead, and before embarking on a history of sovereignty, we must pay some attention to the relationship between the centrality and ambiguity of the concept of sovereignty.

In political discourse, centrality and ambiguity usually condition each other over time. A concept becomes central to the extent that other concepts are defined in terms of it, or depend on it for their coherent meaning and use within discourse. These linkages—whether inferential or rhetorical—saturate the concept in question with multiple meanings that derive from these linkages, which make it ambiguous; an ambiguity that is open to further logical and rhetorical exploitation.

The concept of sovereignty is an emblematic example of this; by being essentially uncontested as the foundation of modern political discourse, it is essentially contested as to its meaning within the same discourse. We can note how the centrality of the concept of sovereignty in modern political discourse has enabled it to soak up a multitude of meanings through its various functions, this gradual saturation going hand in hand with rhetorical and metaphorical capitalizing on the resulting ambiguity, so that it has 'crystallized into a kind of unity that is hard to disentangle and analyse'.

Nor does this chapter aspire to outline any comprehensive theory of sovereignty; instead, it is devoted to the problems that arise when a scientific understanding of sovereignty is attempted. What makes the concept of sovereignty philosophically problematic is not any inherent opacity resulting from the multiplicity of its usages across the history of political ideas, nor any intrinsic ambiguity in the portions of political reality to which it is supposed to refer. My contention is that the problems confronted by conceptual analysis are intrinsic to the meta-language guiding this analysis, and that sovereignty represents a crucial case in this respect. Rather than dismissing the concept of sovereignty because of its ambiguity, we should take a suspicious glance into the practices of definition.

As it is a central assumption in this book that the problem of sovereignty is both logically and historically connected to the possibility of knowledge in general, a critical look at the practices of definition behind the frustrated attempts quoted above may prove instructive, both since the methods adopted when defining a concept often nicely reflect underlying assumptions—whether made explicit or taken for granted as part of the philosophical folklore—about the relation between language and world in general, and since these practices themselves are to be subjected to historical investigation in later chapters.

Conceptual analysis typically begins by closing the concept, while opening up its field of application to divergent interpretations. One begins by isolating ideal instances of the concept to be defined, in order to make it a 'distinguishing mark' or to discover 'a genus of which the species can be distinguished'. When it comes to the case of sovereignty, this is done by identifying a class of properties as 'essential' to statehood, thus demarcating 'sovereignty' from deviant cases and eliminating obnoxious borderline cases by searching for ever more finegrained qualitative differences. The desired outcome is a clarified concept, evident in its logical purity and by the empirical givenness of its referent.

Now this attitude towards concepts is heavily indebted to the codes of semantic conduct drawn up by post-Kantian empiricists, and which have gradually become part of scientific common sense. The underlying assumptions necessary to render this definitory practice defensible go something as follows: since language ought to be a transparent medium for representing what takes place in the world outside the knowing subject, the proper *a priori* meaning of a concept must be fixed through an analysis and determination of its referent. Meaning and reference are interdependent, insofar as their mutual determination is necessary if the concept is to be used in a phrase aspiring to *a posteriori* truth-value. Without the possibility of empirical reference, there is no clear-cut meaning. Without clear-cut meaning, there is no possibility of settling a dispute over truth rationally. Without this possibility, science is lost, rhetoric bursts in and the civil society of political scientists is plunged into civil war.

Applied to sponge concepts such as sovereignty, procedures based upon this essentially *representative* view of language and the world run into considerable difficulties. Conflicting conceptual pressures inherent in the very metavocabulary of conceptual analysis beg the question: does sovereignty refer to the empirical reality of political science, or does it denote a set of juridical rules, such as 'the presupposed assumption of a system of norms whose validity is not to be derived from a superior order', and whose reality therefore is wholly at the level of intersubjectivity? Since there is a strong temptation to get the best out of the two conceptual worlds in order to cover the various usages of sovereignty in modern political and legal discourse, definitions and theories of sovereignty are inclined to reproduce this inherited ambiguity by splitting the difference between the conceptual worlds of empirical political science and normative jurisprudence.

One way to get around those obstacles is to approach sovereignty as an essentially contested concept, by opening it up to divergent interpretations while closing its field of application. Behind this strategy is the assumption of an expressive relation between language and world common to Kant and the romantics. Within this view, language is still ideally transparent, but as a medium for *expressing* the identity and will of a prior subject, rather than for representing what is outside him. Instead of attempting a decontextualized analysis of sovereignty, one analyses the discourse of sovereignty as an expression of the underlying identity of states, and decodes the latter by means of the former, and conversely. Departing from its role in international rhetoric and in the justification of foreign policy, James subsequently strips the concept of sovereignty of a host of 'surface connotations' in order to arrive at a minimal consensus behind its divergent uses by political actors in an international context. What is at stake in this analysis is 'how, nowadays, sovereign states give meaning to the word when they refer to that which makes them eligible for international life'. According to James, sovereignty ultimately refers to a condition of constitutional independence, which is the secret behind all other practices, domestic and international alike.

The implicitly transcendental method employed by James permits an easy leap from 'objective' political reality to the realm of intersubjectivity. Sovereignty is nothing but a set of rules and resources embedded in a collectively held legal understanding in the state system. While sensitizing us to the rhetorical functions of the concept, this quasi-phenomenology of sovereignty suffers from genesis amnesia. The historical question of how this politico-legal intersubjectivity came into being and became constitutive of international and domestic life is simply impossible to answer within James's framework. Making a legal rule foundational begs the question of how it was founded in political practice, and with political practice defined in terms of the same rule, the circle is closed; a history of either except in the terms of the other would have been impossible, had it been James's intention to write one, which it fortunately is not.

Apart from the more or less unsuccessful attempts to furnish a clear-cut and theoretically and empirically fruitful definition of sovereignty, we have in recent years witnessed an increasing emphasis on its constitutive role in modern political reality as well as in our understanding of it. This upsurge of interest in sovereignty ranges from macrosociology to international political theory.

This effort at reproblematization has focused on the fact that the concept seems to connote two contradictory ideas simultaneously, something which has been almost self-evident to historians, but simultaneously philosophically enigmatic. In political sociology and in empirical international political theory, these efforts have had many implications, one being the reification of sovereignty into an organizing principle or a constitutive rule, endowed with powers of its own. As Giddens has pointed out, 'sovereignty simultaneously provides an ordering principle for what is "internal" to states and what is "external" to them'. This double and constitutive character of sovereignty has been touched upon by Ruggie, to whom sovereignty is a principle of legitimacy peculiar to the post-medieval international system. Similarly, Kratochwil emphasizes the impact of territorial sovereignty in the formation of the modern state as the constitutive unit in the modern state system.

Also, the push towards the reification of sovereignty has been fuelled by the 'agent-structure debate' in international relations theory and structurationist macrosociology. Moving the concept of sovereignty away from its merely descriptive connotations, both Wendt and Dessler turn sovereignty into a basic constitutive rule of the international system, upon which the surface practices of statehood, such as security dilemmas and war, depend.

This dual and constitutive character of sovereignty points in an important direction, and partly explains why it has been so difficult to grasp analytically. At a minimum, sovereignty seems to connote a unified political condition, but turns out to be extremely recalcitrant when thought to refer to something 'internal' or 'external' to states. Sovereignty as a concept seems to float free of its instances in the 'domestic' and 'international' spheres. Instead, it cuts across these levels of analysis, and seems to be the condition behind their separation and interdependence; it forms the crucial link between anarchy and hierarchy.

But while structuration theorists in both disciplinary camps have turned sovereignty into an organizing principle or a constitutive rule, they have also simultaneously withdrawn sovereignty itself from study; the more sovereignty is thought to explain, the more it itself is withdrawn from explanation. The theoretical sovereignty of sovereignty leaves sovereignty itself essentially unquestioned; the more constitutive sovereignty appears to be, the less unconstituted it becomes.

The duality of sovereignty has also spurred a critical inquiry into the discourse on sovereignty in international political theory. To Ashley, this duality entails an ethical paradox. Through its function in the discourse of power politics, it effectively separates the domestic from the international sphere by defining the margins of a political community spatially as well as temporally; thus, international theory and practice are rendered immune to criticism. As such, the concept of sovereignty has provided international political theory with a cachet of chic dissidence:

> What is at stake is nothing less than the *question* of sovereignty: whether or not this most paradoxical question, alive in all the widening margins of a culture, can be taken seriously in international studies today. More pointedly, the issue is whether and to what extent the discipline of international studies will be able to exercise its critical resources to engage and analyze the problem of and resistance to sovereignty as it unfolds in all the multiplying deterritorialized zones of a culture in crisis—including that extraterritorial zone called international politics.

Thus, and quite automatically, the question of sovereignty spills over into a questioning of disciplinary identity and cohesion. But while critical theorists have contributed many valuable insights into the logic of sovereignty and its ethical and cultural significance in the present, they cannot be said to have studied sovereignty—whether as a concept or a discursive practice—rigorously. They have limited their investigation to critical reflection upon its present consequences, but without asking how we got into this present, derelict as it appears to them.

It is my contention that the duality of sovereignty has hitherto escaped attention in modern political science and in the history of ideas, and that the main reason for this has to do with what it means to be 'scientific' in political science and 'historical' in the history of ideas. I shall argue that the problem of sovereignty is inexorably intertwined with the possibility of knowledge; in this chapter, I shall demonstrate that the incapacity of contemporary research practices to make sense of sovereignty has to do with their unanimous acceptance of the modernist assumption that theoretical vocabularies are more or less transparent mediums for representing a ready-made reality outside themselves.

Within the view expounded in this book, discourse is not primarily a medium for representing the world more or less accurately, or to express the unthought habits of a subject. Instead, discourse—whether political or scientific—is actively involved in the construction of reality through—as Nietzsche put it—the mobile army of metaphors. In this chapter, this means that the problems confronted by conceptual analysis give us a strong case for shifting philosophical strategy, if we later are to make sense of sovereignty in its full historicity. Thus, before embarking on the task of writing a genealogy of sovereignty, a critical inquiry into the contemporary empirical discourse on sovereignty is necessary.

Deconstructing Sovereignty

Far from being homogeneous the contemporary empirical discourse on sovereignty flows from two distinct but complementary fields of knowledge, their separation to an extent reflecting the divide between the external and internal aspects of sovereignty inherent in the concept. Thus, while concern with the former aspect is the traditional privilege of international political theory, macrosociology of state formation aims to explain the latter.

As I shall argue, these explanatory priorities put international political theory and macrosociology in an inverse but symmetrical relationship to each other; each discourse takes for granted exactly that which the other takes to be problematic. Sampling from the exemplars in each field, the following sections aim to provide a brief sketch of what is presupposed in the current empiricist understanding of sovereignty in both fields, and to explore the possibility of a more integrated conceptualization of sovereignty as proposed by structuration theory.

The choice of these two discourses also reflects two secondary objectives of this chapter. Since they both are empiricist in outlook, the critical inquiry permits us to judge the impact of this empiricism on the conceptualization of sovereignty. The second reason pertains to their complementary yet opposed character. The theoretical and empirical integration *across* these fields of knowledge is a promise held out by structuration theorists and scientific realists within both fields; the present chapter also aims to evaluate this promise, and to explore the reconceptualization of sovereignty it implies.

The general approach of this chapter is deconstructive. As a philosophical strategy, deconstruction addresses itself precisely to that which is taken for granted or regarded as unproblematic by a scientific analysis. In the present context, deconstruction is a way of exposing the possibility of reference and meaning of concepts to internal criticism. Instead of taking the possibility of reference and meaning for granted, deconstruction asks questions about their relation to *presence*, thus turning semantic problems into ontological ones: what must be regarded as real, basic or original, and what must be considered as absent, derivative or supplementary when making sense of sovereignty in empirical discourse?

Above all, assumptions of simple and firm ontological foundations—a minimum starting point for every discourse that aspires to scientific status—are always targets for deconstructive criticism, which recognizes every ontological foundation as something contingent. This habit of presupposing underlying essences is intimately related to the conceptual zero-sum games that organize and govern all theoretical vocabularies. Typically, a scientific or philosophical language is organized and made possible by a set of binary oppositions, conceptual categories defined as mutually exclusive. It is in and through the play of these categories that theoretical meaning is constructed; the upshot of deconstruction is that the terms involved in each such opposition are hierarchically arranged, so that the term which enjoys logical, ontological, or ethical privilege signifies what is present or foundational, while the other, inferior term, marks off its negation or supplement.

As an antidote to uncritical conceptual analysis, deconstruction involves a demonstration of the metaphysical or ideological character of the presuppositions relied on, and the determination of their place in a wider system of metaphysical or ideological values. Furthermore, deconstruction implies a reversal of the conceptual oppositions discovered in a text, rather than an attempt to criticize them from an allegedly external or neutral perspective. In the words of Derrida, to deconstruct a theory does not consist of 'moving from one concept to another but of reversing and displacing a conceptual order as well as the nonconceptual order with which it is articulated.... It is on this condition alone that deconstruction will provide the means of intervening in the field of oppositions it criticizes.' That is, deconstruction is an immanent form of critique: it borrows its resources from the same theory it deconstructs, and the oppositions and concepts criticized are simultaneously maintained and employed in the deconstructive argument, but reinstated with a different status and meaning in the actual context.

What lies ahead is a deconstructive tour through a vast theoretical territory which of course cannot be covered completely; instead, I will go for the milestones along the road to scientification followed by international political theory and macrosociology respectively. In so doing, I shall limit my inquiry to three related questions concerning the status of the concept of sovereignty in these texts. All of them are key questions to classical political philosophy which take on a different sense when posed within a deconstructivist framework; their formulation is not expected to yield final answers, but to unmask the conceptual problems which a scientific discourse runs into when trying to answer them.

The first and most basic question in this triad concerns the *source* of sovereignty: what kind of origin or foundation is invoked when explaining or justifying the existence of the sovereign state by international political theory and macrosociology respectively? Second, what is the *locus* attributed to sovereignty by these theories? Where, and with whom, does sovereignty reside inside the state? Third, what is the *scope* of sovereignty; exactly what is encompassed and brought under its sway? While the first question concerns the philosophical legitimacy of the state, the second concerns its status as an acting subject, while the third concerns the objective conditions of its unity.

Perhaps partly because of its ambiguity, the theme of sovereignty is marked by its relative absence in contemporary scientific texts, and a reading of them must pay attention to elements rendered marginal by the interpretations encouraged or authorized by the texts themselves, and sometimes ask how this silencing and marginalization take place. A deconstructive reading cannot give the author any interpretative privilege on the basis of what his text tells us to do with it or on the basis of arty intentions ascribed to him or declared by him; authorized readings and stated intentions are part of the text, and have to be interpreted as such. Hence, the author is never sovereign within and over the text: he writes in a language and in a logic which he cannot dominate, using them only by letting himself, up to a point, be governed by the system of statements he sets in motion.

International Political Theory and the Givenness of Sovereignty

During the last decades, it has been commonplace to note two things about international political theory. While being 'state-centric', it lacks an accurate understanding of its basic unit of analysis. That is, explicit and falsifiable theories of the state as a political actor are nowhere articulated in the literature on international politics.

To be sure, this line of criticism is valid but in a sense trivial. The very term 'international', taken as a mark of disciplinary identity, makes up both for the centrality and unproblematic character of the state in international political theory. Thus Raymond Aron was anxiously guarding his intellectual territory, when stating that 'a complete science or philosophy of politics would include international relations as one of its chapters, but this chapter would retain its originality since it would deal with the relations between political units'. International relations theory is thus 'entitled to take for granted...the political units'.

No one criticizes chemistry for taking the existence of atoms for granted, lower or higher levels of complexity are simply left to physicists and biologists respectively. Therefore, we should better view criticism along the above lines not as an ontological dispute going on within a preconstituted and homogeneous field of knowledge, but as a contest over a problematic disciplinary identity. For example, during the period when the interdependence of states was emphasized in international relations theory, it became commonplace to insist that the distinction between domestic society and international system was blurred or about to be dissolved. But interdependence theorists could not have it both ways; either they were right in their talk about blurring, with the inevitable consequence that their theories ceased to be theories of international politics, or, as was more often the case, talk about blurring was mere lip-service, this being so since talk about blurring and dissolution always presupposes that that which is blurred *essentially* is distinct; in the end one was tacitly reaffirming the same distinction which one so valiantly criticized.

Every scientific practice has to start somewhere, and international political theory happens to take the existence of the state as foundational for its intellectual enterprise. Nevertheless, even if the state is taken to be ontologically primitive, and its primitiveness is integral to the field of knowledge as such, questions about the state as a political actor have not been avoided by international political theory, even if they occupy a somewhat marginal position.

For what makes a state a state? What is the crucial property behind its capacity for unitary action? What distinguishes it from other forms of political organization?

Facing these questions, sovereignty is introduced both as the defining property of the state and in explaining the presence of an international system. For since the state is regarded as historically and ontologically prior to the system of states in the discourse on international politics, the essence of statehood appears to be the necessary condition also of the larger whole, the international system.

In the more traditional exemplars of international political theory, this foundational character of sovereignty is grasped historically, as a result of the fall from a primordial political unity. According to Wight, 'international politics... came into existence when medieval Christendom dissolved and the modern sovereign state was born'. To Bull, the presence of international relations is conditioned—logically as well as historically—by sovereignty:

> The starting point of international relations is the existence of *states*, or independent political communities, each of which possesses a government and asserts sovereignty in relation to a particular portion of the earth's surface and a particular segment of the human population. On the one hand, states assert, in relation to this territory and population, what may be called internal sovereignty, which means supremacy over all other authorities within that territory and population. On the other hand, they assert what may be called external sovereignty, by which is meant not supremacy but independence of outside authorities.

This traditionalist awareness of the historical roots of sovereignty is replaced by abstraction in the course of scientification. In Waltz's seminal *Theory of International Politics*, sovereignty is stripped of its historical origin and reinstated ahistorically as an organizing principle. What appeared to traditionalists as the outcome of political fragmentation and alienation within Christianity, now carries the burden of explaining 'the striking sameness in the quality of international life through the millennia'.

Here, sovereignty and anarchy are tied together ontologically at the level of definition, the former term being logically privileged, since it signifies that which is foundational to international politics. The state is conceptualized as an individual, in the sense of being indivisible. Further, by giving epistemic priority to the systemic level of analysis, Waltz creates a watertight circular connection between anarchy and sovereignty; their logical interdependence is conditioned by a gesture outside history but inside the theory itself, by splitting the difference between ontological and epistemic priorities. All this is done in order to extend the explanatory scope to cover everything that looks international from the dawn of history up to the present; Waltz has furnished us with a recipe for explaining the past in terms of the present, in which 'anarchy' and 'sovereignty' seem to be two sides of the same coin, but one cannot, from within this perspective, ever hope to explain how this connection was forged; coming from nowhere, consolidated in the deep structure of international politics, sovereignty is here to stay.

Christine Sylvester, "Empathetic Cooperation: A Feminist Method for IR"*

Empathetic Cooperation and Feminism

Feminist constructions of politics reveal and defy the ban on 'women'. They deconstruct and interpret the conventions of sovereign citizens and states that routinely put people called women in apolitical places *vis-à-vis* the sacralised realms reserved for liberal 'individuals'. They interpret from the other side—the side of women and children—or conduct genealogical tracings of the social construction of gender-occluding political power in unsighted and, therefore, uncited realms of the international.

Sometimes they simply and eloquently evoke possibilities for theorising that are currently foreclosed by our guiding premises of human and international behaviour. Trinh Minh-ha, for example, matter-of-factly inserts 'women' into a hypothetical village meeting in an unnamed third world country, showing us how a variety of standards of gender can be present in the politics of village life: 'A mother continues to bathe her child amidst the group; two men go on playing a game they have started; a woman finishes braiding another woman's hair. These activities do not inhibit listening or intervening when necessary'. That is, 'women' need not put aside their usual activities in order to be public and political. Elshtain, by contrast, serves up 'women' as the experienced post-moderns of contemporary western politics, the ones who cannot go on braiding each other's hair as in the past while listening in on the usual patriotic business of modern statecraft.

There is a sense of urgency about bringing real women into view and into village meetings everywhere, finally valorising women's experiences of knowing and being as alternatives to exclusionary citations. There is also evidence of scepticism about the very boundaries of gender identity that we chant like a mantra, wear like birthday suits, and turn into articles of ideological faith—or high patriotic purpose. The urgencies of the debate have often played out as a seeming struggle for feminist hegemony, something Elshtain decries:

> Of course, there are feminisms that push for hegemony, some all encompassing narrative, theory, or model—I call them 'narratives of closure' because they leave no room for ambiguity; instead, they aspire to hard and fast truths on the grand scale and eliminate complexity, irony and paradox as corrosive of totalised ideological commitment…. I…criticize any and all such theories, whether feminist, nonfeminist, antifeminist, political economy, rational choice, realist, neorealist—I don't care.

* *Millenium: Journal of International Studies*. This article first appeared in *Millenium*, Vol. 23, No. 2, 1995, and is reproduced with the permission of the publisher.

There are other struggles at the fulcrum of feminist insights however, that are non-hegemonic in style. What happens, asks Kathy Ferguson, when 'we simultaneously put women at the center and decenter everything including women'? What happens when we ride the hyphens of feminisms that accord women agency as knowers, and those that are radically sceptical of women? Is it possible to arrive at some location of commensurability or must one feminism be hegemonic?

Feminist standpoint epistemology researches and interprets the life experiences of women in order to bring them to bear on knowledge. Much as classical Marxism valorised the experiences of proletarians in places dominated by bourgeois practice, standpoint feminism offers women as a locus both of knowledge and of the agency necessary to correct patriarchal practices (once those knowledges are freed from distortions brought on by life under patriarchy). Women are the mothers, household food preparers, agriculturalists, and caretakers of the world. Their activities sustain the species and provide fertile ground for developing particular knowledges about human relations, relations with 'nature', about struggles for voice, recognition, and status as autonomous beings, and about the intricate ways that societies dominated by people with other assignments can block those knowledges. Through feminist struggles for truth, respect, and dignity, women's ways of knowing can develop into epistemological and political standpoints that are less distorted than the canons that shore up and reproduce the standpointed knowledge of sovereign privilege—the world according to those who create and win wars.

In contrast to the interpretive approach of standpoint feminism, feminist postmodernism is genealogical. It traces the constituted nature of women's life experiences to dominant patterns of knowledge and power that foreclose a vast array of alternative identities. It 'takes up a posture of subversion toward fixed meaning claims' and reveals how men and women, as well as the divisions of labour we associate with them, are constructed as stable statuses. It investigates the social processes that order disorderly currents by asking how power is manifested in the gender stories that conventional society rehearses, and in the substitute stories that standpointers spin. It asks how accidents of life are disciplined to fit a sense of preordination. Its tool of analysis, deconstruction, pulls apart gender in ways that, to use a hackneyed expression, 'open spaces' for new and heretofore ignored identities, ontologies, and epistemologies to emerge. In other words, through this research methodology, women are revealed as subjects tied to subject statuses, and this very revelation enables a multiplication of options.

Standpoint-based research has been accused of seeking alternative perspectives on truth that bubble forth from the experiences of unproblematised women. And yet we do not have to look too far to notice that, rather than discovering something called 'a woman's way of knowing', standpoint feminist research has uncovered so many different experiences of so many different types of people called women that the essentialism implied by *a* standpoint has often gone by the wayside. Indeed, feminist standpoint research has helped to identify many identity communities among people called women, and many standpoints in feminism—African, lesbian, Jewish, peace, womanist, socialist, radical, and so on. By definition, post-modernist research in feminism has done something similar. It has revealed the power and politics laden in local acts of resistance to universalising narratives. It has noted the places people carve out for themselves as they endeavour to decide their identities and knowledges rather than fit themselves to received wisdom.

At this fulcrum of perspectives and positions (in the deliberate plural), there are efforts made to reveal the long histories of inherited statuses that bind women (a genealogical concern), and quests to make alternative readings of those statuses possible. At this fulcrum, 'genealogy keeps interpretation honest, and interpretation gives genealogy direction'. Here there are acts of resistance, insight, and insistency.

At this fulcrum, we the researchers can stand limbs akimbo to suspect and inspect the confining baggage that people called women are routinely meant to carry (*e.g.*, motherhood, peace-lovingness, care). We know that a subject status—a bag carefully labeled—does not necessarily summarise the contents or the subject holding the bag. But we also know to look inside before discarding those burdens. Therein lies treasure troves of experience that have not been tapped for social theory. Therein are indications that the bags have traveled widely and traversed many terrains so that their contents are liminal:

> He blinks twice
> and I realize there is much
> red and browness
> in the 'whites' of his eyes.

Liminality suggests borderlands that defy fixed homeplaces in feminist epistemology, places of mobility around policed boundaries, places where one's bag disappears and reappears before moving on. Feminist standpoint and postmodernist epistemologies are borders to each other, but they also ooze and leak. "The different faces of feminism' simply emphasise different subjectivities, different traveling experiences, which we can think of as mobile rather than fixed, criss-crossing borderlands rather than staying at home.

Empathy taps the ability and willingness to enter into the feeling or spirit of something and appreciate it fully in a subjectivity-moving way. It is to take onboard the struggles of others by listening to what they have to say in a conversational style that does not push, direct, or break through to 'a linear progression which gives the comforting illusion that one knows where one goes'. It is an ability and willingness to investigate questions of 'women' (and other misdeeds in IR) in ways that open us up to the stories, identities, and places that have been by-passed in 'our' field. Along the way, our subjectivities travel to accommodate the new empathies. That is, they shift ranks or parameters of meaning as we listen. We then cooperate when we 'negotiate respectfully with contentious others' around the mobilities that empathy has revealed, jointly probing meaning and action in the face of homelessness in old canons that have slipped their moorings through empathetic readings, modes of listening, and ways of sighting. Together, empathy and cooperation enable 'different worlds and ourselves within them' as we engage in politically difficult negotiations at borderlands of knowledge, experience, differences, and subjectivities.

Interestingly, Kathy Ferguson explicitly rejects the idea that feminist standpoint and post-modernist differences can travel together via empathy. Following Donna Haraway, she argues that approaches to reconciliation that rest on appeals to empathy can go astray: 'empathy can readily be recruited into a gesture of appropriation (as in "I know just what you mean" when I really don't know at all)'. I sympathise with Ferguson's concerns, but that is precisely the point: 'I'ness is a sign of sympathy and not empathy. Sympathy is a self-centred sentiment that allows for little if any slippage, mobility, and hyphenation of subjectivity and identity on the occasion of listening to someone else's tales. Empathy is something rather different. If one 'hears' the different voices of IR empathetically, because one's own identities are less fixed than one thinks and because one is listening respectfully, new field-multiplying identities become possible in the face of shared alienations from master texts (and the homeless wanderings they impose on 'women'). This alienation renders a cooperative negotiation of knowledge both necessary and desirable as many subjectivities, in effect, interparticulate.

Exercises in cooperative knowledge generation would call into question the cooperations that mainstream IR literatures define. Neorealism, for instance, tells us that cooperation is something that can afflict states but that it is less prevalent than self-help, owing to constraints imposed by anarchic system structure. Neoliberal institutionalism presents cooperation as a condition that states submit to in order to avoid suboptimal outcomes of self-help decision-making, while keeping defection as an option. In the idealist tradition, cooperation is a natural human characteristic that can be exported to international relations. Cooperation, in the sense I am using it, is a process of negotiation that (real) theorists join because they have taken on board (rather than strategically calculated) enough of the texture of marginalised identities that their Self-identity with canonical knowledge is disturbed and must be renegotiated by enlarging the social scope of interpretation.

IR theorists need not, in Elshtain's words of caution, 'collapse into empathy—you know, some thoroughgoing identification with "oppressed people everywhere" [in some] rather patronizing [sense that] does not permit the necessary critical distance and analytic acuity'. If our subjectivities are mobile and hyphenated, then no self-sacrifice takes place, no thoroughgoing identity takeover is possible. What is possible is a negotiation that heightens awareness of difference *and* enables us to appreciate that theory can be a range of cooperatively decided or contending positions. Each of these positions can then be tested against demanding standards of empathy to create a 'robust rather than an anemic dialogue'.

Lest the charge of relativism be leveled at this approach, one can only say that relativism seems to be a refusal of cooperation among needed compatibles in favour of an uninvolved position of 'who am I to say'. Relativism is not a position from which one can engage in negotiation. It barricades spaces of difference as off-limits, beyond one's depth. It 'otherises' in the name of tolerance, denying that the invented other to whom one gives space could possibly have anything in common with one's (fixed sense of) Self. It denies mobilities, transversals, commonalities in order to avoid the charge of colonialism; but then it ends up creating exotic and quaint ones that we visit, bomb, or cluck our tongues about. Overcoming relativism entails becoming more comfortable with chronic borderland statuses in ourselves that can tap empathetically into what only seems to be an experience or identity foreign to one-Self. We do not evacuate some subjectivities in a repetition of what happened to 'women' in political theory, or throw away all previous knowledge so that the 'collapse into empathy' can be achieved as a standpoint. Rather, all of us achieve a chastened place in theory-building by recognising that none of us can appeal to *a* Self-evident reason for our endeavours. This is another way of saying that awareness of the identity borderlands we ourselves routinely transverse helps us to focus on relations international as a phenomenon that has eluded IR theory.

Hands-On Empathetic Cooperation in IR

Along with being a method for direct negotiation among theorists of seemingly incommensurable schools of thought, researchers aware of the possibilities of empathetic cooperation can use that knowledge to identify empirical instances of respectful negotiation and identity slippages in International Relations. I outline three such instances below. One is a case of a scholar hosting an empathetically cooperative conversation among two seemingly incommensurable identities—'soldier' and 'mother.' The second case telescopes a situation in which 'women' cooperate empathetically to negotiate themselves into the practice of realist politics. The third is a negotiation, forbidden to usual studies of international political economy, which leads to an entangling of Zimbabwean producer cooperatives—far from even the margins of IR concerns—with international donors.

Jean Bethke Elshtain's discussion of *Women and War* illuminates subtextual conversations occurring at the juncture of war/peace discourses. Elshtain analyzes how commonplace images of Beautiful female Souls, who are socially assigned the domain of peace, and Just Warriors, who are necessary to war stories, ignore the in-between spaces of identity that connect apparent opposites. Her entire book can be thought of as a hosted conversation about these caricatured knowledges of 'men's and 'women's' proper places in war and peace. One section, however, is particularly exemplary of the identity mobility and slippage I associate with empathetically cooperative practice.

Elshtain maintains that two sub-identities of Beautiful Soul and Just Warrior not normally theorised in IR literatures have important common ground that we should investigate. They are 'mothers' and 'soldiers'. A good soldier is like a good mother. Both do their duty but 'both are racked by guilt at not having done it right or at having done wrong as they did what they thought was right': 'One might have acted differently and a buddy been saved. One might have lived up to this ideal and a child spared that trauma or this distress'. Both are terribly concerned with bodily harm and with keeping one's sanity: 'The war lover on a killing binge [is] someone who had "lost it" just as the defensive mother who batters her child has lost it, having gone from protector to attacker'. Many a warrior is sickened by the gung-ho attitudes displayed by noncombatants, just as a mother resents the advice of those who are removed from the daily requirements of children. 'Men conceive of war as a freedom "from" and find themselves pinned down, constrained; women see mothering as the ticket to adulthood and find themselves enmeshed in a dense fabric of responsibility that 'constrains even as it enables'.

Elshtain uncovers a mutuality in difference that exposes commonplace understandings of 'men in war' and 'women in motherhood' as overwrought and lacking in grounding. That mutuality renders masculine soldiers and feminine mothers homeless in assigned places inside and outside of IR respectively. But it does more than that. A simple but profound identity hyphenation of this sort has implications for IR theory. If the definitive test of political manhood has been war and the definitive test of apolitical womanhood has been mothering, but both spaces, identities, and knowledges exist in one person, a good citizen and state is more a mix of gender-ruled assigned traits—more the mother and children—than IR and much of its inherited political theory has acknowledged. An unspoken 'other standard' that realists, in particular, have been admonished to avoid, becomes a mobile position inside rather than outside the realm of state identity and analysis. Lingering Machiavellian nightmares of states ruined on account of 'women' can be turned around to reveal the many ways that citizen and state relations international actually model some of the 'private' mothering activities of 'women.' Where are we then in our studies of international statecraft? Which soldierly and motherly intersections combine to form what types of states seeking what kinds of security? These questions require considerable cooperative conversation to resolve.

Walking 'Home'

In the early 1980s, a small group of mostly 'women' left household places in Cardiff, Wales to walk 120 miles to a US air force base in Berkshire, England, where 96 cruise missiles were scheduled for deployment. They had little intent to be radical. Once they brought pressure to bear on the Thatcher government to submit the deployment decision to parliamentary debate, the 'walkers' planned to return home. Indeed, they initially seemed to be safeguarding the myth of Beautiful Souls, for they called their action 'Women for Life on Earth'. When the media ignored them, however—perhaps because there is no knowledge of 'women' in international relations—they gradually became homeless in their identities as walkers and as Beautiful Souls for Life. They camped on Greenham Common, just outside the US base fences, and determined to maintain a presence there—a politics of resistance—until the missiles were stopped.

   Greenham Common highlights the ways that subjectivities usually refused place in IR can become the basis of empathetically negotiated actions that strike at IR's core—realist defence. These physically homeless refusers of the protector/protected *raison d'être* of security, developed a politics of empathetic cooperation by eschewing usual political conventions, such as voting, designating leaders, and organizing committees in order to conduct their affairs. Negotiating their decisions empathetically, they enlarged the social base of knowledge around each problem that arose, each strategy that was contemplated. Sometimes consensus was reached on the shape of Greenham political actions, and sometimes groups of 'women' acted in ways that vented 'local' or sub-group concerns. For example, some campers put implements of domesticity (potatoes) up exhaust pipes of trucks ferrying nuclear armour around England. Others defied gender place by pinning tea sets, diapers, and recipes to the base fence. In most cases, the usual Greenham style of deciding built empathy for difference through exercises that encouraged participants to listen to each other and cooperate, at minimum, by refusing to interrupt or to force conformity on others in the name of 'the' cause.

Over time, existence on a damp English common turned into a borderland condition between actual physical homelessness and refused homelessness in IR's security scripts. That is, facing daily eviction notices—to vacate homelessness in international politics for proper apolitical place at home—the campers periodically cut down the perimeter fence and surged onto the military base. They made the point that the security of a homebase is chimerical, that soldiers are no more secure behind their fences of defence than the women are in protected English homes: all might as well commingle on the common. Mutual homelessness around the fences pointed to the prospect of respectful negotiation as an alternative to life on either side of the borders. Moreover, daily negotiations at the fences were usually respectful. Rather than denounce or curse the soldiers or women on the other side, each often engaged in 'normal' banter with the other about family, weather, and mutual conditions of security. Defenses came down. Common scripts were (potentially) revealed.

The insubordinations of Greenham Common Women's Peace Camp fit what Pauline Rosenau refers to as an affirmative post-modern movement. As is often the case in such politics, the myriad forms of negotiation at the fences of defence, and within the group of Greenham campers, neither succeeded nor failed. That is, missiles neither left because of the women nor were they finally secured by the soldiers. Instead, the borderlands emerged: the peace camp became a good anarchic system where, in the absence of rule-governed expectations, there was room to change what and where one was properly supposed to be through actions at the fences of assigned place. Alexander Wendt claims that 'Anarchy is What States Make of It'. But anarchy is what a variety of yet-to-be-heard people and their 'strange' politics and conversations and empathies make of it. Rather than think of anarchy as a false projection of that cooperative autonomy from 'women' that disturbs so many feminist analysts, we might rehabilitate 'anarchy' to think about the ways contemporary relations international scramble and refuse IR standards of identity and place.

Good 'Families' Get International Funding?

Through regular trips to Zimbabwe I have learned that a good producer cooperative can be like a good family in the minds of 'women' cooperators who work them, and in the eyes of some international donors. In 1988 I conducted field research for a study on 'women', 'production,' and 'progress' in two provinces of Mashonaland, and came into extended contact with a pair of all-'women' cooperatives in the process of petitioning the European Commmunity (EC) Microprojects Fund for $200,000 to improve their operations. The sponsors of the cooperatives were two locally-resident Greek 'women' who had imported silk worms and weaving machines from Greece and were teaching approximately 40 local African 'women' to tend the worms properly and to spin silk thread.

On several occasions while I was present, the EC team visited the cooperatives and interrogated their business practices, asking about marketing and pricing procedures, book-keeping methods, and possibilities for export trade. The team told me they were seeking to ascertain whether these cooperatives maintained viable business standards. In each case, the Greek patrons answered all the questions, as though perpetuating yet another case of donor-directed development, of western knowledge steamrolling third world 'women,' silencing them in the name of standards of business, turning them into spectators in their own lives. What I learned in contrast to this impression was that the 'women' cooperators and the EC were developing the rudiments of an empathetically cooperative conversation that would lead to unusual hyphenations and, especially, to renegotiated donor standards of appropriate projects to aid.

The members of the cooperatives were the ones who suggested to me that a good cooperative is like a good family. They said that both families and cooperatives teach skills to members and nourish dreams. Our dream, they said, is to turn these cooperatives into one big extended family—a factory that makes silk and other related products. For now they claimed to be asking the EC for money to buy Mulberry trees, because silk worms thrive on Mulberry leaves. They also needed fencing materials and transportation. From there, they said, we will expand into making mulberry jam and selling berries while doing silk. The Europeans may speak to each other about the funding, but the 'women' cooperators think 'our own thoughts'.

The conflation of 'families' with 'cooperatives' and 'factories' blurred the boundaries of identity and place, while the emphasis on 'own thoughts' left some subjectivities open to further negotiation. As the private became public, domestic dreams mingled with international donor agendas, and 'women's' agency was softly proclaimed.

I then talked to EC Microprojects team members and found, quite unexpectedly, that they too were slipping the boundaries of their usual identity. They told me they knew full well that it was risky to fund cooperatives in Zimbabwe because members frequently used the money for other than grant-designated things. They expressed annoyance at instances of local refusals of the rules. But the EC gave these two cooperatives the money anyway. Why? I was told that the cooperatives had been visited so often that they were now 'like family'.

The presence of Greek women may account for the conflation of 'cooperatives' with 'family'. But the EC is not supposed to be funding families, only businesses. Moreover, unlike in parts of West Africa, 'women' are outside business circles in Zimbabwe in ways analogous to being outside politics in the West. This means that the EC donors had to cross borderlands of usual professional identity in order to fund 'families' on the advice of Greek 'women'.

The case of a business-minded intergovernmental organisation negotiating in tacit empathy with local 'women', who see themselves as sitting the fence of 'enterprises' and 'families', prompts me to ask what other cooperative slippages may be occurring 'out there' 'beyond standards'. Where else are the lines smudged between household places and international political economies in ways that reconstitute identities and redistribute resources? Where should we be looking, in other words, for relations of international political economy, and what transversals of place and knowledge might we find there?

Getting Going

In this location in IR time and space, there is considerable discomfiture with an inherited stable of knowledge. Rob Walker goes so far as to claim that:

[t]heories of international relations…are interesting less for the substantive explanations they offer about political conditions in the modern world than as expressions of the limits of the contemporary political imagination when confronted with persistent claims about and evidence of fundamental historical and structural transformation…attempts to think otherwise about political possibilities are constrained by categories and assumptions that contemporary political analysis is encouraged to take for granted.

These are sage words. Arguably there *has* been a profound failure of political imagination in IR, and this article has contended that one failure relates to longstanding conventions, explicitly argued in early political philosophy, that mark out all politics as 'men's' places of knowledge. And yet Walker's words are ripe with irony, since efforts to encourage greater imagination can themselves fail to give proper time and space to the persistent claims of feminist analysts. Andrew Linklater, for example, tells us that we are at a moment in IR when 'critical social theory, post-modernism, and feminism will have left an indelible impression on the field'. In the course of his article he cites the names of post-modernists and critical theorists, but does not cite one feminist contributor to the indelible impression. Can indelibility be "achieved by ghosts with no names, or is it not the case that we have no names because we are still out of place in politics?

The politik thing to do these days may be to tip one's hat in the direction of feminist scholarship in IR. But a long history of staked-out turf prevents even critics of the mainstream from going the full distance to reapportionments of place. Thus the impetus for expanded political imagination is thrown back onto the feminist analysts ourselves. We are the ones who must get going and reach beyond debates to host a variety of conversations with the conventionals of IR, the critics, and those with persistent claims of other types. The goal is not to persuade one side to embrace the other, but to facilitate a process that has each side appreciating that the claims and accounts others present are important to a field of social knowledge. The process imparts a modicum of homelessness in all our inherited positions and assignments, which inspires cooperative ways of reaching across indentity-constituting subjectivities, locations, and skepticisms.

Analysts of IR would be wise to emulate the instances of empathetic cooperation occurring in places remote from usual research gazes—where 'women' make themselves homeless in IR's canon and walk from that position into a politics that in-secures the fences of security, where soldiers and mothers blend stories and assignments in ways that jostle our sense of statecraft, and where local cooperatives teach international donors about the need to aid families that produce—and begin to think theory from 'strange' empirical standpoints. These are the places to visit and the methods to model as the many who are dissatisfied with the current state of IR knowledge endeavour to loosen its old-fashioned corsets.

11

Critical IR Theory and its Response

Introduction

This final chapter features Richard Devetak's essay "The Unfinished Project of Modernity in Critical IR Theory." Habermas, it will be recalled, conceived this unfinished project in terms of the social differentiation associated with flexible reason. Here, Devetak argues that both the pursuit and rejection of rationality and reason are immanent features of an increasingly complex, yet evolving global society, one that valorizes diversity, difference, freedom, and justice. As a result, even the antirationalism and relativism of postmodernism cannot entirely ignore the rationalist foundations of the Enlightenment. What this suggests are the radical possibilities of an expanded dialogue among these approaches, that is, the critical acceptance of reflexive institutional norms understood in terms of an intersubjective framework of interests, values, and identities (an inclusive global community). The question that arises then is whether the metaphorical device of the unfinished project of modernity can furnish us with the conceptual tools for steering beyond the current crisis of the discipline. Can we, in other words, realize a rigorous theoretical pluralism in IR, which is coterminous with a reflexive and empirically sensitive dialectical theory of IR theory? While Devetak addresses these challenges and tensions within the critical theory paradigm, critical IR theorists' response in this case will increasingly turn on this question of advancing a framework that is sensitive to difference.

Richard Devetak, "The Project of Modernity and International Relations Theory"*

The opening sentence of Kal J. Holsti's oft-cited *The Dividing Discipline* announces with some regret that '[i]nternational theory is in a state of disarray'. The long-established consensus about objectives and methodologies which has, until recently, grounded the study of international relations is now under considerable challenge from many directions. For some, the multiplication of theoretical perspectives poses serious problems for the future of the discipline. For others, it is something to be celebrated. Still others have gone beyond the apparent impasse by exploring common thematic concerns in the theoretical profusion.

The so-called 'third debate' is one manifestation of this disciplinary crisis. The stakes are high in this debate, holding ramifications for the meaning and future of the discipline of International Relations. One issue that has come to the fore in this debate is the question of modernity. What modernity refers to and how it relates to the study of international relations remain unclear. Nevertheless, it continues to command attention. It will be contended here that a fruitful approach to the question of modernity and the 'third debate' is to focus on the *project* of modernity. Taking this focus allows international relations theory to reflect on the normative purposes which underwrite political inquiry, as well as take account of two prominent theoretical approaches to the study of international relations: critical theory and post-structuralism.

It has become fashionable in recent times to emphasise the 'crisis of modernity', and modernity's implication in 'relations of domination, control, and power'. The dark underside of modernity has been well exposed not only by the experiences of World Wars, the Holocaust, and the Gulags, but by the critiques of modernity by, *inter alia*, Nietzsche, Weber, Heidegger, Horkheimer, Adorno, and Foucault. The limitations of modernity have been clearly illuminated. What remains unclear, however, is whether we should 'try to hold on to the *intentions* of the Enlightenment...or...declare the entire project of modernity a lost cause?' Have the critiques dealt such a devastating blow that it would no longer be worthwhile trying to rework the intentions, concepts and modes of reasoning that marked the philosophical discourse of modernity?

While the general theme of modernity has been treated in a variety of ways in International Relations, few thinkers have been willing to take seriously Habermas's attempt to reconstruct the Enlightenment for a *renewed project of modernity*. The focus suggested here is intimately related to modernity's new time consciousness, but most especially, to the modern attempt to construct practical political and ethical principles that can find rational approval despite the apparent absence of universal foundations. As explained by Habermas, this is a direct consequence of the delegitimisation of tradition: 'Modernity can and will no longer borrow the criteria by which it takes its orientation from the models supplied by another epoch; *it has to create its normativity out of itself*'. The project of modernity is the foremost expression of this creative

---

* *Millenium: Journal of International Studies*. This article first appeard in *Millenium*, Vol. 24, No. 1, 1995, and is reproduced with the permission of the publisher.

attempt. What is at stake is whether or not the project of modernity is open to critical rethinking, and how this might contribute to the study of international relations.

Reconstructing the Project of Modernity

Against the often caricatured representations of the Enlightenment as monolithic, Habermas insists on a more subtle, differentiated analysis of both its intentions and consequences. He remains sceptical of the supposition that there is a singular Enlightenment which is responsible for the tragedies and disasters of modernity. The project of modernity has not yet been fulfilled, but that does not mean it has been exhausted. Habermas demonstrates that the Enlightenment can be used against itself in order to continue the project of modernity. He makes use of the '200-year old counterdiscourse inherent in modernity itself', to pursue 'the global of enlightening the Enlightenment about its own narrowmindedness'.

The Enlightenment marks something of a cultural and social watershed. This multifaceted, eighteenth century event completed the reorientation in the European worldview that had begun with the Renaissance and Reformation. There are two features of the Enlightenment which are decisive for an understanding of the project of modernity: the ethos of critique, and the spirit of cosmopolitanism.

The Age of Criticism

> Our age is, in especial degree, the age of criticism, and to criticism everything must submit.

In a famous article, Kant posed the question: what is enlightenment? In many ways this question provides the point of departure for the project of modernity. Central to Kant's plea for enlightenment is a defence of the autonomy of reason, and a quest for autonomy itself. For Kant, the problem with humanity thus far is that it does not think for itself. By subscribing to dogmas and traditions humanity remains in a state of 'permanent immaturity'. This immaturity is a symptom of people's dependence on others to authorise and legitimise decisions and actions. It is from this 'self-incurred tutelage' (which Kant also calls heteronomy), that humanity must escape through a process of enlightenment. Only the 'daring of reason' is capable of providing an escape from this tutelage by submitting everything to criticism.

By the end of the eighteenth century, when Kant was writing, the traditional belief that modernity represented a steady decline or fall from grace had been well and truly challenged by Enlightenment thinkers, who believed that modernity represented the steady improvement in the human condition. This was to be realised through the liberating power of reason (*logos*) as it threw off the shackles of tradition (*mythos*). By simply carrying tradition forward as unproblematic, humanity was remaining trapped in the past. Modernity, by contrast, 'revolts against the normalizing functions of tradition'. It resists seeing tradition as exemplary or legitimate in itself. By questioning the authority and legitimacy of tradition, modernity marks the point where tradition is no longer 'passed on' or 'laid down' without question. Central to the Enlightenment was a critique of all authority that dogmatically sought to close itself off from contest. Kant decried the attempt by any authority 'to put the next age in a position where it would be impossible for it to extend and correct its knowledge'. The critical use of reason, Kant thought, would overcome the constraints imposed by tradition and open up unrealised future possibilities.

This modern effort to break with the past signals a perpetual transition to something new. It constitutes a form of *'continuous renewal'* which involves the constant 'dissolution of the exemplary past', and an openness towards what Kant called 'the unbounded future'. By embracing this new relationship with the future, modernity opens up a gulf between what Koselleck has called the 'space of experience' and the 'horizon of expectation'. The future is no longer conceptualised within the parameters set by past experiences; rather, the future is seen as a horizon which can be shaped by forces and ideas yet to be experienced. Indeed, the 'horizon of expectation' is the source of projects and programs aimed at the future. *Project* becomes the distinctive mode of modernity: a mode which looks, acts, and gestures towards the future. Rather than finding social and political legitimation in past experiences, the Enlightenment fosters a modern narrative which is directed towards a future goal: a goal which is normally conceived as the idea of emancipation or freedom. In Kant's historical and political writings, as in other Enlightenment thinkers, there is a strong sense that modernity is preparing the way 'for a great political body of the future, without precedent in the past'.

Critical International Theory: Defending and Extending the Project of Modernity

Critical international theory takes up, modifies, and extends the project of modernity initiated by the Enlightenment. It maintains the Enlightenment's focus on universal normativity and reinforces the global emphasis. It provides resources for a critical inquiry into the conceptual and material constraints on universal emancipation. In particular, it continues the two features of Enlightenment thought that have been highlighted here: the ethos of critique and the spirit of cosmopolitanism. While the element of critique is integral to critical international theory, it has been adequately reviewed elsewhere. What is less well understood, perhaps, is the cosmopolitanism which is rethought under the regulative ideal of universal emancipation. For these reasons the discussion of universal emancipation will be much longer than that of critique.

Critique

The success of critical international theory rests, to a significant degree, on its ability to offer a more self-reflective theory than traditional modes of international theory. It promises to bring to consciousness the material and conceptual constraints on achieving freedom in the modern world by resorting to a method of critique utilised by Kant, Hegel, Marx, and Habermas, amongst others. Of particular importance is the connection between knowledge and values which critical international theory seeks to elucidate. In contrast to traditional approaches, critical international theory inquires into the ways in which knowledge is guided by particular interests or values: it is never neutral. In view of this, critical international theory seeks to provide a theoretical framework which is guided by an interest in universal emancipation. The knowledge it seeks is not neutral. Critical international theory is self-consciously normatively charged.

The normative interest of critical international theory means that it is not only concerned with providing explanations of the existing realities of world politics, it also intends to criticise them in order to transform them. It is interested in knowing how, and to what extent, political transformation is possible. It refutes the 'immutability thesis' that the condition of anarchy in international relations necessarily condemns political communities to the tragedies of power politics. There is nothing natural or necessary about the prevailing form of international relations. In recognising that humans shape their own history, critical international theory allows, as Cox says, 'for a normative choice in favour of a social and political order different from the prevailing order'. The prevailing power-political order, as Cox conceives it, is a hegemonic world order which engenders certain forms of political and economic domination. In short, it is an inadequate resolution of the one and the many since it fails to promote a universal cosmopolitan existence. Critical international theory continues the Enlightenment concern with cosmopolitanism. There are two dimensions to its attempt to re-articulate this Enlightenment vision: autonomy and community, which will be examined in turn.

Taking the question of autonomy first, it will prove helpful to consider the work of Richard Ashley. In accord with Cox's argument, Ashley avers that the maintenance of the prevailing order involves relations of domination. The critical international theorist, therefore, must 'look for the relation of domination *even when the parties to a system are unaware of, or perhaps deny, conflicting interests or possible alternatives to the given order'*. Beyond this consciousness-raising exercise the theorist must inquire into the possibilities of transcending the present system by specifying the historical conditions under which the dominant order might give way to 'alternative oppositional coalitions'. What Ashley is interested in are the possibilities of counter-hegemonic forces developing within and against the dominant order, capable of leading to greater autonomy.

The cognitive interest in emancipation responds to the human interest in, and capacity for, *autonomy*. It explores the prospects 'for extending the human capacity for self-determination'. The quest for autonomy is a quest to make it possible for humans to shape a future free of unnecessary constraints. Ashley elaborates this commitment as an emancipatory cognitive interest in 'securing freedom from unacknowledged constraints, relations of domination, and conditions of distorted communication and understanding that deny humans the capacity to make their future through full will and consciousness'. He invokes this interest against the current order of domination ingrained in the states-system. Although he never fully explicates his notion of domination, it is clear that the states-system itself represents one form of domination in a wider matrix of relations of domination.

Ashley's argument resonates with Kant's. Like Kant, Ashley interprets the prevailing system of states as a form of domination not only because war is an inherent attribute and because powerful states continue to dominate and exploit weaker states, but also because it is linked to a variety of social systems which are global in their threat to human autonomy. Implicit in Ashley's critique of the states-system is an aspiration to move towards a system similar to that envisaged by Kant, who spoke of a 'cosmopolitan system *of general political security*'. It is clear that Kant is not simply alluding to notions of 'common security' or 'security communities' when he uses the phrase 'general political security', but to a much wider idea of security, which takes humans rather than states as the subjects of security. Security in Kant's sense cannot be detached from autonomy and community. Further, it cannot be exclusive to one level, but must be generalised across all levels of human relations. Only the realisation of such an arrangement of general political security can deliver humanity from relations of heteronomy and domination, and ensure the union of the one and the many in a universal cosmopolitan existence.

It might be suggested that such an idea of general political security is implied in Linklater's idea of universal human emancipation. For Linklater, emancipation denotes the abolition of unnecessary constraints on human freedom and the achievement of autonomy. His main concern is to elaborate an argument for overcoming the constraints on emancipation which emanate from the international system. In particular, he identifies 'intersocietal estrangement' as a feature of the states-system that unnecessarily inhibits human freedom. Eschewing the particularism associated with the state, critical international theory defends the 'ideal of the unity of the species'. It offers 'a theoretical position which is committed to the goal of human emancipation', and is grounded in an interest in freedom and universalism.

For critical international theory, freedom and universalism can no longer be confined to the limits of the state or nation. The realisation of the 'good life' is not to be confined to these particularistic limits, but is to be universalised to humanity. To be committed to universalism, as critical international theory is, is to refuse 'total identification with the community to which one belongs' and to accord recognition to humanity as well as citizenship. It would involve a 'redefinition of obligations to outsiders' which would overcome the citizen/human distinction. Citizens could no longer be given automatic privilege over others in all moral and political matters. A shift from the category of citizen to human being as the primary moral and political agent is therefore fundamental to the possibility of achieving emancipation. This new focus necessarily involves rethinking the concept of community; for, if not in the state or nation, in what other community can universalistic value orientations today take root?

The second dimension of critical international theory's attempt to rearticulate the Enlightenment concern with cosmopolitanism is the question of community. This has long been a recurrent philosophical theme in international relations. For the most part it has been associated with the state or nation which is taken to represent an idealised form of community. Although competing understandings of community have tended to be dismissed by Realism, they have not been silenced. Critical international theory facilitates a project of modernity which inquires into the costs of state sovereignty and takes seriously the competing notions of community.

The starting point for a critical international theory is to question the legitimacy of those institutions and practices that define identities or communities *against* others and, as a consequence, implicitly devalue outsiders. The sovereign state, as an example of this exclusion *par excellence*, necessarily becomes the prime target. As one of the strongest exclusionary forces in world politics it remains a considerable barrier to universal emancipation. The source of this problem, as Mark Hoffman remarks, is that the sovereign state is based on the assumption that 'politics is impossible without enclosure'. He adds that it must therefore be 'relinquished because it ignores the possibility that there might be forms of political community which resist or are stifled by enclosure'. Such enclosure restricts the development of community thereby preventing emancipation. Universal emancipation would involve the replacement of such exclusionary social relations by inclusionary ones.

If Linklater's earlier thought seemed to obviate the question of difference in its concern to articulate an inclusionary perspective, this is certainly not the case in his more recent thinking. His version of critical international theory does not opt for what Walker calls an 'easy universalism', which 'generates a reading of History as a move from fragmentation to integration'. It does not ascribe priority to universality at the expense of diversity. Rather, it acknowledges that there ought to be 'limits to universalism, just as there ought to be limits to difference'. This is endorsed by Hoffman, who advances an argument that 'takes seriously the idea of a *cosmopolis* as the embodiment of diversity'. The key question is how to weave the defence of universality and the claim for difference into a single theoretical perspective. For critical international theory this question can only be addressed within the framework of a 'universal cosmopolitan existence': only such a framework can maintain universality and difference while transcending them.

The political task of critical international theory, then, is to extend the framework of normativity beyond the borders of states, or, as Linklater argues, 'to facilitate the extension of moral and political community in international affairs'. This necessarily involves rethinking the ideas of autonomy and community, and contending with the difficult practical issues of resolving the friction between identity and difference, the one and the many. In order to foster this 'universal cosmopolitan existence', critical international theory must reinstate the project of modernity as the framework for international relations theory. For critical international theory, taking the project of modernity seriously means inquiring into the conditions under which it is possible to speak of universal emancipation in world politics. It is a question of how to conceive and plausibly articulate a cosmopolitan vision of world politics without relapsing into the naivety and superficiality that Carr castigated in early idealism, and without compromising normativity by falling back into realism. As Hutchings points out, this is an extremely difficult task as it involves the effort to overcome the apparently intractable division between morality and politics.

The following section elaborates post-structuralist theories of international relations, focusing on themes which feed into the project of modernity. It provides a brief account of post-structuralism's deconstructive mode of critique before elaborating some of the ways in which post-structuralism contributes to the project, of modernity. Of course, the concerns and implications of post-structuralism are by no means limited to the project of modernity. Rather, like critical international theory, it provides strategies for thinking through certain conceptual problems in international relations more generally.

Post-Structuralist International Theory

To begin with, it should be noted that post-structuralism is *not* used here as a synonym of post-modernism, nor to denote a socio-cultural condition, or period following modernity. Most importantly, it should not be presumed that post-structuralism is directed against the project of modernity, that it is anti-modern, or anti-Enlightenment. To be sure, post-structuralism is neither for nor against the project of modernity in any simple sense, for that would imply that either post-structuralism or the project of modernity had a determinate meaning. The post-structuralist attitude gives rise to a double gesture: it tries, as Jacques Derrida says, 'to remain faithful to the ideal of the Enlightenment, the *Aufklärung*, the *Illuminismo*, while yet acknowledging its limits, in order to work on the Enlightenment of this time, this time that is ours—today'. The consequence of this position is that post-structuralism refuses to accept the project of modernity as a pre-packaged set of ideas that can simply be handed down like a tradition. The project of modernity remains an open-ended, on-going project, which is still contested and open to scrutiny. The project of modernity must be an Enlightenment *for today*, not an Enlightenment *from the past*. In this sense, it constitutes a form of the 'continuous renewal' and openness to 'the unbounded future' that began with the Enlightenment of the eighteenth century. It forms an important continuation of the project of modernity through a general rethinking of both the ethos of critique and the spirit of cosmopolitanism. More specifically, it submits the political concepts of sovereignty, identity and difference to critique.

Deconstruction as Critique

Post-structuralism operates with a notion of deconstruction which is a general mode of unsettling concepts and conceptual oppositions which are otherwise taken to be settled. The main point of deconstruction is to try to demonstrate and displace the effects produced by settled oppositions. According to Derrida, conceptual oppositions are not simply neutral: they are hierarchical. One of the two terms is valorised, or governs the other. This privileged term supposedly signifies a presence, propriety, or identity which the other lacks. Deconstruction attempts to show that such oppositions are untenable. The subordinate term is never completely different than the governing term. Each always depends on, and is already contaminated by, the other.

This suggests that, because the boundary that is supposed to keep the two terms separate and distinct is always already breached, the dominant term never achieves the purity or totality to which it aspires. Totalities (conceptual and social) are always impure and incomplete. They always require a supplement, and will never have been properly established to begin with. Consequently, Jean-Francois Lyotard's slogan, 'wage war on totality', is more misleading than helpful, because such a war assumes the very possibility of totalisation, which post-structuralism continuously points out to be impossible. We may find that there is no totality against which to wage war. Nor are there uncomplicated, clear systems of totalisation and exclusion. According to this understanding, then, post-structuralism is most interested in *attempted* closure, in the ways in which theoretical frameworks or circumscribed objects, are not self-sufficient or closed, but vulnerable to pressure from an outside, or supplement. Post-structuralism can be understood as a strategy of interpretation and criticism directed at theories and concepts which attempt closure or totalisation. Against totalisation, post-structuralism seeks to deploy a mode of unsettling or 'decentering that leaves no privilege to any centre'. This holds implications for ontological questions about how subjects and objects are constituted in international relations, as well as ethical and political questions. It suggests a 'form of thought in which the interrogation of the limit replaces the search for totality'. It will be argued here that post-structuralist thought tends to focus on questions of boundaries and closure. How boundaries operate, how they are constituted, what they signify, what they enclose and thereby exclude, and what general and particular effects they produce, will therefore be integral to a post-structuralist inquiry. Just as integral, however, will be a recognition that boundaries fail to absolutely demarcate and constitute a totality; for although closure is constantly attempted, it is also constantly thwarted. Nevertheless, this attempt at closure constitutes a crucial political moment.

In the following section, we will see how the post-structuralist critique of totality becomes a critique of sovereignty in the study of international relations. As Ashley and Walker rightly claim, '[w]hat is at stake is nothing less than the *question* of sovereignty'. Ontologically and ethico-politically, post-structuralist international theory resists the privileging of a sovereign centre which holds everything together. It resists the closure and totalisation associated with sovereignty. Its main focus is to demonstrate the impossibility of establishing permanent boundaries around sovereign centres, showing that there are always competing sovereignties and competing sovereign claims which will frustrate sovereignty. Sovereign closure is constantly undone.

After Sovereignty: Cosmopolitanism With a Différence

It is important to keep in mind that post-structuralist international theory does not just challenge state sovereignty, it questions the concept of sovereignty as such: hence Jean Bethke Elshtain's question, '[a] politics *sans* sovereignty: is it possible?' Her purpose in asking this question is to challenge the assumption that either the sovereign self or the sovereign state are 'unproblematic, unified, sharply bounded phenomena'. The task is not to search for a genuinely sovereign subject to replace the state, but to resist the temptation which presumes that such a subject might be identified or found for either ethical or political purposes. The task is to question the concept of sovereignty itself, and to move towards a 'post-sovereign international relations' as Linklater calls it." As Claude Lefort admonishes, 'we must resolve to abandon the idea of a politics...that would stand over the world in which we live and allow it to be struck by the thunderbolts of the Last Judgement'. Sovereign thunderbolts of supreme and ultimate judgement are no longer to be associated with a single, totalising level of subjectivity. No single subject can be privileged as ethically and politically sovereign, including, or perhaps especially, the state.

Consequently, the post-structuralist concern with boundaries and closure has important implications not only for central concepts in the traditional study of international relations but also for critical approaches. If appeal can no longer be made to a sovereign subject as the foundation of community or ethical judgement, the issue then becomes whether it is possible to continue the project of modernity at all. The underlying premise of post-structuralist international theory, however, is not that the loss of sovereign certitude constitutes a set-back for the project of modernity, but that it actually liberates it from a severe constraint. A brief discussion of post-structuralist implications for the concept of community should help to demonstrate how post-structuralism rethinks a central theme of the project of modernity.

The Question of Community: Beyond Identity and Difference

It might be assumed that because post-structuralism questions sovereignty, identity, and totality, and espouses *différance* and 'de-centring', it must necessarily be antithetical to community. This might even lead to accusations of nihilism, anarchism, or even Realist scepticism: a case of Waltz meeting Zarathustra! Such conclusions, however, would be wrong. Post-structuralism is only critical of community to the extent that it attempts to inscribe fixed, rigid boundaries of enclosure; that is, to the extent that it claims or institutes sovereignty.

The target of post-structuralist international theory is the traditional conception of community which is tied to notions of totality, boundedness and identity, all of which is captured in the notion of sovereignty. The philosophical task then consists in undoing sovereignty by questioning the legitimacy of its closed community and problematising its boundaries and identity. The ethico-political moment in post-structuralism disavows the assertion or imposition of sovereign boundedness. Rather than correlate community with a clearly demarcated social space (territory) that asserts sovereignty, it prefers a position of openness: not just to keep open the boundaries of the community, but to keep open the question of community. The issue is not that of establishing a sovereign community, but of thinking what community without sovereignty might mean.

Beyond simply refusing to fetishise the moment of sovereignty, identity, or totality as the basis of community, post-structuralism also questions the opposition between identity and difference. It is not uncommon to find post-structuralism presented (by critics and adherents alike) as an approach aimed at simply inverting the identity/difference hierarchy and celebrating difference. The whole point of Derrida's neologism *différance*, however, is to resist absolutising difference; that is, making difference into either a prized value, or a disdained one. It must be remembered that the point of post-structuralism is not to valorise difference as an ethical or political value, but to question binary oppositions. There is a danger of making difference into a value in itself, and giving it a special status as superior to identity. Post-structuralism could not simply choose difference over identity, for that would preserve 'the prior framework in which identity and difference are counterposed as mutually exclusive opposites'. The challenge, as understood by Walker, is to resist the urge to define difference as relativistic, and in opposition to identity.

Resisting the traditional presuppositions regarding community, Walker insists that 'whatever community may come to mean, it will necessarily involve a recognition of the claims of both identity and of difference'. It 'must be rooted in an equal respect for the claims of both diversity and unity'. Community is not to be reduced to identity, but neither should it be reduced to the negation of identity. Consequently, post-structuralist international theory allows for a rethinking of community, which is not bound by the limits of traditional conceptions. Instead, it makes possible a cosmopolitan vision free of sovereignty and sovereignty's usual understandings of identity and difference.

This cosmopolitan vision might be thematised in terms of what Connolly calls an 'ironic' attitude toward community. As Connolly describes it, such a community would problematise or question what it is, even while affirming itself. It would be conscious of its contingency and its incompleteness. This attitude is based on an understanding that the community is fundamentally at odds with itself over its own identity. Derrida advances a similar argument in his discussion of European cultural identity, where he affirms that, *what is proper to a culture is to not be identical to itself*'. This is both an ontological assertion and an ethical claim. It implies that community is never entirely selfsame, or 'at-one-with-itself', but also that this lack of fit is essential to ethical relations with what lies beyond the community. Indeed, it means that the referent community is never a clear or distinct entity, for it has no fixed or permanent boundary to distinguish the inside from the outside of community. Without a sovereign centre there will be no sovereign boundary. This post-sovereign politics also resonates with Christine Sylvester's feminist reflections on identity and community. She elaborates a notion of 'homeless homesteading' which is based on the recognition of multiple, hyphenated identities. Rather than presuppose a fixed limit or essence to identity and community, this idea registers the ongoing 'process of identity slippage'. According to Sylvester, this lack of self-sameness makes possible greater empathetic cooperation.

What is at stake for post-structuralism is a politics without sovereignty: a politics without a centre that aspires to hold everything in its place. Post-structuralism is, at a minimum, against sovereignty, which is thought to be misleading as an ontological description and harmful as an ethical prescription. If the project of modernity is concerned with analysing the conditions under which it is possible to speak of emancipation in world politics, post-structuralist theorists insist that the elaboration of these conditions must confront questions of sovereignty, closure, and totalisation. An indispensable condition for emancipation in world politics, from a post-structuralist position, would be the resistance to sovereignty, closure, and totalisation. Post-structuralism rethinks the meaning of a universal cosmopolitan existence under these conditions.

The Question of Closure: Post-structuralism and Critical International Theory

So far, the article has demonstrated that there are common themes which loosely bind the Enlightenment with critical and post-structuralist international theories.

The commonality derives from a focus on the question of emancipation in world politics. For both critical international theory and post-structuralist international theory, this remains an open question, but one that must continually be re-posed. The willingness to re-pose the question and never to assume that the answer has been found is fundamental to rethinking the project of modernity. As Kant said, in the age of criticism everything must be submitted to critique, including our 'answers' to the question of emancipation. The meaning of "emancipation" has to be discovered rather than stipulated in advance'. We must always be prepared to rethink our most cherished visions of the future: As Foucault avers, we must always remain in the position of beginning again. Therefore, the project of modernity demands the 'permanent reactivation' of the critical attitude. There is good reason for this. Whereas the eighteenth century Enlightenment thinkers thought that they had made a successful break from *mythos* to *logos*, critical and post-structuralist theorists doubt that the break is ever clear or complete. As Horkheimer and Adorno, Gadamer, and Derrida, amongst others, have so forcefully argued, it is not a simple task to escape the constraints of myth, tradition, or metaphysics. Although we can never make an unproblematic step beyond tradition we must continue to reflect upon limits. In maintaining this 'limit-attitude', as Foucault calls it, we are no longer inside tradition in any clear or simple sense.

Boundaries and Emancipation

Post-structuralist international theory focuses on the question of totalisation and sovereignty, and in the process raises questions about boundaries. Critical international theory also confronts questions of boundaries, particularly in relation to community. It is precisely on this point that they both converge: the question of the constitution of boundaries and their relation to emancipation. As Ashley and Walker point out, questions of boundaries are inseparable from questions of emancipation, for '[w]ith the hardening of boundaries, one's own domain of freedom is now more limited'. The 'radical interpretation of textual and social closure' that they offer not only gives them a common focus, it also puts them within the same project.

If the project of modernity is concerned with breaking away from the past, and past forms of injustice, in order to shape a universal normative trajectory, then it will need to combine its normative dimension with its historical, empirical and practical political dimensions. Indeed, the project of modernity must develop 'a critical, historical account of *how we came to be what we are*, a reflection on the particulars of our self-formative process'. It would need to provide an analysis and critique of the origins, development, and the normative implications of identity formations. With this in mind, Linklater turns to Foucault who provides resources for explaining how our concepts of 'self' emerged in history by focusing on practices of exclusion. Linklater finds two things interesting about Foucault: first, his analysis of the ways in which societies arrive at particular principles of inclusion and exclusion; and secondly, his analysis of the ways in which subjects recognise themselves as moral subjects. The overall aim of critical international theory, then, is to inquire into the historical constitution of subjects as political and ethical agents. That is, to thematise ideas and practices of exclusion which differentiate the self from the other. The task is to understand how we came to be, and recognise ourselves as, what we are through practices of exclusion and differentiation. Critical theory is no longer exclusively a reflection on the particulars of our 'self-formative process', but equally a reflection on processes which simultaneously constitute the *other*. This has led, in the work of Linklater and Hoffman, to a concern with the logics of inclusion and exclusion, and to what John Gerard Ruggie calls principles of separability. It directs inquiry toward the ways in which communities understand the meaning and significance of their separateness from others, and to the historicity of their separateness.

Linklater proposes that the task is to understand 'how human communities are formed and re-formed, how their boundaries open and close, and how different conceptions of self and other evolve over time'. The question of boundaries becomes crucial because it is boundaries, those 'monstrous partitions' as Derrida calls them, which mark the difference between those included and those excluded from certain rights, duties, or obligations. The historical constitution and legitimation of boundaries which close off moral and political space must be addressed.

Within Linklater's perspective, this would lead to an examination of the conditions under which spurious forms of inclusion and exclusion have developed and been legitimated at certain points in time, and, more importantly, how they have been resisted, de-legitimated, or dismantled. Critical international theory would seek to delineate the historical shifts which have shaped and determined the boundaries that separate inside from outside, us from them, the powerful from the disenfranchised, and the public from the private. Furthermore, it would inquire into the principles that have governed relations across those boundaries and the ways in which these principles have changed over time. The crucial theoretical issue, then, is not exclusively, as in the traditional study of international relations, how already-constituted, bounded communities interact, but also how the inscription of boundaries constitutes separate political communities.

Boundaries in themselves are neither inherently good nor bad. Though 'monstrous' at times, they are probably unavoidable in one form or another. The point, as Richard Bernstein assures us, 'is not that we can get along without demarcating boundaries, but rather there is no "boundary-fixing" that cannot itself be questioned'. It needs to be added that the status and significance attached to boundaries is equally important. It may not be possible to dispense with boundaries, but it may be possible to impute different meanings and status to them. It is the rigidity of the boundaries (and not just territorial ones), and the trust invested in them as indisputable delimitations that is at stake for emancipation.

Conclusion

The project of modernity must therefore rethink boundaries for both ontological and ethico-political reasons. It needs to confront the *'question of the relations between belonging and the opening'*, which Derrida specifies as 'the *question of closure*'. This question of closure is crucial to the project of modernity not just because the closure promised by those boundaries facilitates the closure of community at the expense of others and otherness, but also because this brings us to what Lefort considers the very question of the political: 'the principles that generate society'. The argument advanced in this article is that the inscription of boundaries is a political act *par excellence*. It gives shape to the limits and identity of political units, marking the point of articulation between inside and outside, association and dissociation, attachment and detachment, and the principles of bonding and separability. Extending from the question of the political is a range of important ethical questions pertaining to relations across boundaries. These questions will find no easy answers, but the project of modernity provides the most promising framework in which to think about provisional responses. Indeed, this article contends that critical social theories cannot take a single step in the study of international relations without first paying tribute to the project of modernity, even if it is only to rethink or rework its central features of critique and cosmopolitanism.

Although the present context (the 'third debate') has raised important questions regarding methodology, it has yet to provide any orientation. There is more at stake in these debates than simply getting methodology right. The trajectory of the modern world is also at stake. The intention of this article has been to draw attention to the project of modernity as one attempt to shape this trajectory. More specifically, the project of modernity inquires into the conditions under which it is possible to speak of emancipation in world politics. This is an inquiry in which the Enlightenment, critical international theory and post-structuralist international theory have participated, hence the contention that they all contribute to the project of modernity. This article has attempted to provide a sketch of how they converge on, and contribute to, the project of modernity.

The range of diversity in international relations theory to which the 'third debate' has drawn attention, should not obscure the considerable overlap in thematic concern. At a minimum, feminism, philosophical hermeneutics, Frankfurt School critical theory and post-structuralism, while remaining distinctive modes of interpretation, have nevertheless undertaken critiques of traditional modes of theorising international relations. More substantively, they have reflected, to various degrees, on structures and practices of exclusion, and the general theme of modernity. The 'third debate' presents us with an invitation to think seriously, not just about the future of the discipline, but about the future of the project of modernity. To take up either of these invitations it is imperative to maintain a critical attitude. Neither the discipline nor the project of modernity should have their meaning determined in advance, but should remain open questions, constantly submitted to critical scrutiny.

Index

Index

R

S